lonely planet

Andalucía

**John Noble
Susan Forsyth**

Andalucía

1st edition

Published by
   Lonely Planet Publications
   Head Office: PO Box 617, Hawthorn, Vic 3122, Australia
   Branches: 150 Linden Street, Oakland, CA 94607, USA
                  10a Spring Place, London NW5 3BH, UK
                  1 rue Dahomey, 75011 Paris, France

Printed by
   Colorcraft Ltd, Hong Kong

Photographs by
   Mark Armstrong   John Hay   Damien Simonis
   Bethune Carmichael   John Noble   David Waterman
   Susan Forsyth   Gerry Reilly

   Front cover: Olvera (Hans Wolf, The Image Bank)

First Published
   January 1999

Although the authors and publisher have tried to make the information as accurate as possible, they accept no responsibility for any loss, injury or inconvenience sustained by any person using this book.

National Library of Australia Cataloguing in Publication Data

Noble, John
Andalucia.

   1st ed.
   Includes index.
   ISBN 0 86442 559 7.

   1. Andalusia (Spain) - Guidebooks. I. Forsyth, Susan. II. Title.

914.680483

text & maps © Lonely Planet 1999
photos © photographers as indicated 1999
Málaga climate chart compiled from information supplied by Patrick J Tyson, © Patrick J Tyson, 1999

John Noble & Susan Forsyth

John Noble and Susan Forsyth hail from opposite sides of the globe – he from the Ribble valley in northern England, she from Melbourne, Australia. After completing university degrees John worked in Fleet Street journalism and Susan taught secondary school and adult students. But travel proved too much of a distraction and one year they both found themselves in Sri Lanka – Susan working as a volunteer teacher and John carrying out his first commission for Lonely Planet. They got married three years later in Melbourne, then lived five years in the Ribble valley before moving to an Andalucian hill village. They have continued to travel elsewhere, co-authoring Lonely Planet titles including *Australia*, *Indonesia* and *Sri Lanka* as well as *Spain* and *Mexico*. John co-authored *Central Asia, USSR* and *Russia, Ukraine & Belarus* and wrote *Baltic States* solo. Susan and John's children Isabella and Jack go most places with them, but still manage to attend school in their Andalucian village, thanks to which their command of the Andalucian dialect is somewhat better than that of their parents.

From the Authors

We owe thanks to everyone who answered our questions, gave us tips and shared their experiences and knowledge of Andalucía. Particularly: Nick and Corinna Selby for a great deal of help with Algeciras, Gibraltar, Tarifa, technology and other things; Patricia for e*luce*idating Lorca, being a constant source of information and pointing us in some interesting directions; Tony and Jean Allsop for Ronda help; Jane Warnick for tips on the Granada coast; Paul Covill for musical enlightenment; the helpful staff in Andalucian tourist offices, especially María Angustias Maldonado in Granada; Sara Yorke and Christina at LP London for valuable help on UK-Spain transport. Thanks also to Damien Simonis for all sorts of bits and pieces and use of some of his material from *Spain*, and to Corinne Simcock for blazing the trail on the Costa del Sol and in Huelva and Jaén.

From the Publisher

This book was edited by a team of editors including Rebecca Turner, Ron Gallagher, Janet Austin and Mary Neighbour. Jenny Joy Jones coordinated the design, mapping and layout with great flair and Marcel Gaston used his inimitable calm diplomacy to make sure our brilliant ideas did not blow out the budget. Michael Weldon, Nick Trenerry and Nick Kelly drew on their artistic talents, Darren Elder saved the day with indexing assistance and Quentin Frayne checked our Andalucian Spanish pronunciation. Jamieson Gross designed the front cover and Tim Uden grouped and linked us seamlessly into Quark mode. David Andrew and Clay Lucas rescued us from the brink of insanity with inappropriate wit and we all fought valiantly against Bob.

Warning & Request

Things change – prices go up, schedules change, good places go bad and bad places go bankrupt – nothing stays the same. So if you find things better or worse, recently opened or long since closed, please tell us and help make the next edition even more accurate and useful.

We value all of the feedback we receive from travellers. Julie Young coordinates a small team who read and acknowledge every letter, postcard and email, and ensure that every morsel of information finds its way to the appropriate authors, editors and publishers.

Everyone who writes to us will find their name in the next edition of the appropriate guide and will also receive a free subscription to our quarterly newsletter, *Planet Talk*. The very best contributions will be rewarded with a free Lonely Planet guide.

Excerpts from your correspondence may appear in new editions of this guide; in our newsletter, *Planet Talk*; or in updates on our Web site – so please let us know if you don't want your letter published or your name acknowledged.

Contents

Map Legend

BOUNDARIES

.... International Boundary
.... Regional Boundary
.... Provincial Boundary

ROUTES

..... Freeway, with Route Number
.... Major Road, with Tunnel
.... Minor Road
.... Minor Road - unsealed
.... City Road
.... City Street
.... City Lane
.... Steps on Street
.... Cable Car or Chairlift
.... Ferry Route
.... Walking Track
.... Railway, Train Station

AREA FEATURES

.... Building
.... Cemetery
.... Sand
.... Market
.... Park, Gardens
.... Forest
.... Urban Area

HYDROGRAPHIC FEATURES

.... Coastline
.... Creek, River
.... Flow
.... Lake, Intermittent Lake
.... Rapids, Waterfalls
.... Salt Lake
.... Swamp

SYMBOLS

☼ **CAPITAL** ...... Country Capital
◉ **CAPITAL** ...... Provincial Capital
● **CITY** .... City
● **Town** .... Town
● Village .... Village

■ .... Place to Stay
Å ...... Camping Ground
⌂ .... Shelter

▼ .... Place to Eat
🍺 .... Pub or Bar

.... Airport
.... Ancient or City Wall
.... Bank
.... Beach
.... Castle or Fort
.... Cave
.... Church
.... Cliff or Escarpment
.... Embassy
.... Hospital
.... Lighthouse
.... Lookout
.... Monument
.... Mountain or Hill
.... Museum
.... One Way Street

🅿 .... Parking
)(................................ Pass
.... Picnic Area
★ .... Police Station
.... Post Office
∴ .... Ruins
❖ .... Shopping Centre
.... Ski Field
× .... Spot Height
◎ .... Spring
.... Synagogue
🏛 .... Palace
☎ .... Telephone
▣ .... Tomb
ℹ .... Tourist Information
⊖ .... Transport

Note: not all symbols displayed above appear in this book

Map Index

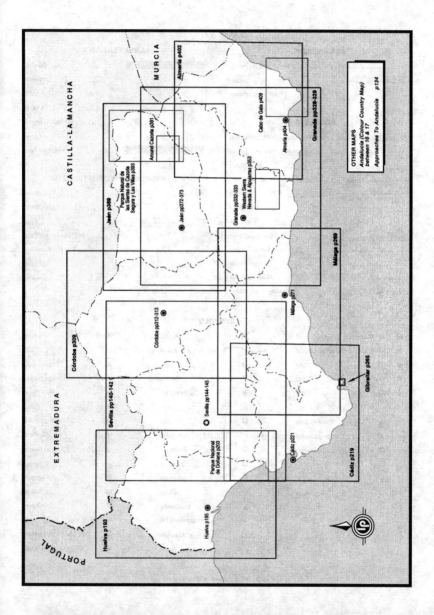

PORTUGAL

EXTREMADURA

CASTILLA-LA MANCHA

MURCIA

Huelva p190

Huelva p195

Sevilla pp140-142

Parque Nacional de Doñana p203

Sevilla p144-145

Córdoba p309

Córdoba pp312-313

Jaén p369

Parque Natural de las Sierras de Cazorla Segura y Las Villas p393

Around Cazorla p391

Jaén pp372-373

Almería p402

Cabo de Gata p409

Almería p404

Granada pp328-329

Granada pp332-333

Western Sierra Nevada & Alpujarras p353

Málaga p269

Málaga p271

Gibraltar p265

Cádiz p221

Cádiz p219

OTHER MAPS
Andalucía (Colour Country Map)
between 16 & 17
Approaches To Andalucía   p134

Introduction

Andalucía – the south of Spain, barely a stone's throw from Africa – has fascinated foreign travellers since the early 19th century when Romantic voyagers and writers were captivated by its people's love of colour, music and *fiesta*; by its state of picturesque decay from an exotic, often splendid past; by the dramatic mountains and the southern heat; and by the unique flamenco music and dance of the Gypsies.

Much of what gripped those early travellers lives on in Andalucía today. Though the region has known some very hard times within living memory, its poverty is now greatly diminished, many of its superb monuments have been rescued from decay and modern life has arrived with a bump. Yet Andalucians remain gregarious, relaxed and in love with life, and time is a much more flexible concept than in most Western cultures. Andalucía's multitudinous fiestas are always full-blooded affairs, full of colour, noise and spectacle – whether it's the relatively solemn processions of Semana Santa (Holy Week) or the unadulterated hedonism of night-long music, dancing and drinking at summer *ferias*.

The Islamic civilisation that swept the Iberian Peninsula in the 8th century flourished longest (until 1492) in this area and Andalucía is perhaps the least European part of western Europe. The Muslim era has left behind magnificent and famous buildings such as the Alhambra palace in Granada and the great Mezquita in Córdoba. It has also left a deep imprint on the landscape, the townscapes, the people and even the food of modern Andalucía. Flamenco, the music which says 'Spain' to the outside world but which is Andalucía's own, has clear Islamic roots, too, though it was only developed later as flamenco *per se* by the Gypsies. The guitar, another Andalucian invention, also has its origin in Islamic times.

The more recent Christian centuries have given Andalucía a great deal of its fascinat-

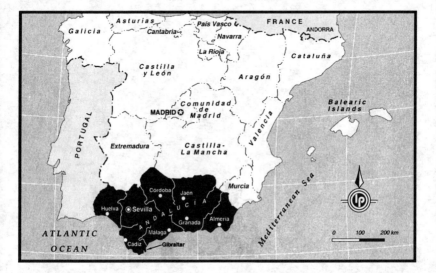

ing folklore and a superb legacy of Gothic, Renaissance and baroque architecture. The great artists Velázquez, Murillo and Picasso all came from Andalucía, as did the great Spanish writer Federico García Lorca and Spain's most celebrated composer, Manuel de Falla. In the 18th century Andalucía was one of the birthplaces of the quintessential Spanish activity of bullfighting, which continues to thrive there today.

Sevilla, Granada, Málaga, Córdoba and Cádiz are cities with a fascinating heritage of history, art and architecture. They also provide vibrant entertainment which often kicks on until dawn. A great start to a night out is to do the rounds of a few bars to sample the varied, often delicious snacks known as *tapas*. An excellent accompaniment to many tapas is sherry, which is produced only in Andalucía.

The region's climate – sizzling in July and August, temperate in winter – is another reason for its appeal. The potent combination of sun, sea and sand has turned the Costa del Sol, west of Málaga, into one of the world's most densely developed package tour destinations. Yet, you'll be delighted to discover, other stretches of the Andalucían coast such as Cabo de Gata in the east and the Atlantic Costa de la Luz in the west have better beaches and far fewer people.

Outside the towns and cities and away from the beaches, much of Andalucía is rugged mountain chains and picturesque white villages where time has ambled along for centuries. From the old-fashioned villages of the rolling Sierra Morena in the north-west to the mysterious, timeless Las Alpujarras valleys in the south-east, from the green, damp Sierra de Grazalema in the south-west to the rocky crags of beautiful Parque Natural de Cazorla in the north-east, you'll find a wealth of excellent walking routes and a profusion of flora and fauna. Seventeen per cent of the region is now under environmental protection. Perhaps most famous of the protected areas is the Parque Nacional de Doñana in the delta of the Río Guadalquivir, a vital refuge for hundreds of thousands of migratory birds and other wildlife.

Almost anywhere you go in Andalucía, fascinating surprises await. And the more you explore it, the deeper its fascination grows.

Facts about Andalucía

HISTORY

Andalucía is situated at the point where the Mediterranean Sea meets the Atlantic Ocean and Europe gives way to Africa. From prehistoric times to the 17th century, this critical location put Andalucía at the forefront of Spanish history – and at times made it a mover of European and even world history. Then Andalucía became a backwater, a condition from which it has only begun to emerge since the 1960s, with its leading place in Spain's tourism industry and the prominent role played by Andalucians in national politics after the Franco dictatorship.

In the Beginning

A bone fragment, perhaps 1.5 million years old, found a few years ago near Orce in Granada province, could be the oldest known human remains in Europe. It is believed to be from the skull of an infant *Homo erectus* – an ancestor of modern *Homo sapiens*. This and other finds in Spain have caused anthropologists to believe the first Europeans came directly from Africa, instead of via Asia as had long been supposed.

From the much later Neanderthal era comes 'Gibraltar Woman', a skull dating from about 50,000 BC, found in 1848. Neanderthals, a now extinct branch of Homo sapiens, were displaced from about 40,000 BC, during the last Ice Age, by the Cro-Magnons, the first real modern humans, who may also have been of African origin.

The Palaeolithic or Old Stone Age, which lasted beyond the end of the Ice Age to about 8000 BC, was somewhat less cold in Andalucía than in more northerly European regions. This enabled thick forests and varied fauna to develop – which in turn allowed hunter-gatherer humans to live here in reasonable numbers. There are plenty of traces of their presence, notably some impressive rock paintings and carvings (see Arts in this chapter).

The Neolithic or New Stone Age reached eastern Spain from Egypt and Mesopotamia in about 6000 BC, bringing a host of innovations such as the plough, crops, livestock raising, pottery, textiles and permanent villages. Some time between 3000 and 2000 BC, what was probably Spain's first metalworking culture arose at Los Millares near Almería. The Los Millares people's ability to smelt and shape local copper deposits was a big breakthrough in agricultural and military terms. This copper or chalcolithic age also saw the arrival in Andalucía of the Megalithic culture, when some people built tombs of large rocks, known as dolmens. Spain's best dolmens are near Antequera, in Málaga province.

The next big technological advance was bronze – an alloy of copper and tin, stronger than copper. In about 1900 BC, El Argar, near Antas in Almería province, became probably the first Bronze Age settlement in the Iberian Peninsula. Between 1700 and 1200 BC bronze technology spread throughout Andalucía.

Tartessos

By about 1000 BC, a flourishing culture had arisen in western Andalucía around the lower Guadalquivir valley, which had agricultural wealth, an abundance of animals and valuable metals, especially in the Sierra Morena. The development of this culture was much influenced by Phoenician and, later, Greek traders, who brought oils, textiles, jewels and ivory to exchange for copper, silver and tin. Both these peoples, but especially the Phoenicians, who were largely from Tyre and Sidon in present-day Lebanon, set up permanent trading colonies. Phoenician colonies included Cádiz (which they called Gadir), Huelva (Onuba), Málaga (Malaca) and Almuñécar (Sexi). Cádiz, believed to have been founded in 1100 BC, may be the oldest city in Europe.

The Phoenicians and Greeks brought to Andalucía the potter's wheel, writing, the olive tree, the vine and domestic animals like the donkey and hen. Around 700 BC, in the lower Guadalquivir valley, iron replaced bronze, methods of working gold improved and a new religion arose. This Phoenician-influenced culture was very likely the fabled Tartessos, mythologised by Greek, Roman and biblical writers as a place of unimaginable wealth. Some believe that the vanished city or state of Tartessos may lie beneath the marshes near the mouth of the Río Guadalquivir. Others even equate it with the lost continent of Atlantis.

Iberians

From about the 6th century BC the Phoenicians and Greeks were pushed out of the western Mediterranean by Carthage, a former Phoenician colony in modern Tunisia which came to dominate the trade and economy of the region. The Phoenician-influenced lower Guadalquivir culture weakened and Iberians from farther north in Spain set up a number of small, often one-village statelets in Andalucía.

Romans

Inevitably the Carthaginians came into conflict with the next rising Mediterranean power – Rome. After losing the First Punic War (264-241 BC), with Rome for control of Sicily, Carthage invaded the Iberian Peninsula. General Hamilcar Barca, who landed at Cádiz in 237 BC, and his successors Hasdrubal and Hannibal succeeded in conquering all of southern Spain and part of the east coast.

The Second Punic War (218-201 BC) not only saw Hannibal march his elephants over the Alps towards Rome but also brought Roman legions to Spain for the first time to open up another theatre of war. Hannibal was eventually forced to retreat and was finally routed by the Roman general Scipio in North Africa in 202 BC. Rome ended Carthaginian ambitions on the Iberian Peninsula with a victory at Ilipa (Alcalá del Río, near Sevilla) in 206 BC. The first Roman town in Spain, Itálica, was founded near the battle site soon afterwards.

Though it took Rome 200 years finally to subdue the rest of the Iberian Peninsula, Andalucía settled quickly into Roman ways and became one of the most civilised and wealthiest areas of the empire outside Italy. Local products such as wheat, vegetables, grapes, olives, copper, silver, lead, fish and garum (a spicy sauce derived from fish and used as a seasoning) were exchanged for luxury goods from Rome. Andalucía gave Rome two emperors – Trajan and Hadrian, both from Itálica.

Initially, Rome divided the Iberian Peninsula (Hispania) into two provinces, Hispania Citerior and Hispania Ulterior, with their capitals at Carthago Nova (Cartagena) and Corduba (Córdoba). In the 1st century BC these were reorganised into three: Baetica, covering most of Andalucía plus southern Extremadura and south-western Castilla-La Mancha, with its capital at Corduba; Lusitania (Portugal and northern Extremadura); and Tarraconensis (the rest including far-eastern Andalucía). The Via Augusta ran from Rome to Gades (Cádiz) passing through Tarraco (Tarragona, Cataluña), Corduba, Astigi (Écija), Carmo (Carmona) and Hispalis (Sevilla).

Rome gave Andalucía and Spain their language (Castillian Spanish is basically colloquial Latin 2000 years on) and the basis of their legal system, plus aqueducts, temples, theatres, amphitheatres, circuses and baths. The Roman era also brought many Jews, who spread throughout the Mediterranean part of the empire. Christianity, which probably came with soldiers from North Africa and merchants in the 3rd century AD, also came with the Romans. It took root in Andalucía – initially among the wealthier urban classes – well before it was established in the rest of Spain and before Emperor Constantine made Christianity the empire's official religion in 313 AD.

Visigoths

By the late 3rd century the Roman empire was weakening and under attack by invaders from northern and eastern Europe. In 324 Constantine made Byzantium (renamed Constantinople) his new capital, and in 395 the empire split into eastern and western halves. When the Huns arrived in eastern Europe from Asia in the late 4th century, displaced Germanic peoples moved west – among them the Suevi and the Vandals, who overran the Iberian Peninsula. The Suevi sacked Sevilla in 409. Another Germanic people, the Visigoths, took Rome in 410. Having spared the Roman emperor, the Visigoths made a pact with him to rid Hispania of other invaders in return for lands in southern Gaul (France). But early in the 6th century yet another Germanic people, the Franks, pushed the Visigoths out of Gaul. The Visigoths then settled on the Iberian Peninsula and Toledo in central Spain became their capital.

The long-haired Visigoths, who numbered about 200,000, had little culture of their own and tended to ape Roman ways. Their rule over the several million relatively sophisticated Hispano-Romans on the peninsula was precarious and was undermined by strife among their own nobility. The Hispano-Roman nobles still ran the fiscal system and their Catholic bishops were the senior figures in urban centres.

In the mid-6th century Emperor Justinian from Constantinople managed to reconquer large parts of the western Roman empire. One of his conquests was a swathe of southern Spain, where he found allies among the Catholic community opposed to the Visigoths' Aryan version of Christianity (which denied that Christ was God). Ties between the Visigoth monarchy and the Hispano-Romans were strengthened in 587 when King Reccared converted to Catholicism. This probably helped the Visigoths expel the Byzantines in 622, but they still had to contend with regular revolts by nobles, bishops and others.

The Muslim Conquest

The Visigoths achieved their success by military superiority. But by 700, with famine and disease in Toledo, strife among the aristocracy and chaos throughout the peninsula, their kingdom was falling apart. This paved the way for the Muslim invasion of 711 which set Spain's destiny quite apart from the rest of Europe.

Following the death of Mohammed in 632, Arabs had spread through the Middle East and North Africa, bringing Islam with them. If you believe the myth, they were finally ushered onto the Iberian Peninsula by the sexual exploits of the last Visigoth king, Roderick. Ballads and chronicles written long after the event relate how Roderick seduced young Florinda, the daughter of Julian, the Visigothic governor of Ceuta in North Africa; and how Julian sought revenge by approaching the Muslims with a plan to invade Spain. In dull fact Julian probably just wanted outside help in a struggle for the Visigothic throne.

In 711 Musa, the Arab governor of northwestern Africa, ordered the governor of Tangier, Tariq ibn Ziyad, across the Strait of Gibraltar. Tariq landed at Gibraltar with around 10,000 men, mostly Berbers (indigenous North Africans). He had some of Roderick's Visigoth rivals as allies. In the same or the following year, probably near the Río Guadalete in Cádiz province, Roderick's army was decimated and he is thought to have drowned as he fled. Visigothic survivors fled north.

Within a few years the Muslims had taken over the rest of the Iberian Peninsula except for small areas in the Asturian mountains in the far north. In many places they were welcomed by Jews and slaves, who had been badly treated under Visigothic rule.

Al-Andalus

The Muslims (often referred to as Moors) were to remain the dominant force on the Iberian Peninsula for nearly four centuries, a potent force for 170 years after that and a lesser one for a further 250 years. Between wars and rebellions, the Muslim areas of the peninsula developed the most cultured society of medieval Europe. The name given to the Muslim territories, Al-Andalus, lives on in the modern name of what was always the Muslim heartland – Andalucía.

Al-Andalus' frontiers were constantly shifting, in a generally southward direction, as the Christians strove to regain territory in the stuttering 800-year Reconquista (Reconquest). But up to the mid-11th century the frontier lay across the north of the Iberian Peninsula, roughly in a line from just south of Barcelona to northern Portugal, with a protrusion up to the central Pyrenees. North of this frontier, a number of small Christian states developed in the north-east and from the initial Visigothic redoubt in Asturias, but they were too weak and prone to internal squabbling to pose a major threat to Al-Andalus for 350 years. Early Christian advances were mainly spearheaded by the kingdom of León.

Al-Andalus also suffered its share of internal conflicts and at times quarrelling Muslims and Christians even struck up alliances against their own kind. Muslim political power and cultural developments centred initially on Córdoba (756-1031), then Sevilla (c1040-1248) and lastly Granada (1248-1492). In these cities the Muslims built beautiful palaces, mosques and gardens, established large, bustling markets *(zocos)* and opened universities. Sticklers for cleanliness, the Muslims built numerous public bathhouses, which most people attended about once a week. A typical bathhouse had masseurs, barbers, and rooms with cold, temperate and hot water.

The Muslims in Spain were great imitators rather than innovators but they imbued their art, architecture and environment with their own style and sensuous nature. They built on the Hispano-Roman agricultural base by improving irrigation and introducing new fruits and crops (oranges, lemons, peaches, sugar cane, rice and more).

Though military raids and campaigns against the northern Christians could be bloodthirsty affairs, Al-Andalus' rulers allowed freedom of worship to Jews and Christians under their rule. Jews, on the whole, flourished, but Christians in Muslim territory (*mozárabes* or Mozarabs) had to pay a special tax, so most either converted to Islam (to be known as *muladíes* or muwallads) or left for the Christian north.

The Muslim settlers themselves were not homogeneous: beneath the Arab ruling class – itself composed of various groups prone to factional friction – was a larger group of Berbers who mainly held second-rank positions and settled on second-grade land. Tension between these two groups broke into Berber rebellion on numerous occasions.

The Arabs and Berbers don't seem to have brought many women with them and, before long, Muslim and local blood merged. This applied as much to the rulers as to the ruled, for as well as the acquisition of women for royal harems, there was frequent intermarriage with the Christian royalty and aristocracy of the north – for tribute, appeasement or even alliance.

Cordoban Emirate (c 756-929) Initially, Muslim Spain was a province of the Emirate of Ifriqiya (North Africa), part of the Caliphate of Damascus which ruled the Muslim world. In 750 the Omayyad caliphal dynasty was overthrown by a rival clan, the Abbasids, who soon shifted the caliphate to Baghdad. One Omayyad, however, escaped the slaughter and somehow made his way to Córdoba, where in 756 he managed to set himself up as an independent emir, Abd ar-Rahman I. It was he who began the construction of the Córdoba Mezquita (mosque), one of the world's greatest Muslim monuments.

Most of Al-Andalus was more or less unified under Cordoban rule for long periods, though the rulers had to fight to stay in charge. Muslim leaders near Christian frontiers often resisted central Cordoban authority, but some of the most prolonged resistance came from closer to home in the shape of Omar ibn Hafsun, a muwallad from near Ronda in Málaga province, who turned to banditry. From a hill-top hideout at Bobastro (Málaga province), ibn Hafsun quickly gained followers and popular support – partly, it's said, because he defended the peasants against taxes and forced labour – and at one stage controlled territory from Cartagena to the Strait of Gibraltar. His rebellion was carried on by his sons for 10 years after his death in 917.

Cordoban Caliphate (929-1031) The ruler who finally subdued Bobastro was Abd ar-Rahman III (912-61). In 929 he bestowed on himself the title caliph to assert his religious authority in the face of a new heterodox Muslim state in Tunisia, ruled by the Shiite Fatimids. Thus he launched what is called the Caliphate of Córdoba (929-1031), during which Al-Andalus reached its peak of power and lustre. Córdoba's population at this time has been estimated at between 100,000 and 500,000, but even at the lowest of those figures it was easily the biggest – and most dazzling and cultured – city in western Europe, thriving on agriculture and the work of its skilled artisans. Astronomy, medicine, mathematics, philosophy, history and botany flourished, and one of the greatest Muslim libraries was established in the city.

Abd ar-Rahman III's court was frequented by Jewish, Arab and Christian scholars and even Christians from northern Spain came to be treated by its renowned medical practitioners. Cordoban learning considerably influenced later Christian Europe. Abd ar-Rahman III built himself a fabulous new palace and centre of government outside the city, the Medina Azahara, which was said by one (imaginative) chronicler to have had fishponds so big that the fish ate 12,000 loaves of bread a day.

Later in the 10th century the fearsome Cordoban general Al-Mansour (or Almanzor) terrorised the Christian north with 50-odd forays in 20 years. In 997 he destroyed the cathedral at Santiago de Compostela in north-west Spain – home of the cult of Santiago Matamoros (St James the Moor-Slayer) which was a crucial inspiration to Christian warriors – and forced Christian slaves to carry its doors and bells to Córdoba, where they were incorporated into the great mosque. Al-Mansour even conquered Morocco and, though not caliph, effectively ruled Al-Andalus. But after the death of his son Abd al-Malik in 1008, rival claimants to the caliphate, one supported by Berber troops, the other by Christian allies from Cataluña, indulged in a devastating civil war. In 1031 the caliphate finally broke up into dozens of *taifas* (small kingdoms) ruled by whoever was strongest.

Rise of Sevilla Such was the disintegration that for Andalucía alone the list of main taifas comes to 12: Granada, Carmona, Morón, Arcos, Ronda, Algeciras, Málaga, Sevilla, Huelva, Niebla, Córdoba and Almería. The first seven of those were set up by Berber generals; Granada and Sevilla were the strongest.

In Sevilla the new Abbadid dynasty, prospering from the trading and agricultural wealth of the lower Guadalquivir valley, was soon able to start absorbing other taifas – by a variety of means including the suffocation of the rulers of Morón, Arcos and Ronda in the bathhouse of the Sevilla Alcázar. By 1078, Sevilla controlled the south of the Iberian Peninsula from southern Portugal to Murcia, returning a large measure of peace and prosperity to Andalucía. The Abbadids patronised the arts – Al-Mutadid (1042-69) and Al-Mutamid (1069-91) were both poets – and presided over a languid, hedonistic court in the Alcázar.

Almoravids Meanwhile, the small Christian states of the north were getting themselves into more threatening shape. Castilla, originally a small principality in eastern León, emerged in its own right as the dominant force. When Toledo fell to Alfonso VI of Castilla in 1085, Al-Mutamid asked the Almoravids, a fanatical Muslim sect of Saharan Berbers who had conquered Morocco, for help against the growing Christian threat. The Almoravids came, defeated Alfonso at Sagrajas (Extremadura) in 1086, and went back to Morocco. They then returned in 1091 to help themselves to Al-Andalus too.

The harsh, unsophisticated Almoravids, aghast at what they saw as the decadence of Al-Andalus, persecuted Jews and Christians (many fled north into Christian territory), unified Al-Andalus and ruled it from Marrakesh as a colony. But their grip eventually weakened, partly, it seems, because the charms of Al-Andalus relaxed their austerity. A wave of revolts spread across Al-Andalus from 1143 and within a few years it was again split up into taifas.

Almohads A new strict Muslim Berber sect, the Almohads from the Atlas Mountains, displaced the Almoravids in Morocco then started nibbling at Al-Andalus – as, too, did the Christians, who had been spurred to a more aggressive crusading posture by the Almoravids' intransigence. Portugal, an emerging western Christian kingdom, took Lisbon in 1147. Alfonso VII of Castilla and León briefly took Córdoba in 1146 and Almería in 1157, but quickly lost them both to the Almohads, who launched a full-scale invasion of Al-Andalus in 1160. They had it under full control by 1173, but what they ruled was considerably less than the Al-Andalus of its 10th century heyday: its frontier ran roughly from south of Lisbon to north of Valencia.

The Almohads made Sevilla capital of their whole realm (which included Algeria, Tunisia and Morocco) and revived arts and learning, glorifying Sevilla with a big new mosque. King Yousouf Yacoub al-Mansour thrashed Castilla's army at Alarcos, south of Toledo, in 1195.

This defeat united most of the Iberian peninsula's increasingly strong but hitherto divided Christian states. The pope called an international crusade, embracing the cult of Santiago Matamoros, and in 1212 the combined armies of three Christian states (Castilla, Aragón-Cataluña and Navarra) routed a large Almohad force at Las Navas de Tolosa in north-eastern Andalucía. This was the beginning of the end for Al-Andalus.

When, after 1224, the Almohad state cracked over a succession dispute, the Christians took full advantage. Castilla's Fernando III (El Santo, the Saint) took the strategic town of Baeza in north-eastern Andalucía in 1227. León took the key towns of Extremadura in 1229 and 1230; Aragón-Cataluña took the Valencia region in the 1230s. Fernando III took Córdoba easily in 1236, triumphantly returning to Santiago de Compostela the bells taken by Al-Mansour in 997.

Fernando won Jaén after a six-month siege in 1246 by agreeing to respect the frontiers of the Muslim Emirate of Granada, a wedge of territory from the Strait of Gibraltar to east of Almería which had been carved out of the disintegrating Almohad realm by a certain Mohammed ibn Yousouf ibn Nasr (also called Mohammed al-Ahmar). Ibn Nasr agreed to pay half his annual income in tribute to Castilla and sent a troop of cavalry to join Fernando's attack on Sevilla, which fell, after a two-year siege, in 1248.

Nasrid Emirate of Granada Portugal's defeat of the Muslims in 1249 left the state of Granada, known as the Nasrid emirate (or kingdom) after ibn Nasr, as the only Muslim state on the Iberian Peninsula. It comprised roughly the modern provinces of Granada, Málaga and Almería, plus bordering bits of Cádiz, Sevilla, Córdoba and Jaén, and had a population of about 300,000, of whom some 50,000 were in Granada itself.

The Nasrids ruled the emirate from Granada's lavish Alhambra palace. The city was the venue for the final flowering in Spain of the Muslim culture and the state prospered with the influx of refugees from conquered Muslim lands. In between outbreaks of fighting, Granada traded with Christian Spain, exporting silk, dried fruits, sugar and spices, and buying salt, oil and other staples. It reached its peak in the 14th century under Yousouf I and Mohammed V, both of whom contributed to the splendours of the Alhambra.

Castilian armies eventually started nibbling at the emirate in the 15th century. Granada's final downfall was precipitated

DAVID WATERMAN

DAVID WATERMAN

GERRY REILLY

GERRY REILLY

GERRY REILLY

BETHUNE CARMICHAEL

Andalucía's many fiestas are celebrated with colour, noise and spectacle, whether they involve solemn processions at religous festivals like Easter Sunday (middle left) or **Corpus Christi** (bottom right) or music, dancing and drinking parties of hot summer days and nights such as the **Feria de Málaga** (top), the feria in Nerja (middle-right and bottom left).

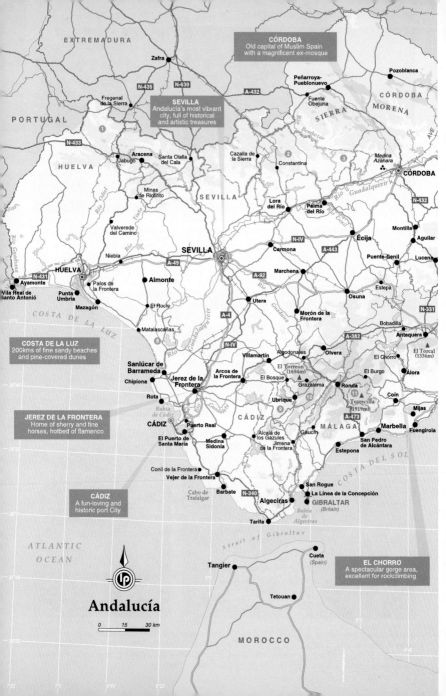

EXTREMADURA

CÓRDOBA
Old capital of Muslim Spain
with a magnificent ex-mosque

Zafra

Pozoblanca

N-435 N-630

Peñarroya-
Pueblonuevo

CÓRDOBA

SEVILLA
Andalucía's most vibrant
city, full of historical
and artistic treasures

Fregenal
de la Sierra

Fuente
Obejuna

SIERRA

MORENA

PORTUGAL

N-433

Aracena
Jabugo

Santa Olalla
del Cala

Cazalla de
la Sierra

Constantina

Medina
Azahara

CÓRDOBA

HUELVA

Minas
de Riotinto

SEVILLA

Lora
del Río

Palma
del Río

N-432

Montilla

Valverde
del Camino

Écija

Aguilar

N-IV

Lucena

Río Guadalquivir

Niebla

SEVILLA

A-49

Carmona

A-443

Puente-Genil

HUELVA

N-431

Palos de
la Frontera

Almonte

A-92

Marchena

Osuna

Estepa

Ayamonte

Punta
Umbría

El Rocío

Utera

Bobadilla

Vila Real de
santo Antonió

Mazagón

Morón de la
Frontera

Antequera

N-331

COSTA DE LA LUZ

Matalascañas

A-4

A-382

El Torcal
(1336m)

COSTA DE LA LUZ
200kms of fine sandy beaches
and pine-covered dunes

N-IV

Villamartín

Algodonales

Olvera

El Chorro

Río Guadalquivir

Sanlúcar de
Barrameda

Arcos de
la Frontera

El Torreón
(1654m)

Grazalema

El Burgo

Álora

Chipiona

Jerez de la
Frontera

El Bosque

Ronda

Coín

Rota

Ubrique

Torrecilla
(1919m)

Mijas

JEREZ DE LA FRONTERA
Home of sherry and fine
horses, hotbed of flamenco

Bahía
de Cádiz

CÁDIZ

A-473

Marbella

Fuengirola

CÁDIZ

Puerto Real

MÁLAGA

Gaucín

San Pedro
de Alcántara

El Puerto de
Santa María

Medina
Sidonia

Alcalá de
los Gazules

Jimena
de la Frontera

Estepona

Conil de la Frontera

Vejer de la Frontera

CÁDIZ
A fun-loving and
historic port City

Cabo de
Trafalgar

Barbate

N-340

San Roque

La Línea de la Concepción

Algeciras

GIBRALTAR
(Britain)

Tarifa

Bahía
de
Algeciras

COSTA DEL SOL

ATLANTIC
OCEAN

Strait of Gibraltar

Cueta
(Spain)

EL CHORRO
A spectacular gorge area,
excellent for rockclimbing

Tangier

Andalucía

Tetouan

0   15   30 km

MOROCCO

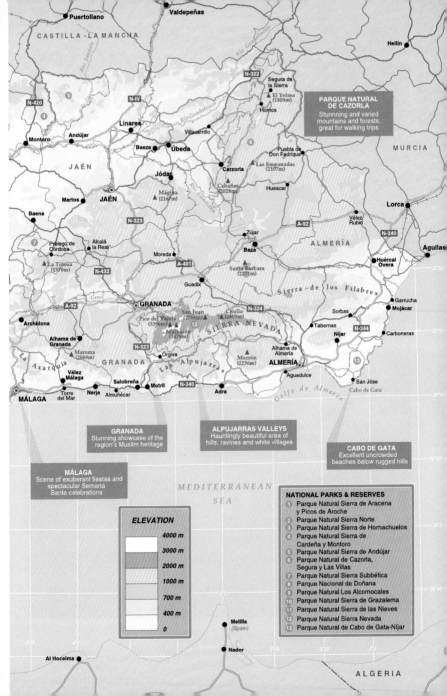

GERRY REILLY

White village of La Axarquía

by Emir Abu al-Hasan's refusal in 1476 to pay any more tribute to Castilla, and by the unification in 1479 of Castilla and Aragón-Cataluña, the peninsula's biggest and most powerful Christian states, after the marriage of their monarchs Isabel and Fernando. Known as the Reyes Católicos (Catholic Monarchs), Isabel and Fernando launched the final crusade of the Reconquista in 1482.

By now Granada's rulers had retreated to a pleasure-loving existence in the Alhambra and were riven by harem jealousies and other feuds. Matters degenerated into a confused civil war and the Christians took full advantage, pushing across the emirate, besieging towns and devastating the countryside. They captured Alhama de Granada in 1482, then Málaga (whose people were mostly sold as slaves) in 1487. Fernando and Isabel finally entered Granada, after an eight-month siege, on 2 January 1492.

The surrender terms were fairly generous to Boabdil, the last emir, who got 30,000 gold coins and the Alpujarras valleys as a personal fiefdom. He stayed there only a year, however, before leaving for Africa. The Muslims were promised respect for their religion, culture and property, but this didn't last long.

Christian Andalucía

Many Muslims fled to Granada or even North Africa from those parts of Andalucía that were conquered by the Christians in the 13th century. The new rulers gave small-holdings to Christian settlers in an attempt to repopulate the countryside. They also handed out large tracts to the nobility and to the knightly crusading orders – such as the Orden de Santiago (Order of Santiago) and Orden de Calatrava – who had played a part in the Reconquista. This was the origin of the *latifundia* (large estates) which have been a problematical feature of rural Andalucía ever since. Muslim raids from Granada often made the lesser settlers flee or sell their lands to the nobility and orders, whose landholdings thus increased. By 1300 rural Christian Andalucía was almost

The Muslim Legacy

The Muslims left a deep imprint on Andalucía – and not just because of the palaces, castles, mosques and bathhouses which rank among the greatest monuments today. Many Spaniards are, through medieval interbreeding, partly descended from the Muslims.

The typical narrow, labyrinthine street plan of Andalucian villages and towns is of Muslim origin, as is the taste for fountains, running water and the use of plants as decoration. Muslim crafts and architectural tastes were adopted by Christians both inside and outside Al-Andalus and many of these techniques and motifs remain in use today. Flamenco song, though brought to its modern form by Gypsies in post-Muslim times, has pretty clear Islamic roots. The Spanish language contains numerous words of Arabic origin – including *arroz* (rice); *alcalde* (mayor); *naranja* (orange); *azúcar* (sugar). Many of the foods eaten in Andalucía today were introduced by the Muslims, and in many places the irrigation and terracing systems on which foods are grown date back to Muslim times. Many Andalucian churches are converted mosques.

It was through Al-Andalus that much of the learning of ancient Greece was transmitted to Christian Europe. The Arabs, in the course of their conquests in the eastern Mediterranean, had absorbed the Greek scientific and philosophical traditions, translating classical works into Arabic and refining and enlarging such sciences as astronomy and medicine. There were two meeting points in southern Europe between the Islamic and Christian worlds where this knowledge could find its way north – one was southern Italy, the other was Al-Andalus.

empty. The landowners turned much of it over to sheep, ruining formerly productive food-growing land.

Fernando III's son Alfonso X (El Sabio, The Learned, 1252-84) made Sevilla one of his capitals and launched something of a cultural revival, gathering around him scholars, particularly Jews, who knew Arabic and Latin and could translate ancient texts into Castilian Spanish. By the 14th century Sevilla was the most important Castilian city.

Initially, those Muslims who stayed on in Christian territory – known as *mudéjares* – faced no reprisals. But in 1264 the mudéjares of Jerez rose up against new taxes and rules that required them to celebrate Christian feasts and live in ghettoes. After a five-month siege they were expelled to Granada or North Africa, along with the mudéjares of Sevilla, Córdoba and Arcos.

Alfonso was plagued by further uprisings and plots, even from within his own family. This unrest continued in Castilla until the 15th century, with the nobility, rich from wool production on their huge estates, repeatedly challenging the crown. This was also an era of growing intolerance towards the Jews and foreigners – especially Genoese – who were taking over Castilian commerce and finance while the Castilians were preoccupied with their low-effort, high-profit wool production.

The Black Death and a series of bad harvests ravaged the population of Christian Andalucía in the 14th century. Discontent eventually found its scapegoat in the Jews – resented for their involvement in tax collecting and money lending – who were subjected to pogroms around the peninsula in the 1390s. As a result, some Jews converted to Christianity (they became known as *conversos*); others moved to Granada.

The Catholic Monarchs

The pious Isabel and Machiavellian Fernando were an unbeatable team. The war against Granada was just one of several steps they took to cement their subjects' loyalty. They checked the power of the Castilian nobility, granting Andalucian land to their supporters and excluding aristocrats from the royal administration. They also reformed a corrupt clergy. By the time Fernando died in 1516 (12 years after Isabel – they are both buried in Granada) Spain had been united under a single rule for the first time since Visigothic days.

Jews & the Inquisition The urge for unity was not just territorial. The Catholic Monarchs revived the almost extinct Inquisition – founded earlier to deal with heretics in France – to root out those who didn't practise Christianity as the Catholic church wished them to. The Spanish Inquisition focused most of all on conversos, accusing many of continuing to practise Judaism in secret. Despite Fernando's part-Jewish background and Jewish loans for the Granada war, Jews were considered Muslim allies. The Inquisition's first tribunal was held in Sevilla in 1481. In its three centuries of existence, the Inquisition was responsible for perhaps 12,000 deaths, 2000 of them in the 1480s.

Under the influence of Grand Inquisitor Tomás de Torquemada, in 1492 Isabel and Fernando ordered the expulsion from their territories of all Jews who refused Christian baptism. Around 50,000 to 100,000 Jews converted, but some 200,000, the first Sephardic Jews (Jews of Spanish origin), left for other Mediterranean destinations. The bankrupt monarchy seized all unsold Jewish property. A talented urban middle class was decimated.

Persecution of the Muslims Cardinal Cisneros, Isabel's confessor and overseer of the Inquisition, took the spirit of the Reconquista to its logical conclusion by trying to eradicate Muslim culture altogether. Given the task of converting the Muslims of the former Granada emirate, he carried out forced mass baptisms, had Islamic books burnt and banned the Arabic language. This, combined with expropriation of land from Muslims, sparked a revolt in 1500 in the

The first tribunal of the Inquisition, which was responsible for 12,000 deaths, was held in Sevilla in 1481.

Alpujarras valleys south of Granada, which spread right across the former emirate, from Ronda to Almería. Afterwards, Muslims were ordered to convert to Christianity or leave. Most – an estimated 300,000 – underwent baptism and stayed. They became known as Moriscos (converted Muslims), but their conversion was barely skin-deep and they never assimilated.

Sevilla & the Americas
In April 1492 the Catholic Monarchs finally granted the Genoese sailor Christopher Columbus (Cristóbal Colón to Spaniards) funds for his long-desired voyage across the Atlantic in search of a new trade route to the Orient. Isabel and Fernando were motivated by the urgent need to fill their empty coffers and the possibility of more Christian conversions. (For the Christopher Columbus story, see the boxed text in the Huelva Province chapter.)

Columbus' discovery of the Americas opened up a whole new hemisphere of opportunity for Spain, and in particular

Sevilla, the river port where the Casa de la Contratación, a government office controlling commerce with the new colonies, was soon established.

The reign of Carlos I (1516-56), the first of the new Habsburg dynasty, saw Spain take over vast tracts of the American mainland. Ruthless but brilliant conquistadors such as Hernán Cortés, who subdued the Aztec empire with a small band of adventurers in 1519-21, and Francisco Pizarro, who did the same to the Inca empire in 1531-33, were, with their odd mix of brutality, bravery, gold lust and piety, the natural successors to the crusaders of the Reconquista.

The new colonies sent hugely valuable cargoes of silver, gold and other treasure back to Spain, where the crown was entitled to one-fifth of the bullion (the *quinto real* or royal fifth). Sevilla became the hub of world trade and one of Europe's biggest and richest cities, a cosmopolitan melting pot of money seekers, from Dutch and Italian bankers and merchants to card sharps and dice tricksters known as *pícaros*, and beggars. Even though little Madrid was made the national capital in 1561, Sevilla remained Spain's major city until late in the 17th century.

The prosperity was shared to some extent by Cádiz and the lower Guadalquivir area, and less so by cities such as Jaén, Córdoba and Granada. But eastern Andalucía continued to depend on agriculture and artisanry, both of which remained technologically backward. In the countryside, a small number of big landowners did little with large tracts of territory except run sheep on them, while those peasants who still lived off the land lacked any way of improving their lot. Though sherry from Jerez and silk from Granada brought in some export earnings, wool was the only serious export and Spain ran a budget deficit because grain had to be imported.

Sevilla's cosmopolitan status opened up Andalucía to new European ideas and artistic movements. Lavish Renaissance and, later, baroque buildings sprouted and Sevilla was a focus of Spain's artistic golden age. New universities in Sevilla (1505), Granada (1531) and Baeza (1542) spread the humanist ideas of the Renaissance which led to a questioning of Roman Catholic dogma by so-called *protestantes* or *alumbrados* (enlightened ones) in a few centres. But these nascent flickers of Protestantism were soon snuffed out by the Inquisition.

Morisco Revolt & Expulsion

Felipe II (1556-98) was, among other things, a fanatical Catholic who, as well as spurring the Inquisition to renewed persecutions, in 1567 forbade Moriscos (ex-Muslims) to use the Arabic language, Arabic names, Morisco dress and certain Morisco customs. The Moriscos were seen – with good reason – as uncommitted Christians, and were also blamed – again with good reason – for some of the frequent raids on Spanish coasts from North Africa. A Morisco revolt in the Alpujarras, which spread across southern Andalucía and took two years to put down, resulted in the ex-

pulsion of the Moriscos from the rebel areas and Granada to western Andalucía and more northerly parts of Spain. Among other things, this ruined the Granada silk industry which depended on thread produced by the Alpujarras Moriscos. The Moriscos were finally expelled from all of Spain by Felipe III between 1609 and 1614.

Decline

Even under Carlos I, Spain had been spending much of its new wealth from the Americas on an endless series of costly European wars, which wrecked any chance of the country developing into an early industrial power. Much the same situated continued under Felipe II. There was no plan to absorb the new wealth, or to cope with the inflation it caused. The gentry's disdain for commerce and industry allowed Genoese and German merchants to dominate trade, and left the countryside dominated by sheep and cattle ranches, with the nation running a trade deficit because grain had to be imported.

In the 17th century, under the last three ineffectual Habsburg kings, these chickens came home to roost. Spain's European wars continued while silver shipments from the Americas shrank disastrously. In Andalucía, epidemics and runs of bad harvests killed some 300,000 people – including half of Sevilla in 1649. Coming after the expulsions of the Jews and Moriscos, this left Andalucía distinctly underpopulated. The lower Guadalquivir – Sevilla's lifeline to the Atlantic – became increasingly silted up and in 1717 the Casa de la Contratación was transferred to Cádiz.

The gentry and the church – which was entitled to one-tenth of all production – led a comfortable existence, but for other Andalucians life was decidedly underprivileged. Most people had no land or property, and the cities had to pay heavy taxes and send soldiers to fight in the kings' wars.

The 18th Century

Under Spain's new Bourbon dynasty – still in place today – the 18th century was one of limited recovery from the ruin of the 17th. This was the age of the Enlightenment, with its faith in reason, science and social planning. The monarchy financed incipient industries such as Sevilla's tobacco factory. A new road, the Carretera General de Andalucía, was built from Madrid to Sevilla and Cádiz, and along the Andalucía section Carlos III's reforming minister Pablo de Olavide founded a couple of dozen new towns, with straight streets, broad plazas and German and Flemish settlers. The idea was both to repopulate empty and rather lawless areas along the important new road and to modernise Andalucía's underproductive agriculture. Opposed by the big landowners (who didn't like releasing land) and the church (because many of the settlers were Protestants), the project had little effect.

New land was opened up for wheat and barley, however, and trade through Cádiz (whose glorious century this was) grew. Free trade decrees in 1765 and 1778 also made it legal, for the first time, for other Spanish ports to carry on commerce with the Americas, which stimulated the growth of Málaga. New settlers came to Andalucía from other parts of Spain and by 1787 the region had a population of about 1.8 million.

Napoleonic Invasion & the Cádiz Cortes

When Louis XVI of France (a cousin of Spain's Carlos IV) was guillotined in 1793, Spain declared war on France. Two years later, with French forces occupying northern Spain, Spain switched sides, pledging military support for France against Britain in return for French withdrawal from Spain. In 1805 a combined Spanish-French navy was beaten by the British fleet under Nelson off Cape Trafalgar (between Cádiz and Gibraltar). This put an end to Spanish sea power.

Two years later, Napoleon Bonaparte and Spain agreed to divide Britain's ally Portugal between them. French forces poured into Spain, supposedly on the way to northern Portugal. By 1808 this had become a French occupation of Spain, with Napoleon forcing Carlos IV to abdicate to his brother Joseph Bonaparte (José I). In what is known

as the Spanish War of Independence, or Peninsular War, the Spanish populace took up arms against the French in guerrilla fashion, with help from British and Portuguese forces led by the Duke of Wellington. The French were eventually driven out in 1813.

During the war, few Spanish cities kept the French at bay, but Cádiz withstood a two-year siege from 1810 to 1812. A national *cortes* (parliament) convened in the city, a strongly liberal gathering which included many politically progressive refugees from other parts of the country. In 1812 the Cádiz Cortes adopted a new liberal constitution for Spain which proclaimed sovereignty of the people and reduced the rights of the monarchy, nobility and church.

Liberals v Conservatives

The Cádiz constitution set the scene for a century of struggle between Spanish liberals, who wanted vaguely democratic reforms, and conservatives who wanted to maintain the status quo.

Fernando VII, son of Carlos IV, quickly revoked the new constitution, persecuted opponents and re-established the Inquisition. In 1820 in Las Cabezas de San Juan, Sevilla province, Colonel Rafael de Riego made the first of the 19th century's many *pronunciamientos* (pronouncements of military rebellion in the name of liberalism. But French troops put Fernando back on the throne in 1823 (Riego was captured in Jaén and taken to Madrid to be hung, drawn and quartered).

Meanwhile, the American colonies had taken advantage of Spain's internal problems to strike out on their own. Mexico and most of South and Central America achieved independence from Spain between 1813 and 1825. This was desperate news for Cádiz, which had been totally reliant on trade with the colonies.

The Disamortisations of 1836 and 1855, when liberal governments ordered church and municipal lands to be auctioned off in an attempt to reduce the national debt, pleased the bourgeoisie, who could now build up new latifundia. But they were a disaster for the peasants who were deprived of municipal grazing lands. Andalucía's large numbers of *jornaleros* – landless agricultural day labourers – hardly had the money to keep their families alive, let alone enough to buy land.

With a quarter of Spain's population of 12 million in 1877, Andalucía declined into one of Europe's most backward areas. Its society was largely polarised between, at one extreme, the very rich, often absentee noble landowners and the bourgeoisie, and at the other extreme, a small number of poor people with regular jobs and a large number of even poorer jornaleros, who were without work for a good half of the year and who, with their families, probably comprised three-quarters of the population.

The Industrial Revolution, which reached northern Spain in the late 18th century, didn't touch the south. Agriculture remained primitive (the Roman model of plough was still in use) and was still largely dependent on the traditional vine, olive and wheat, or else the land was given over to sheep or cattle or stood idle. Illiteracy, disease and hunger were rife. The few successful industries – such as the Río Tinto mines and the Jerez and Málaga wineries – owed a lot to British investment and management.

In 1873 a liberal government proclaimed Spain a federal republic of 17 states. But this First Republic was riven by internal divisions and totally unable to keep a grip on the provinces, where numerous cities and towns declared themselves independent states. Some even declared war on each other, as happened between Sevilla and nearby Útrera. Not surprisingly, the First Republic lasted only 11 months, with the army restoring the monarchy.

Social Unrest

In the face of lost grazing lands, erratic, miserably paid work and constant hunger, some Andalucian peasants emigrated to Latin America. Others staged uprisings, always savagely put down, from the mid-19th century on. The anarchist ideas of the Russian Mikhail Bakunin, which reached

Spain in the late 1860s, gained a big following in Andalucía, especially in the lower Guadalquivir area where the *latifundistas'* monopoly on cultivable land was most complete. Bakunin advocated replacing the state and church with a free society in which autonomous groups of people would voluntarily cooperate with each other – a state of affairs to be prepared for by strikes, sabotage and revolts, and ultimately achieved by a spontaneous, angry revolution of the oppressed.

It was in Sevilla that the powerful anarchist union, the CNT (Confederación Nacional del Trabajo, National Confederation of Labour), was founded in 1910. Anarchist trade unionists, known as syndicalists, saw unionism as the means to achieve an anarchist society, the main weapon being the general strike. But major anarchist actions in Andalucía, such as the occupation of Jerez by 4000 labourers armed with sticks one day in 1891, brought little but violent repression which sent the movement back underground for years at a time. Waves of anarchist strikes occurred in 1902-05 and 1917-18.

Socialism, with its aim of steady change through parliamentary processes, won less support in Andalucía. By 1919 the CNT had 93,000 members in Andalucía (nearly all in the west and Málaga), compared with the socialist UGT's 12,000, and 7000 in Catholic unions. In 1923 an eccentric general from Jerez de la Frontera, Miguel Primo de Rivera, launched a mild six-year military dictatorship. Primo kept a lid on worker discontent by gaining the cooperation of the UGT, while anarchists went underground. Primo's achievements included more industrialisation, better roads, punctual trains, new dams and power plants. He was unseated by an economic downturn following the Wall Street crash and by discontent in the army, with King Alfonso XIII taking the chance to dismiss him.

The Second Republic

When a new republican movement scored sweeping victories in the municipal elections around Spain in April 1931, Alfonso

XIII departed to exile in Italy. The Second Republic (1931-36) that ensued was an idealistic, tumultuous, increasingly violent period that ended in civil war.

The Left in Charge (1931-33) La Niña Bonita (the Pretty Child), as the Second Republic was called by its supporters, was welcomed by leftists and the poor masses, but conservatives were alarmed. National elections in 1931 brought in a mixed government of socialists, centrists and republicans, but the Cortes (Parliament) contained few workers – and no-one from the anarchist CNT, which relied on strikes and violence to bring on the revolution.

A new constitution in December 1931 outraged Catholics by ending Catholicism's status as the official religion, stopping government payment of priests' salaries, legalising divorce and banning clerical orders from teaching. The constitution promised land redistribution, which pleased the Andalucian landless, but failed to deliver much.

The Right in Charge (1933-36) Continuing anarchist disruption, an economic slump, the alienation of big business and disunity on the left all helped the right win the 1933 election. A new Catholic party, CEDA, won more seats than any other party. Another new force on the right was the fascist Falange, led by José Antonio Primo de Rivera, son of the 1920s dictator. The Falange practised blatant street violence. The left, including the emerging communists (who, unlike the socialists, supported the Russian Revolution), now called increasingly for revolution.

By 1934 violence on all sides was spiralling out of control. When workers' committees which had taken over the northern mining region of Asturias were viciously quashed by generals Millán Astray and Francisco Franco and the Spanish Foreign Legion (set up to fight Moroccan tribes in the 1920s), the whole country was finally polarised into left and right.

Popular Front & Army Uprising In the February 1936 elections the Popular Front, a left-wing coalition with the communists to the fore, narrowly defeated the right-wing National Front. Violence continued on both sides of the political divide. Extremist groups grew (the CNT now had over a million members), and peasants were on the verge of revolution.

On 17 July 1936 the Spanish garrison in Melilla in North Africa revolted, followed the next day by some garrisons on the mainland. The leaders of the plot were five generals. On 19 July one of them, Francisco Franco, flew from the Canary Islands to Morocco to take command of his legionnaires. The civil war had begun.

The Civil War
The Spanish Civil War split communities, families and friends. Both sides committed atrocious massacres and reprisals, in the early weeks especially, and employed death squads to eliminate members of opposition organisations. The rebels, who called themselves Nationalists, shot or hanged tens of thousands of supporters of the Republic. Republicans did likewise to those they considered to be Franco sympathisers, including some 7000 priests, monks and nuns around the country. Political affiliation often provided a convenient cover for settling old scores. Around 350,000 Spaniards died in the war.

In Republican areas, anarchists, communists or socialists ended up running many towns and cities. Social revolution followed. In Republican parts of Andalucía this generally tended to be anarchist, with private property abolished and churches and convents often burned and wrecked. Large estates were occupied by the peasants, who were fed from the village store according to their needs. Around 100 agrarian communes were set up. The Nationalist campaign quickly took on overtones of a holy crusade against the enemies of God.

Nationalist Advance The basic battle lines were drawn within a week of the rebellion in Morocco. Cities whose garrisons backed the rebels (most did) and were strong enough to overcome any resistance fell into Nationalist hands – as happened at Cádiz, Córdoba, Algeciras and Jerez. Sevilla was in Nationalist hands within three days and Granada within a few more. Hugh Thomas, in his authoritative *The Spanish Civil War,* gives an estimated figure of 4000 people executed by the Nationalists in and around Granada after they had taken the city, saying that this was probably characteristic of Nationalist Spain generally. In Republican areas there was slaughter too. An estimated 2500 people were murdered in a few months in anarchist Málaga. A gang from Málaga killed over 500 in Ronda in the first month of the war. The bishops of Almería and Guadix were forced to wash the deck of a prison ship before being murdered near Málaga.

From Sevilla, Nationalist troops moved out to mop up most of western Andalucía by the end of July and relieved Granada in August. Ronda fell on 16 September. Málaga was taken, with little resistance, by Italian and Spanish Nationalist troops in February 1937. When the Nationalists captured Republican towns they exacted bloody revenge for any supposed atrocities carried out there: thousands were executed after they took Málaga.

After the fall of Málaga there was little shift in the military position in Andalucía for the rest of the war. Communist Almería and its province, socialist Jaén and most of its province, together with the eastern half of Granada province and the north of Córdoba province all remained in Republican hands till the end of the war came in 1939.

Franco's force of legionnaires and Moroccan mercenaries was airlifted from Morocco to Sevilla by German warplanes in August 1936. Essential to the success of the revolt, this force moved north through Extremadura towards Madrid. In October Franco pulled all the Nationalists into line behind him, styling himself Generalísimo (Supreme General). Before long Franco had declared himself head of state and adopted the title *caudillo*, roughly equivalent to the German *Führer*.

Madrid repulsed Franco's first assault in November 1936 then endured, under communist inspiration, more than two years siege.

Foreign Intervention What really tipped the scales in the Nationalists' favour was support from Nazi Germany and Fascist Italy – weapons, planes and men (75,000 from Italy, 17,000 from Germany). These turned the war into a rehearsal for WWII. The Republicans had some Soviet support – planes, tanks, artillery and advisers – but the rest of the international community refused to get involved, though 25,000 or so French, as well as many other foreigners in the International Brigades, fought on the Republican side.

Republican Quarrels The Republican government moved from Madrid to Valencia in late 1936 to continue trying to preside over the diversity of political persuasions on the Republican side – from anarchists and communists to moderate democrats and regional secessionists.

In 1937 Spain's north coast fell to the Nationalists. Republican counterattacks near Madrid and in Aragón failed, and internal Republican tensions erupted into fierce street fighting in Barcelona in May 1937, with the communists – who under Soviet influence were trying to unify the Republican war effort – crushing the anarchists and Trotskyites. The Republican government moved to Barcelona in autumn 1937.

Nationalist Victory In early 1938 Franco swept eastward, isolating Barcelona from Valencia. The Union of Soviet Socialist Republics (USSR) withdrew from the war in September 1938. The Nationalists took Barcelona unopposed in January 1939 and Madrid in March. Franco declared the war over on 1 April.

Franco's Spain (1939-75)
War's Aftermath Instead of reconciliation, more bloodletting ensued. In Spain as a

whole, an estimated 100,000 people were killed, or died in prison, after the war. Spanish communists and Republicans continued their hopeless struggle in small *maquis* guerrilla units in the Andalucian *sierras* and elsewhere up to 1951.

Franco kept Spain out of WWII but his ambiguous stance during the war won him no friends abroad. Spain was excluded from the United Nations and suffered a UN-sponsored trade boycott which helped turn the late 1940s into the *años de hambre* (years of hunger) – particularly hungry in poor areas like Andalucía. In 1953 Franco agreed to the USA's request for four military bases in Spain – including one at Rota near Cádiz – in return for American aid. In 1955 Spain was admitted to the UN.

Dictatorship Franco ruled absolutely. He was commander of the army and leader of the government and the sole political party, the Movimiento Nacional (National Movement), a development of the old fascist Falange. The army provided many ministers and enjoyed a generous budget. Garrisons were maintained outside every large city. The jails were full of political prisoners and Franco controlled parliament and the press. Catholic orthodoxy was fully restored, with most secondary schools entrusted to the Jesuits, divorce made illegal and church weddings made compulsory. Franco won some working-class support with carrots such as paid holidays, job security and social security, but there was no right to strike. Crime was low.

Recovery – of Sorts In the late 1950s a new breed of technocrats in government engineered an economic boom. But despite some new industries and the rapid takeoff of tourism on the Costa del Sol, improvement was a lot less obvious in Andalucía than elsewhere. Many villages still lacked electricity, reliable water supplies and paved roads to the outside world. Between 1950 and 1970 some 1.5 million Andalucians left to find work elsewhere – some going to other European countries, but more to

Barcelona, Madrid and other Spanish cities. They often lived in shantytowns at first.

Tourism enabled Franco to present the outside world with an amiable image of Spain – sun, beaches, flamenco – when the reality remained rather different. Though tourism certainly created jobs for some Andalucians, it also brought culture shock to what was still an old-fashioned, traditional society. John Hooper, in *The New Spaniards,* notes that, according to a study made in 1971, 90% of all non-chronic mental illness in the rural parts of Málaga province was found in teenage males who had worked on the coast.

New Democracy
Franco, who always made out that he was a monarchist at heart, chose as his successor the Spanish-educated Prince Juan Carlos, grandson of Alfonso XIII. Juan Carlos took the throne, aged 37, two days after Franco's death in 1975. Much of the credit for the ensuing transition to democracy goes to the king. He appointed a former Franco apparatchik, Adolfo Suárez, as prime minister. To general surprise, Suárez pushed through the Francoist-filled Cortes a proposal for a new, two-chamber parliamentary system. In early 1977 political parties, trade unions and strikes were all legalised, and the Movimiento Nacional was abolished.

Suárez's centrist party won nearly half the seats in elections to the new Cortes in 1977. The left-of-centre PSOE (Partido Socialista Obrero Español, Spanish Socialist Worker Party), led by a charismatic young lawyer from Sevilla, Felipe González, came in second.

Personal and social life, too, enjoyed a sudden liberation after Franco. Contraceptives, homosexuality, adultery and divorce were legalised, and it was during this era that the *movida* – the late-night bar and disco scene that enables people almost anywhere in Spain to party till dawn or after – emerged.

Government by the PSOE and the PP
In 1982 Spain made a final break with the past by voting the PSOE into power with a big majority. Felipe González was to be

prime minister for 14 years, taking several other Andalucians into high office with him. The PSOE's young, educated leadership came from the generation that had opened the cracks in the Franco regime in the late 1960s and early 70s. It made big improvements in education and launched a national health system. It legalised the use of narcotics in 1983 and abortion in 1985 (though in the face of major drug and alcoholism problems, public use of narcotics was banned in 1992).

In 1986, Spain joined the EC (now the EU), which brought on its second post-civil war economic boom, lasting until 1991, and cut unemployment to 16%. It was around halfway through the boom that the good life began to go a bit sour. The PSOE began to figure in a series of scandals. Questions were asked about how the party got hold of its substantial funds. González's long-standing No 2, another *sevillano* called Alfonso Guerra, resigned as deputy prime minister in 1991 over an affair involving his wheeler-dealer brother's use of a government office. Most damaging was the GAL affair, named after the Grupos Antiterroristas de Liberación, death squads that had murdered over 20 suspected Basque terrorists in the mid-1980s. By 1996 a dozen senior police and PSOE men had been charged in connection with GAL.

In the face of all this and a post-1991 economic slump, the PSOE lost the 1996 general election to the PP (Partido Popular, People's Party), a centre-right party under the leadership of an Elton John fan and former tax inspector, José María Aznar.

Andalucía since Franco The PSOE eradicated the worst of Andalucian poverty with a series of grants and community works schemes and a much more generous dole system. But despite tourism and gradual industrial growth, Andalucía is still economically a long way behind most of Spain.

The 1992 Expo world fair in Sevilla – held the same year as the Barcelona Olympic Games, exactly five centuries on from the pivotal year of Spanish history, 1492 –

brought not only hundreds of thousands of visitors and a big boost to the international image of Sevilla and Andalucía, but also the new superfast AVE (Alta Velocidad Española) rail link from Madrid and a big improvement in Andalucía's roads. Hopes that Expo would somehow spark further economic growth, however, have come to little.

Nevertheless, any Andalucian returning home today after 40 years on Mars would scarcely recognise much. The bright lights and large high-rise public housing blocks in the cities, the transformation of long stretches of formerly useless, barren coast into international honey (and money) pots, the relaxation of old codes of dress and morality, the loud new music, the motorcycles instead of donkeys, the rarity of hunger, youth literacy – all these would startle. Yet not everything would be unfamiliar. Andalucians remain a close-knit bunch, or rather an agglomeration of close-knit bunches, oriented first to their family, second to their *pueblo* (village or town), third to their *comarca* (district), fourth to their province, and then, equally to Andalucía and Spain. They know they have to stick together because the relatively good times have not lasted long enough to obliterate the memory of the bad ones.

GEOGRAPHY

Andalucía stretches 550km from east to west and between 90 and 250km from north to south. Its 87,000 sq km area – about the same size as Portugal – comprises 17% of Spain. The region has 460km of coastline along the Mediterranean Sea, and a 240km seaboard on the Atlantic Ocean. The two meet at the Strait of Gibraltar, where the town of Tarifa, just 15km from Africa, is continental Europe's most southerly point.

Andalucía is divided into eight provinces, all named after their capital cities – from west to east, across the north, Huelva, Sevilla, Córdoba and Jaén, and across the south Cádiz, Málaga, Granada and Almería. The city of Sevilla is the capital of Andalucía and the seat of the regional government.

Andalucía has four main geographic regions, all running roughly east-west across it – the Sierra Morena, the Guadalquivir valley, the mountains, and the coastal plain.

The Sierra Morena

The Sierra Morena, a range of low, mostly rolling hills that rarely top 1000m, stretches across the north of Andalucía, straddling the borders with neighbouring Extremadura and Castilla-La Mancha. The sierra has a few mining towns but most of it is very sparsely populated and divided between evergreen oak woodlands and scrub and rough pasture used for grazing. Different bits of the Sierra Morena have their own names such as the Sierra del Viento in Sevilla province and the Sierra de Aroche and Sierra de Aracena in Huelva province.

Guadalquivir Valley

South of the Sierra Morena is the valley of the 660km Río Guadalquivir, Andalucía's longest river. The Guadalquivir flows roughly westward from Jaén province through Córdoba, then turns south through Sevilla to enter the Atlantic at Sanlúcar de Barrameda. Its valley, the most fertile area in Andalucía, broadens out from east to west and from its lower end a broad plain stretches west across Huelva province and south-east into Cádiz province. Near its mouth, the Guadalquivir splits into a marshy delta known as Las Marismas del Guadalquivir which includes the Parque Nacional de Doñana.

The Guadalquivir used to be navigable from the Atlantic as far upstream as Córdoba (it's still navigable up to Sevilla), and its valley has always been the great artery of Andalucía. The two big cities along it, in the midst of rich agricultural country, have been the main seats of political power in the region since at least Roman times. The name Guadalquivir derives from the Arabic Wadi al-Kabir (Great River): the Romans called it the Betis, and the ancient Greeks the Tartessos.

The plains rolling north and south from the river as far down as Sevilla are known as *La Campiña*. From about Córdoba downstream, the valley is referred to as the lower Guadalquivir basin: this is the territory of the huge estates known as latifundia, which have been the source of some of Andalucía's greatest social problems.

The Mountains

Between the Guadalquivir valley and the Mediterranean coast stretches the Cordillera Bética, a band of rugged mountain ranges. This mountain system widens out from modest beginnings in Cádiz province's Sierra del Aljibe to a breadth of 125km or so in the east. Beyond Andalucía it continues across the Murcia and Valencia regions then dips under the Mediterranean to re-emerge as the Balearic islands of Ibiza and Mallorca.

In Andalucía the mountains divide into two main chains: the more northerly Sistema Subbético and southerly Sistema Penibético. These are separated by a series of valleys, plains and basins such as the Llanos de Antequera, the Vega de Granada, the Hoya de Guadix and the Hoya de Baza.

Each of the two chains is composed of numerous semi-joined ranges. Both emerge from the green, rainy mountains west and south-west of Ronda such as the Sierra de Grazalema and the Sierra del Aljibe. The Sistema Subbético includes the Sierra de Cabra and Sierra de Priego in the south of Córdoba province and the Sierra Mágina in the south of Jaén province (where it first reaches 2000m). In the north-east of Jaén province it turns into the complicated collection of picturesque ranges – here running almost north-south – which make up the Parque Natural de Cazorla, among them the Sierra de Cazorla, Sierra del Pozo and Sierra de Segura. The Río Guadalquivir rises between the Sierra de Cazorla and Sierra del Pozo. South-east of the Parque Natural de Cazorla are sierras such as the Sierra de Castril and Sierra de la Sagra in Granada province, both also topping 2000m.

The Sistema Penibético starts with the

Serranía de Ronda, south and south-east of Ronda. The Serranía de Ronda includes the Sierra de las Nieves and has the Sierra Bermeja and Sierra Blanca, rising behind the Costa del Sol, among its outliers. Eastward, the Sistema Penibético crosses the Sierra de Huma east of the 400m-deep Garganta del Chorro, Andalucía's most awesome gorge, and the weirdly eroded limestone of the Sierra de Chimenea south of Antequera, before topping 2000m at Maroma in the Sierra Tejeda. South-east of Granada city it becomes the 75km-long Sierra Nevada, with a series of peaks including Mulhacén (3478m) which is the highest mountain in mainland Spain. Between the Sierra Nevada and the coast are the lower Sierra de Contraviesa and Sierra de Gádor. Farther north-east are the Sierra de Baza in Granada province, extending into the Sierra de los Filabres in Almería province (both above 2000m) and, in the north of Almería province, the Sierra de las Estancias and Sierra de María.

The Coastal Plain
Andalucía's coastal plain varies in width from 50km in the far west to virtually nothing in parts of Granada and Almería provinces where the Sierra de Contraviesa and Sierra de Cabo de Gata drop away in sheer cliffs to the Mediterranean. Where the plain is wide enough, it supports much productive vegetable and fruit growing.

Along the coast are important ports such as Almería, Málaga, Algeciras, Cádiz and Huelva. Tourist development has turned the 75km Costa del Sol from Málaga to Estepona into one almost continuous developed strip. Elsewhere the coast runs between smaller fishing, farming or resort towns, with – especially around the Cabo de Gata promontory east of Almería and along the Atlantic coast (called the Costa de la Luz) – plenty of fine, long, sandy beaches which for much of the year are distinctly underpopulated. As well as the Marismas del Guadalquivir, further *marismas* (wetlands) mark the mouths of several rivers along the Atlantic coast – among them the

Río Odiel at Huelva and the Río Guadalete flowing into the Bahía (Bay) de Cádiz.

The coastline is curving rather than indented and Algeciras and Cádiz are sited on the only two significantly indented bays.

Desert
Nearly all Andalucía's rivers are dammed at least once in their course to provide the region with water and hydroelectricity, and you'll come across large reservoirs almost throughout the region. The exception is the very dry Almería province which contains extensive semi-desert areas of bare, eroded terrain with enough of a resemblance to the Arizona badlands to have been used as the location of many Western movies!

CLIMATE
There's a marked difference between the climate along the coasts and the inland climate. On the coasts, temperatures are temperate in winter and not quite so hot in summer. Inland, it can be pretty inclement from November to February and baking hot in July and August.

Climatically, the ideal times to visit Andalucía are April to June and September and the first half of October – when temperatures are warm but not too warm, and you'll avoid the winter rains.

In July and August, daytime temperatures typically reach 36°C in Sevilla and Córdoba and only a little less in Granada and Jaén. Along the coasts expect about 30°C. Winter weather (November to February) is unpredictable: several dry, warm winters (and drought) in the early 1990s were followed by much wetter, cooler winters from 1995 to 1998. From December to February, average daytime highs hover round 16°C on the coasts and in Sevilla, and around 13°C in Granada and Jaén. Granada gets close to freezing at night.

Rain falls mainly from October to March (50 to 100mm a month, a similar amount to London). There's little rain anywhere from June to September. With the prevailing winds coming from the Atlantic Ocean,

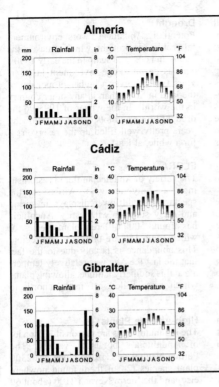

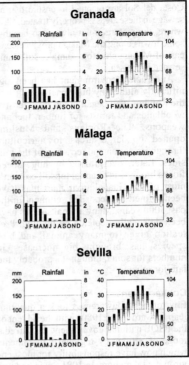

eastern Andalucía is drier than the west. The Sierra de Grazalema west of Ronda is the wettest part of Spain and the town of Grazalema receives over 2200mm of rain a year. The Cabo de Gata promontory in Almería province is the driest place in Europe with just 100mm a year. Tarifa, at Andalucía's southernmost point, where the Atlantic meets the Mediterranean Sea, has strong winds most of the time – a Mecca for windsurfers.

In the mountains, temperatures are always several degrees cooler than down on the plains and you can expect more rain and, in winter, some snow. The Sierra Nevada, above about 3000m, is snow-covered most of the year.

Sea temperatures hover around 20°C along most of the coast from July to

October, and around 15°C from December to April.

ECOLOGY & ENVIRONMENT

Andalucía's relative lack of industry and, until recently, fairly primitive agriculture have left it with a pretty clean environment. There are, however, occasional incidents such as the damage to areas around the Parque Nacional de Doñana caused by a leakage of poisonous mining wastes in 1998. There have also been scares over fertilisers which may have polluted the drinking water of the lower Guadalquivir basin.

Each year, around 50 or 60 Andalucian beaches are awarded the EU's blue flag for hygiene and facilities. Improvements to sewage treatment plants in Málaga and on the

Costa del Sol are planned to ensure that all sewage in these areas is properly treated. Elsewhere, the picture is not always so healthy: some towns along the Málaga province coast east of Málaga city, for example, still dump sewage in the sea.

Andalucía's environment has been significantly altered by human activity. It was the Romans who began to cut its extensive woodlands and forests for timber, fuel and weapons. The Romans and Muslims opened up large areas to agriculture through irrigation and terracing of the hillsides. Later, overgrazing by huge sheep flocks brought substantial topsoil erosion – most of the Guadalquivir marismas have been formed by deposited sediment in the past 3000 years. Many animal species have been drastically depleted by hunting. Protection given to many animal and bird species has brought big increases in numbers for some, though it's probably too late for others.

Conservation

Environmental awareness took a quantum leap forward in the 1980s with the advent of the PSOE national government. It spurred a range of actions by regional governments which now have responsibility for most environmental matters. In 1981 Spain had just 35 environmentally protected areas, covering 2200 sq km. Today there are over 400, covering more than 25,000 sq km, and Andalucía is the leader in this field (see National Parks & Reserves). Not that protected areas are always perfectly protected. The Parque Nacional de Doñana in western Andalucía, for instance, whose wetlands are a bird habitat of huge international importance, has had to fight an ongoing battle since its creation in 1969 against agricultural and tourism schemes around its fringes which threaten to reduce or pollute its water supplies. At the time of writing Spain's national government was fighting a legal battle against the Andalucian regional government to try to stop a new tourism development near Sanlúcar de Barrameda on the park's fringes.

Drought

Potentially, Andalucía's worst environmental problem is drought, which struck in the 1950s and 60s, and again in the early 1990s. This is despite huge investment in reservoirs (which cover a higher proportion of the land in Spain than in any other country in the world). In the winter of 1995-96 the drought broke and lots of rain in following years pretty well filled up the reservoirs – for a while, at least.

FLORA

The variety of Andalucian flora is astonishing, as anyone who witnesses the spectacular wildflower displays in spring and early summer will testify. Andalucía has around 5000 different plant species, of which some 150 are unique to the region. This abundance is largely due to the fact that the last Ice Age was relatively temperate at this southerly latitude, allowing plants which were killed off farther north to survive here.

High-Altitude Plants

The mountain areas are responsible for a lot of Andalucía's botanical variety. The Parque Natural de Cazorla alone has 2300 plant species (24 of them found nowhere else) and the Sierra Nevada 2100 (about 60 unique to it). When the snows melt, the alpine and subalpine zones above the tree line bloom spectacularly with small rock-clinging plants and high pastures full of gentians, orchids, crocuses and narcissi.

Mountain Forests

The lower slopes of many of Andalucía's mountains are clothed in forests of pine (pino), often commercial. The rare Spanish fir (pinsapo), a relic of forests more than 2 million years old, exists only in the mountainous area around Ronda and in northern Morocco. Many pine forests are threatened by the hairy, pine-needle-devouring caterpillars of the Pine Processionary Moth – best steered clear of (see Cuts, Bites & Stings under Health in Facts for the Visitor).

Lowland Forests

Along river valleys you'll often find a rich variety of deciduous trees such as the poplar *(álamo)*, ash *(fresno)*, willow *(sauce)*, maple *(arce)*, elm *(olmo)* and alder *(aliso)*, as well as reeds *(juncos)* and bullrushes *(eneas)*.

In areas such as the Sierra Morena and Parque Natural Los Alcornocales there are extensive woodland pastures known as *dehesas*, with stands of two types of useful evergreen oak – the cork oak *(alcornoque)* and the holm or ilex oak *(encina)*. The cork oak's thick outer bark is stripped every nine years for cork *(corcho)* – you'll see the scars on some trees, a bright terracotta colour if they're new. The holm oak can be pruned about every four years and the offcuts used for charcoal. Meanwhile, livestock can graze the pastures and in autumn pigs are turned out to gobble up the fallen acorns *(bellotas)* – a diet considered to produce the best ham of all. Dehesas were mostly created long ago by the felling or burning-off of the original Mediterranean forest for pasture which was replanted with these useful trees.

In some areas, especially in Jaén and Córdoba provinces, there's nothing but lines of olive trees *(olivos)* as far as the eye can see (see the boxed text Essential Oil in the Jaén Province chapter).

Scrub & Steppe

Where there's no woodland and no agriculture, the land is likely to be either scrub or steppe-like. Scrub occurs where forests were felled and the land was then abandoned. Herbs like lavender *(lavanda)*, rosemary *(romero)*, fennel *(hinojo)* and thyme *(tomillo)* are typical plants, as are shrubs of the cistus *(jara)* family and gorse *(tojo)*, juniper *(enebro)* and heather *(brezo)*. Orchids, gladioli and irises may flower beneath these shrubs, which themselves can be quite colourful in spring. Steppe is produced by overgrazing or occurs naturally in hot, very dry areas such as the south-east of Almería province. Here, plant life is sparse and scrubby, often with cacti, but the area bursts into colour after rain.

FAUNA

Andalucía's wildlife is among the most varied in Europe, thanks to its wild, varied terrain, which has allowed the survival of several species that have died out in other countries – though some are now in perilously small numbers. Many animals are nocturnal and you need to be dedicated and/or lucky to track down even the more common ones. Naturally they tend to be most common in the wilder country areas, especially protected areas.

Mammals

A small number of wolves (called *lobos* in Spanish) survive in the eastern Sierra Morena, in protected areas such as the Parques Naturales Sierra de Despeñaperros and Sierra de Andújar. In 1986 the wolf was declared to be in danger of extinction in Andalucía and, to protect it from hunting, farmers are now entitled to compensation if their animals are attacked by wolves. Between 1986 and 1998 there were 90 such compensation claims – mostly from within the parques naturales. But the wolf population – almost certainly less than 100 – is apparently continuing to diminish. There are up to 1000 wolves in other parts of Spain.

Things are better for the ibex *(cabra montés)*, a stocky high-mountain goat whose males have distinctive long horns. It spends summer hopping agilely around high-altitude precipices and descends lower in winter. Almost hunted to extinction in Spain by 1900, the ibex was protected by royal decree a few years later and there are now an estimated 70,000 in the country. Around 5000 are in the Sierra Nevada, and there are sizeable populations in the Parque Natural de Cazorla and Parque Natural Sierra de las Nieves.

The pardel lynx *(lince ibérico)*, a uniquely Spanish species smaller than the lynx of northern Europe, is considered the world's most endangered feline. Its numbers have been reduced to between 600 and 800 by hunting and by a decline in the numbers of rabbits, its staple diet. Around 40 or 50 of these animals survive in Andalucía's Parque

Nacional de Doñana. There are others of the species in Sierra Morena.

Less uncommon beasts include the mainly nocturnal wild boar *(jabalí)*, which likes thick woods, marshes and farmers' root crops; the red deer *(ciervo)*, roe deer *(corzo)* and fallow deer *(gamo)* in forests and woodlands of all types; the nocturnal genet *(gineta)*, rather like a short-legged cat with a black-spotted white coat and a long, striped tail, in woodland and scrub; the red squirrel *(ardilla)* in mountain forests; the nocturnal badger *(tejón)*, in woods with thick undergrowth; the mainly nocturnal Egyptian mongoose *(meloncillo)* in woods, scrub and marshes; the fox *(zorro)*, common in scattered areas; the otter *(nutria)*; and the beech marten *(garduña)* in deciduous forests and on rocky outcrops and cliffs. The mouflon, a wild sheep, has been introduced to the Parque Natural de Cazorla and a couple of other areas for hunting.

Other Fauna

Gibraltar is famous for its colony of Barbary macaques, the only wild monkeys in Europe. The Bahía de Algeciras and Strait of Gibraltar have plenty of dolphins (common, striped and bottle-nosed) and some whales (pilot, killer or even sperm), and boat trips to see them are an increasingly popular attraction from Gibraltar.

From spring to autumn, Andalucía is a paradise for butterfly and moth enthusiasts. Most of Europe's butterflies are found in Spain. There are several bat species, salamanders, chameleons (most numerous in the Axarquía region), numerous lizards, and snakes. See Health in Facts for the Visitor for information on dangerous beasts.

Birds

Andalucía is a magnet for birdwatchers (see Birdwatching under Activities in Facts for the Visitor for more information).

Raptors Andalucía has 13 resident raptor species and several other summer visitors

from Africa. You can see some of them circling or hovering over the hills in many parts of Andalucía.

The Sierra Morena is a stronghold of Europe's biggest bird, the rare black vulture *(buitre negro)*. The few hundred pairs in Spain are probably the world's biggest population, and one of the biggest colonies of these birds is in the Paraje Natural Sierra Pelada y Rivera del Aserrador, south of Aroche in Huelva province.

Another emblematic and rare bird is the Spanish imperial eagle *(águila imperial)*. Its white shoulders distinguish it from other imperial eagles. Of the 100 or so pairs remaining, about 20 are in the Parque Nacional de Doñana.

Other large birds of prey include the golden eagle *(águila real)* and several other eagles, and the griffon vulture *(buitre leonado)* and Egyptian vulture *(alimoche)*, all found in mountain regions. Among smaller birds of prey, many of them found around deciduous or lowland woods and forests, are the common kestrel *(cernícalo)* and buzzard *(ratonero)*, the sparrowhawk *(gavilán)*, various harriers *(aguiluchos)*, and the acrobatic red kite *(milano real)* and black kite *(milano negro)*. Black kites may be seen over open ground near marshes, rivers and rubbish dumps.

Storks The large, ungainly white stork *(cigüeña blanca)*, actually black and white, nests from spring to summer on electricity pylons, trees and towers – sometimes right in the middle of towns – in western Andalucía. The much rarer black stork *(cigüeña negra)*, all black, also nests in western Andalucía, typically on cliff ledges. Both types migrate from Africa across the Strait of Gibraltar to breed in Spain.

Water Birds Andalucía is a haven for water birds, mainly thanks to some large wetlands along the Atlantic coast – notably the Parque Nacional de Doñana and Paraje Natural Marismas del Odiel. Hundreds of thousands of migratory birds, including an estimated 80% of western Europe's wild ducks, winter in Doñana and many more call in during spring and autumn migrations.

Laguna de Fuente de Piedra near Antequera is Europe's main breeding site for the greater flamingo *(flamenco)*, with as many as 13,000 pairs rearing chicks in spring and summer. This beautiful pink bird can be seen in several other places including Cabo de Gata, Doñana and the Marismas del Oriel.

Other Birds Among the most colourful of Andalucía's many other birds are the golden oriole *(oropéndola)* seen in orchards and deciduous woodlands in summer (the male has an unmistakable bright yellow body); the orange, black and white hoopoe *(abubilla)*, with its distinctive crest, common in open woodlands, on farmland and golf courses; and the gold, brown and turquoise bee-eater *(abejaruco)*, which nests in sandy banks in summer. Various woodpeckers *(pitos* or *picos)* and owls *(búhos)* inhabit mountain woodlands.

NATIONAL PARKS & RESERVES
Much of Spain's most spectacular and ecologically important country is under some kind of official protection and Andalucía has 60% of the total protected area in Spain – over 80 protected areas covering some 15,000 sq km (17% of Andalucian territory). All these areas can be visited, but degrees of conservation, access and facilities vary. The most interesting usually have visitor centres with ample information on features of interest and on where you can and can't go.

Parques Nacionales
National parks are declared by the national parliament and administered by the national and regional governments. At the time of writing mainland Spain has just four, of which one, the Parque Nacional de Doñana, is in Andalucía. However, several other areas are due to be raised to national park status – including, in Andalucía, the upper reaches of the Sierra Nevada (in 1998), and parts of Cabo de Gata and the nearby Almerian deserts (by about 2002).

National parks are areas of exceptional importance for their fauna, flora, geomorphology or landscape and are generally the most strictly controlled protected areas. They tend to have a very sparse human population and may include reserves *(reservas)* which are closed to the public and restricted areas *(zonas restringidas)* which can only be visited with permission. Camping is banned.

Parques Naturales
Natural parks are declared and administered by regional governments. In Andalucía they are administered by the Junta de Andalucía's Agencia de Medio Ambiente (Environmental Agency). The 23 in Andalucía account for most of the region's protected territory and include most of its most spectacular country – from the great cork oak forests of Los Alcornocales to the beautiful mountains and valleys of Cazorla (at 2140 sq km the largest protected area in Spain) and the Sierra de Grazalema, or the rolling Sierra Morena country of the Sierra Norte or Sierra de Aracena y Picos de Aroche.

Parques naturales are intended to protect not only nature but also human cultural heritage. They are also designed to promote economic development that's compatible with conservation. Many of them include paved roads, villages or even small towns, with accommodation often available within the park. Camping is usually not allowed outside organised campsites. In some there are networks of marked walking trails. Like national parks, they may include areas which can only be visited with permission.

Other Protected Areas
The two other protected areas in Andalucía are Paraje Natural (31 of these) and Reserva Natural (28). These are smaller, usually little-inhabited areas, with much the same goals as parques naturales. Parajes naturales include many of the lesser Atlantic coast wetlands. Reservas naturales are the smallest areas and include many inland lakes.

Reservas Nacionales de Caza
Some wilderness areas – about 900 sq km in Andalucía – are National Hunting Reserves.

These are usually well conserved for the sake of the wildlife that is to be hunted – which has to be exploited in a 'rational' manner. Hunting, though subject to restrictions, is a deeply ingrained side of Spanish life. Public access to the reserves is usually pretty open and you might walk or drive across one without even knowing it. If you hear shots, though, caution is advisable!

GOVERNMENT & POLITICS

Since 1978 Spain has been a constitutional monarchy. The national parliament, the Cortes Generales, is bicameral and comprises the Congreso de los Diputados (lower house) and Senado (upper house). Both houses are elected by free universal suffrage. From 1982 to 1996 government was by the left-of-centre PSOE (Partido Socialista Obrero Español, Spanish Socialist Worker Party), led by the sevillano Felipe González. In 1996 the PSOE finally lost out to the centre-right PP (Partido Popular, People's Party), led by José María Aznar.

The 1978 constitution also provided for substantial devolution of power to Spain's regions – largely in response to long-standing desires for autonomy in the northern regions of Cataluña and the País Vasco (Basque Country). As a result, Spain is now divided into 17 comunidades autónomas (autonomous communities), each with its own parliament, president, government and supreme court. The policy areas controlled at comunidad level vary. In general, the larger, more important comunidades and those that were most autonomy-minded when all this was being negotiated have greater powers. Andalucía, the most populous comunidad, has more powers than most, including powers over industry, agriculture, tourism, education, health, social security, environmental conservation and non-national roads and railways. But since the national government has a far larger budget than that of the comunidades, a great many of the important decisions are still made in Madrid.

Andalucía's parliament sits in Sevilla and its 109 members are chosen by universal suffrage every four years. The executive government, called the Junta de Andalucía, is headed by a president, with a cabinet called the Consejo de Gobierno. The parliament and Junta de Andalucía have been controlled by the PSOE ever since autonomy began in 1982 – though recently the PSOE has been governing without an absolute parliamentary majority after the breakup of a coalition with the communist IU (Izquierda Unida, United Left), which usually gets around 15% to 20% of the vote. The junta's current president is Manuel Chaves.

Each autonomous region consists of one or more provinces. Andalucía has eight, all named after their capital cities – Almería, Cádiz, Córdoba, Granada, Huelva, Jaén, Málaga and Sevilla. The provinces are further subdivided into city, town and village administrative units called municipios, each with an elected council headed by an alcalde (mayor).

ECONOMY

Andalucía has long been one of Spain's economically retarded regions. The roots of the problem go back to the Reconquista when a lot of cultivated land was abandoned and the Castilian nobility was awarded huge estates (latifundia), which in many cases they turned over to sheep. At the same time, the gentry's reluctance to get involved in trade and industry meant that silver and gold which came from the Americas was not used to found any solid economic base which would continue after the treasure shipments stopped coming.

By the 19th century Andalucian society consisted basically of a small number of very rich, often absentee landowners and a large number of very poor peasants, many of whom had no land of their own. Agriculture was technologically primitive and industry barely existent. In the late 19th and early 20th centuries this led to much unrest, culminating, as elsewhere in Spain, in the civil war of 1936-39.

Under Franco

In the 1940s años de hambre (years of

hunger), with the economy blighted by the civil war and a UN-sponsored trade boycott of Spain, Andalucian peasants at times subsisted on soup made from grass and wild herbs. In Spain's 1960s boom – funded chiefly by the tourism surge on the Costa del Sol and Cataluña's Costa Brava – industry at Huelva and the Cádiz shipyards was developed and agriculture moved forward a little with new dams providing irrigation (and hydroelectricity), and conservation and reforestation schemes reclaiming land.

But Andalucians' earnings were one-third below the national average and remained at 'developing nation' levels, as defined by the UN, until well into the 1960s. This was the time of the great Andalucian migration to Barcelona and elsewhere, in search of work.

After Franco

Spain's entry into the European Community (now the European Union) in 1986 opened new export markets and brought a flow of funds into infrastructure projects (roads, railways, airports etc). In the resulting boom, Spaniards had more money than ever before and the middle class grew rapidly. Spain's traditionally stay-at-home women poured into higher education and jobs. But the EC also opened up Spain to competition from outside which contributed to the boom's eventual change to slump, with national unemployment reaching 24% in 1994. Growth has since returned and by 1997 unemployment had fallen to 20% – still easily the highest in the EU. Unemployment among the under-26-year-olds reached an alarming 40%.

Andalucía has followed the curves of the national economy – at a distance. Things are better than they were, but worse than in most of Spain. Back in the 1970s, the prime minister Adolfo Suárez told John Hooper, then *The Guardian* correspondent in Madrid, that if one thing made him lose sleep it was the centuries-old problem of Andalucía's landless, seasonally employed, agricultural day-labourers, the jornaleros. Even today, just 2% of Andalucian landowners still own about half of Andalucía's land and the 'big five' – the Duques de Arcos, Infantado, Medinaceli, Medina Sidonia and Osuna – retain truly vast estates. The estates now tend to be efficiently and profitably farmed rather than trampled by sheep or left idle, but mechanisation has not provided many new jobs. There are still perhaps 200,000 jornaleros. In Suárez's nightmares, the threat of a peasant revolt still loomed. To stave this off, he set up a community works programme for Andalucian farm workers who were out of work between harvests.

The left-of-centre Andalucian-dominated PSOE national government of the 1980s went further, raising the percentage of unemployed people entitled to the dole from 26% in 1983 to 70% in 1993. The PSOE also channelled generous amounts of EU aid to Andalucía. The Expo 92 world fair in Sevilla brought big improvements in road and rail communications, but hopes that Expo would also somehow spark a take-off of high-tech industries in Andalucía have not been realised. Andalucía remains an industrial laggard. Industry is concentrated mainly in the western Sevilla-Huelva-Cádiz triangle, with some in Málaga, Córdoba and Granada.

Agriculture still provides one job in seven (one in five in some provinces). Successful intensive hothouse farming under acres of plastic sheeting in Almería and Huelva provinces, with most of the products exported to northern Europe, has joined traditional – if now more efficient – agricultural sectors such as pork, wool, beef, wine, grains and olives (Andalucía produces about 10% of the world's olive oil – see the boxed text on Essential Oil in the Jaén Province chapter). Fishing is still important. Andalucía has one of the biggest fishing fleets in Spain which, as a whole, has the largest in the EU. But much of the profit on Andalucian products continues to be made outside Andalucía: Sevilla oranges are turned into marmalade in Britain; Andalucian asparagus is canned in northern Spain; Andalucian cork is processed in Extremadura, Cataluña, Portugal, and even

Argentina. The value of Andalucian production, per head of population, is not much more than half that of prosperous Spanish areas such as Cataluña and Madrid.

Tourism accounts for over 10% of the Andalucian economy, providing over 100,000 jobs directly. Around 15 million tourists a year come to Andalucía, just over half of them foreigners. Málaga province, where the Costa del Sol lies, gets nearly half this business.

Average Andalucian wages are still, at under 200,000 ptas a month, well below the national average. And unemployment – 31% in 1997 – is still the highest in Spain. The jobless rate varies across Andalucía – it's highest in Cádiz province (40%), lowest in Almería (25%) and Málaga (28%) provinces – and it also changes through the year as seasonal tourism and agricultural work comes and goes.

Such statistics may conflict with the impression many visitors get of Andalucía, whose people on the whole appear, if not rich, not desperately poor either. One explanation is that tourists don't generally frequent the rougher areas of cities or the more desolate country towns and villages. It's also certainly true that the dole and other help for the unemployed has eradicated most of the worst poverty. The strength of the family helps too – several generations may share housing and share whatever income they get. Finally, many of the jobless supplement their government money by doing temporary cash-in-hand work.

POPULATION & PEOPLE
Population
Andalucía has a population of 7.23 million – almost exactly one for every foreign tourist per year. The figure is 19% of the Spanish total and Andalucía is the most populous of Spain's 17 regions. Of its eight provinces, Sevilla has most people (1.7 million), followed by Málaga (1.25 million), Cádiz (1.11 million), Granada (808,000), Córdoba (761,000), Jaén (649,000), Almería (502,000) and Huelva (455,000). The 10 cities which

have over 100,000 people are the eight provincial capitals – Sevilla (697,000), Málaga (549,000), Córdoba (306,000), Granada (246,000), Almería (171,000), Cádiz (146,000), Huelva (141,000) and Jaén (105,000) – plus Jerez de la Frontera (182,000) and Algeciras (102,000).

In most provinces the population is very much weighted to the capital. The cities of Sevilla, Málaga, Córdoba, Granada and Huelva are all at least five times as big as any other town in their provinces. This reflects a drift in recent decades from the countryside to the cities in many areas. Like most other Spaniards, Andalucians like to live together, in cities, towns or *pueblos* (villages). Country farmsteads and cottages (*fincas* or *cortijos*) are rarely actually lived in these days – their owners will travel out to them daily from their villages by car, motorcycle, mule or donkey, or just use them at weekends.

People
The ancestors of today's Andalucians include prehistoric hunters from Africa; Phoenicians, Jews and Arabs from the Middle East; Carthaginians and Berbers from North Africa; Visigoths from the Balkans; Celts from central Europe; Romans; and northern Spaniards who were themselves descended from a similar mix of ancient peoples. By the time the remaining identifiable Jews and Muslims were expelled in the 15th to 17th centuries, all these influences were intermingled. In the past 1000 years there have been just two significant additions to the Andalucian ethnic picture: the Gypsies, who arrived in the 15th century, and the northern Europeans whose 19th century trickle turned into a tide in the 1960s. Spain never received any significant immigration from its overseas empire.

Gypsies Some consider Spain's Gypsies (*gitanos*) to be its only ethnic minority. More than half of the country's roughly 500,000 Gypsies live in Andalucía. Their origins are uncertain, but they are thought to have come from India, from where they headed west in the 9th century AD. One migration route led to Istanbul and then into Europe, where some eventually reached Spain in the 15th century, most heading to the south. It's postulated that they came south because of some kind of affinity with the Muslims of the Emirate of Granada. Another Gypsy route from the east, it is thought, led to Egypt (hence, some reckon, the word Gypsy) and across North Africa to Andalucía.

Spain began enacting laws against the Gypsies in 1499 and went on doing so for a long time. Early ones were chiefly intended to stop them wandering. Others tried to extinguish the Gypsy identity by forbidding them to use Gypsy names, language or dress, or banning them from traditional activities such as owning horses or working as blacksmiths. King Carlos III in 1783 permitted Gypsies to do whatever work they could on condition that they abandon their customs (which of course they could not do). They remained on the fringes of society. Along the way they created flamenco music, which emerged in something like its current form in the 19th century.

Today, most Andalucian Gypsies lead a settled life, in cities, towns and villages across the region, though the heartland of flamenco is the lower Guadalquivir basin, especially in and around Sevilla, Jerez de la Frontera and Cádiz. In many, but not all places, Gypsy quarters are among the poorest parts of town. Gypsies rub along all right with other Spaniards but still tend to keep – and be kept – to themselves. Marriages between Gypsies and non-Gypsies, for instance, are unusual.

Expatriates Officially, Andalucía has 132,000 foreign residents, mostly from Britain, Germany, Scandinavia and France, and almost half of them are on the Costa del Sol. A good proportion of them are retired. In addition, there are probably at least the same number of northern Europeans living in Andalucía temporarily who don't appear on the censuses.

Africans An estimated 80,000 Africans, chiefly from Morocco and neighbouring countries, live in Spain. Most of them enter the country through Andalucía but tend to head north in search of work. Many come illegally, and numbers drown in the attempt when their overloaded boats capsize in the treacherous Strait of Gibraltar or when they can't manage to swim the last few hundred metres to the shore after their boats dump them. Thousands more are intercepted by the police and sent back.

ARTS
Painting, Sculpture & Metalwork
Early & Muslim Art The earliest known Andalucian art was by Stone Age hunter-gatherers who left impressive rock paintings and carvings, of animals, people and mythical or divine figures, in caves such as the Cueva de la Pileta and Cueva de Ardales in Málaga province and the Cueva de los Letreros in Almería province (all three caves can be visited).

The later Tartessians were notable goldsmiths – witness the Carambolo gold in Sevilla's Museo Arqueológico – and their successors the Iberians left a wealth of fine stone sculptures of animals, deities and other figures, often with influence from the Carthaginians and Greeks who were around at the same time. Fine Iberian collections are on view in the Museos Arqueológicos in Sevilla and Córdoba, and Jaén's Museo Provincial. The most famous piece is the *Dama de Baza*, a lifesize goddess figure from near Baza in Granada province.

The Roman artistic legacy is at its best in the form of mosaics, with some wonderful examples at Itálica, Carmona and Écija (all in Sevilla province), Córdoba's Alcázar de los Reyes and the Museos Arqueológicos in Córdoba and Sevilla.

Visigothic artistic output was limited, and at most you'll see a few Visigothic-era carvings or fonts incorporated into later buildings. Some museums contain pieces of gaudy Visigothic jewellery.

Islam frowns on the artistic representation of living beings, so the art of Muslim

Andalucía – and of the mudéjares, Muslims living or working under Christian rule – is chiefly a matter of intricate carved or tilework geometric and plant patterns, or calligraphic inscriptions from the Qur'an. There's some stupendous work of this type in the Alhambra in Granada and the Alcázar in Sevilla.

Gothic & Renaissance Art Sevilla, the most powerful and richest city of early Christian Andalucía, was long the region's artistic epicentre. By the time the Christians had settled in, the prevailing artistic style was Gothic. There's plenty of Gothic architecture in Andalucía, but less in the way of painting. The huge main *retablo* (altarpiece) in Sevilla's cathedral was designed and begun by a Flemish sculptor, Pieter Dancart, in 1482 and carved with more than 1000 gilded and painted biblical figures.

Around Dancart's time, the Frenchman Lorenzo Mercadante de Bretaña, followed by his local disciple Pedro Millán, began to work a new naturalism and detail into Sevillan sculpture. Then Sevilla's 16th century boom opened it right up to the humanist and classical trends of the Renaissance. In sculpture, the Italian Pedro Torrigiano

---

Retablos

A retablo – a Spanish invention in church adornment – is a large, often three-part, sculptural altarpiece, elaborately carved and painted with detailed biblical scenes, saints, angels and so on. A church's main retablo can fill the whole width of the nave behind the altar, and there are often smaller ones for side altars too. The retablo's basic function is to illustrate Christian stories and teachings for the benefit of worshippers.

The first retablos appeared in the 14th century, in Gothic style, and they reached their peak of lavish, gilded, colourful elaboration in the baroque era.

(1472-1528) was the key figure. Having been a rival of Michelangelo in Florence, he went to Sevilla in 1522. Alejo Fernández (1470-1545), an artist of probable German origin who moved to Sevilla in 1508, ushered in the Renaissance in painting. Southern Spain, however, produced no-one in the 16th century of the stature of El Greco, the great Greek-born painter who spent his career in Toledo. Another major Spanish Renaissance figure, Alonso Berruguete (1488-1561), did a lot of paintings in the Capilla Real in Granada but spent most of his career elsewhere.

A 16th century master artisan known as Maestro Bartolomé created some of Spain's loveliest *rejas* (wrought iron grilles) in churches in Granada and Jaén province. Another noted metalsmith of the period was Juan de Arfe (1535-1603), who made large, almost architectural monstrances for several Spanish cathedrals including Sevilla's.

Siglo de Oro The later 16th century saw a decline into the stiff, idealised schemes of Mannerism, a transition from Renaissance to baroque art. But early in the 17th century – the dawn of Spain's artistic *Siglo de Oro* (Golden Century) – a more naturalistic approach, heralding baroque, was taken by Sevillans led by Juan de Roelas (1560-1625), who travelled in Italy, and Francisco Pacheco (1564-1654), who was more of a teacher than an artist. His studio was the centre of a humanist circle that influenced most of Andalucía's leading artists of the century. Pacheco advised his pupils to 'go to nature for everything'. Roelas' 'two-level' style – depicting heavenly realms in the upper parts of his large canvases and earthly matters below – was very influential.

These and the greater Sevillan artists of the 17th century are very well represented in the city's Museo de Bellas Artes, which is the best art museum in Andalucía.

The mystically-inclined Francisco de Zurbarán (1598-1664), a Basque born in Extremadura who lived most of his life in and around Sevilla, carried naturalism into the mid-17th century. Zurbarán's clear, detailed and spiritual paintings of saints, churchmen and monastic life are often highlighted by strong light/shadow contrasts comparable with two contemporaries, the Italian Caravaggio and José de Ribera, a Spaniard who spent most of his life in Italy. Zurbarán received many commissions in and around Sevilla, though he eventually died in poverty in Madrid. There are notable collections of his paintings in Sevilla's Museo de Bellas Artes and Catedral, and in the Museo de Cádiz.

Pacheco's son-in-law, Sevilla-born Diego Rodríguez de Silva y Velázquez (1599-1660), also showed a strong naturalistic leaning and masterly light/shadow effects in the early works he painted in Sevilla – kitchen scenes, portraits and religious scenes – before leaving in 1623 to become an official court painter in Madrid and, ultimately, *the* major artist of Spain's cultural golden age. In his early religious paintings, he used models drawn from the streets of Sevilla.

Velázquez's friend Alonso Cano (1601-77) also studied under Pacheco. In the course of a turbulent life he moved to Madrid, which he left after being wrongfully accused and tortured for the murder of his wife, and later to Granada. Cano was a gifted painter, sculptor *and* architect. Some of his best work is to be seen in Sevilla's Museo de Bellas Artes and the Granada and Málaga cathedrals.

Bartolomé Esteban Murillo (1618-82) and his friend Juan de Valdés Leal (1629-90), both Sevilla-born, led the way to full-blown baroque art. With its large, colourful, accessible images, the baroque movement took deep root in Andalucía. The prolific Murillo was the youngest of 14 children and was orphaned at the age of nine. His fine technique and soft-focus, at times sugary, beggar images and religious scenes (he did seemingly dozens of versions of the *Concepción Inmaculada*) were very popular in a time of economic decline. He died from injuries received in a fall while painting the retablo of the Iglesia de los Capuchinos in Cádiz. He had many artistic

disciples. The greatest works of the passionate Valdés Leal, who could be both humorous and bitingly pessimistic, can be seen – alongside several Murillos – in Sevilla's Hospital de la Caridad.

Baroque Sculpture Sevilla's Juan Martínez Montañés (1568-1649), known in his day as El Dios de la Madera (The God of Wood), produced many dramatic, lifelike sculptures and reliefs in polychromed wood. His crucifixions, immaculate conceptions, infant Christs and retablos with diverse carvings of saints provided models which were later followed by generations of sculptors. Martínez Montañés' work crops up in many Sevillan and Andalucian churches and among the images carried by Sevilla's processional brotherhoods during Semana Santa. His career coincided with the first organisation of the Semana Santa rituals along something like their current lines, bringing numerous commissions for images to be carried in the procession. Among Martínez Montañés' many disciples, Juan de Mesa stands out for the pathos of his images, particularly his crucifixions.

The leading Sevilla sculptor of the second half of the 17th century was Pedro Roldán (1624-1699). Some of his work (in wood) was painted by Valdés Leal and, like the latter, Roldán's best work is in the Hospital de la Caridad. Several of his children and grandchildren were sculptors too. His daughter, María Luisa Roldán or La Roldana (1654-1704), according to tradition, created La Macarena, the powerful image of the Virgin which takes the place of honour in Sevilla's Semana Santa.

Pedro de Mena (1628-1688), the most sought-after Andalucian sculptor of his age, produced a welter of saints, child Christs and other religious work. The last major Andalucian baroque sculptor was José de Mora (1642-1724) from Granada, who seems to have had only one model for his numerous Virgin sculptures – his wife Luisa de Mena.

The 18th & 19th Centuries An impoverished Spain in this period produced just one outstanding artist – the great Francisco José de Goya y Lucientes (1746-1828) from Aragón. Goya recorded bullfights at Ronda and may have been a guest at a royal hunting lodge in what is now the Parque Nacional de Doñana where, tradition has it, he painted his famous *La Maja Vestida* and *La Maja Desnuda* – identical portraits of the same woman, clothed and unclothed. It was also on a visit to Andalucía, in 1792, that Goya went deaf – an event which cast a much bleaker aspect over his work. A few of Goya's works are on view in Andalucía in places such as the Sevilla Catedral, the Oratorio de la Santa Cueva in Cádiz and Córdoba's Museo de Bellas Artes.

The 19th century *costumbrista* painters of Sevilla – chief among them José Domínguez Bécquer – turned out sentimental pictures of Gypsies, dancers and so on for a largely tourist market.

The 20th Century Like Velázquez, Pablo Ruiz Picasso (1881-1973) was born in Andalucía (Málaga) but did not stay long. When Picasso was nine his family moved to Galicia and then a few years later to Barcelona, which happened to be about the only environment in an otherwise depressed Spain where creative artists could hope to flourish. Having shown prodigious aptitude at an early age and having already absorbed lessons from his greatest forerunners – Goya, Velázquez and El Greco – Picasso started visiting Paris in 1900 and opened himself to the riches of Gauguin, Toulouse-Lautrec and Van Gogh. He settled for good in France in 1904. He had revisited Málaga for holidays every year from 1891 to 1900, painting landscapes and fishing scenes, but never returned thereafter.

Picasso's career involved many abrupt changes and periods. The rather sombre Blue Period (1901-04) was followed by the merrier Pink Period; later, with Georges Braque, Picasso pioneered cubism. His best known work is *Guernica*, portraying the horror of war and inspired by the German bombing of the Basque town Gernika, in 1937. A new Museo Picasso, largely con-

Andalucía's famous son, artist Pablo Picasso

sisting of 138 works donated by the artist's daughter-in-law Christine Ruiz-Picasso, is due to open in Málaga in 2000, finally giving the city of his birth a slice of the Picasso pie.

Probably the two most notable 20th century artists who actually worked in Andalucía were Julio Romero de Torres (1880-1930) from Córdoba, a painter of dark, sensual female nudes, and Huelva's Daniel Vázquez Díaz (1882-1969), a portraitist who also did a set of murals on the Columbus story in the Monasterio de La Rábida.

Architecture

Apart from a few Phoenician tombs (as at Almuñécar) and megalithic dolmens such as those at Antequera, the only significant pre-Muslim structures are Roman – notably at Itálica near Sevilla with the biggest of all Roman amphitheatres, a bathhouse and a theatre. The Roman town sites of Baelo Claudia and Ronda la Vieja are worth a visit, as is the necropolis at Carmona. The

Romans bequeathed to Andalucía the happy invention of the interior patio in houses and other buildings (an idea later taken up by the Muslims). The Visigoths left little lasting imprint – most of their churches have been built over.

Muslim Architecture Muslim cities had at their heart a main mosque *(mezquita)* and a large market *(zoco)*, around which would spread the tangled streets of the *medina* or inner city. A mosque is composed of three main parts: the minaret, a tower (always square in Andalucía) from which the faithful are called to prayer; the prayer hall; and the ablutions courtyard, for ritual washing before entering the prayer hall.

Relatively few major Muslim buildings in Andalucía survived the Christian era intact, but those that did include some of the greatest Muslim buildings in the world: the Mezquita in Córdoba, the Alhambra palace at Granada, and the Giralda minaret in Sevilla. A fourth great construction, the Medina Azahara palace-city outside Córdoba, has been partly restored. To the Muslim list can be added the Alcázar in Sevilla, whose beautiful Palacio de Don Pedro was created in the 14th century for a Christian king but by mainly Muslim artisans. A marvellous example of a well preserved small mosque is the Mezquita in the village of Almonaster la Real, Huelva province.

In addition, there are numerous impressive Muslim castles and fortifications in varying states of preservation at places like Almería, Málaga and Baños de la Encina. Many other castles and forts are of Muslim origin but were rebuilt later. Many Andalucian churches are either converted mosques or were built on the sites of ruined mosques, and many church towers were originally minarets. In civil architecture, dozens of town centres and villages incorporate portions of Muslim buildings and have labyrinthine Muslim-era street plans. Granada's Albayzín district is just one case in point. Also of interest are the Muslim bathhouses in places like Jaén and Ronda.

One very distinctive architectural feature

DAMIEN SIMONIS

Muslim masterpiece: The Alhambra, Granada

used throughout the Muslim period was the horseshoe-shaped arch – though this wasn't brought to Spain by the Muslims. The Visigoths and even the Romans had used it before. Another common Muslim thread was the use of beautiful decorative tilework and, from the 10th century, carved stucco, forming intricate patterns with geometric or plant motifs or calligraphic verses from the Qur'an.

Muslim architecture in Andalucía falls into two broad periods. First was the caliphal style emanating from Córdoba and brought by the Arabs from the Middle East. The Córdoba Mezquita is the pre-eminent example of this style, with its double rows of arches supporting the roof. Tenth century innovations at the Mezquita such as intersecting and multifoil arches, and domes with star-pattern stone ribs, even spread into churches in Christian Spain.

The second period was that of the Maghreb style, developed by Muslims in Morocco and neighbouring areas, brought to Spain by the 12th century Almohad invaders and developed as contact with North Africa spread over the next three centuries. The Giralda, built in 1184-98, with its beautiful proportions and trellis-like brick patterning, is considered the finest of all Maghreb minarets. Later, the style became increasingly elaborate and decorative, culminating in the Alhambra's Palacio Nazaries and Sevilla's Palacio de Don Pedro.

Mozarabic & Mudéjar These are the names given to the derivatives of Muslim architecture developed by, respectively, Christians in Muslim areas and Muslims in Christian areas. Christians who fled Al-Andalus for the north took their Mozarabic style with them and, in fact, there's much more Mozarabic architecture in northern Spain than in Andalucía, where the only significant remaining example is the church at Bobastro.

Mudéjar architecture is much more common. Some mudéjar buildings are almost indistinguishable from Muslim buildings, as is the case with Sevilla's Palacio de Don Pedro (see Muslim Architecture, above). However, mudéjar builders did develop a few distinguishing features of their own. One was the use of brick for many churches and mansions. Extravagantly decorated timber ceilings, often ornately carved, are also a mark of the mudéjar hand. The term *armadura* refers to any of these wooden ceilings, especially when they have the shape of an inverted boat. *Artesonado* ceilings are characterised by interlaced beams leaving regular spaces (triangular, square or polygonal) for the insertion of decorative *artesas*. The truly mudéjar ones generally bear floral or simple geometric patterns, but later Renaissance variations with less oriental patterns also abound.

Mudéjar style is often found side by side with Christian Gothic in the same building.

Romanesque By the time the Reconquista reached Andalucía in the 13th century, the first major architectural style of Christian Spain, Romanesque, was just about on its way out. One of the very few Romanesque buildings in Andalucía is the Iglesia de la Santa Cruz in Baeza, the first significant Andalucian town to fall to the Christians. This church's round arches and semicircular apse make it quite distinct from the Gothic buildings that came later.

Gothic The Gothic style (nothing to do with Spain's Visigoths), with its pointed arches, ribbed ceilings, flying buttresses and fancy window tracery, began to infiltrate Spain from France in the 12th century and was carried to north and west Andalucía with the Reconquista in the 13th. It lasted to the 16th century. These technical innovations enabled much bigger buildings – notably big cathedrals. Sevilla's cathedral is the biggest in Spain and almost entirely Gothic in structure. Spanish Gothic cathedrals have a number of differences from French and English ones. They are often wider (in some cases because they were built on the sites of square mosques); place the choir *(coro)* and a chapel containing the high altar (the *capilla mayor*) in the middle of the church; they usually have many side chapels off the aisles; they feature retablos – big, elaborate altarpieces; and frequently use star-patterned vaulting, which arrived from Germany in the 15th century.

There are dozens of Gothic or part-Gothic churches in Andalucía. Many of its innumerable castles were built or rebuilt in Gothic times; so were some town mansions. Many buildings that began life in Gothic times were finished, or added to, later so that they ended up as (often successful) stylistic hotch-potches. Such are the cathedral at Jerez de la Frontera (Gothic, baroque and neoclassical, with a mudéjar belfry too); Málaga cathedral (Gothic, Renaissance, baroque); and the Iglesia de Santa María La Mayor in Ronda (Gothic, Renaissance and baroque along with remnants of the mosque that had occupied the site).

The final flourish of Spanish Gothic was the Isabelline Gothic style from the time of the Catholic Monarchs. This features sinuously curved arches and tracery and façades with low-relief sculptures (including a lot of heraldic shields) and lace-like ornament. The Catholic Monarchs' own burial chapel, the Capilla Real in Granada, is one of the finest creations of Isabelline Gothic. Another is the façade of the Palacio de Jabalquinto in Baeza.

Renaissance The Renaissance in architecture can be described as an Italian-originated return to disciplined ancient Greek and Roman ideals of harmony and proportion, with columns and classical shapes like the square, circle and triangle predominating. A fine feature of many Andalucian Renaissance buildings is elegant interior courtyards surrounded by two tiers of wide, rounded arcades.

The Renaissance in Spanish architecture can be roughly divided into three distinct styles. Firstly, the Italian-influenced special flavour that was *plateresque*. Taking its name from the Spanish for silversmith, *platero*, because its decorative effects resembled those of silverware, this genre was more one of decoration than of structure. Façades were generally given round-arched portals bordered by classical columns and stone sculpture (often including heraldry, in a carryover from Isabelline Gothic). Next is the more purist Renaissance style that has its maximum expression in the Palacio de Carlos V in Granada's Alhambra, designed by the Rome-trained Spaniard Pedro Machuca.

The last, most austere phase was Herreresque, after Juan de Herrera (1530-97), creator of the grand, almost ornamentation-free palace-monastery complex of San Lorenzo de El Escorial near Madrid, and of Sevilla's Archivo de Indias.

All three phases were spanned by the architecture in Jaén province of Andrés de Vandelvira (1509-75), who gave the town of Úbeda one of the finest ensembles of Renaissance buildings in the country (see the boxed aside on Vandelvira in the Úbeda section of the Jaén Province chapter). Vandelvira was much influenced by the Burgos-born Diego de Siloé (1495-1563), one of Spain's major Renaissance architects, who had studied in Italy and was chiefly responsible for the cathedrals of Granada, Málaga and Guadix. Hernán Ruiz, who specialised in 'improving' on surviving Islamic buildings, stuck a Renaissance bell tower atop Sevilla's Giralda, and plonked an entire cathedral *inside* the Mezquita at Córdoba.

Baroque The reaction to Renaissance sobriety came in the form of the curves, colours, sense of motion and dramatic, top-heavy effect of baroque, a movement which gathered steam in the later 17th century and reached a peak of elaboration (some say over-elaboration) in the 18th century. Andalucía was one of the places where baroque blossomed most brilliantly.

Baroque was at root classical but crammed a great deal of ornament onto façades, especially portals, and stuffed interiors full of ornate stucco sculpture and gilt paint. This was the era when the retablo reached its apogee of opulence.

Before full-blown baroque was reached there was a kind of transitional stage from the Renaissance, exemplified by more sober, simple works such as Alonso Cano's 17th century façade for Granada cathedral. Then came an outburst of greater exuberance, of which the most elaborate work is termed Churrigueresque after a family of Barcelona sculptors and architects called Churriguera. One of Churrigueresque's hallmarks, helping to give its typical top-heavy effect, is the *estípite* – a pilaster (pillar projecting only partly from the wall) in the form of a very narrow upside-down pyramid.

Sevilla has probably as many baroque churches per square kilometre as any city in the world – and elaborate is certainly the word for many of them. Two of the most outstanding are the Iglesia de la Magdalena and the Capilla de San José. The Monasterio de La Cartuja at Granada, by Francisco Hurtado Izquierdo (1669-1728), is one of the most lavish baroque creations in all

Spain. Hurtado's followers adorned the small town of Priego de Córdoba with seven or eight baroque churches. Écija is another small place that received a disproportionate share of baroque attention because of its prosperity. Elsewhere, the baroque style often appears as additions rather than complete buildings.

Neoclassicism Throughout Europe, in the mid-18th century, the cleaner, restrained lines of neoclassicism came into fashion – another return to Greek and Roman ideals in keeping with the Enlightenment philosophy that prevailed in learned circles. Cádiz, whose heyday straddled the baroque and neoclassical eras, has one of Andalucía's biggest neoclassical heritages. But the most notable neoclassical building in the region is Sevilla's very large, almost monastic Antigua Fábrica de Tabacos (Old Tobacco Factory), built to house an early state-supported industry.

19th & 20th Centuries Neoclassicism survived into the early 19th century. Thereafter the most noticeable trend was revivalism – a return to earlier styles in a sort of yearning for past glories. There was some neo-Gothic, even a bit of neobaroque, but most prevalent were neomudéjar and neo-Islamic. Private mansions such as the Palacio de Orleans y Borbón at Sanlúcar de Barrameda and public buildings ranging from railway stations in Sevilla and Almería to markets in Málaga and Tarifa were constructed in imitation (often pleasing) of past Muslim architectural styles. For the 1920s Exposición Iberoamericana, fancy buildings in almost every past Andalucian style were constructed in Sevilla.

The Franco era was an architectural trough. In Sevilla, historic buildings were demolished to make way for new roads and developments. Drab, Soviet-style blocks of workers' housing sprang up in many cities. New public buildings exhibited a bit of Stalinist classicism here, a touch of art deco there.

Since Franco, the major impetus has been Expo 92 in Sevilla, which brought the city several spectacular new bridges over the Guadalquivir and a sea of avant-garde exhibition pavilions on the Isla de la Cartuja. Sadly, many of the latter are now falling into neglect and dilapidation.

Literature

Roman Andalucian literature begins with two Cordobans, the Stoic philosopher Seneca and his poet-historian nephew Lucan. They rose high in imperial circles in Rome but were both condemned to death by suicide for their parts in a 65 AD conspiracy against emperor Nero, their former mentor.

Muslim Period The 11th century saw a flowering of both Arabic and Hebrew poetry. The Arabic was chiefly love poetry (platonic and otherwise), by such as Ibn Hazm and Ibn Zaydun from Córdoba, and Ibn Ammar and Al-Mutamid, a king, from Sevilla. The latter pair, initially friends, fell out and Al-Mutamid hacked Ibn Ammar to death with an axe. Of the Jewish poets, Judah Ha-Levi, considered one of the greatest of all post-biblical Hebrew writers, divided his life between Granada, Sevilla, Toledo and Córdoba before deciding that a return to Palestine was the only solution for Spanish Jews. Samuel Ha-Nagid's work dealt a lot with war because he was also Granada's top general.

Of the many Muslims who wrote on weightier themes, outstanding was the philosopher Averroës or Ibn Rushd (1126-98), from Córdoba. He expressed the Almohads' inward, spiritual approach to Islam, and his commentaries on Aristotle, trying to reconcile science with religious faith, had great influence on European Christian thought in the 13th and 14th centuries. This remarkable polymath was also a judge, astronomer, mathematician and personal physician and adviser to two Almohad rulers.

Siglo de Oro In Andalucía the Spanish literary Golden Century, roughly the mid-16th to the mid-17th centuries, began with the circle that gathered in Sevilla around Christopher Columbus' great-grandson Álvaro Colón. It included the playwrights

Juan de la Cueva and Lope de Rueda as well as Fernando de Herrera, who addressed his love poetry to Colón's wife. The great Spanish playwright of the age, Lope de Vega (1562-1635), didn't have very much to do with Andalucía but did set his best-known play here. *Fuente Obejuna* treats themes of honour and revenge against the background of a 1489 peasant rebellion in the Cordoban town of that name.

Córdoba's Luis de Góngora (1561-1627) is considered the greatest Spanish sonneteer and, by many, the greatest Spanish poet. Learned and classical-influenced, but largely unconcerned with theories, morals or lofty sentiments, Góngora manipulated words with a majesty that has defied attempts at critical explanation; his metaphorical, descriptive verses are above all intended as a source of sensuous pleasure. Some of them celebrate the more idyllic aspects of the Guadalquivir valley.

Góngora's contemporary Miguel de Cervantes Saavedra (1547-1616) was not an Andalucian but he did, in the course of an eventful life, spend 10 troubled years here procuring oil and wheat for the Spanish navy and as a collector of unpaid taxes. The unfortunate Cervantes also procured for himself an indecent number of lawsuits, spells in jail and even excommunications – which were no doubt grist to the mill of the man commonly thought of as the inventor of the novel. Cervantes' *El Ingenioso Hidalgo Don Quijote de La Mancha* started life as a short story designed to make a quick peseta, but Cervantes had turned it into an epic tale by the time it appeared in 1605. Quijote and his companion Sancho Panza conducted most of their comically deranged ramblings on the plains of La Mancha but did stray into the Sierra Morena for a few crazed episodes. Some of Cervantes' short *Novelas Ejemplares* (Exemplary Novels) chronicle turbulent 16th century Sevilla.

19th Century The next burst of Andalucian literary creativity didn't come till the time of the intriguing Jose María Blanco White (1771-1841), who was born into an Irish Catholic merchant family in Sevilla. A rebellious, restless soul, he fled from the Napoleonic invasion to England, where he converted to Protestantism. His *Letters from Spain* (1822), widely read in England, chronicled Andalucian life and customs in a detail that didn't disguise his contempt for local 'superstition' and 'fanaticism'. The one place in Andalucía that he remembered favourably was liberal Cádiz – 'one of the few Spanish cities which for their good taste can be compared with the English of the second rank'.

The so-called *costumbrista* writers Serafín Estébanez Calderón, with his *Escenas Andaluzas* (1846), and Fernán Caballero (actually a Swiss-born *sevillana* called Cecilia Böhl de Faber Morges), with her novel *La Gaviota* (1849), portrayed Andalucian manners and customs in a manner influenced by the foreign Romantics' interest in 'exotic' Andalucía. Sevilla's Gustavo Adolfo Bécquer (1836-70), son of a costumbrista painter, produced the most popular Spanish poem collection of the day, *Rimas*.

Generations of 98 & 27 The Generation of 98 was a loose collection of intellectuals whose common thread was a deep disturbance about the national decline symbolised by Spain's loss of its last overseas colonies in 1898. Its best known figure was the northern novelist, poet, academic and political writer Miguel de Unamuno. Antonio Machado (1875-1939), the leading poet, was born in Sevilla but spent most of his adult life outside Andalucía, except for a few years as a teacher in Baeza. In Baeza he completed *Campos de Castilla*, a set of poems evoking the landscape of Castilla, home of his beloved wife who had died young, and ruminating on the national malaise. His brother Manuel Machado (1874-1947), however, loved Andalucía – bullfighting, Semana Santa, the lot – and wrote poetry often based on flamenco songs.

Antonio Machado's friend Juan Ramón Jiménez (1881-1958), from Moguer near Huelva, touchingly and amusingly brought to life his home town and its countryside in *Platero y Yo* (Platero and I). This prose-poem tells of his childhood wanderings around Moguer with his donkey and confidant, Platero. For this, and later work which concentrated on rhythm rather than content, he was awarded the 1956 Nobel literature prize.

Juan Ramón stands as a kind of link between the Generation of 98 and the last great wave of Andalucian writers in the Generation of 27. The name comes from the readings and talks they organised in Sevilla for the tercentenary of the death of their icon Luis de Góngora. The loose-knit grouping included the poets Rafael Alberti, from El Puerto de Santa María, and Vicente Aleixandre (the 1977 Nobel laureate) and Luis Cernuda, both from Sevilla. The composer Manuel de Falla was also closely associated with them, but the outstanding figure was Federico García Lorca from Granada.

Federico García Lorca For many, *the* major Spanish writer since Cervantes, Lorca (1898-1936) was a musician, artist, theatre director, poet, playwright and more. Though charming and popular, he felt alienated – by his homosexuality, his leftish outlook and, probably, his talent itself – from his stuffy home town, Granada (which in 1936 he called 'a wasteland populated by the worst bourgeoisie in Spain'), and from contemporary Spanish society at large. Lorca identified with Andalucía's marginalised Gypsies and empathised with women stifled by conventional mores. He longed for spontaneity and vivacity and he eulogised both Granada's Islamic past and what he considered the 'authentic' Andalucía (to be found in Málaga, Córdoba, Cádiz – anywhere except Granada). But he was inspired by, and nostalgic about, the countryside he had grown up in around Granada.

As a student in Madrid in the early 1920s Lorca met Jiménez, Alberti and others associated with the Generation of 27 including the artist Salvador Dalí and the film maker Luis Buñuel. Lorca won major popularity with *El Romancero Gitano* (Gypsy Ballads), a 1928 collection of colourful verses on Andalucian Gypsy themes, full of startling metaphors and with

the simplicity of flamenco song. This was followed between 1933 and 1936 by the three tragedies for which he is best known: *Bodas de Sangre* (Blood Wedding), *Yerma* (Barren) and *La Casa de Bernardo Alba* (The House of Bernardo Alba) – brooding, dark but dramatic works dealing with themes of entrapment and liberation, passion and repression. Lorca was executed by the Nationalists early in the civil war.

Music

The flamenco tradition so permeates Andalucian sensibilities that even classical and rock music are often imbued with its influence. (For information on flamenco see the Flamenco special section on pages 49-56.)

Classical Arguably the finest Spanish classical composer of all, Manuel de Falla, was born in Cádiz in 1876. He grew up in Andalucía before heading off to Madrid and Paris, then returned in about 1919 to live in Granada till the end of the civil war, when he left for Argentina. His three major works were all intended as ballet scores. One, *Noches en los Jardines de España* (Nights in the Gardens of Spain), was never performed as a ballet, but *El Amor Brujo* (Love the Magician) – a Gypsy love story with a supernatural touch – was the mainstay of Spanish dancers for decades. *El Sombrero de Tres Picos* (The Three-Cornered Hat) caused a sensation in its 1919 London production by the famous Ballets Russes, with sets by Picasso. All three works had deep Andalucian roots: the last two in flamenco, while *Noches* evokes the Muslim past and the sounds and sensations of a hot Andalucian night.

Falla's friendship with Federico García Lorca was instrumental in the staging of the 1922 Concurso de Cante Jondo in the Alhambra in Granada (see the Flamenco special section). One guitarist who played at the *concurso* – but not flamenco – was Andrés Segovia from Jaén province, who was en route to becoming one of the major classical guitarists of the 20th century.

That, however, exhausts the list of important Andalucian contributions to classical music. The region is actually more notable for the music it has inspired from outside composers. This includes Rossini's opera *Il Barbiere di Siviglia* (The Barber of Seville), and Mozart's opera *Don Giovanni* which drew on a 17th century Spanish play by Tirso de Molina and which presented the immortal character of Don Juan. (See the boxed text Don Juan & Carmen Through Rose-Coloured Glasses.)

Major works by two of the more prominent Spanish composers before de Falla, the Catalans Isaac Albéniz and Enrique Granados, were also inspired by Andalucía.

Don Juan and Carmen Through Rose-Coloured Glasses

The backwardness and poverty of 19th century Andalucía prompted travellers and writers from northern Europe, escaping from the realities of their own lands, to develop the Romantic image of Andalucía as an exotic, mysterious, exciting, sensuous, materially poor but spiritually rich land of almost oriental adventure. The picturesque decay of Andalucía's cities and monuments; its Gypsy flamenco music and dance; its semi-oriental, legend-filled past; its people's love of pageant, fiesta, fun and bullfight; its narrow, crooked streets; its rugged, picturesque mountains; its heat; its dark-haired, dark-eyed women; even the brigands who roamed its remoter regions – contributed to an image that acted like a pair of glitter-spangled spectacles and is hard to shake off even today. Many Andalucians themselves believe it. This is hardly surprising because it's partly accurate and more acceptable now because the poverty has disappeared.

One of the first Romantic writings to be set in Andalucía (Sevilla, in this case) was *Don Juan*, the masterpiece of Britain's Lord Byron, who came to Andalucía in 1809 and wrote the mock epic near the end of his life in the early 1820s. In 1826 the French Viscount Chateaubriand published a melancholic, highly imaginative novella, *Les Aventures du Dernier Abencerage* (The Adventures of the Last Abencerraj), in which a Granada Muslim prince returns to his city after the Christian conquest. The Alhambra was established as *the* symbol of exotic Andalucía by *Les Orientales* (1829), written by Victor Hugo (who didn't visit Granada) and *Tales of the Alhambra* (1832) by the American Washington Irving (who lived in the palace for a few months). Another Frenchman, Théophile Gautier, took the Alhambra as his focus in *Voyage en Espagne* (1841). *Carmen*, a violent story of Gypsy love and revenge in Sevilla, written in the 1840s by yet another Frenchman, Prosper Mérimée, added subtropical sensuality to the Andalucian mystique. Georges Bizet's 1875 opera based on Mérimée's novella watered down the plot but firmly fixed the stereotype of Andalucian women as full of fire, guile and flashing beauty.

The Russian composer Mikhail Glinka went to Granada in 1845. Fascinated by Gypsy song and guitar, he returned home to write Spanish-flavoured music that influenced many of his successors, among them Rimsky-Korsakov who popped into Cádiz for three days' shore leave from the Russian navy – resulting in his delightful *Capriccio Espagnol* (1887).

Falla's friendship in Paris with the French composers Ravel (of *Bolero* fame) and Debussy *(Ibéria)* no doubt encouraged their Hispanic leanings, too.

Pop & Rock The Spanish rock and pop scene is busy and vibrant. Andalucian summers seem filled with happy, danceable pop, about half of it Spanish, half foreign. The Sevilla duo Los del Río had a hit in discos around the world with *Macarena* in the mid-1990s, but with many of its best young musicians drawn to flamenco fusion, Andalucía has produced less than its share of straight rock and pop stars.

Easily the most interesting character is the singer-songwriter Kiko Veneno. Born in Cataluña in 1952, Kiko has spent most of his life around Sevilla and Cádiz. Though also a practitioner of flamenco fusion, he's more in a rock/R&B/folk camp now. After his 1970s collaboration with Raimundo Amador (see Nuevo Flamenco, in the Flamenco special section) Kiko accompanied El Camarón de la Isla for a while, including on the classic hit rumba *Volando Voy*, then disappeared from the music scene for a while. He eventually found his way back, and to success, with three 1990s albums, *Échate un Cantecito*, *Está muy bien eso del Cariño*, and *Punta Paloma* – the latter recorded in Tarifa and London and named after one of the finest spots on the coast near Tarifa. With the help again of Raimundo Amador and others, Kiko mixes rock, blues, African and flamenco rhythms with lyrics that range from humorous, *simpático* snatches of everyday life to Lorca poems.

The Granada trashmetal band Lagartija Nick made waves in 1997 and 1998 through a partnership with flamenco ace Enrique Morente. The band then announced its next project would be a homage to Lorca with Joe Strummer (ex-The Clash).

Other groups worth watching out for are Perdidos Sin Control from Fuengirola, who play funky Latin stuff with rock and flamenco touches; the punkish Sevillans Amphetamine Discharge; and Los Hermanos Dalton, an energetic rock trio from San Fernando with distant influences from the Ramones and Jimi Hendrix.

Andalucian performers apart, there's usually a chance to see some of the top Spanish bands at the many concerts and festivals staged in summer. Popular ones to keep an eye open for include El Último de la Fila, a fine Barcelona duo; Australian Blonde, an indie trio from Gijón in Asturias; and heavy rockers Extremoduro from Extremadura. A whole Spanish subterranean world of loud and, for many, unbearable dance noise is most commonly known as *bakalao*. A subcategory (for those capable of discerning a difference) is *mákina*.

SOCIETY & CONDUCT

Andalucians have a big capacity for enjoying themselves, but their reputation for being lazy seems entirely unjustified. As someone put it, they work, but they don't have a work ethic.

They can be economical with etiquette and thank-yous but this does not signify unfriendliness. One small way in which you may notice people expressing their fellow-feeling is a general *'Buenos días'* to all present when they enter a shop or bar, or an *'Adiós'* when they leave. Andalucians are generally tolerant and easygoing, often welcoming, towards the millions of foreigners who descend upon their land each year, and now have several decades experience in making life easy for them. They don't expect foreigners to speak much Spanish – though you need some words to get by outside tourist centres. Equally, most Andalucians don't expect more than superficial communication with transient visitors. Invitations to their homes are something special.

Andalucians are highly gregarious and the family is of paramount importance, with children always a good talking point. At the same time they're an individualistic, proud people. But short of blatantly insulting someone, it's not easy to give offence. Disrespectful behaviour in churches – including excessively casual dress – doesn't go down well, though.

continued on page 57

flamenco

Passion play (*above*). Andalucians love dancing; this *bailaora* flaunts her skill and traditional 19th century dress, the *bata de cola*

Right: Most flamenco song and dance is performed to a blood-rush of virtuoso guitar accompaniment by a *tocaor* such as this one

(*All photographs by Gerry Reilly*)

THE GYPSY'S LAMENT

Spain pulsates with music and Andalucía is, in many ways, the country's musical heart. Flamenco, the music that outsiders most readily associate with Spain, has Andalucian roots.

Flamenco is a type of song, music and dance that emerged among Andalucian Gypsies in the lower Guadalquivir valley in the late 18th and early 19th centuries. It grew out of existing song forms whose forerunners may have included music and verses from Al-Andalus, song forms brought by the Gypsies themselves, and even the Byzantine chant used in Visigothic churches.

The earliest flamenco was *cante jondo* (deep song), an anguished lament that grew from the experience of the marginalised Gypsy. Jondura is still considered the essence of flamenco today. Some early jondo forms are still sung – notably the *martinete* whose only accompaniment is the sound of a hammer striking an anvil, as in the smithies where many Gypsies worked.

A flamenco singer is called a *cantaor* (*cantaora* if she's a woman); a dancer is a *bailaor/a*; most of their songs and dances are performed to a blood-rush of guitar from the *tocaor/a*.

Flamenco songs, called *coplas*, are made up of one or more short, rhyming bursts of two to five lines called *tercios*, permitting a certain amount of prolongation, repetition or improvisation. Their underlying rhythms are known as the *compás*.

Although flamenco's rhythms and scales – different from those of most Western music – can make it a little hard for the uninitiated to deal with, it is difficult not to be moved by what is a very

Flamenco song and dance have their origins in the anguished lament of Spain's marginalised Gypsies, like those shown in this 19th century illustration.

physical, at its best visceral, experience. (To be technical, flamenco uses the Phrygian mode, in which the interval between the first and second notes of an eight-note scale is a semitone. In conventional Western music the interval is a whole tone.)

Dance (called *baile* in flamenco contexts) soon accompanied cante, and the guitar, the third component of flamenco, was invented in Andalucía. Its origin lay in an ancient Middle Eastern stringed instrument, the cithara, which the Arabs developed into a four-string strummed lute. The 9th century Córdoba court musician Ziryab added a fifth string and this instrument became popular and its use very widespread in Spain for centuries. In about the 1790s a sixth string was added, probably by a Cádiz guitarmaker called Pagés. In the 1870s Antonio de Torres of Almería brought the instrument to its modern shape by enlarging its two bulges and placing the bridge centrally over the lower one to give the guitar its carrying power. In flamenco, guitar-playing (*toque*) for a long time functioned solely as an accompaniment to singing and dance.

From the mid-19th to early 20th centuries, establishments called *cafés cantante* literally gave flamenco its first platform – a small, low stage in a bar with tables and chairs so that customers could be entertained as they drank and ate. This was when castanets first put in an appearance in flamenco (they're not essential to it, percussion being essentially provided by tapping feet or clapping hands). Typical 19th century clothing – for women the long, frilly *bata de cola* dress, the shawl and the fan; for men, Cordoban hats and tight black trousers – became fixed as flamenco costume.

The lute, depicted in this illustration from a music book that belonged to Alfonso X, was a precursor to Andalucía's guitar.

Song Forms

There are several types of song, or *palo*. The *siguiriya*, a song of intense sorrow or loss or death, is the most despairing and is considered the biggest test of a singer's ability. It's thought to have originated in Jerez de la Frontera, one of the three key cities of flamenco's lower Guadalquivir heartland.

The **soleá**, only marginally less anguished, probably came from the Triana district of Sevilla, for centuries a Gypsy barrio until it was gentrified in the 1960s and 70s. The happier, livelier *alegría* is a contribution from the third city, Cádiz. Jerez is also now the home of the *bulería*, the fastest, most upbeat palo – though it may have originated in Triana.

Non-jondo forms (in other words lighter ones, though they can still be intense) include the *tango* from Cádiz and its derivatives the *guajira*, *rumba* and *colombiana*. The tango is nothing to do with the Argentine tango dance, though its origin may have been in

Latin America or the Caribbean. The home of the *fandango* is Huelva but many other areas have their own varieties of fandango – the *malagueña* from Málaga, the *granaína* from Granada and the *rondeña* from Ronda. Almería's *taranta* is not dissimilar.

The *saeta*, an outburst of adoration by an onlooker at a Semana Santa procession, was not originally a flamenco form but was flamenco-ised around the start of the 20th century. Saetas, traditionally spontaneous, are these days usually stage-managed.

The very popular *sevillana* is not, most pundits agree, really flamenco at all. Primarily a folk dance form for couples, with high, twirling arm movements and consisting of four parts each coming to an abrupt halt, it's probably an Andalucian version of a Castilian dance called the *seguidilla*.

Legends of Flamenco

The first person to make a living from flamenco was El Fillo from the Cádiz area, born about 1820. His name lives on in the term *voz afillá* which refers to the classic raw, powerful, booze-and-baccy-soaked jondo voice.

The first two great singers of the cafés cantante era of the mid-19th to early 20th century were Silverio Franconetti from Sevilla and Antonio Chacón from Jerez. Their successors in the early 20th century were Manuel Torre from Jerez – whose singing could, legend has it, drive people to rip their shirts open and upturn tables – and Sevilla's La Niña de los Peines, the first great cantaora.

La Macarrona from Jerez and Pastora Imperio from Sevilla, the first great bailaoras, took flamenco to Paris and South America. Their style concentrated on movements of the torso and arms, rather than on the feet and on moving around the stage.

The flamenco of the cafés cantante tended to be of the non-jondo sort and from this developed, in the 1920s, a type of light, operetta-like show called opera flamenca. The singer Pepe Marchena, its chief exponent, went on until the 1950s, by which time cante jondo had almost disappeared. In 1922 the composer Manuel de Falla, the writer Federico García Lorca and others organised a famous Concurso (competition) de Cante Jondo in Granada to try to revive pure jondo singing. Though the event launched the career of Manolo Caracol, the leading jondo singer of the mid-century, it did not stop cante as a whole from continuing to get more commercial and less jondo.

The *baile* (dance), however, flourished in the persons of La Argentina and the younger La Argentinita, two female dancers of Argentine origin who turned it into a theatrical show, forming the first Spanish dance troupes and triumphing in Paris, South America and New York in the late 1920s and 30s. Their contemporary Vicente Escudero was the first great male dancer. La Argentina and Escudero mixed classical dance with flamenco, but La Argentinita was strictly flamenco – and so was Carmen Anaya (1913-63) from Barcelona, whose fast, dynamic, unfeminine dancing and wild lifestyle made her the Gypsy dance legend of all time. She too toured successfully in the Americas and Europe – as did Antonio Ruiz Soler (1921-96) from Sevilla, internationally the best known bailaor of the century. Antonio's footwork was famous but he was also the first male flamenco dancer to really use his arms.

Sabicas, born in 1912 in Pamplona in northern Spain and a long-time partner and lover of Carmen Anaya, was the father of the modern solo flamenco guitar, inventing a host of techniques now considered indispensable. He never returned to live in Spain after leaving during the civil war.

Modern Flamenco

In the 1950s and 60s the flame of pure flamenco was kept alive by Antonio Mairena from Sevilla, who not only sang cante jondo but campaigned for it, collecting and recording old songs and spurring a new wave of concursos and festivals. At the same time the lightweight strand of flamenco reached its most debased form with the *tablaos* set up to entertain the new wave of foreign tourists – 'clubs' with second-rate shows dwelling on the sexy and jolly. The tablaos continue today but there has also been, since the late 1960s, a new lease of life for *flamenco puro*.

The legendary singer El Camarón de la Isla had duende – the spirit.

Singers who flourished in the 70s included Terremoto (Earthquake) from Jerez; El Chocolate, with one of the real afillá voices of recent times; Enrique Morente from Granada, with a clearer, tenorish voice, who has been referred to as 'the last Bohemian'; Fernanda de Útrera, from Sevilla province (another important nest of flamenco), famous for her soleás; and La Paquera from Jerez, renowned for her bulerías. The latter four are, to varying extents, still singing today, and Morente is the leader of contemporary male cante.

The 70s was, however, above all the decade of El Camarón de la Isla, the 'Shrimp of the Island' – the island being his home town of San Fernando on the Cádiz peninsula. Camarón's screaming, raucous voz afillá, great range of styles and wayward unreliability made him a flamenco legend even before his early death in 1992 after years of an uncontrollable drug problem. He was one who had *duende* (the spirit), an undefinable transforming magic possessed by the great flamenco performers – the kind of thing that made Manuel Torre's listeners tear open their shirts.

The biggest dance name in the 70s and 80s was the Madrid-based Antonio Gades. He and his erstwhile partner Cristina Hoyos, from Sevilla, now both have their own successful dance companies.

The one flamenco name likely to be known to the uninitiated is Paco de Lucía. Hailing from Algeciras and born in 1947, de Lucía absorbed forms and techniques with such Picasso-like rapidity that by the time he was 14 his teachers found they had nothing left to do. Since then he has transformed the guitar – formerly the junior partner of the flamenco trinity – into an instrument of solo expression with a raft of new techniques, scales, melodies and harmonies which have taken him far beyond the limits of traditional flamenco. De Lucía's virtuosity is such that he can sound like two or three people playing together. The innovation of his playing was perfectly suited to the post-Franco social liberation of the 1970s and early 1980s.

In the 1970s, de Lucía accompanied El Camarón de la Isla and several albums of them playing together have resulted. Since then, he has, among other things, interpreted

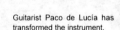

Guitarist Paco de Lucía has transformed the instrument.

Manuel de Falla with an electric backing band; collaborated with jazz players such as John McLaughlin, Larry Coryell and Al di Meola; and (in the 1990 album *Ziryab*) looked back to the Islamic roots of Andalucian music. He has attained international acclaim through extensive foreign tours and a steady flow of varied albums. The double album *Paco de Lucía Antología* is a pretty good introduction to his work, ranging from 1967 to 1990.

Contemporary Flamenco

In addition to those mentioned above who are still performing, big-name singers include Carmen Linares from Jaén province, a versatile ambassador of jondo whose 1996 double album *Carmen Linares en Antología* is a journey through the past 150 years of female cante; El Cabrero (a goatherd, as his name says), does the sterner stuff well; the big-voiced, big-gestured El Lebrijano (Juan Peña) from Lebrija, another Guadalquivir valley town that has given much to flamenco; the versatile Calixto Sánchez; José Mercé; and Miguel Poveda.

Among guitarists, look out for the top-flight soloist Manolo Sanlúcar; Manuel Morao from Jerez, who played with many past greats; Pedro Bacán; Moraíto Chico; Juan Habichuela and Pepe

Habichuela from Granada's voluminous Montoya family of flamenco performers; and Rafael Riqueni and Tomatito from Almería, who accompanied El Camarón de la Isla after Paco de Lucía.

Nuevo Flamenco

 Given a cue perhaps by Paco de Lucía, a new generation of musicians appeared who adventurously mixed flamenco with jazz, rock, blues, rap and other idioms. At first reviled by traditionalists, this New Flamenco greatly broadened flamenco's appeal, especially among the young.

The seminal work was a 1977 flamenco/folk/rock album called *Veneno* by the group of the same name, centred on Kiko Veneno (see Pop & Rock under Music in the Facts for the Visitor chapter) and Raimundo Amador, both from Sevilla. The album was virtually ignored but has since acquired legendary status. Amador and his brother Rafael then formed Pata Negra which produced four fine flamenco/jazz/blues albums culminating in *Blues de la Frontera* in 1986. Since then, Raimundo has gone solo, veering towards blues and playing with BB King.

Ketama, named after a Moroccan hashish town and whose three key members are all from the Montoya flamenco family, have fused flamenco with African, Cuban, Brazilian and other rhythms. Two of their most successful albums were *Songhai* (1987) and *Songhai 2* (1995) on which they collaborated with Malian kora player Toumani Diabate and British folk bassist Danny Thompson.

In the early 1990s, Radio Tarifa emerged with a mesmerising mix of flamenco, North African and medieval sounds. The first CD, *Rumba Argelina*, was a great hit.

More recently, Cádiz's Niña Pastori has become hugely popular, singing flamenco with an electric jazz-rock band backing. Her 1997 album *Entre dos Puertos* with its hit 'Tu Me Camelas' is well worth looking out for. Tomasito, from Jerez, *'el breaker flamenco'*, does sort of robotised bulerías with an avalanche of rumba and hiphop rhythm. Navajita Plateá, two brothers from Jerez, are successful with what's been described as 'blues de la frontera', between flamenco and pop.

Oddly, the most successful modern flamenco-style music is the rumba-rock of the Gipsy Kings – who happen to be from southern France, not Spain.

Established flamenco artists are experimenting too. El Camarón de la Isla was as much a pop star as a flamenco star by the time of his death. Guitarist Manolo Sanlúcar, in the de Lucía mould, encompasses rock, jazz and classical. El Lebrijano has done appealing combinations with classical Moroccan music. Perhaps most astonishing of all was Enrique Morente's 1997-98 collaboration with the Granada metallic rockers Lagartija Nick on *Omega*, an interpretation of Lorca's poetry collection *Poeta en Nueva York* (Poet in New York), which also includes songs by the Lorca-influenced Leonard Cohen.

Dance

Always the readiest of the flamenco arts to cross boundaries, dance has reached out to yet more adventurous (outrageous, say some) horizons in the person of Joaquín Cortés, born in Córdoba in 1969. Cortés sees himself as the dance follow-up to Paco de Lucía and El Camarón de la Isla, and says he is not really a flamenco dancer but a Gypsy who dances. With an immensely popular touring ensemble, he fuses flamenco with contemporary dance, ballet and jazz, with music at rock-concert amplification, to which he dances naked from the waist up using lyrical arm movements.

Antonio Canales, born in Triana in 1962, is more of a flamenco purist. His company has done shows on bullfight and Gypsy themes, and plans further ones around Lorca and Picasso's *Guernica*. A rising star is Javier Barón, a sevillano who launched his own company in 1997.

Top names in more traditional flamenco dance include Miguel El Funi and Concha Vargas, both from Lebrija.

Wooden castanets such as these are clicked together rhythmically by the *bailaoras* as they dance, and complement their expressive hand movements and tapping feet.

Flamenco dancers: it is difficult not to be moved by this very physical, at times even visceral, experience. *(photographs by David Waterman)*

Flamenco Films

 Carlos Saura, one of the leading Spanish film makers since the early 1970s, has dedicated several films to flamenco. His flamenco versions of Lorca's *Bodas de Sangre*, Bizet's *Carmen* and de Falla's *El Amor Brujo*, made between the late 1970s and 1986, feature dancers Antonio Gades and Cristina Hoyos. *Carmen* has a soundtrack by Paco de Lucía. Saura's *Flamenco* (1995) is as good an introduction as any to flamenco, less a film than an exciting review of the best in the field – among them Paco de Lucía, Manolo Sanlúcar and Joaquín Cortés. A double CD set of the music is available. Saura has also made *Sevillanas*, celebrating the various forms of this idiom.

Seeing Flamenco

See the Public Holidays & Special Events and Andalucian Festivals sections and Entertainment in the Facts for the Visitor chapter for tips on where and when to catch live flamenco.

The following Web sites are also useful resources: Centro Andaluz de Flamenco, Jerez de la Frontera (caf.cica.es); and Music Spain, an excellent, wide-ranging site (www.music-spain.com/indice.htm)

continued from page 48
Gender roles are more defined in Spain than in northern Europe and north America and perhaps particularly so in Andalucía. While a respectable number of women have jobs outside the home, they tend to do most of the domestic work too. Things are less extreme in the bigger cities and among the young, but in the villages you'll notice that nearly all motorcycle riders are men and nearly all pushchair pushers are women. It's not common to see a man shopping for food, or a woman sitting at a bar! It still seems to be the case that many men can get away with extramarital affairs, while their wives are expected to remain 100% faithful – even to the point of not being seen to converse with unfamiliar men.

Most people like to look their best and take every opportunity to dress up well – though not often to the extent of a formal suit and tie. They know that foreigners don't go to quite the same lengths, but you may feel uncomfortable in an unfresh T-shirt, jeans and trainers in some restaurants or discos – some of the latter wouldn't let you in, in any case.

Time
The Spanish attitude to time *is* more relaxed than in most western cultures. But things that need a fixed time – trains, buses, cinemas, bullfights – get one, and it's generally stuck to. Waiters may not always be in a hurry, but they come eventually.

What is different is the daily timetable. The Spanish *tarde* (afternoon) doesn't really starts till 4 or 5 pm and goes on till 9 or 10 pm or later. Shops and offices close from around 2 to 5 pm, then mostly open again till around 8 pm. In hot summer months people stay outside till very late at night, enjoying the coolness. At fiestas, don't be surprised to see a merry-go-round packed with tiny children at 3 am. And, of course, Friday and Saturday nights all year round barely begin till midnight for those doing the rounds of bars and discos.

Siesta Contrary to popular belief, most Spaniards do not sleep in the afternoon. The siesta, if taken, is generally devoted to a long lunch and lingering conversation. Then again, if you've stayed out until 6 am ...

RELIGION
Roman Catholicism
It's impossible not to notice the importance of the Roman Catholic church in Spain. So many of the country's great occasions are religious fiestas; so many of its most magnificent buildings are cathedrals or churches, lavishly adorned and lovingly tended by the faithful. The great majority of Spaniards have church baptisms, weddings and funerals. According to surveys, around 85% of them say they are Catholics.

All this is hardly surprising in a nation whose very existence is the result of a series of medieval anti-Muslim crusades. Under Franco, the church and state were so closely tied that the government appointed bishops, paid priests' salaries and granted the church numerous other privileges, including lots of money. The government still subsidises the church heavily, and one-sixth of schools are still run by religious orders and groups, even though Spain has had no official religion since 1978.

Yet the country has a long-standing and deep-rooted *anti*clerical tradition too, going back to the days when the church and nobility were very rich and most other people very poor. In the 19th century the church became identified with conservative opposition to political change, and it was considered one of the main enemies by the Andalucian anarchists and other revolutionaries of the period. This enmity reached a bloody crescendo in the civil war, when some 7000 priests, nuns and monks were killed in Spain. The revolutionary spirit still lives in Andalucía (15% to 20% of people vote communist) and so does the anti-church tradition – especially, it seems, among men. One villager said to us: 'Look at the people who go to church. They're the *bad* people.'

The church's hold is also challenged by the usual distractions of modern life. Only some

40% of Spaniards now go to church once a month or more. Those who do go are often old, poor, female and live in rural areas. Catholicism is so deeply ingrained, however, that men who hardly ever go to church vie for membership of the brother-hoods that carry holy images in Easter processions, and families spend an average of 300,000 ptas on special clothes and fes-tivities for a child's first communion. The early 20th century philosopher Miguel Unamuno's quip, 'Here in Spain we are all Catholics, even the atheists', still holds.

Other Faiths

Protestantism was eradicated by the Inqui-sition in the 16th century. Today, the few Protestants in Andalucía nearly all come from northern Europe. The Jehovah's Wit-nesses have a sizeable presence.

Muslims and Jews played an enormous role in medieval Spain but were firmly stamped on at the end of that period (see History). Today, mainland Spain has around 80,000 Muslims. Most are Muslim immi-grants, not many of whom live in Andalucía, though there are a few hundred native-born converts living in Granada's old Muslim quarter, the Albayzín.

The Jewish community numbers a few thousand people (1500 in Málaga), many of them from Morocco. In 1982 Sephardic Jews (Jews of Spanish origin) were offi-cially invited to return to Spain, 490 years after expulsion by the Catholic Monarchs.

LANGUAGE

Spanish is spoken throughout Andalucía. See the Language Guide at the back of the book for details and local pronunciation.

Facts for the Visitor

PLANNING
When to Go
Andalucía can be enjoyable any time of year, though the weather from November to February is a hit-or-miss affair. Climatically, the ideal months to visit are April, May, June, September and October. At these times you can rely on good to excellent weather, yet avoid the sometimes extreme heat and the main crush of Spanish and foreign tourists of July and August, when temperatures may climb to 45°C inland. The countryside is at its most colourful in spring and autumn too. July and August are the peak months for colourful fiestas, though there are plenty of these at almost any time between Semana Santa (the week leading up to Easter Sunday) and October.

If you plan to pursue some specific activity such as hiking, you may need to choose your time carefully – see Activities in this chapter and destination sections in the regional chapters.

Maps
Small-Scale Maps Michelin's 1:400,000 *Southern Spain* is good. A new edition is published each year. It's widely available in and outside Andalucía: in Spain, petrol stations and bookshops are the places to look, and the maps cost 785 ptas.

Road Atlases See Car & Motorcycle in the Getting Around chapter.

City Maps For finding your way around cities and towns, the maps provided by tourist offices are often adequate. If you want something more comprehensive, most cities are covered by one of the Spanish series such as Telstar, Alpina and Everest, with street indexes – available in bookshops, but check their publication dates.

Large-Scale Maps Two organisations publish large-scale maps of parts of Spain.

The CNIG (Centro Nacional de Información Geográfica) covers most of the country, including about three-quarters of Andalucía, in 1:25,000 (1cm to 250m) sheets, most of which are recent. The CNIG and the Servicio Geográfico del Ejército (SGE, Army Geographic Service) each publishes a 1:50,000 series; the SGEs, published in the mid-1980s, tend to be more up to date. The CNIG also has a *Mapa Guía* series for national and natural parks, mostly 1:50,000 or 1:100,000 and published in the 1990s. Until a few years ago the CNIG was called the IGN (Instituto Geográfico Nacional) and some of its maps still bear that name.

CNIG and SGE maps are hard to come by in Andalucía's hiking areas – you're more likely to find the CNIG Mapas Guía than the others – so it's best to try to obtain them in advance. Edward Stanford (☎ 0171-836 1321), 12-14 Long Acre, Covent Garden, London WC2E 9LP, UK, has a good range of Spain maps. The CNIG (☎ 91 597 95 14; fax 91 553 29 13), Calle General Ibáñez de Íbero 3, 28003 Madrid, will send you a free catalogue of its maps, which you can then purchase by mail: the standard 1:25,000 and 1:50,000 maps are 330 ptas each plus postage. The CNIG also has sales points in Andalucía's eight provincial capitals, including:

Granada
 Avenida Divina Pastora 7 & 9 (☎ 958 29 04 11)
Málaga
 Avenida de la Aurora 47, 7ª (☎ 95 231 28 08)
Sevilla
 Avenida San Francisco Javier 9, Edificio Sevilla 2, 8º (módulo 7) (☎ 95 464 42 56)

The SGE has one map shop at Calle de Darío Gazapo 8 (Cuartel Alfonso X), 28024 Madrid (☎ 91 711 50 43; fax 91 711 50 32), open Monday to Friday, 9 am to 1.30 pm. The SGE can send maps to Spanish addresses if you prepay by postal giro or cash.

HIGHLIGHTS

Most parts of Andalucía are well worth visiting. Here are a few highlights to help you with your itinerary.

Cities & Towns

Sevilla is Andalucía's most vibrant city. Málaga is not far behind in terms of its people's capacity for fun, though it lacks Sevilla's range of great historical and artistic treasures. Granada is a must because of its Muslim heritage. It has perhaps the most international atmosphere of Andalucía's cities thanks to the many foreign students and travellers it attracts. Córdoba too has a fascinating Muslim heritage.

Among smaller cities and towns, our favourites include down-to-earth, fun-loving Cádiz; Jerez de la Frontera, the sherry capital also famed for its horses and flamenco; Tarifa, with fine beaches and an international windsurfing scene; Ronda, astride a dramatic gorge with beautiful hill country close by; Arcos de la Frontera, a white town which spills over a rocky ridge; and Cazorla, an old-fashioned place that's also the gateway to the beautiful Parque Natural de Cazorla. All these places, except Cádiz, have a clear imprint from the Islamic past. Near Cazorla, the towns of Baeza and Úbeda are full of magnificent architecture dating from the early post-Reconquista centuries.

Coasts

Andalucía's best coasts are near its extremities. East of Almería, the dry, sparsely populated Cabo de Gata promontory is strung with excellent and, by Spanish standards, underpopulated beaches, backed by some stark, rugged coastal hills.

In western Andalucía, the so-called Costa de la Luz (Coast of Light) stretches almost 200km from Tarifa to the Portuguese border. The slightly cooler Atlantic waters and breezes are a small price to pay for many fine, long, sandy beaches, backed by pine-covered dunes. Small places like Bolonia, Zahara de los Atunes, Los Caños de Meca, Sanlúcar de Barrameda, Mazagón and La Antilla are among the most enjoyable and laid-back resorts of the region – most of them relatively unknown to the outside world, though popular enough with Andalucians. The beaches and resorts are interspersed with cities and ports such as Cádiz, Huelva and Isla Cristina and with extensive wetlands which are vital to wildlife – most famously the Parque Nacional de Doñana.

Hill Country

Andalucía has some marvellously beautiful mountain and hill areas, good for walking or just cruising around. The thickly forested Parque Natural de Cazorla in Jaén province is perhaps the most stunning – its mountains are among the most rugged, varied and spectacular, and in Segura de la Sierra you'll find one of the most dramatically sited villages in Spain.

The Alpujarras valleys on the southern flank of the Sierra Nevada, south-east of Granada, are an otherworldly, hauntingly beautiful zone of arid hillsides and ravines, dotted with oasis-like white villages.

The Sierra Morena, rolling along Andalucía's northern rim, rarely more than 1000m high, attains surprising levels of abruptness, verdure and beauty towards its western end, in areas like the Parque Natural Sierra Norte and especially the Parque Natural Sierra de Aracena y Picos de Aroche. These areas are well off the regular foreign tourist's trail.

Further beautiful, green mountainous areas lie west and east of the town of Ronda, mostly in the Parque Natural Sierra de Grazalema and Parque Natural Sierra de las Nieves. East of the latter Andalucía's most awesome gorge, El Chorro, has been carved out by the Río Guadalhorce.

The 1:50,000 maps are 303 ptas, plus postage. It advises people in other countries, however, to contact local specialists.

What to Bring
Everything you bring, you have to carry. You can buy most things you need in Spain.

Luggage If you'll be doing any walking at all with your luggage, a backpack is the sensible answer. One with straps and openings that can be zipped inside a flap is more secure and there's less risk of getting it trapped in escalators, caught on door handles etc. A small daypack is a useful addition.

Inscribing your name and address on the inside of your luggage, as well as labelling it on the outside, increases your chances of getting it back if it's lost or stolen.

Clothing In high summer you may not need more than one layer of clothing even at 4 am. At cooler times, layers of thin clothing, which trap warm air and can be peeled off if necessary, are better than a single thick layer. It's a good idea to pack a set of good clothes for some discos and restaurants – they don't have to be *too* formal, though.

You need a pair of strong shoes – at least strong trainers – no matter what type of trip you're making. If you plan on going to smart discos or restaurants, you'll need something other than trainers.

Useful Items Apart from any special personal needs, or things you might require for particular kinds of trips (camping, hiking, windsurfing etc), consider the following:

- an under-the-clothes money belt or shoulder wallet, useful for protecting your money and documents in cities
- a small towel and soap, often lacking in cheap accommodation
- sunscreen lotion, which can be more expensive in Spain than elsewhere
- a small Spanish dictionary and/or phrasebook
- books, which can be hard to find
- photocopies of your important documents, kept separate from the originals

- a pocket knife
- minimal unbreakable cooking, eating and drinking gear if you plan to prepare your own food and drinks
- a medical kit (see Health)
- a padlock or two
- an adapter plug for electrical appliances
- a torch (flashlight)
- an alarm clock
- sunglasses
- binoculars if you plan to do any wildlife spotting

TOURIST OFFICES
All cities and many smaller towns and even villages have at least one *oficina de turismo* or *oficina de información turística*. On the whole, these are helpful, knowledgable and well equipped with give-away or for-sale printed material. There's nearly always someone on hand with at least some English. Opening hours vary widely.

The regional government, the Junta de Andalucía, maintains tourist offices in all eight provincial capitals and several other towns. The Junta's environmental department, the Agencia de Medio Ambiente, has visitor centres in many environmentally protected areas – *parques naturales* and so on. If a place has no tourist office, the *ayuntamiento* (town hall) will often be able to help with information.

Tourist Offices Abroad
Information on Andalucía is available from Spanish national tourist offices in 19 countries, including:

Canada
  2 Bloor St West, 34th floor, Toronto, Ontario M4W 3E2 (☎ 416-961 3131)
France
  43 rue Decamps, 75784 Paris, Cedex 16 (☎ 01 45 03 82 50)
Germany
  Kurfürstendamm 180, 10707 Berlin (☎ 030-8 82 65 43)
Portugal
  Edificio Monumental, Avenida Fontes Pereira de Melo 51- 4º andar D, 1000 Lisbon (☎ 01-354 1992)

UK
22-23 Manchester Square, London W1M
5AP (☎ 0171-486 8077; brochure request
☎ 0891-669920 at 50p a minute)
USA
666 Fifth Ave, 35th floor, New York, NY 10103
(☎ 212-265 8822)
Also Chicago (☎ 312-642 1992),
Los Angeles (☎ 213-658 7188) and Miami
(☎ 305-358 1992)

VISAS & DOCUMENTS
Passport
Citizens of the 15 European Union (EU)
member states and Switzerland can travel to
Spain with their national identity card alone.
If such countries do not issue ID cards – as is
the case with the UK – travellers must carry
a full valid passport (UK Visitor passports are
not acceptable). All other nationalities must
have a full valid passport.

Check that your passport's expiry date is at
least some months off, as otherwise you may
not be granted a visa should you need one.

By law, you are supposed to have your ID
card or passport with you at all times in
Spain. You will usually need one of these
documents for registration when you take a
hotel room.

Visas
For tourist visits to Spain of up to 90 days,
nationals of many countries – including the
EU states, Australia, Canada, Israel, Japan,
New Zealand, Norway, Switzerland and the
USA – require no visa.

South Africans are among those who *do*
need a visa for Spain – unless they are resident in a 'Schengen country' (see below).
Options include 30-day and 90-day single-
entry visas (in London these cost UK£17.75
and UK£21.30 respectively), 90-day multi-
ple-entry visas (UK£24.85) and various
transit visas (people who need a visa for
Spain may do so even if just changing
planes at a Spanish airport). A multiple-
entry visa will save you a lot of time and
trouble if you plan to leave Spain – say to
Gibraltar or Morocco – and then re-enter it.
You are allowed to use only one 90-day visa
of either type in any six-month period. It's

best to apply for the visa in your country of
residence to avoid possible bureaucratic
delays and/or refusal of a 90-day visa.

The Schengen 'System' Spain is one of
the 'Schengen countries' which have theo-
retically done away with passport control
on travel between member countries. (The
others are Portugal, France, Germany, Italy,
the Netherlands, Belgium, Luxembourg and
Austria, with Greece, Sweden, Denmark,
Norway, Iceland and Finland expected to
join up soon.) In fact, the Schengen countries reserve the right to make spot passport
checks and these occur fairly regularly at
Spanish airports and have been known to
occur on Lisbon-Madrid trains.

Nationals of Australia, Canada, Israel,
Japan, New Zealand, Norway, Switzerland,
the USA and the non-Schengen EU countries require no visa for tourist visits of up
to 90 days to any Schengen country. South
Africans do. Though it is sometimes possible for people who are required to have a
visa to reach Spain and travel there without
one, it is illegal and can lead to deportation.
Travellers who arrive in France by boat or
train from the UK may not have their passports checked but those arriving by air,
however, have no such chance .

One good thing about the Schengen
system is that a visa for one Schengen
country is valid for all other Schengen countries too – so, for instance, a French visa is
good for Spain too. Compare validity periods,
prices and the number of permitted entries
before you apply. Schengen visas are free for
spouses and children of EU nationals.

Legal residents of one Schengen country
do *not* require a visa for another Schengen
country.

Visa Extensions & Residence Nationals
of EU countries, Norway and Iceland can virtually (if not technically) enter and leave
Spain at will. Those wanting to stay in Spain
longer than 90 days are supposed to apply
during their first month in Spain for a resident's card *(tarjeta de residencia)*. This is a
lengthy bureaucratic procedure: if you intend

to subject yourself to it, consult a Spanish consulate before you go to Spain, as you will need to take certain documents with you.

Other nationalities who want to stay in Spain longer than 90 days are also supposed to get a resident's card, and for them it's a truly nightmarish process, starting with a residence visa issued by a Spanish consulate in your country of residence: begin the process light years in advance.

Non-EU spouses of EU citizens resident in Spain can apply for residence too. The process is lengthy, and those needing to travel in and out of the country in the meantime could ask for an *exención de visado* – a visa exemption. In most cases, the spouse is obliged to make the formal application in his/her country of residence. A real pain.

Photocopies

It is a wise precaution to keep photocopies of the data pages of your passport and any other identity cards, and even your birth certificate if you can manage it. This will help speed up replacement if the originals are lost or stolen. If your passport is stolen or lost, notify the police and obtain a statement, and contact your embassy or consulate as soon as possible.

Other worthwhile things to photocopy include airline tickets, travel insurance documents with emergency numbers, credit cards (and phone numbers to contact in case of card loss), driving licence and vehicle documentation. Keep all of this, and a list of your travellers' cheque numbers, separate from the originals. Leave extra copies with someone reliable at home.

Travel Insurance

A travel insurance policy to cover theft, loss of luggage or tickets, medical problems, and perhaps cancellation or delays in your travel arrangements, is a good idea. (But see Health later in this chapter for further information on medical insurance.)

A wide variety of travel policies is available and travel agents will be able to make recommendations. The policies handled by STA Travel and other student travel organisations are usually good value. Check the small print: some policies specifically exclude 'dangerous activities', which can include scuba diving, motorcycling, even trekking. You may prefer a policy which pays doctors or hospitals directly rather than you having to pay on the spot and claim later. If you have to claim later make sure you keep all documentation.

Buy travel insurance as early as possible. If you buy it in the week before you leave home, you may find, for example, that you are not covered for delays to your trip caused by industrial action.

Paying for your ticket with a credit card often provides limited travel accident insurance, and you may be able to reclaim payment if the operator doesn't deliver. Ask your credit card company what it will cover.

Driving Licence & Permits

EU licences (pink or pink and green) are fully recognised in all EU member states, including Spain. (But note that the old-style UK green licence is not accepted.) Other foreign licences are supposed to be accompanied by an International Driving Permit (although in practice, for renting cars or dealing with traffic police, your national licence will suffice). The International Driving Permit is available from automobile clubs in your country and is valid for 12 months. For other documents needed to drive to or in Spain, see The UK in the Land section of the Getting There & Away chapter.

Hostel Card

A valid hostel card is needed at all the 17 youth hostels of Inturjoven, the official Andalucía hostel organisation – see Accommodation in this chapter.

Student, Teacher & Youth Cards

These kinds of cards can get you worthwhile discounts on travel, and reduced prices at some museums, sights and entertainments.

The International Student Identity Card (ISIC), for full-time students, and the International Teacher Identity Card (ITIC), for full-time teachers and professors, are issued by more than 5000 organisations around the world – mainly student travel-related, such as STA Travel, Campus Travel, Council Travel and Travel CUTS (see Air in the Getting There & Away chapter for more on these). The same offices usually sell student air, train and bus fares.

Anyone under 26 can apply for a GO25 card or a Euro26 card. Both these give similar discounts to the ISIC and are issued by most of the same organisations. The Euro26 has a variety of alternative names in different countries including the Under 26 Card in England and Wales and the Carnet Joven Europeo in Spain. For information you can contact Under 26, 52 Grosvenor Gardens, London SW1W OAG, UK (☎ 0171-730 7285).

As an example of the sort of discounts you can expect in Spain, the more useful things on offer for Euro26 card holders include 20% to 25% off most 2nd-class train fares; 10% or 20% off some international bus fares; and 20% to 50% discounts at several theatres in Sevilla.

EMBASSIES
Spanish Embassies Abroad
Here is a list of Spanish embassies in selected countries:

Australia
    15 Arkana St, Yarralumla, Canberra, ACT 2600 (☎ 02-6273 3555)
Canada
    74 Stanley Ave, Ottawa, Ontario K1M 1P4 (☎ 613-747 2252)
    Consulates in Toronto (☎ 416-977 1661) and Montreal (☎ 514-935 5235)
France
    22 Ave Marceau, 75008 Paris Cedex 08 (☎ 01-44 43 18 00)
Germany
    Schlossstrasse 4, 53115 Bonn (☎ 0228-21 70 94)

Consulates in Berlin (☎ 030-261 60 81), Düsseldorf (☎ 0211-43 90 80), Frankfurt/Main (☎ 069-96 10 41), Munich (☎ 089-98 50 27) and other cities
Ireland
    17A Merlyn Park, Balls Bridge, Dublin 4 (☎ 01-269 1640)
Morocco
    105 Ave Allal ben Abdellah, 3 Zankat Madnine, Rabat (☎ 07-707600, 07-707980)
New Zealand
    The Spanish embassy in Australia handles New Zealand too
Portugal
    Rua do Salitre 1, 1200 Lisbon (☎ 01-347 2381)
UK
    Embassy: 39 Chesham Place, London SW1X 8SB (☎ 0171-235 5555)
    Consulates: 20 Draycott Place, London SW3 2RZ (☎ 0171-581 7888, 0171-589 8989)
    Suite 1A, Brook House, 70 Spring Gardens, Manchester M2 2BQ (☎ 0161-589 5842, 0161-236 1233)
    63 North Castle St, Edinburgh EH2 3LJ (☎ 0131-226 4568, 0131-220 1843)
USA
    2375 Pennsylvania Ave NW, Washington, DC 20037 (☎ 202-728 2330)
    Consulates in Boston (☎ 617-536 2506), Chicago (☎ 312-782 4588), Houston (☎ 713-783 6200), Los Angeles (☎ 213-938 0158), Miami (☎ 305-446 5511), New Orleans (☎ 504-525 4951), New York (☎ 212-355 4080) and San Francisco (☎ 415-922 2995)

Embassies & Consulates in Spain
All the embassies are in Madrid, but many countries also have consulates in Andalucía – most often in Sevilla or Málaga (see city sections of this guide). Embassies and consulates in Madrid include:

Australia
    Plaza del Descubridor Diego de Ordás 3-2, Edificio Santa Engracia 120 (☎ 91 441 93 00)
Canada
    Calle de Núñez de Balboa 35 (☎ 91 431 43 00)
France
    Calle Salustiano Olózaga 9 (☎ 91 435 55 60)
Germany
    Calle de Fortuny 8 (☎ 91 557 90 00)
Ireland
    Calle de Claudio Coello 73 (☎ 91 576 35 00, 91 435 16 77)

BETHUNE CARMICHAEL

BETHUNE CARMICHAEL

BETHUNE CARMICHAEL

SEVILLA
Top left: The Alcázar
Top right: Shopfronts in Sevilla
Bottom: El Catedral

CÓRDOBA

Top and right: The Mezquita, with its mesmerising stripes of red brick and white stone and rows of twin tier arches is one of the most magnificent of Islamic buildings

Bottom: The Puerta de Almódovar, an Islamic gate in a restored section of the old city walls

Morocco
 Calle de Serrano 179
 (☎ 91 563 79 28, 91 563 10 90)
 Consulate: Calle de Leizaran 31
 (☎ 91 561 89 12, 91 561 21 45)
New Zealand
 Plaza de la Lealtad 2
 (☎ 91 523 02 26, 91 531 09 97)
Portugal
 Calle Castillo 128 (☎ 91 561 78 00)
 Consulate: Paseo de General Martínez Campos
 11 (☎ 91 445 46 00)
South Africa
 Calle de Claudio Coello 91
 (☎ 91 435 66 88, 91 576 34 63)
UK
 Calle de Fernando el Santo 16
 (☎ 91 319 02 00)
 Consulate: Centro Colón, Calle del Marqués
 de la Ensenada 16 (☎ 91 308 52 01)
USA
 Calle de Serrano 75 (☎ 91 587 22 00)

CUSTOMS

People entering Spain from outside the EU are allowed to bring in duty-free one bottle of spirits, one bottle of wine, 50 ml of perfume and 200 cigarettes. If you are travelling from one EU country to another, you can bring 2L of wine and 1L of spirits, but the same limits apply on the rest. However, duty-free allowances for travel between EU countries are due to be abolished on 30 June 1999. For duty-paid items bought at normal shops in one EU country and taken into another, the allowances are 90L of wine, 10L of spirits, unlimited quantities of perfume and 800 cigarettes.

MONEY

A combination of travellers' cheques and plastic is the best way to take your money.

Currency

Spain's currency, the peseta (pta), comes in coins of one, five, 10, 25, 50, 100, 200 and 500 ptas, and notes of 1000, 2000, 5000 and 10,000 ptas.

A five ptas coin is widely known as a *duro*, and it's fairly common for small sums to be quoted in duros: *dos duros* for 10 ptas, *cinco duros* for 25 ptas, even *veinte duros* for 100 ptas.

Sometimes it's hard to get change for a 5000 or 10,000 ptas note. If you're getting cash from a bank or ATM, requesting a sum that's not a multiple of 5000 ptas will prevent you being stuck with 5000 or 10,000 ptas notes only.

The Euro When the new common currency for most EU countries, the euro, is launched on 1 January 1999, Spain will be among the first countries to adopt it. However, its use will at first be restricted to things like share prices and inter-bank transfers. Actual euro coins and notes will not appear until 1 January 2002. The euro will then circulate alongside the peseta for a few months. By 1 July 2002 the peseta will cease to be legal tender.

The euro will have a fixed peseta value (probably about 165 ptas), and will be divided into 100 cents.

Exchange Rates

Currencies of the developed world can be changed without problems, except queues, in any bank or exchange office. But get rid of any dirham before you leave Morocco – you can change them for pesetas in Ceuta and Melilla but rates are worse than in Morocco.

The peseta has been fairly stable since its last devaluation in 1993.

Australia	A$1	=	90 ptas
Canada	C$1	=	100 ptas
France	1FF	=	25 ptas
Germany	DM1	=	84 ptas
Japan	¥100	=	104 ptas
New Zealand	NZ$1	=	76 ptas
Portugal	100$00	=	83 ptas
UK	UK£1	=	245 ptas
USA	US$1	=	152 ptas

Exchanging Money

You can change cash or travellers' cheques at virtually any bank or exchange office. International airports usually have both, and road border crossings into Spain will have one or the other close by. Banks tend to offer the best rates. They're very common in cities, and even small villages often have one. They're mostly open Monday to Friday from about 8.30 am to 2 pm, and Saturday from 9 am to 1 pm. A great many banks have ATMs.

Exchange offices – usually indicated by the word *cambio* (exchange) – exist mainly in tourist resorts and other places that attract high numbers of foreigners. Generally they offer longer opening hours and quicker service than banks, but significantly worse exchange rates (though American Express is an honourable exception here).

Travellers' cheques usually bring a better exchange rate than cash, and in many places, the more money you change, the better the exchange rate you'll get.

Wherever you change, it's well worth asking about commissions first, and confirming that exchange rates are as posted. Every bank seems to have a different commission structure: commissions may be different for travellers' cheques and cash, and may depend on how many cheques, or how much in total, you're cashing. A typical commission is 3%, with a minimum of 300 to 500 ptas, but there are places with a minimum of 1000 and sometimes 2000 ptas. Places that advertise 'no commission' may offer poor exchange rates to start with (American Express is again an honourable exception.)

Carrying Money

Spain has a high rate of theft from tourists. According to the British organisation Card Protection Plan, no fewer than 200,000 British credit cards and cash cards went missing in Spain in just four months (June to September) in 1995. Consolation for visitors to Andalucía is that Barcelona and Madrid are the country's worst cities for card theft.

Keep only a limited amount of money as cash, and the bulk in more easily replaceable forms such as travellers' cheques or plastic. If your accommodation has a safe, use it. If you have to leave money in your room, divide it into several stashes and hide them in different places.

For carrying money on the street – it's in cities and tourist resorts that you have to take most care – the safest thing is a shoulder wallet or under-the-clothes money belt. An external money belt is only safe if it can't be sliced off by a quick knife cut. Watch out for people who touch you or seem to be getting unwarrantedly close, in any situation.

Travellers Cheques

These protect your money because they can be replaced if they are lost or stolen. In Spain they can be cashed at the many banks and exchange offices and usually attract a higher exchange rate than cash. American Express and Thomas Cook are widely accepted brands with efficient replacement policies. For American Express travellers' cheque refunds you can call ☎ 900-99 44 26 from anywhere in Spain.

It doesn't really matter whether your cheques are denominated in pesetas or in the currency of the country you buy them in: most Spanish exchange outlets will change most non-obscure currencies. Get most of your cheques in fairly large denominations (the equivalent of 10,000 ptas or more) to save on any per-cheque commission charges. American Express exchange offices charge no commission to change travellers' cheques (even other brands).

It's vital to keep your initial receipt, and a record of your cheque numbers and the ones you have used, separate from the cheques themselves.

Take along your passport when you go to cash travellers' cheques.

Plastic Money

You can use plastic to pay for many purchases (including meals and rooms, especially from the middle price range up, and long-distance trains), and you can use it to withdraw cash pesetas from banks and automatic teller machines (ATMs). Among the most widely usable cards are Visa, MasterCard, Eurocard, Eurocheque, American Express, Cirrus, Plus, Diners Club and JCB.

Once you consider the exchange rates and

commissions involved in depending on travellers' cheques or cash, you'll find that you usually win by using plastic, even taking into account any charges levied on foreign transactions and cash advances. Some foreign cash cards, for accessing money in personal bank accounts, can be used in Spain and do not attract any cash-advance fee.

A very high proportion of Spanish banks, even in small towns and some villages, have an ATM *(cajero automático)* which will dispense cash pesetas at any time if you have the right piece of plastic to slot into it. This will save you having to queue at a bank counter.

Check with your card's issuer before you come to Spain how widely usable your card will be, how to report a lost card, withdrawal/spending limits, and whether your personal identification number (PIN) will be acceptable (some European ATMs don't accept PINs of more than four digits).

American Express cardholders can get cash or at least travellers' cheques – up to various maximums depending on the type of card – from American Express offices around Spain by writing a personal cheque drawn on their home bank account.

American Express are among the easiest cards to replace – you can call ☎ 91 572 03 03 or 91 572 03 20 (in Madrid) at any time. Always report a lost card straight away. You can ring the following Madrid telephone numbers to do so: Visa, MasterCard or Access (☎ 91 519 21 00), Eurocard (☎ 91 519 60 00) and Diners Club (☎ 91 547 40 00).

A recently introduced option worth considering, for travellers from Britain at least, is Visa TravelMoney, a prepaid disposable credit card which you can buy from selected banks or travel agencies for amounts from £100 to £5000. It works for ATM withdrawals wherever the Visa sign is displayed. Inquire at Thomas Cook or call Visa before you travel.

International Transfers

To have money transferred from another country, you need to organise someone to send it to you (through a bank there or a money-transfer service such as Western Union) and a bank (or Western Union office) in Spain to collect it at. If there's money in your bank account at home, you may be able to instruct the bank yourself.

For information on Western Union services in Andalucía, call ☎ 902-11 41 89.

To set up a transfer through a bank, either get advice from the bank at home on a suitable pick-up bank in Spain, or check with a Spanish bank about how to organise it. You'll need to let the sender have full, exact details of the Spanish bank branch – its name, address, city and any contact or code numbers required.

A bank-to-bank telegraphic transfer typically costs the equivalent of 3000 or 4000 ptas and should take about a week. Western Union is likely to be quicker but a bit more expensive.

It's also possible to have money sent by American Express.

Costs

If you are very frugal, it's just about possible to scrape by on 2500 to 3000 ptas a day; if you stay in the cheapest possible accommodation, avoid eating in restaurants or going to museums or bars, and don't move around too much. Places like Sevilla will put a greater strain on your money belt.

A more comfortable budget would be 5000 ptas a day. This could allow you 1500 to 2000 ptas for accommodation; 300 ptas for breakfast (coffee and a pastry); 800 to 1000 ptas for a set lunch; 250 ptas for public transport (two metro or bus rides); 500 ptas for a major museum; and 600 ptas for a light dinner, with a bit over for a drink or two and intercity travel.

If you've got 20,000 ptas a day you can stay in excellent accommodation, rent a car and eat some of the best food Andalucía has to offer.

Ways to Save Two people can travel more cheaply (per person) than one by sharing rooms. You'll also save money by avoiding the peak tourist seasons, when most room prices go up: these vary from place to place, depending on local festivals and climate, but run from about July to mid-September in most places. A student or youth card, or a document such as a passport proving you're over 60, brings worthwhile savings on some travel costs and entry to some museums and sights (see Visas & Documents, above). A few museums and sights are cheaper for EU passport holders.

Tipping & Bargaining
The law requires restaurant menu prices to include service charge, and tipping is a matter of personal choice – most people leave some small change if they're satisfied, and 5% is usually plenty. Hotel porters will generally be happy with 200 ptas, and most won't turn their noses up at 100 ptas.

The only places in Spain where you are likely to bargain at all are markets – though even there most things have fixed prices – and, occasionally, cheap hotels, particularly if you're staying for a few days.

Taxes & Refunds
In Spain, value-added tax (VAT) is known as IVA (EE-ba, *impuesto sobre el valor añadido*). On accommodation and restaurant prices, it's 7% and is usually – but not always – included in quoted prices. On retail goods and car hire, IVA is 16%. To check whether a price includes IVA, you can ask *'¿Está incluido el IVA?'* ('Is IVA included?').

Visitors are entitled to a refund of the 16% IVA on purchases costing more than 15,000 ptas from any shop if they are taking them out of the EU within three months. Ask the shop for an invoice showing the price and IVA paid for each item and identifying the vendor and purchaser. Then present the invoice to the customs booth for IVA refunds when you leave Spain. The officer will stamp the invoice and you hand it in at a bank in the airport or port for the reimbursement.

POST & COMMUNICATIONS
Stamps & Post Offices
Stamps are sold at most *estancos* (tobacconist shops with 'Tabacos' in yellow letters on a maroon background), as well as at all post offices *(oficinas de correos)*. Main post offices in cities and towns are usually open Monday to Friday from about 8.30 am to 8.30 pm, Saturday from about 9 am to 1.30 pm. Village offices may be open shorter hours. Estancos usually open for normal shop hours.

Postal Rates
At 1998 rates a postcard or letter weighing up to 20 grams cost 70 ptas from Spain to other European countries, 115 ptas to North America and 185 ptas to Australasia or Asia. An aerogram costs 85 ptas to anywhere in the world.

Certificado (registered mail) costs an extra 175 ptas for international mail. *Urgente* service, which means your letter may arrive two or three days quicker, costs an extra 230 ptas for international mail. You can send mail both certificado and urgente.

Sending Mail
It's quite safe and reliable to post mail in the yellow street postboxes *(buzones)* as well as at post offices. Delivery times are erratic but ordinary mail to other Western European countries normally takes up to a week; to North America up to 10 days; to Australia or New Zealand up to two weeks.

Receiving Mail
Delivery times are similar to those for outbound mail. All Spanish addresses have a five-digit postcode, use of which may help your mail arrive a bit quicker. Poste restante mail can be addressed to you at poste restante (or better, *lista de correos*, the Spanish name for it), anywhere in Spain that has a post office. It will be delivered to the place's main post office unless another one is specified in the address. Take your passport when you go to pick up mail. It helps if people writing to you capitalise or underline your surname. Postcodes for poste restante/lista de correos at some main post offices are given in this book's destination sections. A typical lista de correos address looks like this:

```
Jenny JONES
Lista de Correos
29780 Nerja
Málaga
Spain
```

American Express card or travellers cheque holders can use the free client mail-holding service at American Express offices in Spain. You can obtain a list of these from American Express. Take your passport when you go to pick up mail.

Telephone

Andalucía is very well provided with street pay phones, which are blue and easy to use for both international and domestic calls. They accept coins and/or Spanish phonecards *(tarjetas telefónicas)*. Phonecards come in 1000 and 2000 ptas denominations and, like postage stamps, are sold at post offices and estancos.

Public phones inside bars and cafés, and phones in hotel rooms, are a good deal more expensive than street pay phones. Managements set their own rates for these; always ask the cost before using one.

Costs Calls from pay photos cost 30% to 35% more than calls from private lines. A three-minute pay-phone call should cost around 25 ptas within your local area, 75 ptas to other places in the same province, 180 ptas to other Spanish provinces, 260 ptas to other EU countries, 350 ptas to North America and 600 ptas to Australia. All calls are cheaper between 10 pm and 8 am, and domestic ones also after 2 pm on Saturday and all day Sunday and holidays.

Calls to numbers starting ☎ 900 are free. Calls to numbers starting ☎ 902 cost around 140 ptas for three minutes. Calls to mobile phones – numbers starting ☎ 907, ☎ 908, ☎ 909, ☎ 929, ☎ 939 or ☎ 970 – cost about 200 ptas for three minutes.

Domestic Calls Since April 1998, Spain has had no telephone area codes. All numbers now have nine digits and you just dial that nine-digit number, wherever in the country you are calling from. Since it takes time for such changes to sink in, many people still give their number in the old style of area code followed by number (eg ☎ 95-345 67 89). This isn't a problem, as the new nine-digit numbers simply consist of the old area code followed by the old number. So the old ☎ 95-345 67 89 is now just ☎ 95 345 67 89.

Dial ☎ 1009 to speak to a domestic operator, including for a domestic reverse-charge (collect) call *(una llamada por cobro revertido)*. For directory inquiries dial ☎ 1003; calls cost about 60 ptas.

International Calls The access code for international calls from Spain is ☎ 07 at the time of writing but was due to change to ☎ 00 by 1999. To make an international call dial the access code, wait for a new dialling tone, then dial the country code, area code and number you want. International collect calls are simple: dial ☎ 900 99 00 followed by a code for the country you're calling: ☎ 61 for Australia; ☎ 44 for the UK; ☎ 64 for New Zealand; ☎ 15 for Canada; and for the USA, ☎ 11 (AT&T) or ☎ 14 (MCI); codes for other countries are usually posted up in pay phones. You'll get straight through to an operator in the country you're calling. If for some reason this doesn't work, in most places you can get an English-speaking Spanish international operator on ☎ 1008 (for calls within Europe) or ☎ 1005 (rest of the world).

Calling Spain from Abroad Spain's country code is ☎ 34. Follow this with the full nine-digit number you are calling.

Fax

Most main post offices have fax service: sending one page costs about 350 ptas within Spain, 920 ptas to elsewhere in Europe and 1700 to 2000 ptas to other countries. However, you'll often find cheaper rates at shops or offices with 'Fax Público' signs.

Email & Internet Access

The Internet and email are burgeoning in Spain. Using email and the Internet while travelling with your own computer is a matter of having a server to which you can connect from Spain, and of being able to plug your computer into a phone line – which generally means staying in accommodation which has a phone. Check what connection procedures and pay rates you can expect through your server before leaving home. CompuServe has a 28,800 bps node (access number) in Málaga (☎ 95 204 85 89) and a 9600 bps node in Sevilla (☎ 95 442 53 11).

Andalucía also has a number of Internet cafés and other public Internet and email services, which you can use for a few hundred ptas an hour. You'll find some mentioned in city sections of this guide.

INTERNET RESOURCES

The following are just a few of the huge number of useful Web sites for travellers to Andalucía. Many of them are available in English.

Andalucía There's Only One
    www.andalucia.org/ing/homepage.html
    (official tourism site of Junta de Andalucía)
Estación de Esquí Sierra Nevada
    www.cetursa.es/ (click on 'Parte de Nieve'
    for conditions and weather in Spanish)
Guía de Semana Santa
    www.andal.es/guiaSemanaSanta/
    (links to dozens of sites about Semana Santa)
Instituto Cervantes
    www.cervantes.es/
Lonely Planet
    www.lonelyplanet.com (includes recent
    travellers' tips and links to a number of other
    sources on Spain)
Parques Naturales Andaluces
    www.cma.caan.es/parques/idxparques.htm
    (introductions in Spanish to Andalucía's 22
    parques naturales, with good locator map)
The Real Spain Directory
    realspain.com (huge number of links)
Sherry
    www.sherry.org (history, production, varieties,
    visits)
Todo Sobre España
    www.red2000.com/spain/1index.html
    (with sections on cities, bullfighting, flamen-
    co, fiestas, food, nightlife and more)

Tourist Office of Spain (Tokyo)
    www.spaintour.com/ (good site)
TURESPAÑA
    www.tourspain.es/inicio.htm (official Web Site
    of Spain's Board of Tourism)
Tourist Office of Spain in the USA
    www.okspain.org/ (includes long list of
    organised tour possibilities)
Toros, Links
    www.sol.com/list/toros.htm (bullfighting
    sites)

CompuServe's Spanish Forum has a data library with copious info on various aspects of Spanish travel, and you can post messages asking for specific tips.

BOOKS

Andalucía has fascinated foreign writers for two centuries. There's a wealth of literature on the region, in English and other languages. For any reading material you particularly want, stock up before you go: local availability of foreign-language books is patchy. Books on Spain (☎ 0181-898 7789, keith_harris books@compuserve.com), PO Box 207, Twickenham TW2 5BQ, UK, can send you mail-order catalogues of hundreds of old and new titles on Andalucía.

Lonely Planet

Those with trekking or hiking on their agenda will find route descriptions for some areas in Andalucía and the rest of Spain, plus practical and informative background, in Lonely Planet's *Walking in Spain*. If you're travelling in Spain beyond Andalucía, Lonely Planet's *Spain*, *Canary Islands* and *Barcelona* guides will point you in the right directions. *Spain* covers the mainland and the Balearic Islands.

Other Guidebooks

Of the many guides in Spanish to different parts and aspects of Andalucía and Spain, those published by El País/Aguilar stand out for their concise, lively, honest coverage and handy format. They range from city guides and guides to tapas bars, to one-offs such as the excellent *Pequeños Hoteles con Encanto* (Charming Small Hotels) and *Pueblos con Encanto de Andalucía* (Charming Villages of Andalucía). See also Walking under Activities in this chapter.

Travel

19th Century Classics Washington Irving was an American who took up residence in Granada's Alhambra palace when it was in an abandoned state in the 1820s. His *Tales of the Alhambra*, easy to find in Granada, weaves a series of still enchanting stories around the folk with whom he shared his life there. Irving was largely responsible, along with French writers of the same period, for the Romantic image of Al-Andalus which persists to this day.

A Handbook for Travellers in Spain by Richard Ford, first published in 1845, remains a classic not only for telling us how things were then in places we see now, but also for its irascible, witty English author. Ford spent much of his time in Andalucía, including three summers in Sevilla. Unfortunately, the most easily available edition costs around £75.

The Bible in Spain by George Borrow is an English clergyman's view of 19th century Spain in which he tried to spread the Protestant word. It's amusing both for the man himself and for his experiences. You stand a chance of tracking this down relatively cheaply.

20th Century In the 1920s Englishman Gerald Brenan settled in Yegen, a remote village in Las Alpujarras south of Granada, aiming to educate himself unimpeded by British mores and traditions. *South from Granada* is his absorbing account of local life and visits from members of the Bloomsbury set. In 1949 Brenan returned to Andalucía to explore Franco's Spain, an experience recounted in *The Face of Spain*.

Laurie Lee, meanwhile, walked off from his Gloucestershire home, aged 19, in 1934. He walked from northern Spain to Andalucía, playing his violin for a living, before the civil war broke out when he was in a village he calls Castillo (probably Almuñécar) and he was rescued by the Royal Navy. *As I Walked Out One Midsummer Morning*, his delightful account of these adventures, evokes the sights, smells and contrasting moods of turbulent pre-civil war Spain. Lee returned to his old haunts in Andalucía in the 1950s, a trip recorded in *A Rose for Winter*.

Among recent writings, David Gilmour's *Cities of Spain* and Adam Hopkins' *Spanish Journeys*, both culture and history-focused, give decent coverage to Andalucía in books ranging over all Spain. Gilmour paints good portraits of Sevilla, Córdoba and Cádiz.

History

Michael Jacobs in *A Guide to Andalusia* and James Woodall in *In Search of the Firedance* (see Culture & Arts, below) both admirably relate and elucidate Andalucía's history in books of broader compass.

Most histories of Spain as a whole pay major attention to pre-1700 Andalucía, since it was the hub of Islamic Spain and then of early imperial Spain. Among these are *The Story of Spain* by Mark Williams, a colourful and not over-long survey of the whole story, and Juan Lalaguna's concise *A Traveller's History of Spain*.

Moorish Spain by Richard Fletcher is a fascinating short history of the Islamic era, concentrating to a large extent on Andalucía.

Andalucía since 1700 is less written about, but Gerald Brenan works much about the region's problems and politics into *The Spanish Labyrinth*, an unravelling of the tangled political and social movements in the half-century or so before the civil war.

The murky story of one of the civil war's more infamous atrocities, the killing near Granada of the writer Federico García Lorca, is chillingly and fascinatingly pieced together in *The Assassination of Federico García Lorca* by Ian Gibson, who also gives background on Lorca and the war.

On the civil war in general, Hugh Thomas' *The Spanish Civil War* is probably the classic account in any language; long and dense with detail, yet readable and humane. Ronald Fraser's *Blood of Spain* is a fascinating, voluminous collection of eyewitness accounts of the war.

Life in Andalucía

Inside Andalusia by David Baird is a lively, always interesting, recent collection of portraits of people and places. Alastair Boyd's *The Sierras of the South* evokes life in the hill country around Ronda in the 1950s and 60s, when foreigners were a rarity. Nicholas Luard does a similar job for the valleys behind Tarifa in *Andalucia: A Portrait of Southern Spain* (1984). Ronald Fraser's *The Pueblo*, about the village of Mijas, gives an insight into local attitudes to the changes of recent decades, among them tourism.

James Michener's *Iberia*, first published in 1968, is not an epic novel in his usual mode, but an absorbing treatise reflecting a long love affair with Spain – including chapters on the Doñana wetlands, Sevilla, Córdoba and bullfighting.

Two of the best overall introductions to modern Spain are *The New Spaniards* by John Hooper, a former Madrid correspondent for *The Guardian*, which ranges comprehensively from the arts through politics and bullfighting to sex, and *Fire in the Blood* by Ian Gibson.

Death in the Afternoon is Ernest Hemingway's book on bullfighting.

Culture & Arts

It would be hard to better James Woodall's *In Search of the Firedance* as an introduction to flamenco. Woodall explains the different forms of flamenco, tells us about the great artists, visits all the main flamenco hubs and explores flamenco's Gypsy and Islamic roots. He also weaves in some history to set everything in a wider context. Ian Gibson's *Federico García Lorca* is an excellent biography.

Michael Jacobs' *A Guide to Andalusia* runs comprehensively through all the important cultural and historical aspects of Andalucía, from Muslim architecture to Lorca and the Sevillan golden age to flamenco, adding informed comment on today's Andalucía, plus a 120-page gazetteer of places and sights. It's great for those of us who wonder whether the street we're

staying on is named after a 16th century playwright or a 19th century general.

Fiction

Ernest Hemingway's *For Whom the Bell Tolls* (1941) – probably the most-read of all English-language books set in Spain – only touches on Andalucía but it repays reading in any Spanish context. This gripping tale of the civil war, which Hemingway experienced as a journalist, is full of Spanish atmosphere and all the emotions unleashed in the war. Another civil war journalist was Arthur Koestler, who was imprisoned by the Nationalists when they took Málaga, and almost executed – an experience on which his excellent novel *Darkness at Noon* (1940) is based.

See the Literature section in Facts about Andalucía for information on Andalucian literature.

Fauna

Wildlife Travelling Companion Spain by John Measures covers 150 of the country's best sites for viewing flora and fauna – many of them in Andalucía – with details of how to reach them and what you can hope to see. It also contains a basic field guide to some common animals and plants. Serious birdwatchers will find *Where to Watch Birds in Southern Spain* by Ernest Garcia and Andrew Paterson invaluable, but will also want a field guide such as *Collins Field Guide to the Birds of Britain and Europe* by Roger Peterson, Guy Mountfort & PAD Hollom, or *Collins Pocket Guide Birds of Britain and Europe* by H Heinzel, RSR Fitter & J Parslow.

For botanists, there's *Flowers of South-West Europe, A Field Guide* by Oleg Polunin & B E Smythies, and *Wild Flowers of Southern Spain* by Betty Molesworth Allen.

Food

A Flavour of Andalusia by Pepita Arias gives you recipes for some 50 typical Andalucian recipes, plus interesting background on the region's food. Numerous books on the diverse field of Spanish cookery include plenty of Andalucian material: among the best are *The Foods and Wines of Spain* by Penelope Casas and *The Best of Spanish Cooking* by Janet Mendel.

NEWSPAPERS & MAGAZINES
Spanish Press
Spain has a thriving and free press. Spaniards have never taken to the idea of 'popular' newspapers so there's no equivalent of the *Sun* or the *New York Daily News* here. Among the major daily national newspapers, the liberal *El País* is hard to beat for solid reporting. Every sizeable city in Andalucía has at least one daily paper of its own and these are often useful for what's-on and transport information. Among the best are Sevilla's *El Correo* and Málaga's *Sur*. *El Giraldillo* has a useful Web site at www.elgiraldillo.es.

Foreign-Language Press
The Málaga-published weekly free newspaper *Sur in English* reviews local news and has good small ads. You can often pick it up at tourist offices, hotels and some shops, especially in Málaga province and the western half of Andalucía. *Lookout* is a glossy monthly magazine, usually with plenty of interesting features and news on Andalucía and Spain. Look for it in bookshops and other shops patronised by English speakers. *The Coastal Gazette* from La Herradura is an expat freebie 'dedicated to the restoration of beer-drinking as a true art form'.

Newspapers from Western European countries and international press such as the *International Herald Tribune*, *Time* and *Newsweek* reach major cities and tourist areas on the day of publication.

RADIO & TV
Radio
The *costas* have at least four English-language radio stations, all a mix of music and talk. Most have BBC news on the hour several times a day; sometimes, particularly in the evenings or at weekends, they broadcast the World Service for a few hours. Brightest is Central FM (98.6MHz FM). Onda Cero International (101.6MHz FM) is middle of the road, and Coastline Radio (97.7MHz FM) – broadcasting from Nerja, unlike the other two which are Costa del Sol-based – is even staider. Radio Gibraltar is on 91.3MHz FM. Somewhere around 99 or 100MHz FM you can often pick up BBC Radio 4 or 5, broadcast for British forces.

Spanish radio stations, of which there are dozens in Andalucía, are good for music and trying to improve your Spanish. *El País* publishes local wavelength guides in its *'Cartelera'* (What's-on) section. The most listened-to stations in Andalucía are Canal Sur Radio and the commercial pop and rock stations 40 Principales and M-80 ('M-ochenta'). The state network Radio Nacional de España (RNE) has four stations including RNE 2 (classical music) and RNE 3 (or 'Radio d'Espop'), with varied pop and rock music, both on FM only. For flamenco and other exclusively Spanish music, find Radio E around 91MHz FM.

TV
Spaniards are Europe's greatest TV watchers after the British. Most TVs receive between five and seven channels – two from the state-run Televisión Española (TVE1 and La 2), three independent (Antena 3, Tele 5 and Canal Plus) and a couple of regional or local ones, including the all-Andalucía Canal Sur. Most of them broadcast round the clock, or nearly. Apart from news (of which there's a respectable amount), programming consists largely of game and talk shows, sport, *telenovelas* (soap operas) and English-language films dubbed into Spanish. Canal Plus is a pay channel: non-subscribers get only fuzzy reception on most programmes.

Satellite TV is popular too – mainly in private homes, though some bars, cafés and hotels have it too. Foreign channels you may come across include BBC World (mainly news and travel), BBC Prime (other BBC programmes), CNN, Eurosport, MTV, Sky News, Sky Sports, Sky Movies and the German SAT 1.

VIDEO SYSTEMS

If you want to record or buy video tapes to play back home, you won't get a picture if the image registration systems are different. Spanish television and nearly all prerecorded videos in Spain, use the PAL (phase alternation line) system common to most of Western Europe and Australia. France uses the incompatible SECAM system, and North America and Japan use the incompatible NTSC system. PAL videos can't be played on a machine that lacks PAL capability.

PHOTOGRAPHY

Most main brands of film are widely available, and processing is fast and generally efficient. A roll of print film (36 exposures, ISO 100) costs around 650 ptas and can be processed for around 1700 ptas – there are often better deals if you have two or three rolls developed together. The equivalent in slide *(diapositiva)* film is around 850 ptas plus 850 ptas for processing.

Your camera and film will be routinely passed through airport x-ray machines. These shouldn't damage film but you can ask for hand inspection if you're worried. Lead pouches for film are another solution.

Some museums and galleries ban photography, or at least flash, and soldiers can be touchy about it. It's common courtesy to ask – at least by gesture – when you want to photograph people.

Bright middle-of-the-day sun tends to bleach out your shots. You get more colour and contrast earlier and later in the day.

TIME

All Spain is on GMT/UTC plus one hour during winter, and GMT/UTC plus two hours during the daylight-saving period which runs from the last Sunday in March to the last Sunday in October. Most other Western European countries have the same time as Spain year round, the major exceptions being Britain, Ireland and Portugal. Add one hour to these three countries' times to get Spanish time.

Spanish time is normally USA Eastern Time plus six hours, and USA Pacific Time plus nine hours. But the USA tends to start daylight saving a week or two later than Spain, so you must add one hour to the time differences in the intervening period.

In the Australian winter subtract eight hours from Sydney time to get Spanish time; in the Australian summer subtract 10 hours. The difference is nine hours for a few weeks in March.

ELECTRICITY
Voltages & Cycles

Electric current in Spain is 220V, 50 Hz, as in the rest of continental Europe, but a few places are still on 125V or 110V (sockets are often labelled where this is the case). Voltage may even vary in the same building. Don't plug 220V (or British 240V) appliances into 125V or 110V sockets unless they have a transformer. North American 60 Hz appliances with electric motors (such as some CD and tape players) may perform poorly.

Plugs & Sockets

Plugs have two round pins, again like the rest of continental Europe.

WEIGHTS & MEASURES

The metric system is used. Like other continental Europeans, the Spanish indicate decimals with commas and thousands with points.

LAUNDRY

Self-service laundrettes are rare. Small laundries *(lavanderías)* are fairly common: they will usually wash, dry and fold a load for 1000 to 1200 ptas. Some youth hostels and a few budget hostales have washing machines for guests' use.

TOILETS

Public toilets are not particularly common in Andalucía, but it's OK to wander into many bars and cafés to use their toilet even if you're not a customer. It's worth carrying some loo paper with you as many toilets lack it. If there's a bin beside the loo, put paper etc in it – it's there because the local sewerage system can't cope otherwise.

HEALTH
Andalucía is a pretty healthy place. Your main potential risks are likely to be sunburn, dehydration, foot blisters and insect bites, or mild gut problems at first if you're not used to olive oil. Most travellers experience no problems.

Health Insurance
EU citizens are entitled to free Spanish national health medical care on provision of an E111 form, which you must get in your home country before you come. Even with an E111, you still have to pay for medicines bought from pharmacies, even if a doctor has prescribed them, and perhaps for a few tests and procedures.

An E111 is no good, however, for private consultations or treatment in Spain, which includes virtually all dentists and some of the better clinics and surgeries, or for emergency flights home. If you want to avoid paying for these, you'll need to take out medical travel insurance. See Travel Insurance under Visas & Documents earlier in this chapter for more information. In Britain, E111s are issued free by post offices. Just supply name, address, date of birth and National Insurance number.

Most, but not all, US health insurance policies stay in effect, at least for a limited period, if you travel abroad. Most non-European national health plans (including Australia's Medicare) don't, so you must take out special medical insurance.

Other Preparations
If you wear glasses take a spare pair and your prescription. If you need a particular medication carry an adequate supply, as it may not be available locally. Take part of the packaging showing the generic name, rather than the brand, to make getting replacements easier. It's a good idea to have a legible prescription or letter from your doctor to show you use the medication legally.

Water
Domestic, hotel and restaurant tap water is safe to drink virtually everywhere in Spain.

Medical Kit Check List
☐ Aspirin or paracetamol (acetaminophen in the US) – for pain or fever.
☐ Antihistamine (such as Benadryl) – useful as a decongestant for colds and allergies, to ease the itch from insect bites or stings and to help prevent motion sickness. Antihistamines may cause sedation and interact with alcohol: if possible, take one you have used before.
☐ Loperamide (eg Imodium) or Lomotil for diarrhoea; prochlorperazine (eg Stemetil) or metaclopramide (eg Maxalon) for nausea and vomiting.
☐ Antiseptic such as povidone-iodine (eg Betadine) – for cuts and grazes.
☐ Calamine lotion or aluminium sulphate spray (eg Stingose) – to ease irritation from bites or stings.
☐ Bandages and Band-aids.
☐ Scissors, tweezers and a thermometer (note that mercury thermometers are prohibited by airlines).
☐ Insect repellent, sunscreen, chap stick and water purification tablets.

Ask '¿Es potable el agua?' if you're in any doubt. Water from public spouts and fountains is not reliable unless it has a sign saying 'Agua Potable'. Often there are signs saying Agua No Potable: don't drink here.

Natural water, unless it's straight from a definitely unpolluted spring, or running off snow or ice with no interference from people or animals, is not safe to drink unpurified.

Safe bottled water is available everywhere, generally for 40 to 75 ptas for a 1.5L bottle in shops and supermarkets.

Medical Services
For serious medical problems and emergencies, the Spanish public health service provides care to rival that anywhere in the world. Seeing a doctor about something more mundane can be less than enchanting, because of obscure appointment systems,

queues and grumpy personnel, though you should still get decent attention in the end. The expense of going to a private clinic or surgery often saves time and frustration: you'll typically pay between 3000 and 6000 ptas for a consultation (not counting medicines). All dental practices are private in any case.

If you need to see a doctor quickly, or need emergency dental treatment, one way is to go along to the *urgencias* (emergency) section of the nearest hospital. Many towns also have a Centro de Salud (Health Centre) with an urgencias section.

Take along as much documentation as you can muster when you deal with medical services – passport, E111, insurance papers, ideally photocopies too. Tourist offices, the police and usually your accommodation can all tell you where to find medical help, or how to call an ambulance. You could also contact your country's consulate for advice. Many major hospitals and emergency medical services are mentioned and/or shown on maps in this book's city sections.

Pharmacies *(farmacias)* can help with many ailments. A system of duty pharmacies *(farmacias de guardia)* operates so that each district has one open all the time. When a pharmacy is closed, it posts the name of the nearest open one on the door. Lists of farmacias de guardia are often given in local papers, too.

Environmental Hazards

Altitude Sickness Lack of oxygen at altitudes over 2500m affects most people to some extent. The effect may be mild or severe and occurs because less oxygen reaches the muscles and the brain, requiring the heart and lungs to compensate by working harder. Mild symptoms include headache, lethargy, dizziness, difficulty sleeping and loss of appetite. Acute Mountain Sickness (AMS) has been fatal at 3000m, although 3500 to 4500m is the usual range.

Treat mild symptoms by resting at the same altitude until recovery, usually a day or two. Paracetamol or aspirin can be taken

for headaches. If symptoms persist or become worse, however, *immediate descent is necessary*, even 500m can help.

Fungal Infections Fungal infections occur most commonly in hot weather and are usually found on the scalp, between the toes or fingers, in the groin and on the body (ringworm). You get ringworm (which is a fungal infection, not a worm) from infected animals or other people. Moisture encourages these infections.

To prevent fungal infections wear loose, comfortable clothes, avoid artificial fibres, wash frequently and dry carefully. If you get an infection, wash the area at least daily with a disinfectant or medicated soap and water. Apply an antifungal cream or powder like tolnaftate (Tinaderm). Try to expose the area to air or sunlight as much as possible, and wash all towels and underwear in hot water, change them often and let them dry in the sun.

Heat Exhaustion Dehydration and salt deficiency can cause heat exhaustion. Take time to acclimatise to high temperatures, drink sufficient liquids and don't do anything too physically demanding.

Salt deficiency is characterised by fatigue, lethargy, headaches, giddiness and muscle cramps; salt tablets may help, but adding extra salt to your food is better.

Heat Stroke This serious, occasionally fatal, condition can occur if the body's heat-regulating mechanism breaks down and the body temperature rises to dangerous levels. Long, continuous periods of exposure to high temperatures and insufficient fluids can leave you vulnerable to heat stroke.

The symptoms are feeling unwell, not sweating very much (or at all) and a high body temperature (39°C to 41°C or 102°F to 106°F). Where sweating has ceased, the skin becomes flushed and red. Severe, throbbing headaches and lack of coordination will occur, and the sufferer may be confused or aggressive. Eventually the victim will become delirious or convulse. Hospitalisation is essential, but in the interim get victims out of the sun, remove their clothing, cover them with a wet sheet or towel and then fan continually. Give fluids if they are conscious.

Hypothermia Too much cold can be just as dangerous as too much heat. Though unlikely in Andalucía, it could occur in the mountains in winter. Hypothermia occurs when the body loses heat faster than it can produce it, and the body's core temperature falls. It is surprisingly easy to progress from very cold to dangerously cold due to a combination of wind, wet clothing, fatigue and hunger. It is best to dress in layers: silk, wool and some of the new artificial fibres are good insulating materials. A hat is important. Carry basic supplies, including food containing simple sugars to generate heat quickly and fluid to drink.

Symptoms of hypothermia are exhaustion, numb skin (particularly toes and fingers), shivering, slurred speech, irrational or violent behaviour, lethargy, stumbling, dizzy spells, muscle cramps and violent bursts of energy. Irrationality may take the form of sufferers claiming they are warm and trying to take off their clothes.

To treat mild hypothermia, first get the person out of the wind and/or rain, and replace wet clothes with dry, warm ones. Give them hot liquids – not alcohol – and some high-kilojoule, easily digestible food. Do not rub victims, instead allow them to slowly warm themselves. The early recognition and treatment of mild hypothermia is the only way to prevent severe hypothermia, a critical condition.

Prickly Heat This itchy rash, caused by excessive perspiration trapped under the skin, usually strikes people who have just arrived in a hot climate. Keeping cool, bathing often, drying the skin and using a mild talcum or prickly heat powder, or resorting to air-conditioning, may help.

Sunburn You can get sunburnt surprisingly quickly, even through cloud. Use a sunscreen (taking care to cover areas which don't normally see sun – eg your feet), a hat, and barrier cream for your nose and lips. Calamine lotion or Stingose are good for mild sunburn. Protect your eyes with good quality sunglasses, particularly if you will be near water, sand or snow.

Infectious Diseases

Diarrhoea Simple things like a change of water, food or climate can all cause a mild bout of diarrhoea, but a few rushed toilet trips with no other symptoms are not indicative of a major problem.

Dehydration is the main danger with any diarrhoea, particularly in children or the elderly. Under all circumstances *fluid replacement* is the most important thing to remember. Weak black tea with a little sugar, soda water, or soft drinks allowed to go flat and diluted 50% with clean water are all good. With severe diarrhoea a rehydrating solution is preferable to replace minerals and salts lost. Commercially available oral rehydration salts (ORS) are very useful; add them to boiled or bottled water.

In an emergency you can make up a solution of six teaspoons of sugar and a half teaspoon of salt to a litre of boiled or bottled water. You need to drink at least the same volume of fluid that you are losing in bowel movements and vomiting. Urine is the best guide – if you have small amounts of concentrated urine, you need to drink more. Keep drinking small amounts often. Stick to a bland diet as you recover.

Lomotil or Imodium can be used to bring relief from the symptoms, but they do not cure the problem. Only use these drugs if you do not have access to toilets, eg if you *must* travel. For children under 12 years Lomotil and Imodium are not recommended. Do not use these drugs if the person has a high fever or is severely dehydrated.

Hepatitis Hepatitis is a general term for inflammation of the liver. It is common worldwide. The symptoms are fever, chills, headache, fatigue, feelings of weakness, and aches and pains, followed by loss of appetite, nausea, vomiting, abdominal pain, dark urine, light-coloured faeces and jaundiced (yellow) skin. The whites of the eyes may turn yellow. **Hepatitis A**, transmitted by contaminated food and drinking water, is not common in Spain. There are almost 300 million chronic carriers of **Hepatitis B** in the world and Spanish children are routinely vaccinated against it. It is spread through contact with infected blood, blood products or body fluids, for example through sexual contact, unsterilised needles and blood transfusions, or contact with blood via small breaks in the skin. Other risk situations include having a shave, or your body pierced or tatooed with contaminated equipment. The symptoms of type B may be more severe than type A and may lead to long-term problems. **Hepatitis C** can lead to chronic liver disease. The virus is spread by contact with blood, usually via contaminated transfusions or shared needles. Avoiding these is the only means of prevention.

HIV & AIDS HIV, the Human Immunodeficiency Virus, develops into AIDS, Acquired Immune Deficiency Syndrome, a fatal disease. Any exposure to blood, blood products or body fluids may put the individual at risk. Intravenous drug use is the major reason for Spain having the highest AIDS rate in Europe (about 50,000 cases since 1981). The disease can also be transmitted through sexual contact, vaccinations, acupuncture, tattooing, body piercing or infected blood transfusions.

If you do need an injection, ask to see the syringe unwrapped in front of you, or take a needle and syringe pack with you. Fear of HIV infection should never preclude treatment for serious medical conditions.

HIV and AIDS are VIH and *sida*, respectively, in Spanish. All Andalucian provincial capitals have AIDS information and support organisations. One in Sevilla is the Comité Ciudadano Anti-Sida de Sevilla (☎ 95 43719 58), Calle San Luís 50 bajo. Many gay organisations (see Gay & Lesbian Travellers in this chapter) can provide AIDS information.

Sexually Transmitted Diseases Gonorrhoea, herpes and syphilis are among these diseases; common symptoms are sores, blisters or rashes around the genitals, discharges or pain when urinating. In some STDs, such as wart virus or chlamydia, symptoms may be less marked or not observed at all, especially in women. Syphilis symptoms eventually disappear but the disease continues and can cause severe problems in later years. While abstinence from sexual contact is the only 100% effective prevention, using condoms *(condones, preservativos)* is also effective. The different sexually transmitted diseases each require specific antibiotics. There is no cure for herpes or AIDS.

Cuts, Bites & Stings
Wash well and treat any cut with an antiseptic such as povidone-iodine. Where possible, avoid bandages and Band-aids, which can keep wounds wet.

Insects, Scorpions & Centipedes Bee and wasp stings are usually painful rather than dangerous. However, in people who are allergic to them severe breathing difficulties may occur and require urgent medical care. Calamine lotion or Stingose spray will give relief; ice packs will reduce pain and swelling.

Scorpion stings are notoriously painful but Spanish scorpions are not considered fatal. Scorpions often shelter in shoes or clothing, so shake these out before you put them on when camping. Some Andalucian centipedes *(escolopendras)* have a very nasty, but not fatal, sting. The ones to steer clear of are those composed of clearly defined segments, which may be patterned with, for instance, black and yellow stripes.

Also beware of the hairy, reddish-brown caterpillars *(procesionarias)* of the pine processionary moth, which live in easily discernible silvery nests in pine trees in many parts of Andalucía and have a habit of walking around in long lines. Touching the caterpillars' hairs sets off a severely irritating allergic skin reaction.

Mosquito and other insect bites can be a nuisance but Spanish mosquitoes don't carry malaria. You can avoid bites by covering your skin and using an insect repellent.

Ticks Check all over your body if you have been walking through a potentially tick-infested area, as ticks can cause skin infections and other more serious diseases. If a tick is found attached, press down around its head with tweezers, grab the head and gently pull upwards. Avoid pulling the rear of the body.

Snakes The only venomous snake that is even relatively common in Spain is the hog-nosed viper (*víbora hocicuda* in Spanish). It's a triangular-headed creature, rarely more than 50cm long, and grey with a zigzag pattern. It lives in dry, rocky areas, away from humans. Its bite can be fatal and needs to be treated as soon as possible with a serum which state clinics in major towns keep in stock.

To minimise the chance of snake bites, wear boots, socks and long trousers where snakes may be present. Don't put your hands into holes and crevices, and be careful when collecting firewood. Snake bites do not cause instantaneous death and antivenenes are usually available. Immediately wrap the bitten limb tightly, as for a sprained ankle, and attach a splint to immobilise it. Keep the victim still and seek medical help, if possible with the dead snake for identification. Don't attempt to catch the snake if there is a possibility of being bitten again.

Jellyfish Jellyfish *(medusas)*, with their stinging tentacles, generally occur in large numbers or hardly at all, so it's fairly easy to know when not to go into the sea. Dousing in vinegar will deactivate any jellyfish stingers which have not 'fired'. Calamine lotion, antihistamines and analgesics may reduce the reaction and relieve the pain.

Leishmaniasis This is a group of parasitic diseases found in many parts of the Mediterranean. The strain found in Spain – mainly in country areas near the Mediterranean coasts – is called leishmania infantum and is a form of visceral leishmaniasis which is characterised by irregular bouts of fever, substantial weight loss, swelling of the spleen and liver, and anaemia. It can be fatal for children under five and people with deficiencies of the immune system such as AIDS sufferers. It is transmitted when sandflies bite dogs carrying leishmaniasis, then bite humans. Avoiding sandfly bites is the best precaution: cover up and apply repellent. Sandflies are most active at dawn and dusk. The bites are usually painless but itchy. If you suspect leishmaniasis, seek medical advice as laboratory testing is required for diagnosis and treatment.

Women's Health

Gynaecological Problems Sexually transmitted diseases are a major cause of vaginal problems. Symptoms include a smelly discharge, painful intercourse and sometimes a burning sensation when urinating. Male sexual partners must also be treated. Medical attention should be sought, and remember that HIV or hepatitis B may also be acquired during exposure. Besides abstinence, the best thing is safe sex using condoms.

Antibiotic use, synthetic underwear, sweating and contraceptive pills can lead to fungal vaginal infections in hot climates. Good personal hygiene, loose-fitting clothes and cotton underwear will help prevent them. Fungal infections, characterised by a rash, itch and discharge, can be treated with a vinegar or lemon-juice douche, or with yoghurt. Nystatin, miconazole or clotrimazole pessaries, or vaginal cream, are the usual treatment.

Pregnancy Most miscarriages occur during the first three months of pregnancy. They can occasionally lead to severe bleeding. The last three months should also be spent within reasonable distance of good medical care. A baby born as early as 24 weeks stands a chance of survival, but only in a good modern hospital. Pregnant women should avoid all unnecessary medication, but vaccinations should be taken where needed. Additional care should be taken to prevent illness and particular attention should be paid to diet and nutrition. Alcohol and nicotine, for example, should be avoided.

WOMEN TRAVELLERS
Women travellers should be ready to ignore any stares, catcalls and unnecessary comments, though in fact harassment is much less frequent than you might expect. Men under about 30, who have grown up in the post-Franco era, are less sexually stereotyped and less diverted by foreign women than their older counterparts. But you still need to exercise common sense about where you go on your own. Think twice about going alone to isolated stretches of beach or lonely country areas, or down empty city streets at night. It's highly inadvisable for a woman to hitchhike alone – and not a great idea even for two women together.

Topless bathing and skimpy clothes are in fashion in many coastal resorts, but people tend to dress more modestly elsewhere.

Recommended reading is the *Handbook for Women Travellers* by M & G Moss.

Seeking Help
All police headquarters *(jefaturas de policía)* have a special Servicio de Atención a la Mujer (Service of Attention to Women).

The Asociación de Mujeres Víctimas de Malos Tratos (☎ 958 29 25 03) in Granada offers advice and help to rape victims, and can advise of similar centres in other cities, though only limited English may be spoken. There's also a free 24-hour national emergency phone line for victims of physical abuse: ☎ 900-10 00 09. You'll get through to the Comisión de Investigación de Malos Tratos a Mujeres (Commission of Investigation into Abuse of Women).

GAY & LESBIAN TRAVELLERS
Gay and lesbian sex are both legal in Spain: the age of consent is 16, the same as for heterosexuals. Lesbians and gay men generally adopt a fairly low profile except in gay locales: Andalucía's liveliest scenes are in Sevilla, Granada and Torremolinos.

Organisations A good source of information on gay places and organisations throughout Spain is Coordinadora Gai-Lesbiana, Carrer Buenaventura Muñoz 4, 08018 Barcelona, Cataluña (☎ 93 309 79 97; cogailes@pangea.org). It has a good English-language Internet site and a telephone information line (☎ 900-60 16 01 for free calls in Spain, ☎ 34-93 300 40 48 from outside Spain), daily from 6 to 10 pm, on which you can find out about gay and lesbian bars, cafés, discos, hotels and organisations, as well as about AIDS and AIDS organisations.

NOS (Asociación Andaluza de Lesbianas y Gais) at Calle Lavadero de las Tablas 15, Granada, runs the Teléfono Andaluz de Información Homosexual (☎ 958 20 06 02). It's open Monday to Friday from 10 am to 2 pm and 4 to 8 pm.

Some useful Web sites:

COLEGA
　　www.arrakis.es/~colega (Colectivo de Lesbianas y Gays de Andalucía)
Coordinadora Gai-Lesbiana
　　www.pangea.org/org/cgl/inde.htm (Barcelona-based; site includes Gay Spain travel guide and details of gay associations Spain-wide)
Gayscape
　　www.jwpublishing.com/gayscape/spn.html (links to information on gay and lesbian Spain)
Gay Spain, Feel the Passion
　　www.geocities.com/WestHollywood/1007/ www.pangea.org/org/cgl/inde.htm (a partly updated version of a guide to gay Spain which was distributed from some Spanish Tourism Information Offices in the USA in 1996 and 1997; information on bars, hotels, discos, associations and tours)
NOS (Asociación Andaluza de Lesbianas y Gais)
　　www.lander.es/~chema/

DISABLED TRAVELLERS

Some Spanish tourist offices in other countries (including the one in London) can provide a basic information sheet with some useful addresses for disabled travellers, and give details of accessible accommodation in specific places.

Wheelchair accessibility in Andalucía is improving, but it's still rare enough in budget accommodation. One Sevilla disabled association estimates that 80% of Spanish hotels that claim to be accessible actually retain problem features. A handful of Andalucía's youth hostels – among them Córdoba and Cazorla – have rooms adapted for the disabled. All new public buildings are required to have wheelchair access, but most of them predate the law.

The British-based Royal Association for Disability & Rehabilitation (RADAR, ☎ 0171-250 3222), 12 City Forum, 250 City Rd, London EC1V 8AF, publishes the useful *Holidays & Travel Abroad*, with a section on Spain covering contact addresses, transport, services and accommodation for the disabled. Mobility International (☎ 02-410 6297, mobint@dproducts.be), Rue de Manchester 25, Brussels 1070, Belgium, has researched facilities for disabled tourists in Spain.

SENIOR TRAVELLERS

There are reduced prices for people over 60, 63 or 65 at some museums and sights, and occasionally on transport (see Train Passes & Discounts in the Getting There & Away chapter). Some of the luxurious *paradores* (see Accommodation later in this chapter) sometimes offer discounts for people over 60.

TRAVEL WITH CHILDREN

Andalucians as a rule are very friendly to children. Any child whose hair is less than jet black will get called *rubia* (blonde) if she's a girl, or *rubio* if he's a boy. Accompanied children are welcome at all kinds of accommodation, and in virtually every café, bar and restaurant. Andalucian children stay up late and at fiestas it's commonplace to see even tiny ones toddling the streets at 2 or 3 am. Visiting kids like this idea too – but can't cope with it quite so readily.

Try to tailor your trip partly to what the kids like and can cope with. Most of them don't like moving around too much and are happier if they can settle into places and make new friends. It's easier on the parents too if you don't have to pack up and move on every day or two. Spanish street life and bustle, and the novelty of being in new places, provide some distraction for most kids but they'll get bored unless some of the time is devoted to their own favoured activities. Children are likely to be more affected by unaccustomed heat and need time to acclimatise, and care should be taken to avoid sunburn.

Apart from the obvious attractions of beaches, playgrounds are fairly plentiful in Andalucía, and in many places there are excellent special attractions such as amusement parks (for example Sevilla's Isla Mágica, and Tivoli World on the Costa del Sol), aquaparks, aquariums – and let's not forget Mini-Hollywood and other Western movie sets in the Almería desert.

Most children are fascinated by the ubiquitous street-corner *kioscos* selling sweets or *gusanitos* (corn puffs) for a few pesetas. The magnetism of these places often overcomes children's inhibitions enough for them to carry out their own first Spanish transactions.

Nappies, creams, lotions, baby foods and so on are as easily available in Spain as in any other Western country, but if there's some particular brand you swear by it's best to bring it with you. Calpol, for instance, isn't easily found.

Children benefit from cut-price or free entry at many sights and museums. Those under four travel free on Spanish trains and those aged four to 11 normally pay 60% of the adult fare.

Lonely Planet's *Travel with Children*, by Maureen Wheeler, has lots of practical advice on this subject, and first-hand stories from many Lonely Planet authors, and others.

USEFUL ORGANISATIONS

The Instituto Cervantes exists to promote

the Spanish language and the cultures of Spain and other Spanish-speaking countries. It's mainly involved in Spanish teaching and has library and information services. It has branches in over 30 cities around the world, including at 102 Eaton Square, London SW1W 9AN, UK (☎ 0171-235 0353).

DANGERS & ANNOYANCES

Andalucía is generally a pretty safe place. The main thing you have to be wary of is petty theft (which may of course not seem so petty to you if your passport, money and camera go missing). But with a few simple precautions you can minimise the risk.

For some specific hints about looking after your luggage, money and documents, on travel insurance and on safety for women, see the Planning, Visas & Documents, Money and Women Travellers sections in this chapter.

Theft & Loss

Most risk of theft occurs in tourist resorts, big cities, and when you first arrive in the country or a new city and may be unaware of danger signs.

The main things to guard against are pickpockets, bag snatchers and theft from cars. Carry valuables under your clothes if possible – certainly not in a bag which could be snatched away easily – and watch for people who get unnecessarily close to you at airports, at stations, on trains or buses or on the street. Don't leave baggage unattended, and avoid crushes. Also be cautious with people who come up to offer or ask you something, or start talking to you for no obviously good reason. These could be attempts to distract you and make you an easier victim.

Car contents are sitting ducks for thieves. It's safest to remove any radio or cassette player from your car before you go to Spain. When you leave the car, don't leave visible anything that looks even remotely valuable – and preferably don't leave anything at all. Even if thieves who get into your car end up taking nothing, they will probably have broken a window first.

Take care with your belongings on the beach; anything lying on the sand could disappear in a flash when your back is turned. Also avoid dingy, empty city alleys and backstreets, or anywhere that just doesn't feel 100% safe, at night.

Don't leave anything valuable lying around your room, especially in any hostel-type place. Use a safe if there's one available.

If anything valuable does get stolen or lost and you want to make an insurance claim, you'll need to report it to the police, and get a copy of the report. If your passport has gone, contact your embassy or consulate for help with a replacement.

Other Emergencies

A new single emergency telephone number for ambulance, police or fire – ☎ 112 – is due to come into use throughout Spain, but no one knows when. In the meantime, throughout Andalucía you can call ☎ 061 for an ambulance. In many cities, the Cruz Roja (Red Cross) number is ☎ 22 22 22 or ☎ 222 22 22 preceded by whatever three or two digits other numbers in the city start with. Other medical emergency numbers and locations of many hospitals and clinics are given in this book's city and town sections. See Health in this chapter for more on Spanish medical facilities and health problems. If you're seriously ill or injured, someone should tell your embassy or consulate.

See the boxed aside Police – Who Does What? for police information.

Terrorism

The Basque terrorist organisation ETA occasionally explodes small bombs in Andalucía, sometimes in places like Granada and Málaga with the intention of scaring off tourists. Before travelling to Spain, you can consult your country's foreign affairs department for any current warnings. For Foreign Office travel advice in Britain, ring ☎ 0171-238-4503. For State Department travel warnings and consular advice sheets in the US, call ☎ 202-647-5225. For DFAIT travel information reports in Canada, call ☎ 613-944-6788 or ☎ 800-267-6788. In Aus-

Police – Who Does What?

Spanish police are more of a help than a threat to the average law-abiding traveller. Unpleasant events such as random drug searches do occur, but not with great frequency.

There are three main types of *policía*: the Policía Nacional, the Policía Local (sometimes called Policía Municipal) and the Guardia Civil.

Guardia Civil The main responsibilities of the green-uniformed Guardia Civil include roads, the countryside, villages and international borders.

Policía Nacional This force covers cities and bigger towns. Those of its number who wear uniforms are in blue. There is also a large contingent to be found shuffling paper in bunker-like police stations called *comisarías*.

Policía Local or **Policía Municipal** are controlled by city and town councils and deal mainly with minor matters such as parking, traffic and bylaws. They wear blue-and-white uniforms.

Contacting the Police If you need to go to the police, any of them will do, but you may find the Policía Local are the most helpful. A new single emergency telephone number for ambulance, police or fire (☎ 112) is due to be introduced throughout Spain. Meanwhile, anywhere in Spain you can call ☎ 091 for the Policía Nacional or ☎ 092 for the Policía Local. Further police numbers, and locations of main stations, are given in city and town sections of this book.

---

tralia the Department of Foreign Affairs & Trade (☎ 02-6261-3305) can advise on risks in specific countries. Most of these services are also available on the Internet.

Annoyances

Andalucía is a pretty mellow place and there isn't much to get annoyed about. That said, there may be a few attempts to short-change you – and you must be prepared for more noise than you're probably used to! There's some sort of legislation about motorcycle silencers but it's rarely enforced.

El Libro de Reclamaciones

Most public establishments have a sign up saying that they have a complaints book *(libro de reclamaciones)*. If you have a serious gripe or are in dispute about a bill, asking for the libro de reclamaciones might just bring a change of attitude from whoever you're at odds with. If you actually go as far as making an entry in the book, there'll be a copy for you and a copy for the establishment concerned. On the back of your copy will be instructions on how to take the matter further.

The books are supposedly checked from time to time by government consumer agencies.

LEGAL MATTERS

If you're arrested you will be allotted the free services of a duty solicitor *(abogado de oficio)*, who may speak only Spanish. You're also entitled to make a phone call. If you use this to contact your embassy or consulate, it will probably be able to do no more than refer you to a lawyer who speaks your language. If you end up in court, the authorities are obliged to provide a translator.

Drugs

Spain's liberal drug laws were severely tightened in 1992. The only legal drug is cannabis, and only for personal use – which means very small amounts. There are some bars where people smoke joints openly, although public consumption of any drug is supposedly illegal. The only sure guideline is to be very discreet if you do use cannabis. It would be very unwise in hotel rooms or guesthouses.

Travellers entering Spain from Morocco should be ready for intensive drug searches.

BUSINESS HOURS

Generally, people work Monday to Friday from about 9 am to 2 pm and then again from 5 pm for another three hours. Shops are usually open these hours on Saturday too. Big supermarkets and department stores often stay open all day Monday to Saturday, from about 9 am to 9 pm. A lot of government offices don't bother with afternoon opening any day.

The Times They Are A-Changing

Opening hours of museums, sights and information offices in Andalucía change frighteningly often, and can be thrown into utter confusion around public holidays. Many tourist offices give out lists of opening hours but these don't always keep track of the latest changes. The only sure way to check opening hours is to phone ahead, or get a tourist office to phone for you.

Major museums tend to open for something like normal business hours (with or without the afternoon break), but often have their weekly closing day on Monday, not Sunday.

PUBLIC HOLIDAYS & SPECIAL EVENTS
Holidays

Everywhere in Spain there are 14 official holidays a year – some observed nationwide, some very local. When a holiday date falls on a weekend, sometimes the holiday is moved to the Monday. The list of holidays may change a bit from year to year.

The two main periods when Spaniards go on holiday are Semana Santa (the week leading up to Easter Sunday) and the six weeks from mid-July to the end of August. At these times accommodation in resorts can be scarce and transport heavily booked, but other cities are often half-empty.

In 1998 the seven official national holidays were:

1 January
  Año Nuevo (New Year's Day)
March/April
  Viernes Santo (Good Friday)
1 May
  Fiesta del Trabajo (Labour Day)
15 August
  La Asunción (Feast of the Assumption)
12 October
  Fiesta Nacional de España (National Day)
8 December
  La Inmaculada Concepción (Feast of the Immaculate Conception)
25 December
  Navidad (Christmas)

In addition, regional governments set five holidays and local councils a further two. In 1998 Andalucía's five regional holidays were:

6 January
  Epifanía (Epiphany) or Día de los Reyes Magos (Three Kings' Day). Children receive presents – in many towns, Reyes Magos cabalgatas (cavalcades) tour the streets, tossing out sweets to the crowds.
28 February
  Día de Andalucía (Andalucía Day)
March/April
  Jueves Santo (Holy Thursday) The day before Good Friday.
1 November
  Día de Todos Santos (All Saints' Day). The traditional day for paying respects to the dead.
6 December
  Día de la Constitución (Constitution Day)

Local holidays in some places include:

Late May or June
  Corpus Christi (3 June in 1999, 22 June in 2000)
24 June
  Día de San Juan Bautista (Feast of St John the Baptist) King Juan Carlos I's saint's day.
25 July
  Día de Santiago Apóstol (Feast of St James the Apostle) The feast day of Spain's patron saint.

ANDALUCÍA FESTIVALS

Andalucians indulge their love of colour, noise, crowds, pageant, dressing up and partying at innumerable exuberant local fiestas. Even small villages will have at least one festival (probably several) in the year, each with its own own unique twist. Many fiestas are religion-based but still highly festive.

Most places hold their main annual *feria* (fair) in summer, with concerts, parades, fireworks, bullfights, fairgrounds, dancing and an all-night party atmosphere.

The calendar is peppered with music festivals (any excuse for a party). Summer is a big time for flamenco festivals (and music generally), with many towns staging one or two-day *fiestas de flamenco* in June, July or August.

Main local festivals are noted in city and town sections of this book, and tourist offices can supply detailed information. The monthly what's-on magazine *El Giraldillo* (see the Entertainment section) also has a section devoted to fiestas.

There's always a festival happening somewhere in Andalucía. A few outstanding events include:

Corpus Christi Festival in Granada *(photograph by Bethune Carmichael)*

Spring

Carnaval (Carnival) – fancy-dress parades and merrymaking in many places (wildest in Cádiz), usually ending on the Tuesday 47 days before Easter Sunday

Semana Santa (Holy Week, the week leading up to Easter Sunday) – parades of lavishly bedecked holy images, long lines of penitents (*nazarenos*, who sometimes go hooded), and big crowds, in almost every city, town and village. In major cities there are daily processions from Palm Sunday to Easter Sunday; smaller places tend to omit Monday and Tuesday. Sevilla has the most famous celebrations; Málaga, Granada, Córdoba, Arcos de la Frontera, Jaén, Baeza, Úbeda and Huércal-Overa also stage big or spectacular processions. Village events can be just as unique and touching.

Espárrago Rock Festival – held in Granada over a weekend in late March or early April, highlighting Spanish and foreign alternative rock

Feria de Abril – a week-long party held in Sevilla in late April, counterbalancing the religious fervour of Semana Santa

Romería de la Virgen de la Cabeza – hundreds of thousands of people make a mass pilgrimage to the Santuario de la Virgen de la Cabeza near Andújar, Jaén province, on the last Sunday in April

Festival de Jerez – two-week fiesta of music and dance, especially flamenco, in Jerez de la Frontera in late April

Corpus Christi Festival in Granada *(photograph by Bethune Carmichael)*

Feria de Málaga Festival in Málaga *(photograph by Bethune Carmichael)*

Summer

Feria del Caballo (Horse Fair) – held in Jerez de la Frontera in early May; includes colourful equestrian activities and other festivities in Andalucía's horse capital

Cruces de Mayo (May Crosses) – crosses in plazas and patios in many towns, notably in and around Granada, are decorated with flowers early in the month and become the focus for temporary bars, food stalls, music and dancing

Concurso de Patios Cordobeses – scores of beautiful private courtyards open to the public for two weeks in early May in Córdoba

Romería del Rocío – festive pilgrimage of up to one million people to the village of El Rocío in Huelva province, focused on Pentecost weekend, the seventh after Easter (22-24 May 1999; 10-12 June 2000)

Corpus Christi – processions in Sevilla and Jaén, and a general fiesta in Granada (3 June 1999; 22 June 2000)

Hogueras de San Juan – midsummer bonfires and fireworks, notably along the coasts (23 June)

Potaje Gitano (Gypsy Stew) – flamenco festival in Utrera in June, one of the three big annual one-night events for *aficionados*, all in Sevilla province (the others are in La Caracolá and the Gazpacho – see below)

Festival Torre del Cante – flamenco event in June, in Alhaurín de la Torre near the Costa del Sol, attracting some top performers

La Caracolá (caracol means snail) – flamenco festival in Lebrija, Sevilla province, in June or July

Festival Internacional de la Guitarra – held in Córdoba for two weeks in late June or the first half of July

Festival Internacional de Música y Danza – held in Granada; runs for two weeks in late June or early July

Día de la Virgen del Carmen – on the feast day (16 July) of the patron of fisherfolk, her image is carried into the sea, or paraded on it amid a flotilla of small boats, at many coastal towns

Gazpacho – flamenco festival in Morón de la Frontera (July or August)

Feria de Málaga – one of the most animated summer ferias, for nine days from about 15 August

Autumn

Moros y Cristianos (Moors and Christians) – re-enactment on 14 and 15 September of the 1568 Muslim rebellion in Válor, Granada province. This is one of the most colourful of several events commemorating Muslim/Christian conflicts.

Bienal de Flamenco – held in Sevilla in September of even-numbered years, this event attracts the largest assembly of big flamenco names

Fiestas de Otoño (Autumn Festival) – Jerez de la Frontera's grape harvest celebrations, mid-September to mid-October, with horse races and parades, flamenco and an air show

Festival Internacional de Jazz – this event is held in several Andalucian cities during November

ACTIVITIES

There's a great deal to do in Andalucía apart from seeing sights and lying on the beach. Spanish tourist offices – locally and in other countries – usually have information or useful contact addresses/numbers for most activities. Junta de Andalucía tourist offices sell useful *Marinas*, *Golf* and *Horse* leaflets, in several languages, for a few hundred pesetas.

Walking

Andalucía has some beautiful walking areas, among them Parque Natural de Cazorla in Jaén province; the Sierra Nevada & Las Alpujarras in Granada province; Parque Natural Sierra de Aracena y Picos de Aroche in Huelva province; the Cabo de Gata promontory in Almería province; Parque Natural Sierra de Grazalema and other hill areas near Ronda (Cádiz and Málaga provinces); Parque Natural Sierra Norte in Sevilla province; and the Sierras de Tejeda and Almijara along the border of Málaga and Granada provinces.

In some of these areas you can string together day walks into a trek over several days, using a variety of hostales, mountain refuges, camping grounds and occasionally wild camping for accommodation.

Paths Andalucía's many walkable trails are erratically signposted. In some areas, paths are well signed with route numbers. In others just the odd spot of paint on a stone might tell you you're heading in the right direction. Elsewhere, you're left entirely to your own devices.

The two main categories of path in Spain are the *senderos de Gran Recorrido* (GRs, long-distance footpaths, some several hundred kilometres long) and the *senderos de Pequeño Recorrido* (PRs, shorter routes suitable for day or weekend hikes). Not all, however, are marked or maintained over their full length – or even for much of their length in some cases. In addition there are plenty of paths which are neither GRs nor PRs.

The GR-7, a long-distance path which is being created across Europe from Greece to Algeciras, enters Andalucía near Almaciles in north-east Granada province, then divides at Puebla de Don Fadrique, with one branch heading through Jaén province and the other through Las Alpujarras southeast of Granada. Signposting of this path throughout Andalucía was due to be completed in 1998 (the section through Las Alpujarras is already marked).

Natural and national parks and other protected areas may restrict visitors to limited zones and routes – and ban wild camping – but usually they have marked walks through some of their most interesting areas.

Seasons April to mid-June, and September through to mid-October, are generally the most pleasant times for walking, but the high Sierra Nevada is only really accessible from mid-July to September. The weather in high mountains is never predictable.

Sources of Information Tourist offices – especially visitor centres in natural parks and other protected areas – can help. A number of hiking guidebooks are available in English: Lonely Planet's *Walking in Spain* covers several Andalucian walking areas, and has advice on equipment, preparation and so on. In Spanish, Libros Penthalon's handy *El Búho Viajero* series of hiking guides includes about a dozen volumes on areas of Andalucía. Anaya Touring Club's *Ecoguía* series has walking guides on the Sierras de Cazorla and on the Sierra Nevada and Las Alpujarras. You may find some of these Spanish guides available in walking areas, but it's also a good idea to check out city bookshops.

For information on maps, see Planning at the beginning of this chapter.

Climbing

Mountainous Andalucía is full of rocky crags that invite climbing *(escalada)*. More than 3000 climbs – over half of them in Málaga province – are equipped with bolts. The sheer walls of El Chorro gorge in north-west Málaga province are the main magnet, with over 400 charted climbs of every degree of difficulty. Other climbing areas and centres include El Torcal near Antequera, Benaoján and the Sierra de las Nieves near Ronda, Casares near Estepona, the Sierra de Grazalema and the Parque Natural de Cazorla. *Andalusian Rock Climbs* by Chris Craggs is a good guide.

Cycling

Mountain bikers can test their muscles on many kilometres of good and bad tracks and roads in Andalucía. Tourist offices often have info on routes: some of them sell an English-language booklet, *120 Itineraries around Andalusia on a Mountain Bike*, for 400 ptas. The Spanish for mountain bike is *bici todo terreno* (BTT).

See this book's sections on Parque Natural Los Alcornocales; El Chorro, Ardales & Around; Las Alpujarras; and Parque Natural de Cazorla for mountain bike rental possibilities.

Skiing

The Sierra Nevada ski resort south-east of Granada is Europe's most southerly, and its runs and facilities are good enough to have staged the world alpine skiing championships in 1996. The season normally lasts from December to April.

Windsurfing

Tarifa, west of Gibraltar, is one of Europe's top windsurfing spots, with strong breezes all year, a big windsurfing scene and long, sandy beaches.

Diving

Many of the rockier parts of the Mediterranean coast offer interesting snorkelling. The best diving spots include La Herradura, near Almuñécar (with underwater cliffs); Castell de Ferro east of Almuñécar; Punta del Plomo on Cabo de Gata (good for beginners); and Tarifa. You'll find diving trips, and gear rental, available in all these places.

Sailing

Sailing is naturally a popular activity along Andalucía's coasts and there are over 40 marinas and mooring places between Ayamonte on the Portuguese border and Garrucha in Almería province. The biggest are the flashy Puerto Banús and Benalmádena on the Costa del Sol, and Almerimar near Almería, each with over 900 moorings.

Golf

Andalucía's profile in the golfing world was so heightened by the 1997 Ryder Cup at the Valderrama course at Sotogrande (near Gibraltar) that the Costa del Sol now subtitles itself 'Costa del Golf' on road signs. This was the first time that the illustrious Ryder Cup, a contest between Europe and the USA, had been held anywhere in Europe except Britain. (Europe, captained by the Spaniard Severiano Ballesteros, won.) Thirty-six golf courses are dotted along and near the Costa del Sol between Gibraltar and Málaga. A further 17 courses are scattered around Andalucía. Most courses are 18 holes. Green fees at most clubs are between 4000 and 8000 ptas, with Estepona and La Duquesa on the Costa del Sol, Guadalhorce near Málaga, and Añoreta at Rincón de la Victoria among those at the low end of the scale. Top courses, such as Valderrama, Sotogrande, and Las Brisas and Aloha at Marbella are more expensive (around 20,000 ptas at Valderrama). There are several Internet sites devoted to golf in Spain.

Horseriding

Chief breeding ground of the Spanish thoroughbred horse (also known as the Andalusian), Andalucía is steeped in equestrian tradition. There are plenty of fine trails to ride in many areas, and a growing number of stables which will rent you a mount, or take you on a guided ride or even a long-distance trek. Check this book's sections on Aracena, Arcos de la Frontera, El Rocío, Grazalema, Las Alpujarras, Parque Natural de Cazorla, Parque Natural Los Alcornocales, San José (Almería province), Tarifa and Zahara de la Sierra. The cost is usually around 3000 ptas for two hours or 5000 ptas for four hours.

Anyone with an interest in horses should put Jerez de la Frontera on their itinerary. The town holds a number of exciting annual equine events and its Royal Andalucian School of Equestrian Art and the nearby Yeguada del Hierro breeding centre are fascinating to visit at any time.

Birdwatching
Andalucía is a magnet for birdwatchers. It attracts ornithologists year round. March and April, when you can see many wintering species *and* some arriving summer visitors, are particularly good times. You'll find information on birdwatching sites and areas – including where and when to see the greater flamingo, which to nonspecialists is probably Andalucía's most spectacular bird

– in several sections of this book, including Flora & Fauna (in Facts about Andalucía), Isla Cristina, Laguna de Fuente de Piedra, Paraje Natural Marismas del Odiel, Parque Nacional de Doñana, Parque Natural de Cazorla, Parque Natural Sierra de Grazalema, Parque Natural Sierra Norte, San Miguel de Cabo de Gata and South of Córdoba. See also Books in this chapter.

COURSES
Undertaking a spot of study is a great way not only to learn something but also to meet people and get an inside angle on local life.

Language
Branches of the Instituto Cervantes (see Useful Organisations) can send you long lists of places offering Spanish-language

High-Fliers at the Strait of Gibraltar

Most serious birdwatchers in Andalucía will want to head at some point for the Strait of Gibraltar, a key point of passage for raptors, storks and other birds migrating between Africa and Europe. In general, northern migrations occur between mid-February and early June and southbound flights happen between late July and early November. When a westerly wind is blowing, Gibraltar itself is usually good for birdwatchers but when the wind is calm or easterly, the Tarifa area (including the Mirador del Estrecho 7km east of town) is usually better.

Soaring birds such as raptors and storks cross at the Strait of Gibraltar because they rely on thermals and updrafts, which don't happen over wider expanses of water. White storks sometimes congregate in flocks of up to 3000 to cross the strait (January and February northbound, July and August southbound).

Flocks of white storks often soar over the strait.

From mid-July to mid-September every year, the Sociedad Española de Ornitología (SEO/BirdLife) organises a watch of migrating soarers (raptors, vultures, storks) over the strait. If you're interested in volunteering, send a brief resumé of your ornithological experience, and your preferred dates, to the Programa Migres (☎ & fax 956 67 91 61, migres@tnet.es), Centro Ornitológico del Estrecho de Gibraltar, Parque Natural Los Alcornocales, Carretera Nacional N-340 Km 96, 11390 Algeciras, Cádiz, Spain.

courses in Spain. Or you can contact the Servicio Central de Cursos de Español (☎ 91 593 19 49; fax 91 445 69 60), Calle Trafalgar 32, 28010 Madrid. Most places cater for a wide range of levels (from beginners up). Many courses have a cultural component as well.

Sevilla and Granada are the most popular places in Andalucía to study Spanish. University courses often last a term, though some are as short as two weeks or as long as a year. Private language schools can be more flexible about when you can start and how long you stay.

Costs vary widely. University courses offer some of the best value, with a typical four-week course of 20 one-hour classes a week for around 40,000 or 50,000 ptas. Many places offer accommodation with families, in student lodgings or in flats, if you want it – generally from around 30,000 ptas a month with no meals to about 60,000 ptas for full board.

Other things to think about when choosing a course include intensiveness (intensivo means different things at different schools), class sizes, who the other students are likely to be and whether you want organised extracurricular activities. It's also worth asking whether a course will lead to any formal certificate. The Diplomas Oficiales de Español como Lengua Extranjera (DELE) are qualifications recognised by Spain's Ministry of Education and Science.

It's easy to arrange private classes in many places: check notice boards in universities and language schools, or small ads in the local press. Expect to pay around 2000 ptas per hour for individual private lessons.

Arts & Culture

Some places offering language courses also offer other aspects of Spanish culture. See the Sevilla, Granada, Las Alpujarras and Jerez de la Frontera sections for information on courses in Spanish dance or guitar. The Instituto Cervantes and Spanish tourist offices are good places to start asking about further possibilities.

Some foreigners living in Andalucía have set up residential centres where you can combine a learning experience with comfortable surroundings and, often, extras like excursions. These include:

Cortijo Romero, Apartado 31, 18400 Órgiva, Granada – personal development and alternative living centre in Las Alpujarras, with vegetarian food and week-long programmes ranging from dance to yoga; typical price around 60,000 ptas; in the UK contact Little Grove, Grove Lane, Chesham, Bucks HP5 3QQ (☎ 01494-782720)

Learning for Pleasure (☎ & fax 95 248 62 10), Apartado 150, 29650 Mijas, Málaga – courses in painting, gardening, cooking (led by well-known cooks) and more, at a farmhouse at Jimena de la Frontera in Cádiz province

Los Pinos Centro de Fotografía (☎ 95 203 02 90), Molino Becerril, 29710 Periana, Málaga – one-week workshop/holidays led by well-known British photographers, emphasising architecture, festivals, landscape and nature; around 90,000 ptas

The Spirit of Andalusia (☎ 95 215 13 03, 95 215 12 22), Apartado 20, 29480 Gaucín, Málaga – cooking courses with 'name' cooks, painting courses

WORK

With high unemployment even by Spanish standards, Andalucía doesn't exactly have a labour shortage. But there are a few possible ways of earning your keep (or almost) while you're here. If you have any contacts – perhaps among the many foreigners living in Andalucía – follow them up. Word of mouth counts for a lot.

Regulations

Nationals of EU countries, Norway and Iceland are allowed to work in Spain without a visa, but if they plan to stay for more than three months, they are supposed to apply within the first month for a tarjeta de residencia (see Visas & Documents). Virtually everyone else is supposed to obtain a work permit from a Spanish consulate in their country of residence and, if they plan to stay more than 90 days, a residence visa. These procedures are well-nigh impossible unless you already have a job contract, and you should set things rolling long before you aim to go to Spain. That said, numerous people do work, discreetly, without bothering to tangle with the bureaucracy.

Opportunities

Tourist Resorts Summer work, especially on the Costa del Sol, is a distinct possibility, particularly if you get in early in the season and are prepared to stay a while. Many bars, restaurants and other businesses are run by foreigners. Follow up any contacts you have, look at notice boards, and check the local press, including *Sur In English* which carries some ads for waiters, nannies, chefs, baby sitters and cleaners – as well as 'closers', 'liners' and others wanted to hawk time-share properties to foreign holiday-makers.

Language Teaching Language-teaching qualifications and some knowledge of Spanish would obviously help for this option. There are several language schools in most cities and often one or two even in smaller towns. Getting a job is harder if you're not an EU citizen. Giving private lessons is another option, though unlikely to bring you a living wage very soon.

Sources of information on possible teaching work – school or private – include universities, language schools and foreign-language bookshops. Some of these have notice boards where you may find work opportunities, or where you can advertise your own services. The local press is also worth scanning or advertising in. Language schools are listed under 'Academias de Idiomas' in the yellow pages.

Boat Crew Gibraltar is the best place to look for a crew place on a yacht or cruiser. In high summer, a few places a week come up here on craft sailing the Mediterranean, and from November to January there's the chance of working your passage to the Caribbean. Puerto Banús is the next best place to try. You're unlikely to be paid for this work.

ACCOMMODATION

The Junta de Andalucía's annual *Guía de Hoteles, Pensiones, Apartamentos, Campings, Casas Rurales y Agencias de Viajes*, available from some tourist offices and bookshops in Andalucía for 800 ptas, lists most of the region's places to stay, including camp sites, and their facilities and approximate prices.

These Web sites might be useful:

RurALandalus
    adves.com/ruralandalus/
Paradores de Turismo
    www.parador.es/

Camping

Andalucía has over 130 officially graded camp sites *(campings)*. Some are well located in woodland or near beaches or rivers, but others are stuck away near main roads on the edges of towns and cities. Very few are near city centres.

Sites are officially rated as 1st class (1^a C), 2nd class (2^a C) or 3rd class (3^a C). There are also a few not officially graded, usually equivalent to 3rd class. Facilities range from reasonable to very good, though any site can be crowded and noisy at busy times. Even a 3rd-class site is likely to have hot showers, electrical hook-ups and cafeteria. The best sites have heated pools, supermarkets, restaurants, laundry service and children's playgrounds. Sizes vary; some cater for under 100 people, others can take over 5000 people.

Camp sites usually charge per person, per tent and per vehicle – anywhere between 250 and 800 ptas for each, though 500 ptas is typical. Children usually pay a bit less than adults. Many sites are open all year, but some close from around October to Easter. Here and there you come across a *zona de acampada* or *área de acampada*, a country site with no facilities, no supervision and no charge. Tourist offices can always direct you to the nearest camp site.

With certain exceptions – such as many beaches and environmentally protected areas – it is legal to camp outside camp sites (though not within 1km of official ones). Signs may indicate where wild camping is not allowed. You'll need permission to camp on private land.

Camping Gaz is the only common brand of camping gas: screw-on canisters are near-impossible to find.

Hostels
Most of Andalucía's approximately 20 youth hostels (*albergues juveniles*, not to be confused with *hostales* – see the next section) are affiliated to Inturjoven, the official Andalucía youth hostel organisation. They are mostly good, modern places with a high proportion of twin rooms as well as small dormitories with bunks. Sheets are provided and many rooms have private bathrooms. The hostels don't have cooking facilities but they do have *comedores* (dining rooms), usually serving all meals at good prices. Inturjoven has a central booking office (☎ 95 455 82 93, fax 95 455 82 92) at Calle del Miño 24, Los Remedios, 41011 Sevilla – open Monday to Friday from 9.30 am to 2 pm and 5 to 7.30 pm. You can also book with the hostels themselves.

Prices in all Inturjoven hostels are 900/1300 ptas in the low/high season for under-26s (1075/1475 ptas with breakfast), and 1200/1600 ptas (1375/1775 ptas with breakfast) for 26 and overs – plus IVA in all cases. At the Córdoba, Granada, Huelva, Málaga, Almería and Sevilla hostels, high season is all year; at Jerez de la Frontera it's April to September; at Sierra Nevada it's when the ski station is open (normally from about the beginning of December to early May); and at the other hostels it's from mid-June to mid-September, long weekends year round and Semana Santa.

To stay in an Inturjoven hostel you need a youth hostel card. If you haven't already obtained one from a youth hostel or hostel organisation in your own country, you can get an HI (Hostelling International) Card, valid till 31 December of the year you buy it, at any Inturjoven hostel or the Sevilla office, or at any of the 140 or so other hostels in the Red Española de Albergues Juveniles (REAJ), which is the Spanish affiliate of HI. For the HI card, you pay in instalments of 300 ptas for each night you spend in a hostel, up to 1800 ptas.

Some hostels are often heavily booked by school or youth groups. Inconvenient nighttime curfews or daytime closing hours seem rare in Andalucian hostels.

The annual HI European hostels directory contains details of all Inturjoven and other REAJ hostels.

Just a few hostels are run by organisations other than Inturjoven. Some of these do not require hostel cards.

Hostales, Hospedajes, Pensiones, Hotels, Paradors etc
Officially all these establishments are classified as either *hoteles* (from one to five stars) or *pensiones* (one or two stars). In practice, places to stay use all sorts of titles, especially at the budget end of the market.

In broad terms, the cheapest are places which just advertise *camas* (beds), *fondas* (traditionally a basic eatery and inn combined, though one or other function is now often missing) and *casas de huéspedes* or *hospedajes* (guesthouses). A *pensión* (basically a small private hotel) is usually a small step up from these, but in any of them bathrooms are likely to be shared, with single/double rooms costing 1000/2000 to 1500/3000 ptas. All such places will be bare and basic. Your room may be small, possibly lacking a window, towel and (probably) soap, and it may have alarmingly inventive electrical fittings and erratic hot water – but in most cases it will be kept pretty clean. The beds may make you feel as though you're lying diagonally across a bumpy hillside – or they may be firm, flat and comfortable. In winter don't hesitate to ask for extra blankets.

Next up the scale are *hostales*, essentially little different from pensiones, except that some are considerably more comfortable, and more rooms tend to have private bathrooms. Hostal prices range from pensión levels up to 6000 ptas or so for a

When the Price is Right

Prices at any type of accommodation may vary with the season. Many places have separate price structures for the high season *(temporada alta)*, mid-season *(temporada media)* and low season *(temporada baja)*, all usually displayed on a notice in reception or close by. (Hoteliers are free to charge less than the posted prices, which they quite often do, or more, which happens less often.)

High season depends on where you are, but in most places it's in summer – which can mean a period as short as mid-July to the end of August or as long as Easter to October. The Christmas-New Year period, Semana Santa and local festivals which attract lots of visitors are also high season or at least mid-season in some places.

Differences between low and high-season prices tend to be biggest – typically 30% – in coastal resorts. Occasionally, there are bigger differences: some places in Sevilla, for instance, charge three times as much during Semana Santa and the Feria de Abril as they do in winter.

Room prices in this book are generally high-season prices, so you can expect some pleasant surprises at other times. Major seasonal trends are noted. Prices include the 7% IVA tax unless stated otherwise.

In the low season there's generally no need to book ahead, but when things get busier it's advisable to do so, and at peak periods it can be essential if you want to avoid a wearisome search for a room. At most places, a phone call is all that's needed, giving your approximate time of arrival.

---

double. Some hostales are bright, modern and pleasant; others are less so.

Establishments calling themselves *hoteles* range from simple places where a double room could cost 4000 ptas or less up to wildly luxurious, five-star places where you could pay 50,000 ptas. Even in the cheapest, rooms are likely to have an attached bathroom and there'll probably be a restaurant.

Paradores, officially *paradores de turismo*, are a state-run chain of 80-odd high-class hotels around Spain (about 16 of them in Andalucía). Many are in converted castles, mansions or monasteries and they can be wonderful places to stay if you have 14,000 ptas or more for a double room. Occasional special offers may make paradors more affordable. You can book a room at any parador through their Central de Reservas (☎ 91 516 66 66, fax 91 516 66 57), Calle Requena 3, 28013 Madrid.

Many places of all these types have a range of rooms at different prices. At the bottom end prices will vary according to whether the room has a washbasin *(lavabo)*, shower *(ducha)* or full bathroom *(baño completo)*. At the top end you may pay more for a room on the outside of the building or with a balcony, and will often have the option of a suite.

Casas Rurales

The burgeoning interest of Spaniards in their own countryside has led to the opening of many new places to stay in rural areas. These *casas rurales* are usually comfortably renovated country houses or farmhouses, with just a handful of rooms. Some have meals available; some just provide rooms; some offer self-catering accommodation. Prices typically range between 1500 and 3000 ptas per person per night.

Tourist offices can often provide leaflets listing local country accommodation. Two organisations which can send you catalogues of casas rurales are the Red Andaluza de Alojamientos Rurales (RAAR, Andalucian Country Lodgings Network,

☎ 950 26 50 18, fax 950 27 04 31, 100705.106@compuserve.com), Apartado 2035, 04080 Almería; and RurALandalus (☎ 95 227 62 29, fax 95 227 65 56, rural-landalus@adv.es), Calle Don Cristián 10, 29007 Málaga. The RAAR has over 200 places all over rural Andalucía, most with a high-season minimum stay of one week (two nights minimum out of season). Rur-ALandalus focuses chiefly on Málaga province and its catalogue is also available on the Internet.

Refugios

Except in the Sierra Nevada, *refugios* – mountain shelters for hikers and climbers – are not as plentiful in Andalucía as in other mountainous areas of Spain. Refugios belong to walking and climbing organisations, but are generally open to the public, and at a minimum provide space to spread out a sleeping bag. Some are in a semi-ruined state but at least provide a roof over your head. The best are permanently staffed and have meals and drinks available. A *refugio vivac* usually has nothing but sleeping space. In busy seasons refugios can fill up quickly, so you should try to book ahead where possible.

Apartments, Houses & Villas

In many places there are equipped, self-catering apartments, houses and villas to rent. A simple one-bedroom apartment for two or three people might cost as little as 1500 ptas a night, though more often you're looking at twice that, and prices can jump further in peak seasons. These options are most worth considering if you plan to stay several days or more, in which case there will usually be discounts from the daily rate.

Tourist offices can supply lists of places for rent, and in Britain the *Sunday Times* carries a lot of private ads for such places. Companies such as Magic of Spain (see Organised Tours in Getting There & Away) can also fix you up with a house or villa, but their prices are not low. Also see Casas Rurales, above.

ENTERTAINMENT

You need never go short of entertainment in Andalucía. If nothing else, just sitting in a café and watching the animated street life go on around you can be fun enough.

Listings

Local papers often carry fairly thorough entertainment listings. Try to pick up *El Giraldillo*, a good monthly what's-on guide for all Andalucía, from tourist offices. It's in Spanish but decipherable. It's also available on the Internet (though it doesn't appear there till about the 10th of the month!). Tourist offices can help with specific inquiries and may have other what's-on publications.

Bars & Discos

If you're up to it, wild and *very* late nights, especially on Friday and Saturday, are an integral part of the Andalucian experience. Even small towns often have lively scenes. Many young Andalucians don't think about going out till midnight or so. Bars, in all shapes, sizes and themes, are the main attractions until around 2 or 3 am. Some play great music, which will get you hopping before you move on to a disco, if you can afford it, till 5 or 6 am – or later! Some discos won't let you in wearing jeans or trainers. Techno, in various guises, is the go in many of them. Spain's contributions to it are the frenzied *bakalao* and *mákina*.

Live Pop, Rock & Jazz

Most towns have at least one bar or café with live music on weekends. In the cities there's a big choice most nights of the week.

The Spanish rock and pop scene is large and lively, and foreign touring bands put in fairly frequent appearances in Andalucía, especially in summer. Live music of many types is an essential ingredient of many fiestas. Jazz and blues have good followings, with venues in most big cities.

Flamenco

Flamenco is easiest to catch in the summer,

when a number of towns stage flamenco festivals and others put on one-night events, often as part of a feria or fiesta. These are typically long-drawn-out open-air affairs, maybe scheduled to start at 10 pm but not really getting going till midnight. They can last till dawn and copious quantities of alcohol are usually drunk.

The rest of the year there are intermittent big-name performances in theatres, but also regular flamenco nights at bars and clubs in some cities – often just for the price of your drinks. Flamenco fans also band together in clubs called *peñas* which stage live performance nights – most will admit genuinely interested visitors and the atmosphere here can be very intimate and informal.

Unless asked otherwise, tourist offices will tend to steer you towards *tablaos*, regular shows for a tourist audience, usually with high prices. Some of these are reasonably good; others are tacky.

See Public Holidays & Special Events in this chapter, and city and town Entertainment sections for more on flamenco venues and events. Places like Sevilla and Jerez de la Frontera in the lower Guadalquivir basin are flamenco hotbeds, but you'll often be able to find something in other places such as Málaga, Granada, Cádiz and Córdoba.

Cinemas

Cinemas abound and are inexpensive, though foreign films are almost always dubbed into Spanish. In the major cities a few cinemas show foreign films with Spanish subtitles – look for the letters v.o. *(versión original)* in listings.

Classical Music, Dance & Theatre

For the culturally inclined, there are plenty of these going on in Andalucía's cities. They often take the form of festivals (see Public Holidays & Special Events). Theatre is nearly all in Spanish, of course.

Festivals

Andalucía's myriad fiestas (see Public Holidays & Special Events) provide heaps of colourful spectacle and, more often than not, a celebratory atmosphere.

SPECTATOR SPORT
Football

Fútbol (soccer) rivals bullfighting as Spain's national sport. Every weekend from September to May, millions follow the national Primera División (First Division) on TV. Spaniards take their favoured teams' fortunes very seriously!

Andalucía currently has only one decent team – Real Betis of Sevilla, which in recent years has been occupying a respectable position in the Primera División. Sevilla's other big team, FC Sevilla, has been in the Segunda División. Teams from other main Andalucian cities tend to go up and down between the Segunda División and the next league down, the Segunda División B (which is divided into four regional groups). Andalucian soccer fans often care more about Real Madrid or Barcelona than about their local club.

League games are mostly played on Saturday and Sunday. Games in the Copa del Rey (Spain's FA Cup equivalent) are held midweek at night. Watch the local press and the sports paper *Marca* for upcoming fixtures.

SHOPPING

You can find some very attractive and reasonably priced handicrafts in Andalucía if you look in the right places. In some crafts there's wide regional variation and many products tend not to be found very far afield from where they are made. Apart from craft shops – abundant in producing and tourist areas – you may pick up crafts at weekly or daily markets in villages or towns, and even in department stores such as the nationwide El Corte Inglés chain. There are also flea markets and car boot sales *(rastros)* around the region where you can at times find incredible bargains.

Pottery

This comes in many attractive regional varieties – crockery, tiles, plant pots and more

GERRY REILLY
Andalucian crafts displayed in a Frigiliana street

– and is cheap. Islamic influence on design and colour is strong. In Granada, the dominant colours are white splashed with green and blue, often with a pomegranate as the centrepiece of the pattern. In Córdoba the product is finer, with black, green and blue borders on white. Úbeda, another noted pottery centre, typically employs a green glaze. Gaudier colours are used in some other areas. Some excellent, more individual pieces are made in Níjar in Almería.

Rugs
Inexpensive, colourful rugs and blankets are made in several areas, among them Las Alpujarras and Níjar.

Leather
Andalucian leather goods used to be quite a bargain and, though prices have gone up, you can still get good deals on jackets, bags, belts, shoes and boots in many places. Exquisite riding boots can be purchased in 'horsey' places like Jerez de la Frontera and El Rocío. Embossed, polychrome leather products such as poufs make a good, not-too-bulky present: you simply roll up the leather and insert the filling back at home.

Other Crafts
Gold and silver jewellery abound; some of the best is the filigree made in Córdoba. There's some pleasing woodwork available, such as Granada's marquetry boxes, chess sets and more. Basketwork is most evident on the coasts.

JOHN HAY

FOOD

Andalucía's cooking is typically Mediterranean in its liberal use of olive oil, garlic, onions, tomatoes and peppers. Traditionally, it is simple peasant fare based on fresh ingredients with a hint of herbs and spices, reflecting Roman, Jewish, New World and Arabic influences, the latter being the most distinctive.

Seafood and meat are eaten almost everywhere and there are many excellent varieties of seafood, especially from the Atlantic coast. Unfortunately they don't usually come very cheap. A quick deep-fry in very hot olive oil is the most common method of cooking seafood in Andalucía. A good **sopa de mariscos** (seafood soup) can be almost a meal in itself.

Everywhere the fruit and vegetables are delicious and fresh, for the growing season is year round.

Many varieties of soaked dried beans have, for reasons of economy, traditionally made up the bulk of stews, with meat only added for flavour if available.

Provincial Specialities

Andalucía's varied local cuisines reflect its geographical diversity. In the sierras, hams are cured and game dishes abound. On the coasts, seafood predominates. Seafood soups, fried fish, and sardines grilled on spits (**espetos**) over driftwood fires, are all common.

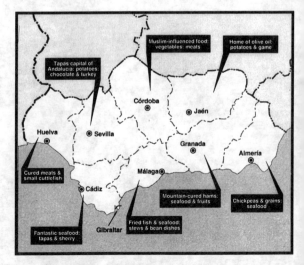

Previous page: Andalucía's version of Spain's most famous dish, paella. *(photograph by Gerry Reilly)*

Here is a brief look at some of the gastronomic traditions of Andalucía's eight provinces.

Almería This arid eastern province has a simple cuisine using chickpeas, grains, seafood and plenty of irrigation-grown fresh vegetables.

Cádiz The coastline has fantastic seafood, with a multitude of mouth-watering tapas. The city of Cádiz is home to the **pescaíto frito**, take-away fried fish. Sherry is added to meat dishes in Jerez de la Frontera. The French and English, who played a big role in the sherry industry in Jerez, have also influenced its cuisine.

Córdoba Córdoba was at the heart of the culinary changes introduced by the Muslims. Today, some of its classy restaurants prepare food in the medieval Muslim and Sephardic (Jewish) styles. At grassroots level, Córdoba is strong on vegetable dishes and has good cured meats.

Granada The province of Granada includes Spain's highest peaks and a semi-tropical coastline. It's known for its warming meat dishes but seafood and tropical fruits feature too. Granada's mountain-cured hams are justly famous.

Huelva There's more excellent seafood here at the western end of Andalucía – **chocos** (small cuttlefish) are a local passion. But Huelva is best known for its cured meats, especially hams from Jabugo.

Jaén On the southern slopes of the eastern Sierra Morena, Jaén is the home of olive oil, added liberally to many dishes. The province is also known for its potato and game dishes.

Málaga This province is known for its fried fish and seafood, especially **boquerones** (anchovies), often eaten raw marinated in vinegar, oil and garlic. Seafood soups are common. Ronda, in Málaga's sierras, has tasty game, cured meats, stews and bean dishes. **Migas** is a Málaga speciality. At its most basic, this dish consists of crumbly fried flour and water but is often enlivened with fish, garlic, capsicum or dried tomato.

Sevilla Cuisine here is a touch more sophisticated than elsewhere in Andalucía. Sevilla city was the first port of arrival for all the new foodstuffs from the Americas that radically changed European cookery – potatoes, avocados, chocolate, turkey, tomatoes, peppers, dried beans and more. It's also the tapas capital of Andalucía.

Olive oil – an important export of Andalucía. A vast range of olive oils are available in the region.

Mejillones a la Marinera – one example of the many seafood dishes in Andalucía.

Meals

The Spanish eating timetable is at its most extreme in Andalucía. So it's a good idea to reset your stomach clock, unless you want to eat alone or only with other tourists.

Breakfast Andalucians, like most Spaniards, start the day with a light breakfast (**desayuno**) – usually coffee with a **tostada** (a toasted roll or slice of bread).

You can put an almost infinite variety of things in or on your tostada. Andalucian toppings include olive oil (**aceite**), maybe with garlic (**ajo**); **manteca**, pork lard, maybe coloured red with paprika; **sobrasada**, a lard made from pork sausages; and **tomate frotado**, crushed tomato. Likely to appeal more to most

Tostada con aceite – a typical breakfast of sliced toast drizzled with olive oil.

The Menú is not Always on the Menu

Menú del Día Most restaurants offer a **menú del día** (daily set menu) – the budget traveller's best friend – typically for 800 to 1200 ptas. You normally get a starter, main course, dessert (**postre**), bread and wine. Often there's a choice of two or three dishes for each course. The menú is usually posted up outside – if it makes no mention of drinks, dessert, bread, coffee or 'IVA incluido', your meal may cost more.

Platos Combinados The **plato combinado** is a near relative of the menú del día. It literally translates as 'combined plate' – maybe a steak and egg with chips and salad, or fried squid with potato salad. Insipid photos of what's available can be offputting, but more often than not a plato combinado is fine.

À la Carte You'll pay more for your meals if you order à la carte but the food will be better. The Spanish menu (**la carta** – not **el menú** which means the menú del día) begins with starters such as **ensaladas** (salads), **sopas** (soups) and **entremeses** (hors d'oeuvres). Entremeses can range from a mound of potato salad with peppers, olives, asparagus, anchovies and a selection of cold meats – almost a meal in itself – to simpler cold meats, slices of cheese and olives.

Later courses on the menu will probably be listed under headings like chicken (**pollo**), meat (**carne**), seafood (**mariscos**), fish (**pez/pescado**), rice (**arroz**), eggs (**huevos**) and vegetables (**vegetales/verduras/legumbres**). Meat may be subdivided into pork (**cerdo**), beef (**vaca**) and lamb (**cordero**).

Desserts have a low profile – ice cream (**helado**), fruit and flan are often the only choices. There may be **arroz con leche** (cold rice pudding) or **tocino del cielo** (heavenly bacon), a type of caramel custard with a vaguely bacon-like appearance.

visitors are options such as ham; bacon (**beicon** or **tocino**); a slice of grilled pork loin (**lomo a la plancha**); a slab of omelette (**tortilla**); cheese (**queso**); or plain old butter (**mantequilla**) and jam (**mermelada** or **confitura**).

You may get the chance to specify what type of bread you want – we thoroughly recommend **molletes**, tasty soft rolls, if they're available. You can have a whole (**entera**) or half (**media**) roll or slice of bread.

Churros con chocolate – long, deep-fried doughnuts to dip in thick hot chocolate – make a rich, calorie-laden breakfast.

If you're hungry, a tortilla (omelette) is a good option. **Huevos fritos** are fried eggs and **huevos revueltos** are scrambled eggs; **huevos pasados por agua** are lightly boiled eggs; ask for **huevos cocidos** if you want hard-boiled eggs.

Churros con chocolate (chocolate-dipped doughnuts) – a rich breakfast snack

Lunch This is usually the main meal of the day, eaten between about 1.30 and 4 pm and known as **comida** or **almuerzo**. It can consist of several courses including a soup and/or salad, meat or fish with vegetables or a rice dish or bean stew, followed by fruit, ice cream or flan. You can try a **plato combinado,** order **a la carte** or try the **menú del día**

Dinner The evening meal, **cena**, tends to be lighter than lunch, and may be eaten as late as 10 and 11 pm. But lots of people also go out to a bigger dinner in restaurants – though before about 9 pm you're unlikely to see anyone but foreigners doing this. Only a few restaurants offer their menú del día in the evening.

In-Between Times It's common (and a great idea!) to go to a bar or café for a **merienda** (snack) around 11 am and again around 7 or 8 pm. Tapas apart, one great Spanish snack is a **bocadillo**, a long white bread roll filled with cheese or ham or salad or sometimes tortilla ... the list goes on.

Tortilla de Patatas (Potato Omelette) – a hearty meal of fried potatoes, onions and salted eggs.

Put a Lid on it – Tapas & Raciones

The saucer-sized mini-snacks known as tapas are part of the Spanish way of life and come in infinite variety. You can make a meal of tapas, or go on to a meal afterwards, or hop on to another bar to sample more tapas. In Andalucía, Sevilla is the place to tapear – to tour bars to sample their tapas.

'Tapa' translates as 'lid'. Today's snacks supposedly originated in the sherry area of Andalucía in the 19th century when bar owners placed a piece of bread on top of a drink to deter flies; this developed into the custom of putting a titbit, something salty to encourage drinking, such as olives or a piece of sausage, on a lid to cover the drink. Today, tapas have become a cuisine in their own right and each

Spanish region and city has its specialities. Sometimes they're free, though this custom has all but disappeared in many areas. A typical tapa costs between 100 and 200 ptas (check before you order as some are a lot dearer).

Typical tapas include olives, slices of cured meats or cheese, potato salad, diced salad, bite-sized portions of fried fish, **albóndigas** (meat or fish balls), chickpeas with spinach, rabbit stew, **callos** (tripe), **gambas** (prawns) in garlic, and **boquerones** (anchovies) marinated in vinegar or rebozados (fried in batter).

Bars often display a range of tapas on the counter, or chalk a list on a board. There may even be a tapas menu. Otherwise, it seems you're expected to know what's available and the situation can be rather confusing. A place that appears not to have tapas may actually specialise in them! You just have to ask what tapas are available then try to recognise a few words in the long answer you're likely to get.

A **ración** is a meal-sized serving of these snacks, a media-ración is a half-ración. Two different **media-raciones** amount to pretty much a full meal. When ordering, make it clear if it's a tapa you're after, not a ración or media-ración, or you'll end up paying three or five times what you planned.

Types of Eatery

Cafés & Bars If you want to live like the locals, you'll spend plenty of time in cafés and bars. The latter come in various guises such as **bodegas** (old-fashioned wine bars), **cervecerías** (beer bars), **tascas** (bars specialising in tapas), **tabernas** (taverns) and even **pubs**. In many of them you'll find tapas. Others may serve more substantial fare too. You'll often save 10% to 20%

Andalucian Tapas Specialities

Charcutería or **chacinas** (pork products), feature everywhere. **Lomo embuchado**, pork loin cured and stuffed in a sausage skin, also called **caña de lomo** or **cinta** in Andalucía, and **chorizo**, a marbled salami-type sausage, are also common. Offal such as **sesos** (brains), **callos** (tripe), **criadillas** (bull or sheep testicles), **riñones** (kidneys) and **hígado** (liver) may appear in a small earthenware dish (cazuelita), simmering in a tomato sauce or gravy, like **albóndigas** (meatballs). Meat eaters can also enjoy ham croquettes (**croquetas**) or **flamenquines** which are rolled and crumbed veal or ham, deep-fried.

Seafood tapas are possibly the highlight of Spanish cookery. Sample Andalucía's best shellfish in the sherry triangle of Cádiz province – from Atlantic **conchas finas** (Venus shell, the biggest of the clams) or **langostinos** (striped jumbo prawns from the mouth of the Río Guadalquivir) to **cangrejos** (tiny crabs, cooked whole) or **búsanos** (sea snails or whelks). **Langostinos a la plancha**, grilled with coarse-grained salt, can be a taste sensation.

Cádiz city has its own special array of seafood tapas. Elsewhere, standard seafood tapas include **boquerones**; **mejillones** (mussels); **cazón en adobo** and **pavía**, chunks of deep fried fish (pre-seasoned and marinated); and **gambas al pil pil**, small prawns cooked in oil with garlic and chilli.

The plump manzanilla type of olives, with or without anchovy stuffing, are sometimes a free tapa. Salads are common tapas: varieties include **pipir-rana** (based on diced tomatoes and red peppers), **salpicón** (the same with bits of seafood), **ensal-adilla** (Russian salad) and **aliño**, any salad in a vinegar-and-oil dressing.

by eating at the bar rather than at a table. (The outside table area of a cafe, bar or restaurant is known as a **terraza**.)

Restaurants Throughout Andalucía, you'll find plenty of **restaurantes** serving good, straightforward food at affordable prices, often featuring local specialities. There are also some ordinary to woeful places, particularly in tourist haunts.

A **mesón** is a simple eatery with home-style cooking, attached to a bar, while a **comedor** is usually a dining room attached to a bar or hostal – here the food is likely to be functional and cheap. A **venta** is usually a family-run establishment, probably previously a roadside inn, often off the beaten track – the food can be delectable and cheap. A **marisquería** or **merendero** is a seafood restaurant. A **chiringuito** is a small open-air bar or kiosk, or sometimes a more substantial beachside restaurant.

From Little Acorns, Great Hams Grow

In Spanish bars you'll often see dozens of pigs' back legs hanging from the ceiling. To the uninitiated, it may look a bit gruesome but this cured ham (**jamón**) is mouth watering for a Spaniard. Try two or three slices as a tapa, or have it in a bocadillo for 300 or 400 ptas, or get a ración for around 600 to 1000 ptas. Hard cheeses such as Manchego from La Mancha go well with jamón.

JOHN NOBLE

Most of these hams are **jamón serrano** (mountain ham). Even better (and more expensive) is **jamón ibérico**, from the black (or dark brown) Iberian breed of pig, and the best jamón ibérico is **jamón ibérico de bellota**, from pigs fed on acorns (**bellotas**). A glass of fino sherry is the traditional accompaniment to jamón ibérico.

Considered to be among the best jamones are those from Trevélez in Las Alpujarras and, above all, the jamón ibérico of Jabugo in Huelva province, from pigs free-ranging in the Sierra Morena oak forests. The best Jabugo hams are graded from one to five jotas (Js), and JJJJJ (cinco jotas) hams are said to come from pigs that have never eaten anything but acorns.

For 1kg of jamón serrano in a shop expect to pay about 2000 ptas. Ibérico ham can cost double that price.

Ordinary, uncured cold ham, by the way, is called jamón York. It's dull as ditchwater after you've tasted serrano or ibérico.

Talking of Eating ...

Here are a few basic words that will come in handy:

bill (check) – **cuenta**	menu – **carta**
breakfast – **desayuno**	olive oil – **aceite de oliva**
cold – **frío/a**	plate – **plato**
cup – **taza**	pepper – **pimienta**
dinner – **cena**	salt – **sal**
food, meal, lunch – **comida**	sauce – **salsa**
fork – **tenedor**	spoon – **cuchara**
glass – **vaso** or **copa**	sugar – **azúcar**
hot (temperature) – **caliente**	table – **mesa**
hot (spicy) – **picante**	vinegar – **vinagre**
knife – **cuchillo**	waiter/waitress – **camarero/a**
lunch – **almuerzo** or **comida**	water – **agua**

Few authentic recipes survive from the Muslim era but there is enough information to approximate. Some Andalucian restaurants do just that. Try Córdoba's upmarket *El Caballo Rojo* if you're interested in sampling dishes from the time of the caliphs. A close relation to Muslim fare is Mozarabic fare *(cocina mozárabe)*, the food of the Christians who lived under Muslim rule. Some restaurants offer Mozarabic desserts or meat in a Mozarabic sauce with ingredients like figs, cinnamon, raisins and cloves.

JOHN HAY

Spanish Onions – used in many dishes in Andalucia. You'll also find them in the mercado – a fun place to visit.

Ethnic Restaurants Andalucía has many Chinese restaurants, generally mundane but cheap. Some of the bigger cities and tourist resorts have other Asian restaurants including Indian. Italian restaurants are common and vary in quality: pizzas are mostly tasty and filling. There are some good Arabic restaurants in Málaga and Granada.

Markets Andalucía's food markets (**mercados**) are fun places to visit. Buy a selection of fruits, vegetables, cold meat or sausage, olives, nuts and cheese, pick up some bread from a bakery, stop in at a supermarket for a bottle of wine and head for the nearest picturesque spot. This can make a pleasant change from sitting in restaurants and, if you shop carefully, you could put together a filling meal for as little as 500 ptas.

Popular Dishes

Stews In the past, the cocido or stew, a one-pot feast of meat, sausage, beans and vegetables, was a mainstay of the local diet. It's time-consuming to prepare, but in Andalucian villages the smell of cooking chickpeas still wafts through the narrow streets around comida time. Cocido can constitute a three-course meal, with the broth eaten first followed by the vegetables and then the meat.

More usual nowadays is a simpler kind of stew, the **guiso**, which comes in three traditional types in Andalucía – **las berzas** with cabbage and either beef or pork; **el puchero**, with chicken and bacon broth, **nabo** (a type of turnip) and mint; and **los potajes**, with dried beans and chorizo sausage.

Gazpacho True gazpacho, a typical Andalucian dish, is a cold soup of blended tomatoes, capsicums, onion, garlic, breadcrumbs, lemon and oil. It's often served in a jug with ice cubes, with side dishes of chopped raw vegetables such as cucumber and onion. There are a number of close relatives – all cold soups containing oil, garlic and breadcrumbs – such as salmorejo cordobés, Cordoban gazpacho cream with hard-boiled eggs as a garnish, or ajo blanco con uvas, pounded almond and garlic soup with grapes, popular in Málaga province.

Gazpacho developed in Andalucía among **jornaleros** – agricultural day labourers – who were given rations of bread and oil. They soaked the bread in water to form the basis of a soup then added oil and garlic plus whatever fresh vegetables were to hand. All the ingredients were pounded using a mortar and pestle. The resulting dish was relatively refreshing and nourishing.

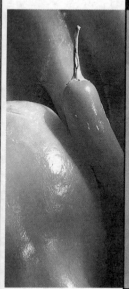

JOHN HAY

Helpful Hints for Vegetarians

In a few places, such as Málaga, Granada and Tarifa, there are Arabic eateries that prepare tasty vegetarian dishes.

Andalucian fruits and vegetables are wonderfully fresh year round, so salads in most restaurants are a good bet. To be on the safe side when you order, add something like 'Soy vegetariano/a, no me gusta carne/jamón/pollo/atún/huevos' ('I'm a vegetarian, I don't like meat/ham/chicken/tuna/eggs'), or whatever it is you don't want in your salad. Or simply say 'Sin ...' ('Without ... '). More generally, you need to ask '¿Que hay sin carne, jamón, pollo, marisco o pescado?' ('What is there without meat, ham, chicken, seafood or fish?').

A good vegetarian dish is **pisto**, similar to ratatouille, a fry-up of courgettes, green peppers, onions and potatoes. **Menestra** is a dish of artichokes, chard, peas and green beans – but you might have to ask that no **chorizo** (sausage), ham or egg be included. **Garbanzos con espinacas** (chickpeas with spinach) is a filling and tasty stew. You'll often see **setas** (wild mushrooms) on menus; usually they're cooked in olive oil and garlic but are better in a sauce (**salsa**). **Pimientos rellenos** (stuffed peppers) are available in some restaurants but the filling is likely to have meat or prawns. Tofu and seitán, a miso-like vegetable protein, usually only crop up in vegetarian restaurants.

Paella Spain's most famous dish often includes seafood and/or chicken in Andalucía. On the Costa del Sol, peas, clams, mussels and prawns and a garnish of red peppers and lemon slices are a popular combination, while in Sevilla and Cádiz, big prawns, and sometimes lobster, are added. Paella takes its name from the wide, two-handled metal pan in which it's cooked – best on a wood fire outdoors – and served. The rice absorbs the juices of the other ingredients as it simmers. The bright yellow colour traditionally comes from saffron but, since saffron is expensive today, food colouring or paprika (pimentón) are more commonly used. A lot of restaurants will only serve paella to a minimum of two people because it's not worth the effort to prepare a single portion.

RECIPE FOR PAELLA

Ingredients

Olive oil
1 onion, chopped
3 cloves garlic, chopped
500g (approx) rabbit or chicken, cut roughly
250g clams

125g cubed pork
1 chorizo sausage (or salami), sliced
100g peas
1 large tomato, chopped
250g mussels
150g peeled prawns
250g mussels

250g clams
650 ml chicken or seafood stock
250g short grain white rice
¼ teaspoon saffron threads (or paprika)
Salt & pepper to taste

Method

Several hours before cooking, put the unshelled prawns, mussels and clams in cold water with a handful of porridge oats. This flushes out the shellfish. Fry the onion, garlic and red pepper in olive oil until soft. Add the tomatoes and simmer for five minutes. Take the mixture out of the pan and put to one side. In more olive oil, fry the rabbit/chicken and pork until half-cooked. Add the onion/tomato mix, chorizo slices, stock, rice and saffron. The paella now needs to cook slowly with the lid on for a total of 20 minutes. Stir as little as possible. (Meanwhile, the shellfish need to be cooked quickly in boiling water. Take them out as soon as they are open. Keep the mussel shells for garnish.) After 10 minutes, add the peeled prawns and peas to the paella. Five minutes later, add the cooked shellfish then simmer for a further five minutes. Your paella is now ready to garnish and serve! Arrange the mussel shells around the edge of the pan and decorate with unshelled prawns and lemon wedges.

WINE

Wine production in Spain began in Andalucía when the Phoenicians, who founded Cádiz around 1100 BC, introduced vines. **Vino**, white, (**blanco**), red (**tinto**) or rosé (**rosado**), accompanies many a meal in Spain where it is strong because of the sunny climate. Andalucía is most famous for sherry, which is produced nowhere else.

In general, wine remains cheap. A 500 ptas bottle from a supermarket or wine merchant will be better than average. The same money in a restaurant will get you an average drop. Cheap **vino de mesa** (table wine) sells for less than 200 ptas a litre in shops.

JOHN HAY

You can order wine by the glass (**copa**) in bars and restaurants: the **vino de la casa** (house wine) may come from a barrel or jug at 125 ptas, sometimes less, a glass.

Wine Terminology Spain regulates its wine fairly carefully, so you can judge its quality to a certain extent from the label. The letters DOC stand for **Denominación de Origen Calificada** and refer to wine from areas that have maintained consistent high quality over a very long period. Rioja, in northern Spain, is the only DOC at present, though Andalucía's Jerez (sherry) may join it. DO, **Denominación de Origen**, is one step down from DOC. There are 50-odd DO areas around Spain. A DOC or DO label tells you that the wine has been produced to certain supervised standards by serious wine growers – though each DOC and DO covers a wide range of wines of varying quality (usually indicated by the price), and it's also true that some good wine growers and areas haven't bothered with trying to get DO status.

Vino joven is wine made for immediate drinking, while **vino de crianza** has to have been stored for certain minimum periods: if red, two full calendar years with a minimum of six months in oak; if white or rosé, one calendar year. **Reserva** requires longer storage – three years for reds and two for whites and rosés. **Gran reserva** is a title permitted for particularly good vintages which must have spent at least two calendar years in storage and three inside the bottle. They're mostly reds.

Sherry & Manzanilla The Jerez DO, which produces sherry, and the Manzanilla DO, producing manzanilla (to nonexperts, effectively another type of sherry), come under one regulatory council which glories in the catchy title Jerez-Xéres-Sherry y Manzanilla-Sanlúcar de Barrameda.

These wines are produced in the towns of Jerez de la Frontera, El Puerto de Santa María and Sanlúcar de Barrameda, plus five other areas in the province of Cádiz, and Lebrija in Sevilla province. There are 103 sq km of vineyards. A combination of climate, chalky soils that soak up the sun but retain moisture, and a special ageing process called the **solera** system produce this unique wine.

The main distinction in sherry is between **fino** (dry and straw-coloured, with an alcohol content of around 15%) and **oloroso** (sweet and dark, with a strong bouquet and an alcohol content of 18%). An **amontillado** is an amber, moderately dry fino with a nutty flavour and a higher alcohol content. A **manzanilla** is a camomile-coloured, unfortified fino from Sanlúcar de Barrameda: its delicate flavour is reckoned to come from sea breezes wafting into the **bodegas** (wineries) there. An **oloroso** combined with a sweet wine results in a 'cream sherry', containing up to 25% alcohol. Sherry, especially fino, goes brilliantly with many tapas, but it can also accompany a meal: manzanilla is great with seafood, amontillado with white meat, and olorosos with red meat and game. Cream sherry goes best with cakes or tipped over a glass of ice on a hot day.

Statue of Manuel María González, founder of the González Byass sherry house, Jerez de la Frontera. *(photograph by John Noble)*

Once sherry grapes have been harvested, they are pressed and the resulting must is left to ferment. Within a few months a frothy veil of yeast called **flor** appears on the surface. The wine is fortified then transferred to the bodegas in big barrels of American oak.

Wine enters the solera process when it is a year old. The barrels, about five-sixths full, are lined up in rows, called **escalas**, at least three barrels high: the barrels on the bottom layer, called the solera (from **suelo**, floor), contain the oldest wine. From these, around three times a year, 10% of the wine is drawn off. This is replaced with the same amount from the barrels in the layer above, which is in turn replaced from the next layer. The wines are left to age for between three and seven years.

Sherry houses are often beautiful buildings in attractive gardens. A tour will take you through the bodegas where the wine is stored and aged, inform you about the process and the history of the sherry producers, and allow you a tasting. You'll also be shown the use of a **venencia**, a long-handled cup for sampling sherry from the barrel. The venencia is expertly manipulated, so the sherry cascades from head level into a glass held at waist level.

Famous sherries include Tio Pepe, the world's best selling fino, made by González Byass; Domecq's fino La Ina; La Gitana, a manzanilla by Vinícola Hidalgo; Williams & Humbert's Dry Sack, a blend of oloroso, amontillado and sweet wine; and Harvey's Bristol Cream, a cream sherry.

Málaga wine – famous and sought-after for centuries.

Other Sherry-Like Wines The Montilla-Moriles DO comprises 106 sq km of vineyards in Córdoba province, centred on the towns of Montilla and Moriles. This wine is similar to sherry but not fortified – the fino is the most acclaimed. The fermented wine is stored in huge Ali Baba-type earthenware jars (**tinajas**) until the wine is ready for the solera process.

Málaga Wine Sweet and velvety Málaga Dulce pleased the palates of the famous from Virgil and Shakespeare to the ladies of Victorian England, for whom it was a favourite tipple. Unfortunately, the vines were blighted around the beginning of the 20th century and today Málaga DO area is Andalucía's smallest, at only 9 sq km. Drier wines are also produced. You can sample Málaga wine straight from the barrel in one of the city's numerous bars.

A Taste of the Sweet Life

Andalucía's Islamic past has had quite an effect on its strong tradition of elaborate sweets, cakes and pastries. Almonds, honey, anis, wine, white sugar and egg yolks are common ingredients. Locals eat these delectables (often simply called dulces) especially on holidays or feast days, with coffee, brandy or sweet wine.

Some of the best sweets are made and sold at convents – a tradition developed in some places from donations of egg yolks, by-products of the sherry process. Other sweets, cakes and pastries are more readily available at bars, panaderías (bakeries), and patisserías (cake shops). Some city folk travel out to villages on weekends just to procure their favourite dulces.

Yemas (candied egg yolks), pestiños (sweet fritters), sugared almonds or pine nuts, marzipan and candied fruits are found throughout Spain. Turrón basically means almond nougat but also describes a variety of other rich, sweet, chocolatey things which appear in the shops just before Christmas.

Typical Andalucian dulces:

Borrachuelos – 'little drunkards', deep-fried fritters soused in a honey syrup spiked with anis or wine
Empanadillas de cabello de ángel – 'angel hair pasties', deep fried and stuffed with angels' hair jam, made from **cidra**, a type of melon
Polverones – small crumbly cakes that look like biscuits
Mantecados – traditionally lard cakes, but more likely to be made from butter these days
Roscones – ring-shaped biscuits; a **roscón de reyes** is a cake specially prepared for Three Kings' Day, 6 January

Other Andalucian Wines Almost every village has its own wine – cheap country wine is simply known as **mosto**. In addition to the DOs, eight further areas produce a range of distinctive, good wines which can be sampled locally. These are Aljarafe and Los Palacios (Sevilla province), Bailén, Lopera and Torreperogil (Jaén province), Costa Albondón (Granada province), Laújar de Andarax (Almería province), and Villaviciosa (Córdoba province).

Beer

The most common way to order a beer (**cerveza**) is to ask for a **caña**, which is a small draught beer. A larger beer (about 300mL) is called a **tubo** and comes in a straight glass. Bars around streets and squares where the **movida** – the late night teen drinking scene – gathers sometimes sell large plastic mugs of beer called **macetas** (literally plantpots). All these words apply to draught beer (**cerveza de barril** or **cerveza de presión**); if you just ask for a cerveza you may well get bottled beer, which tends to be more expensive. A small bottle of beer is called a **botellín** or a **quinto**; a bigger one is a **tercio** or a **mediana**. San Miguel, Cruzcampo and Victoria are all decent Andalucian beers.

A **clara** is a shandy, a beer with a dash of lemonade.

Mixed Drinks, Spirits & Liqueurs

Sangría is a wine and fruit punch sometimes laced with brandy. It's refreshing going down but can leave you with a sore head. You'll see jugs of it on tables in restaurants but it also comes ready-mixed in bottles at around 300 ptas for 1.5L.

Tinto de verano is a mix of wine and Casera, a brand of lemonade or sweet fizzy water. A **chupito** is a spirit-and-mixer combination – some bars specialise in highly inventive chupito concoctions.

Coñac (Spanish brandy) is popular and cheap. Most of it is made in Andalucía – mainly in the sherry towns but also in Málaga and in Córdoba province. In bars, you'll notice locals starting the day with a coffee and a brandy, or a glass of **anís** (aniseed liqueur).

Spirits produced in Spain are generally much cheaper than imports. Málaga's Larios gin is an example. Rum (**ron**) is produced in Málaga and Motril (Granada province), the only areas in Europe that grow sugar cane.

Andalucía also produces a wide range of liqueurs (**licores**). **Aguardiente** is a colourless grape-based liqueur. When spiked with aniseed, it becomes an **anís** or **anisado** (anisette). **Pacharán** is a red liqueur made with aniseed and sloes, the fruit of the blackthorn. Though not specific to Andalucía, it's very popular here – the favourite brand is Zoco.

Non-Alcoholic Drinks

Coffee Addicts should specify how they want their fix, and expect it to be strong. A **café con leche** is about 50% coffee, 50% hot milk; ask for **grande** or **doble** if you want a large cup, **en vaso** if you want it in a glass, or **sombra** if you want lots of milk. A **café solo** is a short black; **café cortado** is a short black with a little milk.

Tea Tea (**té**) in cafés and bars is invariably weak. Ask for milk to be separate (**leche aparte**); otherwise, you'll end up with a cup of milky water with a tea bag thrown in. Most places also have camomile tea (**té de manzanilla**). **Teterías** (Islamic-style tearooms) have become fashionable in some cities, though they are expensive. They serve all manner of teas, including herbal (**infusiones**).

Chocolate Spaniards brought chocolate back from Mexico and adopted it enthusiastically. As a drink, it's served thick; sometimes it even appears among **postres** (desserts) on menus. Generally it's a breakfast drink consumed with churros; see Food.

Soft Drinks Orange juice (**zumo de naranja**) is the main freshly squeezed juice available, but expensive at around 200 ptas a glass. Boxed juices come in all varieties in shops and are good and cheap.

Refrescos (cool drinks) include the usual international brands of soft drinks, local brands such as Kas, and expensive **granizado** (iced fruit crush).

Clear, cold water from a public fountain or tap is a Spanish favourite – but check that it's **potable** (drinkable). For tap water in restaurants, ask for **agua de grifo**. Bottled water (**agua mineral**) comes in innumerable brands, either fizzy (**con gas**) or still (**sin gas**). A 1.5L bottle of still water costs between 40 and 75 ptas in a supermarket.

A **batido** is a flavoured milk drink or milk shake. **Horchata** is made from the juice of **chufa** (tiger nuts), sugar and water: it tastes like soya milk with a hint of cinnamon. You'll come across it both fresh and bottled: Chufi is a delicious brand.

GLOSSARY

a la brasa – char-grilled
a la parrilla – grilled
a la plancha – grilled on a hotplate
aceite – oil
aceituna – olive
adobo – a marinade of vinegar, salt, lemon and spices, usually for fish before frying
aguacate – avocado
aguja – swordfish
ahumado/a – smoked
ajo – garlic
albóndiga – meatball, fishball
alcachofa – artichoke
aliño – anything in a vinegar and oil dressing
alioli – garlic mayonnaise
almejas – clams
almendra – almond
alubia – bean
anchoa – tinned anchovy
apio – celery
arroz – rice
asado – roasted
atún – tuna

bacalao – salted cod, soaked before cooking. (It can be succulent and is prepared in many ways.)
beicon – bacon (usually thin-sliced and pre-packaged; see tocino)
berenjena – aubergine, egg-plant
bistek – thin beef steak
bocadillo – bread roll with filling
bollo – bread roll
boquerones – fresh anchovies
butifarra – thick sausage (to be cooked)

caballa – mackerel
cabeza – head

cabra – goat
cabrito – kid
cacahuete – peanut
calabacín – zucchini, courgette
calabaza – pumpkin
caldereta –stew
caldo – broth, stock
callos – tripe
calamares – squid
camarón – shrimp
cangrejo – crab
caracol – snail
carne – meat
carne de **monte** – 'mountain meat': venison or wild boar
casero/a – homemade
caza – hunt, game
cazuela – casserole
cebolla – onion
cerdo – pig, pork
cereza – cherry
chacinas – pork products
champiñones – mushrooms
chanquetes – whitebait (illegal, but not uncommon)
charcutería – cured pork meats, or a shop selling them
chipirón – small squid
chirimoya – custard apple, a tropical fruit
choco – cuttlefish
chorizo – red sausage
chuleta – chop, cutlet
churro – long, deep-fried doughnut
cigala – crayfish
cocido – cooked; also hotpot/stew
cocina – kitchen
codorniz – quail
col – cabbage
coliflor – cauliflower
conejo – rabbit
confitura – jam
cordero – lamb
crudo – raw

dorada – sea bass
dulce – sweet

embutidos – the many varieties of sausage
empanada – pie
ensalada – salad
entremeses – hors d'oeuvres
escabeche – a marinade of oil, vinegar and water for pickling perishables, usually fish or seafood
espagueti – spaghetti
espárragos – asparagus
espinacas – spinach
estofado – stew

faba – type of dried bean
faisán – pheasant
fideo – vermicelli noodle
filete – fillet
flamenquín – rolled and crumbed veal or ham, deep-fried
flan - caramel custard
frambuesa – raspberry
fresa – strawberry
frito – fried
fritura – a mixture of deep-fried seafood
fruta – fruit

galleta – biscuit, cookie
gamba – prawn
garbanzo – chickpea
gazpacho – cold, blended soup of tomatoes, peppers, cucumber, onions, garlic, lemon and breadcrumbs
gazpachos – game dish with garlic and herbs
girasol – sunflower
granada – pomegranate
gratinado/a – au gratin (with grated cheese)
guindilla – hot chilli pepper
guisante – pea
guiso – stew

haba – broad bean
hamburguesa – hamburger
harina – flour
helado – ice cream
hierba buena – mint
hígado – liver
higo – fig
hongo – wild mushroom
horno – oven
horneado – baked
hortalizas – vegetables
huevo – egg

jabalí – wild boar
jamón (serrano) – (mountain-cured) ham
judías blancas – butter beans
judías verdes – green beans

langosta – lobster
langostino – large prawn
lechuga – lettuce
legumbre – pulse
lengua – tongue
lenguado – sole
lentejas – lentils
lima – lime
limón – lemon
lomo – loin (unless otherwise specified it will be of pork – usually the cheapest meat dish on the menu)

macarrones – macaroni
maíz – sweetcorn
mandarina – tangerine
mantequilla – butter
manzana – apple
manzanilla – camomile; also a type of sherry and a type of olive
marisco – shellfish
mayonesa – mayonnaise
media-ración – half a ración
mejillones – mussels
melocotón – peach
menta – mint
merluza – hake
mermelada – jam

miel – honey
migas – simple dish basically composed of fried flour and water
mojama – cured tuna
mollete – soft, tasty bread roll
montadito – small bread roll with filling, or a small sandwich, or open sandwich – all usually toasted
morcilla – blood sausage, ie black pudding

naranja – orange
nata – cream
natilla – custards
nuez – nut, walnut (plural: nueces)

olla – pot
ostra – oyster

paella – rice, seafood and meat dish
paloma – pigeon
pan – bread
panecillo – bread roll
pasa – raisin
pastel – pastry, cake
patata – potato
patatas a lo pobre – poor man's potatoes – potato dish with peppers and garlic
patatas bravas – spicy fried potatoes
patatas fritas – chips, French fries
pato – duck
pavía – battered fish or seafood
pavo – turkey
pechuga – breast, of poultry
perdiz – partridge
peregrina – scallop
pescado – fish
pescadilla – whiting
pez espada – swordfish
picadillo – minced meat
pierna – leg
pil pil – garlic sauce sometimes

spiked with chilli
pimiento – pepper, capsicum
pinchito – Moroccan-style kebab
pincho – can mean the same as pinchito, or the same as tapa
piña – pineapple
pipirrana – salad of diced tomatoes and red peppers
pitufo – small filled baguette
plátano – banana
platija – flounder
potaje – stew
pollo – chicken
postre – dessert
puerro – leek
pulpo – octopus
puntillita/o – small squid, fried whole

queso – cheese

rabo (de toro) – (ox) tail
ración – meal-sized serving of a tapas dish
rape – monkfish
rebozado/a – battered and fried
relleno – stuffed
revuelto de – eggs scrambled with ...
riñón – kidney
rosada – ocean catfish, wolf-fish

salado – salted, salty
salchicha – fresh pork sausage
salchichón – cured sausage
salmón – salmon
salmonete – red mullet
sandía – watermelon
sardina – sardine
seco – dry, dried
sepia – cuttlefish
sesos – brains
seta – wild mushroom
sobrasada – pork sausage lard
soja – soy
solomillo – sirloin
sopa – soup

tapa – snack on a saucer
tarta – cake
ternera – veal, beef
tierno/a – tender, fresh
tocino – bacon (usually thick; see beicon)
tomate – tomato
torta – round flat bun, cake
tortilla – omelette
tortilla española – potato omelette
tostada – toasted roll
trigo – wheat
trucha – trout
trufa – truffle
turrón – almond nougat or rich, chocolatey sweets

uva – grape

vaca, **carne de** – beef
vegetal – vegetable (adjective)
vegetariano/a – vegetarian
venado – venison
venera – scallop
verdura – green vegetable

yema – yolk, or candied yolk

zanahoria – carrot
zarzuela – fish stew

Getting There & Away

Andalucía is one of Europe's top holiday destinations and is well linked to other European countries and the rest of Spain by air, rail and road. From Europe, you save a lot of time, hassle and often money by flying rather than going overland or by sea, unless of course you want to enjoy the journey to Andalucía as much as your travels within it.

If you are coming from North America, there should be direct flights from New York to Málaga by the time you read this book. Otherwise, you have to change planes in Madrid or elsewhere. There are some reasonable deals available.

However you're travelling, it's worth taking out travel insurance (see Visas & Documents in the Facts for the Visitor chapter).

AIR

Always reconfirm your return or onward flight by the specified time – at least 72 hours before departure on international flights. Otherwise you risk finding you've missed your flight because it was rescheduled, or that you've been classified as a 'no-show'.

The peak season for travel to Andalucía is mid-June to mid-September, with Easter also busy.

Airports & Airlines

Málaga is the main international airport in Andalucía and the cheapest flights available usually go there. Almería, Sevilla, Jerez de la Frontera and Gibraltar also receive some international flights. Andalucía's other airport, Granada, receives internal Spanish flights only (you can fly there from other countries with a change at Madrid or Barcelona).

National airlines – such as British Airways (BA), Alitalia, Swissair, Lufthansa, Sabena, SAS and Spain's Iberia, all of which fly into Málaga and in some cases other Andalucian airports – are generally one of the most expensive ways to fly, though they're worth checking for special offers. Other scheduled airlines, often cheaper, include Monarch (from Luton, England to Málaga and Gibraltar), and two Spanish airlines, Air Europa and Spanair, which fly direct from the USA to Spain. The lowest fares are usually to be found on the numerous charter flights from a variety of airports in Britain, France, Germany, Italy, Scandinavia, Russia and elsewhere. Most charters go to Málaga, though Almería gets some too.

Iberia and/or one of its subsidiaries, Aviaco, fly domestic routes to/from all five of Andalucía's airports (not Gibraltar). Other Spanish airlines – Air Europa, Spanair, Pauknair – provide further domestic flights.

Buying Tickets

Start your ticket search early: some of the cheapest tickets have to be bought months in advance, and some popular flights sell out early. Look at the ads in newspapers and magazines (including any Spanish press in your home country), and watch for airline special offers. Then phone around travel agents for bargains and consult the Internet if you can. Find out fares, routes and any restrictions on the tickets (in general the cheapest fares carry the most restrictions, such as that you have to book ahead, or you have to pay when you make the booking, or you can't change dates). You may discover that those wonderfully cheap advertised flights are 'fully booked, but we have another one that costs a bit more ...' Or agents claim only to have the last two seats available for Málaga for the whole of July, which they will hold for you for a maximum of two hours. Don't panic – keep ringing around. Then sit back and decide which is best for you.

Use fares quoted in this book as a guide only. They are approximate and based on

AIR TRAVEL GLOSSARY

Apex Apex, or 'advance purchase excursion', is a discounted ticket which must be paid for in advance. There are penalties if you wish to change it.

Baggage Allowance This will be written on your ticket; you are usually allowed one 20kg item to go in the hold, plus one item of hand luggage.

Bucket Shops At certain times of the year and/or on certain routes, many airlines fly with empty seats. It's more cost-effective for them to fly full, even if that means having to sell a certain number of drastically discounted tickets. They do this by off-loading them to bucket shops (UK) or consolidators (USA), travel agents who specialise in discounted fares. The agents sell them to the public at reduced prices. These tickets are often the cheapest you'll find, but you can't purchase them directly from the airlines. Bucket-shop agents advertise in newspapers and magazines.

Bumped Just because you have a confirmed seat doesn't mean you're going to get on the plane – see Overbooking.

Cancellation Penalties If you have to cancel or change a discount ticket, there may be heavy penalties involved; insurance can sometimes be taken out against these penalties. Some airlines impose penalties on regular tickets as well, particularly against 'no-show' passengers.

Check In Airlines ask you to check in a certain time ahead of the flight departure (usually two hours on international flights). If you fail to check in on time and the flight is overbooked, the airline can cancel your booking and give your seat to somebody else.

Confirmation Having a ticket written out with the flight and date on it doesn't mean you have a seat until the agent has confirmed with the airline that your status is 'OK'. Prior to this confirmation, your status is 'on request'.

Economy-Class Tickets Economy-class tickets are usually not the cheapest way to go, though they do give you maximum flexibility and they are valid for 12 months. If you don't use them, most are fully refundable.

the rates advertised at the time of going to press. Quoted fares do not necessarily constitute a recommendation for the carrier. If you are travelling from the UK or the USA, you will probably find that the cheapest flights are advertised by obscure bucket shops whose names haven't yet reached the telephone directory. Many such firms are honest and solvent, but there are a few rogues who will take your money and disappear. If you feel suspicious, don't pay all the money at once – leave a deposit of 20%

or so and pay the balance when you get the ticket. And once you have the ticket, ring the airline to confirm that you are actually booked on the flight.

You may decide to pay more than the rock-bottom fare by opting for a better-known travel agent. Firms such as STA Travel, which has offices worldwide, Council Travel in the USA or Travel CUTS in Canada are not going to disappear overnight but they do offer good prices to most destinations.

Lost Tickets If you lose your airline ticket, an airline will usually treat it like a travellers' cheque and, after inquiries, issue you with a replacement. Legally, however, an airline is entitled to treat it like cash, so if you lose a ticket, it could be forever.

No-shows No-shows are passengers who fail to show up for their flight for whatever reason. Full-fare no-shows are sometimes entitled to travel on a later flight. The rest of us are penalised (see Cancellation Penalties).

Overbooking Airlines hate to fly with empty seats, and since every flight has some passengers who fail to show up (see No-shows), they often book more passengers than they have seats available. Usually the excess passengers balance those who fail to show up, but occasionally somebody gets bumped. If this happens, guess who it is most likely to be? The passengers who check in late.

Reconfirmation You must contact the airline at least 72 hours prior to departure to 're-confirm' that you intend to be on the flight. If you don't, the airline can delete your name from the passenger list and you could lose your seat.

Standby This is a discounted ticket where you fly only if there is a seat free at the last moment. Standby fares are usually available only at the airport, but sometimes may also be handled by an airline's city office. To give yourself the best possible chance of getting on the flight you want, get there early and have your name placed on the waiting list. It's first come, first served.

Transferred Tickets Airline tickets cannot be transferred from one person to another. Travellers sometimes try to sell the return half of their ticket, but officials can ask you to prove that you are the person named on the ticket. This may not be checked on domestic flights, but on international flights, tickets are usually compared with passports.

Travel Periods Some officially discounted fares, Apex fares in particular, vary with the time of year. There is often a low (off-peak) season and a high (peak) season. Sometimes there's an intermediate, or shoulder, season as well. At peak times, when everyone wants to fly, both officially and unofficially discounted fares will be higher, or there may simply be no discounted tickets available. Usually the fare depends on your outward flight – if you depart in the high season and return in the low season, you pay the high-season fare.

Once you have your ticket, make a note of its number, the flight number and other details. If it's lost or stolen, this information will help you get a replacement.

Round-the-World Tickets Travellers from outside Europe who are including Andalucía in a longer trip should look into the possibility of a round-the-world (RTW) ticket. Airlines' official RTW tickets are often real bargains, and can even work out cheaper than an ordinary return ticket. They are usually put together by two airlines and allow you to fly anywhere you want on their route systems so long as you do not backtrack. An alternative type of RTW ticket is one put together by a travel agent using a combination of discounted tickets.

Travellers with Special Needs
If you have special needs of any sort – you've broken a leg, you're vegetarian, travelling in a wheelchair, taking the baby – you should tell the airline early so that they can

make arrangements accordingly. Remind them when you reconfirm your booking and again when you check in. Airports and airlines can be surprisingly helpful, but they do need advance warning. Most international airports will provide escorts from check-in desk to plane where needed, and there should be ramps, lifts, accessible toilets and reachable phones. Aircraft toilets, on the other hand, are likely to present a problem; travellers should discuss this with the airline at an early stage.

Guide dogs for the blind often have to travel in a specially pressurised baggage compartment with other animals, away from their owner. They will be subject to the same quarantine laws as any other animal when returning to countries currently free of rabies such as Britain.

Deaf travellers can ask for airport and in-flight announcements to be written down for them.

Children under two generally travel for 10% of the standard fare (or free, on some airlines), as long as they don't occupy a seat. They don't get a baggage allowance. 'Skycots' for babies and infants should be provided by the airline if requested in advance. Children between two and 12 can usually occupy a seat for half to two-thirds of the full fare (though they may be charged full fare on charter flights), and do get a baggage allowance. Pushchairs can often be taken as hand luggage.

The UK & Ireland

Some of the best sources of information about cheap fares are the weekend editions of the national newspapers. In London try also the *Evening Standard*, *Time Out* and *TNT*, a free magazine which comes out every Monday and is found in dispenser bins outside underground stations. The Internet is another source of information.

Most British travel agents are registered with ABTA (Association of British Travel Agents). If you have bought a flight ticket from an ABTA-registered agent which then goes out of business, ABTA will guarantee a refund or an alternative. Unregistered bucket shops are riskier but also sometimes cheaper.

Scheduled Airlines On BA and Iberia, regular economy return fares from London to Málaga or Sevilla range from about £230 (low season) to £285 (high season), but there may be special offers, especially in the low season, under £150. BA flies from London to Jerez de la Frontera and Gibraltar for similar fares. Many BA flights are operated by a franchise carrier, GB Airways.

Monarch Airlines flies from Luton to Málaga and Gibraltar several times a week. Fares to either place range from £150 to £240 return, depending on season.

Discount & Charter Flights One of the most reliable, but not necessarily the cheapest, discount agencies is STA, which has several offices in London (☎ 0171-361 6161) and branches in several other cities. The main London branches are:

86 Old Brompton Rd, London SW7 3LH
117 Euston Rd, London NW1 2SX
11 Goodge St, London W1

A similar place is Trailfinders (☎ 0171-937 5400), 215 Kensington High St, London W8 7RG. It also has offices in Bristol, Birmingham, Glasgow and Manchester.

Campus Travel is in much the same league and has branches in 23 UK cities including these in London (☎ 0171-730 3402):

52 Grosvenor Gardens, Victoria, London SW1W 0AG
YHA Adventure Shop, 174 Kensington High St, London W8 7RG
YHA Adventure Shop, 14 Southampton St, Covent Garden, London WC2E 7HY

All the above agencies sell student fares and/or other tickets at worthwhile discounts on the scheduled airlines, but the cheapest deals of all – usually on charter flights – are advertised by bucket shops. Spanish Travel

Services (☎ 0171-387 5337), 138 Eversholt St, London NW1 1BL, often has a good range of charter flight options.

In the low season you should be able to get a bucket-shop return from London to Málaga for between £80 and £125; in summer you might have to pay up to £150, though booking well ahead may get you a lower fare. Return fares as low as £49 are often advertised: these tend to be long-weekend charter flights around Easter and from September to November. Even if they don't fit your dates, it may be worthwhile to buy the ticket and ditch the return leg, getting a one-way ticket back from Spain.

Many good deals are available from other UK airports besides London. If you're coming from Ireland, it might be worth comparing what is available direct and from London; getting across to London first may save you a few quid.

Check the arrival and departure times of charter flights, as they can often be inconvenient. If they're delayed, as they often are at peak travel periods, a flight that was supposed to take off at 11 pm may not actually do so till 4 am. And remember that if you miss a charter flight, you have lost your money.

Non-European passport-holders should note that some charter flights running between Britain and Spain will accept only EU passport holders as passengers.

Fly-Drive Packages including flights and pre-booked car hire can be an attractive option, especially in the high season when local car hire prices will exceed those of pre-booked cars. Numerous travel agents can make arrangements.

Continental Europe
Very short hops can be expensive, but for longer journeys you can often find airfares that beat overland alternatives on cost.

Germany In Munich, a great source of travel information is the Därr Travel Shop (☎ 089-28 20 32) at Theresienstrasse 66. In Berlin, ARTU Reisen (☎ 030-31 04 66), at Hardenbergstrasse 9, near Berlin Zoo (with five branches around the city), is a good travel agent. In Frankfurt/Main, try SRID Reisen (☎ 069-43 01 91), Bergerstrasse 118.

Netherlands & Belgium In Amsterdam, the student travel agency NBBS Reiswinkels (☎ 020-620 5071), with seven branches, has fares comparable to London bucket shops. NBBS Reiswinkels has branches in Brussels too.

Italy The best place to look for cheap flights is the CTS (Centro Turístico Studentesco), which has branches all over the country. The one in Rome (☎ 06-46791) is at Via Genova 16.

France In Paris, Voyages et Découvertes (☎ 01 42 61 00 01), 21 rue Cambon, is a good place to start hunting down the best airfares, although given the proximity to Spain you should compare the advantages of travelling overland.

Portugal There are no direct flights between Portugal and Andalucía.

Morocco
Iberia flies Málaga-Casablanca for around 20,000/40,000 ptas one-way/return. Royal Air Maroc flies Málaga-Casablanca twice a week for a little less. GB Airways flies Gibraltar-Casablanca for £99/146 one way/return.

The Spanish airlines Binter Mediterráneo and Pauknair fly to Melilla, the Spanish enclave on the Moroccan coast, from Málaga and Almería (and from Granada too in Binter's case). Binter's return fares are between 20,000 and 25,000 ptas.

The USA
A direct New York-Málaga service by a Spanish airline called Air Plus Comet was about to start at the time of writing. The only other alternative is to fly to Madrid or some other European city and make a connection there. Airlines flying New York-Madrid include TWA, Delta and the Spanish airlines

Iberia and Air Europa; another Spanish airline, Spanair, flies Washington-Madrid. London and Paris are other common transfer cities. Further possibilities are via Zurich with Swissair, or via Copenhagen with SAS. Fares via London, Paris or other cities may be cheaper than via Madrid.

The *New York Times*, *LA Times*, *Chicago Tribune* and *San Francisco Examiner* produce weekly travel sections in which you'll find any number of travel agents' ads. The Internet is another good source of fare information, chat and bookings.

Scheduled Airlines Standard fares on commercial airlines are expensive, but special offers are worth looking into. BA's regular New York-Málaga economy return fare (via Madrid, London etc) is between about US$1200 and US$1800 depending on the season, but it has shoulder-season special deals as low as US$475. Iberia's standard fare is US$1836 plus taxes, but special offers and youth fares can cut this to under US$700.

At the time of writing, the most exciting deal was with Spanair, which was offering return flights from Washington DC to Málaga for around US$350, including taxes. This was an opening offer on a new four-times-weekly service but, who knows, it may be the beginning of a price war! There are also good fares on Air Europa, which flies to Málaga via Madrid from New York and Miami. Air Europa Málaga-New York fares are 60,000 ptas one way and from 72,900 ptas return, plus taxes.

Standby, Courier, Charter & Discount Flights Standby one-way fares are often sold at 60% of the normal price. Airhitch (π 800-326-2009), 2641 Broadway, 3rd Floor No 100, New York, NY 10025, specialises in this sort of thing, with one-way fares from the USA or Canada to Western Europe of US$169 to US$269 depending on how far west you start. Airhitch has other offices in the USA, a European office at 5 rue de Crussol, F-75011 Paris, France (π 01 47 00 16 30), and a peak-season representative in Madrid.

On courier flights you accompany freight or a parcel to its destination. A New York-Madrid low-season return on a courier flight can cost under US$200. Generally courier flights require that you return within a specified period (sometimes one or two weeks, often one month). You will need to travel light, and you may have to be a US resident and have an interview before they take you on. Now Voyager (π 212-431 1616), 74 Varick St, Suite 307, New York, NY 10013, specialises in courier flights: you pay an annual membership fee (around US$50), which entitles you to take as many courier flights as you like.

Reliable travel agents specialising in charter flights, discounted tickets on scheduled flights and budget travel for students include STA Travel (π 800-781 4040) and Council Travel (π 800-226 8624).

Both have offices in big cities, including:

STA Travel
  10 Downing St, New York, NY 10014 (π 212-627 3111)
  920 Westwood Blvd, Los Angeles, CA 90024 (π 310-824-1574)
  51 Grant Ave, San Francisco, CA 94108 (π 415-391 8407)
Council Travel
  205 East 42nd St, New York, NY 10017 (π 212-822 2700)
  10904 Lindbrook Drive, Los Angeles, CA 90024 (π 310-208 3551)
  530 Bush St, Ground Floor, San Francisco, CA 94108 (π 415-421-3473)

On a charter or discounted flight you should be able to get a New York-Málaga return fare for between US$450 and US$550 in the low seasons. From the west coast add US$125 to US$150. In summer, you're looking at a minimum of US$800 to US$1000 (up to US$1150 from the west coast).

Canada

Iberia has direct flights to Madrid from Montreal, with round-trip fares to Málaga from around C$1000. Routings via other European cities with other airlines often offer better fares. Travel CUTS, which specialises in discount fares for students, has offices in all major cities. Otherwise, scan the ads in the *Toronto Globe & Mail*, *Toronto Star* and *Vancouver Sun*.

For courier flights originating in Canada, contact FB Onboard Courier Services (☎ 604-278-1266 in Richmond, British Columbia). Airhitch (see The USA) has standby fares to/from Toronto, Montreal and Vancouver.

Australia

As a rule there are no direct flights from Australia to Spain. You will have to change flights, if not airlines, and fly to Europe via Asia or America. Aerolíneas Argentinas is one airline that connects with Spain indirectly this way.

On some flights between Australia and main European destinations such as London, Paris and Frankfurt, a return ticket between that destination and another European city is thrown in. Madrid and Barcelona are generally both possible choices for such a deal.

Discounted return tickets to Europe on mainstream airlines through reputable agents can be had for A$1600 to A$1800 return (low season) and up to A$2500 (high season).

The Saturday Melbourne *Age* and *Sydney Morning Herald* have many cheap-fare advertisements. STA Travel and Flight Centres International are major dealers in cheap airfares, although heavily discounted fares can often be found at the travel agent in your local shopping centre. Addresses include:

STA Travel
   222 Faraday St, Carlton, Melbourne, Vic. 3053 (☎ 03-9349 2411)
   9 Oxford St, Paddington, Sydney, NSW 2021 (☎ 02-9360 1822)
Flight Centres International
   Bourke Street Flight Centre, 19 Bourke St, Melbourne, Victoria 3000 (☎ 03-9650 2899)
   Martin Place Flight Centre, Shop 5, State Bank Centre, 52 Martin Place, Sydney, NSW 2000 (☎ 02-9235 0166)

New Zealand

STA Travel and Flight Centre are popular travel agents. The cheapest fares to Spain are generally routed through the USA or Latin America. Useful addresses include:

Flight Centres International
   Auckland Flight Centre, Shop 3A, National Bank Towers, 205-225 Queen St, Auckland (☎ 09-309 6171)
STA Travel
   2nd floor, Student Union Building, Princes St, Auckland University, Auckland (☎ 09-307 0555)
Campus Travel
   Gate 1, Knighton Rd, Waikato University, Hamilton (☎ 07-856 9139)

The Rest of Spain

Competition between Spain's several domestic airlines produces some fares which can make flying worthwhile if you're in a hurry, especially for longer or return trips.

Iberia & Aviaco The national airline, Iberia, and one of its subsidiaries, Aviaco, between them have direct daily flights from Madrid and Barcelona to all Andalucía's airports, except that the Barcelona-Jerez de la Frontera service is only three days a week. There are direct flights to Málaga or Sevilla from several other cities too. On both airlines, the cheapest return fare is the 'Estrella', for which you must buy your ticket at least two days before departure and return between four and 14 days after departure; for longer stays you need a 'Supermini' which you must buy at least four days ahead. Estrella/Supermini/one-way fares are 23,800/26,200/24,100 ptas for Barcelona-Málaga, and 14,300/18,400/14,950 ptas for Madrid-Sevilla.

Other Airlines Air Europa undercuts Iberia/Aviaco by a few thousand pesetas on most of its routes. Its direct flights (three to six days a week) include: Barcelona-Granada/Málaga/Sevilla; Bilbao-Málaga; Gran Canaria-Sevilla; Madrid-Málaga; Palma de Mallorca-Sevilla; Santiago de Compostela-Sevilla; and Tenerife-Málaga/Sevilla.

Spanair flies to Málaga direct from Madrid and Barcelona. It's especially worth checking for its last-minute offers which can give you, for example, a Madrid-Málaga return for 10,000 ptas.

Pauknair has a few flights a week to Málaga from Barcelona, Bilbao, Madrid, Santiago de Compostela and Palma de Mallorca, and from Barcelona to Almería.

Useful Numbers Here are some useful airline phone numbers:

Air Europa
    Spain (☎ 902-24 00 42 or contact Halcón Viajes, ☎ 902-30 06 00)
    New York (☎212-921 2381)
    Miami (☎ 305-372 8880)
Air Plus Comet
    Spain (☎ 971 46 74 60)
Binter Mediterráneo
    UK (☎ 0171-830 0011)
    Spain (☎ 902-40 05 00)
    US (☎ 800-772-4642)
British Airways
    UK (☎ 0345-222111)
    Spain (☎ 902-11 13 33)
    US (☎ 800-AIRWAYS)
    Gibraltar (☎ 79300)
GB Airways
    UK (☎ 0345-222111)
    Spain (☎ 902-11 13 33)
    US (☎ 800-AIRWAYS)
    Gibraltar (☎ 79300)
Iberia/Aviaco
    UK (☎ 0171-830 0011)
    Spain (☎ 902-40 05 00)
    US (☎ 800-772-4642)
Monarch Airlines
    UK (☎ 01582-398333)
    Spain (☎ 95 204 82 03)
    Gibraltar (☎ 47477)
Pauknair
    Spain (☎ 902-33 88 33)
Royal Air Maroc
    UK (☎ 0171 439 8854)
    Spain (☎ 91 541 51 58)
    US (☎ 800-344-6726)
Spanair
    Spain (☎ 902-13 14 15)
    US (☎ 888-545 5757)

Youth Fares In Andalucía the student and youth travel organisation TIVE is at Calle Jesús de la Veracruz 27, Sevilla (☎ 95 490 60 22), and Calle Huéscar 2 Bajo, Málaga (☎ 95 227 84 13).

Flights from Andalucía

If you need a flight out of Andalucía, check the ads in local English-language papers like *Sur in English*. Agencies like Servitour (☎ 95 256 60 00) and Flight-Line International (☎ 95 204 83 40) offer some of the best deals from Málaga, with occasional one-way flights to London, for instance, as cheap as 6500 ptas (but more often 10,000 to 12,000 ptas). TIVE (see Spain, above) may have youth fares.

LAND

If you are travelling by bus, train or car to Spain, check whether you require visas for the countries you intend to pass through.

Train Passes & Discounts

Passes for unlimited train travel over varying periods in Spain and other European countries are an attractive option for some, but you should consider carefully how much train travel you'll really be doing. Also look closely into any restrictions on the use of the passes on some Spanish trains, and supplements to be paid on others, and bear in mind that cardholders usually have to pay 500 ptas each time they reserve a seat – which is advisable on all long-distance trains, and compulsory on some.

Euro<26 This European youth card for the under-26s, known as the Carnet Joven in Spain, gives 20% off Spanish *largo recorrido* and *regional* train fares, including couchette supplements but not sleeping cars, and 25% off *turista* class fares on the fast AVE and Talgo 200 trains. The GO25 card may also get you discounts.

Inter-Rail Inter-Rail passes are for people who are resident in the UK or any other European country in the Inter-Rail network. The Inter-Rail map of Europe is divided into zones, one of which comprises Spain,

Portugal and Morocco. There are tickets for those under 26 and those aged 26 or over. Twenty-two days unlimited 2nd-class travel in one zone costs about £150/220 for under-26s/26-and-overs. A one-month ticket for two zones (which could get you across France too) is about £200/270.

Inter-Rail's usefulness for Andalucía is curtailed, however, by the fact that it is not valid on any train using the high-speed AVE line from Madrid to Sevilla – which means you must pay the full fare on all Madrid-Sevilla trains and AVE and Talgo 200 trains from Madrid to other places. Inter-Railers must also pay part of the fare on certain other high-speed trains like Talgos.

Places you can buy Inter-Rail cards in Britain include Campus Travel and STA Travel offices (see The UK & Ireland under Air in this chapter), and several main-line stations.

Eurail These passes are for non-European residents, which means you are not entitled to one if your passport shows you have been in Europe continuously for six months or more. For some reason, people aged 26 and over pay for a 1st- class pass and those under 26 for a 2nd- class pass. Eurailers can use their cards on all Spanish trains, but have to pay supplements on some – for instance 15% of the normal fare in turista class on AVE and Talgo 200 trains.

There's a gamut of different Eurail versions – Eurail Pass, Flexipass, Saverpass and more – but for those who intend to hang around in places a bit, rather than spend all their time rushing from one place to another, the Eurail Europass is probably the best bet. This gives between five and 15 days unlimited travel within a two-month period in Spain, France, Germany, Italy and Switzerland. Five days for under-26s/26-and-overs costs US$216/326, and you add US$29/42 for each extra day up to the maximum of 15. Adults can save a little on the standard prices by purchasing a pass for two people. You can also pay to add other countries to the pass. You might consider the Europass/Drive, for combined rail travel and car rental.

People generally purchase Eurail passes

in their country of origin (US outlets include Council Travel and STA Travel), but they are also available at Campus Travel branches in Britain.

Freedom/Euro-Domino Pass This pass, called the Freedom Pass in Britain and Euro-Domino everywhere else, entitles you to three, five or 10 days travel over a month in any one of 25 European countries. For Spain, a youth (under-26) five-day card costs £109; for 26-and-overs, five days is £139 in 2nd class or £169 in 1st class. Like other cards, this is subject to some restrictions and supplements.

Rail Europ Senior This pass gives the over-60s up to 30% off train trips that cross at least one border, and rail-connected sea crossings. UK citizens pay £5 for it, and they must already have a British Rail card (£16). It's not valid on Madrid-Lisbon trains.

Spain Flexipass RENFE (Spanish National Railways) issues the Spain Flexipass (or Tarjeta Turística), valid for three to 10 days travel in a two-month period: in 2nd class, four days costs around 23,000 ptas; 10 days, about 49,000 ptas.

Explore Rail Available from RENFE to holders of ISIC, Euro<26 or GO25 cards, this allows unlimited 2nd-class travel on Spanish trains except the AVE or Euromed trains for seven/15/30 days for 19,000/23,000/30,000 ptas.

The UK
Bus Bus fares from Britain to Andalucía are more expensive than the cheapest flights. Eurolines (☎ 0990-143219), 52 Grosvenor Gardens, Victoria, London SW1 (the terminal is a couple of blocks away), runs buses to Granada (32 hours), Málaga, Torremolinos and Algeciras twice a week. The one-way and return fares to all stops in Andalucía at the time of writing were, respectively, £79 and £144 (£72 and £129 for 13 to 25-year-olds and 60-or-overs).

In Málaga, Eurolines is on ☎ 95 223 23 00.

Train Getting from London to Andalucía involves changing trains at least twice and takes anything from 27 hours up. The simplest and quickest routings involve using the expensive Eurostar service from London Waterloo to Paris through the Channel Tunnel, changing from the Gare du Nord to the Gare d'Austerlitz in Paris (take the RER B to St Michel and change there to the RER C to Austerlitz), taking the 'Francisco de Goya' sleeper-only train to Madrid's Chamartin station, then taking another train from Madrid to your destination in Andalucía. You may also have to change stations in Madrid: the best services to most of Andalucía use the expensive high-speed AVE line from Madrid's Atocha station. (The quickest way between Chamartin and Atocha stations is a *cercanía* local train for 130 ptas.) Leaving Waterloo at about 2 pm, you reach Sevilla at 5.25 pm the next day, or Málaga at 6.35 pm. Fares vary according to the time of year, day of the week and whether or not you're under 26, but you're looking at about £120 and £205 one way to Málaga or Sevilla in 2nd class (returns are from about £215 to £315). It's worth asking about the 'joker fare' which gives you up to 45% off if you book 30 days in advance for selected trains in France and Spain.

To cut costs – and add time – you can cross the English Channel by ferry or hovercraft, take a more economical Paris-Madrid service such as the 10.58 pm (changing at Irun on the France-Spain border), and use a cheaper train between Madrid and Andalucía. Trains connecting with cross-Channel ferries and hovercraft from Dover run from Charing Cross and Victoria stations in London. Using these, London-Paris in low season costs about £25/40 one way/return for under-26s, or £40/60 for 26-and-overs.

For international train information in Britain, call ☎ 0990-848848.

Car & Motorcycle Driving yourself is in many ways the ideal way to get around Andalucía. Using a rental car is easy and fairly inexpensive: two people should be able to get return flights to Málaga and two weeks car hire for a total of £350 to £500, depending on the time of year (see below for more on rentals). Driving all the way yourself works out cheaper if you plan to stay several weeks and want a car all the time.

The options for getting your vehicle from Britain to continental Europe are threefold: you can use Le Shuttle, the Channel Tunnel car train from Folkestone to Calais; or put your vehicle on a cross-channel ferry or hovercraft to France; or use the direct vehicle ferries from England to northern Spain (from which it's possible to reach Andalucía in one long day).

Using Le Shuttle or a ferry to France, then driving quickly down to Andalucía, should cost in the region of £275 to £350 for a return trip for two people, including petrol, food and one night's accommodation each way en route. To this, add about £70 *each way* for road tolls if you use the French autoroutes and the Spanish A-7 through Cataluña and along the Mediterranean coast.

Le Shuttle (☎ 0990-353535) runs around the clock, with up to four crossings (35 minutes) an hour. You pay for the vehicle only. One-way fares range from £65 to £90 for a car and £37.50 to £42.50 for a motorcycle, depending on the season.

Refer to the Sea section later in this chapter for more details of the ferry options.

It's possible to put your car or motorcycle on the train from Barcelona or Bilbao to Málaga. Contact a travel agent or RENFE (Spanish National Railways) about these *autoexpreso* and *motoexpreso* services.

Paperwork & Preparations Proof of ownership of a private vehicle (Vehicle Registration Document for UK-registered cars) should always be carried when driving in Europe. See Visas & Documents in the Facts for the Visitor chapter for information on driving licences. Third party motor insurance is a minimum requirement in Spain and throughout Europe. For travellers who are not citizens of EU countries, Switzerland or Norway, it is compulsory to have a Green

Card, an internationally recognised proof of insurance, which can be obtained from your insurer. Also ask your insurer for a European Accident Statement form, which can simplify matters in the event of an accident.

A European breakdown assistance policy such as the AA Five Star Service or the RAC Eurocover Motoring Assistance is a good investment. In Spain, assistance can be obtained through the RACE (see the Getting Around chapter).

Every vehicle crossing an international border should display a nationality plate of its country of registration. A warning triangle (to be used in the event of a breakdown) is compulsory throughout Europe. Recommended accessories are a first-aid kit, spare bulb kit and fire extinguisher. If the car is from the UK or Ireland, remember to adjust the headlights for driving in continental Europe (motor accessory shops sell stick-on strips which deflect the beams in the required direction).

In the UK, further information is available from the RAC (☎ 0990-722722) or the AA (☎ 01256-20123).

Rental If you want to use one of the international car rental companies, which will provide a reliable service and good standard of vehicle, you'll almost always save a lot of money by booking the car before leaving home – or even calling back home from Spain and making the booking in your home country, rather than from the same company in Spain.

Also worth looking into is Malaga Car Hire (in the UK ☎ 0181-398 2662), which offers cars to be picked up at Málaga airport from £90 a week all inclusive in summer (from £65 from November to January).

Wherever you rent, make sure you understand what is included in the price (unlimited kilometres, tax, insurance, collision damage waiver etc) and what your liabilities are. The minimum rental age in Spain is 21. A credit card is usually required. See Visas & Documents in Facts for the Visitor for information on driving licences; and Car & Motorcycle in the

Getting Around chapter for more on rental rates and options within Spain.

Bicycle People do make their way to Andalucía by bike – best in spring, early summer or autumn. Bicycles can also travel by air: usually you can check them in as a piece of baggage, but check this with the airline well in advance, preferably before you pay for your ticket.

European Bike Express (☎ 01642-240020 in England) is a bus service that enables cyclists to travel with their machines to Calella de Palafrugell in north-east Spain. It runs in summer from north-east England, with pickup/drop-off points en route. The return fare is £160, plus £24 if you stay more than 17 days.

France
Bus Eurolines (☎ in Paris 01 49 72 51 51) runs buses from several French cities to Granada and Málaga. Enatcar (☎ in Madrid 91 754 20 04) is another bus company linking France with Andalucía.

Train Most routes enter Spain at Irún, on the Bay of Biscay, or Portbou on the Mediterranean, and involve at least one change of train (usually in Madrid). Of several possible daily connections from Paris to Madrid, the easiest and most expensive is the 8 pm 'Francisco de Goya' train from the Gare d'Austerlitz. This is a sleeper-only train and costs around 700/1200FF one way/return in 2nd-class. Cheaper options involve at least one change of train between Paris and Madrid.

Trains from Madrid can get you to most main Andalucian cities in a few hours for 4000 or 5000 ptas, though some trains, including the super-fast AVEs to Córdoba and Sevilla, are more expensive.

Car & Motorcycle See the UK section earlier for general information on taking a vehicle across Europe. The main highways from France into Spain run to Barcelona and San Sebastián at either end of the Pyrenees. The Mediterranean coast road is excellent all the way from the border at La

Jonquera to Andalucía – but see the section The Rest of Spain for a warning on tolls.

Portugal

Bus Transportes Agobe (☎ in Spain 958 63 52 74), based in Almuñécar, Granada province, runs three buses a week from Porto, Lisbon and Albufeira to Huelva, Sevilla, Málaga, Almuñécar and Granada. Departures from Porto are at 6 am on Tuesday, Thursday and Saturday; return buses leave Granada at 6 am on Monday, Wednesday and Friday. The buses make the trip in about 17 hours. Porto-Granada costs 10,600 ptas; Lisbon-Sevilla is 4500 ptas. Departure and ticket points in Portugal include:

Porto
    Viagens Resende, Rua Carmelitas 7
    (☎ 02-20 84 70 47)
Lisbon
    Viagens Samar, Avenida do Brasil, corner of
    Avenida Roma (☎ 01-796 61 48)
Albufeira
    Rua 1º Dezembro 32 (☎ 089-58 98 49)

In Spain, Agobe's departures are from main city bus stations.

From Lisbon there's another daily 10-hour service to Aracena and Sevilla at 7 am. You change to the Spanish Casal line at Rosal de la Frontera on the Spanish side of the border. In the other direction the bus leaves Sevilla (Plaza de Armas) at 9 am (2875 ptas to Lisbon).

On Saturday and Sunday there are Eurolines buses each way between Lisbon's main long-distance bus station at Avenida Casal Ribeiro 18 (metro: Saldanha) and Málaga bus station, via Badajoz, Sevilla (Plaza de Armas), Cádiz (Glorieta Ingeniero La Cierva), Algeciras (Estación Marítima) and the Costa del Sol. Departures from Lisbon are at 7 am; from Málaga at 7.15 am (Sevilla at 1.35 pm). From April to September, this service has also been running westbound on Tuesday and eastbound on Wednesday. Málaga to Lisbon one way is 7750 ptas, Sevilla-Lisbon 4350 ptas. In Málaga Eurolines is on ☎ 95 223 23 00.

Portugal's EVA Transportes and Spain's Damas line run a joint service once or twice daily each way between Faro (Terminal Eva, Avenida da República 5, ☎ 089-89 97 60) and Ayamonte, Huelva and Sevilla in Andalucía. Sevilla-Faro takes four hours for 1570 ptas.

Several other EVA services run daily between Lisbon, Faro, Tavira and Vila Real de Santo António, where there's a frequent ferry service across the Río Guadiana to Ayamonte in Andalucía.

Train No railway line crosses from Portugal into Andalucía. You can travel from Lisbon to Sevilla, or vice versa, in about 16 hours by changing trains at Cáceres in Spain's Extremadura. Departure from Lisbon's Santa Apolónia station is at 10 pm daily. The 2nd-class fare from Sevilla to Lisbon is 6800 ptas.

Trains run at least seven times a day along the Algarve from Lagos to Vila Real de Santo António, where there's a ferry service to Ayamonte in Andalucía. From Ayamonte you'd need to take a bus to the nearest train station, Huelva, 50km east.

Car & Motorcycle From Lisbon, head for Beja and Serpa and cross into Spain at Rosal de la Frontera, where the N-433 runs 160km to Sevilla. From the Algarve a modern road bridge crosses the Río Guadiana just north of Vila Real de Santo António (Portugal) and Ayamonte (Andalucía). There's no toll, and no customs or immigration presence, on this border. See the UK section above for general information on taking your own vehicle across Europe.

Elsewhere in Europe

Bus Eurolines (☎ in Berlin 030-301 8028, ☎ in Basel 061-157 37 47) operates buses to Granada and Málaga from several German and Swiss cities. Starbus (☎ 020-624 10 10 in Amsterdam, ☎ 02-513 41 50 in Brussels, ☎ 95 234 16 08 in Málaga) runs from the Netherlands and Belgium to Almería, Granada, Málaga, the Costa del Sol and Algeciras.

Train Direct trains run at least three times a week from Geneva, Zürich, Turin and Milan to Barcelona, where you can pick up direct trains to Granada, Córdoba, Sevilla, Málaga or Cádiz.

Morocco

Eurolines (☎ in Málaga 95 223 23 00) runs several weekly buses from Córdoba, Granada, Málaga and the Costa del Sol to Casablanca, Marrakesh, Fès and other places in Morocco, via Algeciras-Tangier ferries. Granada to Casablanca costs 9400/16,100 ptas one way/return.

You can transport vehicles by ferry from several Andalucian ports (see Sea).

The Rest of Spain

You can reach Andalucía in a day, if you wish, from most corners of Spain by bus, train or your own vehicle.

On some long-haul runs bus is cheaper and/or quicker than train; on others it's the opposite.

Bus For most buses you can turn up at the bus station half an hour or so before departure and get a seat. But it's advisable during Semana Santa, July and August to buy tickets in advance.

In most larger towns and cities, buses leave from a single main bus station (estación de autobuses). In Madrid, buses to Andalucía leave from the Estación Sur de Autobuses (☎ 91 468 42 00), Calle Méndez Álvaro (metro: Méndez Álvaro). In Barcelona, buses go from the Estació del Nord (☎ 93 265 65 08), Carrer d'Alí Bei 80 (metro: Arc de Triomf).

Daily buses operated by a plethora of companies run, among other routes, from Madrid to all main and many of the smaller Andalucian cities and towns; from Barcelona, Valencia and other Mediterranean coast cities to Almería, Jaén, Granada, Córdoba, Sevilla, Málaga, Algeciras and places en route. Buses also run to Sevilla from cities in Extremadura and in Galicia and Castilla y León in northern Spain.

Here are some journey times and one-way fares for bus travel within Spain:

Departure	Destination	Fare	Duration
Barcelona	Granada	7600 ptas	14 hrs
Cáceres	Sevilla	2200 ptas	4 hrs
Madrid	Málaga	2750 ptas	8½ hrs

Occasionally, a return ticket is cheaper than two singles. People under 26 should always inquire about discounts.

Train Generally, the main-line trains of RENFE (Red Nacional de Ferrocarriles Españoles, Spanish National Railways) are reliable, if not always super fast – an exception being the AVE (Tren de Alta Velocidad Español) which covers the 471km from Madrid to Sevilla, via Córdoba, in just 2½ hours, reaching speeds of 280km/h. (If an AVE arrives more than five minutes late due to a delay attributable to RENFE, you get your money back – but don't get excited: this only happens on one train in 250.)

For train information you can go to the station or RENFE's city centre ticket offices, or call the local RENFE office (in Madrid ☎ 91 328 90 20, in Barcelona ☎ 93 490 02 02). Schedules for *salidas* (departures) and *llegadas* (arrivals) are generally posted at stations. RENFE also has a good Internet site giving schedules and fares.

Routes From Madrid, the high-speed AVE line runs to Córdoba and Sevilla. Another line from Madrid runs to Linares-Baeza, north of Jaén, where it divides into branches for Córdoba and Sevilla to the west, and Granada to the south. Between Linares-Baeza and Granada, at Moreda, another branch heads south-east to Almería. Málaga trains pass through Córdoba; Cádiz and Huelva are reached through Sevilla. At Bobadilla, between Córdoba and Málaga, a branch heads off south-west to Ronda and Algeciras.

Trains from Barcelona either funnel through Madrid or head down the Mediterranean coast to Valencia, where they turn inland and enter Andalucía through Linares-Baeza.

Finally, there's a line from Cáceres and Mérida in Extremadura to Sevilla.

Types of Train A host of different train types coast the Spanish network. A saving of a couple of hours on a faster train can mean a big hike in the fare.

Most long-distance *(largo recorrido)* trains have 1st and 2nd class carriages. All except some night trains have a cafeteria.

The standard inter-regional trains are the daytime *diurnos* and overnight *estrellas*. Estrellas usually have seats as well as couchettes and sleeping compartments; some of them are 2nd class only. More comfortable daytime trains with fewer stops are called InterCity – marginally more expensive than a diurno. Even more comfy and expensive is a Talgo, which can come in the variations of Talgo Pendular (which leans into curves and travels faster as a result) or a Talgo 200 (a normal Talgo which uses part of the AVE line for trips between Madrid and such destinations as Málaga and Cádiz). On a Talgo 200, Madrid-Málaga takes less than five hours.

A *tren hotel* is a sleek, comfortable, expensive sleeping-car train. First class on these tends to be called *gran clase*, and 2nd class (if it exists) *turista*.

The most expensive way to go is to take the AVE itself along the Madrid-Córdoba-Sevilla line. Even in the cheapest class (turista), AVE passengers have access to everything from videos and telephones to children's games and facilities for the disabled.

Couchettes & Sleepers Couchettes are known as *literas* and are fold-out bunk beds (generally six to a compartment). The standard price in addition to your 2nd-class ticket is 1300 ptas.

If you want a proper sleeper, you have half a dozen choices, ranging from shared cabins through to luxury singles. Prices depend on the distance you travel.

Reservations On most trains you don't need to book in advance. If you want to be sure of a place, it may nevertheless be wise to do so. Bookings can be made at stations, RENFE offices and many travel agents. There is usually no booking fee unless you have the ticket(s) mailed to you.

Costs The variety of possible fares is just as confusing as the number of train types. Fares quoted elsewhere in this guide are basic 2nd-class seat fares.

Your fare depends first on the type of train. Among long-distance daytime trains, a diurno is usually the cheapest, followed by an InterCity, then the Talgos and Talgo 200s, with AVEs the most expensive. At night, a tren hotel generally costs more than an estrella.

As for classes, on daytime trains you generally have the easy choice of 2nd or 1st-class seats (called *turista* and *preferente* on Talgo 200s and AVEs). AVEs also have a super-1st class called *club*. Night trains offer varied combinations of 1st and 2nd-class seats, couchettes and in some cases *camas* (sleeping compartments) – see Couchettes & Sleepers, above.

In some cases, the fare also depends on the time of day you travel – this mainly applies to the fast Talgo 200 and AVE trains. The cheapest times of day are called *valle* and the most expensive *punta*, but most trains fall into the in-between category, *llano*.

Children under four travel free and those from four to 11 get 40% off the cost of seats and couchettes. Return fares are generally 20% less than two one-ways if you're coming back within 60 days.

As an example of the range of possible fares, Madrid to Sevilla costs 5400 ptas in a 1st-class seat on a tren hotel (3¾ hours); 7000/10,100 ptas for 2nd/1st- class seats on a Talgo Pendular (3¼ to 4¼ hours); 7900/11,400 ptas for turista/preferente seats on a Talgo 200 (3¼ hours); 8100/11,700/14,100 ptas for turista preferente/club seats on valle-period AVEs (2½ hours); and 9500/13,800/16,600 ptas on llano-period AVEs.

Other one-way 2nd or turista-class train-seat fares within Spain include:

Departure	Destination	Fare	Duration
Barcelona	Granada	6200 – 6300 ptas	12 – 14½hrs
Cáceres	Sevilla	2165 ptas	6 hrs
Madrid	Málaga	4500 – 8000 ptas	4 – 9½hrs

See Train Passes & Discounts for ways to reduce the cost of Spanish train travel.

Car & Motorcycle Spain's main roads are good. Friends say they drive from Málaga to Barcelona in eight hours. We believe them, but at a sane pace it's more like 11 or 12.

The main highway from Madrid is the N-IV to Córdoba, Sevilla and Cádiz. Branch off this at Bailén for Jaén, Granada, Almería or Málaga. Another road, the N-401 becoming the N-420, heads from Madrid to Córdoba via Toledo and Ciudad Real. If you're coming from the ferry at Santander or Bilbao, the direct route is to head for Burgos, from which it's a pretty straight 240km to Madrid. The main Bilbao-Burgos highway is subject to about 3000 ptas of tolls.

The A-7 leads down the east side of Spain from La Jonquera on the French border as far as Murcia. It has several toll stretches between La Jonquera and Alicante which total about 8000 ptas. The toll-free alternative roads tend to be busy and slow. At Murcia the toll-free N-340 takes over as the main road and continues to Almería and Málaga.

The N-630 heads all the way down to Sevilla from Gijón on Spain's north coast, through Castilla y León and Extremadura.

See the Getting Around chapter for some general information on driving in Spain.

Hitching Hitchhiking is never entirely safe and we don't recommend it. Travellers who decide to hitch should understand that they are taking a small but potentially serious risk. Women should avoid hitching alone, and even men should consider the safer alternative of hitching in pairs.

Hitching is illegal on the best Spanish roads – autopistas and autovías – and difficult on other major highways. You can try to pick up lifts before the tollbooths on tollways. Otherwise, you need to choose a spot where cars can safely stop prior to highway slipways, or use minor roads. The going can be slow on the latter, as traffic is often light.

There are one or two organisations, such as Compartecoche in Sevilla (see the Sevilla Getting There & Away section), that organise car pooling – a kind of organised hitching service for which you pay a contribution to petrol and often a small fee.

Bicycle If you get tired of pedalling, it is possible to take your bike on the train, but you have to be travelling overnight in a sleeper or litera (couchette), in order to have the (dismantled) bike accepted as normal luggage. Otherwise, it can only be sent separately as a parcel.

SEA
The UK
Portsmouth-Bilbao P&O European Ferries (in Britain ☎ 0990-980555) operates a ferry from Portsmouth to Bilbao on Spain's north coast throughout the year, except for a couple of weeks in January. As a rule, there are two sailings a week and the one-way voyage time is about 34 hours.

The standard one-way/return fares for two people with a car are £245/460 in the cheapest period (October to March) and £420/600 in the most expensive (mid-July to mid-August from Britain, August from Spain). This includes the cheapest available form of cabin accommodation. Cabins are compulsory – all have private shower and toilet.

In Spain, inquiries and reservations can be made at P&O's office (☎ 94 423 44 77), Calle de Cosme Echevarrieta 1, Bilbao. The ferries dock at Santurtzi, about 14km north-west of central Bilbao.

Plymouth/Portsmouth-Santander Brittany Ferries (in Britain ☎ 0990-360360) operates a twice-weekly car ferry from Plymouth to Santander, also on Spain's north coast (24 hours sailing time), from mid-March to mid-November. In other months, the service is once a week or less and departs from Poole or Portsmouth (28 to 31½ hours).

Standard return fares for two people with a car range from £359 (October to March) to £644 (mid-July to mid-August from Britain, August from Spain). In addition you must pay for a seat (£6 each way) or cabin. Fares apart, Brittany Ferries has the edge over the Bilbao route when it comes to the food available on board.

In Santander, buy tickets at the port, or make reservations on ☎ 942 36 06 11.

Via France You can transport your vehicle by ferry or hovercraft to France then drive to Spain. Cross-Channel routes include Dover-Calais, operated by ferries of P&O Stena Line (☎ 0990-980980) and SeaFrance (☎ 0990-711711), and hovercraft of Hoverspeed (☎ 01304-240241); Folkestone-Boulogne (Hoverspeed); Newhaven-Dieppe (P&O Stena Line); Portsmouth- Caen (Brittany Ferries, ☎ 0990-360360); and Portsmouth-Cherbourg (P&O European Ferries, ☎ 0990-980980). Dover-Calais is the quickest and busiest, with as many as 60 crossings a day.

One-way England-France fares for a car and two people range from around £45 to £180, depending on the route and time of year. Peak summer fares can be almost double winter fares. P&O Stena Line's summer standard Dover-Calais return for a car with two people is £159. Of the longer routes, Portsmouth-Cherbourg is among the cheapest. For the Le Shuttle car train service through the Channel Tunnel, see the UK in the Land section earlier in this chapter.

Morocco
You can sail to Tangier or to Ceuta or Melilla (Spanish enclaves on the Moroccan coast) from Almería, Málaga, Gibraltar, Algeciras or Tarifa. All routes take vehicles as well as passengers. The cheapest are those that cross the Strait of Gibraltar from Algeciras, Gibraltar and Tarifa, and by far the

most frequent are from Algeciras. Usually at least 14 sailings a day go from Algeciras to Tangier and 20 or more to Ceuta, most of them by two Spanish companies, Trasmediterránea (☎ 902-45 46 45) and Isleña de Navegación SA (Isnasa, ☎ 956 65 20 00). To Tangier, a passenger pays 2960 ptas one way on a ferry (taking two hours) or 3440 ptas on a hydrofoil (one hour). A car costs 9300 ptas. To Ceuta it's 1801 ptas on a ferry (1½ hours), 2945 ptas on a hydrofoil (40 minutes), and 8223 ptas for a car.

For more details see the Getting There & Away entries for Algeciras, Almería, Málaga, Gibraltar and Tarifa.

Canary Islands
A weekly car ferry sails from Cádiz – see the Cádiz section.

DEPARTURE TAXES
Departure taxes for leaving Spain by air (around 1000 ptas for European flights and rising to as much as 5000 ptas beyond Europe) are included in the price of the ticket at purchase. For European flights they are generally only charged if you are taking a *return* flight.

Taxes on ferry services are also included in ticket prices.

ORGANISED TOURS
Numerous companies offer tours to Andalucía, sometimes combining it with other parts of Spain. Special interest tours include horse riding, wildlife, cycling or wine trips. There are also holidays which cater for the disabled, non smokers, gays, naturists as well as music and dance holidays. Spanish tourist offices can often provide long lists of tour operators, as can the Internet. The following examples are just a tiny sample of tours available.

Short Breaks
Kirker Travel Ltd (☎ 0171-231 33 33), 3 New Concordia Wharf, Mill St, London SE1 2BB, offers fairly pricey short breaks from London in good hotels in Sevilla, Granada and Córdoba. As a rule, they will

set you back from £250 per person for three nights, breakfast only included.

Under-35s Tours

Contiki (☎ 0181-290 6777 in Britain, ☎ 800-266-8454 in the USA) does a range of European tours for 18 to 35-year-olds – its 12-day Spain and Portugal jaunt (US$829) spends much of its time in Andalucía. Bravo Tours (☎ 800-272 8674), 215 East Ridgewood Ave, Suite 201, Ridgewood, NJ 07450, USA, runs one-week or 10-day Spain tours for students, several of which include Andalucía.

Coach Tours

The all-in price for a one-week Andalucía tour with Mundi Color Holidays (☎ 0171-828 6021), 276 Vauxhall Bridge Rd, London SW1V 1BE, hovers around the £800 mark.

Saga Holidays (in Britain ☎ 0800-300500, in the USA ☎ 800-343-0273) takes in a good slice of Andalucía in all-Spain coach tours costing from £800 for 10 to 12 nights.

Magic of Spain (☎ 0181-748 4220), 227 Shepherds Bush Rd, London W6 7AS, does a one-week tour of Andalucía for £625 to £699 including flights from Britain.

Saranjan Tours (☎ 800-858 9594), 12865 NE 85th St, No 102, Kirkland, WA 98033, USA, does a deluxe small-group tour of several of Andalucía's most interesting cities and towns, staying in classy hotels.

Walking Holidays

Explore Worldwide (☎ 01252-34 41 61), 1 Frederick St, Aldershot, Hants GU11 1LQ, UK, runs two-week small-group summer trips which include nine days walking in the Alpujarras and Sierra Nevada, south of Granada. Cost is in the region of £360 plus flights. Explore does a slightly more expensive Granada, Córdoba and Sevilla trip with a few days in the Cazorla natural park.

Headwater Holidays (☎ 01606-48699), 146 London Rd, Northwich, Cheshire CW9 5HH, UK, does a one-week walking holiday in the Sierra de Aracena for around £700 including flights.

Country Walkers (☎ 800-464 9255), PO Box 180, Waterbury, VT 05676, USA, offers a week of Alpujarras walking and Granada for US$2050.

Golf Tours

Companies running Andalucía golf holidays – usually including some of the region's best courses, and not cheap – are: Atlantic Golf, 26 Crown Rd, St. Margrets, Twickenham, Middlesex TW1 3EE, UK; Executive Golf Tours (☎ 0131-226 2830), 21 Lansdowne Crescent, Edinburgh EH12 5EH, UK; and, in the USA, Classic Golf & Leisure (☎ 800-283 1619) and Perry Golf (☎ 800-344 5257).

Riding Tours

Andalucía Trails (☎ 956 68 51 36), Cortijo Las Piñas, 11380 Tarifa, Cádiz, Spain, will give you a week's riding on the coast or in the hinterland of Cádiz province for around £450 to £600.

Birdwatching Tours

Gourmet Birds (☎ 01959-563 627), Windrush, Coles Lane, Brasted, Westerham, Kent TN16 1NN, is one British firm that has taken birdwatchers to Andalucía. Another worth contacting is Ornitholidays (☎ 01243-821 230), 1-3 Victoria Drive, Bognor Regis, West Sussex PO21 2PW, UK.

WARNING

The information in this chapter is particularly vulnerable to change: prices for international travel are volatile, routes are introduced and cancelled, schedules change, special deals come and go, rules are amended. You should check directly with the airline or a travel agent to make sure you understand how a fare (and ticket you may buy) works. Get opinions, quotes and advice from as many airlines and travel agents as possible before you part with your hard-earned cash. The details given in this chapter should be regarded as pointers and are not a substitute for your own careful, up-to-date research.

Getting Around

AIR

There are no direct flights between Andalucian cities.

BUS

Long-distance or local bus services reach just about every town or village in Andalucía. The comments on Spanish long-distance buses in the Getting There & Away chapter also apply to long-distance services within Andalucía. Services to small villages may run just once a day – or not at all on Saturday or Sunday.

In smaller places, buses tend to operate from a set street or plaza, which is often unmarked. Ask around; everyone generally knows where to go. Usually a specific bar sells tickets and has timetable information.

One-Way Bus Journeys			
Departure	*Destination*	*Fare*	*Duration*
Cádiz	Sevilla	1200 ptas	1 hr
Granada	Almería	1285 ptas	2¼ hrs
Granada	Pampaneira	620 ptas	2½ hrs
Granada	Sevilla	2700 ptas	4 hrs
Jaén	Cazorla	930 ptas	2 hrs
Málaga	Sevilla	2245 ptas	3½ hrs

TRAIN

Long-distance trains linking Andalucía with other parts of Spain (see Spain in the Land section of the Getting There & Away chapter) can sometimes be used for getting from one part of Andalucía to another – for example from Córdoba to Sevilla or Málaga.

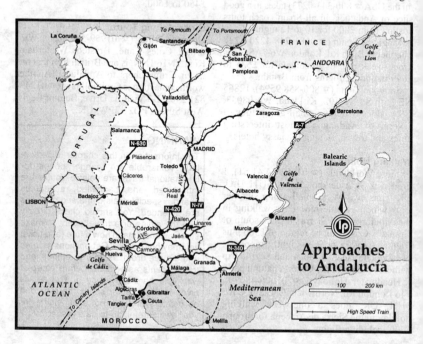

Approaches to Andalucía

Regional & Long-Distance Train Journeys				
Departure	*Destination*	*Type of Train*	*Duration*	*2nd Class Fare*
Granada	Almería	Andalucía Express	2¼ hrs	1550 ptas
Málaga	Córdoba	Andalucía Express	3 hrs	1550 ptas
		InterCity/Talgo 200	2 to 2¼ hrs	2000 to 2200 ptas
Sevilla	Cádiz	Regional	2 hrs	1085 ptas
		Andalucía Express	1¾ hrs	1240 ptas
		Diurno/Estrella/Talgo	1½ to 1¾ hrs	1600 ptas

But more often you'll use the generally cheaper shorter-distance trains. These are of two basic types: *regionales*, regional trains between main towns and cities; and *cercanías*, local trains linking Sevilla, Málaga and Cádiz with their suburbs and nearby towns. An Andalucía Express is a superior kind of regional train, a little quicker and a little dearer than other regionales.

The regional routes, with some main stops, are:

Sevilla–Jerez de la Frontera–El Puerto de Santa María–Cádiz
Sevilla–Córdoba–Jaén
Sevilla–Osuna–Bobadilla–El Chorro–Málaga
Sevilla–Osuna–Bobadilla–Antequera–Granada
Sevilla–Huelva
Sevilla–Cazalla–Constantina
Bobadilla–Ronda–Jimena de la Frontera–Algeciras

Córdoba–Montilla–Fuente de Piedra–Bobadilla–El Chorro–Málaga
Granada–Moreda–Guadix–Almería
Granada–Moreda–Linares–Baeza
Huelva–Almonaster–Cortegana–Jabugo–Galaroza

On most of these routes there are three or four regional trains a day each way. The most important interchange station is Bobadilla, where lines from five directions meet.

The rail authority RENFE has an excellent Web site for Spanish train schedules and fares (in Spanish but easy to use) at www.renfe.es/index.html. Click on 'Horarios y Precios', then select your stations of departure (origen) and destination (destino), and click on 'Realizar Consulta'. If your stations are small ones that don't appear in the initial lists, click on 'Formulario General con Todas las Estaciones'.

See Train Passes & Discounts in the Getting There & Away chapter for information on European and Spanish rail passes.

CAR & MOTORCYCLE
Touring Andalucía with your own vehicle offers maximum flexibility. The main intercity highways are, in general, good and quick; country roads can be badly surfaced. Parking in cities is sometimes a minor headache but not enough to put you off. There's only one toll road in Andalucía – the A-4 from Sevilla to Cádiz (783 ptas).

The Land section in the Getting There & Away chapter covers ways of getting a vehicle to Andalucía from Britain and from other parts of Spain, and the paperwork needed to take a vehicle to Spain.

Trenes Regionales Diésel (New Fast Trains)

A new, faster type of regional train, the Tren Regional Diésel (TRD), was due to be introduced as this book was going to press. These trains will cut 35 to 45 minutes off journeys such as Granada-Sevilla, Málaga-Sevilla and Almería-Granada, and will shorten the Almería-Sevilla trip from nearly seven hours to five by removing the need to change trains in Granada. Owing to lack of advance detail, information on regional trains in this book does not cover TRDs.

Road Rules
If fitted, rear seat belts must be worn; fines for failure to comply range from 50,000 to 100,000 ptas. The minimum driving age is 18.

Motorcyclists must use headlights at all times. Crash helmets are obligatory on bikes of 125cc or more – although you wouldn't think so to judge by the way some locals behave. The minimum age for riding bikes and scooters under 75cc is 16 (no licence is required).

The speed limit is 50km/h in built-up areas, rising to 100km/h on major roads and 120km/h on *autopistas* and *autovías*. Cars towing caravans are restricted to 80km/h.

The blood-alcohol limit is 0.08% and breath-testing is carried out on occasion. Fines ranging up to 100,000 ptas are imposed if you are caught driving under the influence.

Fines for many traffic offences range from 50,000 to 100,000 ptas. Nonresident foreigners can be fined on the spot – minor compensation being that they get 20% off normal fines for immediate settlement.

Road Maps & Atlases
Many road numbers in Andalucía have been changed in the last few years and mapmakers have a hard time keeping up with all the changes. However, Michelin's *Southern Spain* map (see Planning in Facts for the Visitor) is pretty good for finding your way round Andalucía. Michelin also publishes the good *Michelin Motoring Atlas – Spain & Portugal* (called *Michelin Atlas de Carreteras España Portugal* in Spain). Both these are widely available in and outside Spain. In Spain, petrol stations and bookshops are the places to look: the map costs 785 ptas and the atlas about 2600 ptas. Several other road atlases of Spain are available, including the *Mapa Oficial de Carreteras*, put out by the Ministry of Public Works, Transport & Environment for around 1900 ptas.

Road Assistance
The head office of Real Automóvil Club de España (RACE) (☎ 91-447 32 00) is at Calle de José Abascal 10 in Madrid. For RACE's 24-hour, countrywide emergency breakdown assistance, call ☎ 900-11 81 18. This service is available to members of foreign motoring organisations such as the RAC and AA.

City Driving & Parking
Driving in the bigger cities can be a little nerve-racking at the start. Road rules and traffic lights are generally respected, but the pace and jostling take a little getting used to.

Avoid leaving anything which looks even remotely valuable in unattended vehicles. If you must leave luggage in vehicles, use paid car parks (around 100-150 ptas per hour). If you double park or leave your vehicle in a designated no-parking zone, you risk being towed – and recovering the vehicle costs about 10,000 ptas.

Petrol
Gasolina is as expensive in Spain as just about anywhere else in Europe. Prices vary slightly between service stations and fluctuate with oil tariffs and tax policy. Lead-free *(sin plomo)* usually comes in two versions: 95 octane, sometimes called Eurosuper, at around 112 ptas/L, and 98 octane, with names like Súper Star, at about 122 ptas/L. The 95 octane is often hidden away unadvertised at one of the rear pumps. Leaded super costs around 118 ptas/L and the increasingly popular diesel (or *gasóleo*) about 87 ptas/L.

Rental
All the major international car rental companies are well represented in Andalucía, and there are plenty of local operators too. At Málaga airport and on the Costa del Sol and in Nerja and the Almería resorts, you can get a small car from a local firm for around 20,000 ptas a week (even 16,000 ptas in winter), including collision damage waiver, insurance and 16% IVA (value-added tax). Elsewhere, and from the multinational firms, rates are often double that – though many companies offer better rates on weekends. In general it's more economical to organise your rental car before you come to Spain (see The UK in

the Land section of the Getting There & Away chapter).

If you do decide to hire after arriving, shop around. You need to be at least 21 (23 with some companies) and to have held a driving licence for a minimum of one year (often two years). It's easier, and with some companies obligatory, to pay with a credit card.

Rental outlets for motorcycles and mopeds are rare and tend to be expensive.

BICYCLE

Bicycle rental is rare in Andalucía, so if you want to tour by bike – which can be enjoyable in spring and autumn if you're not averse to a few hills – you should bring your own. See The UK and Spain in the Land section of the Getting There & Away chapter for a couple of hints on getting a bike to Andalucía, and Activities in Facts for the Visitor for one or two hints on mountain biking.

HITCHING

See Land in the Getting There & Away chapter.

LOCAL TRANSPORT

Cities and larger towns have efficient bus systems but in most places accommodation,

attractions and main-line bus and train stations are usually within fairly comfortable walking distance of each other. All Andalucía's airports except Jerez de la Frontera are linked to city centres by bus – and in Málaga's case also by train. Gibraltar airport is within walking distance of downtown Gibraltar.

Taxis are plentiful in larger places and even many villages have a taxi or two. Fares are reasonable – a typical 3km trip should cost about 400 ptas, though airport runs are a bit extra. Many taxis will take you on inter-city runs too: expect to pay around 90 ptas a kilometre. You don't have to tip taxi drivers but a little rounding up doesn't go amiss.

ORGANISED TOURS

Guided tours of the major cities are an option, but as a rule it's cheaper and not a great deal more trouble to do it under your own steam. Of more potential use are trips in national and natural parks, some of which are hard to penetrate if you don't have your own vehicle. Guides' local knowledge can be illuminating. The only way the general public is permitted to enter the Parque Nacional de Doñana is by guided tour.

Sevilla Province

The wonderful city of Sevilla is the highlight of the province, but country lovers will enjoy heading out to the Parque Natural Sierra Norte. In the east, travellers have the option of stopping off at interesting old towns such as Carmona, Écija, Osuna and Estepa.

SEVILLA

Sevilla, with 697,000 people, is Andalucía's biggest and most exciting city. It takes a stony heart not to be captivated by its unique atmosphere – stylish, confident, ancient, proud, yet also convivial, intimate and fun-loving. One of the first people recorded to have fallen in love with Sevilla was the Muslim poet-king Al-Mutamid in the 11th century. The place is working its enchantment every bit as well today.

Except along the Río Guadalquivir – navigable to the Atlantic Ocean 100km away and source of Sevilla's greatness in times past – this is not a city of great long vistas. Its flat, crowded centre unfolds more subtly as you wend your way around narrow streets and small plazas, stopping for a drink or a bite in some of the wonderful bars and cafés. The city's two great monuments – the Muslim Alcázar and the Christian Catedral – reveal most of their glories only once you're inside them.

A great city in Muslim times and again in the 16th and 17th centuries, Sevilla has known bad times too, so it knows how to enjoy the good ones when they come. The year 1992, when the eyes of the world turned on Sevilla's world Expo, was one of the best. You might think the atmosphere today was just a carryover from 1992 if you didn't know that Sevilla has been throwing one of Spain's biggest parties, the Feria de Abril, every April for more than a century. Or that a couple of weeks before the feria, the town's Semana Santa processions are among the most magnificent in Spain.

Aside from its fascinating inner city,

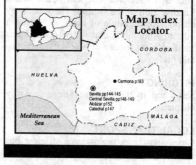
Sevilla enjoys some good green parks on the fringes of the centre. It's also one of the homes of flamenco and bullfighting, and has wonderful nightlife. But above all, Sevilla is an atmosphere. Being out among its happy, celebratory crowds on a warm night is a not-to-be-forgotten experience. To put it in one Spanish word, the city has *alegría*.

There are a couple of catches, of course. Sevilla is expensive. You might pay 5000 or 6000 ptas here for a room that would cost 3000 ptas in some other towns. And prices go even higher during the two big festivals (if you can get a room). Another thing to bear in mind is that Sevilla gets obscenely hot in July and August: locals, sensibly, leave the city then.

History

Beginnings It was Phoenician influence in the Sevilla area that gave rise to the fabled ancient culture of Tartessos, when iron replaced bronze for the first time in Andalucía, and a new method of working gold was developed.

The Roman town of Hispalis, probably founded in the mid-2nd century BC, was a significant port, but overshadowed by Córdoba. Visigothic Hispalis was a bit of a cultural centre, especially in the time of St Isidoro (565-636), the leading scholar of the Visigothic period in Spain.

The Taifa Kings Under the Muslims, who called it Ishbiliya, Sevilla played second fiddle to Córdoba until the collapse of the Córdoba Caliphate in 1031, when the city became the most powerful of the taifa states of Al-Andalus. By 1078 it controlled the south of the Iberian Peninsula from the Algarve to Murcia. Its Abbadid dynasty rulers Al-Mutadid (1042-69) and Al-Mutamid (1069-91) were both poets too, and Al-Mutamid was the first of a long line of rulers to succumb to the city's powers of enchantment, presiding over a languid, hedonistic court in the Alcázar.

Almoravids & Almohads When Toledo in central Spain fell to the Christians in 1085, Al-Mutamid asked the Muslim fundamentalist rulers of Morocco, the Almoravids, for help against the growing Christian threat. The Almoravids came, defeated Alfonso VI of Castilla at Sagrajas (Extremadura) in 1086, and went back to Morocco – but then returned in 1091 to help themselves to Al-Andalus too, ruling it harshly as a colony. But by the mid-12th century Al-Andalus was again breaking up into taifas.

A new strict Muslim Berber sect, the Almohads, displaced the Almoravids in Morocco then moved on into Al-Andalus, which they controlled by 1173. Arts and learning revived under the Almohads: Caliph Yacoub Yousouf rather liked Sevilla and made it capital of the whole Almohad realm, building a great mosque where the city's Catedral

now stands. His successor Yousouf Yacoub al-Mansour added the Giralda tower and thrashed the Christian armies at Alarcos (Castilla-La Mancha) in 1195. The Christians, however, bounced back with their pivotal victory at Las Navas de Tolosa (1212).

Reconquista After this, Almohad power in Spain dwindled, enabling the Castilian king Fernando III (El Santo, the Saint) to capture several major Andalucian cities including Sevilla, after two years' siege, in 1248.

Fernando brought 24,000 Castilian settlers to the city. His intellectual son Alfonso X made Sevilla one of his capitals and by the 14th century it was the most important Castilian city. But the reign of the monarch who perhaps loved it more than any other, Pedro I (1350-69), was plagued by bloody feuds in the royal family and conflict between the monarchy and nobles (see the Alcázar section). Pedro's court included many Jewish financiers and tax collectors, which brought racial jealousies. A pogrom which emptied the Jewish quarter in 1391 signalled the end of 'three cultures' tolerance.

The Catholic Monarchs, Fernando and Isabel, set up court in the Alcázar for several years as they prepared for the conquest of the Emirate of Granada, the last Muslim stronghold on the peninsula, which fell in 1492.

The Golden Age Sevilla's biggest break of all followed Columbus' discovery of the Americas in 1492. In 1503 the city was given an official monopoly on Spanish trade with the new continent. Galleons disgorged cargos of gold and silver at its port (in the El Arenal area around the Plaza de Toros) and the city rapidly became one of the most cosmopolitan places on the planet, a multi-faceted hotbed of poverty and wealth, vice and virtue (with over 100 monasteries and other religious institutions). Sevilla was labelled the *puerto y puerta de Indias* (port and gateway of the Indies), the Babylon of Spain and even the New Rome. Its population exploded from about 40,000 in 1500 to 150,000 in 1600, lavish Renaissance and

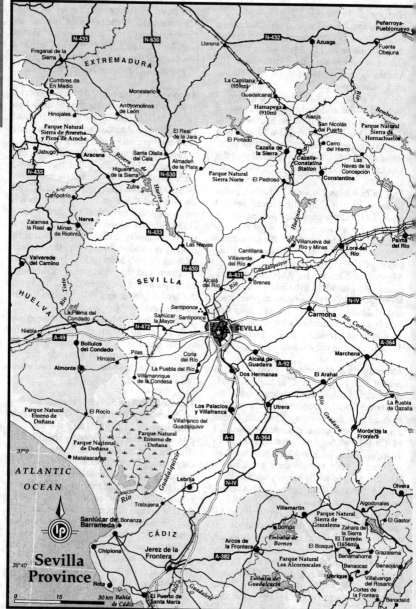

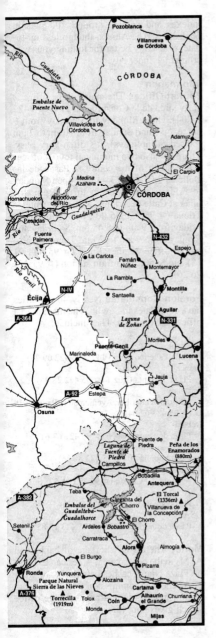

baroque buildings sprouted and many leading figures of Spain's artistic golden age did the bulk of their work here.

The Not-so-Golden Age But a plague in 1649 killed half the city and, as the century wore on, the Guadalquivir became more and more silted up and difficult for big ships, many of which foundered on a sandbar at its mouth near Sanlúcar de Barrameda. Cádiz began to take much of the American trade. By 1700 Sevilla's population was down to 60,000 and in 1717 the Casa de la Contratación, the government body which controlled the American commerce, was transferred to Cádiz. Another plague in 1800 killed 13,000. The Napoleonic troops who occupied the city from 1810 to 1812 stole, it's said, 999 works of art when they left.

A certain prosperity returned in the mid-19th century with the beginnings of industry. The first bridge across the Guadalquivir, the Puente de Triana (or Puente de Isabel II), was built in 1845 and the old Almohad walls were knocked down in 1869 to let the city expand. Romantics were attracted by Sevilla's air of faded grandeur, but the majority in the city and countryside remained very poor.

The 20th Century Middle class optimism was expressed by Sevilla's first international fair, the Exposición Iberoamericana of 1929. The fair's architects tried to inspire a new future with buildings that looked back to the city's glorious past.

Sevilla fell very quickly to the Nationalists at the start of the Civil War despite resistance in working class areas (which brought savage reprisals). Urban development in Franco's time did little for the look of the city, with numerous historic buildings being demolished. Things looked up in the early 1980s with the naming of Sevilla as capital of the new Andalucía autonomous region and the coming to power in Madrid of the PSOE, led by *sevillano* Felipe González. The city was given another big thrust forward by Expo 92, on the 500th anniversary of the discovery of America. As well as millions of extra visitors and a boost to its international image, Sevilla got eight new bridges across the Guadalquivir, the new superfast AVE rail link to Madrid, and several thousand new hotel rooms.

Almost inevitably, Expo was a source of controversy too. Costs escalated in the run-up to 92, and no one seemed to know what to do with the site afterwards. In 1997, the national Accounts Tribunal reported Expo had lost around 35 billion ptas instead of making a profit of 17 billion ptas. Large sums were alleged to have disappeared into private pockets and PSOE coffers, and, at the time of writing, the men in charge of Expo were facing court hearings.

Orientation

Sevilla straddles the Río Guadalquivir with most of the interest on the east bank. The central area is mostly a tangle of narrow, twisting old streets and small plazas, with the exceptions of Plaza Nueva and Avenida de la Constitución which runs south from Plaza Nueva to Puerta de Jerez, a busy intersection marking the south edge of the centre. Just east of Avenida de la Constitución are the Catedral, the Giralda tower and the Alcázar fortress-palace, the city's major monuments. The quaint Barrio de Santa Cruz, immediately east of the Catedral and Alcázar, has many budget lodgings. The true centre of Sevilla (El Centro) is a bit farther north, around Plaza de San Francisco, Plaza Salvador and Calle Sierpes.

The main transport terminals are on the periphery of the central area: Santa Justa train station is 1.5km north-east of the Catedral at Avenida Kansas City s/n; Plaza de Armas bus station is 1km north-west of the Catedral near the Puente del Cachorro bridge; and Prado de San Sebastián bus station is 750m south-east of the Catedral on Plaza San Sebastián.

Maps The main tourist office sells a reasonable street map for 100 ptas, though parts are obscured by drawings of buildings. Better are the city maps published by Almax and Plaza & Janes, both with street indexes and costing around 700 ptas in bookshops. The Almax, though less up-to-date, is actually better for finding your way around the inner city.

Information

Tourist Offices The main tourist office is at Avenida de la Constitución 21 (☎ 95 422 14 04). Open Monday to Saturday from 9 am to 7 pm and Sunday from 10 am to 2 pm (closed on holidays), it's often very busy. There are also two municipal tourist offices – one south of the centre at Paseo de las Delicias 9 (☎ 95 423 44 65), open Monday to Friday from 8.30 am to 6.30 pm; the other at Calle de Arjona 28 by the Puente de Triana (☎ 95 450 56 00), open Monday to Friday from 9 am to 8.45 pm, Saturday and Sunday from 9 am to 2 pm. There are also tourist offices at the airport (☎ 95 444 91 28) and Santa Justa train station (☎ 95 453 76 26).

Foreign Consulates Nearly 40 countries have consulates in Sevilla. The main tourist office has a full list. They include:

Australia
    Calle Federico Rubio 14 (☎ 95 422 09 71)
France
    Plaza de Santa Cruz 1 (☎ 95 422 28 96)
Germany
    Edificio Winterthur, Avenida de la Palmera 19 (☎ 95 423 02 04)
Ireland
    Plaza de Santa Cruz 6 (☎ 95 421 63 61)
Italy
    Calle Fabiola 10 (☎ 95 422 85 76)
Portugal
    Avenida del Cid s/n (☎ 95 423 11 50)
UK
    Plaza Nueva 8B (☎ 95 422 88 75)
USA
    Paseo de las Delicias 7 (☎ 95 423 18 85)

Money There's no shortage of banks and ATMs in the central area. American Express on Plaza Nueva cashes banknotes and travellers cheques commission free. Santa Justa station has ATMs and an exchange office which gives poor rates.

Post & Communications The main post office (postcode 41080) is at Avenida de la Constitución 32, opposite the Archivo de Indias. It's open Monday to Friday from 8.30 am to 8.30 pm, Saturday 9.30 am to 2 pm.

Finding an unvandalised coin pay phone in the city centre can take a long time, so a phonecard comes in handy.

Public Internet and email services include Alfalfa 10 (☎ 95 421 38 41), a café at Plaza de la Alfalfa 10, and the Cibercenter (☎ 95 422 88 99), Calle Julio Cesar 8. At Alfalfa 10 you can go online for 500 ptas an hour from around noon to 2.30 pm and 6 pm to midnight (except Sunday evenings).

Internet Resources The following Web sites could be useful:

Sevilla Cultural
    www.sevillacultural.com/ (good for what's on and arts and music background)
Sevilla Online
    www.sol.com/index_i.htm (sights, language schools, tours, entertainment, bars and nightlife, festivals, transport etc)

Bookshops Librería Beta at Avenida de la Constitución 9 and 27, and Calle Sierpes 81, has guidebooks and novels in English, and maps. Librería Internacional Vértice, Calle San Fernando 33, has a large range of books in English, French and German. There's also The English Bookshop (☎ 95 465 57 54), east of the centre at Avenida de Eduardo Dato 36.

Laundry Tintorería Roma at Calle Castelar 4 will wash, dry and fold a load of washing in one hour for 1000 ptas. It's open weekdays from 9.30 am to 1.30 pm and 5 to 8.30 pm, Saturday from 10 am to 2 pm.

Medical & Emergency Services There's a first aid post (☎ 95 441 17 12) on Calle de Menéndez Pelayo at the corner of Avenida Málaga. The main general hospital is the Hospital Virgen del Rocío (☎ 95 424 81 81) at Avenida de Manuel Siurot s/n, 1km south of the Parque de María Luisa. For an ambulance call ☎ 95 442 55 65.

The Policía Municipal (☎ 95 461 54 50) are in the Pabellón de Brasil, Paseo de las Delicias 15, at the south end of the Parque María Luisa; the Policía Nacional (☎ 95 422 88 40) are on Plaza Concordia, 900m north of the Catedral.

Dangers & Annoyances Sevilla has a reputation for petty crime against tourists – pickpockets, bag snatchers and the like – so take care.

La Catedral & La Giralda
Sevilla's immense cathedral stands on the site of the main Almohad mosque. After Sevilla fell to the Christians in 1248 the mosque was used as a church until 1401, when in view of its decaying state the church authorities decided to knock it down and start again. 'Let us create such a building that future generations will take us for lunatics,' they agreed – or so legend has it. They certainly got themselves a big church. Some 160m wide and 140m long, it's surpassed in cathedral floor space only by St Peter's (Rome) and St Paul's (London). The building, whose architect is unknown, was completed by 1507 – all Gothic, though work done after its central dome collapsed in 1511 was mostly in Renaissance style.

Exterior The bulky exterior of the cathedral, seen from ground level, gives few hints of the treasures within, apart from the Puerta del Perdón on Calle Alemanes (a survival from the Islamic building) and the one neo-Gothic and two Gothic doorways on Avenida de la Constitución. These last are sculpted with 15th century terracotta reliefs and statues by Lorenzo Mercadante de Bretaña and Pedro Millán.

More impressive from outside is La Giralda, the tower on the cathedral's east side. Over 90m high, La Giralda was the minaret of the mosque, constructed in brick in 1184-98 at the height of Almohad power. Its proportions and decoration and its colour, which changes with the light, make it perhaps Spain's most perfect Islamic building. Each of its four sides is divided

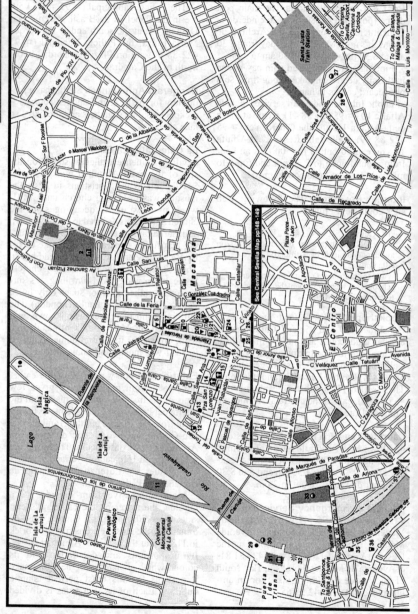

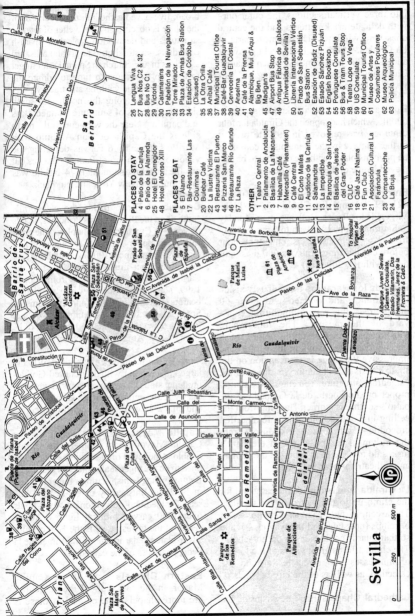

PLACES TO STAY
4 Patio de la Cartuja
6 Patio de la Alameda
25 Hotel El Corregidor
48 Hotel Alfonso XIII

PLACES TO EAT
5 El Álamo
17 Bar-Restaurante Las Columnas
20 Bulebar Café
22 La Ilustre Victima
43 Restaurante El Puerto
44 Pizzería San Marco
46 Restaurante Río Grande
57 La Raza

OTHER
1 Teatro Central
2 Parlamento de Andalucía
3 Basílica de La Macarena
7 Habanilla Café
8 Mercadillo (Fleamarket)
9 Café Central
10 El Corto Maltés
11 Auditorio de la Cartuja
12 Salamandra
13 La Imperdible
14 Parroquia de San Lorenzo
15 Basílica de Jesús del Gran Poder
16 CLIC
18 Café Jazz Naima
19 Fun Club
21 Asociación Cultural La Farándula
23 Compartecoche
24 La Bruja
26 Lengua Viva
27 Bus Nos C2 & 32
28 Bus No C1
29 Victoria
30 Catamaranes
31 Pabellón de la Navegación
32 Torre Mirador
33 Plaza de Armas Bus Station
34 Estación de Córdoba (Disused)
35 La Otra Orilla
36 Aníbal Café
37 Municipal Tourist Office
38 Café-Bar Guadalquivir
39 Cervecería El Costal
40 Anselma
41 Café de la Prensa
42 Alambique, Mui d'Aquí & Big Ben
45 Madigan's
47 Airport Bus Stop
49 Antigua Fábrica de Tabacos (Universidad de Sevilla)
50 Librería Internacional Vértice
51 Prado de San Sebastián Bus Station
52 Estación de Cádiz (Disused)
53 Estadio Sánchez Pizjuán
54 English Bookshop
55 Portuguese Consulate
56 Bus & Tram Tours Stop
58 Teatro Lope de Vega
59 US Consulate
60 Municipal Tourist Office
61 Museo de Artes y Costumbres Populares
62 Museo Arqueológico
63 Policía Municipal

into three vertical sections, the outer ones with delicate brick patterns and the central ones with windows. The topmost parts of La Giralda – from the bell level up – were added in the 16th century, when Spanish Christians were busy 'improving on' surviving Islamic buildings.

The bronze weathervane representing Faith, a symbol of Sevilla known as El Giraldillo, which had topped the Giralda for four centuries, was removed in 1997 to prevent further damage by the elements. A copy is to be put in its place, with the original to be displayed in one of the city's museums.

Entry The entrance to the Catedral (☎ 95 421 49 71) and La Giralda is on Plaza Virgen de los Reyes. Both are open Monday to Saturday from 10.30 am to 6 pm, Sunday from 2 to 5 pm, with last entry one hour before closing time. Entry is 600 ptas (students with ID, 200 ptas).

Patio de los Naranjos Immediately inside the entrance and planted with over 60 orange trees, this was originally the courtyard of the mosque. The font where Muslims performed ablutions before entering the mosque remains in the centre. The impressive Puerta de la Concepción on the south side is a 20th century addition to the cathedral's structure. You enter the Catedral proper by the Puerta de la Granada in the patio's south-east corner. Hanging from the ceiling just outside this entry are a stuffed crocodile – a gift in 1260 to Alfonso X from the Sultan of Egypt – and an elephant's tusk, said to have been found in the Roman amphitheatre at nearby Itálica.

La Giralda Turn left inside the cathedral for the climb up to the belfry of the Giralda. The ascent is quite easy as there's a series of ramps (not stairs) all the way up – made so that guards could ride up on horseback. The climb affords great views of the forests of buttresses and pinnacles around the cathedral, as well as of the city beyond.

Cathedral Chapels Back down inside the broad, five-naved cathedral, the sheer size of the place is obscured by the welter of interior structures and decoration typical of Spanish cathedrals – a storehouse of art and artisanry as rich as in any church in Spain. Don't forget to look up from time to time to admire the marvellous Gothic vaulting and tracery.

The chapels along the north and south sides hold riches of sculpture, stained glass and painting. Near the west end of the north side is the Capilla de San Antonio with Murillo's large 1666 canvas depicting the vision of St Anthony of Padua – thieves cut out the kneeling saint in 1874 but he was later found in New York and put back.

Columbus' Tomb Inside the cathedral's south door, the Puerta de los Príncipes, stands the tomb of Christopher Columbus. The great sailor's remains – or rather, his probable remains, for no one's 100% sure that the real ones didn't get mislaid somewhere in the Caribbean – were brought here from Cuba in 1899. The monument shows four sepulchre-bearers representing the four kingdoms of Spain at the time of Columbus' voyage: Castilla (carrying Granada on the point of its spear), León, Aragón and Navarra.

Coro In the middle of the cathedral is the large *coro* (choir) with 117 carved Gothic-mudéjar stalls. The lower ones have marquetry representations of La Giralda. Vices and sins are depicted on their misericords.

Capilla Mayor East of the Coro is the Capilla Mayor (main chapel). Its Gothic retablo is the jewel of the cathedral and reckoned to be the biggest altarpiece in the world. Begun by the Flemish sculptor Pieter Dancart in 1482 and finished by others in 1564, the sea of gilded and polychromed wood holds over 1000 carved biblical figures. At the centre of the lowest level is the 13th century silver-plated cedar image of the Virgen de la Sede, patroness of the cathedral.

Eastern Chapels East of the Capilla Mayor, in the east wall of the cathedral, are more chapels. The central of these is

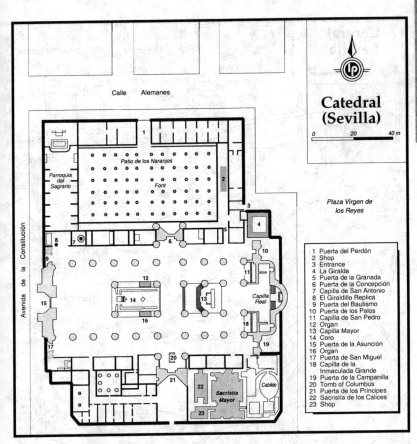

Catedral (Sevilla)

0   20   40 m

Calle   Alemanes

Patio de los Naranjos

Parroquía del Sagrario

Font

Plaza Virgen de los Reyes

Avenida de la Constitución

Capilla Real

Cabildo

Sacristía Mayor

1 Puerta del Perdón
2 Shop
3 Entrance
4 La Giralda
5 Puerta de la Granada
6 Puerta de la Concepción
7 Capilla de San Antonio
8 El Giraldillo Replica
9 Puerta del Bautismo
10 Puerta de los Palos
11 Capilla de San Pedro
12 Organ
13 Capilla Mayor
14 Coro
15 Puerta de la Asunción
16 Organ
17 Puerta de San Miguel
18 Capilla de la Inmaculada Grande
19 Puerta de la Campanilla
20 Tomb of Columbus
21 Puerta de los Príncipes
22 Sacristía de los Cálices
23 Shop

the Capilla Real (Royal Chapel) containing the tombs of two great Castilian kings. The silver and bronze tomb of Fernando III stands in front of the altar (he's mummified inside); the tombs of his son, Alfonso X, and wife, Beatrice of Swabia, are at the sides. The Capilla de San Pedro, immediately north, has a retablo with nine fine Zurbarán paintings of St Peter's life.

Sacristía de los Cálices South of the Capilla Mayor is the entrance to rooms which hold some of the Catedral's main art treasures. The westernmost room is the Sacristía de los Cálices, built in 1509-37. Goya's painting of the Sevilla martyrs *Santas Justa y Rufina* (1817) hangs above the altar. The two potters died at the hands of the Romans in 287 AD. Other works of art from the 16th and 17th century include Zurbarán's *San Juan Bautista* (1640).

Sacristía Mayor This large domed room east of the Sacristía de los Cálices is a plateresque creation of 1528-47: the arch over its portal has carvings of 16th century

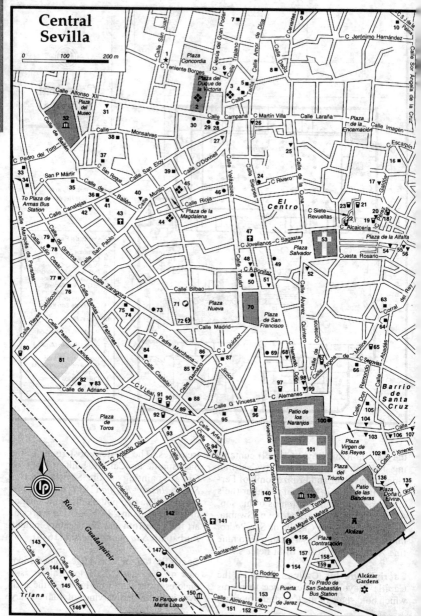

Central Sevilla

0   100   200 m

Plaza Concordia
Plaza del Duque de la Victoria
Plaza del Museo
Plaza de la Encarnación
El Centro
Plaza de la Alfalfa
Plaza Salvador
Cuesta Rosario
Plaza Nueva
Plaza de San Francisco
Barrio de Santa Cruz
Plaza Virgen de los Reyes
Plaza del Triunfo
Patio de los Naranjos
Plaza de Toros
Plaza Doña Elvira
Patio de las Banderas
Alcázar
Alcázar Gardens
Plaza Contratación
Río Guadalquivir
Triana
To Parque de María Luisa
Puerta de Jerez
To Prado de San Sebastián Bus Station
To Plaza de Armas Bus Station

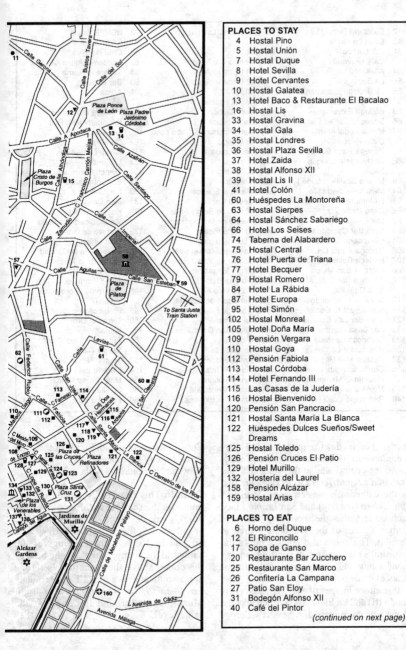

PLACES TO STAY
- 4 Hostal Pino
- 5 Hostal Unión
- 7 Hostal Duque
- 8 Hotel Sevilla
- 9 Hotel Cervantes
- 10 Hostal Galatea
- 13 Hotel Baco & Restaurante El Bacalao
- 16 Hostal Lis
- 33 Hostal Gravina
- 34 Hostal Gala
- 35 Hostal Londres
- 36 Hostal Plaza Sevilla
- 37 Hotel Zaida
- 38 Hostal Alfonso XII
- 39 Hostal Lis II
- 41 Hotel Colón
- 60 Huéspedes La Montoreña
- 63 Hostal Sierpes
- 64 Hostal Sánchez Sabariego
- 66 Hotel Los Seises
- 74 Taberna del Alabardero
- 75 Hostal Central
- 76 Hotel Puerta de Triana
- 77 Hotel Becquer
- 79 Hostal Romero
- 84 Hotel La Rábida
- 87 Hotel Europa
- 95 Hotel Simón
- 102 Hostal Monreal
- 105 Hotel Doña María
- 109 Pensión Vergara
- 110 Hostal Goya
- 112 Pensión Fabiola
- 113 Hostal Córdoba
- 114 Hotel Fernando III
- 115 Las Casas de la Judería
- 116 Hostal Bienvenido
- 120 Pensión San Pancracio
- 121 Hostal Santa María La Blanca
- 122 Huéspedes Dulces Sueños/Sweet Dreams
- 125 Hostal Toledo
- 126 Pensión Cruces El Patio
- 129 Hotel Murillo
- 132 Hostería del Laurel
- 158 Pensión Alcázar
- 159 Hostal Arias

PLACES TO EAT
- 6 Horno del Duque
- 12 El Rinconcillo
- 17 Sopa de Ganso
- 20 Restaurante Bar Zucchero
- 25 Restaurante San Marco
- 26 Confitería La Campana
- 27 Patio San Eloy
- 31 Bodegón Alfonso XII
- 40 Café del Pintor

(continued on next page)

42	Cafetería Donald	157	Cafetería Las Lapas	73	RENFE Office
48	Casa La Viuda			78	Cibercenter
51	Bar Laredo		**OTHER**	80	Café Isbiliyya
52	Café Universal	1	Policía Nacional	82	Academia Atlántika
54	Alfalfa 10	2	El Corte Inglés	88	Tintorería Roma
55	La Bodega	3	El Corte Inglés	90	Bar Populus
56	La Bodega Extremeña	11	CLIC	91	Arena
57	La Trastienda	14	Quitapesares	92	A3
59	Bodega Extremeña	15	Café Lisboa	96	Hijos de E Morales
68	Bodegón El Pez Espada	18	La Rebótica	97	P Flaherty Irish Pub
81	Mercado del Arenal	19	Bare Nostrum & Cabo Loco	100	La Giralda
83	Casa Pepe-Hillo	21	El Mundo	101	Catedral
85	Bodega Paco Góngora	22	Bar Europa	111	Italian Consulate
86	Restaurante Enrique	23	Sur	123	El Tamboril
	Becerra	24	Z Zulategui	124	French Consulate
89	Mesón Sevilla Jabugo I	28	Cortefiel	128	Bar Entrecalles
93	Mesón del Serranito	29	Marks & Spencer	130	Los Gallos
94	La Infanta	30	Sevilla Rock	131	Irish Consulate
98	Casa Robles	32	Museo de Bellas Artes	134	Hospital de los
99	Las Escobas	43	Iglesia de la Magdalena		Venerables Sacerdotes
103	Café-Bar Campanario	44	El Corte Inglés	139	Archivo de Indias
104	Cervecería Giralda	45	El Corte Inglés	140	Post Office
106	Bodega Santa Cruz	46	La Teatral (ticket agency)	141	Hospital de la Caridad
107	Bodega Belmonte	47	Capilla de San José	142	Teatro de la Maestranza
108	Pizzería San Marco	49	Virgin Megastore &	144	Café La Pavana
117	Altamira Bar-Café; Alta-		Librería Beta	147	Bus & Tram Tours Stop
	Mira Café Bar	50	Halcón Viajes	148	Centro de Información
118	Bar Casa Fernando	53	Parroquia del Salvador		Juvenil
119	Restaurant El Cordobés	58	Casa de Pilatos	149	Embarcadero (boats)
127	Café Bar Las Teresas	61	La Carbonería	150	Torre del Oro
133	Bar Casa Román	62	Australian Consulate	151	Iberia
135	El Rincón de Pepe	65	L'Image	152	Autos Mínguez, Ata &
136	Restaurant La Cueva	67	La Subasta &		Sevilla Car
137	Restaurante Giralda		Antigüedades	153	Triana Rent A Car
138	Corral del Agua	69	Librería Beta	154	Librería Beta
143	Pizzería O Mamma Mia	70	Ayuntamiento	155	Main Tourist Office
145	Mex-Rock	71	British Consulate	156	Sevilla Mágica
146	Ristorante Cosa Nostra	72	American Express	160	First Aid Post

foods. Pedro de Campaña's 1547 *Descendimiento* (Descent from the Cross), above the central altar at the south end, and Zurbarán's *Santa Teresa* to its right, are two of the cathedral's masterpieces. Murillo's *San Isidoro* (reading) and *San Leandro* face each other across the room (the pair were leading figures of the Visigothic church in Sevilla). This room also holds some of the cathedral's most important treasures, among them a huge 475kg silver *custodia* (monstrance) made in the 1580s by Juan de Arfe; 17th century images of San Fernando (Fernando III) and La Inmaculada which, like the monstrance, are carried in Sevilla's Corpus

Christi processions; and, in one of the glass cases, the city keys handed over to Fernando III when he captured Sevilla in 1248.

Cabildo This beautifully domed chapter house, in the south-east corner of the Catedral, was designed by Hernán Ruiz, architect of the Giralda belfry, and created in 1558-92 for meetings of the cathedral hierarchy, to the . At the base of the dome, above the archbishop's throne at the south end, is a Murillo masterpiece, *La Inmaculada*. There are also eight Murillo saints around the dome at the same level.

THE ALCÁZAR

South of the Catedral across Plaza del Triunfo, the Alcázar (Fortress) is more palace than castle. It's an intriguing and beautiful place that shouldn't be missed, not least for its associations with the lives and loves of several famous rulers, above all the extraordinary Pedro I (1350-69), who was known either as El Cruel or as El Justiciero – the Justice-Dispenser – depending which side you were on.

History The Alcázar was founded as a fort for the Cordoban governors of Sevilla in 913. As Sevilla prospered as a taifa capital in the 11th century, its rulers built themselves a palace called Al-Muwarak (The Blessed) in what's now the western part of the Alcázar. East of this, the 12th century Almohad rulers added another palace around the Patio del Crucero. When Sevilla fell to the Christians in 1248, Fernando III moved into the Alcázar, dying here in 1252. Several later Christian monarchs used the Alcázar as their main residence. Fernando's son Alfonso X replaced much of the Almohad palace with a Gothic one, now called the Salones de Carlos V. In 1364-66 Pedro I created the Alcázar's crown jewel, the sumptuous mudéjar palace known as the Palacio de Don Pedro, partly on the site of the old Al-Muwarak palace.

The whole complex was further adapted and expanded by several later rulers, who also created the Alcázar's beautiful gardens. The repeated modifications make the Alcázar rather complicated to understand but in the end only add to its fascination. As recently as 1995 the Alcázar was used for the wedding feast of the Infanta Elena, daughter of King Juan Carlos I, after her marriage in Sevilla's Catedral.

Information The entrance is the Puerta del León at the southern corner of Plaza del Triunfo. The Alcázar (☎ 95 422 71 63) is open Tuesday to Saturday from 9.30 am to 7 pm (to 5 pm from October to March), Sunday and holidays from 9.30 am to 5 pm (to 1.30 pm from October to March). Entry is 600 ptas (free for students).

Patio del León This was the garrison yard of the original Al-Muwarak palace. Off its south-east corner is the Sala de la Justicia, with beautiful mudéjar plasterwork and an artesonado ceiling – built in the 1340s by Christian king Alfonso XI, who disported here with his mistress Leonor de Guzmán, reputedly the most beautiful woman in Spain. Alfonso's sexual exploits left his heir Pedro I with five illegitimate half-brothers and a severe case of sibling rivalry. Pedro is said to have had a dozen relatives and friends murdered in his efforts to stay on the throne. One of the half-brothers, Don Fadrique, met his maker right here in the Sala de la Justicia.

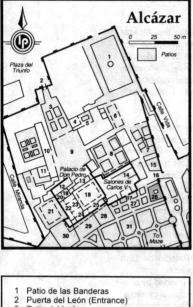

Alcázar

0 25 50 m

Patios

Plaza del Triunfo

Calle Vida

Palacio de Don Pedro

Salones de Carlos V

Calle Miranda

To Maze

1   Patio de las Banderas
2   Puerta del León (Entrance)
3   Patio del León
4   Sala de la Justicia
5   Patio del Yeso
6   Apeadero
7   Jardín de la Alcabilla
8   Patio del Crucero
9   Patio de la Montería
10 Salón del Almirante
11 Sala de Audiencias
12 Cuarto del Príncipe
13 Cámara Regia
14 Salón de Tapices
15 Jardín del Chorrón
16 Puerta del Palacio de los Duques de Arcos
17 Baños de Doña María de Padilla (Entrance)
18 Patio de las Doncellas
19 Patio de las Muñecas
20 Cuarto del Techo de los Reyes Católicos
21 Jardín del Príncipe
22 Salón del Techo de Felipe II
23 Salón de Embajadores
24 Sala de Infantes
25 Salón del Techo de Carlos V
26 Estanque de Mercurio
27 Jardín de las Danzas
28 Jardín de Troya
29 Jardín de las Galeras
30 Jardín de las Flores
31 Jardín de las Damas

The room gives on to the pretty Patio del Yeso, one of the few surviving parts of the 12th century Almohad palace.

Patio de la Montería The rooms on the west side of this courtyard were part of the original Casa de la Contratación founded by the Catholic Monarchs in 1503. The Salón del Almirante has 19th and 20th century paintings showing historical events associated with Sevilla. The Sala de Audiencias is hung with the shields of admirals of the Spanish fleet and the 16th century Virgen del Buen Aire by Alejo Fernández, the earliest known painting on the subject of the discovery of the Americas. Columbus, Fernando El Católico, Carlos I, Amerigo Vespucci and American Indians can all be seen sheltered beneath the cloak of the Virgin in her role as protector of sailors. This room also contains a model of Columbus' ship the *Santa María*.

Patio del Crucero The passage off the Patio de la Montería's east side gives on to this garden, which was originally the upper level of the central patio of the 12th century Almohad palace. At first it consisted only of walkways along the four sides and two cross-walkways which met in the middle. Below grew orange trees, whose fruit could be plucked at hand height by the lucky folk strolling along the upper walkways. The whole lower level had to be built over in the 18th century after earthquake damage.

Pedro I, ever a man of extremes and notwithstanding the fact that he was married to a French princess, loved to distraction a woman called María de Padilla to whom he gave the Salones de Carlos V, on the south side of this patio, to live in. María must have liked strolling around picking oranges because the patio is also known as the Patio de María de Padilla.

Palacio de Don Pedro Whatever else Pedro I may have done, posterity owes him a big thankyou for creating this palace, which rivals Granada's Alhambra in the magnificence of its design and decoration. The entrance is on the south side of the Patio de la Montería.

Though (or perhaps because) he couldn't trust many of his fellow 'Christians' from closer to home, Pedro did maintain a long-standing alliance with the Muslim Emir of Granada, Mohammed V, the man responsible for much of the decoration of the Alhambra's Palacio Nazaríes. So when, in 1364, Pedro decided to build himself a new palace in the Alcázar, Mohammed sent along many of his best artisans to help. These were joined by Jews and Muslims from Toledo, and others, mainly Muslim, from Sevilla. Their work not only represented the best of contemporary architecture and design but also drew on the earlier traditions of the Almohads and caliphal Córdoba. What resulted is a unique synthesis of Iberian Muslim art.

Inscriptions on the palace's relatively austere façade, on the Patio de la Montería, encapsulate the unusual nature of the whole enterprise. While one records that the building's creator was 'the very high, noble and conquering Don Pedro, by the grace of God king of Castilla and León', another tells us repeatedly that 'There is no conqueror but Allah'.

From the vestibule, the left-hand passage leads to the wonderful **Patio de las Doncellas**, surrounded by beautiful arches and with some exquisite plasterwork and tiling. The doors at the two ends are among the finest ever made by Toledo's carpenters. The upper galleries were added in 1540.

The Alcázar, more palace than castle, is an intriguing place that shouldn't be missed. *(photograph by Bethune Carmichael)*

The **Cámara Regia** on the north side of the patio has two rooms with incredibly beautiful ceilings and more wonderful plaster and tilework. The rear room was probably the monarch's summer bedroom.

From here you can move west into the small **Patio de las Muñecas**, the heart of the palace's private quarters, with delicate Granada-style decoration on its lowest level. The mezzanine and top gallery were added in the 19th century for Queen Isabel II, using plasterwork brought from the Alhambra. The **Cuarto del Príncipe** to the north has superb ceilings and was probably the queen's bedroom.

The spectacular **Salón de Embajadores** (Hall of Ambassadors), on the west side of the Patio de las Doncellas, was the throne room of Pedro I's palace – as it had been, in earlier form, of the Al-Muwarak palace. Its fabulous wooden dome of multiple star patterns, symbolising the universe, was added in 1427. The dome's shape gives the room the alternative name Sala de la Media Naranja (Hall of the Half Orange). The coloured plasterwork is equally magnificent. The door arches, heavily reminiscent of the ruined 10th century Medina Azahara palace near Córdoba, were retained by Pedro from the Al-Muwarak building. On the west side the beautiful **Arco de Pavones** – named after its peacock motifs – leads into the **Salón del Techo de Felipe II**, with a Renaissance ceiling (1589-91). The **Salón del Techo de Carlos V** along the south side of the Patio de las Doncellas has another fine ceiling (1540s) and used to be the palace chapel.

Salones de Carlos V Reached by a staircase from the southeast corner of the Patio de las Doncellas, these are the much-remodelled rooms of the 13th century palace built by Alfonso X. It was here that Alfonso's intellectual court gathered and, a century later, Pedro I installed his mistress María de Padilla. The Salón de Tapices or Sala Grande has a collection of huge tapestries showing Carlos I's 1535 conquest of Tunis from the Turkish-backed pirate Barbarossa.

Gardens From the Salones de Carlos V you can make your way out into the Alcázar's large gardens, the perfect place to ease your body and brain after some intensive sightseeing. The gardens (jardines) in front of the Salones de Carlos V and Palacio de Don Pedro go back to Muslim times but were mostly brought to their present form in the 16th and 17th centuries, while those to the east, beyond a long Almohad wall, are 20th century creations.

Immediately in front of the Salones de Carlos V and Palacio de Don Pedro is a series of small linked gardens, some with pools and fountains. From one, the Jardín de las Danzas, a passage runs beneath the Salones de Carlos V to the so-called Baños de Doña María de Padilla. Here you can see the vaults beneath the Patio del Crucero and a grotto which replaced that patio's pool – in which, we imagine, María de Padilla liked to bathe.

Farther out in the old gardens there's a maze (laberinto). From the new gardens you can return to the corner of the Salones de Carlos V, from where a passage leads north to the Apeadero, built in 1607-09 as an entrance hall for the palace and now housing a collection of carriages. From here you leave the Alcázar via the Patio de las Banderas.

Archivo de Indias

This building on the west side of Plaza del Triunfo has been, since 1785, the main archive on Spain's American empire. Its 8km of shelves hold 80 million pages of documents dating from 1492 through to the end of the empire in the 19th century. Most of the archive can only be consulted with special permission but there are rotating displays of fascinating maps and documents, often including manuscripts written by Columbus or Cervantes or conquistadors such as Cortés or Pizarro. Entry to the Archivo de Indias (☎ 95 421 12 34) is free, and the archive is open Monday to Friday from 10 am to 1 pm. The 16th century building, which was designed by Juan de Herrera, was originally Sevilla's Lonja (Exchange) for commerce with the Americas.

Barrio de Santa Cruz

This area immediately east of the Catedral and Alcázar was Sevilla's medieval Judería (Jewish quarter). Today it is a tangle of quaint winding streets and lovely plazas with flowers and orange trees. If you're not staying in the area, wander through it anyway: there are some good places to stop off for food or drink as you go.

The Judería, which extended to just east of Calle Santa María La Blanca, came into existence after the Reconquista and was emptied after a pogrom in 1391. Its most characteristic plaza is **Plaza de Santa Cruz**, which has a central cross that was made in 1692. The cross is one of the finest examples of Sevilla wrought iron work. **Plaza Doña Elvira** is another quaint spot, with tiled benches beneath the orange trees.

On Plaza de los Venerables is the **Hospital de los Venerables Sacerdotes** (☎ 95 456 26 96). Used from its inception in the 17th century until the 1960s as a residence for aged priests, it's now open most of the year for guided visits (600 ptas) daily from 10 am to 2 pm and 4 to 8 pm. You'll visit the lovely central courtyard as well as the old living quarters, several art exhibition rooms (one with an interesting collection of

Sevilla prints), and the church with murals by Juan de Valdés Leal and fine sculptures by Pedro Roldán.

El Centro

The real centre of Sevilla stretches north of the Catedral. It's a densely packed zone of narrow, crooked streets, broken up here and there by plazas around which the life of the city has revolved for aeons.

Plaza de San Francisco & Calle Sierpes
Site of a market in Muslim times, Plaza de San Francisco has been Sevilla's main public square since the 16th century. Once the scene of Inquisition burnings, today it's the place where the city's upper echelons sit on special viewing stands to watch the Semana Santa processions.

The **Ayuntamiento** (City Hall) on the west side is a building of two distinct characters: its southern end is encrusted with lovely Renaissance carving from the 1520s and 1530s, while its northern end, a 19th century extension, is bare.

Pedestrianised Calle Sierpes, which heads north from the plaza, is Sevilla's fanciest shopping street. Take a few steps off Sierpes along Calle Jovellanos to the **Capilla de San José** (open for mass daily at 8 pm, and Monday to Saturday at 9, 10 and 11 am and noon). This small 18th century chapel, created by the city's carpenters' guild, is a world unto itself of intense, almost suffocating baroque ornamentation. The main altarpiece and those either side of it are absolute riots of gilded, curving, carved wood, with cherubim popping out all over the place.

Plaza Salvador A couple of blocks northeast of Plaza de San Francisco, this was the main forum of Roman Hispalis. The plaza is dominated by the Parroquia del Salvador, a big red baroque church built in 1674-1712 on the site of the Muslim city's first main mosque. Inside are three huge and profuse baroque retablos; on the north side, the mosque's small patio remains, with orange trees, font, and a few half-buried Roman columns. The church is open daily from 6.30 to 9 pm.

Plaza de la Alfalfa Some 200m east of Plaza Salvador, this was once the site of the Muslim silk exchange and a later medieval market. It's an animated place with good bars, though it can be rather traffic-infested.

Casa de Pilatos Some 300m east of Plaza de la Alfalfa, on Plaza de Pilatos, this is the finest of Sevilla's noble mansions, still occupied by the ducal Medinaceli family. The building is a mixture of mudéjar, Gothic and Renaissance architecture and decoration, with some beautiful tilework and artesonado ceilings, though the overall effect is similar to that of the Alcázar.

There are rival explanations for the building's name (Pilate's House). One is that its 16th century creator, Don Fadrique Enríquez de Ribera, was trying to imitate Pontius Pilate's palace in Jerusalem, to which city he had made a pilgrimage. Another is that the house served as the first station – representing Christ's appearance before Pilate – of a *Via Crucis* (Way of the Cross), in which penitents would symbolically retrace Christ's steps to the crucifixion.

The Casa de Pilatos (☎ 95 422 52 98) is open daily from 9 am to 7 pm and entry is 500 ptas for each of the two floors – if time or money are short, skip the top floor.

A plan on your ticket helps you find your way round. From the **Apeadero**, a courtyard for boarding and alighting from carriages, you pass into the **Patio Principal** which has lots of wonderful, colourful 16th century tiles, intricate mudéjar plasterwork and a Renaissance fountain. In each corner stands a classical statue: the armless Athene, on the far side from the entrance, is Greek, from around the 4th century BC; the others are Roman. Around the walls are busts of Roman historical and mythical figures plus King Carlos I of Spain.

The names of the rooms off the Patio Principal recall the mansion's supposed connection with Pontius Pilate's palace. The **Descanso de los Jueces** (Judges' Retiring Room), **Salón Pretorio** (Palace Hall) and **Gabinete de Pilatos** (Pilate's Study) all have fine artesonado ceilings. Beyond the Salón Pretorio are the **Zaquizami**, a corridor with Roman sculptures and inscriptions on display, and the **Jardín Chico** (Small Garden). The Gabinete de Pilatos leads into the leafy **Jardín Grande** (Big Garden), with Italian-style Renaissance loggias on three of its sides.

The **staircase** leading from the Patio Principal to the upper floor has the most magnificent tiles in the building, with a great golden artesonado dome above. Visits to the **upper floor** itself, partly inhabited by the Medinacelis, are accompanied by a rather hurried guide. Of interest are the several centuries' worth of Medinaceli portraits and a small Goya painting of a bullfight, in the Salón Oviedo.

Along the River
A short walk west from Avenida de la Constitución brings you to the bank of the Río Guadalquivir, a pleasant place for a stroll.

Torre del Oro This 13th century Almohad watchtower, on the riverbank just north of the Puente de San Telmo, once crowned a corner of the city walls that stretched here from the Alcázar. It was supposedly originally covered in golden tiles, hence its name. Inside is a small, crowded maritime museum, open Tuesday to Friday from 10 am to 2 pm, Saturday and Sunday from 11 am to 2 pm (100 ptas).

Hospital de la Caridad A block back from the river at Calle Temprado 3, this hospice for the elderly was founded in the 17th century by Miguel de Mañara who, legend has it, was a notorious libertine who changed his ways after experiencing a vision of his own funeral procession. The interest lies in the hospital's church for which in the 1670s Mañara commissioned a collection of top-class Sevillan art and sculpture on the theme of death and redemption, by Valdés Leal, Murillo and Pedro Roldán. The Hospital de la Caridad (☎ 95 422 32 32) is open Monday to Saturday from 9 am to 1.30 pm and 3.30 to 6.30 pm, Sunday and holidays from 10 am to 1 pm. Entry is 400 ptas.

The two masterworks of Valdés Leal, chillingly illustrating the futility of worldly success in the face of death, are at the west end of the church. In *Finis Gloriae Mundi*, above the door by which you enter, a bishop, a king and a knight of Calatrava are devoured in their coffins by worms and cockroaches, while Christ's hand weighs their virtues and their sins (represented by animals) in the balance. *In Ictu Oculi* (In the Blink of an Eye), on the opposite wall, shows a skeletal Death figure extinguishing the candle of life while trampling symbols of power, glory, wealth and knowledge. Also on this side of the church are *San Juan de Dios* (St John of God, caring for an invalid) and *Moises Haciendo Brotar el Agua de la Roca* (Moses Drawing Water from the Rock), two of eight large Murillo canvases painted for this church on themes of compassion and mercy – ways of transcending death. (Only four of the eight remain, the others having been looted by Napoleonic troops.) To the left of the high altar a flight of steps descends to the crypt in which Miguel de Mañara is buried.

The sculpture on the high altar illustrates the ultimate act of compassion – the burial of the dead (in this case Christ). The tableau, with its strong sense of movement, is Pedro Roldán's masterpiece. It was polychromed (coloured) by Valdés Leal.

On the south side of the church are Murillo's *La Multiplicación de Panes y Peces* (The Miracle of the Loaves and Fishes) and *Santa Isabel de Húngria* (St Isabel of Hungary, caring for the diseased and poor), plus another fine Roldán sculpture, of Christ praying before being nailed to the cross.

Plaza de Toros de la Real Maestranza
Sevilla's bullring (☎ 95 422 45 77) on Paseo de Cristóbal Colón is one of the most handsome and important in the country, and probably the oldest (building began in 1758). It was in this ring and the one at Ronda in Málaga province that bullfighting on foot took off in the 18th century. The site had originally been a practice ground for Sevilla's Real Maestranza de Caballería (Royal Cavalry Masterhood) – hence its name today.

You can visit the ring and its museum, and peep into its mini-hospital for bullfighters who have come off second best, daily from 10 am to 1.30 pm, plus Monday to Friday (except holidays) from 4 to 5.30 pm. The interesting visits are guided, in English and Spanish, and happen every 20 minutes (300 ptas). For more on bullfights, see the Spectator Sport sections in this chapter and the special section on Bullfighting.

Iglesia de la Magdalena A jewel among Sevilla's many baroque churches stands farther north, on Calle San Pablo. Built in 1691-1709, the Iglesia de la Magdalena has a fine crucifixion sculpture of 1612, *El Cristo del Calvario* by Francisco de Ocampo, in the chapel to the right of the main altar, and two paintings by Zurbarán in the Capilla Sacramental.

The church is the home of Hermandad de la Quinta Angustia, whose 17th century *Descendimiento* tableau, depicting the taking down of Jesus from the cross, is borne through Sevilla's streets during Semana Santa. This can usually be seen in the chapel immediately on the left as you enter the church: the Christ is attributed to Pedro Roldán. The church is open at service times – normally 8 to 11 am and 6.30 to 9 pm.

Museo de Bellas Artes As Spain's leading city for most of the 16th and 17th centuries, Sevilla played an important role in the country's artistic golden age, which ran from roughly the late 16th to the late 17th centuries. The Fine Arts Museum (☎ 95 422 07 90), housed in the beautiful former Convento de la Merced at Plaza del Museo 9, does full justice to this period, and a visit is a big help to understanding the context of much of the other art you see in Sevilla and Andalucía.

The 17th century Sevillan masters Murillo, Zurbarán and Valdés Leal are particularly well represented, but the museum also holds interesting Sevillan antecedents to the golden age and some works by great artists who worked elsewhere such as El Greco and José de Ribera. It's open Tuesday from 3 to 8 pm, Wednesday to Saturday from 9 am to 8 pm, Sunday from 9 am to 3 pm, and is free for EU citizens with passport or identity card (250 ptas for others).

Room I exemplifies the 15th century beginnings of the Sevillan school: the outstanding exhibits are Pedro Millán's terracotta sculptures, displaying a realism rare in Spanish art before that time.

Room II was the dining hall of the convent and displays Renaissance work from Flanders, Sevilla and elsewhere, including El Greco's piercing portrait of his son Jorge Manuel, Alejo Fernández's *La Anunciación*, and sculptures by Pedro Torrigiano. Torrigiano, an Italian who came to Sevilla from Florence in 1522, was the major artistic figure of the early Renaissance

in Sevilla. His lifesize *San Jerónimo Penitente*, with its expressive head and finely studied anatomy, was very influential.

Room III exhibits Sevillan Renaissance retablos and early 17th century baroque Sevillan paintings – including Velázquez's portrait of Don Cristóbal Suárez de Ribera and Alonso Cano's *San Francisco de Borja*. Cano's striking *Las Ánimas del Purgatorio* (Souls in Purgatory) is in the corner between rooms III and IV.

In room IV, devoted mainly to Mannerism – a rather stiff, idealised transition between Renaissance and baroque art – Alonso Vázquez's large *Sagrada Cena* (Last Supper) of 1588 stands out. From here you move through the convent's beautiful main cloister to room V, the convent church, which is hung with paintings by masters of Sevillan baroque. Here you'll see Zurbarán's masterpiece, the *Apoteosis de Santo Tomás de Aquinas*, but the room is dominated by Murillo, whose *Inmaculada Concepción Grande*, depicting the Virgin borne aloft by cherubim, displays all the curving, twisting

JOHN NOBLE

Columbus received by the Catholic Monarchs in Barcelona: relief sculpture (1893) by Antonio Susillo in the Museo de Belles Artes, Sevilla

movement that is central to baroque art. This painting hangs as part of the main retablo at the head of the church, along with other Murillo works which were, like it, originally painted for other churches.

Upstairs, the most arresting images in room VI are Ribera's very Spanish-looking *Santiago Apóstol* (St James the Apostle) and Zurbarán's small *Cristo Crucificado Expirante* (Christ Crucified, Expiring), which is perhaps the most disturbing picture in the whole museum. Room VII is devoted to Murillo and his disciples, room VIII to Valdés Leal, and room IX to baroque art from elsewhere in Europe.

Room X is all Zurbarán: the *Cristo Crucificado* is one of his greatest achievements. In one of several monastic scenes, the contrast he draws between the worldly Pope Urban II and the ascetic St Bruno in *Visita de San Bruno a Urbano II* is masterly.

Room XI displays Sevillan and Spanish painting of the 18th century, a time when Sevilla (and Spain) had lost its creative verve. Rooms XII to XIV are given over to 19th and 20th century painting, mainly Sevillan, with the works of the Romantic Antonio María Esquivel and the historical painter Eddo Cano among the most interesting.

South of the Centre
Antigua Fábrica de Tabacos Sevilla's massive former tobacco factory on Calle San Fernando – workplace of Bizet's operatic heroine Carmen – was built in the 18th century and served its original purpose until the mid-20th century. For a long time a cornerstone of the city's economy, the factory had its own jail, stables for 400 mules, 21 fountains, 24 patios and even a nursery, since most of its workers were women. Measuring 250 by 180m, it covers a larger area than any building in Spain except El Escorial.

The old tobacco factory is now part of the Universidad de Sevilla and you can wander round it daily between 9 am and 9 pm.

Neoclassical in style, it's an impressive, if rather gloomy building. The most curious feature is the main portal which sports carvings which are concerned with the theme of the discovery of the Americas, the original source of tobacco – among them Christopher Columbus (Cristóbal Colón), Hernán Cortés (conqueror of the Aztecs) and two American Indians – one of them smoking a pipe. At the top of the portal is Fame blowing a trumpet.

Parque de María Luisa & Plaza de España A large area south of the Fábrica de Tabacos was transformed for the 1929 Exposición Iberoamericana. It's spattered with all sorts of fancy and funny buildings, many of them harking back to Sevilla's eras of past glory. In its midst, the Parque de María Luisa is a fine respite from the hustle of the city, with its maze of paths, flowers, fountains, shaded lawns and 3500 trees. It's open daily from 8 am to 10 pm.

Facing the north-east side of the park across Avenida de Isabel la Católica, Plaza de España is one of the city's favourite relaxation spots, with fountains and minicanals. Around it is the most grandiose of the 1929 buildings, a semicircular brick and tile confection featuring Sevilla tilework at its gaudiest, with a map and historical scene for each of Spain's provinces.

On Plaza de América at the south end of the park are a large flock of white pigeons (they will clamber all over you if you buy a 200-ptas bag of seed from vendors), and two interesting museums. Among the highlights of the big **Museo Arqueológico** (☎ 95 423 24 01) are a room of gold jewellery from the mysterious Tartessos culture and fine collections of Iberian animal sculptures and beautiful Roman mosaics. Among large quantities of Roman sculpture are, in room XX, sculptures of the two emperors from Itálica near Sevilla, Hadrian (Adriano) and Trajan (Trajano, with the top half of his head missing). The Museo Arqueológico is open Tuesday from 3 to 8 pm, Wednesday to Saturday from 9 am to 8 pm, Sunday and holidays from 9 am to 2.30 pm. Tuesday mornings are for group visits only. Entry is free with an EU passport or identity card and for students (250 ptas otherwise).

Facing the Museo Arqueológico is the **Museo de Artes y Costumbres Populares** (☎ 95 423 25 76), in the 1929 exhibition's mudéjar pavilion, which appeared as an Arab palace in the film *Lawrence of Arabia*. Its collection includes mock-up workshops of several local crafts (among them guitar-making, ceramics and wrought iron), and some beautiful old bullfight and feria costumes. Hours and prices are the same as the Museo Arqueológico's.

North of the Centre

The more working-class area north of Calle Alfonso XII and Plaza Ponce de León is an interesting contrast to the city centre. The city's most bustling fleamarket (*mercadillo*, see Things to Buy) is to be found up here.

Alameda de Hércules This dusty 350m-long paseo was created in the 1570s by the draining of a marsh. Two columns from a ruined Roman temple elsewhere in the city were erected at its south end and topped with statues of Hercules and Julius Caesar by Diego de Pesquera.

Planted with avenues of *álamo* (poplar) trees – hence the name – the Alameda became a fashionable meeting place in the 17th century. By the 1980s, however, the area was little more than a red light zone. But it has since come back up in the world and is now one of the city's busiest nightlife areas – still with a raffish touch.

Basílica de Jesús del Gran Poder This church behind a large baroque portal in the corner of Plaza de San Lorenzo was built in the 1960s, but houses, above its main altar, a famous and far older sculpture of a cross-bearing Christ (after which it is named). This almost wizened image, sculpted in 1620 by Juan de Mesa, inspires much devotion among sevillanos and takes an honoured place in the Semana Santa processions. On either side of the altar are a sculpture of St John the Evangelist, also by de la Mesa, and an anonymous *Virgen del Mayor Dolor* (Virgin of the Deepest Grief) of the 18th century or earlier. The church is

open daily from 8 am to 1.30 pm and 6 to 9 pm.

Basílica de la Macarena & Around If you're not in Sevilla for Semana Santa, you can get an inkling of what it's about at the Basílica de la Macarena (☎ 95 437 01 95) at Calle Bécquer 1, off Calle S. Luis, open daily from 9 am to 1 pm and 5 to 9 pm. This 1940s church contains the most adored religious image in Sevilla, the *Virgen de la Esperanza* (Hope), believed to have been created by an unknown sculptor in the mid-17th century. Commonly known just as La Macarena, she is patron of bullfighters and the city's supreme representation of the grieving, yet hoping, mother of Christ. She stands in appropriate splendour behind the main altarpiece, adorned with a golden crown, lavish vestments and five diamond and emerald brooches donated by a famous early 20th century matador, Joselito El Gallo.

In front of and below La Macarena stands a beautiful 1654 statue of *El Cristo de la Sentencia* by Felipe Morales. Both statues are carried from the church at midnight at the start of every Good Friday: their journey through the city the climax of Semana Santa in Sevilla. Their return to the church around 1.30 pm is attended by enormous crowds.

In the church's museum – open daily from 9.30 am to 1 pm and 5 to 8 pm (300 ptas) – are displayed rich vestments of La Macarena and the lavish Semana Santa *pasos* on which both images are carried. The paso of El Cristo de la Sentencia is in fact a tableau of the scene of Pontius Pilate washing his hands; that of La Macarena bears 90 silver candlesticks.

Bus Nos C1, C2, C3 and C4 (see Getting Around) stop near the Basílica de la Macarena, on Calle de Resolana. East of the church extends the longest surviving stretch of Sevilla's 12th century **Almohad walls**. On the far side of a small park across the road is the **Parlamento de Andalucía**, Andalucía's regional parliament (not generally open to visitors).

(continued on page 165)

bullfighting

...rior permiso y si el tiempo no lo impide, se picarán, banderillearán y serán muertas a estoque...

...AGNIFICOS Y BRAVOS TOROS

...amosa ganadería de **D. GERMAN GERVAS DIEZ** de Mad...

divisa: Encarnada, azul y caña. Señal: Brincadas en ambas orejas, para los grandes ESPADAS:

Previous page: Poster art, Mijas *(photograph by Gerry Reilly)*

The killing of a fighting bull is a ritual which involves several players and many skillful manoeuvres. First, the peones (junior bullfighters) distract the animal with great capes to bring it to the desired position. Then, bandilleros attempt to plunge their sharp prods into the beast before the matador returns to the ring to wield his heavy silk cape, performing several passes until finally he moves in for the kill with his sword.

(All photographs on this page by Mark Armstrong)

A PERFORMANCE TO DIE FOR

The *corrida* (bullfight) is a spectacle and pageant with a long history and many rules. It is not, as many would suggest, simply a ghoulish alternative to the slaughterhouse. Many people feel ill at the sight of the kill, and the preceding few minutes' torture is cruel, but aficionados will say that fighting bulls have been bred for conflict and that prior to the fateful day they are treated like kings. The bull is better off, it is said, dying at the hands of a matador (killer) than in the *matadero* (abattoir). The corrida is about many things – a direct confrontation with death, bravery, skill, performance. Although many Spaniards themselves consider it a cruel and 'uncivilised' activity (few would call it a sport), there is no doubting its popularity.

Contests of strength, skill and bravery between man and beast are no recent phenomenon. The ancient Persians and Etruscans liked a good bullfight, and the Romans probably staged Spain's first bullfights. *La lidia*, as the modern art of bullfighting on foot is known, took off in an organised fashion in Spain in the mid-18th century. (Andalucía was one of its birthplaces and has been one of its hotbeds ever since.) Before then, bullfighting was performed from horseback as a kind of cavalry training-cum-sport for the gentry. (Horseback bullfights, known as *corridas de rejones*, still crop up here and there – and the horsemanship can be enthralling.)

Bred for conflict, the *toro bravo*, or fighting bull, is nevertheless treated like a king until the final fatal day.

Three generations of the Romero family from Ronda in Málaga province are credited with having established most of the basics of bullfighting on foot. In the 1830s King Fernando VII appointed Pedro Romero, the third of the line, director of the Escuela de Tauromaquia de Sevilla, the country's first college for bullfighters. It was around this time, too, that breeders succeeded in creating the first reliable breeds of *toro bravo* or fighting bull.

El Matador & La Cuadrilla

Only champion matadors make good money, and some actually make a loss. The matador must pay a *cuadrilla* (supporting team), pay for the right to fight a bull, and rent or buy an outfit and equipment.

If you see a major fight, you will notice the cuadrilla is made up of quite a few people. Firstly, there are several *peones*, junior *toreros* (bullfighters) under the orders of the matador. The peones come out to distract the bull with great capes, manoeuvre him into the desired position, and so on. Then come the *banderilleros*. At a given moment one or two banderilleros race towards the bull and attempt to plunge a pair of colourfully decorated *banderillas* (short prods with harpoon-style ends) high into the withers of the bull. This is intended to goad the animal into action. The horseback *picadores* play a different role. Charged by the bull, which tries to upend or eviscerate the horse, the picador shoves a lance into the withers in an attempt to weaken the bull. Animal-lovers will take small consolation from the fact that, since the 19th century, the horses have been protected by heavy padding that bulls rarely manage to penetrate.

Then there is the matador. The matador's dress could be that of a flamenco dancer. At its simplest, in country fiestas, it is generally a straightforward combination of black trousers or tights, white shirt and black vest. At its most extravagant, the *traje de luces* (suit of lights) can be an extraordinary display of bright, spangly colour. All the toreros (matadors, banderilleros etc) wear the black *montera*, the hat that looks a little like a set of Mickey Mouse ears. The torero's standard weapons are the *estoque* or *espada* (sword) and the heavy silk and percale *capa* (cape). The matador alone also employs a different cape with the sword – a smaller piece of cloth held with a bar of wood called the *muleta* and used for a number of different passes.

The mounted picador goads the bull and tests its courage by shoving a lance into its withers to weaken it.

La Corrida

Bullfighting usually begins about 6 pm and, as a rule, six toros are on the day's card, with three different matadors fighting two bulls each. If a bull is considered not up to scratch, it is booed off (to the shame of the ranch which bred it) and a replacement is brought on. Each fight takes about 15 minutes.

Fights begin with the bull charging out into the arena, then being moved about and calmed down a little by the peones. The matador then appears and executes *faenas* (moves) with the bull. The more closely and calmly the matador works with the bull, pivoting and virtually dancing before the bull's horns, the greater will be the crowd's approbation. After a little of this, the matador strides off and leaves the stage first to the banderilleros, then to the picadores, before returning for the final session. At various moments during the fight, the brass band will strike up, adding to the air of grand spectacle.

When the bull seems tired out and unlikely to give a lot more, the matador chooses the moment for the kill. Facing the animal head-on, the matador aims to sink the sword cleanly into its neck for an instant kill – the *estocada*. It's an awful lot easier said than done.

A good performance followed by a clean kill will have the crowd on its feet waving handkerchiefs in appeal to the president to award the matador an *oreja* (ear) of the animal. The president usually waits to gauge the crowd's enthusiasm before finally flopping a white handkerchief on to his balcony. If the fight has been exceptional, the matador might *cortar dos orejas* – cut two ears off. And a matador who does really *really* well may be awarded the tail too.

The sad carcass is meanwhile dragged out by a team of drayhorses and the sand raked in preparation for the next *toro*. The meat ends up on general sale at the market or a butcher's.

Matadors

 If you are spoiling for a fight, it is worth looking out for the big names among the matadors. A big name is no guarantee you'll see a high-quality corrida, as that also depends on the animals themselves, but it is a good sign. Names to look for include: Jesulín de Ubrique, a true macho whose attitudes to women don't go down well with everyone; Enrique Ponce, a serious class act; Joselito; Rivero Ordóñez; Litri; Curro Romero, born in the 1920s and still fighting; Cristina Sánchez, born in 1972 and the only woman to have fought her way into the upper echelons of this macho world in the 20th century; and El Cordobés, one of the biggest names, although for some, his style borders on mocking the animal and is considered unnecessarily cruel.

Ethics of the Fight

 Anyone in any doubt about the danger to the human participants in this contest of bravery should remember that people *do* die in the ring. That it no longer happens often is perhaps to be welcomed, but there are those who cry foul. Time and again corrida reviewers lament the poor quality of the bulls and matadors. The most fraudulent practice, however, is the *afeitado* – the filing down of the bull's horns. Filing not only makes the bull a little bit less anxious to attack its tormentors but also impairs its judgement of distance and angle. When moves were made to stop this practice in 1997, the matadors went on strike.

The corrida has a long history and the confrontation with death, bravery, skill and performance is still popular.

Manolete, though one of the most famous of Spain's great matadors, was gored to death by a bull named Islero at Linares, Jaén in 1947.

When & Where

The official bullfighting year in Andalucía runs from Easter Sunday to October, though it's possible to see a corrida at other times of the year on the Costa del Sol. Most corridas are held as part of a city or town fiesta. Few rings have regular fights right through the season, Sevilla being an exception.

The big bang that launches Andalucía's bullfighting year is Sevilla's Feria de Abril (April Fair), with fights almost every day during the week of the feria and the week before it. It's Sevilla, too, where the year ends with a corrida on the Día de la Hispanidad, 12 October. In addition to the top corridas, which attract 'name' matadors and big crowds, there are plenty of lesser ones in cities, towns and villages. These are often *novilleras*, in which immature bulls *(novillos)* are fought by junior matadors *(novilleros)*. In small places the Plaza Mayor may serve as a makeshift bullring. When fights are coming up locally, gaudy posters advertise the fact and give ticket information.

Bullfighting as an art form

ANDALUCÍAN BULLFIGHT CALENDAR

Late April/early May
Fiesta de Jerez de la Frontera

Late May/early June
Feria de Nuestra Señora de la Salud in Córdoba, a big bullfighting stronghold
Feria de la Manzanilla, Sanlúcar de Barrameda

Late May/June
Corpus Christi, Granada

June to August, most Sundays
El Puerto de Santa María
Costa del Sol – mainly frequented by tourist crowds but most weeks there's a respectable fight in one of the rings (Fuenirola, Marbella, Torremolinos, Mijas etc)

Approx 3 to 9 August
Fiestas Colombinas, Huelva

Mid-August
Feria de Málaga

Last week of August
Feria de la Virgen del Mar, Almería

Around 6 to 8 September
Corrida Goyesca, Ronda – select, stylish matadors fight in costumes of the type shown in Goya's bullfight engravings

Mid to late September
Corridas in Jaén province, including Úbeda, Cazorla and Linares, site of the 1947 death of the very famous matador Manolete

(continued from page 160)
Triana
Across the Guadalquivir from the Torre del Oro and Plaza de Toros is Triana, a barrio which used to be Sevilla's Gypsy quarter and was one of the birthplaces of flamenco. The Gypsies, however, were moved out to suburban dormitory estates in the 1960s and 70s, and Triana is now rather yuppified. The riverfront streets Calle del Betis and Paseo de Nuestra Señora de la O make a very pleasant stroll. There are views back across the river to the city centre, and popular bars and cafés.

Isla de La Cartuja
North of Triana, the northern part of the island formed by two branches of the Guadalquivir, this was the site of Expo 92. Since the big year, this area has had a chequered history and expanses of it now lie decaying, victims of political squabbles and lack of funds and purpose. But there's still plenty to see and do. The easiest approach from the city centre is by the Puente del Cachorro, which takes you to Puerta de Triana, the southern end of the site. Bus Nos C1, C2 and C3 (see Getting Around), and No 5 from the Puerta de Jerez, all go to Puerta de Triana.

Puerta de Triana This area (☎ 95 446 00 89) features a Pabellón de la Navegación (Shipping Pavilion), with exhibits on sea exploration, (500 ptas); a replica of Magellan's ship the *Victoria* (250 ptas); and a Torre Mirador (Lookout Tower, 250 ptas). The site is open Tuesday to Friday from 10.30 am to 1 pm and 4.30 to 7 pm; Saturday, Sunday and holidays from 11 am to 2.30 pm and 4.30 to 8 pm. Visits to the Pabellón de la Navegación are in one-hour sessions starting at fixed times.

From here, you can also take half-hour trips on the Guadalquivir in motorised catamarans (250 ptas), daily except Monday.

Conjunto Monumental de La Cartuja
Just north of Puerta de Triana is this former monastery, built in the 15th century, where Columbus used to stay. The explorer's remains lay here from 1509 to 1536. In 1836 the monks were finally expelled during the Disamortisation, (when church property was auctioned off by the state) and the monastery's many art treasures were moved elsewhere. Three years later the complex was bought by a Liverpudlian, Charles Pickman, who turned it into a porcelain factory. Pickman built the five tall bottle-shaped kilns which stand incongruously beside the monastery buildings, and the porcelain factory functioned till 1982. The whole complex was restored for Expo.

Highlights of a visit include the mudéjar-style Capilla de Santa Ana (off the monastery church) which was built as the Columbus family tomb; the pretty 15th century Claustro Mudéjar (Mudéjar Cloister); an artesonado ceiling – used by Napoleonic troops for shooting practice – in the Refectorio (Dining Hall); and the close-up view of the Pickman kilns, of which there were originally 10. The complex (☎ 95 448 06 11) is open daily except Monday from 11 am to 9 pm (October to March to 7 pm). Entry costs 300 ptas (free for EU citizens on Tuesday).

Exhibition Pavilions Further north, some of the exotic Expo pavilions are slowly being turned into a technology industries park. Others are being converted for use by the Universidad de Sevilla, and some are simply rotting away. A road leads past some of these areas from the monastery, but when we checked, some of the more interesting parts could only be accessed, inconveniently, from the western side.

Isla Mágica On the eastern side of the island near the Puente de la Barqueta, Isla Mágica (☎ 902-16 17 16) is a big 15 billion-peseta amusement/theme park which opened in 1997. The theme is the 16th century Spanish colonial adventure. Highlight rides include the Anaconda and El Jaguar roller-coasters (the latter with high-speed 360-degree turns) and the Iguazú in which you descend an Amazon jungle waterfall. You may have to wait 45 minutes at busy times for the big attractions.

There are also set-piece events such as music and pirate shows and the *cine-simulador*, a cinema with tilting seats and a giant screen in which you re-live an explorer's adventures.

Isla Mágica is open from March to October, daily from 11 am to midnight or 1 am (climaxing with firework, music and laser show). The entry charge of 3100 ptas for adults, and 2100 ptas for children from five to 12 and over-65s, includes all the main attractions. *Tarde* tickets, valid from 5, 6 or 7 pm depending on the season, are 2100/1500 ptas. There are 20-odd places to eat and drink in the park.

Bus Nos C1 and C2 (see Getting Around) stop at Isla Mágica.

Courses

Language For information on Spanish-language courses at the university, contact the Instituto de Idiomas, Universidad de Sevilla (☎ 95 455 14 93, fax 95 456 04 39), Calle Palos de la Frontera s/n, 41004 Sevilla. The main tourist office can give you a list of private colleges. Three that we have heard good things about are CLIC at Calle Santa Ana 11 near the Alameda de Hércules (☎ 95 437 45 00) and at Calle Sor Ángela de la Cruz 18 near Plaza de la Encarnación (☎ 95 456 15 14, 95 456 19 96); Lengua Viva (☎ 95 490 51 31), Calle Viriato 22 near the Alameda de Hércules; and Academia Atlántika (☎ & fax 95 421 08 22), Calle de Adriano 32-5º. The Atlántika has mainly French and German students.

Dance & Guitar The main tourist office has a list of several *academias de baile* which you can contact if you're looking for a course in flamenco or other Spanish dance, or guitar. You'll also find ads in the *Música*, *Cursos* and *Enseñanza* 'sections of *El Giraldillo* magazine.

Organised Tours

Open-topped double decker buses run by Sevirama/Guide Friday, and the converted trams of Compañía Hispalense de Tranvías, both do several daily city tours of about one hour – you can board on Paseo de Cristóbal Colón (100m north of the Torre del Oro), or on Avenida de Portugal behind Plaza de España. Price for either is 1300 ptas, but you can usually pick up discount coupons worth 200 or 300 ptas at the main tourist office and elsewhere. Children under 12 go free on Sevirama; children and students pay 500 ptas on Hispalense. Sevirama has earphone commentary in a choice of eight languages, while Hispalense has commentary by real live guides (who speak English as well as Spanish). Sevirama runs from 10 am to 8 pm, about every 30 minutes; Hispalense goes from 10 am to 6.15 pm, every 45 minutes. Their routes are broadly similar – Antigua Fábrica de Tabacos, Parque de María Luisa, Plaza de España, Plaza de Toros, Expo 92 site, etc.

There are one-hour cruises (1200 ptas) on the river at least hourly from 11 am to 7 pm run by Cruceros Turísticos Torre del Oro from the *embarcadero* (jetty) by the Torre del Oro.

The horse-drawn carriages which hang around near the Catedral and Plaza de España charge 4000 ptas for a one-hour trot around the Barrio de Santa Cruz and Parque de María Luisa areas (up to four people).

Special Events

Sevilla's Semana Santa processions (see the boxed text) and its Feria de Abril, the fair which follows a week or two later, are two of Spain's most famous and exciting festivals.

Feria de Abril Sevilla's April Fair, in the second half of the month, is a kind of release after the solemnity of Semana Santa. It takes place on a special *recinto* (site), El Real de la Feria, in the Los Remedios area on the west side of the Guadalquivir. The ceremonial lighting up of the feria grounds on the Monday night is the starting gun for six nights of eating, drinking, talk, fabulous flouncy dresses, and music and dancing till dawn. Much of the recinto is taken up by private *casetas*, marquees for clubs, associations, families and groups of friends. But there are public casetas, too, where much the same fun goes on. There's also a huge fairground.

In the afternoons, from about 1 pm, those who have horses and carriages *(enganches)* parade about the feria grounds – and the city at large – in their finery (many of the horses are dressed up too). Sevilla's major bullfight season also takes place during the feria.

Other Festivals Other Sevilla events include:

5 January
Cabalgata de los Reyes Magos – a big evening parade of floats in which the Reyes Magos (Three Kings) and their retinues throw some 60,000kg of sweets to the crowds

Late May/June
Corpus Christi – important early morning procession of the Custodia de Juan de Arfe and accompanying images from the Catedral

September, even-numbered years
Bienal de Flamenco – one of Spain's major flamenco festivals, with events most nights for about three weeks, in various Sevilla locations

Places to Stay
Room prices in many places go up by anything from 20% to 200% during and around Semana Santa and the Feria de Abril (a period which can last as long as two months at some hotels), and you should book far ahead, too. Even at normal times, accommodation in Sevilla is fairly expensive – and often in heavy demand, so it's advisable to ring ahead. But the summer prices given here can come down significantly from October to March. Some middle and top-end places cut prices significantly in July and August.

Places to Stay – Budget
Camping *Camping Sevilla* (☎ 95 451 43 79) is about 6km out on the N-IV to Córdoba – on the right, just before the airport, if you're approaching from Sevilla. It's open all year and prices are 460 ptas per person and per car, and 400 ptas per tent, plus IVA. *Camping Club de Campo* (☎ 95 472 02 50) and *Camping Villsom* (☎ 95 472

08 28) are in Dos Hermanas, 15km south of Sevilla on the N-IV towards Cádiz.

Youth Hostel The recently renovated *Albergue Juvenil Sevilla* (☎ 95 461 31 50) is south of the centre at Calle Isaac Peral 2, just off Avenida de la Palmera. It has room for 188 people, mostly in twin rooms, and is about 10 minutes by bus No 34 from opposite the main tourist office (ask for the *albergue juvenil*).

Hostales & Pensiones The attractive Barrio de Santa Cruz, close to the Catedral, has lots of places, some of them reasonably good value. There are many more places north of Plaza Nueva, a mostly quieter area but still pretty central.

Barrio de Santa Cruz & Around The 14-room *Hostal Santa María La Blanca* (☎ 95 442 11 74), Calle Santa María La Blanca 28, has clean, modern singles/doubles for 1500/3000 ptas, or doubles with bath for 4000 ptas. *Huéspedes Dulces Sueños/Sweet Dreams* (☎ 95 441 93 93), at Calle Santa María La Blanca 21, is a friendly place with eight clean rooms of varied sizes for about 2000/3500 ptas, and singles with private bath for 3000 ptas.

Calle Archeros, a narrow street off Calle Santa María La Blanca, has four hostales. One, the friendly, 13-room *Hostal Bienvenido* (☎ 95 441 36 55) at No 14 has singles for 1600 or 1700 ptas, and doubles for 3200 ptas, with shared bathrooms. A little farther east, the small *Huéspedes La Montoreña* (☎ 95 441 24 07), Calle San Clemente 12, has clean, simple singles/doubles with shared baths at 1500/3000 ptas.

Just west of Calle Santa María La Blanca, *Pensión San Pancracio* (☎ 95 441 31 04), at Plaza de las Cruces 9, has poky singles for 1800 ptas and bigger doubles for 3200 ptas, or 4000 ptas with bath. *Pensión Cruces El Patio* (☎ 95 422 96 33), Plaza de las Cruces 10, has a dorm room with beds at 1300 ptas, singles at 2500 ptas, and doubles at 4000 and 5000 ptas. Some rooms have shower and toilet.

SEMANA SANTA

Every day from Palm Sunday to Easter Sunday, large, richly bedecked images and life-size tableaux of scenes from the Easter story are carried from Sevilla's churches through the streets to the Catedral. They're accompanied by long processions, which may take more than an hour to pass, and are watched by vast crowds. These rites go back to the 14th century but they took on their present form in the 17th, when many of the images – some of them supreme works of art – were created.

The processions are organised by over 50 different *hermandades* or *cofradías* (brotherhoods, some of which include women). There are normally two *pasos*, as the lavishly decorated platforms bearing the images are called. The first paso carries an image of Christ, crucified, bearing the cross, or in a tableau representing a scene from the Passion; the second holds an image of the Virgin. The pasos are carried by teams of about 40 bearers called *costaleros*, who work in relays. The pasos are heavy – each costalero normally carries about 50kg – and they move with a hypnotic swaying motion to the rhythm of their accompanying bands and the commands of their *capataz* (leader), who strikes a bell to start and stop the paso. Each pair of pasos has between 400 and 2500 costumed followers, known as *nazarenos*. Many of these wear tall Ku Klux Klan-like capes which cover their heads except for narrow eye slits. The most contrite go barefoot and carry crosses. Membership of a hermandad is a keenly sought honour, even by some who wouldn't dream of attending mass at other times. These events, with their combination of splendour and anguish, spectacle and solemnity and overriding adoration of the Virgin can give a special insight into the nature of Spanish Catholicism.

Each day from Palm Sunday to Good Friday, seven or eight hermandades leave their churches in the afternoon or early evening and arrive between 5 and 11 pm at Calle Campana at the north end of Calle Sierpes. This is the start of the *carrera oficial* along Calle Sierpes, through Plaza San Francisco and along Avenida de la Constitución to the Catedral. The processions enter at the west end and leave at the east, emerging on Plaza Virgen de los Reyes, returning to their churches some time between 10 pm and 3 am.

The climax of the week is the *madrugada* (early hours) of Good Friday, when some of the most respected and/or popular hermandades file through the city. The first of these to reach the carrera oficial, about 1.30 am, is the oldest hermandad, El Silencio, which goes in complete silence. Next, at about 2 am, comes Jesús del Gran Poder, whose 17th century Christ is one of the masterpieces of Sevillan sculpture. This is followed at about 3 am by La Macarena, whose Virgin is the most passionately adored of all. Then come El Calvario from the Iglesia de la Magdalena, Esperanza de Triana, and finally, at about 6 am, Los Gitanos, the Gypsy hermandad.

Pensión Fabiola (☎ 95 421 83 46), at Calle Fabiola 16, with a plant-filled courtyard, has simple, well kept singles/doubles, for 2000/4000 ptas, and doubles with bath for 6000 ptas. The singles are small. *Hostal Córdoba* (☎ 95 422 74 98), nearby at Calle Farnesio 12, has a plant-draped atrium and 12 nice air-conditioned rooms for 2500/4000 ptas (3500/5000 ptas with a small shower room).

Some of the cheapest rooms in Sevilla are at the little *Pensión Vergara* (☎ 95 422 47 38), Calle Ximenez de Enciso 11, with only a 'Camas Rooms Chambres' sign outside. Adequate singles/doubles, with shared bathrooms, go for as little as 1300/2500 ptas.

The friendly, well kept *Hostal Toledo* (☎ 95 421 53 35), Calle Santa Teresa 15, has 10 clean rooms, all with bath, for 2500/5000 ptas. Except during Semana Santa and the

On the Saturday evening just four hermandades make their way to the Catedral, and finally, on Easter Sunday morning, the Hermandad de la Resurrección. In contrast to their fascination with the anguish of the Crucifixion and the events leading up to it, Sevillanos show relatively little interest in the Resurrection.

There are marked differences between the styles of the hermandades. City centre hermandades, such as El Silencio, are traditionally linked with the bourgeoisie. They're serious and austere, use little or no music, and wear black tunics, usually without capes, and tied with esparto grass. Hermandades from the working class barrios outside the centre, such as La Macarena, have brass and drum bands accompanying more brightly bedecked pasos. Their nazarenos wear coloured, caped tunics, often of satin, velvet or wool. They also have to come from farther away, and some are on the streets for more than 12 hours.

Programmes giving each hermandad's schedule and route are widely available during Semana Santa. The best source of information is *ABC* newspaper, which has maps showing the churches, recommended viewing spots *(lugar recomendado)* and other details.

La Macarena, Sevilla's most adored image of the virgin and the city's patron saint

It's not too hard to work out which procession will be where and when, so you can pick one up on the way through its barrio or as it leaves or re-enters its church, always an emotional moment.

Crowds along most of the carrera oficial make it hard to get much of a view there, unless you manage to get a seat., These go for anything from about 900 ptas on Plaza Virgen de los Reyes behind the Catedral to 3000 ptas on Good Friday morning at the top of Calle Sierpes. But if you arrive early enough in the evening, you can usually get close enough to the cathedral to see plenty without paying.

Feria de Abril, they lock the door at 1 am. *Hostal Monreal* (☎ 95 421 41 66), Calle Rodrigo Caro 7, is one of the bigger places, with 20 varied rooms (a few with Giralda views), at 2650/4028 ptas for singles/doubles, or 6360 ptas for doubles with bath.

The 20-room *Hostal Goya* (☎ 95 421 11 70), Calle Mateos Gago 31, has nice, clean singles/doubles with bathroom at 4175/6500 ptas, doubles with shower for 5775

ptas, and a pleasant downstairs sitting area. A bit farther north at Corral del Rey 22, 36-room *Hostal Sierpes* (☎ 95 422 49 48) has a restaurant, bar, garage space, and singles/doubles with shower or bath for 3000/5000 ptas plus IVA. Across the street, the friendly 11-room *Hostal Sánchez Sabariego* (☎ 95 421 44 70), Corral del Rey 23, with a nice little courtyard, has decent, individually decorated rooms, most with bath, for around 2000/4500 ptas.

Pensión Alcázar (☎ 95 422 84 57), on a peaceful little plaza just west of the Alcázar at Calle Deán Miranda 12, has good rooms for 3500/5000 ptas, or 4000/6000 ptas with private bath. There's a little terrace near the top with Giralda views. Round the corner at Calle Mariana de Pineda 9, the friendly, well-kept *Hostal Arias* (☎ 95 422 68 40; reina@arrakis.es) has 15 decent rooms, all with private shower, for 4850/6050 ptas.

North of Plaza Nueva *Hostal Central* (☎ 95 421 76 60), Calle Zaragoza 18, a three minute walk from Plaza Nueva, has well-kept, decent-sized singles/doubles with bath for around 3500/5000 ptas.

Hostal Lis II (☎ 95 456 02 28), in a beautiful house at Calle Olavide 5, a narrow street between Calle O'Donnell and Calle San Eloy, charges 1700 ptas for singles and 3500 ptas for doubles with toilet. The singles are on the small side.

The good *Hotel Zaida* (☎ 95 421 11 38), Calle San Roque 26, occupies an 18th century house with a lovely mudéjar-style arched patio. The 27 rooms, some with wrought-iron balconies, are plain but decent, with air-conditioning, TV and bath, and cost 3000/5000 ptas plus IVA.

The 23-room *Hostal Londres* (☎ 95 421 28 96), Calle San Pedro Mártir 1, has a pleasant tiled lobby and plain but decent rooms with private bath, some with little balconies, at around 3500/5000 and 4000/6100 ptas.

The small, friendly *Hostal Romero* (☎ 95 421 13 53), Calle Gravina 21, has bare and simple but clean rooms with shared baths for 2000/3000 ptas, and doubles with small private shower and toilet for 5000 ptas. Prices can double in August, though. *Hostal Gravina* (☎ 95 421 64 14), Calle Gravina 46, has adequate singles/doubles with shared bath for 2500/4000 ptas. The slightly bigger *Hostal Gala* (☎ 95 421 45 03), Calle Gravina 52, has the same prices, plus doubles with bath for 5000 ptas.

The friendly 10-room *Hostal Alfonso XII* (☎ 95 421 15 98), in a nice old building at

Calle Monsalves 25, has singles for 2000 ptas and doubles with bath for 4000 ptas, but is often full.

Farther east, the 10-room *Hostal Lis* (☎ 95 421 30 88), Calle Escarpín 10, is owned by the same family as the Lis II. It has a nice tiled lobby, and singles/doubles with shower for 2000/3500 ptas.

Near Plaza del Duque de la Victoria, a bustling square surrounded by classy stores, *Hostal Pino* (☎ 95 421 28 10), Calle Tarifa 6, in an old building with a small courtyard, has decent, sizeable rooms for 1700/2700 ptas or 2200/3500 ptas with shower. The friendly *Hostal Unión* (☎ 95 422 92 94), next door at Calle Tarifa 4, has good clean rooms at 5000 ptas a double, or 6000 ptas with private bath. *Hostal Duque* (☎ 95 438 70 11), Calle Trajano 15, is another friendly place, in an old house with fine antique lobby/patio. The 36 varied singles/doubles cost 1800/3500 ptas, or 3000/5000 ptas with private bath. You're best with a room off the noisy street. *Hotel Sevilla* (☎ 95 438 41 61), Calle Daóiz 5, is past its best but has 30 clean, plain, medium-sized rooms with bath for 3745/5885 ptas. There's a large lobby with a small greenery-filled patio.

A few blocks east, the small, friendly *Hostal Galatea* (☎ 95 456 35 64), Calle San Juan de la Palma 4, has 12 varied rooms, at 3424 ptas for singles with shared bathrooms and 5992 ptas for doubles with private bath. Popular with international travellers, it's well kept, with a pleasant plant-draped lobby and sitting area downstairs.

Places to Stay – Mid-Range
Barrio de Santa Cruz *Hostería del Laurel* (☎ 95 422 02 95), above a characterful old bar at Plaza de los Venerables 5, has 21 simple, attractive air-conditioned rooms with TV and bath or shower. Singles/doubles are 7000/9500 ptas plus IVA (but 5000/7500 ptas plus IVA in July and August). *Hotel Murillo* (☎ 95 421 60 95), Calle Lope de Rueda 7, has a lobby like an antique showroom but its 57 rooms are a little tired, if clean. They cost 4500/7800 ptas plus IVA (less from mid-June to early September).

Hotel Fernando III (☎ 95 421 73 07), Calle San José 21, has 156 comfy if unimaginative rooms with TV and bath for 9200/11,500 ptas plus IVA. It also has a restaurant, bar, spacious lounge, garage and rooftop pool.

West of Avenida de la Constitución This is a good central location. *Hotel Simón* (☎ 95 422 66 60), in a fine 18th century house at Calle García de Vinuesa 19, has 29 very pleasant rooms at 5500/7500 ptas for singles/doubles with bathroom. It's extremely popular so you should always book ahead. Breakfast is available. *Hotel Europa* (☎ 95 421 43 05), Calle Jimios 5, has 16 decent, quite sizeable rooms with TV from 5600/7000 to 7200/9000 ptas plus IVA. The bigger *Hotel La Rábida* (☎ 95 422 09 60), Calle Castelar 24, has an impressive lobby with a fountain, a restaurant, and good rooms with bath, at 5700/8750 ptas plus IVA.

North & West of Plaza Nueva *Hotel Puerta de Triana* (☎ 95 421 54 04), Calle Reyes Católicos 5, is a good larger (65-room) hotel in an old house that has been well modernised but maintains a traditional style. Singles/doubles are 6500/10,000 ptas plus IVA.

The pleasant 40-room *Hostal Plaza Sevilla* (☎ 95 421 71 49), Calle Canalejas 2, has well-kept if not huge rooms with bath and TV for 5500/8000 ptas plus IVA (coming down to 4000/6000 ptas plus IVA at slow times). Some rooms have little balconies. There are comfy sitting areas on the two upper floors.

To the east, *Hotel Baco* (☎ 95 456 50 50), Plaza Ponce de León 15, has 25 good rooms with old-fashioned trimmings for 6500/ 9000 ptas plus IVA. All have private bathroom, satellite TV and air-conditioning. You're probably best with an off-street room, because of the bus stop outside.

Farther north towards the Alameda de Hércules, the 77-room *Hotel El Corregidor* (☎ 95 438 51 11), on a quiet little street at Calle Morgado 17, has comfy, clean, moderate-sized, air-conditioned rooms with TV and bath for 6420/9630 ptas. Downstairs are spacious sitting areas, a bar and a little open-air patio. There's parking 200m away.

Patio de la Cartuja (☎ 95 490 02 00) at Calle Lumbreras 8-10, just off the north end of the Alameda de Hércules, occupies a former *corral*, a three-storey community of apartments around a patio which was once the typical form of Sevillan lower middle-class housing. Renovated into 30 very pleasant, cosy apartments with double bedroom, kitchen, bathroom, and sitting room with double sofa bed, it's a pleasant place to stay if you don't mind being this far north. The apartments cost 7200/9000 ptas plus IVA for single/double use (less in July and August). There's a café too. *Patio de la Alameda* (☎ 95 490 49 99), nearby at Alameda de Hércules 56, is similar, with the same ownership and prices.

Places to Stay – Top End
In the Barrio de Santa Cruz, *Las Casas de la Judería* (☎ 95 441 51 50), Callejón de Dos Hermanas 7, are a group of charmingly restored old houses around several patios and fountains, with lots of pretty tiles and plants. The 56 cosy rooms and suites cost from 8500/14,500 to 11,000/17,000 ptas plus IVA for singles/doubles (less in July and August). Breakfast is available, and there's a bar.

A few steps from La Giralda at Calle Don Remondo 19, *Hotel Doña María* (☎ 95 422 49 90) has 60 varied rooms and suites in comfy, old-fashioned style from 11,000/18,000 to 13,000/23,000 ptas plus IVA (less in July and August). There's a nice big lobby-lounge, but no restaurant.

Also close to the main sights is the luxurious *Hotel Los Seises* (☎ 95 422 94 95), Calle Segovias 6, set around what was the rear patio of the Palacio del Arzobispo (Archbishop's Palace). The 43 rooms cost 20,000/25,000 ptas plus IVA (less in July and August). The hotel has a good restaurant.

Taberna del Alabardero (☎ 95 456 06 37), just west of Plaza Nueva at Calle Zaragoza 20, is a 19th century house beautifully restored as a classy hotel of just seven rooms. They cost 12,000/15,000 ptas plus IVA. Nearby, the *Hotel Becquer* (☎ 95 422 89 00), Calle Reyes Católicos 4, has 120 comfy, modern rooms for 8000/13,000 ptas plus IVA. A little farther north, *Hotel Colón* (☎ 95 422 29 00), Calle Canalejas 1, is one of the city's top hotels, a 200-room place modernised but with old-fashioned furniture and trimmings. Rooms are 17,850/22,000 ptas plus IVA.

Up north towards the Alameda de Hércules, *Hotel Cervantes* (☎ 95 490 02 80), Calle Cervantes 10, is a charming medium-sized hotel in modern style with 50 rooms at 9500/13,000 ptas plus IVA (less at weekends and in July and August). It's on a quiet street in a rather quaint old part of the city.

You can break the bank in style at the *Hotel Alfonso XIII* (☎ 95 422 28 50), just south of the centre at Calle San Fernando 2, a magnificent 1920s confection of old Sevillan styles in marble, mahogany and tiles. Doubles start at 34,000 ptas plus IVA.

Places to Eat
Sevilla is one of Spain's tapas capitals, with scores and scores of bars serving all sorts of varied and tasty light bites. To catch the atmosphere of the city, you should certainly do some of your eating in bars.

Breakfast, Lunch & Dinner Don't bother looking for dinner till at least 8 pm – very few kitchens get going for the evening before then.

Barrio de Santa Cruz & Around The narrow streets and plazas just east of the Alcázar are dotted with numerous, mainly tourist-oriented, restaurants. *Restaurant La Cueva*, a pleasant courtyard place at Calle Rodrigo Caro 18, does a lunch menú of gazpacho, salad, paella and dessert for 1350 ptas plus IVA (minimum two people). *El Rincón de Pepe* nearby at Calle Gloria 6 has the same menú, except that it's gazpacho *or* salad, for 1050 ptas. *Restaurante Giralda*, Calle Justino de Neve 8, is one of the more economical places in the vicinity, with platos combinados for 700 ptas. For some-

thing fancier, *Corral del Agua*, Callejón del Agua 6, has good, inventive food and its cool, green courtyard is great on a hot day, if you can get a table. Main courses (1800 to 2500 ptas) include some good fish choices, and varied dishes of the day; for starters you might go for the puddin de verduras (vegetable mousse, 700 ptas).

At Plaza de los Venerables 5, *Hostería del Laurel* has an atmospheric old bar with herbs and hams dangling from the ceiling, and efficient, friendly waiters serving a wide range of good media-raciones (550 to 1450 ptas) and raciones (850 to 2250 ptas).

Cervecería Giralda, Calle Mateos Gago 1 in an old Muslim bathhouse, is a good spot for breakfast close to the Catedral and Alcázar. Tostadas are from 95 to 275 ptas depending what you have on them, or there's bacon and eggs for 450 ptas. *Café-Bar Campanario*, across the street, does good raciones such as tortilla de patatas or revuelto de espárragos, both 550 ptas.

Pizzería San Marco, in another old Muslim bathhouse – stylishly refurbished – at Calle Mesón del Moro 6, is extremely popular but portions are on the mean side. Most pizzas and pastas are around 800 ptas plus IVA, and it's open daily except Sunday from 1.15 to 4.30 and 8.15 to 10.30 pm (to 1 am on Friday and Saturday nights).

Calle Santa María La Blanca has several good-value places. At the *Alta-Mira Café Bar*, No 6, a media-ración of tortilla Alta-Mira (with potatoes and vegetables) is almost a meal for 600 ptas. Next door at No 4, *Altamira Bar-Café* (we don't know if they are related) has similarly priced media-raciones, plus platos combinados for around 950 to 1100 ptas. Busy little *Bar Casa Fernando* around the corner has some good-value *platos del día* for 350 ptas, and a decent 800-ptas lunch menú; *Restaurant El Cordobés* at No 20 is good for breakfasts such as eggs, bacon, bread and coffee for 350 ptas.

Cafetería Las Lapas at Calle San Gregorio 6, just off Plaza Contratación near the Alcázar, is a typically bustling spot at breakfast/morning-coffee time with office workers and students crowding in for the good molletes. It closes on Sunday.

Among a clutch of somewhat touristic restaurants just off Calle Alemanes, north of the Catedral, *Las Escobas* has a menú for 1000 ptas and offers some reasonable *platos especiales* – such as chicken with chips, salad and vegetables – for around 850 ptas including bread and wine. The classier *Casa Robles*, Calle Álvarez Quintero 58, does raciones (1100 to 1500 ptas) and media-raciones, and unusual revuelto combinations such as algas, erizos y gambas (seaweed, sea urchins and prawns), in its bar. It also has a restaurant section with lots of lamb, beef, venison and fish for around 1500 to 2500 ptas, or a menú for 2500 ptas plus IVA. *Bodegón El Pez Espada*, Calle Hernando Colón 8, specialises in fried fish and does some decent 650 to 850-ptas menús of main course and paella or salad.

West of Avenida de la Constitución
Mesón del Serranito, Calle Antonio Díaz 9, has a good selection of platos combinados from 750 ptas – plus interesting bullfight photos and some impressive bulls' heads. The busy *Bodega Paco Góngora* at Calle Padre Marchena 1 does a huge range of good seafood at decent prices – media-raciones of fish a la plancha (grilled) are mostly 600 ptas. It's open daily from 11 am to 4 pm and 7 pm to midnight. *Restaurante Enrique Becerra*, nearby at Calle Gamazo 2, is a smarter place with good, varied Andalucian fare. Two courses with drinks will usually set you back 4000 ptas or more (closed Sunday).

The tasty tapas at the pleasant *Casa Pepe-Hillo*, Calle de Adriano 24 (see Tapas), are all available as media-raciones (500 to 950 ptas) or raciones (1000 to 1900 ptas).

El Centro On Calle Sierpes, *Bar Laredo* at the south end is a popular breakfast stop, and *Confitería La Campana* at the north end is the city's most famous bakery, in operation since 1885. It still turns out scrumptious cakes and pastries and has a small coffee shop.

Restaurante San Marco, in an 18th century mansion at Calle de la Cuna 6, one

block east of Sierpes, is the parent of Pizzeria San Marco in the Barrio de Santa Cruz, and it's a better and more expensive place. It serves pizza and pasta for around 1000 ptas, plus a big choice of fish and meat from 1000 to 2000 ptas. It's open daily from 1.30 to 4.30 pm and 8.30 pm to 12.30 am.

Alfalfa 10, Plaza de la Alfalfa 10, is good for a tranquil breakfast. As well as the usual tostadas, it has more sophisticated offerings like juice, croissant, muesli, ham and cheese for 500 ptas. *Restaurante Bar Zucchero* on Calle Golfo, a short alley near Plaza de la Alfalfa, is a little haven for vegetarians, doing a lunch menú Monday to Friday for 950 ptas. Good soups, croquettes, salads and potatoes with varied sauces go for around 400 ptas, and mains such quiche, aubergine lasagne and (for non-vegies) chicken tandoori, cost around 700 ptas. It's open daily except Tuesday from 1.30 to 4.30 pm and 9 pm to midnight.

The handsomely blue-tiled *Restaurante El Bacalao*, up at Plaza Ponce de León 15, specialises in bacalao, which is a Sevilla favourite. You can have your bacalao a dozen or so ways for 1100 to 1800 ptas plus IVA, or as a media-ración for 600 to 800 ptas plus IVA.

West of Sierpes, *Café del Pintor* at Calle Murillo 8, a relaxed little tiled, arched and wood-beamed place, is pleasant for breakfast (coffee and mollete 185 to 235 ptas), or baguettes (300 to 400 ptas), tapas or drinks any time. It's open daily from about 8.30 am to midnight (Sunday 11.30 am to 5 pm). The popular *Bodegón Alfonso XII*, Calle Alfonso XII 33 near the Museo de Bellas Artes, is excellent value with deals like scrambled eggs with mushrooms, ham and prawns for 475 ptas, a breakfast of bacon, eggs and coffee for 400 ptas and a good-value menú for 800 ptas.

On Plaza del Duque de la Victoria, the *Horno del Duque* is a fine, busy café for breakfast, or for snacks or light meals later in the day. Solid wood tables (and bar) and leather-upholstered stools appeal to shoppers from nearby El Corte Inglés. A coffee and mollete with butter and jam is 250 ptas if you sit inside; platos combinados are around 900 to 1300 ptas (more expensive outside).

The *Mercado del Arenal*, on Calle Pastor y Landero, is the only food market in the central area.

South of the Centre Opposite the entrance to the Antigua Fábrica de Tabacos at Calle San Fernando 27, *Baguettería La Merienda* is popular with students and serves hot baguettes and croissants with varied fillings for 275 to 475 ptas.

La Raza, Avenida de Isabel la Católica 2 at the north end of Parque María Luisa, is a good stop for breakfast (café con leche and mollete, butter and jam for 275 ptas). Later in the day it does a 1500-ptas menú. There are tables outside under the trees.

Triana *Restaurante Río Grande* serves good meals – 1700 to 2400 ptas for most meat and fish main courses – in a great location on the bank of the Guadalquivir opposite the Torre del Oro, at the south end of Calle del Betis. But *Restaurante El Puerto* next door has just as good a location and much lower prices. Calle del Betis also boasts several popular pizzerias: at No 68, across the street from the Río Grande, is another *Pizzería San Marco* (see Barrio de Santa Cruz & Around). Farther north up the street are the good *Ristorante Cosa Nostra* (pizza 550 to 900 ptas, pasta 600 to 1000 ptas) and the slightly more economical *Pizzería O Mamma Mia* at No 33 (see the Central Sevilla map). Between these two, *Mex-Rock* at No 40-41 dishes up *botanas* (sort of Mexican tapas) for 250 to 500 ptas, and servings of tacos, quesadillas, etc, for 350 to 700 ptas.

Tapas An evening of tapas-hopping round Sevilla's bars with a couple of friends is one of the most enjoyable experiences in the city. Most of these places are good for popping into at other times of day, too, though from about 4 to 8 pm only cold tapas are available at many. In many Sevilla bars, instead of charging for each item as you go along, they chalk your bill

on the counter in front of you and add it up when you leave.

Though many bars helpfully have a tapas menu – or at least a blackboard – you'll certainly find that you don't know what many things are.

Favourite Tapas
Caña de lomo – pork loin
Cazón en adobo – a white fish marinated in vinegar, salt, lemon and spices, then deep fried (delicious)
Espinacas con garbanzos – spinach and chick peas
Papas aliñás – sliced potatoes and boiled eggs, with vegetable garnish and a vinegar-and-oil dressing
Pavía – battered fish or seafood
Puntillitas – baby squid, usually deep fried

Barrio de Santa Cruz *Bodega Santa Cruz* on Calle Mateos Gago, a bar popular with visitors and locals, has a big choice of decent-sized tapas, most at 185 to 210 ptas. *Cervecería Giralda*, Calle Mateos Gago 1, has a wonderful variety of good tapas, some pretty exotic, for 250 to 300 ptas. Some are tiny, but the pimientos bechamel and pechuga bechamel are decent value. Other bars on this street with good tapas include *Café-Bar Campanario* and *Bodega Belmonte* – the latter is a bit dearer and has a fine array of sherry and wine.

Café Bar Las Teresas, Calle Santa Teresa 2, is an atmospheric old-style bar with lots of hanging hams, good tapas from 160 to 200 ptas and media-raciones around 600 ptas. The atmospheric old *Bar Casa Román* specialises in fine jamón tapas, and has tables outside on pleasant Plaza de los Venerables. Next door, the *Hostería del Laurel* does good tapas too, mostly for around 225 ptas.

West of Avenida de la Constitución *Mesón Sevilla Jabugo I*, Calle Castelar 1 at the south end of Calle de Adriano, specialises in expensive Jabugo ham though there's lots of other choice. It's a no-frills place, busy most of the day (closed Sunday). The relaxed *Casa Pepe-Hillo* at Calle de Adriano 24 does some mouth-watering tapas from 250 to 325 ptas – try mushroom-filled artichoke hearts or chicken in bechamel sauce with spinach.

La Infanta, Calle Arfe 36, with sherry barrels for tables, is a haunt of the tweed jacket young Sevilla smart set. If you feel well enough dressed, the tapas, from 200 ptas, are exotic and great. *Bodega Paco Góngora* and *Restaurante Enrique Becerra* (see Breakfast, Lunch & Dinner) are good for tapas too.

El Centro Just off the south end of Plaza Salvador, *Café Universal* is thronged at tapas times with people tucking into delicious, generous offerings such as pinchos de solomillo a la pimienta (pepper steak kebabs) or gambas fritas con verduras (prawns and vegetables), for 300 to 375 ptas, or patatones (fried potato chunks served with a variety of succulent dips).

Calle General Polavieja, a short street off Plaza de San Francisco, has a good cluster of tapas bars including the bright, pine-tabled *Casa La Viuda* where the temptations include solomillo al whisky or al ajo for around 200 ptas. There's lots of manzanilla to wash them down with.

Plaza de la Alfalfa is a hub of the tapas scene. *Alfalfa 10*, Plaza de la Alfalfa 10, has some good tapas for 250 to 350 ptas. *Sopa de Ganso*, just to the north at Calle Pérez Galdós 8, and *Restaurante Bar Zucchero* on Calle Golfo, off Calle Pérez Galdós, do vegetarian tapas. Just off the east end of the plaza on Calle Alfalfa, *La Bodega* deals in jamón and sherry, *La Bodega Extremeña* sticks to cheese, and *La Trastienda*, with a smartish clientele, offers crabs. For succulent grilled meat, head a little farther east to another *Bodega Extremeña*, Calle San Esteban 17, which serves some great tapas a la brasa (grilled tapas) such as solomillo ibérico (Iberian pork sirloin) and chuletas de cordero (lamb chops) – for 250 ptas.

To the north, *Restaurante El Bacalao* (see Breakfast, Lunch & Dinner) does

bacalao tapas, and the nearby *El Rinconcillo*, Calle Gerona 40, is Sevilla's oldest bar, founded in 1670 and still popular. The tapas are fairly straightforward – espinacas con garbanzos, tortilla de jamón – and good with a *coronel*, a big glass of house wine.

Westward, *Patio San Eloy* at Calle San Eloy 9 is a bright, busy place, popular with a young crowd. Tapas of ham, cheese, smoked salmon, pork and more go for 110 to 185 ptas. It's open daily from 11.30 am to 4 pm and 6.30 to 11.30 pm (to midnight on Friday and Saturday). Not far west at Calle Canalejas 5, *Cafetería Donald* also does fine tapas such as cazón en adobo for around 250 ptas.

North of the Centre The Alameda de Hércules area has a few good tapas stops. *Bulebar Café*, Alameda de Hércules 83, serves up unusual home-made tarts and sweet tapas: pastel de verduras – a type of vegetable flan – is good. It's open daily from 4 pm to the early hours. *El Álamo*, on the corner of the Alameda and Calle Relator, does Latin American tapas. *Bar-Restaurante Las Columnas*, on the west side of the Alameda, is a less fancy place for varied tapas and raciones.

A couple of minutes walk east of the Alameda, *La Ilustre Víctima*, Calle Dr Letamendi 35, is a cool bar serving some great pinchos a la brasa and vegetarian tapas such as calabacines al roque (courgettes with Roquefort cheese) for 250 to 350 ptas. It's open daily from 4 pm to 2 or 3 am.

Entertainment
Sevilla's nightlife is among the liveliest in Spain. It really starts to get going about midnight or 1 am, and the best action is on Friday and Saturday nights. But bars begin to fill from 10 pm most nights, and you can find a range of live music any day except perhaps Monday. On fine nights, throngs of people block the streets outside popular bars and crowd the banks of the Guadalquivir, while the teenagers of the *movida* just bring their own *litronas* or *botellonas* (plastic litre bottles filled with liquor or some cocktail) to mass open-air

gathering spots such as the Mercado del Arenal. Sevilla also has some great music bars, often with dance space.

To find out what's on in the way of music and the other arts, consult: *Casco Antiguo*, a free fortnightly newspaper distributed around the central areas; *El Giraldillo*, a monthly what's-on magazine often available free at tourist offices, hotels or museums; the free tourist magazines *Sevilla Welcome & Olé* and *The Tourist Sevilla* which you'll find in some hotels; and the *Sevilla On Line* and *Sevilla Cultural* sites *on the Internet*. None of these is fully comprehensive or completely up-to-date, but they'll give you a good start. There's also some information in the newspapers *El Correo*, *ABC* and *El País*. Tickets for some music events are sold at the Sevilla Rock music shop, Calle Alfonso XII 1.

Drinking, Music & Dancing Of course you can eat while you drink: for some bars where the tapas are an attraction in themselves, see the preceding section. Schedules for live music are changeable, of course.

Barrio de Santa Cruz & Around There are some hugely popular bars just north of the Catedral: *P Flaherty Irish Pub* on Calle Alemanes gets packed with locals and visitors alike – 500 ptas for your pint of Guinness or bitter. *La Subasta* and *Antigüedades* on Calle Argote de Molina are very popular with a slightly older, straighter crowd. On the same street, *L'Image* offers some inventive *chupito* concoctions including a vodka, gin, rum, martini and lime thunderbolt named Tocame los Huevos (Touch my Balls).

In the heart of the Barrio de Santa Cruz, a variety of small bars such as *Bodega Santa Cruz* on Calle Mateos Gago, *Bar Entrecalles* on Calle Ximenez de Enciso and *Café Bar Las Teresas*, Calle Santa Teresa 2, can all get pretty lively, usually with a mixed crowd of visitors and locals. *El Tamboril* bar on Plaza de Santa Cruz packs in jolly crowds enjoying its live Sevillana and rumba music every night from midnight.

La Carbonería (☎ 95 421 44 60), Calle Levíes 18, is a converted coalyard with two large rooms, each with a bar, that gets thronged nearly every night. Locals and visitors alike come to enjoy the social scene and hear varied live music – including, at our last check, blues on Wednesday, flamenco on Thursday and rock on Saturday. The music usually starts at 10 or 11 pm (9 pm on Sunday) and La Carbonería closes about 4 am.

West of Avenida de la Constitución Calle García de Vinuesa has a few bare, old-fashioned but popular bodega-type bars with wine and/or sherry from the barrel (and beer, of course). One of the best is *Hijos de E Morales* at No 3, with a large back room where old wine casks serve as tables. A little further west, on Calle de Adriano, the scene changes again: the mostly young crowds here some nights have to be seen to be believed. This scene merges with the *litrona* mob around the nearby Mercado del Arenal. Busy music bars with inexpensive drinks on Adriano itself include *A3*, *Bar Populus* and *Arena*. There are several more very lively bars on and just off nearby Calle Arfe. Just to the south, Calle Dos de Mayo has some more relaxed bars and bodegas, with an older crowd.

Café Isbiliyya, Paseo de Colón 2 near the Puente de Triana, is a bustling gay music bar – mostly men – overflowing on to the street on busy nights.

El Centro From mid-evening to around 1 am, Plaza Salvador is a very popular spot for an open-air drink, with a studenty crowd and a couple of little bars selling carry-out drinks. People stand around the plaza or sit on the steps of the Parroquia del Salvador church, where hashish fumes may mingle incongruously with the smell of incense from the church. Just off the plaza at the corner of Calle Alcaicería and Calle Siete Revueltas, the long-established *Bar Europa* is a pleasant place for a sit-down drink, bright with colourful tiling. *Sur* bar, Calle Siete Revueltas 10, is a bastion of house, funky, dance and other recent musical tendencies. Tuesday is its international night. It's open daily except Monday from 10.30 pm.

Calle Pérez Galdós, off Plaza de la Alfalfa, has at least four throbbing music bars – *Bare Nostrum*, *Cabo Loco*, *La Rebótica* and *Sopa de Ganso*. If you're in a partyish mood, you should find at least one with a scene and music to your fancy. A bit farther east, *Café Lisboa*, Calle Alhóndiga 43, is a shiny music bar with minimalist decor and live blues, jazz or flamenco most Thursdays and Fridays from around 11 pm. A beer is 200 ptas.

Quitapesares on Plaza Padre Jerónimo Córdoba, off Plaza Ponce de León, is a small, earthy place run by a famous *saeta* singer, Pepe Peregil. Flamenco posters and photos dot the walls and you might hear Pepe do a song.

Alameda de Hércules Several excellent bars and some live music attract an offbeat, studenty, young-but-not-too-young crowd to this area. It used to be a red-light district and there are still a few seedy characters lurking around.

Just south of the Alameda, the mellow *Café Jazz Naima* (☎ 95 438 24 85), Calle Trajano 47, has occasional live jazz or blues from around 10 pm.

The *Fun Club*, Alameda de Hércules 86, is a small dance warehouse with a long bar and a little stage, open Thursday to Sunday from 11.30 pm (9.30 pm on live-band nights) till late. There's live rock Friday and/or Saturday (500 to 1000 ptas entry). Other nights entry is free and it usually gets pretty full (drinks 250 ptas-plus). The *Bulebar Café*, Alameda de Hércules 83, is a more relaxed place for a drink or some unusual tapas, with comfy old-fashioned furniture and a good courtyard out front. Farther along this east side of the Alameda, *El Corto Maltés*, *Café Central* and *Habanilla Café* are all busy pub-like places that spill out on to the street: at the Corto Maltés all drinks are free on the 32nd of every month The Habanilla is distinctly aromatic.

There are more great bars in the streets east of the Alameda. *La Ilustre Víctima*, Calle Dr Letamendi 35, is one of the more respectable and plays a lot of jazz and does some great tapas. It's open daily from 4 pm

to 2 or 3 am (beer 125 ptas). Round the corner at Calle Cruz de la Tinaja 5, the quaintly named *Asociación Cultural La Farándula* is a slightly seedy and secretive little dive with live blues on Tuesday, flamenco on Wednesday, pop/rock on Thursday, and pounding recorded sounds other nights. It pulls in all sorts, from Rastas to clean-cut leather-jacketed types and is open daily from 10 pm till very late (beer 125 ptas). *La Bruja*, upstairs in a corner of little Plaza Europa, is a haunt of the long-haired heavy-rock crowd, who sit around on the floor rolling joints – cool and mellow despite the loud, fast music (beer 150 ptas).

West of the Alameda, *La Imperdible* (☎ 95 438 82 19), Plaza San Antonio de Padua 9, is an epicentre of experimental arts in Sevilla, with a mellow bar, called the Almacén, where you'll often find free live jazz on Tuesday, Friday and Saturday nights from 10.30 pm, and a small theatre, the Sala La Imperdible, which stages lots of contemporary dance and a bit of experimental drama, usually at 9 pm for 800 to 1000 ptas. The *Salamandra* (☎ 95 490 28 38), at Calle del Torneo 43, across the road from the Río Guadalquivir, is one of Sevilla's top live music spots, with varied bands – soul, blues, Latin, ethnic – on Thursday and/or Friday from around 10.30 pm (usually 600 to 1000 ptas).

Triana Calle del Betis, on the west bank of the Guadalquivir, has a string of bars from which you can carry your drink across the street and sit on the wall above the river. On the way to Calle del Betis, you could stop in at *Madigan's*, Plaza de Cuba 2, another of Sevilla's popular Irish pubs – open daily from noon. Clustered side by side at Calle del Betis 54, *Alambique*, *Mui d'Aqui* and *Big Ben* all play good music and attract an interesting mix of students and travellers. They open at about 9 pm. Big Ben has live music after midnight on Friday and Saturday – as does *Café La Pavana* at Calle del Betis 41. Bars towards the north end of the street get a bit mellower – among them *Café de la Prensa* at Calle del Betis 8.

North of Calle del Betis, Calle Castilla

has yet more good bars, overflowing with a mixed twenties-ish crowd on weekend nights, including *Cervecería El Costal*, No 7, *Café-Bar Guadalquivir*, No 17, and *Aníbal Café*, No 98. A couple of passages lead through to Paseo de Nuestra Señora de la O on the riverbank, where you'll find *La Otra Orilla*, a buzzing music bar blessed with a great outdoor terrace.

Summer Nights by the River In summer, dozens of temporary open-air late-night bars *(terrazas de verano)*, many of them with live music and plenty of room to dance, spring up along both banks of the river. They change names and ambience from year to year.

Flamenco Sevilla is one of Spain's flamenco capitals and its Triana barrio on the west bank of the Guadalquivir, once the city's Gypsy quarter, was one of flamenco's birthplaces. Though impromptu flamenco in small, smoky bars in Triana or around the Alameda de Hércules is pretty much a thing of the past, there are plenty of spots where you can catch live flamenco (or sevillana) song, dance or guitar. Hotels and tourist offices will steer you towards one of the expensive tourist-oriented flamenco *tablaos* which put on nightly shows, sometimes including dinner. These can be fairly unauthentic and lacking in atmosphere, but *Los Gallos* (☎ 95 421 69 81), at Plaza de Santa Cruz 11 in the Barrio de Santa Cruz, is an honourable exception. Some top-notch flamenco performers have trodden Los Gallos' boards in the early stages of their careers. There are two-hour shows at 9 and 11.30 pm nightly for 3000 ptas including one drink.

In general, you'll catch a more genuine atmosphere in one of the growing number of bars that stage regular nights of flamenco or sevillanas, usually with no entry charge. However, the quality is unpredictable. At the time of writing these bars include (see Drinking, Music & Dancing, above, for more details on some):

Anselma Calle Pages del Corro 49, Triana (☎ 95 433 40 03) – decor and atmosphere redolent of

El Rocío, with flamenco and sevillana guitar, singing and dancing most nights (open from 8 pm to about 1 am except Sundays); the sign over the door says 'Joaquín Arenas Comestibles Finos'

Asociación Cultural La Farándula Calle Cruz de la Tinaja 5, Alameda de Hércules – flamenco on Wednesday night

Café Lisboa Calle Alhóndiga 43, El Centro – flamenco most Thursdays around 11 pm

El Mundo Calle Siete Revueltas 5, El Centro – flamenco on Tuesdays around 11 pm (300 ptas including one drink)

El Tamboril Plaza de Santa Cruz, Barrio de Santa Cruz – sevillanas and rumba every night from midnight

La Carbonería Calle Levíes 18, Barrio de Santa Cruz (☎ 95 421 44 60) – flamenco on Thursday and Monday nights (entry free)

Salamandra Calle del Torneo 43 west of the Alameda de Hércules (☎ 95 490 28 38) – flamenco Wednesdays from around 10.30 pm (entry free)

In addition there are fairly frequent appearances by big-name flamenco artists at some theatres (see below), especially the Teatro Central which runs flamenco seasons under the name Flamenco Viene del Sur. Sevilla also stages one of Spain's major flamenco festivals, the Bienal de Flamenco (see Special Events, above), and, if you're present for the Feria de Abril, you'll find plenty going on there.

Theatres The *Teatro de la Maestranza* (☎ 95 422 65 73), Paseo de Cristóbal Colón 22, the *Teatro Lope de Vega* (☎ 95 459 08 53), Avenida de María Luisa s/n, and the *Teatro Central* (☎ 95 446 07 80) and *Auditorio de la Cartuja* (☎ 95 450 56 56), both on Isla de La Cartuja, all stage varied programmes of music, dance and drama events. The Maestranza is big on opera and classical music.

Spectator Sport
Sevilla failed in its bid for the 2004 Olympics but gained the consolation prize of the World Athletics Championships – to be held in July or August 1999 in a new 60,000-seat, 15 billion peseta Estadio Olímpico at the north end of the Isla de La Cartuja.

La Teatral ticket agency (☎ 95 422 82 29) at Calle Velázquez 12 in El Centro sells tickets for bullfights, soccer games and some concerts at a markup of a few hundred pesetas.

Bullfights Fights at Sevilla's Plaza de Toros de la Real Maestranza, on Paseo de Cristóbal Colón, are among the best in Spain. The ring, which holds 14,000 spectators, is one of the country's oldest and most elegant, and its crowds some of the most knowledgeable. The season runs from Easter Sunday to early October, with fights every Sunday, usually at 6.30 pm, and almost every day during the Feria de Abril and the week before it.

From the start of the season until late June/early July, nearly all the fights are by fully-fledged matadors (all the big stars in the bullfighting firmament appear at least once in the Maestranza every year). These are the *abono* (subscription) fights, for which locals buy up the best seats on season tickets. Often only *sol* seats (those which are in the sun at the start of proceedings) are available to non-subscribers for these fights. They start at 3000 ptas. The most expensive tickets, if available, are 13,000 ptas. Most of the rest of the season, the fights are *novilleras* (noovice bullfights) with young bulls and junior toreros. Tickets for these cost from 1500 to 6500 ptas.

For more on the Plaza de Toros de la Real Maestranza, see the Along the River section earlier in this chapter.

Football Sevilla has two professional clubs, Real Betis and Sevilla. Recently, Betis has been doing nicely in the Spanish First Division while Sevilla has been in the Second Division. Betis signed the Brazilian midfield player Denilson for a world record transfer fee of US$35 million in 1997.

The city authorities have been trying to persuade both clubs to move to the new Estadio Olímpico on the Isla de La Cartuja but, for now, Betis plays at the Estadio Villamarín beside Avenida de Jerez in the suburb of Heliopolis, 1.5km south of the Parque María Luisa (bus No 34 southbound from op-

posite the main tourist office), and Sevilla's home is the Estadio Sánchez Pizjuán on Calle de Luis Morales, east of the centre.

Except for the biggest games – against the Madrid clubs or Barcelona, or when the two Sevilla teams meet each other – you can pay at the gate, from about 2500 ptas. For the big matches, prices may rise to a minimum 3500 or 4000 ptas, and it's advisable to get tickets in advance.

Things to Buy
There are lots of tourist-oriented craft shops in the Barrio de Santa Cruz just east of the Alcázar. Several sell some excellent local pottery with colourful Islamic designs or scenes of old rural life.

Pedestrianised Calle Sierpes, running north from Plaza de San Francisco in the city centre, is the fanciest shopping street, lined with smallish shops devoted to a wide range of everyday and luxury goods, from photo supplies or fashion clothes to antiques or polkadot *trajes de flamenca* (flamenco dresses). Z Zulategui at No 41 has a good stock of backpacks and outdoor gear. The Virgin Megastore at No 81 has probably the biggest range of recorded music in Andalucía. There's more of much the same in streets near Sierpes such as Velázquez, Tetuán and Cuna.

The large El Corte Inglés department store – the best single shop to look for almost anything – occupies four separate buildings a little to the west: two on Plaza de la Magdalena and two on Plaza del Duque de la Victoria. On the latter square you'll also find Marks & Spencer and the classy clothing store Cortefiel, while Sevilla Rock, just off it at 1 Calle Alfonso XII, is another good music store.

Street Markets The large Thursday *mercadillo* (flea market) on Calle de la Feria, east of the Alameda de Hércules, is a colourful event well worth a visit. Plaza del Duque de la Victoria and Plaza de la Magdalena both stage markets of leather bags and belts, hippie-type necklaces and jewellery, and other clothes, Thursday to

Saturday. On Plaza de la Alfalfa there's a Sunday morning pet market.

Getting There & Away

Air Sevilla's San Pablo airport (☎ 95 451 25 78) has quite a range of international and domestic flights. Iberia flies daily to/from London, Amsterdam, Brussels, Dusseldorf, Frankfurt, Munich and Rome, and most days to/from Paris. Within Spain, Iberia has several daily flights to/from Madrid (from around 14,000 ptas one way or return), Barcelona (22,000 ptas) and Valencia. Air Europa flies most days to/from Barcelona (19,200 ptas one way, from 20,150 ptas return) and Palma de Mallorca.

Iberia is at Calle Almirante Lobo 2 (☎ 95 422 89 01) and the airport (☎ 95 467 29 81). Air Europa's local reservations number is ☎ 95 465 28 00, and you can also get tickets at Halcón Viajes (☎ 95 421 44 56), Calle Almirante Bonifaz 3, off Calle Sierpes.

Bus Sevilla has two bus stations. Buses to/from the north of Sevilla province, Huelva province, Extremadura, Madrid and Portugal use the Plaza de Armas bus station (☎ 95 490 80 40) on Avenida del Cristo de la Expiación, just east of the Puente del Cachorro. Buses to/from most other places in Andalucía and places up the Mediterranean coast use the Prado de San Sebastián bus station (☎ 95 441 71 11) on Plaza San Sebastián, just south-east of the Barrio de Santa Cruz.

From Plaza de Armas there are frequent buses to Huelva (1¼ hours, 875 ptas); a few a day to La Antilla, Isla Cristina and Ayamonte west of Huelva, and to El Rocío and Matalascañas; and 11 to Madrid (six hours, 2715 ptas). For Extremadura and beyond, about 12 daily go to Mérida (3¼ hours, 1600 ptas), and five or more to Cáceres (four hours, 2170 ptas) and Salamanca, plus a few to Valladolid and Galicia. For information on buses to/from Portugal, see Land in the introductory Getting There & Away chapter.

Plaza de Armas is also the station for frequent buses to Santiponce (for Itálica), and

buses to the Parque Natural Sierra Norte and Minas de Riotinto, Aracena and other places in northern Huelva province.

From Prado de San Sebastián there are nine or more daily buses to Córdoba (two hours, 1200 ptas), Granada (four hours, 2710 ptas), Málaga (3½ hours, 2245 ptas), Jerez de la Frontera, Sanlúcar de Barrameda and Cádiz (one hour, 1200 to 1300 ptas); and a few to Arcos de la Frontera and Ronda (2½ hours, 1235 ptas). This is also the station for frequent buses to Carmona, and a few daily to Tarifa, Algeciras, La Línea, the Costa del Sol, Osuna, Estepa, Antequera, Écija, Jaén, Almería, Valencia and Barcelona.

Train Sevilla's Santa Justa train station (☎ 95 454 02 02) is about 1.5km north-east of the centre on Avenida Kansas City. There's also a city centre RENFE information and ticket office at Calle Zaragoza 31, open Monday to Friday from 9 am to 1.15 pm and 4 to 7 pm. Luggage lockers at the station cost 300 to 600 ptas for 24 hours.

There are four types of train to/from Madrid. The best and costliest are the 14 daily superfast AVEs, taking just 2½ hours. (See Spain in the Land section of the Getting There & Away chapter for fares.) Inter-Rail cards are not valid on trains from Madrid to Sevilla or vice versa; Eurail passholders pay 1200 ptas in Turista on AVEs.

Other daily trains from Sevilla include about 20 to Córdoba (45 minutes to 1¼ hours, 1050 to 2700 ptas); up to 15 to Jerez de la Frontera and Cádiz (1½ hours to two hours, 1085 to 1600 ptas); three each to Granada (four hours, 2280 ptas), Málaga (three hours, 1825 ptas), Huelva (1½ hours, 820 to 945 ptas), Ronda (three hours, 1860 ptas) and Algeciras (five hours, 2635 ptas), with a change at Bobadilla for the last two places; two north to Cazalla-Constantina (two hours, 615 ptas) and one to Mérida (4½ hours, 1720 ptas) and Cáceres; and one to Jaén (three hours, 2125 ptas). Other destinations include Osuna, Antequera, El Chorro, Valencia and Barcelona. For Lisbon (16 hours, 6800 ptas in 2nd-class), you must change at Cáceres.

Car & Motorcycle Parking in central Sevilla can be a problem. If you're staying in the Barrio de Santa Cruz, don't park in the nearby Jardines de Murillo – your car will probably be towed away which will cost you over 10,000 ptas. You can usually find a place five minutes walk away, east of Calle de Menéndez Pelayo in streets such as Avenida de Cádiz.

Rental Good deals are hard to come by. The cheapest car we came across was a Seat Marbella for 5800 ptas a day or 32,480 ptas a week from Autos Mínguez (☎ 95 422 46 78), Edificio Cristina, Calle Almirante Lobo 1 (just off the Puerta de Jerez). Several other local rental firms hang out in the same street. Buizauto (☎ 95 421 18 58), Paseo de las Delicias 1, and Avis (☎ 95 421 65 49), Avenida de la Constitución 15B, are also central. Other international firms – such as Budget (☎ 95 458 03 53), Europcar (☎ 95 467 38 39) and Hertz (☎ 95 451 47 20) – mostly have offices at the airport and/or outside the city centre.

Car Pooling Compartecoche (☎ 95 490 75 82) at Calle González Cuadrado 49 is an intercity car-pooling service. Its service is free to drivers, while passengers pay an agreed transfer rate. Ring or visit them between 10 am and 1.30 pm or 5 to 8 pm for details.

Boat There are no regular passenger services along the Guadalquivir, but from around April to October round-trip day cruises sail to Sanlúcar de Barrameda, 100km away at the river's mouth. Early and late in the season, cruises may only go at weekends. Several companies make the trips, from the *embarcadero* by the Torre del Oro, for around 3500 ptas. It's 4½ hours each way, usually with 4½ hours in Sanlúcar in between.

Getting Around
To/From the Airport Sevilla airport is about 7km from the centre on the N-IV Córdoba road. Buses of the Amarillos line (☎ 902-21 03 17) make the 30-minute trip (750 ptas)

between the airport and the Puerta de Jerez, in front of the Hotel Alfonso XIII, at least nine times daily. A taxi is about 1200 ptas.

Bus Bus Nos C1, C2, C3 and C4 do useful circular routes linking the main transport terminals and the city centre. However, there's been talk of changing their routes, so check that they're going where you want to go. The C1, going east from in front of Santa Justa train station, follows a clockwise circular route via Avenida de Carlos V (close to Prado de San Sebastián bus station), Avenida de María Luisa, Triana, Puerta de Triana, Isla Mágica and Calle de Resolana. No C2, heading west from in front of Santa Justa train station, follows the same route in reverse. Bus No 32, from the same stop as No C2, runs to/from Plaza de la Encarnación in the northern part of the city centre.

The clockwise No C3 will take you from Calle de Menéndez Pelayo (near Prado de San Sebastián bus station) to the Puerta de Jerez (the south end of Avenida de la Constitución), Triana, Puerta de Triana, Plaza de Armas bus station, Calle del Torneo, Calle de Resolana and Calle de Recaredo. The C4 does the same circuit anti-clockwise except that from Plaza de Armas bus station it heads south along Calle de Arjona and Paseo de Cristóbal Colón to the Puerta de Jerez, instead of going across the river to Puerta de Triana and Triana.

A single bus ride is 125 ptas. You can pick up a route map, the *Guía del Transporte Urbano de Sevilla*, from tourist offices or from information booths at major stops including Plaza Nueva, Plaza de la Encarnación, and the corner of Avenida de Carlos V and Calle de Menéndez Pelayo.

Bicycle Pedalling your way around Sevilla can be a pleasant way of exploring the city. Sevilla Mágica (☎ 95 456 38 38) at Calle Miguel de Mañara 11B, near the main tourist office, rents out decent bikes for 1200 ptas a half-day or 1800 ptas a day. It's open daily.

Taxi Taxis start with 129 ptas on the meter, rising by 88 ptas per kilometre. There's a minimum charge of 354 ptas. From 10 pm to 6 am and on holidays rates go up about 25%.

AROUND SEVILLA
Itálica & Santiponce
Itálica, about 8km north-west of Sevilla on the north-west edge of the small town of Santiponce, was the first Roman town in Spain. It was founded in 206 BC for soldiers wounded in the Battle of Ilipa, nearby, when Rome finally extinguished Carthaginian ambitions in the Iberian Peninsula. Itálica was also the birthplace of the 2nd century AD Roman emperor Trajan, and his adopted son and successor Hadrian received some of his education here. Most of the Roman *vetus urbs* (old town) now lies beneath Santiponce. The partly reconstructed ruins you visit are mainly in the *nova urbs* (new town), which was added by Hadrian. They include one of the biggest of all Roman amphitheatres, able to hold 25,000 spectators; a large public bathhouse, the Termas Mayores; and some excellent mosaics. To the west, in the vetus urbs, you can also visit a restored Roman theatre.

The site (☎ 95 599 73 76) is open Tuesday to Saturday from 9 am to 5.30 pm, Sunday and holidays from 9 am to 2 pm (free for EU citizens with passport or identity card, 250 ptas otherwise).

At the south end of Santiponce, on Avenida de San Isidoro, the **Monasterio de San Isidoro del Campo** is due to open to visitors in 1999 after renovation work. In the 16th century this was one of the most cosmopolitan centres of learning in Spain, and monks here did the first translation of the Bible into Spanish. The community was dissolved by the Inquisition after the monks developed Lutheran ideas from reading too many dangerous foreign books. Later, the monastery was used as a women's prison. Its Claustro de los Muertos (Cloister of the Dead), in Renaissance style, is one of the finest cloisters in Andalucía, and the main retablo in the church is one of the masterpieces of Juan Martínez Montañés who also carved the effigies on the tomb of the founder, Guzmán El Bueno, and his wife.

Frequent buses run to Santiponce from Plaza de Armas bus station.

La Campiña

This is the rolling area east of Sevilla and south of the Río Guadalquivir, crossed by the N-IV to Córdoba and the A-92 towards Granada and Málaga. Despite its fertility it can be strangely bleak country, with hardly a soul in sight in the long distances between the few towns. La Campiña is still a land of huge estates belonging to a few landowners, with modern farming methods doing little to relieve the plight of Andalucía's centuries-old stratum of landless labourers. Today's successors to the rural revolutionaries of the past are led by the communist villagers of Marinaleda, between Écija and Estepa, who stage periodic occupations of estates to draw attention to the need for land reform.

If you're not in a hurry there are four towns (two on the N-IV and two on the A-92) whose surprisingly grand architecture – though clear evidence of the area's long-standing wealth gap – makes them well worthy of a stop.

CARMONA
Just off the N-IV, 38km east of Sevilla, Carmona (population 25,000) stands on a low hill. Fortified as early as the 8th century BC, its strategic position was important to the Carthaginians as well as to the Romans, who laid out a street plan which survives to this day. The Via Augusta, which ran from Rome to Cádiz, entered Carmona by the eastern Puerta de Córdoba and left by the western Puerta de Sevilla.

The Muslims built a strong defensive wall around the town but Carmona fell in 1247 to Fernando III (El Santo). In the 14th century, Pedro I (the Cruel) turned Carmona's main *alcázar (*fortress) into a

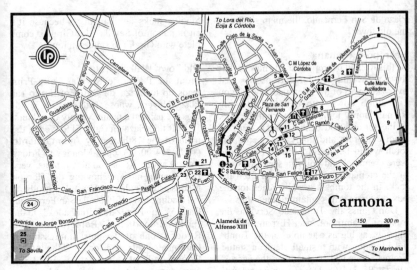

Carmona

0   150   300 m

PLACES TO STAY
5   Casa de Carmona
10 Parador Alcázar del
    Rey Don Pedro
19 Pensión Comercio
21 Casa Carmelo
23 Hostal San Pedro

PLACES TO EAT
11 Cafetería La Farola
13 Restaurante San
    Fernando
14 Café Bar El Tapeo
15 Mercado
16 Molino de la Romera

OTHER
1   Puerta de Córdoba
2   Iglesia de Santiago
3   Capilla de la
    Caridad
4   Convento de Santa
    Clara
6   Palacio de los Ruedas
7   Iglesia Prioral de
    Santa María
8   Museo de la Ciudad
9   Alcázar
12 Ayuntamiento
17 Iglesia de San Felipe
18 Iglesia de San Bartolomé
20 Puerta de Sevilla;
    Tourist Office
22 Iglesia de San Pedro
24 Roman Amphitheatre
25 Necrópolis Romana

splendid residence. The town was later adorned with numerous churches, convents and mansions by mudéjar and Christian artisans.

Information

The old part of Carmona stands on the hill at the east end of the town: the Puerta de Sevilla marks its western end. At the time of writing getting into old Carmona from the Sevilla direction was complicated by construction work on Calle Sevilla, the main approach street. Buses, which normally stop on Paseo del Estatuto about 300m west of the Puerta de Sevilla, were being forced to terminate on Avenida de Jorge Bonsor, 500m farther west (close to the Necrópolis Romana). In your own vehicle, you had to make a big loop around to the north from Avenida de Jorge Bonsor.

The helpful tourist office (☎ 95 419 09 55), in the Puerta de Sevilla, is open Monday to Saturday from 10 am to 6 pm, Sunday and holidays from 10 am to 3 pm. There are banks with ATMs on Calle San Pedro, west of the Puerta de Sevilla, and on

Plaza de San Fernando, the main square of the old town.

Necrópolis Romana

At this Roman necropolis in the new part of town at Avenida de Jorge Bonsor 9, just over 1km west of the Puerta de Sevilla, you can climb down into a dozen or more Roman family tombs, hewn from the rock in the 1st and 2nd centuries AD, some of them elaborate and many-chambered. (A torch would be useful.) Most of the dead were cremated and you can see, too, some of the cremation pits, also hewn from the rock. In the tombs are wall niches for the boxlike stone urns containing the ashes.

Don't miss the Tumba de Servilia, the tomb of a family of local Hispano-Roman bigwigs, as big as a temple, or the Tumba del Elefante, with a small elephant statue. From 15 June to 15 September, the necropolis (π 95 414 08 11) is open Tuesday to Friday from 9 am to 2 pm, and Saturday from 10 am to 2 pm; the rest of the year it's open daily except Monday from 10 am to 2 pm, plus Tuesday to Friday from 4 to 6 pm (closed holidays). Entry is free to EU passport holders, 250 ptas for others. Across the street from the entrance is a large Roman amphitheatre, but it's not open to visitors – you can only look from the road.

Puerta de Sevilla & Around

This impressive main gate of the old town has been fortified for millenia. Today it also houses the tourist office which sells tickets (200 ptas) for visits to the interesting upper levels of the structure, the Alcázar de la Puerta de Sevilla (open the same hours as the tourist office). The Alcázar affords fine views and includes an upstairs Almohad patio with traces of a Roman temple. An informative leaflet enables you to differentiate between the various Carthaginian, Roman, Muslim and Christian stages of the Alcazar's construction.

From the Puerta extend lengthy sections of Carmona's mainly Muslim **walls**. If the tower on the **Iglesia de San Pedro** on Calle San Pedro, west of the Puerta de

Sevilla, looks familiar, that's because it's an imitation of Sevilla's La Giralda, complete with Giraldillo statue on top.

Old Town Walking Tour

From the Puerta de Sevilla, Calle Prim leads up to **Plaza de San Fernando** (or Plaza Mayor), whose 16th century buildings are painted a quaint variety of colours. Just off this plaza on Calle El Salvador, the patio of the 18th century **Ayuntamiento** (π 95 414 00 11), open Monday to Friday from 8 am to 3 pm, contains a large, very fine Roman mosaic showing the Gorgon Medusa surrounded by four other heads.

Heading east off Plaza de San Fernando, Calle Martín López de Córdoba leads to the finely proportioned **Palacio de los Ruedas**, one of the most impressive of Carmona's noble mansions, and the **Iglesia Prioral de Santa María** (π 95 414 13 30), Carmona's most splendid church. Santa María was built, mainly in the 15th and 16th centuries, in a typical Carmona combination of brick and stone on the site of the Muslim town's main mosque. Especially to be admired inside are the fine Gothic pillars and ceiling tracery, the plateresque main retablo, and the Patio de los Naranjos (formerly the mosque's ablutions courtyard) with a 6th century Visigothic calendar carved into one of its pillars. The church is open daily from 9 am to noon and 6 to 9 pm.

Behind Santa María at Calle San Ildefonso 1 is the **Museo de la Ciudad** (City Museum) with archaeological and ethnographic displays, open daily except Tuesday from 4 to 6 pm (5 to 7 pm in summer), plus Saturday, Sunday and holidays from noon to 2 pm. Entry is 200 ptas.

Moving on along Calle Santa María de Gracia you reach the 16th century **Convento de Santa Clara**, with an ornamental brick tower, open for visits daily from 10 am to 12.30 pm and 5 to 7 pm. At the beginning of Calle de Dolores Quintanilla is the little 16th century **Capilla de la Caridad**, with a nice brick façade. This street continues downhill to the **Puerta de Córdoba**, originally a Roman gate, through which there are panoramas over the country to the east.

Moving back uphill and turning southwest up Calle Calatrava you come to the **Iglesia de Santiago,** with a pretty mudéjar tower tiered in red brick and blue tiles. South from here along Calle María Auxiliadora and Calle General Freire is the **Alcázar**, the Almohad fort which Pedro the Cruel turned into a country palace in a mudéjar style similar to his parts of the Sevilla Alcázar. Ruined by an earthquake in 1504, part of the alcázar was restored as a parador in the 1970s. With excellent views and a lovely patio, this is a good place to stop for a drink or (if you can afford it) a meal. There are more fortifications up to the left.

From here you can start back along the street called Puerta de Marchena on the southern rim of the town, with more good views over the country around Carmona. Head into the tangle of streets to look at the 14th century **Iglesia de San Felipe** at the head of Calle San Felipe, with a pretty brick mudéjar tower and Renaissance façade, and the 15th-to-18th century **Iglesia de San Bartolomé** on Calle San Bartolomé.

Places to Stay
Easily the best budget option is *Pensión Comercio* (☎ 95 414 00 18) at Calle Torre del Oro 56, just north of the Puerta de Sevilla. It's a lovely tiled old building with a mudéjar-style entrance arch and brick-pillared patio. The 14 clean, well-kept rooms cost 2000/3500 ptas plus IVA a single/double, or 4500 ptas plus IVA for doubles with bath. It also has a restaurant with very reasonable prices (400 to 600 ptas for most main dishes), open daily except Sunday for all meals. The smaller *Casa Carmelo* (☎ 95 414 05 72), Calle San Pedro 17 outside the Puerta de Sevilla, has doubles from 4000 ptas. *Hostal San Pedro* (☎ 95 414 16 06), Calle San Pedro 3, has comfy if bare doubles with bath, TV and air-con for 6000 ptas.

From there, it's a big jump in price and quality to the historic *Parador Alcázar del Rey Don Pedro* (☎ 95 414 10 10) at the southeast corner of town, with 63 rooms at 18,000

ptas plus IVA for doubles. Even more charming and luxurious is the *Casa de Carmona* (☎ 95 414 33 00) in a 17th century mansion at Plaza de Lasso 1. The 30 rooms cost from 22,000 to 34,000 ptas, plus IVA, a double.

Places to Eat
The bars and cafés around Plaza de San Fernando do raciones and tapas, and two of them – *Café Bar El Tapeo* and *Cafetería La Farola* – have menús for around 950 ptas. *Restaurante San Fernando*, overlooking the plaza though access is from Calle Sacramento, is a much classier place with a good 3500-ptas menú of several courses. It's open for lunch and from 9 pm for dinner (closed Sunday evening and all Monday). A meal in the fine restaurants of the *Parador Alcázar del Rey Don Pedro* or the *Casa de Carmona* is likely to cost the same or a bit more.

Another place where you might stop to eat is the *Molino de la Romera*, in an interesting 15th century oil mill building on Puerta de Marchena. You can choose between restaurant and café sections; it's open daily for lunch and dinner.

There are more tapas bars on Calle La Fuente off Calle San Pedro, just outside the Puerta de Sevilla.

Getting There & Away
Frequent buses run to Carmona from Sevilla (Prado de San Sebastián) for 265 ptas. See Orientation for the location of the stop in Carmona.

ÉCIJA
Écija (population 37,000) stands on the Río Genil, 53km east along the N-IV from Carmona. It's known both as La Ciudad de las Torres, for its many fine – if often dilapidated – baroque church towers, studded with colourful tiles and visible from some distance away, and as La Sartén de Andalucía (the Frying-Pan of Andalucía) for its summer temperatures, which have been known to top 50°C. The town owes its splendours to the 18th century, when the local nobility splashed out on large mansions, and

the church towers were rebuilt following a 1757 earthquake.

The tourist office (☎ 95 590 29 33) at Calle de Cánovas del Castillo 4 near the leafy, arcaded main square, Plaza de España, gives out good printed material which will help to guide you around all the sights.

Things to See

As in Carmona, the **Ayuntamiento**, on Plaza de España, boasts a Roman mosaic. Two of the most spectacular towers are on the **Iglesia de Santa María** just off Plaza de España, and the **Iglesia de San Juan Bautista** to the east on Plaza San Juan. Calle Castillo beside Santa María leads to one of Écija's most magnificent mansions, the Palacio de Benamejí, housing a fine **Museo Histórico Municipal** (☎ 95 590 29 19) with lovely patios and good archaeological and equestrian sections (Écija is a noted horse breeding centre).

The museum is open daily except Monday from 9 am to 2 pm (October to May: Tuesday to Friday 9.30 am to 1.30 pm and 4.30 to 6.30 pm, Saturday and Sunday 9 am to 2 pm).

Another highlight is the huge **Palacio de Peñaflor** on Calle Castellar, two blocks south of San Juan, with frescos on its curved façade and an elaborate baroque portal. You can visit the patio and ground floor Monday to Friday from 10.30 am to 1 pm and 5 to 8 pm.

Places to Stay

The only options in the centre, but both good, are *Pensión Santa Cruz* (☎ 95 483 02 22), Calle Practicante Romero Gordillo 8, charging 2400 to 3000 ptas for rooms with shared bathrooms, and the *Hotel Platería* (☎ 95 483 50 10), Calle Garcilópez 1A, where doubles with bath are 7000 ptas plus IVA.

Getting There & Away

Sevibús runs five buses a day to Écija from Sevilla (Plaza de Armas). There are three or more a day from Córdoba.

OSUNA

Osuna (population 17,000), 91km southeast from Sevilla just off the A-92, doesn't look much from the highway but if you penetrate the town you'll find it a handsome old place with many lovely stone buildings from the 16th to 18th centuries. Several of the most impressive of these were created by the ducal family of Osuna, one of Spain's richest since the 16th century.

The tourist office (☎ 95 481 16 17), next to the Ayuntamiento on the central Plaza Mayor, hands out useful little guides in various languages detailing the town's monuments. It's open Monday to Friday from 9 am to 2 pm and 5 to 7 pm.

Plaza Mayor

The fine, leafy central square has the partly modernised 16th century Ayuntamiento on one side, a large market building on the other, and the 16th century church of the Convento de la Concepción at the end.

Baroque Mansions

You can't go inside but four of these mansions have fine façades worth hunting out. One is the **Palacio de los Cepeda** on Calle de la Huerta behind the Ayuntamiento, with rows of Churrigueresque columns topped by stone halberdiers holding the Cepeda family coat of arms. The 1737 portal of the **Palacio de Puente Hermoso** at Calle Sevilla 44, a couple of blocks west of Plaza Mayor, has twisted pillars encrusted with grapes and vine leaves.

Moving north from Plaza Mayor up Calle Caballos and its continuation Calle Carrera, you pass the **Iglesia de Santo Domingo** (1531) before you reach the corner of Calle San Pedro (marked by an El Monte bank). At Calle San Pedro 16 the **Palacio del Cabildo Colegial** bears a sculpted representation of Sevilla's La Giralda, flanked by the Sevilla martyrs Santa Justa and Santa Rufina. Farther down this street, on the corner of Calle Jesús, the **Palacio de los Marqueses de La Gomera** has elaborate clustered pillars, and the family shield at the top of the façade.

Museo Arqueológico

On Plaza de la Duquesa, just east of the Plaza Mayor, the Torre del Agua, a 12th century Almohad tower, houses Osuna's Archaeological Museum. The mainly Iberian and Roman collection includes copies of local Iberian bronzes and reliefs whose originals are now in the Louvre in Paris and Spain's national archaeological museum in Madrid. The museum (300 ptas) is open daily except Monday from 11.30 am to 1.30 pm and 4.30 to 6.30 pm (May to September, 5 to 7 pm).

Colegiata de Santa María & Around

Osuna's most impressive monuments overlook the centre from the hill above the Museo Arqueológico. Pre-eminent is the Colegiata de Santa María de la Asunción (☎ 95 481 04 44), a 16th century church which contains a wealth of fine art collected by the Duques de Osuna. It's open for guided tours (300 ptas) daily except Monday from 10 am to 1.30 pm and 4 to 7 pm (October to April: 11.30 am to 1.30 pm and 3.30 to 5.30 pm). In the main body of the church are José de Ribera's *Cristo de la Expiración*, a marvellous example of this 17th century painter's use of light/dark contrast; an elaborate baroque main retablo; a contrasting 14th century retablo in the Capilla de la Virgen de los Reyes; and, in the Capilla de la Inmaculada, a Crucifixion sculpture attributed to the Sevillan 17th century master Juan de Mesa. The church's sacristy contains, amid much more religious art, another four Riberas. The tour also includes the lugubrious underground Sepulcro Ducal, created in 1548 as the family vault of the Osunas, who are entombed in wall niches. There's more art down here including work by the Sevilla sculptor Pedro Torrigiano and the painter Luis 'El Divino' Morales from Extremadura, two leading figures of the Renaissance in Spain.

Down the steps in front of the Colegiata is the **Convento de la Encarnación** (☎ 95 481 11 21), now a museum with mainly religious art and artefacts, and beautiful old tiles in the cloister – open daily except Monday from 10 am to 1.30 pm and 3.30 to 6.30 pm (250 ptas). Behind the Colegiata, the **Antigua Universidad** (Old University), a square building with pointed towers, was founded in 1549. It was closed on our visit, for adaptation as a pre-university college.

Places to Stay & Eat

Pensión-Residencia Esmeralda (☎ 95 582 10 73), two minutes walk south of Plaza Mayor at Calle Tesorero 7, has respectable singles/doubles with toilet from 1500/3000 to 2000/4000 ptas.

Hostal 5 Puertas (☎ 95 481 12 43), five minutes' walk north of Plaza Mayor at Calle Carrera 79, has smallish but decent singles/doubles with shower and toilet for 2000/4000 ptas (more in April and May). *Hostal Caballo Blanco* (☎ 95 481 01 84), an old coaching inn across the street at Calle Granada 1, is slightly more expensive at 3000/5000 ptas with bathroom, TV and parking in the courtyard. Both these places have restaurants, and at the 5 Puertas there are also good-value platos combinados in the bar for around 500 ptas, and many tapas for a cheap 75 ptas.

Restaurante Doña Guadalupe at Plaza Guadalupe 6, on a small square between Calle Quijada and Calle Gordillo off Calle Carrera, does a four-course menú for 1500 ptas, and à la carte main courses for around the same price, all plus IVA. You can sit in green wicker chairs in the bar area, or in the restaurant behind.

Getting There & Away

The bus station (☎ 95 481 01 46) is on Plaza de San Agustín, from which it's a few minutes' walk north-west along Calle Capitán and Calle San Agustín to the central Plaza Mayor. Half a dozen daily buses run to/from Sevilla (Prado de San Sebastián), four to/from Estepa and Antequera, and there's also service to/from Málaga.

Three trains a day run to/from Sevilla, Antequera, Granada and Málaga: the station (☎ 95 481 03 08) is on Avenida de la Estación in the south-west of town, about 15 minutes walk from the centre.

ESTEPA

Picturesque Estepa (population 12,000), which climbs up a hill above the highway 24km east of Osuna, was the scene of a mass suicide back in 207 BC when its inhabitants, who had picked the wrong (Carthaginian) side in the Second Punic War, decided not to throw themselves on the mercy of their Roman conquerors. The town has a tourist office (☎ 95 591 27 71) at Calle Saladillo 12.

The most impressive buildings in the lower part of town are baroque: the lavish **Iglesia del Carmen** by the central Plaza del Carmen, and the 18th century **Palacio de los Cerverales**.

In the upper part of the town – still surrounded by walls and towers constructed by the medieval Knights of Santiago – are the **Torre del Homenaje**, the 14th century castle keep; the fortlike Gothic **Iglesia de Santa María de la Asunción**, built in the 15th century on the site of a mosque and with quite an art collection; and, next door to the church, the 16th century **Convento de Santa Clara** with a lovely patio. Also up here, the **Balcón de Andalucía** mirador has fine views over the Campiña and much of the town – including the 18th century **Torre de la Victoria**, 50m high, which once adorned another convent.

The *Hostal Balcón de Andalucía* (☎ 95 591 26 80), Avenida de Andalucía 11, has doubles for 5000 ptas.

The buses mentioned for Osuna also serve Estepa.

Parque Natural Sierra Norte

This 1648 sq km natural park, stretching across almost the whole of the north of Sevilla province, is rolling Sierra Morena country, with no great mountains, but it is attractive, remote and often wild. Much of it is covered in *dehesas*, woodlands of scattered evergreen oaks rising from scrub or pasture. The valleys tend to be more richly vegetated.

A number of charming, old-fashioned villages and small towns bear a clear Islamic imprint, with forts or castles that go back to Muslim times, part-mudéjar churches and narrow, zig-zagging white streets. A second good reason to come here is the ample opportunity for walks, especially around Cazalla de la Sierra and in the lovely valley of the Río Huéznar. Most visitors are *sevillanos* in search of fresh air and rural calm.

The heart of the park is around the two main towns, Cazalla de la Sierra and Constantina, which are 20km apart.

Getting There & Away

There's no public transport to/from Carmona, or east or west into Córdoba or Huelva provinces.

Bus Linesur/Bética runs buses between Sevilla (Plaza de Armas) and Cazalla de la Sierra, Constantina (both 1¾ hours, 725 ptas), El Pedroso, San Nicolás del Puerto, Alanís and Guadalcanal twice or more daily each way (but on Sunday and holidays there's only one bus back from Cazalla, at 6.15 pm at the time of writing). To/from Las Navas de la Concepción there's one bus daily except Sunday.

Train Cazalla-Constantina station is on the A-455 Cazalla-Constantina road, 7km from Cazalla and 12km from Constantina. There are three or four trains daily to/from Sevilla (two hours, 615 ptas), all stopping at El Pedroso. Two a day go on to/from Guadalcanal, and one to/from Mérida and Cáceres in Extremadura.

Buses to/from Cazalla meet the trains at Cazalla-Constantina station (leaving Cazalla about 30 minutes before the train is due), but there's no bus service linking the station with Constantina.

Getting Around

Buses between the *pueblos* have complicated, changing schedules. For up-to-date details contact Linesur/Bética in Sevilla (☎ 95 498 82 20) or Bar Gregorio (where the buses stop in Constantina), or try one of the tourist offices. At the time of writing there's a bus from Cazalla de la Sierra to Constantina Monday to Friday at 11.45 am and Saturday at 2.30 pm; and from Constantina to Cazalla de la Sierra daily at 9 am. Buses also run at least once daily between Constantina and San Nicolás del Puerto, Alanís and Guadalcanal; and between Constantina and Las Navas de la Concepción Monday to Friday. Most buses between Sevilla and Cazalla de la Sierra or Constantina stop at El Pedroso.

CAZALLA DE LA SIERRA

This pretty little white town of 5000 people, 85km north-east of Sevilla, is the best geared up for visitors in the region. Tourist information and free town maps are available Monday to Friday from 9 am to 2 pm at the Ayuntamiento (☎ 95 488 40 00), Plaza de Manuel Nosea 1. There's an intermittently open tourist office (☎ 95 488 45 60) at Paseo del Moro 2.

Things to See

The most impressive building in Cazalla's tangle of old-fashioned streets is the enormous fortress-like **Iglesia de Nuestra Señora de la Consolación** on Plaza Mayor, a 14th century mudéjar and Gothic construction in the typical brick and stone of the region. It was badly damaged in the civil war but has been restored. If its main door on Plaza Mayor is not open, the one on the other side often is.

La Cartuja de Cazalla (☎ 95 488 45 16) is a large, ruined 15th century monastery in a beautiful, secluded nook of the Sierra Morena, 4km from Cazalla (take the A-455 Constantina road for 2.5km, then turn along a signposted side road). Built on the site of a Muslim mill and mosque, the monastery fell into ruin in the 19th century. In 1977 it was bought by a redoubtable art lover called Carmen Ladrón de Guevara, who is devotedly restoring it – in part as an arts centre (there are exhibition and concert rooms) – and has opened a guesthouse to help pay for the project. La Cartuja is open for visits daily from 10 am to 2 pm and 5 to 9 pm (500 ptas).

Walks

Two tracks lead from Cazalla down to the Huéznar valley and by combining them you can enjoy a round trip of about 8km. They pass through typical Sierra Norte evergreen oak woodlands, olive groves and small cultivated plots, and the odd chestnut wood and vineyard. Overhead look for eagles, griffon vultures and the rare black vulture (sometimes the two types of vulture fly together).

One track is the Sendero de las Laderas (also called the Vereda del Valle) which starts at a fountain called El Chorrillo on the eastern edge of Cazalla at the foot of Calle Parras. The path leads down to the Puente de los Tres Ojos bridge on the Huéznar, from which you go up the west bank of the river a short way, then head up the Arroyo del Castillejo stream which enters the Huéznar from the west. Shortly after the Puente del Castillejo bridge, bear left and return to Cazalla by the Camino Viejo (the Old Road) from Cazalla-Constantina station.

You can also join this walk from Cazalla-Constantina station by following the 'Molino del Corcho' path down the Huéznar for about 1km to the Arroyo del Castillejo.

Places to Stay

Hospedaje La Milagrosa (☎ 95 488 42 60) at Calle Llana 29, on the main road heading north from the town centre, has rather suspicious owners and half a dozen small singles/doubles for 2000/3500 ptas. Much nicer is *Posada del Moro* (☎ 95 488 43 26), near the southern entrance to the town at Paseo El Moro s/n, where comfortable rooms with tiled floors and cork-topped furniture are 5000/8000 ptas with bathroom. The rooms overlook a patio and garden with a pool.

Two kilometres south of Cazalla on the Sevilla road, then 1km east down a dirt road (signposted), *Las Navezuelas* (☎ 95 488 47 64) is a restored 17th century olive oil mill with rooms for around 8000 ptas a double. Short courses in crafts such as pottery, jam-making and gardening are available, and there's a pool.

Hospedería La Cartuja (☎ 95 488 45 16) is the guesthouse at La Cartuja de Cazalla (see Things to See). The eight rooms are simple and modern, with bath, and hung with work by artists who have been invited to pay for stays here by donating some of their art. Singles/doubles for one night are 8500/12,000 ptas including breakfast, but the rate goes down if you stay longer. Dinner is 3000 ptas – much of the food is home grown and the dining rooms are in the monastery's old pilgrims' hostel. There's a nice pool too.

Places to Eat
For tapas and raciones, there are bars on and near the central pedestrian street La Plazuela. *Cafetería-Bar Gonzalo* at Calle Caridad 3, a few steps off La Plazuela, does inexpensive meals too. If you fancy Italian, head for *Pizzería Mediterránea*, Calle Daóiz 30. The *Posada del Moro* has a good restaurant with lunch or dinner for around 2000 ptas.

Things to Buy
Cazalla is known for its *anisados*, aniseed-based liqueurs. Two places you can sample and buy them are Anís Miura, Calle Virgen del Monte 54, and Anís del Clavel, Calle San Benito 8. Miura's *guinda* (wild cherry) anisado is a rich, tasty, heart-warming concoction.

CONSTANTINA
With a population of 7000, the likeable valley town of Constantina is the 'capital' of the Sierra Norte.

Orientation & Information
Buses stop at the Bar Gregorio on Calle El Peso in the centre.

The Parque Natural's information centre, Centro de Interpretación El Robledo (☎ 95 588 15 97), is 1km west along the A-452 El Pedroso road from the petrol station at the south end of Constantina. It's open daily from 9 am to 2 pm and 5 to 8 pm (4 to 6 or 7 pm in winter).

There are several banks with ATMs on the pedestrianised main street Calle Mesones, just north of the bus stop.

Things to See & Do
The west side of Constantina is topped by a Muslim **fort** surrounded by shady gardens (always open). Below are medieval streets and 18th century mansions of the **Barrio de la Morería**. The **Iglesia de Santa María de la Encarnación**, just off Calle El Peso, has a mudéjar tower topped by a belfry, added in 1568 by Hernán Ruiz, who also did the one atop La Giralda in Sevilla.

The marked walk to **Los Castañares**, north-west from the town's bullring (by the Cazalla road in the north of town), takes you in about 1½ hours up to a hilltop viewpoint, through thick chestnut woods.

Places to Stay
The *Albergue Juvenil Constantina* youth hostel (☎ 95 588 15 89) at Cuesta Blanca s/n has room for 93, all in single or twin rooms. Cuesta Blanca leads uphill behind the petrol station at the south end of town. The friendly *Pensión Angelita* (☎ 95 588 17 25), Calle El Peso 28, has four rooms for 1500/2200 ptas without bath, 2500/3700 ptas with. There are also economical rooms in the *Casa Mari Pepa* (☎ 95 588 01 58), a private house at Calle José de la Bastida 25.

Places to Eat
Most options are on or near the pedestrianised main street Calle Mesones. Probably the best meals are at the *Restaurant Las Farolas* at Calle Mesones 14: the tortilla espárragos silvestre (wild asparagus omelette, 650 ptas) followed by the solomillo de cerdo ibérico al roquefort (Iberian pork sirloin in Roquefort sauce, 1450 ptas) make a pretty good meal, but there are cheaper options too, including pizzas for around 700 ptas. *Cafetería Mesones 39* at Calle Mesones 39 is a decent spot for breakfast. The local sweet red wine, called *mosto*, is a good drop – and cheap.

SIERRA NORTE VILLAGES

The other main settlements in the park are **El Pedroso**, 16km south of Cazalla de la Sierra; **Las Navas de la Concepción**, 22km east of Constantina; **San Nicolás del Puerto**, 17km north of Constantina; **Alanís**, 8km north-west of San Nicolás, with a Muslim castle; and **Guadalcanal**, a further 11km north-west, an ancient mining centre with a castle, medieval walls and mudéjar churches. There are fine views from 910m **Pico Hamapega**, 5km south-east of Guadalcanal, reached by a driveable track from the Alanís-Guadalcanal road.

Walks

Published information on walking routes is rather haphazard. The Paseo del Moro tourist office in Cazalla and the Centro de Interpretación El Robledo have Spanish-language leaflets covering a handful of routes. A 1:100,000 map of the park, *Parque Natural Sierra Norte*, published by the CNIG in 1996, shows 14 marked paths of a few hours each, but it is hard to find.

Huéznar Valley From Cazalla-Constantina station it's about 1km up the valley to the Isla Margarita picnic area on an island in the Río Huéznar. From Isla Margarita a path leads up the east side of the river all the way to San Nicolás del Puerto: after about 4km it meets the line of a disused railway running to San Nicolás and the old mines of Cerro del Hierro – you can walk along this instead of the path, if you like. Two kilometres before San Nicolás are the impressive Cascada Martinete waterfalls.

Cerro del Hierro The village of this name (meaning Hill of Iron) is a dilapidated ex-mining settlement a short distance east of the SE-163 Constantina-San Nicolás del Puerto road. One kilometre south of the village is a parking area which is the starting point of the marked Sendero de El Cerro del Hierro, a 6.5km loop walk through unusual karstic rock formations and old mining tunnels.

Sendero del Arroyo de las Cañas This 11km triangular marked route, around the country west of El Pedroso, is one of the prettiest in the park. The landscape is notable for its large, curiously shaped, granite rocks.

La Capitana The top of this highest hill in the park (959m) affords tremendous long-distance views over much of the Sierra Norte and north into Extremadura. The 7km walk westward to it from Guadalcanal (690m) takes you along the Sierra del Viento, one of the park's most abrupt ranges.

Places to Stay

Camping La Fundición (☎ 95 595 41 17) is beside the Río Huéznar, 2km up the San Nicolás del Puerto road from Cazalla-Constantina station. Price is 250 ptas per person and per car and 300 ptas per tent, plus IVA. *Camping Cortijo* (☎ 95 588 65 98), also called *Camping Batán de las Monjas*, about 5km up the same road in the San Nicolás direction, has just 20 sites.

In El Pedroso, *Hotel Casa Montehuéznar* (☎ 95 488 90 15), Avenida de la Estación 15, has rooms with bath for around 7500 ptas a double, and a good restaurant specialising in meat and game.

At Las Navas de la Concepción, *Hostal Los Monteros* (☎ 95 588 50 62) has rooms for 5000 ptas a double, and a restaurant, and can organise hiking, mountain biking, climbing and donkey-riding trips. San Nicolás del Puerto has a hostal, the *Venta La Salud* (☎ 95 488 52 53), on the Constantina road on the south-east edge of town.

Huelva Province

Most foreigners only pass through Andalucía's westernmost province on the way to or from Portugal's Algarve. But Huelva actually has something for everyone. It includes most of the Parque Nacional de Doñana, whose famous wetlands are a bird habitat of huge international importance. The *lugares colombinos*, (Columbus sites) where Columbus planned his 1492 voyage and from where he set sail, will fascinate anyone with a historical leaning. Also along Huelva's coasts are around half of the excellent, sandy, pine-backed, Atlantic beaches of the Costa de la Luz (Coast of Light).

In contrast to the flat southern half of the province, the Parque Natural Sierra de Aracena y Picos de Aroche in the north is a large area of beautiful, verdant hill country with many good walking routes (and the best *jamón serrano* in Spain). On the way north, the age-old mining centre of Minas de Riotinto makes an unusual and fascinating stop.

HUELVA

The province's capital is a port lying between the Odiel and Tinto estuaries and has a population of 141,000. It was probably founded by the Phoenicians as a trading settlement about 3000 years ago, but much of it was destroyed by the Lisbon earthquake of 1755. Heavy industrial plants line much of its Odiel waterfront and stretch far to the south. The city centre is pleasant enough and Huelva is a convenient base for visiting the nearby Columbus sites or the Marismas del Odiel wetlands.

Orientation & Information

The central area is about 1km square, with the bus station on its western edge on Calle Doctor Rubio, and the train station on its southern edge on Avenida de Italia. From Plaza de las Monjas, the unexciting central square, the main street, Avenida Martín Alonso Pinzón (also called Gran Vía), leads

HIGHLIGHTS

- Parque Nacional de Doñana – a wetland haven for vast numbers of birds and other wildlife
- The Lugares Colombinos – where Christopher Columbus planned his great voyage and from where he set sail
- Walking in the hills and old-fashioned villages of the north
- The long, sandy beaches of the Costa de la Luz
- Paraje Natural Marismas del Odiel – another fine wetland bird site
- The ancient mining area around Minas de Riotinto

Map Locator Index

east and becomes Alameda Sundheim. Parallel to Avenida Martín Alonso Pinzón, one block south, is a long, narrow pedestrianised shopping street running through several names from Calle Concepción to Calle Berdigón.

Tourist Offices If you're planning to do some walking in northern Huelva province, it's worth picking up the *Traveller's Map – Footpaths of the Sierra de Aracena and Picos de Aroche* from the Patronato Provincial de Turismo (☎ 959 25 74 67) in the Diputación Provincial at Calle Fernando El Católico 18, open Monday to Friday from 9 am to 2 pm.

DAVID WATERMAN

GERRY REILLY

MÁLAGA
Top: Rocks of ages at El Torcal, near Antequera
Bottom: Nerja coastline from the Balcón de Europa

MÁLAGA

Top: Looking into Ronda's old Muslim town, La Ciudad, from the Puente Viejo
Bottom: Typical village roofscape, in the sierras behind the Costa del Sol

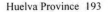

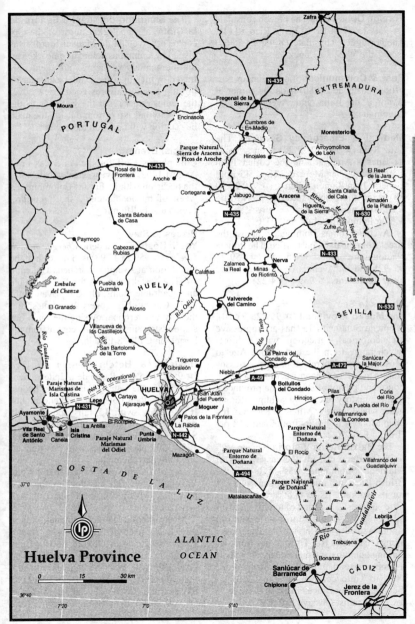

Foreign Consulates The French consulate (☎ 959 25 77 00) is at Calle Rico 53, 1°. The Portuguese consulate (☎ 959 24 55 69) is at Calle Vázquez López 15.

Post & Communications The main post office (postcode 21080) is on the corner of Avenida de Italia and Avenida Tomás Domínguez.

Medical & Emergency Services The Cruz Roja (☎ 959 22 22 22) is on Avenida de Buenos Aires around the corner from Catedral de la Merced. The Hospital General Juan Ramón Jiménez (☎ 959 20 10 88) is on the Ronda Exterior Norte ring road, 4km north of the city centre.

The Policía Local (☎ 959 21 02 21) are on Avenida Tomás Domínguez, across the street from the main post office. The Policía Nacional are on Paseo Santa Fé (☎ 959 24 05 92) and on Avenida de Italia opposite Calle Tendaleras (☎ 959 24 84 22).

Things to See
The **Museo Provincial** (☎ 959 25 93 00), Alameda Sundheim 13, has an impressive archaeological collection with exhibits which range from the early Stone Age to Muslim times. There's abundant Tartessos culture material, a reconstruction of a Celtic house and plenty of stuff on the province's mining history including a huge Roman water wheel found at Minas de Riotinto. It's open Monday to Friday from 9 am to 2 pm (free).

The **Barrio Reina Victoria** (Queen Victoria Quarter), just off the eastern end of Alameda Sundheim, was built by the British Rio Tinto mining company in 1917 for its workers. Its straight streets of cute little cottages – in a kind of hybrid English-Spanish style – make for a curious stroll. Another stroll with Rio Tinto associations is along the **Muelle Río Tinto**, a fine iron pier curving out into the Odiel estuary about half a kilometre south of the port. It was built for the Rio Tinto company in the 1870s by George Barclay Bruce, a British disciple of tower specialist Gustave Eiffel.

The **Santuario de Nuestra Señora de la Cinta**, a chapel 2km north of the city centre off Avenida de Manuel Siurot, was visited by Columbus before he embarked on his momentous voyage – an event portrayed in tiles by artist Daniel Zuloaga. Its hill-top position affords good views over the Odiel estuary and the wetlands to the west. City bus No 6 from outside the main bus station will take you there.

Special Events
Columbus set off for the Americas on 3 August 1492. Each year, Huelva celebrates the occasion with its Fiestas Colombinas, a week of music, dancing, sport, cultural events and bullfighting.

Places to Stay
Youth Hostel The modern *Albergue Juvenil Huelva* (☎ 959 25 37 93) is 2km north of the bus station at Avenida Marchena Colombo 14. The hostel has room for 130 in double and quadruple rooms, all with private bathroom. City bus No 6 (every 25 minutes from the city bus terminal outside the main bus station) stops just round the corner from the hostel, on Calle JS Elcano.

Hostales & Hotels *Pensión La Vega* (☎ 959 24 15 63), Paseo de la Independencia 15 near the Catedral, is the best budget option – albeit noisy on weekend nights. It's friendly, with 15 fairly comfortable rooms, though some are rather airless. Singles/doubles with shared bathrooms are 1750/3500 ptas; doubles with private bath are 4000 ptas. Some have TV.

Hostal Andalucía (☎ 959 24 56 67), Calle Vázquez López 22, has doubles for 3100 ptas plus IVA or 4100 ptas plus IVA with private bath.

Most other budget accommodation is in the streets near the fish market. *Hostal Virgen del Rocío* (☎ 959 28 17 16), Calle Tendaleras 14, is the best of these, with singles for 1800 ptas and doubles with bath for 4500 ptas. *Hostal La Cinta* (☎ 959 24 85 82) at Calle Rascón 29 and *Hostal Calvo* (☎ 959 24 90 16) at Calle Rascón 33 are

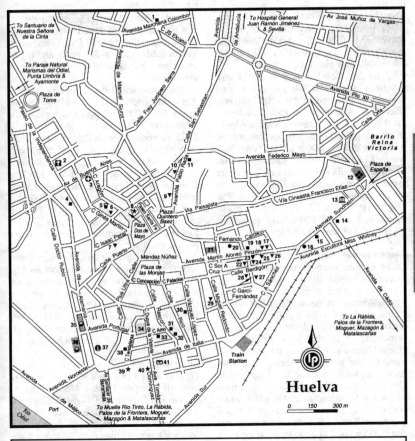

HUELVA PROVINCE

Huelva

0   150   300 m

PLACES TO STAY
1   Albergue Juvenil Huelva
4   Pensión La Vega
11 Hotel Monte Conquero
14 Hotel Luz Huelva
15 Hotel Los Condes
19 Hotel Tartessos
30 Hostal Andalucía
31 Hostal La Cinta
32 Hostal Calvo
33 Hotel Costa de la Luz
38 Hostal Virgen del Rocío

PLACES TO EAT
6   La Casa de la Patata
7   Camillo e Peppone

9   La Mal Donal's
10 La Cabaña
17 La Prensa
18 Cafetería El Punto
22 Taberna El Condado
23 Los Encinares
24 Cafetería Parra I
25 Burger Alameda
26 San Marcos Heladería
27 La Cazuela
28 Oh La La
29 Mesón La Marmita

OTHER
2   Catedral de la Merced
3   Cruz Roja

5   Docklands
8   Policía Nacional
12 El Corte Inglés
13 Museo Provincial
16 Marina Rent A Car
20 Patronato Provincial de
    Turismo
21 Ayuntamiento
34 Fish Market
35 City Bus Terminal
36 Bus Station
37 Tourist Office
39 Policía Nacional
40 Policía Local
41 Post Office

about half that price but very basic. A better place nearby is *Hotel Costa de la Luz* (☎ 959 25 64 22), Calle Alcalde José María Amo 8, where singles/doubles with bath are 4000/6000 ptas plus IVA.

Hotel Los Condes (☎ 959 28 24 00), Alameda Sundheim 14, has 53 air-con rooms with bath and TV for 4200/7500 ptas plus IVA. The modern *Hotel Tartessos* (☎ 959 28 27 11), Avenida Martín Alonso Pinzón 13, has 112 comfy, air-con rooms, with doubles at 12,000 ptas plus IVA. *Hotel Monte Conquero* (☎ 959 28 55 00), not far north at Avenida Pablo Rada 10, is another good modern place, with 168 rooms with outside views at similar prices. *Hotel Luz Huelva* (☎ 959 25 00 11), Alameda Sundheim 26, has over 100 deluxe rooms for 10,980/16,335 ptas plus IVA.

Places to Eat

In the evening many restaurants and tapas places don't open till 8.30 or 9 pm.

Los Encinares bar on the corner of Avenida Martín Alonso Pinzón and Calle Sor Ángela de la Cruz does excellent grills such as brocheta de solomillo ibérico con patatas (brochette of Iberian pork sirloin, with chips, 1700 ptas) – but they do charge (100 ptas) for the olives they bring with your drink. Just south on Calle Sor Ángela de la Cruz, *Taberna El Condado* is an atmospheric bar for tapas (from 250 ptas), while across the street the straightforward *Cafetería Parra I* is popular for its platos combinados (600 to 750 ptas) and tapas. A few steps away at Calle Berdigón 26, *Oh La La* packs 'em in for its baguettes from 350 to 400 ptas and pizza and pasta for 500 to 850 ptas. It's one of the few places where you can find a Sunday morning breakfast. *La Cazuela*, nearby at Calle Garci-Fernández 5, is a classier place specialising in fish, with a menú for 1600 ptas plus IVA.

Mesón La Marmita, at Calle Miguel Redondo 12, is smart but cosy, with a menú for just 850 ptas plus IVA.

Burger Alameda on Avenida Martín Alonso Pinzón does a burger, chips and soft drink special for 560 ptas. At the east end of

Avenida Martín Alonso Pinzón, *La Prensa* is a pleasant café plastered with old newspaper pages; *Cafetería El Punto* specialises in montaditos (125 to 200 ptas); and if you fancy an ice cream, head for *San Marcos Heladería*.

The restaurant at the *Hotel Los Condes*, Alameda Sundheim 14, has platos combinados for 550 to 750 ptas and a menú for 1000 ptas.

To the north, Avenida Pablo Rado is lined with popular eateries, many of them with terrazas, where you can *tapear* or sit down to something more substantial. *La Mal Donal's* is one busy place, turning out montaditos for 250 ptas, revueltos for 500 ptas and grilled meats for 1000 ptas. A little farther up the street, *La Cabaña* is a bit fancier, with a similar menu at higher prices.

Camillo e Peppone on Calle Isaac Peral serves up excellent pasta and pizza for 550 to 1000 ptas – you may have to queue for a table on weekend evenings. Nearby, *La Casa de la Patata* on Calle Ginés Martín specialises in baked potatoes, with varied fillings assiduously mashed into the spud, for 150 to 500 ptas. It's closed Monday.

Entertainment

From around 9 to 11 pm some of the tapas bars off Avenida Martín Alonso Pinzón, such as *Los Encinares*, *Taberna El Condado* and *Cafetería Parra I* (see Places to Eat), get quite lively. Later, crowds flock to the bars and terrazas lining Avenida Pablo Rada and, to a lesser extent, the bars in the streets south of the Catedral such as the Irish pub *Docklands*.

Things to Buy

There's an El Corte Inglés department store on Plaza de España.

Getting There & Away

Bus The bus station (☎ 959 25 69 00) is on the western edge of the centre, on Calle Doctor Rubio. Frequent buses head to Sevilla (875 ptas) and three or four travel daily to Madrid (3240 ptas). For other destinations in Huelva province, see destination sections later in this chapter. For Portugal services, see the introductory Getting There & Away chapter.

Train The train station (☎ 959 24 56 14) is on Avenida de Italia. There are three daily trains to Sevilla (1½ hours; 820 to 945 ptas) and one to Córdoba (two hours; 2700 ptas) and Madrid (4½ hours; 7900 ptas).

Car & Motorcycle For rental cars, Avis (☎ 959 28 38 36) is in the Hotel Luz Huelva, and Europcar (☎ 959 28 53 35) and Hertz are at the train station. One local firm is Marina Rent A Car (☎ 959 25 33 68) at Alameda Sundheim 2.

Getting Around
Drivers should be aware that Andalucian traffic signage reaches its nadir in this city of at best ambiguous signals and apoplexy-inducing one-way systems.

Around Huelva

PARAJE NATURAL MARISMAS DEL ODIEL
This 72 sq km wetlands reserve lies across the Odiel estuary from Huelva. The Odiel *marismas* (marshes) are remarkably wild and peaceful, with a large, varied bird population. Some of these birds are easily viewed from a 20km road that runs the length of the marshes. In winter there are up to 1000 greater flamingoes, and 400 pairs of spoonbill – about one-third of the European population – are resident. Other birds you may see include the osprey, grey heron and purple heron.

For those with their own vehicle, access to Odiel marismas is much easier than to the more famous Doñana national park. Take the A-497 Punta Umbría road west from Huelva and at the far end of the Odiel bridge fork right for 'Ayamonte, Corrales, Dique Juan Carlos I' then immediately left for 'Aljaraque, Espigón'. This curves you

back towards Huelva, but before re-crossing the estuary take the right turn marked 'Dique Juan Carlos I'.

At the southern end of the first of the islands which make up most of the reserve, the road reaches the Centro de Visitantes Calatilla (☎ 959 50 03 25), open daily, except Monday, from 9.30 am to 1.30 pm and 3.30 to 7 pm. It's advisable to ask here which of the several paths *(senderos)* that strike off from the road farther south are open. Ranging from 1km to 4.5km in length, the paths lead to birdwatching sites and to the Excavaciones Arqueológicas del Almendral, where the Almohad town of Shalthis is being excavated. It's possible to drive several kilometres along the breakwater *(espigón)* which is at the end of the southernmost island, Isla de Saltés, but signs warn you to beware of high seas which sometimes cover the road.

Huelva Turística at the Centro de Visitantes Calatilla runs guided trips in the reserve by boat (1500 to 3000 ptas per person), 4WD (2500 ptas) or horse. If there are enough people, they will usually pick you up by boat at Huelva port.

LUGARES COLOMBINOS
La Rábida, Palos de la Frontera and Moguer, three of the key sites in the Columbus story, lie along the eastern bank of the Río Tinto estuary and can all be visited in a fascinating 40km return trip from Huelva. At least 10 buses a day run from Huelva bus station to La Rábida and Palos de la Frontera, many of them continuing to Moguer. The last one back to Huelva leaves Moguer at 8.15 pm. There are several decent accommodation options if you fancy staying here rather than in Huelva.

La Rábida
Monasterio de La Rábida This 14th century monastery, which Columbus visited several times during his attempts to win royal patronage for his projected voyage, is about 9km from central Huelva.

Just off the main road is a tourist office, the Centro de Recepción (☎ 959 53 10 64),

The Four Voyages of Christopher Columbus

The *Santa Maria*

Christopher Columbus (Cristóbal Colón to Spaniards) was born in Genoa, Italy, in 1451, and gained his early sailing experience in the Mediterranean and on trips to Portugal, England, Iceland and Madeira. Portugal was then at the forefront of attempts to find a sea route to the spice-rich Orient and in 1484 Columbus presented to King João II his idea of reaching the Orient by sailing west. The notion that the world was round was widespread but Columbus was the first to test the theory. His proposal was turned down by João, so in 1485 Columbus travelled to the Franciscan monastery of La Rábida near Huelva.

One of the monks, Antonio de Marchena, encouraged Columbus' ambition. Later the abbot, Juan Pérez, who happened to be a former confessor of Queen Isabel La Católica, also took up Columbus' cause. In April 1492, Columbus was finally given a *cédula real* (royal document) ordering the port of Palos de la Frontera, near La Rábida, to put two caravels at his disposal. The crown also paid for the use of his flagship the *Santa María*.

Columbus sailed from Palos on 3 August 1492 with about 100 men. His three vessels – none more than 30m long – were the *Santa María*, a *nao* piloted by its owner Juan de la Cosa from El Puerto de Santa María near Cádiz; the *Niña*, owned by Juan Niño from Moguer and captained by Vicente Yañez Pinzón from Palos; and the *Pinta*, captained by Pinzón's cousin, Martín Alonso Pinzón.

open daily, except Monday, from 10 am to 7 pm. From here it's a short walk to the monastery (☎ 959 35 04 11) which is set among pleasant leafy gardens. Absorbing monk-guided tours of the monastery are given in simple Spanish, Tuesday to Sunday at 10, 10.45 and 11.30 am and 12.15, 1, 4, 4.45, 5.30 and 6.15 pm. You pay by donation at the end of the tour.

The tour starts in a room of interesting 1930 murals on the Columbus story by Huelvan artist Daniel Vázquez Díaz, then moves into the monastery church. Martín Alonso Pinzón is buried in the church, which has a lovely *artesonado* ceiling and a chapel with a 13th century alabaster Virgin before which Columbus prayed. A room where Columbus and Padre Marchena discussed the projected voyage, and the refectory where Columbus ate, are off the peaceful 15th century *mudéjar* cloister.

Upstairs in the Sala Capitular (Chapter House), Columbus and the Pinzóns discussed with Abbot Pérez final plans for their voyage. Other rooms hold art, models and documents on Franciscan and Columban themes. Finally you visit the Sala de Banderas (Flag Room), with the flags of the Latin American nations and a box of earth from each.

Muelle de las Carabelas Down on the waterfront below the monastery is the Wharf of the Caravels (☎ 959 53 05 97), where you can visit accurate replicas of Columbus' three ships, plus an exhibition on his life. It's open daily, except Monday, from 10 am to 2 pm and 5 to 9 pm (late September to late April from 10 am to 7 pm); 420 ptas.

Places to Stay *Hostería de La Rábida* (☎ 959 35 03 12) next to the monastery has

After a month in the Canary Islands, Columbus and his crew sailed west in early September. For 31 days they sighted no land and the rebellious crew gave Columbus just two more days. Then, on 12 October, Columbus landed on the island of Guanahaní, Bahamas, which he named San Salvador. The expedition went on to discover Cuba and Hispaniola, where the *Santa María* sank and its timbers were used to build a fort, Fuerte Navidad.

In January 1493 the remaining two ships left for home, leaving 33 Spaniards at Fuerte Navidad. On 15 March, Columbus returned to Palos with six Caribbean Indians as well as animals, plants and gold ornaments. In Barcelona the next month he received a hero's welcome from the Catholic Monarchs. Everyone was under the impression he had reached the East Indies – no one yet imagined that another continent lay between Europe and Asia.

Late in 1493 Columbus sailed from Sevilla and Cádiz on his second voyage, this time with 17 ships and about 1200 men. The *Niña* was now his flagship. Still in search of Cathay and the Great Khan, he came across Jamaica and other Caribbean islands. On his return to Fuerte Navidad he found it in ruin, its 33 Spaniards killed. He went back to Cádiz in June 1495.

Columbus sailed west for the third time, with six ships, from Sanlúcar de Barrameda near Cádiz in May 1498. This time he reached Trinidad and the mouth of the Orinoco but his failings as a colonial administrator led to a revolt by settlers on Hispaniola. Before he could suppress this uprising he was arrested by a royal emissary from Spain in 1500 and sent home a prisoner (though he was released on arrival).

On Columbus' fourth and last voyage, from Sevilla and Cádiz in April 1502, he reached Honduras and Panama before returning to Sanlúcar de Barrameda in November 1503.

Columbus died in 1506 in Valladolid, northern Spain – poor and apparently still believing he had reached Asia. His remains lay at La Cartuja monastery in Sevilla for a couple of decades before being moved to Hispaniola in 1536. They were transported to Cuba, then back again to Sevilla in 1899 and their current resting place in the cathedral.

just five rooms, with bath, at 7500 ptas a double. It's a nice place but often booked up.

Palos de la Frontera

Four kilometres north-east of La Rábida, the small town of Palos was the port from which Columbus set sail, and which provided two of his ships and more than half his crew. Palos' access to the Tinto estuary is now silted up, but the town remains proud of its role in the discovery of the Americas – especially the part played by the Pinzón cousins.

Buses stop on the central plaza, from which Calle Colón leads north-east (uphill) to the Columbus sites.

Things to See The central plaza has a statue of Martín Alonso Pinzón. Moving up Calle Colón you soon reach the **Casa Museo Martín Alonso Pinzón** (☎ 959 35 01 99) at No 24 (between Nos 32 and 36!). Open Monday to Friday from 10 am to 2 pm (free), this was the home of the captain of the *Pinta* and the place where, an inscription proudly claims, the discovery of America was organised.

Farther along Calle Colón (now heading downhill) is the 14th century **Iglesia de San Jorge**, open Monday to Friday from 10.30 am to 1 pm and 7 to 8 pm. Columbus and his men took communion here before embarking on 3 August 1492, and left the church by the mudéjar portal facing the small plaza. Ten weeks earlier the *cédula real* ordering Palos to help Columbus had been read out in the plaza, where a monument now lists 35 Palos men who sailed with Columbus.

A little farther down the street, in a park that's still being built, is **La Fontanilla**, a brick well where Columbus' crews drew water for their voyage. A viewing platform has a **plaque** marking the site of the *embarcadero* (jetty) from which the three ships sailed.

Places to Stay & Eat Just off the central plaza, *Pensión Rábida* (☎ 959 35 01 63), Calle Rábida 9, has rooms with shared bath at 3000 ptas a double and a cafetería with platos combinados for 700 ptas. Farther along the same street at No 79 is the better *Hotel La Pinta* (☎ 959 35 05 11), with doubles at 10,000 ptas plus IVA, and a good restaurant.

One kilometre south of the centre on the Mazagón road, *Hostal La Niña* (☎ 959 53 03 60), Calle Juan de la Cosa 37, and *Hostal Los Príncipes* (☎ 959 35 04 22), behind the La Niña at Calle Brasil 4, both have doubles with bath for around 4000 ptas plus IVA.

Getting There & Away In addition to buses to/from Huelva, La Rábida and Moguer, there are also a few a day to/from Mazagón. Huelva bus station and the Damas office on Palos' plaza have details.

There are three turnings into central Palos from the main road; the northernmost is right by La Fontanilla.

Moguer

Moguer, 7km north-east of Palos, provided many of Columbus' crew. This pleasant town was also the birthplace and long-time home of the 1956 Nobel literature laureate Juan Ramón Jiménez (1881-1958). The streets are dotted with plaques which bear quotes from Jiménez's *Platero y Yo* (see Literature in Facts about Andalucía) and his old home is now a museum.

Orientation & Information Finding your way into town is a little tricky thanks to a typically Huelvan paucity of signs, but once you've located the central Plaza del Cabildo, with its statue of Juan Ramón Jiménez, things are straightforward. There's a tourist office in the Casa de la Cultura at Calle Andalucía 5, a few steps off the plaza.

Things to See The pretty, arcaded cream-and-brown **ayuntamiento** on Plaza del Cabildo is a classic western Andalucian building.

The 14th century **Convento de Santa Clara** (☎ 959 37 01 07) on Plaza de las Monjas – up the side street almost opposite the Calle Andalucía tourist office – is where Columbus kept vigil the night after returning from his first voyage, having vowed to do so if he survived a particularly bad storm off the Azores. It's open for guided visits (250 ptas) Tuesday to Saturday at 11 am, noon, and 1, 4.30 and 7.30 pm on Sunday and holidays at 11 am, noon and 1 pm. You'll see a lovely mudéjar cloister, some of the old nuns' quarters and a worthy collection of religious art.

The **Casa Museo Juan Ramón Jiménez** (☎ 959 37 21 48) is on Calle Juan Ramón Jiménez, a five-minute walk from Plaza del Cabildo (start along Calle Burgos y Mazo and keep going). It's full of interesting memorabilia of the writer's life and times, and it's open for 45-minute guided visits (250 ptas) daily at 10.15 and 11.15 am and 12.15, 1.15, 5.15, 6.15 and 7.15 pm (except on Sunday afternoons and holidays).

Places to Stay & Eat Moguer has three solidly decent hostales. *Hostal Lis* (☎ 959 37 03 78), Calle Andalucía 6 opposite the tourist office, has double rooms for 2300 ptas plus IVA (2800 ptas plus IVA with private bath) in a sturdy old house with a nice patio. *Hostal Pedro Alonso Niño* (☎ 959 37 23 92) at Calle Pedro Alonso Niño 13 (1½ blocks straight on from the far end of Plaza de las Monjas) charges 2200 ptas for doubles with shower. Best is *Hostal Platero* (☎ 959 37 21 59) at Calle Sor Ángela de la Cruz 4 (turn left just before the Hostal Pedro Alonso Niño) where doubles with bath are 3000 ptas plus IVA.

Mesón La Parrala on Calle Fray Andrés de Moguer, just off Plaza de las Monjas, serves up excellent grills and fish, many for under 900 ptas. *Cafetería Canaria* on Calle Archipreste Borrego, near Hostal Platero, does economical platos combinados.

South-East of Huelva

A wide, sandy, dune-and-pine-backed beach runs 60km south-east from the outskirts of Huelva to the mouth of the Río Guadalquivir. Apart from the seaside resorts of Mazagón and Matalascañas, it's almost uninhabited and the final 25km lie within the Parque Nacional de Doñana. The N-442, becoming the A-494 beyond Mazagón, runs a kilometre or two behind the coast to Matalascañas.

MAZAGÓN
Of the two resorts, the fairly low-key Mazagón is the more pleasant. It has a tourist office on Carretera de la Playa, the main street which runs 1km down from the N-442 to the beach, and a large marina to the right at the bottom of Carretera de la Playa. Mazagón stretches nearly 3km east of here along the beach but is only two or three streets wide.

East of Mazagón, you can access the beach easily from the A-494 at the Parador de Mazagón, 3km from the eastern end of town, and at Costa de Maneli, 9km beyond, where boardwalks lead across the dunes.

Places to Stay & Eat
Camping Playa Mazagón (☎ 959 37 62 08), Cuesta de la Barca s/n, is a couple of minutes walk from the beach at the east end of Mazagón – reachable by a second turning off the main road, 3km east of the first one. Despite its 3000-person capacity it can get crowded. Prices are 475 ptas plus IVA per adult, per car and per tent. This stretch of coast has a few minor cliffs but the beach is as glorious as ever. *Camping La Fontanilla* (☎ 959 53 62 37), a few hundred metres farther east, is smaller, with marginally higher prices. Seven kilometres farther on, the huge *Camping Doñana Playa* (☎ 959 53 62 81) has room for 6000, at 550 ptas plus IVA per adult, per car and per tent. All these camping grounds are open all year.

Mazagón has only a few hostales. A good one to try first is *Hostal Álvarez Quintero* (☎ 959 37 61 69) at Calle Hernández de Soto 174 just off Carretera de la Playa, a two-minute walk from the beach. It's plain but decent, with doubles for 2900 ptas or 4300 ptas with bath. *Hostal Hilaria* (☎ 959 37 62 06), farther back up Carretera de la Playa, has doubles for 6000 ptas plus IVA and a restaurant. *Hostal Acuario* on Avenida Fuentepiña, east off Carretera de la Playa a bit north of the Hilaria, is a cheap, basic option.

The nice *Hotel Albaida* (☎ 959 37 60 29) on the main road about 500m east of the town centre has 24 air-con rooms, with bath, for 8500 ptas plus IVA a double, and a restaurant. The luxurious, modern 43-room *Parador de Mazagón* (☎ 959 53 63 00), 3km east of the east end of Mazagón, is set in cliff-top gardens with easy access to the beach below. It has doubles from 16,500 ptas plus IVA.

Places to eat are mainly on Carretera de la Playa and Avenida Fuentepiña.

Getting There & Away
At least three buses run daily from Huelva bus station to Mazagón and a few from Palos de la Frontera.

MATALASCAÑAS
This modern resort with a number of tall hotels could hardly be in greater contrast to the protected wildernesses of the Doñana national park which it adjoins, but it *is* set on an excellent beach. It attracts few foreigners.

Orientation & Information
Matalascañas extends 4km south-east from the junction of the A-494 with the A-483 from El Rocío. From this junction Avenida de las Adelfas heads south straight to the beach, passing the tourist office (☎ 959 43 00 86), which is open Monday to Friday from 10 am to 2 pm and 3.30 to 6 pm and on Saturday from 10 am to 2 pm. Matalascañas' bus stop is at the roundabout at the beach end of Avenida de las Adelfas.

HUELVA PROVINCE

Places to Stay & Eat

The huge *Camping Rocío Playa* (☎ 959 43 02 38), open all year and with room for 4000, is just above the beach 1km west of Avenida de las Adelfas. It charges 525 ptas plus IVA per adult, per car and per tent. *Pensión Rocío* (☎ 959 43 01 41), a minute's walk north of the tourist office at Avenida El Greco 60 (no sign), has rooms with bath for 4000 ptas a double. *Hostal Los Tamarindos* (☎ 959 43 01 19), Avenida de las Adelfas 31, and *Hostal El Duque* (☎ 959 43 00 58), Avenida de las Adelfas 34, have doubles with bath for 7000 ptas. *Hotel Flamero* (☎ 959 44 80 20) on Ronda Maestro Alonso 1km east along the beach, is one of the more appetising of the bigger hotels, with doubles for 10,550 ptas plus IVA.

There are several restaurants just behind the beach near the end of Avenida de las Adelfas, among them *Restaurante El Pichi* with a three-course menú for 950 ptas, platos combinados from 500 ptas and good-value raciones. You'll find more places in the Centro Comercial off Avenida de las Adelfas.

Getting There & Away

There's one bus from Huelva via Mazagón daily, except Saturday, leaving Huelva Monday to Friday at 2.45 pm and Sunday at 10 am. Going back, the bus leaves Matalascañas Monday to Friday at 7.30 pm and Sunday about 5.30 pm. Buses also link Matalascañas with El Rocío and Sevilla (see Getting There & Away in the Parque Nacional de Doñana section).

PARQUE NACIONAL DE DOÑANA

The Doñana national park, one of Europe's most important wetlands, covers 507 sq km in the south-east of Huelva province and neighbouring Sevilla province. It's vital not only as one of the last refuges for such endangered species as the pardel lynx and Spanish imperial eagle (both with populations of about 40 here), but also as a crucial major habitat for hundreds of thousands of other birds.

Bordering the park are four separate zones, known as Parque Natural Entorno de Doñana, totalling 540 sq km. Two of these zones (265 sq km) are designated *preparque*, buffer zones for the national park.

Visiting the national park itself requires booking ahead – and paying for – a guided tour. Tours go from the Centro de Recepción El Acebuche on the western side of the park (see the Centro de Recepción El Acebuche section), from Sanlúcar de Barrameda near the park's south-eastern tip (see Sanlúcar de Barrameda in the Cádiz Province chapter). But there are also some interesting surrounding areas for which you don't need to pay or book.

A good base for the tours from El Acebuche and trips to the surrounding areas is the village of El Rocío at the north-western corner of the park. Another possibility is the beach resort of Matalascañas, 16km south of El Rocío (see the Matalascañas section).

Perhaps once the site of fabled Tartessos, and in latter centuries a favourite hunting ground of Spanish royalty, Doñana was made a national park in 1969, following concern over threats to its wetlands from rice-growing, road and tourism schemes. The Worldwide Fund for Nature raised much of the cash for the land purchases. James Michener, in *Iberia*, wrote about how members of one Danish shooting club were persuaded to dig into their pockets: 'Gentlemen,' they were told, 'if the lakes of [Doñana] are allowed to disappear, within five years there will be no ducks in Denmark'.

Since its creation the park has had to continue battling against agricultural and tourism schemes around its fringes which threaten to reduce its water supplies. But the biggest threat to its delicate balance came in 1998, when a dam broke at a mine at Aznalcóllar, 50km north. Five million cubic metres of water and mud loaded with acids and heavy metals flooded into the Río Guadiamar, one of the chief waterways feeding Doñana's wetlands. Hastily erected dykes prevented the flood entering the national park itself, but up to 100 sq km of wetlands to its north-east were contaminated and agricultural land bordering about 45km of the river was devastated. Biologists and environmentalists fear that the effects may be

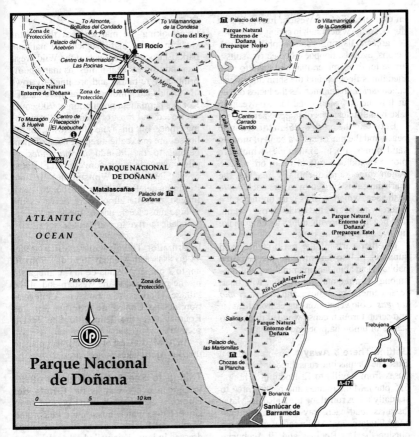

felt for decades to come through poisons entering Doñana's water table and the food chain of its birds and animals.

A good detailed map covering the national park and most of the parque natural is the IGN's *Parque Nacional de Doñana* (1:50,000), sold for 800 ptas at the Centro de Recepción El Acebuche.

Flora, Fauna & Ecosystems

Doñana counts 125 resident and 125 migratory bird species and is a major habitat for many of them.

Half the national park consists of *marismas*, the marshes of the delta of the Río Guadalquivir, which enters the Atlantic Ocean at the south-eastern corner of the park. The park contains only about one-tenth of the Guadalquivir marismas but most of those outside it have been drained and/or channelled for agriculture.

The park's marismas are almost dry from July to October. In autumn they start to fill with water, eventually leaving only a few islets of dry land. Around 300,000 water birds arrive from the north to winter here, including an estimated 80% of Western Europe's wild ducks. As the waters sink in spring, other birds – greater flamingoes, spoonbills, storks, herons, avocets, hoopoes, bee-eaters, stilts – arrive for the summer, many of them to nest. Fledglings flock around the shrinking ponds, called *lucios*, in summer. As the lucios dry up in July, herons, storks and kites move in to take bountiful catches of trapped perch.

Between the park's 25km of Atlantic beach and the marismas is a band of moving sand dunes, up to 5km wide, which are blown inland at a rate of up to 6m a year. When dune sand eventually reaches the marismas, it is carried by rivers back down to the sea, which washes it up on the beach where wind begins the cycle all over again. The beach and moving dunes together make up 102 sq km of the park.

In other parts of the park, stable sand supports 144 sq km of *coto*, the favoured habitat of an abundant mammal population – among them red and fallow deer, wild boar, feral camels, mongoose and a few *Homo sapiens*. Coto vegetation ranges from heather and scrub through dense wooded thickets to stands of umbrella pine and cork oak.

Getting There & Away

Bus The Damas line runs three or four daily buses from Sevilla to El Rocío (1½ hours; 615 ptas), Matalascañas and back. Three to six daily buses run along the El Rocío-Matalascañas road each way between Almonte and Matalascañas. All these buses will stop outside the Las Rocinas and El Acebuche national park centres.

The bus at 10 am on Sunday from Huelva to Matalascañas continues to El Rocío (605 ptas), from which it sets off back to Huelva at 5 pm. On other days you can travel between Huelva and El Rocío by changing buses at Almonte or Matalascañas.

Car & Motorcycle El Rocío is 27km south of the A-49 Sevilla-Huelva highway. Turn off the A-49 at Bollullos del Condado, 51km from Sevilla. From Huelva you can go along the coast road to Matalascañas, then north.

El Rocío

Overlooking the marismas at the northwestern corner of the fenced-off national park, El Rocío has a touch of the Wild West. Its sandy streets bear almost as many hoofprints as tyre marks and are lined by rows of verandahed buildings – far more than El Rocío's permanent population of 700 could ever need and most of them usually standing empty. But this is no ghost town, for the houses are in excellent repair: most of them belong to the 90-odd *hermandades* of pilgrim-revellers who converge on El Rocío every Pentecost (Whitsuntide) in the Romería del Rocío (see the boxed text). Indeed, a fiesta atmosphere pervades the village most weekends of the year as hermandades arrive to carry out lesser rituals.

Information There's a tourist office (☎ 959 44 26 84), open Monday to Friday from 10 am to 2 pm, at Avenida de la Canaliega s/n by the main road at the western end of the village. There's also national park information at the Centro de Información Las Rocinas (see the Things to See & Do section).

An ATM just west of the Ermita, opposite the Bar Ajolí, takes major cards.

Things to See & Do The heart of the village in every way is the **Ermita del Rocío**, a church built in its present form since 1964, which houses the celebrated Virgen del Rocío – a tiny wooden image dressed in long, bejewelled robes. It's open daily from 8.30 am to 7.30 pm, with people arriving to pay their respects to the Virgin every day of the year.

El Rocío overlooks a section of the **marismas** which has water all year, thanks to the Río Madre de las Marismas which flows through here, so it's nearly always a good place to spot some birds and animals. Deer and horses graze in the shallows and you may be lucky enough to see a flock of flamingoes wheeling through the sky in a great pink cloud. The Spanish Ornithological Society's observatory, the **Observatorio Madre del Rocío**, is about 150m east along

The Romería del Rocío

Like most of Spain's holiest images, Nuestra Señora del Rocío – aka La Blanca Paloma (White Dove) – has legendary origins. Back in the 13th century, the story goes, a hunter from the village of Almonte found her in a tree in the marismas and decided to carry her home. But when he stopped for a rest, the Virgin made her way back to the tree.

Before long, a chapel was built on the spot where the tree had been (El Rocío) and it became a place of pilgrimage. By the 17th century hermandades were forming in nearby towns to make an annual pilgrimage to El Rocío at Pentecost. This happens the seventh weekend after Easter (22-24 May in 1999, 10-12 June in 2000). Today, the Romería del Rocío (Pilgrimage to El Rocío) is a vast festive cult that pulls people from all over Spain. There are over 90 hermandades, some with several thousand men and women, and they still travel to El Rocío on foot, on horseback and in gaily decorated covered wagons pulled by cattle or horses, along cross-country tracks.

Solemn is the last word you'd apply to this quintessentially Andalucian event. In an atmosphere similar to Sevilla's Feria de Abril, participants dress in fine Andalucian costume and sing, dance, drink, laugh and romance their way to El Rocío. The total number of people in the village on this special weekend can reach about a million.

The weekend comes to an ecstatic climax in the very early hours of Monday. Members of the hermandad of Almonte, which claims the Virgin for its own, barge into the church and bear her out on a float. Violent struggles ensue as others battle with the Almonte lads for the honour of carrying La Blanca Paloma. The crush and chaos is immense but somehow good humour survives and the Virgin is carried round to each of the hermandad buildings, before being finally returned to the Ermita in the afternoon.

the waterside from the Hotel Toruño. It's open to the public Monday to Thursday from 9 am to 3 pm and Friday to Sunday from 10.30 am to 1.30 pm and 2.30 to 5.30 pm.

The bridge over the river on the A-483 1km south of the village is another good viewing spot. Just past the bridge is the **Centro de Información Las Rocinas** (☎ 959 44 23 40), open daily from 10 am to 7 or 8 pm, which has national park information and short paths to birdwatching hides by a year-round creek. Though outside the national park proper, this is in a special *zona de protección* and has abundant bird life.

Six kilometres along a road west from Las Rocinas, in the same zona de protección, is the **Palacio del Acebrón**, with a 1.5km walking track through riverbank woodland.

For a longer walk from El Rocío, cross the Puente del Ajolí at the north-eastern edge of the village and head along the track into the woodland ahead. This is the begin-

ning of the **Coto del Rey**, a large woodland zone where you can wander freely for hours. It's crossed by numerous tracks which vehicles might manage in dry seasons. In early morning or late evening you may spot deer or boar.

You can rent **horses** at various places in El Rocío including Turismo a Caballo (☎ 959 44 20 84), Calle Boca del Lobo 3, one block back from the waterfront at the eastern end of the village, and Doñana Ecuestre (☎ 959 44 24 74) at the Hotel Puente del Rey. Doñana Ecuestre charges 3000/5000 ptas for two/four hours.

Places to Stay & Eat Don't bother even trying for a room at Romería time. *Hostal Vélez* (☎ 959 44 21 17) at Calle Algaida 2, with no sign but next to Cerámicas La Carreta one block north of Ermita, has clean, basic singles/doubles with shared bath for 1500/2500 ptas. *Pensión Cristina*

(☎ 959 40 65 13), Calle Real 32, a short distance east of the Ermita, has reasonable singles/doubles with bath for 3000/4000 ptas and a decent restaurant where paella, or veal/lamb/venison and chips, cost 700 ptas. Just along towards the Ermita, *Casa Rural El Real 38* (☎ 959 44 20 35) has doubles at 7490 ptas including breakfast.

Hotel Toruño (☎ 959 44 23 23), a little farther east at Plaza Acebuchal 22, is a nice modern place with 30 attractive air-con rooms at 5500/7500 ptas. All have bath and some have marismas views. *Hotel Puente del Rey* (☎ 959 44 25 75), Avenida de la Canaliega s/n by the main road, is a larger place with rooms at 6800/8600 ptas plus IVA and a restaurant.

Café Bar El Pocito on Calle Ermita just east of the Ermita does good tapas for 200 ptas and main platters for 900 ptas. *Bar Ajolí* on the other side of the Ermita has tapas for 200 ptas and media-raciones for 600 ptas. *Bar-Restaurante Toruño* on Plaza Acebuchal has most meat and fish main dishes for around 1200 ptas.

Centro de Recepción El Acebuche
Twelve kilometres south on the A-483 from El Rocío, then 1.6km west along an approach road, El Acebuche (☎ 959 44 87 11) is the national park's main visitor centre and the starting point for tours into the park. Open daily from 8 am to 7 or 8 pm, it also has footpaths to hides overlooking a lagoon with plenty of birds.

National Park Tours Trips from El Acebuche into the national park are run in all-terrain vehicles by the Cooperativa de Guías Marismas del Rocío (☎ 959 43 04 32). These are the only way for ordinary folk to get inside the park except for trips from Sanlúcar de Barrameda. You need to book ahead by telephone – for spring, summer and holiday times the trips can get booked up more than a month ahead but otherwise a week or less is usually adequate. The trips go twice daily (around 8.30 am and 4 pm), except Monday, last about four hours and cost 2500 ptas per person.

They normally stick to the south of the park, as far as the mouth of the Guadalquivir, and begin with a long beach drive before taking in moving dunes, marismas, and woods where you can be pretty certain of seeing a good number of deer and boar.

Monday to Saturday, the first morning bus from El Rocío towards Matalascañas should get you to El Acebuche just in time for the morning tour.

Centro Cerrado Garrido
Some of the best birdwatching in the Doñana area is at this relatively unfrequented visitor centre, overlooking a year-round lucio on the northern fringe of the national park. Also known as the Centro de Visitantes José Antonio Valverde, the centre is some 20km south of the town of Villamanrique de la Condesa by minor roads and driveable tracks (60km from El Rocío).

West of Huelva

The coast between Huelva and the Portuguese border, 53km west, alternates between estuaries, wetlands, good sandy beaches, and small and medium-sized resorts and fishing ports. The main road to Portugal, the N-431, runs some distance inland from the coast.

PUNTA UMBRÍA
Punta Umbría, on a point of land between the Atlantic and the Marismas del Odiel, is Huelva's summer playground, 21km from the city by road. It's a modern and pleasant enough resort, though very busy in July and August.

Places to stay include two camp sites a few kilometres out, off the road from Huelva, and the *Albergue Juvenil Punta Umbría* youth hostel (☎ 959 31 16 50), close to the Atlantic beach at Avenida Océano 13. *Hostal Playa* (☎ 959 31 01 12), Avenida Océano 95, *Hostal Emilio* (☎ 959 31 18 00), Calle Ancha 21, and *Hotel Aya-*

montino Ría (☎ 959 31 14 58), Paseo de la Ría 1, have doubles with bath for around 6000 ptas. The last two are near the estuary on the eastern side of town.

From Huelva there are buses to Punta Umbría every hour from 8 am to 9 pm. In summer there are also hourly ferries, known as *canoas*, from Huelva port.

EL ROMPIDO

Some 16km north-west of Punta Umbría on the Río Piedras estuary, El Rompido is a fishing and yachting village cum minor resort, with several seafood restaurants. The estuary is divided from the ocean by a long spit of land and there are sandy beaches on both sides of it. *Camping Catapum* (☎ 959 39 91 65), which can get pretty crowded, is at the eastern end of the village.

There are a few buses a day to El Rompido from Huelva. Drivers who want to continue west along the coast must go inland to the N-431 and turn south at Lepe.

LA ANTILLA

La Antilla's holiday chalets and apartments are stretching farther and farther along the wide, sandy beach which runs all the way from the Río Piedras to Isla Cristina, but the place only extends a couple of blocks inland. Out of season it's virtually empty. At its western end, the Islantilla development includes a 27-hole golf course and one of the largest hotels on this coast.

Camping Luz (☎ 959 34 11 42) at the western end of town charges 2750 ptas plus IVA for two adults with car and tent. There are two other camp sites. At least six hostales are bunched near the beach on Plaza La Parada, most with doubles for around 6000 ptas plus IVA in summer (but you'd be lucky to get a room in August). The *Confortel Islantilla* (☎ 959 48 60 17) in Islantilla is a handsome modern beachfront resort hotel with 344 rooms at around 10,000 ptas a double.

A few buses a day run to La Antilla from Huelva, Isla Cristina and Sevilla.

ISLA CRISTINA

Isla Cristina (population: 17,000), as well as being a beach resort (packed in August), is enlivened by a sizeable fishing fleet.

Orientation & Information

The main road running east to La Antilla and north to the N-431 passes through the north of town. The bus station – a large white garage with 'Damas SA' on it – is beside this, just south of the bridge where the fishing fleet moors. The town centre, around Plaza del Caudillo Franco, is a few minutes walk away. Gran Vía Román Pérez heads about 1km south from the plaza to the western end of Isla Cristina's beach.

In your own vehicle, turn off the main road just west of Camping Giralda on the eastern edge of town. For Playa Central (the best beach), and the best hotels, turn left almost immediately at a roundabout. If you continue ahead at the roundabout you'll approach the town centre along Avenida de España. The Oficina Municipal de Turismo is at Avenida de España 4, just off Gran Vía Román Pérez.

Things to See & Do

The **Puerto Pesquero** (Fishing Port), a couple of blocks west from Plaza del Caudillo Franco, is a lively scene in the morning and evening as fishing boats check in with their catches.

North of town, the road towards the N-431 crosses the **Marismas de Isla Cristina**, which have a rich bird life including greater flamingo and spoonbill.

Two kilometres from Isla Cristina, signs indicate the **Sendero de Molino Mareal de Pozo del Camino**, a 1km walking track across the marismas and the **Centro de Interpretación El Hombre y La Marisma**, a rarely open visitor centre.

Places to Stay & Eat

The large *Camping Giralda* (☎ 959 34 32 84), among pines by the main road on the eastern edge of town, has room for 2200 at 585 ptas plus IVA per adult, per tent and per car. Playa Central is close.

The cheaper rooms are in the town centre, about 1.5km from the beaches. *Pensión Maty*, Calle Catalanes 7, just west of Plaza del Caudillo Franco, charges 3500 ptas plus IVA a double in high season. *Hostal Gran Vía* (☎ 959 33 07 94), just south of Plaza del Caudillo Franco at Gran Vía Román Pérez 10, is better: rooms with bath are 5500 ptas plus IVA a double.

The best hotels are on or just off Camino de la Playa near Playa Central: *Hotel Paraíso Playa* (☎ 959 33 18 73), *Hotel Los Geranios* (☎ 959 33 18 00) and, right on the seafront, *Hotel Sol y Mar* (☎ 959 33 20 50). All these have doubles with bath for around 8000 ptas plus IVA in high season.

Acosta Bar-Restaurante on Plaza del Caudillo Franco does good seafood, or you could head over to the seafood bars and restaurants on the plaza outside the Puerto Pesquero, such as *Bar-Restaurante Hermanos Moreno*. There are also eateries at Playa Central.

Getting There & Away
Damas buses (☎ 959 33 16 52) run three or more times a day to/from Ayamonte, La Antilla, Huelva and Sevilla.

AYAMONTE
Ayamonte stands beside the almost 1km-wide Río Guadiana which divides Spain from Portugal. A road bridge across the river was opened 2km north of the town in 1991, so there is no longer any compelling reason to visit the town. But it's an agreeable enough place and, if you like doing things slowly, the ferry to Vila Real de Santo António (Portugal) still runs.

Orientation & Information
The bus station is on Avenida de Andalucía, 700m east of the central square, Paseo de la Ribera. The ferry dock *(muelle transbordador)* is on the riverfront street, Avenida Muelle de Portugal, 300m north-west of Paseo de la Ribera.

The tourist office (☎ 959 47 09 87) is 300m off Avenida de Andalucía on Avenida Alcalde Narciso Martín Navarro, which heads south between the bus station and Paseo de la Ribera. It's open Monday to Friday from 9.30 am to 2.30 pm and 6 to 8 pm and Saturday from 11 am to 2 pm.

Beach
Ayamonte's beach is at **Isla Canela**, 6km south. It's wide, sandy and several kilometres long, with a small, quite tasteful resort of holiday flats and one big hotel being developed. From June to September only, buses run every half-hour from Ayamonte. Drivers should leave Ayamonte by Avenida Alcalde Narciso Martín Navarro and keep going.

Places to Stay
The reasonable *Hostal Los Robles* (☎ 959 47 09 59), just west of the bus station at Avenida de Andalucía 121, has doubles for 3700 ptas, or 4700 ptas with private bath.

Hotel Marqués de Ayamonte (☎ 959 32 01 25), Calle Trajano 14, half a block west of Paseo de la Ribera, has plain but decent singles/doubles with bath for 2500/5000 ptas plus IVA.

The *Parador de Ayamonte* (☎ 959 32 07 00), at El Castillito on the hill 1.5km north of the centre, is in modern style with doubles at 14,500 ptas plus IVA. You pay almost twice as much at the luxurious beachfront *Hotel Riu Canela* (☎ 959 47 71 24), Paseo de los Gavilanes s/n, Isla Canela, which boasts three swimming pools and unusual turreted architecture.

Places to Eat
The restaurants on Paseo de la Ribera cater mainly to a passing tourist trade. *Mesón La Casona*, a block north at Calle Lusitania 2, is a better bet. It has a menú for 900 ptas and main dishes for 800 to 1500 ptas. Calle San Diego, running north from the western end of Paseo de la Ribera, also has several eateries.

Getting There & Away
Bus From the bus station (☎ 959 32 11 71), four or more buses run daily to Isla Cristina, Huelva (520 ptas), Sevilla and Vila Real de Santo António, and one goes to Málaga

at 6.45 am. There are also a few buses along the Algarve and to Lisbon.

Car & Motorcycle The bridge over the Guadiana is toll-free.

Boat The ferry to Vila Real de Santo António runs from 9 am to 8 pm, at least every 40 minutes. One-way fares are 525 ptas for a car and driver, 125 ptas for everyone else. Fairly frequent buses and trains run along the Algarve from Vila Real.

The North

The verdant valleys and at times dramatic hills that form Huelva's portion of the Sierra Morena offer some beautiful walks between old-fashioned villages, especially west of the attractive town of Aracena. This area – relatively rainy and not quite as hot as most of Andalucía in summer – forms the 1840 sq km Parque Natural Sierra de Aracena y Picos de Aroche, Andalucía's second biggest protected area.

MINAS DE RIOTINTO
Minas de Riotinto (population 5000), 68km north-east of Huelva at the heart of one of the world's oldest and most bountiful mining districts, makes a fascinating stop on the way north. You can ride an early 20th century train, visit a huge opencast mine and take in an excellent mining museum.

The Río Tinto, which rises nearby, takes its name (Coloured River) from the hue of the copper and iron oxides washed into it from the ores of the mining zone.

Copper may have been mined in this district as early as 3000 BC; silver was being extracted well before the Phoenicians came here and iron has been mined since at least Roman times. The Romans burrowed away busily for 300 years but after their efforts the lodes were largely neglected till 1725. In 1872 the mines were bought by the British-dominated Rio Tinto Company. The company turned the area into one of the world's great copper-mining centres, diverting rivers, digging away an entire metal-rich hill, Cerro Colorado, and founding the town of Minas de Riotinto to replace a village which they demolished. The mines returned to Spanish control in 1954.

Orientation
Minas de Riotinto is 5km east along the A-461 from the N-435 Huelva-Jabugo road. The Barrio de Bella Vista (see this section later) is on the left of the A-461, opposite the turning into the town centre. Entering the town, veer right at the first roundabout to reach the Museo Minero, about 400m uphill. Buses stop on Plaza de El Minero, a little beyond the first roundabout.

Museo Minero
The museum, at Plaza del Museo s/n, is also the reception centre and main ticket office for visits to the Corta Atalaya and rides on the Ferrocarril Turístico-Minero. All three are run by Aventura Minaparque (☎ 959 59 00 25). There are small price reductions if you opt for more than one of the three. Aventura Minaparque is also restoring an underground mine, Pozo Alfredo, for visits.

The museum (200 ptas) is normally open Tuesday to Friday from 10 am to 2 pm, and Saturday, Sunday and holidays from 10 am to 6 pm, but from 16 June to 30 September it closes at 2 pm. Exhibits cover geology and the archaeology and history of the mines, including some very ancient tools and jewellery and statuary of the peoples who lived here. Two rooms are devoted to the railways which the Rio Tinto Company built to serve the mines. At one time 143 steam engines, mostly British-built, were puffing up and down these tracks. Pride of place goes to the Vagón del Maharajah, a luxurious carriage built in 1892 for a tour of India by England's Queen Victoria. That trip never happened but the carriage was used for a visit to the mines by Spain's Alfonso XIII.

Barrio de Bella Vista

Bella Vista was built in the late 19th century as an exclusive home from home for the Rio Tinto Company's mainly British management, with houses, cottages and Protestant church all in a kind of Hampstead Garden Suburb style. There's nothing to stop you wandering round the barrio, now inhabited by Spaniards.

Corta Atalaya

This terraced, oval basin, 1.2km long and 335m deep, is claimed to be the world's biggest opencast mine, and lies about 1km west of the town. In the past the Corta Atalaya yielded huge quantities of copper-bearing iron pyrites, but there's little activity here today. Guided visits (600 ptas) depart from the Museo Minero Tuesday to Sunday, and holiday Mondays, at 11 am, noon, 1 and 2 pm (4 and 5 pm on Saturday, Sunday and holidays from 1 October to 15 June).

Ferrocarril Turístico-Minero

The mine train takes visitors on a 24km trip through the scarred landscapes of Río Tinto valley in refurbished early 20th century carriages pulled by a steam engine of similar vintage. Trips start 2.5km east of Minas de Riotinto from the Talleres Mina, the old railway repair workshops, just off the road to Nerva. From 16 June to 30 September there are trips daily, except non-holiday Mondays, at 2 pm. The rest of the year the train runs on Saturday, Sunday and holidays only at 4 or 5 pm. The cost is 1100 ptas; you can get tickets at the Museo Minero.

Corta Cerro Colorado

About one kilometre north of Minas de Riotinto, the road towards Aracena passes the Corta Cerro Colorado, a vast opencast mine that is the site of nearly all the area's mining activity. There's a viewing platform (the Mirador Cerro Colorado) across the road. A century ago Cerro Colorado was a hill.

Places to Stay & Eat

Hostal Galán (☎ 959 59 18 52), Calle Romero Villa s/n on the street outside the Museo Minero, has rooms with bath at 4250 ptas plus IVA for doubles; it has a restaurant and bar with decent tapas for 200 to 250 ptas, or raciones for 750 to 1800 ptas. In Nerva, 4km east, *Hostal El Goro* (☎ 959 58 04 37), Calle Reina Victoria 2, has doubles for 3000 to 3500 ptas plus IVA and *Hotel Vázquez Díaz* (☎ 959 58 09 27), Calle Cañadilla 51, has doubles for 4500 ptas.

Getting There & Away

Three or more Damas buses run daily from Huelva to Minas de Riotinto (670 ptas) and Nerva. Casal has a service daily, except Sunday, from Nerva (6 am) and Minas de Riotinto to Aracena (300 ptas), heading back from Aracena at 5.15 pm. There is also a Monday-to-Friday Casal service from Aracena at 9.55 am, heading back from Minas de Riotinto at 12.30 pm.

From Sevilla (Plaza de Armas bus station) there are two or more daily Casal buses to Nerva and Minas de Riotinto.

ARACENA

Beneath a hill topped by a medieval church and ruined castle spreads Aracena, a whitewashed town of 6700 people. This 'capital' of hilly northern Huelva is an interesting place to visit, and although budget accommodation is limited, an obvious initial point to head for in the region.

Orientation & Information

Most of the town lies between the castle hill, Cerro del Castillo, in the south and the N-433 Sevilla-Portugal road round the east and north. The main square is Plaza del Marqués de Aracena, from which the main street, Avenida de los Infantes Don Carlos y Doña Luisa (more simply known as Gran Vía), runs west. The bus station is a few minutes walk south-east of Plaza del Marqués de Aracena, on Avenida de Andalucía.

Aracena's main tourist office is the Centro de Turismo Rural y Reservas (☎ 959 12 83 55, 959 12 82 06) on Calle Pozo de la Nieve (facing the entrance to the Gruta de las Maravillas). It is open daily from 9 am to 2.30 pm and 4 to 7 pm.

The Centro de Visitantes Cabildo Viejo (☎ 959 12 82 25) on Plaza Alta is the main information centre of the Parque Natural Sierra de Aracena y Picos de Aroche. Set in Aracena's 15th century former town hall, it has informative displays in the building's beautiful brick vaults.

The Policía Local (☎ 959 12 62 32) are in the Ayuntamiento on Gran Vía.

Gruta de las Maravillas

Aracena's 'Cave of Marvels' (☎ 959 12 83 55), carved out of the limestone beneath Cerro del Castillo by millennia of water action, ranks among the most spectacular caves in Spain and has long been the town's biggest tourist attraction. The 1.2km route open to visitors, with 12 chambers and six lakes, has all sorts of weird and beautiful stalactites, stalagmites and rock formations, culminating in the aptly named Sala de los Culos (Chamber of Bottoms). Coloured lighting and piped music serve to heighten the romantic-cum-kitsch effect.

The cave entrance is on pedestrianised Calle Pozo de la Nieve, off Plaza San Pedro in the south-west of town. It's open daily from 10.30 am to 1.30 pm and 3 to 6 pm, with visits – by 45-minute guided tour in Spanish – every half-hour on Saturday, Sunday and holidays, every hour on other days. The tours only go when there are at least 25 people: this is no problem in summer but on a wet November Monday you might wait all day. The price for adults is 875 ptas.

Plaza Alta

This handsome, sloping, cobbled plaza on the slopes of Cerro del Castillo was once the centre of town. On one side stands the 15th century **Cabildo Viejo** (Old Town Hall), now a natural park information centre (see Orientation & Information). The huge Renaissance **Parroquia de la Asunción,**

HUELVA PROVINCE

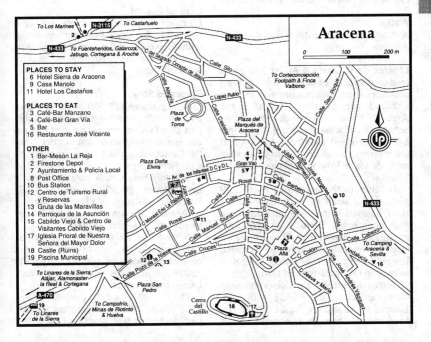

Aracena

0   100   200 m

PLACES TO STAY
6 Hotel Sierra de Aracena
9 Casa Manolo
11 Hotel Los Castaños

PLACES TO EAT
3 Café-Bar Manzano
4 Café-Bar Gran Vía
5 Bar
16 Restaurante José Vicente

OTHER
1 Bar-Mesón La Reja
2 Firestone Depot
7 Ayuntamiento & Policía Local
8 Post Office
10 Bus Station
12 Centro de Turismo Rural y Reservas
13 Gruta de las Maravillas
14 Parroquia de la Asunción
15 Cabildo Viejo & Centro de Visitantes Cabildo Viejo
17 Iglesia Prioral de Nuestra Señora del Mayor Dolor
18 Castle (Ruins)
19 Piscina Municipal

To Los Marines
To Castañuelo
N-3115
N-433 To Fuenteheridos, Galaroza, Jabugo, Cortegana & Aroche
N-433
C del Sagrado Corazón de Jesús
Calle Silo
Calle Alegría
Calle Castelar
C López Rubio
Calle San Roque
To Corteconcepción Footpath & Finca Valbono
Plaza de Toros
Plaza del Marqués de Aracena
Plaza Doña Elvira
Av de los Infantes D C y D L
Calle Julián Calle José Nogales Romero
(Gran Vía)
Rosal
Calle Barbero
Calle Juan del Cid
C Monasterio La Habana
Calle Rosal
Calle Manuel Siurot
Calle Valle
C Blas Infante
C Fco Rincón
Avenida Andalucía
N-433
Calle Cabezo
To Camping Aracena & Sevilla
Calle Cruces
Plaza Alta
C Colón
C Jesús y María
Calle José Andrés Vázquez
Calle Pozo de la Nieve
Plaza San Pedro
To Linares de la Sierra, Alájar, Alamonaster la Real & Cortegana
A-470
To Linares de la Sierra
To Campofrío, Minas de Riotinto & Huelva
Cerro del Castillo

at the foot of the plaza, is built in stone with the brick bands typical of the area's churches. The church was begun in 1528 and work went on into the 17th century, but was never completed. It's normally open for services at 7 pm daily, except Thursday and Sunday.

Cerro del Castillo

A small Muslim fort atop the castle hill was conquered in the 13th century by the Portuguese, who built a castle on the hill before being evicted from the area by Castilla's Fernando III. It was around 1300 that the hilltop **Iglesia Prioral de Nuestra Señora del Mayor Dolor** was built, and the castle rebuilt.

A road from Plaza Alta runs up to the top of Cerro del Castillo. The beautiful Gothic-mudéjar stone-and-brick church has a tower with brick tracery and, inside, three rib-vaulted naves. It's normally open from 10 am to 7 pm. The now-ruined **castle** stretches along the hill top beside the church.

Walks

A couple of attractive day walks start from Aracena.

Linares de la Sierra & Alájar Two paths lead west to Linares de la Sierra (see West of Aracena) and you can combine them in a round trip of about 12km. Leave Aracena by a path which runs down between the Piscina Municipal (Municipal Swimming Pool) and the A-470 road at the western end of town. This is an easy path down a lovely verdant valley to Linares.

To return by the more southerly PRA39 path, find a small stone bridge over the river below Linares, beyond which the path goes round Cerro de la Molinilla, passing old iron mines, then crosses a stream for a stony ascent to Aracena, bringing you out on the Minas de Riotinto road in the south-west of town.

You could extend the walk by continuing 4km west along the PRA38 path from Linares to Alájar, via the hamlet of Los Madroñeros. There are fine views on this stretch. From Alájar you can walk back the way you came or catch the 4 pm bus (daily except Sunday) to Aracena.

Corteconcepción It's a round trip of about 12km to the pretty village of Corteconcepción, east of Aracena. Leave Aracena by Calle San Roque and the Carboneras road, turning right along the marked PRA45 path (Camino del Fuente del Rey) about 300m past the N-433 ring road. The route goes along the valley of the Arroyo del Molino del Bombo. After 3km take a smaller path to the right, crossing the arroyo, towards Corteconcepción, and turn left at a crossing of paths to enter the village. On the way back, carry straight on when you return to this crossing: you're now on the PRA46 path and you'll climb the northern flank of the Sierra de Corteconcepción, with long-distance panoramas, and re-enter Aracena along Calle Cabezo.

Special Events

Carnaval and Semana Santa are both colourful. Aracena's main summer feria, with fireworks, music, dancing, funfairs, bullfights and more, happens in the third week of August.

Places to Stay

Camping Aracena (☎ 959 50 10 05), open all year with room for 270 people at 495 ptas plus IVA per person, per tent and per car, is about 4km south-east of town. Take the Corteconcepción turning from the N-433, 3km out.

The only budget beds are at the friendly *Casa Manolo* (☎ 959 12 80 14), Calle Barbero 6 just south of Plaza del Marqués de Aracena. The seven basic but adequate rooms cost 3200 ptas a double.

Hotel Sierra de Aracena (☎ 959 12 61 75), Gran Vía 21, has 43 well used but comfy singles/doubles, with TV and bath, at 4200/6300 ptas plus IVA. There's a cosy lounge but no restaurant.

The 33-room *Hotel Los Castaños* (☎ 959 12 63 00) on Calle Rosal is the best in town, with doubles at 7000 ptas plus IVA.

Finca Valbono (☎ 959 12 77 71), in the countryside 1km north of Aracena on Carretera de Carboneras, has six double rooms at 8000 ptas plus IVA, plus self-catering chalets for three or more, a café, a pool and horse riding.

Places to Eat

Café-Bar Manzano on Plaza del Marqués de Aracena is a fine spot for varied tapas (125 to 300 ptas), raciones, and platos combinados (800 to 900 ptas). Solomillo, egg and chips will set you back 900 ptas. It plays good music too.

On Gran Vía, the bustling *Café-Bar Gran Vía* has tons of tapas and raciones. You can get a prawn salad for 600 ptas. A nameless, trendier *bar* across the street has pizzas for 700 ptas.

Hotel Los Castaños has a good restaurant with a menú for 1500 ptas, tortillas and salads for 300 to 600 ptas and meat and fish mains for 900 to 1500 ptas – plus IVA.

Several restaurants, many of them with platos combinados for 800 or 900 ptas, line Plaza San Pedro and Calle Pozo de la Nieve near the Gruta de las Maravillas.

The best place for the region's famous ham and pork is *Restaurante José Vicente*, Avenida de Andalucía 53. An excellent menú of three courses and a drink goes for 2300 ptas, or you could specialise in a ración of jamón Jabugo for 2000 ptas. À la carte main dishes are around 1600 to 1800 ptas.

Getting There & Away

Casal (☎ 959 12 81 96) on Avenida de Andalucía runs two or three daily buses to/from Sevilla (Plaza de Armas, 1¼ hours, 760 ptas), plus buses to Minas de Riotinto (see that section), buses to villages around northern Huelva province (see West of Aracena) and a daily bus at 10.30 am to Rosal de la Frontera near the Portuguese border, where you can change to a bus for Lisbon. From the same stop, Damas (also ☎ 959 12 81 96) runs daily buses to/from Huelva (1050 ptas).

WEST OF ARACENA

West of Aracena stretches one of Andalucía's most surprisingly beautiful landscapes, a sometimes lush, sometimes severe hill-country region dotted with old stone villages where time seems to have been proceeding rather slowly for a good long while. Many of the valleys have rich and varied tree canopies, while elsewhere there are expanses of *dehesa* – evergreen oak woodlands – where the region's famed black (or dark brown) Iberian pigs *(cerdos ibéricos)*, raw material of the best *jamón* in Spain, forage for the acorns which constitute most of their diet.

Some of the villages go back a long, long time, but others owe their existence to a Castilian repopulation drive after they had pushed out the Portuguese (who had driven out the Muslims) in the 13th century. Most villages grew up around fortress-like churches, or hill-top castles constructed to deter the Portuguese.

There's an extensive network of marked walking trails throughout the Parque Natural Sierra de Aracena y Picos de Aroche and particularly between Aracena and Aroche. Most villages are served by buses and many of them have accommodation, so you can make day hikes or string together a route of several days.

The main road from Aracena to Aroche is the N-433 through Galaroza and Cortegana (passing close to Fuenteheridos and Jabugo). A more scenic route as far as Cortegana is the A-470 through Santa Ana la Real and Almonaster la Real (passing close to Linares de la Sierra and Alájar). Detours between south and north are quite feasible as there are several roads and paths cutting across.

Getting There & Away

Bus Casal (see Getting There & Away under Aracena) runs buses from Sevilla (Plaza de Armas) and Aracena to many of the *pueblos*. You should be able to pick up a current timetable at either place. At the time of writing there were two buses daily, except Sunday, from Aracena to Cortegana, and vice-versa, via Linares de la Sierra, Alájar, Santa Ana la Real and Almonaster la Real, with one of them continuing to/from Aroche and the other to/from Sevilla. There are three or four buses daily from Aracena to Cortegana, and vice-

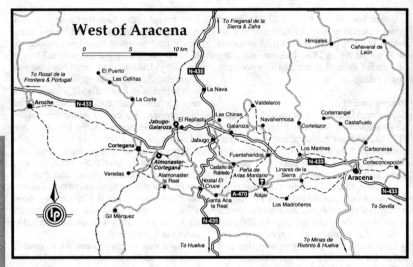

versa, via Fuenteheridos, Galaroza and Jabugo, with two or more continuing to/from Aroche and two to/from Sevilla.

Train Two daily trains run from Huelva to Almonaster-Cortegana and Jabugo-Galaroza stations (and vice-versa), taking about two hours. Almonaster-Cortegana station is 1km off the Almonaster-Cortegana road, about halfway between the two villages. Jabugo-Galaroza station is in El Repilado, on the N-433 about 4km west of Jabugo.

Linares de la Sierra

Seven kilometres west of Aracena on the A-470, a 1km side-road leads down to this poor but pretty little village, surrounded by stone-walled fields in a verdant river valley. The villagers have turned street cobbles into a minor art form by setting patterns of cobbles in front of their doors – rather like stone door mats. The bar on the plaza next to the church has food.

Alájar

Five kilometres west of Linares and also off the A-470 down in a river valley, Alájar is a bigger cobblestoned village clustered round a typical large sierra church.

Almost opposite the Alájar turning on the A-470, another side-road leads uphill towards Fuenteheridos. After 1km you reach the **Peña de Arias Montano**, a spur of the hillside which supports the 16th century Ermita de Nuestra Señora Reina de los Ángeles. This chapel, with a much venerated 13th century carving of the Virgin, is the goal of a hectic *romería* on 7 and 8 September when Alájar villagers race up here on horseback. The crag gets its name from Benito Arias Montano, a remarkable 16th century polymath who, late in life – having among other things produced one of the first maps of the world, learned 11 languages and been a confessor, adviser and librarian to Felipe II – came as parish priest to nearby Castaño del Robledo and made many visits to the peña for retreat and meditation.

There are great views from up here and steps down from the far end of the car park lead to a cave where it's said Felipe II spent time in contemplation when visiting Arias Montano.

The cosy *La Posada* (☎ 959 12 57 12) at

Calle Médico Emilio González 2, near Alájar's church, has nine singles/doubles with bath costing 3500/4500 ptas plus IVA and a restaurant with a menú for 1250 ptas and platos combinados for around 750 ptas.

Santa Ana la Real
Seven kilometres west of Alájar, Santa Ana is nothing special but, 1.5km farther west at the junction of the A-470 and N-435, *Hostal El Cruce* (☎ 959 12 23 33) has singles/doubles for 2000/4000 ptas, and a restaurant.

Almonaster la Real
This picturesque village, 7km west of Santa Ana la Real, is home to one of the most perfect little gems of Islamic architecture in Spain. The **mezquita** (mosque) stands atop a hill on the south side of Almonaster, five minutes walk up from the ayuntamiento on the main square, where you must ask for the key. If the ayuntamiento door is locked, knock on the window to the right of the door – someone will answer. When you reach the mezquita, you need to persevere with the key – push, wiggle and push hard!

The mezquita was built in the 10th century. In the 13th century the conquering Castilians turned it into a church but left the Islamic structure largely intact. The building also incorporates bits of an earlier Visigothic church which had stood here, and of even earlier stonework from Roman times.

At one side stands the original minaret, a square, three-level tower. You can climb up inside it and look down on Almonaster's 19th century bullring which adjoins the Mezquita. As you enter the Mezquita you pass beneath an original Muslim horseshoe arch and a Visigothic lintel carved with a cross and two fleurs-de-lis. The inside is like a miniature version of the great Mezquita in Córdoba, with rows of brick arches supported by varied columns. The capitals of the two columns at the far end of the first row to the left as you enter, and the one at the end of the second row, are Roman. Also at the eastern end is the semi-circular *mihrab* (prayer niche), indicating the direction of Mecca. The Christians

added a Romanesque apse at the northern end – where parts of a broken Visigothic altar, carved with a dove and angels' wings, have been reassembled.

Casa García (☎ 959 14 31 09), on Avenida San Martín at the entrance to the village from the A-470, has rooms for 3000 ptas plus IVA a double, or 5000 ptas plus IVA with bath, and a good restaurant. *Pensión La Cruz* (☎ 959 14 31 35), Plaza El Llano 8, has a few rooms for 3700 ptas plus IVA a double, with bath.

Cortegana
With a population of 5200 people, Cortegana, 6km north-west of Almonaster, is one of the bigger places in the district.

The track up to the hill-top 13th century **Castillo** is just about driveable. Next to the castle, the **Capilla de Nuestra Señora de la Piedad**, which dates from the 16th century, has some curious modern frescos of sweetly smiling angels. The castle should be open Saturday, Sunday and holidays from about 10 am to 2 pm and 4 to 7 pm. On other days you can try asking for the key at the ayuntamiento (open Monday to Friday from 10 am to 1.30 pm) on the central Plaza de la Constitución. The Ayuntamiento also hands out a useful map/leaflet on walks from Cortegana. Also worth a look is the 16th century Gothic-mudéjar **Iglesia del Divino Salvador** on Plaza del Divino Salvador, with the typical regional brick-and-stone construction and pointed tower.

Accommodation is limited to *Pensión Cervantes* (☎ 959 13 15 92) at Calle Cervantes 27B, just off Plaza de la Constitución, with doubles from 2700 to 3500 ptas plus IVA.

Aroche
From Cortegana the N-433 and the PRA2 footpath run 12km west along a broad, open valley to the friendly little town of Aroche, just 10km from the nearest point on the Portuguese border.

Aroche's **castillo**, at the top of the village, was originally built by the Almoravids in the 12th century and has more recently been converted into a bullring. It's open Saturday, Sunday and holidays from 10 am to 2 pm and 4 to 7 pm; at other times you can ask at the Casa Consistorial (ayuntamiento) on the central Plaza de Juan Carlos I, or the Cafetería Lalo, up the steps beside the Casa Consistorial, for a guide to take you up.

Just below the castle, the large **Iglesia de Nuestra Señora de la Asunción** is basically Gothic-mudéjar but has a 16th century Renaissance portal. The **Museo del Santo Rosario**, just before the car park as you drive up from the N-433, has a collection of more than 1000 rosaries from around the world, some donated by the rich and famous.

Hostal Picos de Aroche (☎ 959 14 04 75), at Carretera de Aracena 12 (the road up into town from the N-433), has rooms with bath at 5000 ptas a double. *Pensión Romero* (☎ 959 14 00 22) on Calle Ordóñez Váldez, just off the same road a little higher up, has rooms with bath for 3000 ptas a double. *Centro Cultural Las Peñas* on Calle Real does excellent tapas for 125 to 200 ptas.

Jabugo

Just south of the N-433, 10km east of Cortegana, Jabugo (population 2600) is famous throughout Spain for its *jamón ibérico* (see the boxed text on ham in the Food section of Facts for the Visitor).

The village is the main processing centre for hams from the Huelva sierras, and a line of bars and restaurants along Carretera San Juan del Puerto, on the eastern side of the village, waits for you to sample what's acclaimed as the best jamón in the country. At *Mesón Cinco Jotas*, run by the biggest producer, Sánchez Romero Carvajal, a media-ración of the best ham, *cinco jotas* (5 Js), will set you back 1100 ptas, or you could 'pig out' on cinco jotas and fried eggs for 1500 ptas. In the bars you can get a bocadillo of fine jamón for 700 or 800 ptas. Shops sell jamón to take away for between 3000 and 4800 ptas a kilogram – you might as well go for *jamón ibérico de bellota* (ham of acorn-fed Iberian pig), which is what all the fuss is about. A typical whole ham weighs 7 or 8kg.

Ham apart, Jabugo is unspectacular. *Pensión Aurora* (☎ 959 12 11 46) has six rooms with bath at 4000 ptas plus IVA for a double. It's at Calle Barca 9, between Carretera San Juan del Puerto and the central square, which of course is called Plaza del Jamón.

Galaroza

Little over 1km cross-country north-east of Jabugo, Galaroza is a pretty but unexciting little place, except on 6 September, when villagers chuck a great deal of water at each other in the Fiesta del Jarrito. There are three places to stay: *Hostal Toribio* (☎ 959 12 30 73), in the centre at Calle Iglesia 1, with rooms with bath at 3600 ptas plus IVA a double; *Hostal Venecia* (☎ 959 12 30 98) on the N-433, which is marginally cheaper; and *Hotel Galaroza Sierra* (☎ 959 12 32 37) on the N-433 at the western end of the village, with a pool, garden and doubles for 8000 ptas plus IVA.

Fuenteheridos

Fuenteheridos (population 700), just south of the N-433, is one of the quainter villages in the district. It's reasonably lively down around the wide Plaza del Coso, with its Fuente de los Doce Caños (Fountain of the 12 Spouts), but up around the 18th century church, where grass grows on the narrow streets, you could be in another age.

Camping-Cortijo El Madroñal (☎ 959 50 12 01), 1km west on the Castaño del Robledo road, is set in ancient chestnut woods and has room for just 60 people at 500 ptas plus IVA per adult, per tent and per car. *Pensión Carballos* (☎ 959 12 51 08) at Calle Fuente 16, between Plaza del Coso and the church, has doubles for 2600 ptas, or 3400 ptas with bath.

Just off the N-433, the *Villa Turística Fuenteheridos* (☎ 959 12 52 02) is a quite tasteful development of self-catering chalets which cost 10,000 ptas plus IVA for two people or 14,000 ptas plus IVA for four – plus 500 ptas for rental of pots, pans and cutlery. There's also a pool, restaurant and café.

There are several restaurants and mesones on Plaza del Coso.

Castaño del Robledo

This small, impoverished village, on a minor road between Fuenteheridos and the N-435, has a positively medieval feel, with two large churches in states of advanced disrepair and the tile roofs of houses bending under the weight of the years.

You'll find a couple of bars on Plaza del Álamo behind the Iglesia de Santiago el Mayor, the church with the most pointed tower.

Walking

Information Try to obtain some maps in advance: the best will be in the SGE's 1:50,000 series. Local availability of maps and leaflets on walking routes is erratic – and much of the material is in Spanish only – but you will probably be able to pick up enough from tourist offices to find your way around.

Traveller's Map – Footpaths of the Sierra de Aracena and Picos de Aroche shows in broad outline the routes of many marked paths in and around the Parque Natural Sierra de Aracena y Picos de Aroche; we found it in Huelva city (see Information in the Huelva section) but nowhere in the park itself. The Centro de Turismo Rural y Reservas in Aracena gave out a useful *Senderismo* leaflet mapping and describing 13 routes within about 15km of Aracena (mostly west of the town). The Cortegana Ayuntamiento handed out *Senderos de Pequeño Recorrido en el Entorno de Cortegana*, which maps and describes walks from Cortegana as far as Almonaster la Real, Jabugo and Aroche. These two maps in fact cover most of the main walking areas. Other village ayuntamientos are worth trying for printed information, as is the Centro de Visitantes Cabildo Viejo in Aracena.

Routes The possible permutations along the area's paths are endless. In four or five days you could do a fairly easy circuit of about 100km from Aracena to Aroche and back. An obvious route, nearly all off-road, is: Aracena, Linares de la Sierra, Alájar, Castaño del Robledo, Santa Ana la Real, Almonaster la Real, Cortegana, Aroche, Cortegana, Jabugo, Galaroza, Fuenteheridos, Los Marines, Aracena. One of the most attractive sections of country – with lots of varied woodland, streams and fine views – is between Aracena and Castaño del Robledo. In the west, the more open country between Cortegana and Aroche provides a good contrast. Good north-south trails include Alájar to Fuenteheridos and Castaño del Robledo to Jabugo.

See Walks in the Aracena section for more on the Aracena-Linares de la Sierra-Alájar stretch. From Cortegana to Aroche, the PRA2 leaves the N-433 just after a small group of warehouses, the Polígono Industrial El Pontón, 1km west of the westerly exit from Cortegana. To return from Aroche along the longer, more southerly PRA1, start from the Alto de los Méndez.

Cádiz Province

The province of Cádiz stretches from the mouth of the Río Guadalquivir to the Strait of Gibraltar and inland to the rainy mountains of the Sierra de Grazalema. Its attractions include the historic port of Cádiz, the triangle of sherry-making towns (Jerez de la Frontera, Sanlúcar de Barrameda and El Puerto de Santa María), the long, sandy and little-developed Atlantic beaches along the Costa de la Luz (Coast of Light) and the beautiful, green Sierra de Grazalema with its remote white towns and villages.

The proliferation of 'de la Frontera' place names dates back to the days of the Reconquista. Castilla took most of Cádiz province from the Muslims in the 13th century, but the south was raided repeatedly by the Merenids of Morocco, while to the east lay the Emirate of Granada. Hence, for over two centuries this region was one of the *fronteras* (frontiers) of Christian territory. In the mid-14th century King Alfonso XI offered a free pardon to murderers and criminals who would come here and serve a year and a day in his army. The region still feels untamed today, with windy coasts, large tracts of sparsely-inhabited sierra and big lowland ranches which breed famous fighting bulls.

CÁDIZ

Few people remember Cádiz when they list the great cities of Andalucía, yet this port is as famous and historic as almost any of them. It's just that it's out on a limb, alost as intimate with the oceans and distant continents as with its own land, and with no Muslim or Reconquista heritage whatsoever.

Once past the desolate coastal marshes and grim industrial sprawl around Cádiz, you emerge into a largely 18th century city of decayed grandeur, crammed on to the head of a long peninsula like some huge overcrowded oceangoing ship. The city's 146,000 people, called *gaditano*s, are a mostly unassuming and tolerant lot whose

HIGHLIGHTS

- Windsurfing at Tarifa, an old Muslim town on Spain's southern tip, just across the water from Africa
- The Costa de la Luz – long, sandy Atlantic beaches and laid-back coastal villages
- The fun-loving, historic port city of Cádiz
- Sherry, horses and flamenco in Jerez de la Frontera
- A succulent seafood dinner as the sun goes down over the Guadalquivir at Sanlúcar de Barrameda
- Exploring the white villages and ancient forests of green, mountainous Parque Natural Sierra de Grazalema
- Roaming the tranquil cork oak forests of Parque Natural Los Alcornocales
- The intriguing white hill-top town of Arcos de la Frontera

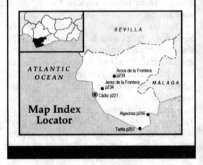

main concern is to make the best of life – whether staying out late to enjoy the after-dark cool in the sweltering summer months, or indulging in Spain's most riotous Carnaval in spring.

History

Cádiz may be the oldest city in Europe. It was founded, tradition says, in 1100 BC by the Phoenicians, who called it Gadir and traded Baltic amber and British tin as well as Spanish silver here. Later, it became a

218

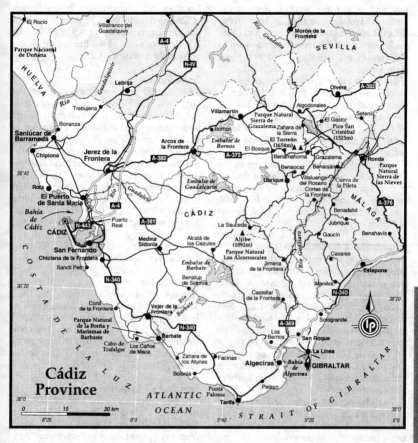

Cádiz
Province

naval base for the Romans, who heaped praise on its culinary, sexual, and musical delights, then it faded into obscurity until 1262 when it was taken from the Muslims by Alfonso X.

Cádiz began to boom with the discovery of America. Columbus sailed from this port on his second and fourth voyages. It attracted Spain's enemies too: in 1587 England's Sir Francis Drake 'singed the King of Spain's beard' with a raid on the harbour which delayed the imminent Spanish Armada. Then, in 1596, Anglo-Dutch attackers burnt almost the entire city.

Cádiz's golden age was during the 18th century when it enjoyed 75% of Spanish trade with the Americas. It grew into the richest and most cosmopolitan city in Spain and gave birth to to the country's first middle class of progressive, liberal inclinations. Most of the city's fine buildings date from this era.

The Napoleonic Wars brought British warships back to blockade and bombard the city and shatter the Spanish fleet at the Battle of Trafalgar, nearby, in 1805. After Spain turned against Napoleon in 1808, Cádiz was one of the few cities not to fall to the French, withstanding a two-year siege from 1810.

During this time a national cortes (parliament) convened here. It was a lopsidedly liberal gathering which adopted Spain's 1812 constitution, proclaiming sovereignty of the people and setting the scene for a century of struggle between liberals and conservatives.

The loss of the American colonies in the 19th century plunged Cádiz into a decline from which it has recovered only in the past few decades. Today, it's an industrial city with shipbuilding among its foremost activities.

Orientation & Information

Breathing space between the huddled streets of the old city is provided by numerous plazas. From Plaza de San Juan de Dios, towards the east end of the old city, Calle Nueva, which becomes Calle San Francisco, leads north-west towards another important square, Plaza de Mina. The train station is in the east of the old city just off Plaza de Sevilla, with the main bus station of the Comes line 800m north-west on Plaza de la Hispanidad. The main harbour lies between the two.

The 18th century Puertas de Tierra (Land Gates) mark the eastern boundary of the old city. Modern Cádiz extends the only way it can – back along the peninsula.

The municipal tourist office (☎ 956 24 10 01) at Plaza San Juan de Dios 11 is open Monday to Saturday from 9 am to 2 pm, and Monday to Friday from 5 to 8 pm. The well-stocked regional tourist office (☎ 956 21 13 13) at Calle Calderón de la Barca 1 opens Tuesday to Friday from 9 am to 7 pm, Saturday and Monday from 9 am to 2 pm.

You'll find banks with ATMs on Avenida Ramón de Carranza and Calle San Francisco, north-west of Plaza de San Juan de Dios. The main post office (postcode 11080) is on Plaza de Topete. The Policía

Local (☎ 092 in emergency) have a station at Campo del Sur s/n. The main hospital is the Residencia Sanitaria (☎ 956 27 90 11), 2.25km south-east of the Puertas de Tierra, at Avenida Ana de Viya 21.

Torre Tavira

This highest and most important of the city's old watchtowers, at Calle Marqués del Real Tesoro 10, is a fine place to get your bearings and a dramatic panorama of Cádiz. Its *cámara oscura* projects moving images of the city on to a screen – absorbing even if you can't understand the 15-minute Spanish commentary. Back in the 18th century Cádiz had no less than 160 towers to watch over its harbours. The Torre Tavira (☎ 956 21 29 10) is open daily, mid-June to mid-September from 10 am to 8 pm, the rest of the year from 10 am to 6 pm. There are cámara oscura sessions (400 ptas) about every 30 minutes.

Plaza de Topete

A couple of blocks south-east of the Torre Tavira, this plaza is one of Cádiz's liveliest, bright with flower and cage-bird stalls and adjoining the large covered Mercado Central (central market). It's still commonly known by its old name Plaza de las Flores (Plaza of the Flowers).

Hospital de Mujeres

The real attraction of the 18th century former women's hospital (☎ 956 22 37 47) on Calle Hospital de Mujeres, is its chapel (capilla), open Monday to Friday from 9 am to 1 pm. One of the many profusely decorated churches from Cádiz's golden century, this contains El Greco's *Extasis de San Francisco*, depicting the grey-cloaked saint experiencing a mystical vision.

Museo Histórico Municipal

The City History Museum (☎ 956 22 17 88), at Calle Santa Inés 9, contains a large and detailed 18th century model of the city, made in mahogany and marble for Carlos III, which would merit a visit even if there were nothing else here. The museum is open Tuesday to

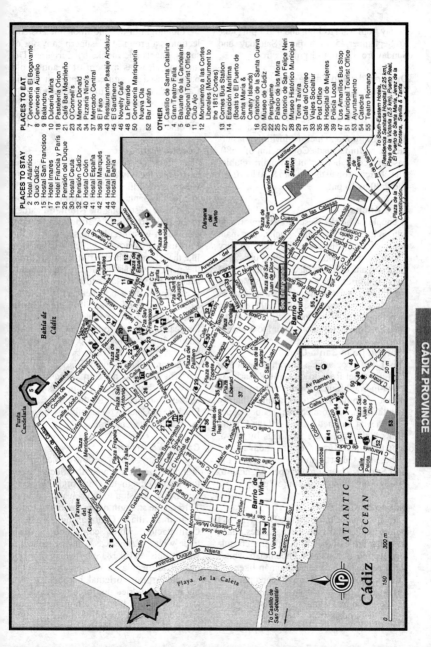

CÁDIZ PROVINCE

Friday from 9 am to 1 pm and 4 to 7 pm (June to September, 5 to 8 pm), Saturday and Sunday from 9 am to 1 pm. It's free.

Oratorio de San Felipe Neri
Also on Calle Santa Inés, this is one of Cádiz's finest baroque churches and was also the meeting place of the 1812 Cortes. The interior has an unusual oval shape and a beautiful dome. One of Murillo's masterpieces, an Inmaculada Concepción of 1680, has a place of honour in the main retablo. The church is open daily from 8.30 to 10 am and 7.30 to 10 pm.

Calle Ancha
A couple of blocks west of the Oratorio de San Felipe Neri is Calle Ancha, the main street of late 18th and early 19th century Cádiz. Its cafés and bars were the unofficial gathering and debating places for members of the 1812 Cortes. The **Palacio de los Mora** at No 28-30 is one of the most sumptuous of Cádiz's urban mansions, built in the eclectic Isabelline style of the mid-19th century. It's open Saturdays only, from 11 am to 1 pm.

Oratorio de la Santa Cruz
This 1780s neoclassical church, attached to the Iglesia del Rosario on Calle Rosario, is a two-in-one affair, with the austere underground Capilla Baja contrasting sharply with the richly decorated oval-shaped upper Capilla Alta. Framed by three of the Capilla Alta's eight arches are paintings by Goya, depicting the Miracle of the Loaves and Fishes, the Guest at the Wedding, and the Last Supper. The church is open Monday to Friday from 10 am to 1 pm (50 ptas).

Museo de Cádiz
The city's major museum (☎ 956 21 22 81) is on one of its most attractive squares, Plaza de Mina. Pride of the ground-floor archaeology section is a pair of Phoenician whitestone sarcophagi carved in human likeness. There's also some beautiful Phoenician jewellery and Roman glassware, and lots of headless Roman statues – plus emperor Trajan, with head, from Baelo Claudia.

A highlight of the 2nd floor fine arts collection is a group of 21 superb canvases of saints, angels and monks by Zurbarán. The museum also has a room of beautiful old puppets used in satirical puppet theatre in Cadíz. It's open daily from 9.30 am to 2.30 pm and Monday to Friday from 5.30 to 8.30 pm. Entry is free for EU citizens, 250 ptas for others.

Coastal Walk
One block north of Plaza de Mina you emerge on the city's northern seafront, with views across the Bahía de Cádiz to El Puerto de Santa María. From here you could head west along the **Alameda** garden to the **Baluarte de la Candelaria** bastion, then south-west beside the sea wall to the **Parque del Genovés**, which was laid out, like the Alameda, in the 19th century. From the park, Avenida Duque de Nájera leads south to **Playa de la Caleta** (very crowded in summer), on a bay between two forts. The star-shaped **Castillo de Santa Catalina**, built in 1598, at the north end of the beach, was for a long time Cádiz's main citadel. It is open for guided visits every 30 minutes, Monday to Friday from 10 am to 6 pm, Saturday and Sunday from 10 am to 2 pm. The **Castillo de San Sebastián**, far out on the south side of the bay, is in military use and closed to the public. From Playa de la Caleta you can follow the coast eastward to the Catedral.

Catedral & Around
The story of Cádiz's yellow-domed cathedral on Plaza de la Catedral reflects that of the whole city in the 18th and 19th centuries. The decision to build it was taken in 1716 on the strength of the imminent transfer from Sevilla to Cádiz of the Casa de la Contratación, which controlled Spanish trade with the Americas. But the cathedral wasn't finished till 1838, by which time not only had neoclassical elements diluted Vicente Arturo's original baroque design, but funds had dried up, forcing cutbacks in size and quality. It's still a big and impressive construction, with little ornamentation

to distract from the grandeur of the marble and stone interior, lit from the 50m-high main dome. The Cádiz-born composer Manuel de Falla is buried in the crypt. The Catedral is open to visitors Monday to Saturday from 10 am to 1.30 pm. The attached **Museo Catedralicio** (☎ 956 28 61 54) contains some very large and lavish monstrances. It's open Tuesday to Saturday from 10 am to noon (400 ptas).

A short distance east of the Catedral along Campo del Sur are the excavated remains of a Roman theatre, the **Teatro Romano**, open Tuesday to Sunday from 11 am to 1.30 pm (free).

Plaza de San Juan de Dios & Around
The shabby **Barrio del Pópulo** district between the Teatro Romano and Plaza de San Juan de Dios was the kernel of medieval Cádiz, a fortified enclosure wrecked in 1596. Its three 13th century gates, the Arco de los Blancos, Arco de la Rosa and Arco del Pópulo, however, remain. Plaza de San Juan de Dios is dominated by the imposing neoclassical **Ayuntamiento**, built at its southern end around 1800.

If by now you're in need of a cool, quiet and leafy resting spot, the bougainvillea-shaded benches in **Plaza Candelaria**, 250m north-west of Plaza de San Juan de Dios, fit the bill very nicely.

Playa de la Victoria
This wide beach stretches many kilometres back down the ocean side of the peninsula, beginning about 1km beyond the Puertas de Tierra. On hot summer weekends almost the whole city seems to be out here. Bus No 1 'Plaza España-Cortadura' from Plaza de España runs along the peninsula one or two blocks inland from the beach.

Courses
Cádiz has at least three language schools. Most popular is Gadir Escuela Internacional de Español (☎ & fax 956 26 05 57; gadir@arrakis.es), Calle Pérgolas 5. The school offers classes in Spanish culture and literature as well as language courses of

varying length and intensity. The cost for two weeks intensive classes in a small group is 22,000 ptas in summer. The postal address is Apartado de Correos 31, Cádiz 11007.

Special Events
No other Spanish city celebrates Carnaval with the verve of Cádiz, where it turns into a 10-day singing, dancing and drinking fancy-dress party that continues until the weekend after the normal Shrove Tuesday close. Everyone – locals and visitors – dresses up, and the fun, abetted by enormous quantities of alcohol, is infectious. Costumed groups called *murgas* tour the city on foot or on floats, singing witty satirical ditties, dancing or performing sketches. In addition to the 300 or so officially recognised murgas, judged by a panel in the Gran Teatro Falla, there are also the *ilegales* – any group that fancies taking to the streets and trying to play or sing.

Some of the liveliest scenes are in the working-class Barrio de la Viña, between the Mercado Central and Playa de la Caleta, and on Calle Ancha and Calle Columela where ilegales tend to congregate.

Rooms in Cádiz for Carnaval time get booked months in advance. Assuming you haven't managed this, you could just go for the night from Sevilla or anywhere else within striking distance. Plenty of people do this – in fancy dress.

Places to Stay – Budget
Youth Hostel Cádiz's excellent independent youth hostel, *Quo Qádiz* (☎ 956 22 19 39), is in a revamped old house at Calle Diego Arias 1, on the corner of Calle Solano just a block south of the Gran Teatro Falla. Cheerful dorms and private singles and doubles occupy several floors topped by an extensive roof terrace which is good for viewing Carnaval. A dorm bed costs 1000 ptas, singles/doubles 2100/3200 ptas. Prices include a decent breakfast. Vegetarian food is served for lunch (450 ptas) and dinner (550 ptas). The energetic owners organise trips to beaches up and down the coast, the sierras of Cádiz province, and even

Morocco. Entertainment happens here some evenings while by day there are classes in tai-chi, flamenco dance, and more.

Hostales & Pensiones Cheaper places mostly cluster just north-west of Plaza de San Juan de Dios. A good choice is the friendly family-run *Hostal Fantoni* (28 27 04) in an old house at Calle Flamenco 5. Very clean and recently renovated and with a roof terrace catching a bit of breeze in summer, it has rooms for 1600/3200 ptas, and doubles with bath for 5000 ptas. *Hostal Marqués* (☎ 956 28 58 54), Calle Marqués de Cádiz 1, has slightly ageing but clean singles/doubles, all with balcony, for 2000/3500 ptas, or doubles with bath for 4500 ptas. *Hostal Colón* (☎ 956 28 53 51) at No 6 on the same street has similar prices. *Hostal España* (☎ 956 28 55 00) at No 9 has nice rooms for 2800/3800 ptas, or doubles with private shower for 4800 ptas.

A bit farther north-west, *Pension Cádiz* (☎ 956 28 58 01), Calle Feduchy 20, is a popular little place with doubles/triples only at 3000/4500 ptas with shared bath. Close by, *Hostal Ceuta* (☎ 956 22 16 54), Calle Montañés 7, has clean doubles with bath for 3500 ptas.

A good choice farther into the old city is the clean *Hostal San Francisco* (☎ 956 22 18 42), Calle San Francisco 12. Singles/doubles are 2300/3900 ptas; doubles with shower are 5400 ptas. Rooms at *Hotel Imares* (☎ 956 21 22 57), across the street at No 9, range from some airless and odorous interior ones to bright and breezy ones overlooking the street. Singles/doubles with bath cost from 2800/4700 to 3500/5700 ptas.

The family-run *Pension del Duque* (☎ 956 22 27 77) at Calle Ancha 13 has decent rooms with bath for 3500/4000 ptas.

Places to Stay – Mid-Range
Hostal Bahía (☎ 956 25 90 61) at Calle Plocia 5 just off Plaza de San Juan de Dios has comfortable air-con rooms with TV at 5200/6500 ptas. *Hotel Francia y París* (☎ 956 21 23 18, 956 22 23 48), very well located at Plaza San Francisco 2, is bigger

(57 rooms) and more luxurious, with singles/doubles for 7100/9500 ptas plus IVA.

Other middle-range options are mostly outside the old city. The good *Hotel Regio II* (☎ 956 25 30 08), Avenida de Andalucía 79, and *Hotel Regio* (☎ 956 27 93 31), Avenida Ana de Viya 11, are both on the main road down the peninsula, 1.5 and 2km respectively from the Puertas de Tierra. Doubles are 8000 ptas plus IVA at the Regio II, 8500 ptas plus IVA at the Regio.

Places to Stay – Top End
The modern *Hotel Atlántico* parador (☎ 956 22 69 05) is on the seafront by Parque del Genovés at Avenida Duque de Nájera 9. Standard rooms are 10,000 ptas or 11,500 ptas, plus IVA, depending on the season. There are off-season deals of 9000 ptas for the same rooms, including IVA and breakfast.

Outside the old city, the large, stylish *Hotel Puertatierra* (☎ 956 27 21 11) at Avenida de Andalucía 34, 750m from the Puertas de Tierra, has doubles for 12,500 ptas plus IVA. *Hotel Meliá Caleta* (☎ 956 27 94 11), Avenida Amilcar Barca s/n, is on the beachfront 1.5km farther south-east with doubles at 15,250 ptas plus IVA. Biggest and best is the 188-room *Hotel Playa Victoria* (☎ 956 27 54 11), Glorieta Ingeniero La Cierva 4, on the beachfront a further 400m along, with doubles at 17,000 ptas plus IVA.

Places to Eat
El Faro, at Calle San Felix 15 in the Barrio de la Viña, the old fishermen's district, around 600m west of the Catedral, is Cádiz's most famous seafood restaurant with a fancy menu and prices to match. However, its attached bar has exquisite seafood tapas from 160 to 225 ptas. There's an extensive list to select from. We enjoyed the frituritas de bechamel con espinacas y gambas, fried pastries with a filling of prawns and spinach in a bechamel sauce, and the albondigas de choco con salsa de mariscos, cuttlefish balls in a shellfish sauce. Raciones or platters of fried fish are 850 to 975 ptas. El Faro is open daily from noon to 4.30 pm and from 8 pm to midnight.

Plaza de San Juan de Dios This central plaza offers plenty of choice. If price is crucial, *Bar Letrán* does *platos combinados* for 550 to 1000 ptas; the menú is 1250 ptas. *Restaurante Pasaje Andaluz* has menús from 850 ptas and main dishes from 500 ptas. *El Sardinero* does similar fare better but for almost twice the price – its menú is 1450 ptas. A few doors east, the *Novelty Café* is a fine place for a light breakfast, cakes or snacks. On the east side of the plaza *Cervecería Marisquería Nueva Ola* has good seafood and fish raciones from 750 ptas and platos combinados from 550 to 1000 ptas. Or you can go for a sherry and tapas. *La Pierrade* one block off the plaza at Calle Plocia 2 is a bit more adventurous. The three-course menú might offer mejillones (mussels) al Roquefort, or brocheta de cordero (lamb kebab) and includes wine and bread.

Plaza de Mina *Café/Bar Madrileño* has a wide choice at reasonable prices: tapas at 150 to 200 ptas, salads around 350 ptas, vegetable raciones for 600 ptas, stuffed peppers or pork brochettes for 700 ptas, fish and seafood raciones from 800 ptas. *Dulcería Mina*, Calle Antonio López 2, has good pastries and excellent filled baguettes, and is a good spot for breakfast (tea/coffee, juice and tostada for 300 ptas, or a bacon and eggs option for 450 ptas).

Off another side of the plaza, it's hard to pass by the mouthwatering fresh seafood tapas at *Cervecería Aurelio*, Calle Zorrilla 1. Try the cazón en adobo (marinated, deep-fried white fish, 150 ptas). Down at the end of this street, enjoy the bay views at *Cervecería El Bogavante* while attentive waiters serve up good scrambled eggs with prawns and asparagus for 900 ptas, big salads for 600 ptas, and fish and meat mains from 800 to 1200 ptas. A few doors east at Alameda Apodaca 22, *Balandro* has sea views from its terrace and upstairs dining room. This place is popular year-round for its good food, cheap prices and attractive old crockery. We liked the pizza-like pan horneado with a smoked salmon, anchovies and cream cheese topping (850 ptas and

enough for two with a salad). Scrambled eggs with fancy fillings cost 650 ptas while meat and fish raciones start at 825 ptas. It's closed Sunday evening and Monday.

Plaza de Topete *Pizzeria Nino's* on Calle Columela just off the plaza does tasty pizzas from 740 ptas, pasta from 625 ptas, and Tex-Mex fare and burgers in the same range. The nearby market (*Mercado Central*) sells, among other things, churros, which you can take to nearby cafés to enjoy with hot chocolate for breakfast.

Plaza San Francisco *Pastelería Orion*, with tables on the plaza opposite the church, is good for a drink and pastry at any time of day. *O'Connell's*, the Irish pub adjacent on Calle Tinte, has Irish beers and food, including baked potatoes with fillings and sandwiches on home-made bread – try the Irish smoked salmon. Around the corner on Calle Sagasta, *Menoc Donald* is *the* place in this part of town for pizzas and burgers.

Entertainment

There's a great atmosphere in some of the old city's plazas on hot summer nights with bars and cafés busy till well after midnight, and kids playing football or cruising on bikes or skates, everyone out enjoying the relative cool.

From midnight or so in summer the real scene migrates to the Paseo Marítimo along Playa de la Victoria – about 3km down the peninsula from the Puertas de Tierra. Here, some 300m past the big Hotel Playa Victoria, you'll find lively music bars like *La Jarra* and *El Cobertizo Pub*; 350m farther on is Calle Villa de Paradas where throngs of people stand in the street with *macetas* (large plastic mugs) of beer for 250 ptas from bars like *H2O* and *Bar Kemedehe*. A lot of people simply mess around on the beach till deep into the *madrugada*. A taxi from the old city to this area costs around 600 ptas. Up to about 1.30 am you can use bus No 1 (see Playa de la Victoria, above) to get there.

A few places in the centre have live music.

Café del Correo at Calle Cardenal Zapata 6 near Plaza Candelaria is a popular spot with good music (closed Monday and Tuesday). *Persígueme* on the corner of Calle Tinte and Calle Sagasta is another popular music bar, with live music on Thursdays. In winter, the bars in the streets west of Plaza de España, such as Calle Dr Zurita, are among the liveliest. *Club Ajo* on Plaza de España is a popular hangout with flamenco on Thursday nights, a disco on Friday and Saturday from around midnight and a Sunday jam session with local musicians from 9 pm.

In the cooler months, Plaza de España is the setting for the Saturday night movida with hundreds of Cádiz youth drinking and socialising under the stars and the watchful eyes of the police. It's impossible to park in the vicinity!

Gran Teatro Falla, in the north-west of the old town, is the main venue for cultural events.

Getting There & Away

Bus Most buses are run by Comes (☎ 956 21 17 63) from Plaza de la Hispanidad. These include at least seven daily to Sevilla (one hour, 1330 ptas), El Puerto de Santa María, Jerez de la Frontera, Tarifa and Algeciras (two hours, 1225 ptas), three or more daily to Arcos de la Frontera, Ronda, and Málaga, and buses at least daily to Zahara de los Atunes (except Sunday), Córdoba and Granada.

Los Amarillos runs up to 10 daily buses to El Puerto de Santa María and Sanlúcar de Barrameda, and two or three daily to Arcos de la Frontera, El Bosque and Ubrique, from its stop by the south end of Avenida Ramón de Carranza. Tickets can be bought at Viajes Socialtur (☎ 956 28 58 52), at Avenida Ramón de Carranza 31.

Buses to Madrid (six hours, 3035 ptas) are run up to six times daily by Sevibús (☎ 956 25 74 15) from Plaza Elios by the Estadio Ramón de Carranza football ground, about 2km south-east of the old city.

Train The station (☎ 956 25 43 01), just off Plaza de Sevilla, has *consigna* lockers. Up to 20 *cercanías* run daily to/from El Puerto de Santa María and Jerez de la Frontera (40 minutes), and up to 12 regionales to/from Sevilla (two hours, 1080 to 1240 ptas) via the same places.

There are four trains daily to/from Córdoba (around three hours, 2325 to 3700 ptas) and two each for Madrid and Barcelona.

Car & Motorcycle The A-4 *autopista* from Sevilla to Puerto Real on the east side of the Bahía de Cádiz carries a toll of 783 ptas. The toll-free alternative, the N-IV, is a lot busier and slower. From Puerto Real the N-443 crosses a bridge over the narrowest part of the bay to join the southern road into Cadiz about 4km short of the old city.

Boat Trasmediterránea (☎ 956 22 74 21) at the Estación Marítima operates a passenger and vehicle ferry to the Canary Islands, leaving Cádiz on Saturday and arriving in Santa Cruz de Tenerife, Las Palmas (Gran Canaria) and Santa Cruz de la Palma (La Palma) respectively 1½, 2 and 2½ days later. The one-way passenger fare is from 29,000 to 35,250 ptas. It's an often bumpy ride.

The Sherry Triangle

North of Cádiz, the towns of Jerez de la Frontera, Sanlúcar de Barrameda and El Puerto de Santa María are best known for being the homes of sherry. But there's a wealth of other good reasons to visit them – beaches, music, horses and access to the Parque Nacional de Doñana. See the special section on Food & Wine for an introduction to the subject of sherry.

EL PUERTO DE SANTA MARÍA

The town of El Puerto de Santa María (population 72,000), 10km north-east of Cádiz across the Bahía de Cádiz (22km by road), makes an interesting side trip, best enjoyed by taking the ferry *Motonave Adriano III*, better known as *El Vapor*. Columbus visited

El Puerto in the 1480s and received some encouragement from the local Duke of Medinaceli for his travel plans. Here, Columbus also met the owner of the *Santa María*, Juan de la Cosa, his pilot on the 1492 journey and who, in 1500, issued the first world map. Later, El Puerto was heavily involved in trade with the Americas and many palaces were built on the proceeds of this trade. From the 16th to the 18th centuries the port was also the base for the Spanish royal fleet. Recent prosperity has come from sherry and you can visit three *bodegas* here.

Orientation & Information

Most of the town is on the north bank of the Río Guadalete, just upstream from its mouth, though development spreads out along the beaches to the east and west. *El Vapor* arrives dead centre at the Muelle del Vapor jetty, beside Plaza de las Galeras Reales. The excellent tourist office (☎ 956 54 24 13), open daily from 10 am to 2 pm and 6 to 8 pm (5.30 to 7.30 pm in winter), is close by at Calle Guadalete 1. Calle Luna, the main drag with shops and banks, is straight ahead of the jetty. Calle Palacios runs parallel, one block to the left. The post office (postcode 11206) is on Plaza del Povorista, a few blocks west of the tourist office.

Buses come and go from stops outside the Plaza de Toros, off Calle Los Moros about 800m north-west of the Muelle del Vapor. Calle Los Moros runs all the way to the riverfront. The train station is to the east on Plaza de la Estación by the Cádiz-Jerez road, a 10-minute walk from the centre.

Things to See & Do

Most of the sights are between the river and Plaza España, seven blocks north of the Muelle del Vapor at the top of Calle Palacios. Stop by the little **Museo Municipal**, Calle Pagador 1, opposite Plaza España, which has interesting archaeological and fine arts sections. It's open Monday to Saturday from 10 am to 2 pm (free). The **Iglesia Mayor Prioral**, with a baroque façade, dominates Plaza España. Back towards the

river, the **Castillo San Marcos** was built by Alfonso X after he took the town in 1260. You can take a guided tour on Saturday between 11 am and 1 pm. Right by the river, **Plaza de las Galeras Reales** takes its name from the America-bound ships *(galeras)* which drew their water supplies from its four-spouted fountain. A couple of blocks to the west on Calle Aramburu de Mora is the lovely old fish exchange, the **Antigua Lonja de Pescado**, now a restaurant.

The tourist office can help with information about visiting the **18th century palaces** which are dotted around town, such as Palacio Medinaceli on Calle Aramburu de Mora and Palacio de Aranibar near the Castillo San Marcos.

El Puerto's **Plaza de Toros**, completed in 1880 and with space for 15,000 spectators, can be visited Tuesday to Sunday from 11 am to 2 pm and 5.30 to 7.30 pm (free).

Phone ahead if you want to visit one of the **sherry bodegas**. Bodegas Osborne (☎ 956 85 52 11) is open for visits (300 ptas) Monday to Friday from 9 am to 1 pm. Bodegas Terry (☎ 956 48 30 00) welcomes visitors (300 ptas) from Monday to Friday at 9.30 and 11 am and 12.30 pm.

Of the town's two **beaches**, the pine-flanked Playa de la Puntilla, a half-hour walk south-west of the centre, is the more appealing. Bus No 26 from Plaza de las Galeras Reales stops here. Bus No 35, from the stop on the north side of the plaza, goes to Playa Fuentebravia, farther west.

Organised Tours

Guided tours of the town set off on Saturday at 11 am from the tourist office.

Special Events

El Puerto's Feria de la Primavera early in May is in large measure dedicated to sherry with around 180,000 half-bottles being drunk in a week.

Places to Stay

Camping Playa Las Dunas (☎ 956 87 22 10), Paseo Marítimo La Puntilla, Playa de la Puntilla, has shade and is open year-round.

Cost is 535 ptas per tent, a further 535 per adult plus 480 ptas per car.

Las Columnas (☎ 956 85 20 19), Calle Vicario (also called Calle Dr Muñoz Seca) 8, a rambling old house a few steps east of Plaza España, has clean rooms with shared bath at 1200 ptas per person. *Hostal Santamaría* (☎ 956 85 36 31), Calle Pedro Muñoz Seca 38, two blocks towards the river from Plaza España, has reasonable singles/doubles at 1500/3000 ptas. The better *Hostal Manolo* (☎ 956 85 75 25), Calle Jesús de los Milagros 18, a block inland from Plaza de las Galeras Reales, has a friendly owner and singles/doubles at 2900/4300 ptas, while nearby *Hostal Loreto* (☎ 956 54 24 10), Calle Ganado 10, just north of Calle Virgen de los Milagros, charges 3000/5500 ptas for rooms with private bath around a leafy courtyard.

The top place is the *Monasterio San Miguel* (☎ 956 54 04 40) at Calle Virgen de los Milagros 27, with singles/doubles from 12,400/17,300 ptas plus IVA.

Places to Eat

El Puerto is an excellent place to sample seafood. Crowds head for the *Romerijo* and *Romerijo 2* on Calle Ribera del Marisco, near the Muelle del Vapor, where you can buy portions of seafood in paper cones to take away or eat at the tables outside. Romerijo specialises in boiled fresh seafood while Romerijo 2 fries it up and you buy by the ¼kg – prawns 700 ptas, choco (cuttlefish) 600 ptas and so on. Just back from here, *Café/Bar Herrera* has good food and prices with a nice little salad at 275 ptas and pinchitos morunos at 800 ptas. *Restaurante El Resbaladero*, in the old fish exchange on Calle Arambura de

---

Sacred Bulls

As you roam the highways of Spain, every now and then you'll observe the silhouette of a truly gigantic black bull on the horizon up ahead. When you get closer to the creature you'll realise it's only two-dimensional, made of metal and held up by bits of scaffolding. But what's it for?

DAMIEN SIMONIS

Well, it's not a silent homage to bullfighting erected by the local folk. Nor is it a sign that you're entering a notable bull-breeding area. It's a sherry and brandy advert for the Osborne company of El Puerto de Santa María. And in recent years the *toros de Osborne* have been raising almost as much passion as bullfighting itself.

At the last count there were 93 of them, looming beside roads all over the country. Why doesn't Osborne put its name on the bulls if it wants to advertise, you might ask? From 1957, when the first bull was erected on the Madrid-Burgos road, until 1988, it did – in big letters. The bulls, which each weigh 50 tonnes and at one time numbered 500, grew into a much-loved national symbol. Then in 1988 a new law banned advertising hoardings beside main roads to prevent drivers being distracted. Osborne left the bulls standing but removed its name, which seemed to pacify the authorities, until 1994 when word got about that the law was going to be enforced strictly, meaning no more bulls. This provoked an enormous outcry, with intellectuals writing to the newspapers about the national heritage, the government of Andalucía talking about declaring the bulls protected monuments, and the El Puerto de Santa María council threatening to take the matter to the supreme court.

The bulls are still standing.

Mora, offers air-conditioned comfort inside and a medium-to-expensive menu with lots of seafood and fish choices.

For breakfast or a drink, head to *Milor*, on the corner of Calle Tie Piury and Calle Virgen de los Milagros, two blocks north of the castle. It's a clone of a comfy English pub, open from 8 am weekdays and 10 am on weekends. *Tortillería Bar*, Calle Palacios 2, a little inland from the tourist office, does a huge variety of *bocadillos* from 175 to 200 ptas including bacalao, chorizo, salmon and roquefort. *Cafetería las Capuchinas* in the Monasterio San Miguel, Calle Virgen de los Milagros, provides welcome air-conditioning on a hot day. Enjoy a drink, or the menú at 1250 ptas plus IVA for three courses. There's a Moroccan-style *tetería* on Calle Luna, 1½ blocks north of the Muelle del Vapor.

Entertainment

El Puerto is a pretty lively place with plenty of bars and quite a lot more going on, especially in summer. On Saturday nights in July and August, there are free concerts in Plaza Colón near the tourist office. Two flamenco clubs – *Tertulia Flamenca Tomás El Nitri* at Calle Diego Niño 1, and *Peña Flamenca El Chumni* – have performances from time to time in their 18th century cellars; ask at the tourist office about forthcoming events. There are also night boat trips (two hours) on the Bahía de Cádiz a couple of nights weekly from July to September (600 ptas). There's more action – bars, discos etc – east of town out at Playa Valdelagrana, reached by Bus No 35 from the stop on Avenida de la Banjamar, just west of the Muelle del Vapor.

Getting There & Away

Bus A timetable is posted on the window of Bar Sol y Sombra, close to the Plaza de Toros bus stops. There are buses for Cádiz almost half-hourly Monday to Friday from 6.30 am to 9.30 pm (fewer at weekends), four to six buses daily to Jerez de la Frontera and four to 10 daily to Sanlúcar de Barrameda. Additional buses for Cádiz and

Jerez and two buses daily to Algeciras and La Línea leave from outside the train station.

Train El Puerto is on the Cádiz-Sevilla line, half an hour from Cádiz, with up to 19 trains daily in each direction leaving from the train station (☎ 956 54 25 85) east of the centre.

Boat *El Vapor* (☎ 956 87 02 70) sails from the Estación Marítima in Cádiz daily, except Monday, from February to November at 10 am, noon and 2, 6.30 and 8.30 pm, with an extra trip at 4.30 pm on Sunday. Trips back from El Puerto are at 9 and 11 am and 1, 3.30 and 7.30 pm, plus 5.30 pm on Sunday. The crossing takes 45 minutes and costs 250 ptas one way.

SANLÚCAR DE BARRAMEDA

The northern tip of the sherry triangle and a flourishing summer resort, Sanlúcar (population 61,000) is 23km north-west of El Puerto de Santa María. It has a likeable atmosphere and a fine location on the Guadalquivir estuary looking across to the Parque Nacional de Doñana, which you can visit from Sanlúcar.

Fears for Doñana have recently provoked strong environmentalist and political opposition to a plan by Alfonso von Hohenlohe, the man who brought the jetset to Marbella, to build a country club near Sanlúcar with two luxury hotels and 1200 holiday apartments.

Columbus, on his third voyage to the Caribbean, set sail from Sanlúcar in 1498. So, on 20 September 1519, did another foreigner sailing under the Castilian flag – the Portuguese Ferdinand Magellan, who set off with five ships and 265 crew to find, as Columbus had been trying to do, a westerly route to the spice islands of Indonesia. Magellan achieved the first known voyage through what is now known as the Magellan Strait, between Tierra del Fuego and the South American mainland, but was killed in the Philippines in a battle with local Indians. By the time Magellan's Basque pilot Juan Sebastián Elcano had completed the first circumnavigation of the globe in 1522 by returning to Sanlúcar via the Cape of Good Hope, just 17 crew members and one ship, the *Victoria*, were left.

Orientation & Information
Sanlúcar stretches about 2.5km along the south-east side of the Guadalquivir estuary. Calzada del Ejército, running 600m inland from the seafront Paseo Marítimo, is the main avenue. A block beyond its inland end is Plaza del Cabildo, the central square. The Los Amarillos bus station is on Plaza La Salle, 500m south-west of Plaza del Cabildo along Calle San Juan.

The old fishing quarter, Bajo de Guía, site of Sanlúcar's best restaurants and Doñana boat departures, is 750m north-east along the riverfront from the end of Calzada del Ejército.

The tourist office (☎ 956 36 61 10) is towards the inland end of Calzada del Ejército. It's open Monday to Friday from 10 am to 2 pm and 6 to 8 pm (5 to 7 pm in winter), Saturday and Sunday from 10 am to 1 pm. You'll find banks and ATMs on Plaza del Cabildo and Calle San Juan.

The Centro de Visitantes Fábrica de Hielo de Bajo de Guía (☎ 956 36 38 13) at the end of Avenida de Bajo de Guía, which runs to Bajo de Guía from near the seaward end of Calzada del Ejército, has displays and information on the Parque Nacional de Doñana and related topics. It's open daily from 9 am to 2.30 pm and 4 to 7 pm (to 8 pm from May to September).

Things to See & Do
Walking Tour A tour of the sights doesn't take long as most of them aren't open to visitors. From Plaza del Cabildo, cross Calle Ancha to Plaza San Roque and head uphill on Calle Bretones, where you can look into the **mercado** (market) just before reaching **Las Covachas**, a set of 15th century wine cellars (closed for restoration). Here, the street turns right and becomes Calle Cuesta de Belén, where, Monday to Friday from 10 am to 2 pm, you can look into the **Palacio de Orleans y Borbon**, now the Ayuntamiento. The creation in the 19th century of this neo-mudéjar fantasy as a sum-

mer home for the aristocratic Montpensier family was what spurred Sanlúcar's growth as a resort.

From the top of Calle Cuesta de Belén, a block to the left along Calle Caballeros is the 15th century **Iglesia de Nuestra Señora de la O**, with a mudéjar façade and ceiling. Adjoining is the **Palacio de los Duques de Medina Sidonia** (not open to visitors), home of the aristocratic family which once owned more of Spain than anyone else. Some 200m farther along the street is the 15th century **Castillo de Santiago** (closed for restoration), amid buildings of the Barbadillo sherry company. From the castle you can return directly downhill to the town centre.

Beach Sanlúcar's sandy beach runs along the riverfront and several kilometres beyond to the south-west.

Sherry Sanlúcar produces a distinctive sherry, manzanilla. Tours of Bodegas Barbadillo, the town's biggest sherry firm, at Calle Luis de Eguilaz 11, are given every Thursday at noon for 200 ptas (book in advance on ☎ 956 36 08 94, or through the tourist office). Other manzanilla houses such as Vinícola Hidalgo (☎ 956 36 05 16), makers of the popular La Gitana brand, at Banda de la Playa 24 off the inland end of Calzada del Ejército, also do some tours on other weekdays between 9 am and 1 pm. You can inquire and book at the tourist office.

Parque Nacional de Doñana Trips to the national park are made by the boat *Real Fernando* from Bajo de Guía. The four-hour trip ventures 10km up the Guadalquivir with stops for short guided walks at some *salinas* (salt lagoons), which attract plentiful birdlife, and a restored farmstead in a pine wood. Guides speak Spanish and English. The trips leave Tuesday to Sunday at 9.30 am and 5 pm from May to October, 10 am the rest of the year. Tickets (2100 ptas, 1050 ptas for children under 10) are sold at the Centro de

Visitantes Fábrica de Hielo (see Information). From May to October and during holiday periods in other months, you need to book one week ahead; at other times book two to three days ahead.

Tourafrica (☎ 956 36 25 40), Calle San Juan 20, operates 3½-hour guided tours (3700 ptas per person) into Doñana on Tuesday and Friday, May to September, leaving Bajo de Guía at 8.30 am and 4.30 pm. After the river crossing, the trip is by 4WD taking in around 70km.

See the Parque Nacional de Doñana section in the Huelva province chapter for information on other access points to the national park.

Special Events
The Sanlúcar summer gets going with a sherry festival, the Feria de la Manzanilla, in late May or early June, and blossoms in July and August with happenings like the Noches de Bajo de Guía flamenco season (late July), jazz and classical music festivals, one-off concerts by some good visiting bands and Sanlúcar's unique horse races (see the boxed text).

Places to Stay
Book well ahead for a room at holiday times. At other times, expect to pay about 20% less than the prices given here. The only budget place seems to be *Hostal La Blanca Paloma* (☎ 956 36 36 44) at Plaza San Roque 15, with adequate singles/doubles for 2500/4000 ptas. *Hostal Bohemia* (☎ 956 36 95 99), Calle Don Claudio 5, off Calle Ancha, 300m north-east of Plaza del Cabildo, has better rooms with bath at 2500/5500 ptas.

Hotel Los Helechos (☎ 956 36 76 55) at Calle Madre de Dios 9, off Calle San Juan 200m from Plaza del Cabildo, is an excellent middle-range choice with rooms around two pretty courtyards and a cosy bar. Singles/doubles with bath are 5000/7000 ptas plus IVA. The welcoming *Hotel Tartaneros* (☎ 956 36 20 44), Calle Tartaneros 8 at the inland end of Calzada del Ejército, is a turn-of-the-century indus-

trialist's mansion with solidly comfortable rooms at 6500/10,000 ptas plus IVA. The modern *Hotel Guadalquivir* (☎ 956 36 07 42), nearby at Calzada del Ejército 10, is also comfortable with similar prices but is much bigger and has less character.

Places to Eat
The line of seafood restaurants facing the riverfront at Bajo de Guía are a reason in in themselves for visiting Sanlúcar. Andalucía holds few more idyllic dining experiences than watching the sun go down over the

---

Horsing Around with the Tides

Sanlúcar's *carreras de caballos*, held every year (bar a couple of interruptions for war) since 1845, may be the only sporting event in the world where police crowd control involves gently persuading the spectators to take off their shoes and stand in an estuary. It's an exciting spectacle in which real racehorses, many of them Irish, French, or British-bred thoroughbreds, thunder along the sands near the water's edge watched by a crowd of spectators.

Two three or four-day meetings are held every August, one in the first half or middle of the month, the other in the second half, usually with four races each day. Exact starting times depend on the tides, but the first race normally begins around 6 pm. The finish is about 1km south-west of Calzada del Ejército and most races start at Bajo de Guía. Prize money for the two meetings totals around 15 million ptas.

Serious racegoers will want to get into the area with spectator stands, bookmakers, paddock and winner's enclosure, up by the finishing post. The rest of the crowd strings itself back along the course. Here, the only bookies, it seems, are children who set up little cardboard-box booths and scrape a line across the track in front, then take money on which horse will cross their 'finish' first!

Guadalquivir while tucking into the succulent fresh fare here and washing it down with a glass or two of manzanilla. Just wander along and pick a restaurant that suits your pocket. The most popular include *Restaurante Poma*, *Restaurante Virgen del Carmen*, *Restaurante Casa Juan* and *Bar Joselito Huerta*. At the Virgen del Carmen most fish mains, plancha (grilled) or frito (fried), are 1000 to 1400 ptas. You shouldn't miss out on the starters: langostinos (king prawns) and the juicy coquines al ajillo (cockles cooked in garlic), both 1000 ptas, are specialities. A half-bottle of manzanilla is 600 ptas.

There are also lots of cafés and bars, many serving manzanilla from the barrel, around Plaza del Cabildo. *Casa Balbino* at Plaza del Cabildo 14 has wonderful seafood tapas – try the *patatas rellenas*, potatoes stuffed with meat or fish, swimming in a delicious tomato salsa. Two short blocks south-west of Plaza Cabildo, *Da Francesco*, at Calle Bolsa 22, doesn't look overly inviting but it does good pizzas and pastas for only 500 to 700 ptas. *Bar El Cura*, Calle Amargura 2, in an alley between Calle San Juan and Plaza San Roque, does some good-value platos combinados for 500 ptas. *Café Tartaneros*, in the hotel at Calle Tartaneros 8, is a pleasant spot to sink into a comfortable chair and enjoy a pot of tea and chocolate cake (475 ptas).

Entertainment
There are some lively music bars and discos on and around Calzada del Ejército and Plaza del Cabildo. *El Pregonero,* a weekly four-page what's-on guide available here and there around town in summer, lists many of them.

Getting There & Away
Bus Los Amarillos (☎ 956 36 04 66) runs up to nine daily buses to/from El Puerto de Santa María, Cádiz, and Sevilla. Linesur-Valenciana (☎ 956 34 10 63), whose stop is at the Bar La Jaula behind the tourist office on Calzada del Ejército, runs at least seven buses daily to/from Jerez de la Frontera.

Boat Though you can visit Sanlúcar on excursion boats from Sevilla (see that section), you can't take a one-way ride upriver from Sanlúcar to Sevilla.

JEREZ DE LA FRONTERA
The large town of Jerez (population 180,000), 36km north-east of Cádiz, is world famous for its wine – sherry – made from grapes grown on the chalky soil surrounding the town. Many people come here to visit its bodegas, but Jerez is also Andalucía's horse capital and, alongside its affluent uppercrust society, supports a Gypsy community which is one of the hotbeds of flamenco.

British money was largely responsible for the development of the wineries from around the 1830s, and Jerez high society today is a mixture of Andalucian and British due to intermarriage among families of wine traders over the past 150 years. Since the 1980s most of the wineries, previously owned by about 15 families, have been bought out by multinational companies. Jerez reeks of money. It has loads of fancy shops, well-heeled residents, wide, spacious streets and old mansions and beautiful churches in its interesting old quarter. It puts on fantastic fiestas with sleek horses, beautiful people and flamenco. The town hopes for a million visitors in 2002 when it will host the World Equestrian Games.

History
The Muslims called the town 'Scheris', from which 'Jerez' (pronounced 'hereth') and 'sherry' are derived. The drink was already famed in England in Shakespeare's time. Jerez had its share of strife during the late 19th century when anarchism gained ground in Andalucía – one day in 1891 thousands of peasants armed with scythes and sticks marched in and occupied the town for a few hours, succeeding only in bringing further repression. The sherry industry has provided greater prosperity in more recent times. Jerez Brandy, consumed widely in Spain, is also a profitable product.

Orientation & Information

The centre of Jerez is between the Alameda Cristina and Plaza del Arenal, connected by the north-south Calle Larga and its continuation Calle Lancería (both pedestrianised). Budget accommodation clusters around two streets east of Calle Larga – Avenida de Arcos and Calle Medina. West of Calle Larga is the old quarter. North-east from Alameda Cristina runs Calle Sevilla, becoming Avenida Álvaro Domecq which has some of the upmarket hotels. Several of the sherry bodegas are north-east and south-west of the centre.

The tourist office (☎ 956 33 11 50), Calle Larga 39, has an energetic multi-lingual staff with mountains of information. In summer, it's open Monday to Friday from 8 am to 2 or 3 pm and 5 to 8 pm, Saturday from 10 am to 2 pm and 5 to 8 pm; in winter, Monday to Friday from 8 am to 3 pm and 4 to 7 pm, Saturday from 10 am to 2 pm and 5 to 7 pm.

There are plenty of banks and ATMs on and around Calle Larga. The post office (postcode 11400) is on the corner of Calle Cerrón and Calle Medina, just east of Calle Larga.

Jerez parking officers show no mercy on vehicles parked in prohibited areas. There are three underground car parks in the centre.

The Old Quarter

The obvious place to start a tour of the old town, of which parts of the walls survive, is the **Alcázar**, the 12th century Almohad fortress slightly south-west of Plaza del Arenal. Inside are the **Capilla Santa María la Real**, a chapel converted from a mosque by Alfonso X in 1264, the **Baños Arabes** (Arab Baths; closed) and an 18th century palace (under restoration). The chapel retains most of the mosque's features including the mihrab. The orange-tree-lined plaza outside has good vistas to the west with, in the foreground, the mainly 18th century **Catedral** which has Gothic, baroque and neoclassical features and was built on the site of the Muslim town's main mosque. Note the 15th century mudéjar belfry, set slightly apart. Behind the cathedral is a large statue of Manuel María González Ángel (1812-1887), the founder of Bodegas González Byass.

A couple of blocks north-east of the cathedral is Plaza de la Asunción with the splendid 16th century **Ayuntamiento** and the lovely 15th century mudéjar **Iglesia de San Dionisio**, named after the town's patron saint.

North and west of here is the **Barrio de Santiago**, a quarter with a sizeable Gypsy population and one of the centres of flamenco. The barrio has churches dedicated to all four evangelists: the Gothic **Iglesia de San Mateo**, with mudéjar chapels, is on Plaza del Mercado, where you'll also find the refurbished **Museo Arqueológico** (☎ 956 34 13 50). The pride of the museum's collection is a 7th century BC Greek helmet (*casco Greco*), found in the Río Guadalete. In summer, the museum (250 ptas) is open daily except Sunday from 10 am to 2.30 pm; in other seasons, Tuesday to Friday from 10 am to 2 pm and 4 to 7 pm, Saturday and Sunday from 10 am to 2.30 pm.

Also in this area is the **Centro Andaluz de Flamenco** (Andalucian Flamenco Centre) (☎ 956 34 92 65; fax 956 32 11 27), in the 18th century Palacio de Pemartín on Plaza de San Juan. Jerez is at the heart of the Sevilla-Cádiz axis where flamenco began and which remains its heartland today. Many great flamenco performers learnt their art here and Jerez is the home of the *bulería*, one of the fastest and most festive flamenco forms. The centre is a kind of museum and school dedicated to the preservation and promotion of flamenco. It has a library with 2500 books on flamenco and other subjects, a music library and a video library. In spring and summer, the centre hosts dance and guitar seminars and performances. There are also dance classes for serious students: for more information, phone or fax Ana Tenorio at the centre, open Monday to Friday from 10 am to 2 pm. In the main tourist seasons an audio-visual introduction to Andalucía and flamenco is screened hourly from 10 am to 1 pm (free).

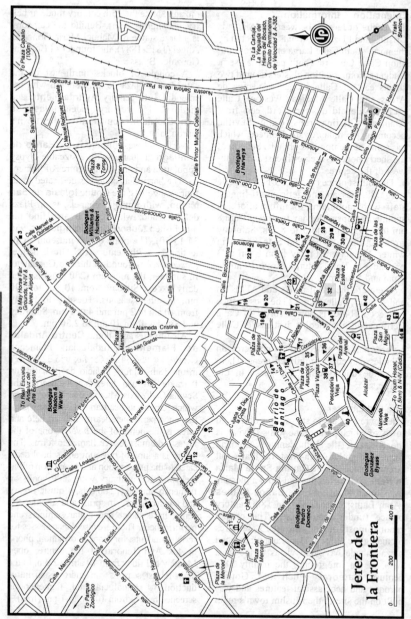

Jerez de
la Frontera

PLACES TO STAY		28	Patissería	13	Cine Astoria
3	Hotel Avenida Jerez	33	Restaurante/Café La	14	Bar
22	Hostal/Hotel San Andrés		Vega	15	16th Century
26	Pensión Los Amarillos	34	Cafetería San Francisco		Ayuntamiento
27	Hotel Trujillo	35	El Almacén	16	Iglesia de San Dionisio
29	Hostal Las Palomas	36	Bar Juanita	18	Tourist Office
30	Hotel Serit	37	Las Almenas	20	RENFE Office
42	Nuevo Hotel			23	Post Office
44	Hostal San Miguel	**OTHER**		24	Teatro Villamarta
		1	Museo de Relojes	31	Bus no 9 to Youth Hostel
PLACES TO EAT		5	La Plaza de Canterbury	32	Mercado
2	Restaurante La Mesa	7	Iglesia de Santiago	38	Bar Dos Deditos
	Redonda	8	Basílica de Nuestra	39	Catedral
4	Telepizza		Señora de la Merced	40	Statue of Manuel María
6	Gaitán	9	El Lago Tío Parrilla		González Ángel
17	Marisquería Cruz Blanca	10	Iglesia de San Mateo	41	Bus No 13 to Youth
19	La Rotonda	11	Museo Arqueológico		Hostel
21	La Canilla	12	Centro Andaluz de	43	Iglesia San Miguel
25	Mesón la Alcazaba		Flamenco		

Just east of Plaza del Arenal is one of Jerez's loveliest churches, the 16th century Iglesia de San Miguel, built in Isabelline Gothic style and featuring superb stained glass windows and a retablo by Juan Martínez Montañés.

Sherry Bodegas

For most of the bodegas, you need to phone ahead to book your visit. Some bodegas, such as Williams & Humbert and Sandeman, are closed from late July through much of August. The two biggest companies, both handily located west of the Alcázar, are González Byass (☎ 956 35 70 00), Calle Manuel González s/n, and Domecq (☎ 956 15 15 00), Calle San Ildefonso 3. González Byass is open for visits Monday to Friday at 10 and 11 am, noon, and 1, 4.30 and 5.30 pm (400 ptas), Saturday 10 and 11 am, noon and 1 pm (500 ptas). Domecq has several tours Monday to Friday from 9 am to 1 pm, Saturday and Sunday from 10 am to 1 pm (375 ptas). The tourist office has a complete list of bodegas that welcome visitors.

Other Things to See

One of Jerez's big attractions is the **Real Escuela Andaluz del Arte Ecuestre** (Royal Andalucian School of Equestrian Art, ☎ 956 31 11 11) on Avenida Duque de Abrantes in the north of town. The school trains horses and riders in dressage and you can watch them being put through their paces in training sessions on Monday, Tuesday, Wednesday and Friday from 11 am to 1 pm (450 ptas). On Thursday at noon there's an official show where the handsome white horses perform to classical music (from 1500 to 2400 ptas).

A short distance from here is the **Museo de Relojes** (☎ 956 18 21 00) on Calle Cervantes 3, an antique clock and watch museum housed in the beautiful Palacio Atalaya. It's open Monday to Saturday from 10 am to 2 pm (400 ptas). Noon is a good time to visit when the hundreds of clocks chime the hour in unison.

A couple of kilometres west of the centre is the **Parque Zoológico** or Zoo Jerez with lovely gardens and a wild animal recuperation centre. It's open Tuesday to Sunday from 10 am to 6 pm, to 8 pm in the summer (adults 600 ptas, children 400 ptas).

Special Events

Jerez's *Feria del Caballo* (Horse Fair) in early May is one of Andalucía's biggest festivals, with music and dance as well as all kinds of horse competitions. Colourful parades of horses pass through the Parque González Hontoria fairgrounds in the north of town, the aristocratic-looking male riders decked out in flat-topped hats, frilly white shirts, black trousers and leather chaps, their female *crupera* (sideways pillion) riders in traditional long, frilly, spotted dresses. The female riders, sporting flat-topped hats, white blouses and cropped woollen jackets with matching longish, full skirts, look as smart as their male counterparts. Preceding the horse fair is the *Festival de Jerez*, a two-week event dedicated to music and dance, particularly flamenco. Many of its events are held in the new Teatro Villamarta (☎ 956 34 47 50) on Calle Medina, near Calle Bodegas.

In early or mid-September there's a one-day festival of flamenco song and dance, the *Fiesta de la Bulería*. The *Fiestas de Otoño* (Autumn Festivals) from mid-September to mid-October, celebrating the grape harvest, range from flamenco and the traditional treading of the first grapes outside the cathedral to horse races on Plaza del Arenal and dressage contests. It concludes with a massive parade of horses and riders and horse-drawn carriages.

Places to Stay

Prices given are for summer unless stated otherwise. Room rates go sky-high during the Feria del Caballo, and you need to book ahead.

Places to Stay – Budget

The modern *Albergue Juvenil Jerez* youth hostel (☎ 956 34 28 90) is 1.5km south of the centre at Avenida Carrero Blanco 30. Bus No 13 from Plaza del Arenal, or bus No 9 with stops near the train and bus stations and Plaza de las Angustias, will take you there. Get off at the Continente stop. (Local buses are painted an eye-catching fluorescent lilac.)

Other budget choices are more conveniently located around Calle Medina and Avenida de Arcos and on Calle Caballeros, which runs south-east off Plaza del Arenal. The friendly *Hostal/Hotel San Andres* (☎ 956 34 09 83), Calle Morenos 12, is a

good choice. Singles/doubles with private bath, TV and winter heating cost 2500/4500 ptas; rooms with shared bath are 1600/2500 ptas. Closer to the bus station at Calle Medina 30, *Pension Los Amarillos* is run by the same family and has cheaper rooms if it's open. *Hostal Las Palomas* (☎ 956 34 37 73), Calle Higueras 17, is another good bet. Spacious, nicely furnished rooms with shared bath go for 1500 ptas per person; there are also doubles with bath for 3000 ptas. *Nuevo Hotel* (☎ 956 33 16 00), Calle Caballeros 23, in an old mansion has roomy singles/doubles with bath, TV and winter heating from 2500/3500 ptas to 3000/6500 ptas. Nearby, *Hostal San Miguel* (☎ 956 34 85 62), Plaza San Miguel 4, costs 1500/3000 ptas with shared bath, 2500/4500 ptas with attached bath.

Places to Stay – Mid-Range & Top End

Add IVA to the following prices. *Hotel Trujillo* (☎ 956 34 24 38), Calle Medina 3, has rooms with all mod-cons at 3500/5500 ptas in the off season, 5900/9800 ptas from May to October. Nearby, *Hotel Serit* (☎ 956 34 07 00) Calle Higueras 7, has similar rooms for 5000/7000 ptas, doubles 8000 to 15,000 ptas during peak periods. At *Hotel Avenida Jerez* (☎ 956 34 74 11), Avenida Álvaro Domecq 10, doubles are 15,000 ptas, 27,000 ptas in April/May. There are more top end places on the same road.

Places to Eat

Not surprisingly, sherry is used to flavour local dishes such as *riñones al jerez* (kidneys in gravy), and *rabo de toro* (oxtail or bull's tail stew). Jerez food combines the usual Andalucian influences – such as the Muslim heritage and proximity to the sea – with English and French touches. English-style roasts, for example, are popular. A good place to try Jerez specialities if you're not on a tight budget is *La Mesa Redonda*, a small restaurant at Calle Manuel de la Quintana 3, north-east of the centre.

The restaurants on Pescadería Vieja, a small alley on the west side of Plaza del Arenal which catches a refreshing breeze on a hot day, are moderate to expensive. *Las Almenas* has menús at 850 ptas and 1350 ptas with two courses, bread and dessert. The *potaje*, a thick vegetable soup, is quite delicious! *Bar Juanita*, and *El Almacén*, round the corner on Calle Ferros, are local tapas haunts and good places to sample a *fino* too.

A short walk north-west, at Calle Consistorio 16, *Marisquería/Cafetería Cruz Blanca* has tables outside on pretty Plaza de la Yerba under tall jacaranda trees. This is a great place to sample seafood tapas (175 to 300 ptas) and raciones – the sushi-style bacalao is sensational!

At Calle Larga 8, *La Canilla* is fine for simple breakfasts, under big canvas sun-shades in summer. Cheaper breakfasts can be had in the *Bar* on the corner of Plaza de Plateros, behind Iglesia de San Dionisio. Our favourite breakfast spot is the stylish *La Rotonda* at the north end of Calle Larga. Breakfasts cost from 475 ptas for tostada (the *molletes* are great), coffee and orange juice to 750 ptas for a full cooked breakfast, and there's a good range of snack and bistro food, tapas, ice creams and cakes. The lunch menú is 1400 ptas.

The *mercado* (produce market) is on Calle Doña Blanca, a stone's throw east of Calle Larga, past Plaza Estévez which has a couple of good places for teas, coffees, pastries, breakfasts and reasonably-priced meals, including *Cafetería San Francisco* at No 2, and *Restaurante/Café La Vega*, right by the market.

Méson la Alcazaba, Calle Medina 19, with a covered patio, has cheap and filling food; menús (800 pts and 1000 ptas) offer plenty of choice and include two courses, a drink and fruit. Platos combinados are 500 ptas. The *Patissería* on the corner of Calles Medina and Higueras, has good cakes, pastries, baguettes and ice creams. *Telepizza* on Calle Salvatierra, north of the bullring in the heart of the small nightlife area, has cheap deals and does a roaring trade.

For a splash-out meal at *Gaitán*, Calle Gaitán 3, two blocks west of the Alameda Cristina, you can expect to pay around 1250 ptas for starters such as seafood cocktails, a

little less for soups, and 1675-2100 ptas for fancy main courses.

Entertainment

Check at the tourist office and watch out for posters advertising upcoming events. The newspaper *Diario de Jerez* has some what's-on information and the Teatro Villamarta puts out a monthly programme. *Cine Astoria* on Calle Francos is an outdoor cinema and concert area where there's often live music from blues to flamenco; there are sometimes concerts in the bullring too. *Bar Dos Deditos*, Plaza Vargas 1, behind Pescadería Vieja, has live music some nights, including blues – if there's something on, the crowd spills out onto the pavement.

North-east of the centre just before the bullring, *La Plaza de Canterbury*, with loads of bars around a central courtyard, attracts a young crowd. Between the bullring and Plaza Caballo is a small nightlife area centred on Calle Salvatierra, with bars and a couple of clubs for dancing until late on weekend nights and fiestas, including *Cairo* on Calle Salvatierra and *Moët* around the corner on Avenida de Méjico. Another area worth investigating at night is on Calle Cádiz, close to the Real Escuela Andaluz de Arte Ecuestre, with more bars and restaurants.

For flamenco, there are several *peñas* in the Barrio de Santiago; sometimes they're listed on the tourist office map – if not, ask at the tourist office. *El Laga Tío Parrilla* (☎ 956 33 83 34) on Plaza del Mercado has more tourist-oriented flamenco performances Monday to Saturday from 11 pm but you never know what you might strike there out of the main tourist seasons. We stopped by and were included in a family party of 20 where everyone either sang, danced, played guitar or a combination of all three – an outstanding display of gutsy flamenco lasting well into the madrugada. The youngest dancer (brilliant) was a rotund seven-year old wearing a tracksuit!

Spectator Sport

Jerez has a motorcycle and car racing track, the Circuito Permanente de Velocidad

(☎ 956 15 11 00) on the A-382, 10km east of town. Motorcycle races are held here throughout the year including – on a Sunday in May – one of the *grands prix* of the World Motorcycle Championship, one of Spain's biggest sporting events with around 150,000 spectators. There are three or four car races annually: occasionally one of them is a Formula One grand prix.

Getting There & Away
Air The airport (☎ 956 15 00 00), the only one serving Cádiz province, is 7km north-east of Jerez on the N-IV. Aviaco (☎ 956 15 00 10) has direct flights daily to/from Madrid and five a week to/from Barcelona. British Airways (☎ 956 15 00 93) has direct flights to/from London twice a week.

Bus The bus station (☎ 956 34 52 07) is on Calle Cartuja, the extension of Calle Medina, about 1km south-east of the centre. Comes has buses for Cádiz (up to 18 daily, 350 ptas), El Puerto de Santa María (up to six daily, 150 ptas) Vejer de la Frontera and Barbate (at least one daily), Ronda (four daily, 1255 ptas) with one continuing to Málaga (2370 ptas), and Córdoba (one daily, 1850 ptas). There are plenty of buses to Sevilla (875 ptas) by Linesur-Valenciana and Comes. Linesur-Valenciana also runs to Sanlúcar de Barrameda (205 ptas) hourly from 7 am to 8 pm. Los Amarillos handles buses to *pueblos* inland and has plenty to Arcos de la Frontera (280 ptas), and up to six daily to El Bosque and Ubrique.

Train The train station is a couple of blocks south-east of the bus station at the end of Calle Cartuja. Jerez is on the Cádiz-Sevilla line with plenty of trains in both directions. The central RENFE office at Calle Larga 34 is open Monday to Friday from 9 am to 2 pm and 5 to 8.30 pm, Saturday from 9 am to 2 pm.

AROUND JEREZ
La Cartuja
The monastery of La Cartuja (☎ 956 15 64 65), founded in the 15th century and with an impressive 17th century baroque facade, is set in attractive gardens on the road to Medina Sidonia, 4km from Jerez. The early Carthusian monks are credited with breeding the much prized Spanish thoroughbred horse, also called the Andaluz or the Cartujano. Around 1950 the former monastery was returned to the Carthusian monks, a closed religious order. Its gardens are open to all (daily from 8 am to 6 pm) but only men are allowed to visit the monastery's interior (Wednesday and Saturday, from 5 to 6 pm, by appointment).

La Yeguada del Hierro del Bocado
Andalucía is ideal for horse breeding. Most of the world's breeds are found in the region, though the major breeding stocks are the Arab, the Crossbred and the Spanish Thoroughbred (Cartujano). It is now possible to visit the stud farm La Yeguada del Hierro del Bocado (☎ 956 16 28 09, 956 23 74 30) at Finca Fuente del Suero, off the A-381 to Medina Sidonia, 6.5km from Jerez. This farm is dedicated to promoting the Cartujano. Turn up any Saturday at 11 am for their two-hour tour (1500 ptas).

Arcos & the Sierra

The mountainous Parque Natural Sierra de Grazalema in the north-east of Cádiz province, dotted with attractive white towns and villages, is the wettest part of Spain and one of Andalucía's most beautiful and green areas. Between it and Jerez is the picturesque old town of Arcos de la Frontera.

ARCOS DE LA FRONTERA
Arcos (population 28,000) is 30km east of Jerez de la Frontera along the A-382 across pretty wheat and sunflower fields, vineyards and fruit orchards. The castle and old town atop a ridge, with the Río Guadalete meandering below, make a striking sight, though the modern suburbs spilling out below are slightly less enchanting. Arcos is said to have a dark, sinister side; there are tales of mad-

ness, interbreeding, covens and witchcraft. Whatever you feel, Arcos is well worth visiting to explore its old town whose street plan has changed little since medieval times. There are some lovely post-Reconquista buildings including Renaissance palaces and two splendid churches.

History

Arcos has always been prized for its strategic location. It was taken from the Visigoths by the Muslims in 711. In the 11th century it was, for a time, an independent *taifa* until absorbed by Sevilla. In 1255 Alfonso X took the town and repopulated it with Castilians and Leonese. Some Muslims stayed but rebelled in 1261 and were evicted by 1264. In 1440 the town passed to the Ponce de León family, known as the Duques de Arcos, who were active in the conquest of Granada. When the last Duque de Arcos died heirless in 1780, his cousin, the Duquesa de Benavente, took over his lands. She was partly responsible for replacing sheep farming with cereals, olives, vines and horse breeding as the dominant economic activities around Arcos. During the period

of liberal rule from 1820 to '23, the so-called *señorío* system of land ownership by noble families was abolished, but the rural poverty that was part and parcel of the system continued well into the 20th century.

Orientation & Information

From the bus station, on Calle Corregidores in the new town, (see inset in the Arcos de la Frontera map) it's a 1km uphill walk to the old town. About halfway up is the leafy Paseo de Andalucía. From Plaza España at the top of Paseo de Andalucía, taken up by a roundabout, Paseo de los Boliches and Calle Debajo del Corral (becoming Calle Corredera) both head east up to the old town's main square, Plaza del Cabildo.

The tourist office (☎ 956 70 22 64), on Plaza del Cabildo, open Monday to Saturday from 9 am to 2 pm and 5 to 7 pm, Sunday from 11 am to 1.30 pm, has lively staff who can provide a useful map and other information.

Banks and ATMs on Calle Debajo del Corral and Calle Corredera and the post office (postcode 11630) on Paseo de los Boliches, near Hotel Los Olivos, are down

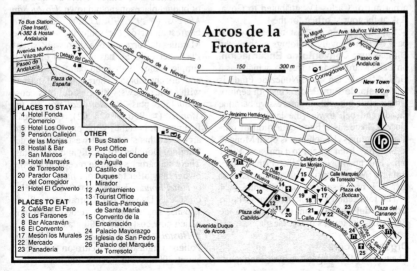

Arcos de la Frontera

0   150   300 m

New Town

0   100 m

PLACES TO STAY
4 Hotel Fonda Comercio
5 Hotel Los Olivos
9 Pensión Callejón de las Monjas
18 Hostal & Bar San Marcos
19 Hotel Marqués de Torresoto
20 Parador Casa del Corregidor
21 Hotel El Convento

PLACES TO EAT
2 Café/Bar El Faro
3 Los Faraones
8 Bar Alcaraván
16 El Convento
17 Mesón los Murales
22 Mercado
23 Panadería

OTHER
1 Bus Station
6 Post Office
7 Palacio del Conde de Águila
10 Castillo de los Duques
11 Mirador
12 Ayuntamiento
13 Tourist Office
14 Basílica-Parroquia de Santa María
15 Convento de la Encarnación
24 Palacio Mayorazgo
25 Iglesia de San Pedro
26 Palacio del Marqués de Torresoto

to the west of the old town. There are telephones by the church on Plaza del Cabildo.

Parking is available around Paseo de Andalucía and on Plaza del Cabildo.

Things to See & Do

The best thing to do in Arcos is simply to wander the old town with its narrow cobbled streets, Renaissance buildings and whitewashed houses. Plaza del Cabildo is surrounded by fine old buildings and has a mirador with panoramic views over the river and countryside. On the west side of the plaza, Arcos' crowning glory, the Castillo de los Duques, dating from the 11th century, is privately owned and not open to the public. On the north side, take a look at the Basílica-Parroquia de Santa María, begun on the site of a mosque in the 13th century but not completed until the 18th century. It's open daily from 10 am to 1 pm and 4 to 7 pm (150 ptas). On the east side, the parador, with striking views from its restaurant and terrace, is a 1960s reconstruction of a 16th century magistrate's house, the Casa del Corregidor. The Ayuntamiento at the south-west corner of the plaza has a mudéjar panelled ceiling and a portrait of Carlos IV attributed to Goya. Ask at the tourist office for the key.

Explore the streets east of here, which pass by some lovely buildings such as the 16th century **Convento de Encarnación**, on Calle Marqués de Torresoto, which has a Gothic façade. On Calle Núñez de Prado is the **Iglesia de San Pedro**, in 15th century Gothic style but with an impressive baroque façade and bell tower (the latter currently closed). Inside is a large collection of religious paintings. The church is open Monday to Saturday from 10 am to 1 pm and 4 to 7 pm (150 ptas). Nearby, the 17th century **Palacio Mayorazgo**, with a Renaissance façade, is now a senior citizens' centre.

The 15th century Gothic/mudéjar **Palacio Conde del Águila**, on Calle Cuesta de Belén, has the town's oldest façade.

Organised Tours

The tourist office organises hour-long guided tours of the old town and its patios from Tuesday to Saturday at 10.30 am, noon, 5 and 6.30 pm (300 ptas).

Special Events

Semana Santa processions through the town's narrow streets are dramatic. At the beginning of August the three-day Fiesta de la Virgen de las Nieves includes late-night music in Plaza del Cabildo. On 29 September, during the feria dedicated to Arcos' patron saint San Miguel in the last few days of the month, there's a hair-raising running of the bulls.

Places to Stay – Budget

Camping *Camping Lago de Arcos* (☎ 956 70 05 14), open year-round, is in El Santiscal near the Lago de Arcos reservoir north-east of the old town. The most straightforward route to drive from the old town is by the A-382 and the Carretera El Bosque y Ubrique. Turn left after the bridge across the dam. A local bus runs out here from Arcos. Cost for two people, a tent and a car is 1575 ptas.

Pensiones & Hostales There are a couple of budget places in the old town. *Hostal San Marcos* (☎ 956 70 07 21), above the bar/restaurant of the same name at Calle Marqués de Torresoto 6, a short walk east of Plaza del Cabildo, has a handful of good, simple rooms with hand-painted furniture and attached bath. There's a roof terrace with fine views. Singles/doubles cost 2500/4500 ptas. *Pension Callejón de las Monjas* (☎ 956 70 23 02), Calle Deán Espinosa 4, is right by the picture-postcard arch over this street, just west of Plaza del Cabildo. Doubles cost 3500 and 4500 ptas. There's a barber's chair in reception and the owner may offer to cut your hair.

Hotel Fonda Comercio (☎ 956 70 00 57), on Calle Debajo del Corral near Plaza España, has recently upgraded its rooms which now cost 4000/6000 ptas.

Hostal Andalucía (☎ 956 70 07 14), at Polígono Industrial El Retiro on the A-382 about 300m south-west of the bus station, offers the best deal in town if you're not too picky about your surroundings; it's above a car yard and backed by workshops. Large rooms with attached bath, fan and TV cost 1500 per person which is excellent value for singles.

Places to Stay – Mid-Range & Top End

Arcos has some charming places to stay in this category. Add IVA to the following prices. *Hotel El Convento* (☎ 956 70 23 33), Calle Maldonado 2, in a 17th century convent just east of Plaza del Cabildo, has similar views to the parador's. Fine singles/doubles are 5000/10,000 ptas. In the same part of town, *Hotel Marqués de Torresoto* (☎ 956 70 07 17) in a converted mansion at Calle Marqués de Torresoto 4, charges 6600/8600 ptas. Down the hill towards Plaza España the attractive *Los Olivos* (☎ 956 70 08 11), Paseo de los Boliches 30, has rooms at 5000/9000 ptas.

Parador Casa del Corregidor (☎ 956 70 05 00), on Plaza del Cabildo, offers typical parador luxury at 13,000/17,500 ptas. *Hacienda El Santiscal* (☎ 956 70 83 13), Avenida El Santiscal 129, Lago de Arcos, (see Camping for directions) costs 7000/12,000 ptas at peak times, 5950/8500 ptas in the off seasons. Activities including horse riding and hot-air balloon trips can be arranged here.

Places to Eat

Arcos has places to eat to suit all pockets. In the old town the homely *Bar San Marcos*, at Calle Marqués de Torresoto 6, does platos combinados from 500 to 900 ptas, tapas around 200 ptas and a menú at 800 ptas. Opposite, *El Convento*, in a 16th century palace, is a classy restaurant turning out interesting fare – the three-course menú is 2500 ptas including a drink. *Mesón Los Murales*, Plaza de Boticas 1, near the Hotel El Convento, has a cheaper menú at 900 ptas and main dishes from 600 to 1400 ptas. The *mercado* (market) is opposite. A little east of here on Calle Núñez de Prado is a good *panadería* (bakery).The cave-like *Bar Alcaraván* at Calle Nueva 1, with tables outside under the castle walls, is good for tapas.

In the new town, there are a couple of options on Calle Debajo del Corral near Plaza España. *Café/Bar El Faro* at No 14 has breakfasts at 225 ptas, main dishes from 500 to 1500 ptas and a menú at 850 ptas. At No 8, *Los Faraones* does cheap breakfasts (150 ptas), platos combinados (600 ptas) and a menú (800 ptas) plus excellent but pricier Arabic food with some tasty vegetarian choices: try the felafel, served with dips, salad and flat bread (1350 ptas).

There are more eateries down by the river, below the castle.

Entertainment

In July and August flamenco happens at the small but atmospheric Plaza del Cananeo, in the old town at the bottom of Calle Cadenas opposite the Palacio del Marqués de Torresoto, on Thursday nights from 10.30 pm. In summer, the flat ground below the castle and near the river is lively with bars, restaurants and music.

Getting There & Away

Buses departing from Calle Corregidores (in the new town) from Monday to Friday include 19 per day to Jerez, six to El Bosque and a few each to Cádiz, Sevilla and Ronda. On most routes there are fewer buses on weekends. For information you can call ☎ 956 70 20 15.

PARQUE NATURAL SIERRA DE GRAZALEMA

This is fine walking country, and there are opportunities for a range of other activities from rock climbing and caving to paragliding and trout fishing. The best times to visit are spring, early summer and autumn. The park extends into the north-west of Málaga province, where it includes the Cueva de Pileta with ancient rock paintings (see Around Ronda in the Málaga Province chapter).

The rare Spanish fir *(pinsapo)*, a relic of forests more than 2 million years old, dominates the land above 1000m. Other vegetation is typically Mediterranean and includes holm oak, cork oak, gall oak, wild olive and riverside forest. Among the park's fauna are the ibex, chamois, roe deer, mongoose, otter and genet. Birds of prey include Bonelli's eagle, golden eagle, Egyptian vulture and one of Europe's largest colonies of common vultures, which feed on the carcasses of the area's sheep, pigs, goats and cattle.

Plenty of maps and printed information on the park are available, including suggested walks and drives. Many of the best walking routes are in the north of the park, around and between the villages of El Bosque, Benamahoma, Grazalema and Zahara de la Sierra, all of which are good bases and can be linked in circuits of three or four days. Highlight walks include the route through the *pinsapar* (pinsapo forest) between Grazalema and Benamahoma; the ascent of the highest peak in Cádiz province, El Torreón (1654m), also called El Pinar, between the same two villages; and the trip into the Garganta Verde gorge south of Zahara.

For some walking routes, including several peaks and entry to the pinsapares, permission is needed. At our last check, entry to the pinsapares was only in groups of 15 accompanied by a guide (900 ptas per person). Places needed to be reserved at the main park information office in El Bosque (☎ 956 71 60 63, 956 72 70 29) at least 48 hours ahead. Contact this office for up-to-date information, or check at the information offices in Benamahoma, Grazalema and Zahara de la Sierra.

El Bosque

From Arcos de la Frontera, the A-372 heads 33km east to El Bosque across rolling country which gradually becomes more treed and dotted with farms and livestock. El Bosque is prettily situated below the wooded foothills of the Sierra de Albarracín, the westernmost section of the natural park. The village grew up around the Palacio de Marcenilla which was owned by the Duques de Arcos. It's better known for sports than its sights: there's a take-off point for hang-gliders and paragliders in the Sierra de Albarracín, plenty of trout to be fished in the streams near the town, and some good walking. Five kilometres along

the A-373 towards Ubrique, on a rocky outcrop opposite Camping Tavizna, you can see the **Castillo de Tavizna**.

Orientation & Information Most places you'll need are close to the A-372 (Avenida Diputación) on the west side of the village, including the park information office, the Centro de Información El Bosque, opposite the Hotel Las Truchas. It's open daily from 9 am to 2 pm, plus Friday to Sunday from 4 to 6 pm. El Bosque's large public swimming pool (adults 350 ptas), with shade, is between the park office and the little stone bridge over the river.

Places to Stay & Eat The *Albergue Campamento El Bosque* (☎ 956 71 62 12), Molino de Enmedio s/n, is pleasantly situated by a trout stream 800m from the A-372 on the west side of the village. Turn off by the Hotel Las Truchas. This youth hostel has bungalows and a shady camping area as well as doubles and triples in the main block. There's a swimming pool too. Various walks, including alongside the Río El Bosque, start on a track beside the hostel; at the beginning of the track there's a board showing the routes. *Camping La Torrecilla* (☎ 956 71 60 95) is on the far side of the village, on Carretera Antigua El Bosque-Ubrique, 1km off the A-372. The cost for two adults, one tent and one car is 1500 ptas. Cabins are available too. Five kilometres south of El Bosque on the A-373 to Ubrique is *Camping Tavizna* (☎ 956 46 30 11) with modern facilities.

Hostal Enrique Calvillo (☎ 956 71 61 05), Avenida Diputación 5, near the park information office, has rooms with bath for 2000/4500 ptas. Reception is in the *Casa Calvillo* restaurant a few doors away. *Hotel Las Truchas* (☎ 956 71 60 61), nearby at Avenida Diputación s/n, has comfy singles/doubles with bath for 4400/7150 ptas plus IVA, and a restaurant terrace overlooking the village and countryside. Try the trout, the local speciality.

Getting There & Away Up to six buses daily run from Arcos de la Frontera and

Jerez de la Frontera, and a few from Cádiz and Grazalema.

Ubrique & Around

The ancient town of Ubrique, 17 kilometres south of El Bosque, sits between the Parque Natural Sierra de Grazalema and the Parque Natural Los Alcornocales. With a backdrop of rocky hills the pretty whitewashed town is best known for its leather goods industry, once a cottage craft. Ubrique is a good base for walks into either of the two natural parks. There's only one hostal, the *Ocurris* (☎ 956 46 39 39) at Calle Solis Pascual 51, with doubles from 6300 to 7875 ptas.

From Ubrique the A-374 runs to Grazalema, skirting a few of the Parque Natural Sierra de Grazalema's higher peaks as it passes through the villages of Benaocaz and Villaluenga del Rosario (highest of the white villages at 870m). There are several possible walks in this area. Benaocaz and Villaluenga del Rosario each have at least one hostal and there's a campsite off the road between the two.

Getting There & Away
There are several buses daily to/from El Bosque, Arcos de la Frontera, and Grazalema via Benaocaz and Villaluenga del Rosario.

Benamahoma

The village of Benamahoma, 4km from El Bosque on the A-372 to Grazalema, is another good base for exploring the sierra. It's known for its market gardens, trout farm and a cottage industry of rush-backed chairs. There's a park information office (☎ 956 71 60 63) and museum in an old mill. Nearby on Camino del Nacimiento is *Camping Los Linares* (☎ 956 71 62 75) which has good facilities including a swimming pool. Benamahoma remembers its past in its Fiestas de Moros y Cristianos (Festival of Moors and Christians), the first Sunday of August.

Grazalema

From Benamahoma the A-372 winds east up to Puerto del Boyar at 1103m, where there's a lookout point, before the descent to Grazalema (823m). When the mist comes down, this road is dangerous. Grazalema nestles into a hillside, surrounded by beautiful mountain country, with the Sierra del Pinar to the north-west and the Sierra del Endrinal to the south. Towering Pico San Cristobal (1525m), to the north-west, provided the first glimpse of home for Spanish sailors returning with their treasure from the Americas.

A haunt of nature-lovers and artists (with a drug rehabilitation centre too), Grazalema is a neat, pretty, picture-postcard village, especially when dusted with snow. Its steep, narrow cobblestone streets, whitewashed houses and flowery window boxes reflect its Muslim heritage. Grazalema's population today (2300) is only one-third of what it was in the 19th century, when it prospered on the wool and textile industries and agriculture. Local products still include pure wool blankets and rugs, as well as pork products, cakes and pastries.

Information The village centre is Plaza de España where you'll find the tourist office (☎ 956 13 22 25) with information about the natural park, details of houses to rent, and local crafts and produce for sale. It's open Tuesday to Sunday from 10 am to 2 pm and 4 to 6 pm (summer 6 to 8 pm). Unicaja bank, right by Plaza de España, has an ATM.

Things To See & Do There are a couple of lovely 17th century churches, the **Iglesia de la Aurora** on Plaza de España and the nearby **Iglesia de la Encarnación**, though, like other buildings, they suffered damage during the 19th century War of Independence and the civil war.

Horizon (☎ 956 13 23 63), Calle Doctor Mateos Gago 12, caters for a range of activities from horse riding and rock climbing to hot-air balloon trips and paragliding. It's open Tuesday to Friday from 10 am to 2 pm and weekends from 3.30 to 5.30 pm. Horse riding costs 1500 ptas per hour.

Grazalema's large public swimming pool, with good views, is below Restaurante El Tajo at the east end of the village.

Special Events From around 12 to 20 July Grazalema celebrates Las Fiestas del Carmen with plenty of late-night music and dance performances. The festivities end on a Monday with a bull-running through the streets.

Places to Stay & Eat *Camping Tajo Rodillo* (☎ 956 13 20 63) is 1km above the village on the A-372 to El Bosque. It's closed in winter. The cost for two adults, a tent and a car is 1515 ptas. There are also *tiendas bengalís*, fancy tents with two bedrooms, kitchen, fridge, etc costing from 4250 ptas to 9950 ptas plus IVA. In the centre, *Casa de las Piedras* (☎ 956 13 20 14), Calle Las Piedras 32, is a long-standing hostal with plenty of rooms, all with winter heating. Singles/doubles are 1500/3000 ptas, or 3600/4800 ptas with attached bath. Its restaurant serves a range of hearty medium-priced breakfasts and *platos del día* such as pisto (mixed vegetables, 450 ptas), gazpacho (400 ptas) and stuffed pork (900 ptas).

The more luxurious *Villa Turística* (☎ 956 13 21 62) is at El Olivar s/n, above the village to the north. It has manicured lawns with a swimming pool and great views. Rooms with all mod-cons cost from 4400/7150 ptas plus IVA. There are also apartments with two double rooms from 13,200 ptas plus IVA.

There are plenty more places to eat and drink on Calle Agua, off Plaza de España. On Calle José Jiménez there's a good *bakery*. *Restaurante El Tajo*, with panoramic views at the east end of the village, has classy airs. The buffet lunch (not available in winter) is around 1100 ptas, salads are 200 to 450 ptas, and hake or trout, both stuffed with ham, are 1250 ptas each.

Getting There & Away There are two buses daily from El Bosque, several from Ubrique, and two from Ronda.

Zahara de La Sierra

The most northerly village in the natural park and topped by a crag with a ruined castle, Zahara de la Sierra is one of the most dramatic and pretty of the white villages. It feels quite otherworldly, especially if you've driven the 18km from Grazalema – another high and potentially dangerous road – through heavy mist. There's a reservoir below the village, to the north and the east. Despite its apparent isolation, Zahara is well set up for those wanting to explore the surrounding country.

History Founded by Muslims in the 8th century, Zahara fell in 1407 to the Castilian prince Fernando de Antequera. Its recapture by Abu al-Hasan of Granada in a daring night raid in 1481 sparked the last phase of the Reconquista which ended in the fall of Granada. Zahara itself was back in Christian hands by 1483. In the late 19th century Zahara was a noted hotbed of anarchism.

Information The village centres on Calle San Juan, a cobblestone street with a church at each end. Here you'll find Turismo Rural Bocaleones (☎ 956 12 31 14), a tourist office-cum-activities cooperative, open daily from 9 am to 2 pm, plus Saturday and Sunday from 4 to 7 pm. For most walks in the park from Zahara you need to get permission here. (See the introduction to this section for information about the pinsapar, which can be accessed from Zahara). The office can organise horse rides, canoe trips, bicycle and 4WD rental and more. Hostal Marqués de Zahara, a few doors away, has printed information about the village and the natural park.

Things to See & Do The obvious thing to do is to climb to the 12th century **castillo**, of which one tower survives, reached by a dirt track beside the 18th century baroque **Iglesia de Santa María de la Mesa** on Calle San Juan – or, more easily, by a new path with steps from the main road below the village. There's a **mirador** on Calle San Juan. Zahara's steep streets invite investigation; there are pretty views across the village and out to the countryside, some framed by tall palm trees or hot-pink bougainvillea in summer, fruited orange trees in winter.

SUSAN FORSYTH
A typical village scene in Zahara de la Sierra.

There are five major walking routes in the natural park, some also open to 4WD vehicles, bicycles and horses. There are also caving possibilites.

Places to Stay & Eat *Camping Cortijo* is 3km from the village at Arroyomolinos, beside the river near the reservoir. There's a picnic place here too. The cost for two adults, a tent and a car is 1000 ptas. The unsigned, friendly little *Pensión González* (☎ 956 17 32 17) at Calle San Juan 9 has a few rooms with shared bath at 2000/3000 ptas. Other hostales include *Los Estribos* (☎ 956 13 74 45), Calle Fuerte 3, and *Los Tadeos* (☎ 956 13 78 86), Paseo de la Fuente s/n. *Hostal Marqués de Zahara* (☎ 956 12 30 61), a converted mansion at Calle San Juan 3, has 10 comfy rooms with winter heating. Singles/doubles are 3750/5650

ptas. The hostal's restaurant, with a menú at 1500 ptas, is for guests only but there are other places to eat on this street, including the welcoming *Bar Nuevo* with homely, cheap food, and a *supermarket* nearby.

Getting There & Away The Comes line operates two buses Monday to Friday to/from Ronda via Algodonales.

The road from Grazalema climbs to the 1331m Puerto de los Palomas (Doves' Pass, but there are more vultures here than doves) before the descent to Zahara (551m). From Zahara one road heads north to Algodonales, crossing the A-382 Arcos-Antequera road. Another road heads south-east towards Ronda.

Costa de la Luz

The 90km coast between Cádiz and Tarifa can be windy, and its Atlantic waters are a shade cooler than those of the Mediterranean. But these are small prices to pay for an unspoiled, often wild shore, strung with long, clean, white-sand beaches and just a few small towns and villages. Andalucians are well aware of its attractions and flock down here in their thousands in July and August, bringing a vibrant fiesta atmosphere to the normally quiet coastal settlements.

From before Roman times until the advent of 20th century tourism this coast was mainly devoted to tuna fishing. Shoals of big tuna, some weighing 300kg, are still intercepted by walls of net several kilometres long as the fish head in from the Atlantic towards their Mediterranean spawning grounds in spring, and again as they head out in July and August. Barbate has the main tuna fleet today.

Apart from Tarifa, the two finest places to head for are the villages of Los Caños de Meca and Zahara de los Atunes, a few kilometres either side of Barbate. It's advisable to ring ahead for rooms in July and August.

CÁDIZ PROVINCE

VEJER DE LA FRONTERA
This isolated, old-fashioned white town looms mysteriously atop a rocky hill 200m above the busy N-340, 50km from Cádiz and 10km inland. It's well worth a wander.

Orientation & Information
The oldest part of town, still partly walled and with narrow winding streets clearly signifying its Muslim origins, spreads over the highest part of the hill. Just below is a small plaza called the *Plazuela,* more or less the heart of town, with the Hotel Convento de San Francisco and, close by, the tourist office (☎ 956 45 01 91) at Calle Marqués de Tamarón 10, open Monday to Friday from 8 am to 3 pm (to 2 pm in summer). When the tourist office is closed you can pick up a town map from the Hotel Convento de San Francisco. Buses stop on Avenida Remedios, the road up from the N-340, about 500m below the Plazuela.

Things to See
Within the walled area, seek out the **Iglesia del Divino Salvador** whose interior is mudéjar at the altar end and Gothic at the other; and the much-reworked **Castillo**, open from 11 am to 2 pm and 5 to 10 pm, with great views from its battlements and a small museum that preserves one of the black cloaks, covering everything but the eyes, that Vejer women wore until just a couple of decades ago.

Places to Eat
Hostal La Janda (☎ 956 45 01 42), across town from the old walled area at the meeting of Calle San Ambrosio and Calle Cerro Clarinas, has singles/doubles with bath for 2000/4000 ptas. Down a side-street nearby, *Hostal Buena Vista* (☎ 956 45 09 69), Calle Manuel Machado 20, has good-value, spotless doubles with bath for 5000 ptas, some with fine views across to the old part of town. The *Hotel Convento de San Francisco* (☎ 956 45 10 01), in a restored 17th century convent at Plazuela s/n, has singles/doubles at 6600/8800 ptas plus IVA. *La Bodeguita*, Calle Marqués de Tamarón

9, near the tourist office, has excellent tapas and meals.

Getting There & Away
Buses of the Comes line run to/from Cádiz and Barbate up to nine times a day. More buses for the same places, plus Tarifa and Algeciras (about 10 daily), La Línea, Málaga and Sevilla (all three or more) stop at La Barca de Vejer, on the N-340 at the bottom of the hill from where, by road, it's 4km uphill to the town; there's a shortcut – follow the locals up the path!

BARBATE
A fishing and canning town of 22,000 people, with a long sandy beach and a big harbour, Barbate becomes a fairly lively resort in summer but it's mostly a drab place. You might need to use Barbate as a staging post if you're travelling by bus. The Comes bus station (☎ 956 43 05 94) is more than a kilometre back from the beach at the north end of the long main street, Avenida del Generalísimo. The only tourist office (☎ 956 43 10 06) for the Los Caños de Meca-Barbate-Zahara de los Atunes area is on Calle Ramón y Cajal, just back from the east end of the beachfront street, Paseo Marítimo.

Hotel Mediterráneo (☎ 956 43 02 43), near the market at Calle Albufera 1, has doubles with bath for 4800 ptas but only opens from July to mid-September. The better *Hotel Galia* (☎ 956 43 04 82), a few blocks from the bus station at Calle Doctor Valencia 5, has doubles from 4500 to 6000 ptas depending on season. There are plenty of seafood eateries with lots of local specialties on Paseo Marítimo.

Buses run to/from La Barca de Vejer (see Vejer de la Frontera, above) and Cádiz up to 12 times daily, Vejer de la Frontera four to nine times daily, Sevilla once (not Sunday) and Tarifa and Algeciras once. There are three buses daily (one on Sunday) to/from Zahara de los Atunes.

LOS CAÑOS DE MECA
Los Caños, once a hippy hideaway, straggles untidily along a series of sandy coves beneath

a pine-clad hill 12km west of Barbate. It maintains its laid-back, off-the-beaten-track air even at the height of summer.

The coast between Barbate and Los Caños is mostly cliffs up to 100m high. The road between the two places runs inland through the La Breña umbrella pine forest. These cliffs and forest, along with wetlands east and north of Barbate, now form the Parque Natural de La Breña y Marismas de Barbate. A couple of walking paths start from the road: one goes to Playa de la Hierbabuena beach just west of Barbate, the other to the Torre del Tajo, a 16th century clifftop lookout tower. Another tower, the Torre de Meca on the hill behind Los Caños, can also be reached from this road.

The road emerges towards the east end of Los Caños' single street, which mostly seems to be called Avenida Trafalgar. The main beach is straight in front of you. Those who want to swim nude do so around the small headland at its east end. At the west end of the village a side-road leads out to a lighthouse on a low spit of land with a famous name – Cabo de Trafalgar. It was off this cape that Spanish naval power was terminated in a few hours one day in 1805 by a British fleet under Admiral Nelson. There are further decent beaches either side of Cabo de Trafalgar.

Places to Stay

There are three medium-sized camping grounds, open from April to September and maybe a couple of weeks either side. They get pretty crowded in high summer. Nearest the centre is *Camping Camaleón* (☎ 956 43 71 54), Avenida Trafalgar s/n, about 1km west from the corner of Barbate road, with a shady site at about 2200 ptas for two people with a car and tent. *Camping Faro de Trafalgar* (☎ 956 43 70 17), another 700m west, and *Camping Caños de Meca* (☎ 956 43 71 20), 1km farther on in the separate settlement of Zahora, are slightly cheaper.

About 10 hostales are strung along Avenida Trafalgar in Los Caños, and there are more at Zahora. Most are pretty similar and have decent rooms with private bath.

The quieter end of the village is east from the Barbate road corner. *Hostal Fortuna* (☎ 956 43 70 75), a couple of hundred metres along, has excellent singles/doubles for 4000/5000 ptas (4000/8000 ptas in August). A bit farther on, the laid-back *Hostal Los Castillejos* (no telephone) is a quaint turreted little place with lingering hippy vibes. It was closed for repairs when we visited but expect doubles to be around 4000 ptas.

Immediately west of the Barbate road corner, *Hostal Villa de Guadalupe* (☎ 956 43 72 29), Avenida Trafalgar 56, is a bit classier with doubles at 10,000 ptas, but only open in summer. Farther in the same direction, *Hostal Mar y Sol* (☎ 956 43 72 55), Avenida Trafalgar 102, open from June to September, has doubles for 5000 or 6500 ptas depending on how busy it is. *Hostal Miramar* (☎ 956 43 70 24), a few doors farther on though numbered Avenida Trafalgar 100, boasts a pool and restaurant and is open from Semana Santa to the end of September. Semana Santa and July rates for singles/doubles with bath are 4000/5300 ptas; it's cheaper at other times. Past the Camping Camaleón turning, *Hostal El Ancla* (☎ 956 43 71 00) has doubles or triples with bath, fridge and TV for around 5000 ptas. It's closed in winter.

At Zahora the *Hostal Alhambra* (☎ 956 43 72 16), opposite Camping Caños de Meca, has Alhambra-esque trimmings, a restaurant and nice rooms with little verandahs at 6000 ptas for doubles (year-round).

Places to Eat

Bar-Restaurante El Caña, a short distance east from the Barbate road corner, has a fine position atop the small cliff above the beach. Most seafood is around 1000 ptas but there are cheaper dishes of chicken, meatballs and so on. You may wait forever for a waiter, though. There's a *supermarket* across the road with an attached *café* which, in winter, is one of the few places to eat right in the village.

El Pirata, overlooking the beach a couple of hundred metres west, is a good bet with salads from 300 ptas and seafood media-raciones at 500 or 600 ptas. The revueltos de gambas y ortigas (scrambled eggs with shrimps and sea anemones), for 900 ptas, are excellent. This place is a hip little bar on winter weekend nights with an open fire and good music. Farther along, just past the Hostal Mar y Sol, *La Ensaladería* offers a variety of sizeable salads for 600 ptas. *Restaurante El Capi*, attached to a hostal on the main road out at Zahora, serves decent tapas and meals; it's another cosy place with an open fire in winter.

Entertainment
In the main tourist season good bars include the cool *Bar Araña* next to Hostal Los Castillejos, *Café-Bar Ketama* across the street from El Pirata and a couple of livelier places with music on the road out to Cabo de Trafalgar. *La Jaima*, in a kind of nomad's tent with red plush seats, overlooking the beach just east of the Barbate road corner, has bellydancing shows.

The *Sajoramí* restaurant/bar on Playa Zahora often has live rock, blues or flamenco on summer nights. Turn left by Camping Caños de Meca, then first right along a sandy road and keep going for 600m.

Getting There & Away
Buses to Los Caños run in summer only. In 1997 the Comes line ran buses from Sevilla, mid-June to early September, daily at 9 am; and from Jerez de la Frontera, July and August, Saturday only, with a return bus on Sunday. Buses continued on to Barbate. From Barbate, there was a daily bus to Los Caños from mid-June to early September at 7 pm.

ZAHARA DE LOS ATUNES
Plonked in the middle of nothing except a broad, 12km-long, west-facing sandy beach, Zahara is an elemental sort of place. At the heart of the village stand the crumbling walls of the old Almadraba, once a depot and refuge for the local tuna *(atún)* fishers, who were an infamously rugged lot. Cervantes, in *La Ilustre Fregona*, wrote that no one deserved the name *pícaro* (low-life scoundrel) unless they had spent two seasons at Zahara fishing for tuna. The pícaros were evidently good at their work for records state that in 1541 no fewer than 140,000 tuna were brought into Zahara's Almadraba. Today the tuna industry here has dwindled out of sight but Zahara has revived as an increasingly popular, almost fashionable, Spanish summer resort. With a little old-fashioned core of narrow streets, it's altogether a fine spot to let the sun, sea, wind – and, in summer, a spot of lively nightlife – batter your senses. Unicaja bank on Calle María Luisa has an ATM.

Places to Stay
The good *Camping Bahía de la Plata* (☎ 956 43 90 40) is near the beach at the southern end of Zahara on Carretera de Atlanterra. It's open all year, charging around 2000 ptas for two people with car and tent.

Otherwise the cheapest place, and the most likely to have a room when everywhere else is full in July and August, is *Hostal Monte Mar* (☎ 956 43 90 47), Calle Peñón 12, at the northern tip of the village. The rooms are fine at 4500 ptas a double with bath. The small *Hotel Nicolás* (☎ 956 43 92 74), Calle María Luisa 13, has simple but attractive singles/doubles with TV and bath for 4000/5700 ptas plus IVA, and a restaurant. Next door is the *Hotel Almadraba* (☎ 956 43 93 32), Calle María Luisa 15, with doubles at 8500 ptas.

The prime beach position is occupied by the *Hotel Gran Sol* (☎ 956 43 93 01), right by the sands and facing the old Almadraba walls at Calle Sánchez Rodríguez s/n, with large, comfortable doubles at 9500 ptas plus IVA. *Hotel Doña Lola* (☎ 956 43 90 09), near the entrance to Zahara at Plaza Thompson 1, is a modern place in attractive old-fashioned style, with good doubles at 10,000 ptas.

Places to Eat
Most restaurants are on or near Plaza de Tamarón near the Hotel Doña Lola, and most offer similar lists of fish, seafood, salads, meat and sometimes pizzas. *Patio la Plazoleta* on Plaza de Tamarón is a good one, open to the air: a media-ración of *pez limón a la plancha* (grilled tuna

with vegetables and lemon) is 600 ptas and there are also good pizzas for around 800 ptas. *Café-Bar Casa Juanita,* off the plaza on Calle Sagasta, is another pleasant place, with similar fare a little cheaper. It's not a bad spot for your morning coffee and tostada, either.

Entertainment
In July and August a line of marquees and makeshift shacks along the beach south of the Almadraba serve as bars, discos and *teterías.* They get busy from about midnight. Some have live flamenco or other music.

Getting There & Away
The Comes line runs two daily buses (one on Sunday) to/from Cádiz, three daily to/from Barbate (one on Sunday), one daily (none on Sunday) to/from Tarifa and, at the time of writing, from mid-June to early September one daily to/from Sevilla via Los Caños de Meca.

BOLONIA
This tiny village, 10km down the coast from Zahara and about 20km from Tarifa, has a fine white sand beach, a handful of restaurants and small hostales, and the ruins of the Roman town of Baelo Claudia. The ruins include substantial remains of a theatre, a paved forum surrounded by remains of temples and other buildings, and the remains of the workshops which turned out the products that made Baelo Claudia famous in the Roman world: salted fish and *garum* paste. The site (☎ 956 68 85 30) is open for guided visits (250 ptas for foreigners) Tuesday to Sunday at 10 and 11 am, 12 noon and 1 pm, also Tuesday to Saturday at 4 and 5 pm (5 and 6 pm from July to mid-September).

Hostal Bellavista (☎ 956 68 85 53), in the centre of the village, has singles/doubles with bath at 3000/5000 ptas, 1500/3000 ptas in winter. *Hostal Villamar* (☎ 956 68 85 61), open from Semana Santa until September, has the plum beach site; doubles with bath and great ocean views cost 4000 and 5000 ptas.

The only road to Bolonia heads west off the N-340, 15km from Tarifa. If you don't have wheels it's a 7km hilly walk from the main road as there's no regular bus service. You can also walk 8km along the coast from Ensenada de Valdevaqueros via Punta Paloma (see Windsurfing in the Tarifa section).

Tunnelling to Africa
Bolonia is the nearest place to the planned Spanish end of a projected Strait of Gibraltar tunnel which could be shuttling vehicle-carrying trains to Tangier by the second decade of the 21st century. After decades of intermittent talk, in 1996 Spain and Morocco finally took a serious step and agreed to seek EU funds for the project. The planned 38km tunnel will begin a couple of kilometres inland, cross the coastline between Bolonia and Punta Paloma and descend to a depth of 450m en route to its southern end just east of Tangier. The railway through it will link up with a new line to be built between Cádiz and Algeciras. The total cost is estimated to be at least 550 billion ptas (US$4.4 billion) – one-eighth of the cost of a bridge.

TARIFA
Even at peak times Tarifa is an attractive and laid-back town. Until 10 years or so ago it was relatively unknown but it has since become a mecca for windsurfers. It's strange to see the international surf scene transported to this European setting with a strong Arabic feel, but if you're Australian, Californian or Hawaiian you'll feel right at home: the beaches have clean, white sand and good waves, and inland the country is green and rolling, though it does get chilly and wet in winter. Then there's the old town to explore with its pretty, narrow streets, whitewashed houses and flowers cascading from balconies and window boxes. Tarifa's

castle is striking too. The only negative – though not for windsurfers or the hundreds of windmills on the hilltops inland – is the wind on which Tarifa's new prosperity is based. For much of the year, either the *levante* (easterly) or *poniente* (westerly) is blowing, ruinous for a relaxed sit on the beach and tiring if you're simply wandering around. August can be blessedly still, hot but not too hot, crowded but not overly so. The windmills, incidentally, are a mainly EU-funded experiment which feed power into Spain's national grid.

History

Tarifa may be as old as Phoenician Cádiz and was definitely a Roman settlement, but it takes its name from Tarik ibn Malik who led a Muslim raid in 710, the year before the main Islamic invasion of the peninsula. Muslims controlled the town from the 8th century, building the castle in the 10th century as fortification against Norse and African raids. (Pirates in the area at this time are said to have extracted a fee from ships wishing to pass safely from the Atlantic through the Strait to the Mediterranean. This could possibly be the origin of the word '*tarifa*', Spanish for tariff or fee.) Christians took Tarifa in 1292 but it was not secure until Algeciras was won in 1344. Later, Tarifa was active in the colonisation of the Americas: many of its people left for Peru in the 16th and 17th centuries.

Orientation & Information

Two roads lead into Tarifa from the N-340. The one from the north-west eventually becomes Calle Batalla del Salado, which ends at east-west Avenida de Andalucía, where the Puerta de Jerez leads through the walls into the old town. The one from the east eventually becomes Calle Amador de los Rios which meets Avenida de Andalucía at the Puerta de Jerez.

The main street of the old town is Calle Sancho IV El Bravo, with the Iglesia de San Mateo at its eastern end. The castle overlooks the port on the southern side of the old town. To the south-west protrudes the

Punta de Tarifa, a military-occupied promontory that is the southernmost point of continental Europe, with the Strait of Gibraltar to the south and east and the Atlantic Ocean to the west.

The tourist office (☎ 956 68 09 93), housed in a little white building surrounded with flower beds, is near the top end of the palm-lined Paseo de la Alameda, which stretches down the west side of the old town from Avenida de Andalucía almost to the port. It's open Monday to Friday from 10.30 am to 1.30 pm and 5 to 7 pm (6 to 8 pm in summer), and Saturday from 11 am to 2 pm. If it's closed, head for the Ayuntamiento on Plaza de Santa María for a map and information.

There are banks and ATMs on Calle Sancho IV El Bravo and Calle Batalla del Salado. The post office (postcode 11380) is at Calle Coronel Moscardó 9, south from the Iglesia de San Mateo. The Policía Local (☎ 956 61 41 86) are in the Ayuntamiento. The Cruz Roja (Red Cross; ☎ 956 64 48 96) is at Calle Alcalde Juan Núñez 5, a short distance west of the bottom of the Paseo de la Alameda. Tarifa's hospital (☎ 956 68 15 15/35) is on Calle Amador de los Rios. There's a pharmacy at Calle Batalla del Salado 22.

International newspapers and books in English and German are available at the News Stand on Calle Batalla del Salado, opposite the Puerta de Jerez. Café Continental on Paseo de la Alameda offers internet access at 1000 ptas per hour (750 ptas per hour at night and on Sunday).

If you want to do your laundry, head to the washer/dryer in SYP supermarket on the corner of Calle San José and General Primo de Rivera. Cost is around 1000 ptas for a load.

Things to See & Do

Tarifa is best enjoyed by strolling about the tangled streets of the old town to the castle walls, checking out the castle, stopping in at the busy port and sampling the beaches.

Old Town The mudéjar **Puerta de Jerez** was built after the Reconquista. Look in at the bustling, neo-mudéjar **market** on Calle Colón before wending your way to the heart of the old town and the mainly 15th century **Iglesia de San Mateo**. The streets south of the church are little changed since Islamic times. Climb the stairs at the end of Calle Coronel Moscardó and go left on Calle Aljaranda to reach the **Mirador El Estrecho** atop part of the castle walls with spectacular views across to Africa.

The **Castillo de Guzmán**, extending west from here, is named after the Reconquista hero Guzmán El Bueno who,

when threatened with the death of his kidnapped son unless he relinquished the castle to Islamic forces, threw down his dagger for his son to be killed. The incident happened in 1294 when the Christians were defending Tarifa against the Merenids of Morocco (Tarifa's Calle Batalla del Salado is named after the 1340 battle, north of Vejer de la Frontera, in which Alfonso XI finally dealt the Merenids a conclusive defeat.) Guzmán's descendants became the Duques de Medina Sidonia, who ran much of Cádiz province as a private fiefdom for a long

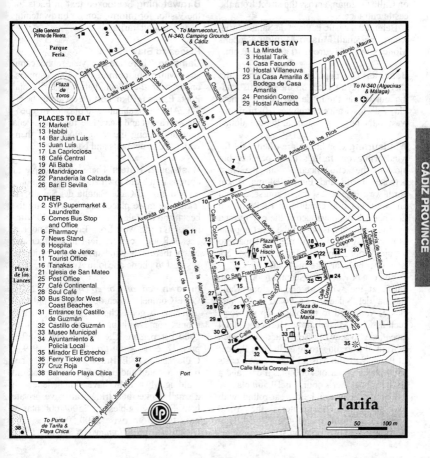

PLACES TO STAY
1 La Mirada
3 Hostal Tarik
4 Casa Facundo
10 Hostal Villaneuva
23 La Casa Amarilla &
   Bodega de Casa
   Amarilla
24 Pensión Correo
29 Hostal Alameda

PLACES TO EAT
12 Market
13 Habibi
14 Bar Juan Luis
15 Juan Luis
17 La Capricciosa
18 Café Central
19 Ali Baba
20 Mandrágora
22 Panadería la Calzada
26 Bar El Sevilla

OTHER
2 SYP Supermarket &
   Laundrette
5 Comes Bus Stop
   and Office
6 Pharmacy
7 News Stand
8 Hospital
9 Puerta de Jerez
11 Tourist Office
16 Tanakas
21 Iglesia de San Mateo
25 Post Office
27 Café Continental
28 Soul Café
30 Bus Stop for West
   Coast Beaches
31 Entrance to Castillo
   de Guzmán
32 Castillo de Guzmán
33 Museo Municipal
34 Ayuntamiento &
   Policía Local
35 Mirador El Estrecho
36 Ferry Ticket Offices
37 Cruz Roja
38 Balneario Playa Chica

Tarifa

CÁDIZ PROVINCE

0   50   100 m

time and remained Spain's largest landowners well into the 20th century. The imposing fortress was originally built in 960 under the orders of the Córdoban Caliph, Abd ar-Rahman III. You can walk along the parapets and stand atop the 13th century Torre de Guzmán El Bueno for 360° views out to sea and Africa and back across the town to the windmills on the hills behind. The castle is open Tuesday to Sunday from 10 am to 1.30 pm and 5 to 8 pm (Sunday 4 to 5 pm). Buy your ticket (200 ptas, free on Sunday) in the *papelería* (stationery shop) on Calle Guzmán, across the street from the castle entrance.

Behind the castle is Plaza de Santa María, where the small **Museo Municipal** opens Monday to Friday from 10 am to 1.30 pm.

Beaches The popular town beach is the sheltered Playa Chica, on the isthmus leading out to the Punta de Tarifa. From here Playa de los Lances stretches 10km north-west to the huge sand dune at Punta Paloma.

Windsurfing Conditions are often right for windsurfing on Tarifa's town beaches but most of the action occurs along the coast between Tarifa and Punta Paloma, 10km north-west. The best spots, of course, depend on wind and tide conditions. El Porro, on Ensenada de Valdevaqueros, the bay formed by Punta Paloma, is one of the most popular as it has easy parking and plenty of space to set up. About 3km from Tarifa, the Río Jara is another popular take-off point.

You can buy new and second-hand gear in Tarifa at the windsurf shops along Calle Batalla del Salado. For board rental and classes you need to try places up the coast such as Club Mistral at the Hurricane Hotel (see Places to Stay), or Spin Out on the beach in front of Camping Torre de la Peña II, near El Porro. At Club Mistral board rental costs 2500 ptas an hour or 7000 ptas a day, and a six-hour beginner's course is 19,500 ptas.

Competitions are held year-round with two big events in summer – the World Speed Cup (July) and the World Cup (Formula 42) (July or August).

Horse Riding On Playa de los Lances, both the Hotel Dos Mares (☎ 956 68 40 35), about 4km from Tarifa, and the Hurricane Hotel (☎ 956 68 49 19), 6km out, rent horses with guides. The cost at both is about 2000 ptas for an hour's ride along the beach.

Whale Watch Three-hour boat trips to track and watch dolphins and whales are run by Whale Watch España (☎ 939-47 65 44 or ☎ 970-79 65 08). Cost is 4000 ptas for adults, 2000 ptas for children.

Birdwatching See boxed text in Facts for the Visitor for information on birdwatching in and around Tarifa.

Places to Stay
Camping There are six year-round camp sites, with room for more than 4000 campers, on or near the beach between Tarifa and Punta Paloma, 10km north-west along the N-340. All charge about 2200 ptas for two people with a tent and a car. The Torre de la Peña sites are among the more modern of them with good restaurants and bars.

Hostales & Hotels There are a couple of options in the old town and plenty of choice on and around Calle Batalla del Salado. At least nine more places are dotted along the beach and the inland side of the N-340 within 10km north-west from Tarifa, but none is cheap. Rooms can be tight in summer and when there are windsurfing competitions. It's best to phone ahead in August.

In Town *Pension Correo* (☎ 956 68 02 03), Calle Coronel Moscardó 9, in the old post office, is a good choice. Brightly painted rooms, some with bath, cost from 1500 to 2500 per person. The best double is 6000 ptas. *La Casa Amarilla* (☎ 956 65 19 93), Calle Sancho IV El Bravo s/n, is an imaginatively restored and beautifully decorated old building. Most rooms have a kitchenette with a small cooker and fridge: all have private bath. Singles/doubles are 3500/7000 ptas at peak times, otherwise 2500/5000 ptas. The friendly *Hostal Villanueva* (☎ 956 68 41 49),

Avenida de Andalucía 11, is built into the old city walls a few doors west of the Puerta de Jerez. Good clean rooms, some with views across to the castle, are 3500/4500 ptas in summer, 2000/4000 ptas at other times. *Hostal Alameda* (☎ 956 68 11 81), at Paseo de la Alameda 4, has doubles with attached bath and air-con for 6000 ptas in August (4000 ptas in winter).

Popular *Casa Facundo* (☎ 956 68 42 98), Calle Batallo del Salado 47, is geared up for windsurfers and even has a storage place for boards. Doubles with private bath and TV are 5000 ptas from July to October; other rooms go for 2500/4000 ptas. *Hostal Tarik* (☎ 956 68 06 48), two blocks west at Calle San Sebastián 32, has doubles with bath for 6000 or 4000 ptas depending on the season. If you're after sea views, *La Mirada* (☎ 956 68 06 26), Calle San Sebastián 48, has doubles for 7500 ptas in the high season.

Along the Coast All these places have rooms with private bath.

Hostal Millón (☎ 956 68 52 46), 5km from the town centre, has a nice little garden giving on to the beach, its own small restaurant, and reasonable doubles at 9000 ptas (7000 ptas from October to June).

The *Hurricane Hotel* (☎ 956 68 49 19), 6km out, is the place to go if money is no object. Set in beachside semi-tropical gardens, it has 33 large comfy rooms, two pools (one heated), a health club, and its own windsurfing school and board rental. Singles/doubles range seasonally from 9000/12,000 ptas to 13,125/17,500 ptas on the ocean side, and 6750/9000 ptas to 10,675/14,500 ptas on the land side. To these prices you must add IVA, but they include an excellent buffet breakfast.

Hostal Oasis (☎ 956 68 50 65) and *Hotel La Ensenada* (☎ 956 68 06 37), both about 8km out, are two of the less pricey places along here, with doubles ranging from 5000 to 8500 ptas depending on season. *Hotel Las Piñas*, 10km out, is the closest hotel to Punta Paloma, with doubles around 7500 ptas.

Places to Eat
Thanks to Tarifa's high number of international visitors, you're guaranteed some variation from typical Spanish fare.

In Town Calle Sancho IV El Bravo has all manner of take-away options. Try *Panadería La Calzada* for filled baguettes, pizza portions and *empanadas*. Across the road, popular *Ali Baba* has cheap, filling and tasty Arabic food, with benches and stand-up tables outside. Vegetarians can enjoy excellent felafels for 375 ptas; carnivores pay a bit extra for the kebabs and kebes (spicy meatballs). A few doors away *Café Central* has good churros y chocolate and a large range of breakfasts from 375 to 600 ptas. Main meals from the long menu are around 950 ptas.

There's excellent food nearby at *Mandrágora*, Calle Independencia 3, on the street behind Iglesia San Mateo. Some of the delicious options are peppers stuffed with bacalao (1000 ptas) and chicken breasts stuffed with cheese (900 ptas). The boquerones (500 ptas) are sensational!

The best-value seafood in town is at *Bar El Sevilla*, the *marisquería* (seafood place) on Calle Invalidos west of the centre. There's no name outside – some locals call it El Gallego. Mixed fish and seafood fry-ups cost 150 ptas for a generous tapa or 850 ptas for a ración (enough for two people) – excellent washed down with a beer!

Juan Luis, Calle San Francisco 15 (with no sign), has fixed price meals (3000 to 4000 ptas) consisting of dish after delicious dish (mainly pork) until you can't fit in any more. *Bar Juan Luis*, opposite at Calle San Francisco 16, does fantastic *lomo* (pork loin) sandwiches (300 ptas) while the Italian restaurant *La Capricciosa*, near the centre on the same street, does very good pizzas (500 to 700 ptas).

Habibi, at the market end of Calle Santísima Trinidad, is another take-away Arabic food bar with cheaper food than the central Ali Baba; the felafels here are 275 ptas, kebabs 225 ptas. The *Hostal Villanueva's* restaurant, on Avenida de

Andalucía, does a brisk trade with its 850-ptas lunch menú.

Along the Coast Most hotels and hostales up here have their own restaurants. The Hurricane Hotel's *Terrace Restaurant*, with ocean views, is good for lunch (homemade pasta, local fish and seafood) or drinks. In the evenings the hotel's interior restaurant does a wonderful beef fillet and very good roast lamb (each around 2000 ptas). *Mesón El Toro*, on the inland side of the road, 4km from Tarifa, is a good steak and fish house with most mains around 1200 to 1500 ptas. It's open from 7 pm to 1 am (closed Monday).

Entertainment

The lovely wine bar *Bodega de Casa Amarilla*, on Calle Sancho IV El Bravo, is open at least Thursday to Sunday from 10 pm, plus Saturday and Sunday from 1 to 4.30 pm for lunch and live flamenco. On Paseo de la Alameda, *Café Continental* has live music on weekend nights in the summer; it's also a good tapas/copa/coffee stop at any time. Nearby, the *Soul Café* on Calle Santísima Trinidad, next to Café Continental's back entrance, is a popular disco/bar in the tourist seasons. Also close by, on Plaza San Hiscio, *Tanakas* is the biggest disco in town, popular with 16 to 20 year-old techno fans, though the crowd gets older as the night wears on. It's open Friday and Saturday until 5 am.

In July and August the open-air disco at Balneario Playa Chica may be worth checking out. Also in summer, a big Moroccan tent pops up on the beach at the town end of Playa de los Lances; by day it functions as tea rooms (try the mint tea at sunset!) but, come midnight, the place turns into a popular disco. About 4km north-west up the *playa*, the *chiringuito* on the beach near the Hotel Dos Mares opens during the summer months with live blues on Friday and Saturday nights.

Getting There & Away

Bus The Comes bus stop and office (☎ 956 68 40 38) is on Calle Batallo del Salado, 1½ blocks north of Avenida de Andalucía.

Comes runs six or more buses daily to Cádiz, Algeciras and La Línea; a few each to Jerez de la Frontera, Sevilla, and Málaga; and one each to Facinas (see Parque Natural Los Alcornocales), Almería and (except Sunday) to Barbate and Zahara de los Atunes.

Car & Motorcycle Stop at the Mirador de El Estrecho, about 7km out of Tarifa on the N-340 towards Algeciras, to take in magnificent views of the Strait of Gibraltar, the Mediterranean, the Atlantic and two continents. Beware of the frequent police speed trap in the 50km/h zone at Pelayo, a few kilometres farther east.

Boat Isleña de Navegación (☎ 956 65 28 00) and Transtour each operate one ferry daily (one hour) between Tarifa and Tangier, leaving Tarifa at 9.30 am and 10 am respectively. The return trips are at 3.30 and 4 pm (Moroccan time). The one-way passenger fare is 2960 ptas; a car and driver is 9300 ptas and a motorcycle 2650 ptas. Buy your ticket in the offices at the port or from Marruecotur (☎ 956 68 18 21), Calle Batallo del Salado 57.

Getting Around

Local buses run from Tarifa up the coast to just beyond Punta Paloma. In town, there's a bus stop at the bottom of the Paseo de la Alameda. Taxis line up on Avenida de Andalucía near the Puerta de Jerez.

The South-East

PARQUE NATURAL LOS ALCORNOCALES

This large (1700 sq km) natural park stretches 75km north from the Strait of Gibraltar to the southern boundary of the Parque Natural Sierra de Grazalema. It's a jumble of sometimes rolling, sometimes rugged sierras of medium height, and much of it is covered in Spain's most extensive cork oak woodlands *(alcornocales)*.

There are plenty of walks and possibilities for other activities in the park, but you need your own wheels to make the most of it as it's sparsely populated and public transport runs mostly along its fringes. The park office (☎ 956 42 02 77) is at Calle José Tizón 5 in the sleepy white town of Alcalá de los Gazules on the park's western fringe. Another information office, the Centro de Visitantes Huerta Grande (☎ 956 67 91 61), is beside the N-340 Tarifa-Algeciras road at Pelayo, about 12km from Tarifa and about 750m east of the modern *Albergue Juvenil Algeciras* youth hostel (☎ 956 67 90 60). There's a bus stop on the N-340 in front of the hostel, which has a few singles, 18 doubles, 16 four-person rooms and a swimming pool.

One road into the south of the park goes through the village of Facinas, off the N-340, 20km north of Tarifa. Turismo Rural, (☎ & fax 956 68 74 29), Calle Divina Pastora 6 in Facinas, offers a wide range of activities in the park including guided walks and cycling trips (each 2000 ptas), horse riding (two hours, 3500 ptas) and four-hour donkey trips (3500 ptas). Bicycle rental is 1000 ptas a day. There's a weekend package for 12,000 ptas including food and accommodation.

The small town of Jimena de la Frontera, on the A-369 on the park's eastern boundary, is a good base for the generally higher and more rugged northern part of the park. Jimena is crowned by a fine Muslim castle, has a couple of hostales, and is served by train and bus from Algeciras and Ronda, and bus from La Línea. The CA-3331 heading northwest from here, a paved but rough road, will take you to La Sauceda, an abandoned village that's now the site of a camping area and cabins (☎ 95 215 02 02).

The La Sauceda area, which is actually a finger of Málaga province jutting into Cádiz province, is beautiful country covered in cork and gall oaks, laurel, wild olives, rhododendrons and ferns. It's a fairly remote area, once a den of bandits, smugglers and even guerrillas during the Spanish Civil War (during which the village was bombed by Franco's planes). Walking possibilities include the ascent of Aljibe (1092m), the park's highest

peak, and nearby El Picacho (883m).

From La Sauceda a road continues to Ubrique (see Parque Natural Sierra de Grazalema).

ALGECIRAS

Algeciras, the major port linking Spain with Africa, is an unattractive, polluted place with little to hold your interest for longer than it takes to organise your crossing to Tangier or Ceuta. During the summer the port is hectic with hundreds of thousands of Moroccans working in Europe who return home for summer holidays. Algeciras is also an industrial town, a big fishing port and a centre for drug smuggling.

History

Algeciras was an important port under the Romans. In 711 it fell to the Islamic invaders. Alfonso XI of Castilla wrested it from the Merenids of Morocco in 1344 but later Mohammed V of Granada razed it to the ground. In 1704 Algeciras was repopulated by many of those who left Gibraltar after the British took it. During the Franco era, industry was developed.

Orientation & Information

Algeciras is on the west side of the Bahía de Algeciras, opposite Gibraltar. Avenida Virgen del Carmen runs north to south along the seafront, becoming Avenida de la Marina around the entrance to the port. From here Calle Juan de la Cierva (becoming Calle San Bernardo) runs inland beside a disused rail track to the Comes bus station (about 350m) and the train station (400m). The central plaza, Plaza Alta, is a couple of blocks inland from Avenida Virgen del Carmen. Plaza Palma, with a bustling daily market (except Sunday), is one block west of Avenida de la Marina.

Tourist Offices The English-speaking main tourist office (☎ 956 57 26 36) at Calle Juan de la Cierva s/n, a block inland from Avenida de la Marina, is open Monday to Friday from 9 am to 2 pm, and on Saturday too in summer. Inside there's a useful message board –

handy if you're planning to meet up with someone for the ferry.

The Spanish-speaking municipal tourist office is in a kiosk outside the main entrance to the port. In July and August it's open Monday to Friday from 10 am to 2 pm and 4 to 8 pm, and sporadically at weekends. In other months it's ostensibly open Monday to Friday from 10 am to 2 pm.

Money Ignore money-changing touts around the port – they're a ripoff for pesetas and you'll get a better deal buying dirham if you wait until you reach Morocco. There are banks and ATMs on Avenida Virgen del Carmen and around Plaza Alta, plus at least one ATM inside the port. Exchange rates are better at the banks than at travel agencies.

Post & Communications There's a post office on Calle José Antonio just south of

Plaza Alta. There are telephones in the port, on Avenida de la Marina, near the market and at the train station.

Medical & Emergency Services The Policía Nacional (☎ 956 66 04 00) are at Avenida de las Fuerzas Armadas 6 next to Parque de María Cristina. For an ambulance dial ☎ 956 65 15 55. The Hospital Cruz Roja (☎ 956 60 31 44) is central at Paseo de la Conferencia s/n, on the southern extension of Avenida de la Marina.

Left Luggage The train station has plenty of *consigna* lockers (400 ptas daily). In the port, storage is available from 7.30 am to 10 pm at 100 ptas a bag; there are no lockers, so bags need to be secured.

Dangers & Annoyances Keep your wits about you in the port, bus terminal and market, and ignore offers from the legions of

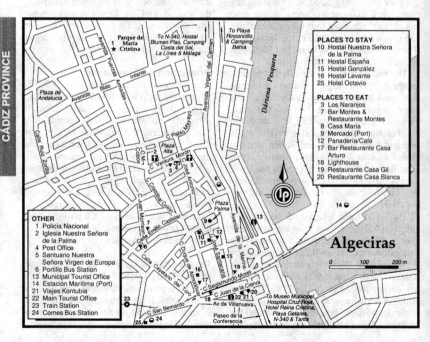

PLACES TO STAY
10 Hostal Nuestra Señora de la Palma
11 Hostal España
15 Hostal González
16 Hostal Levante
25 Hotel Octavio

PLACES TO EAT
3 Los Naranjos
7 Bar Montes & Restaurante Montes
8 Casa María
9 Mercado (Port)
12 Panadería/Café
17 Bar Restaurante Casa Arturo
18 Lighthouse
19 Restaurante Casa Gil
20 Restaurante Casa Blanca

OTHER
1 Policía Nacional
2 Iglesia Nuestra Señora de la Palma
4 Post Office
5 Santuario Nuestra Señora Virgen de Europa
6 Portillo Bus Station
13 Municipal Tourist Office
14 Estación Marítima (Port)
21 Viajes Kontubia
22 Main Tourist Office
23 Train Station
24 Comes Bus Station

Algeciras

money-changers, drug-pushers and ticket-hawkers who approach you. It's nowhere near as bad as in Tangier. Walk purposefully when moving between the Comes and Portillo bus stations in the evening.

Things to See & Do
If you have to spend any time in Algeciras, wander up to the pretty palm-fringed **Plaza Alta**, which has a lovely tiled fountain. On its west side is the 18th century **Iglesia Nuestra Señora de la Palma** and on its east the 17th century **Santuario Nuestra Señora Virgen de Europa**, both worth a look. Some of the houses on the streets around here are delightfully tumbledown.

The leafy **Parque de María Cristina,** a few blocks to the north, also provides a change from the noise and fumes of the port. The new **Museo Municipal**, on Calle Nicaragua just south of the main tourist office, is reasonably interesting. If you've got your own wheels, check out the town's two beaches – **Getares** (south) and **Playa del Rinconcillo** (north).

Special Events
The feria happens in the last week of June. On 15 August the town honours its patroness in the Fiesta del Virgen de la Palma.

Places to Stay
Camping There are two options, both north of the town – *Camping Costa del Sol* (☎ 956 66 02 19) at N-340, Km 108, and *Camping Bahía* (☎ 956 69 19 58) at N-340, Km 109, by Playa Rinconcillo. The cost at the Bahía is 425 ptas per adult and per car, 350 ptas per tent.

Hostales & Hotels There's loads of budget accommodation in the streets behind Avenida de la Marina, but market traffic in the small hours renders a good night's sleep near-impossible. If it's not too hot, try for an interior room.

The friendly *Hostal González* (☎ 956 65 28 43), Calle José Santacana 7, is perhaps the pick of this bunch. Good, clean singles/doubles with shared bath are 1750/3500 ptas

plus IVA in summer. *Hostal España* (☎ 956 66 82 62), Calle José Santacana 4, has large, clean rooms at 1000 ptas per person but it's right by the market. Also near the market, at Plaza Palma 12, *Hostal Nuestra Señora de la Palma* (☎ 956 63 24 81) has comfortable rooms with bath for 2000/4000 ptas plus IVA. *Hostal Levante* (☎ 956 65 15 05), Calle Duque de Almodóvar 21, is a little removed from the thick of things; reasonable rooms with a shower are 1500/3000 ptas though the corridors are a bit musty. The cheerful *Hostal Blumen Plas* (☎ 956 63 16 75), north of town on the N-340 at Km 108, with doubles around 5000 ptas, is a good choice if you want to stay out of the town centre.

The Stalinesque *Hotel Octavio* (☎ 956 65 27 00), Calle San Bernardo 1, with doubles from 15,000 ptas plus IVA, is a big step up in price and unsalubriously located above the main bus station. *Hotel Reina Cristina* (☎ 956 60 26 22), Paseo de la Conferencia s/n, a brisk five-minute walk south of the port, is an old colonial-style hotel set amid tropical gardens. Doubles cost 20,000 ptas, or 14,500 ptas in winter, both plus IVA. This hotel, a suitable place to observe sea traffic in the Strait of Gibraltar, was a haunt of spies in WWII.

Places to Eat
The city *mercado* has a wonderful array of fresh fruit, vegetables, hams and cheese – perfect for packing a picnic lunch. The excellent *Panadería-Café* at the market end of Calle José Santacana is good for breakfast; it's open early. Plaza Alta is dotted with sidewalk cafés; at the southern end, *Los Naranjos* is a smart little spot for a snack, with nice service, good hams and outside tables. A *pitufo* (a filled mini-baguette), with coffee is 250 ptas. English-speaking Christians run the supernaturally-friendly little *Lighthouse*, 200m east of the railway station, with decent breakfasts, generally helpful tourist advice ... and, if you stick around, other information ('Please read this pamphlet ...')

Restaurante Casa Blanca, Calle Juan de la Cierva 1 near the main tourist office, is popular for its 800-ptas menú of two courses, bread, soft drink and dessert; other options are moderately priced. Likewise, *Bar Restaurante Casa Arturo* on Calle Segismundo Moret – the street on the north side of the rail track facing the main tourist office – has a cheapish menú at 900 ptas for three courses plus bread, fruit and a drink; there's also a long list of platos combinados (from 575 to 1000 ptas). On the same street *Restaurante Casa Gil* has similar fare but is more expensive, with an 1100 ptas menú.

In the evening you can sample tapas at *Bar Montes*, Calle Emilio Castelar 36, several blocks north-west. Tapas keep appearing from the kitchen after 7 pm. There are tables out front but the bar is the best place to keep an eye on what tantalising morsel will turn up next. The adjacent *Restaurante Montes*, Calle Juan Morrison 27, has an 1100-ptas menú of tapas, chicken or fish, bread, wine and dessert, and an à la carte seafood list from 1500 ptas. Across the road, the popular *Casa María*, Calle Emilio Castelar 53, has a menú for 975 ptas with quite a wide choice. Tea on the terrace at the *Hotel Reina Cristina* is pleasant.

Entertainment
In summer there are flamenco, rock and other concerts at some of the more attractive spots in town – the Plaza de Toros, Parque de María Cristina, Plaza de Andalucía and Playa Rinconcillo. The main tourist office has a list of events.

Getting There & Away
The daily paper *Europa Sur* has up-to-date transport arrival and departure details.

Bus The main bus station, (☎ 956 65 34 56), is under the Hotel Octavio on Calle San Bernardo. To Tarifa (215 ptas) there are 10 buses daily Monday to Saturday but only four on Sunday and holidays. Buses run to La Línea (40 minutes, 225 ptas) every half-hour from 7 am to 9.30 pm. Other daily buses include 10 to Cádiz (1225 ptas), four to Sevilla, three to Jimena de la Frontera (400 ptas, two on Saturday and one on

Sunday), and two to Madrid (3283 ptas). There's one bus (except Sunday) to Zahara de los Atunes and Barbate (615 ptas).

Portillo (☎ 956 65 10 55), at Avenida Virgen del Carmen 15, operates 10 buses daily (nine on Sunday) to Málaga (1290 ptas, 2½ hours) stopping at Estepona, Marbella, Fuengirola and Torremolinos, and two buses to Granada (2455 ptas).

Bacoma (☎ 956 66 65 89), inside the port, runs up to four services daily to Alicante, Valencia and Barcelona (9785 ptas).There are also buses to France, Germany and Holland from Viajes Kontubia, next to the main tourist office.

Train Three or four trains daily run to/from Ronda and Bobadilla (1395 ptas, 2½ hours) from the station (☎ 956 63 02 02) adjacent to Calle San Bernardo, taking in some dramatic scenery en route. At Bobadilla you can change for Granada, Málaga, Córdoba Sevilla and Madrid. There's a nightly direct train to Madrid at 9.30 pm.

Boat Trasmediterránea (☎ 956 66 52 00), Isleña de Navegación SA (Isnasa, ☎ 956 65 20 00) and Moroccan companies operate frequent daily roll-on, roll-off car ferries and hydrofoils (also called fast ferries or *rápidos*) to/from Tangier and Ceuta, the Spanish enclave on the Moroccan coast. Usually at least 14 sailings a day go to Tangier and 20 or more to Ceuta. From late June to September there are ferries almost round the clock to cater for the Moroccan migration – you may have to queue for up to three hours. Buy your ticket in the port or at the agencies on Avenida de la Marina – prices are the same everywhere.

To Tangier one adult passenger pays 2960 ptas (children 1480 ptas) one way on a ferry taking two hours, or 3440 ptas on a hydrofoil (one hour). A car costs 9300 ptas and a motorcycle over 500cc costs 2650 ptas.

To Ceuta, it's 1801 ptas (children 900 ptas) on a ferry, taking 1½ hours, and 2945 ptas (children 1472 ptas) on a hydrofoil (40 minutes). Cars cost 8223 ptas and motorcycles up to 2801 ptas.

LA LÍNEA DE LA CONCEPCÍON

Twenty kilometres east of Algeciras, round the bay, is the unavoidable stepping stone to Gibraltar. A left turn as you exit La Línea's bus station will bring you out on Avenida 20 de Abril, which runs the 300m or so between La Línea's main square, Plaza de la Constitución, and the Gibraltar border. There's a tourist office (☎ 956 76 99 50) on the corner of the plaza. The bus station has luggage lockers.

Places to Stay & Eat

Pensión La Perla (☎ 956 76 95 13) at Calle Clavel 10, two blocks north of Plaza de la Constitución, has clean and spacious pink-trimmed singles/doubles, with shared bathrooms, for 2000/3000 ptas. *Hostal La Campana* (☎ 956 17 30 59) at Calle Carboneros 3, just off the west side of Plaza de la Constitución, has decent rooms with bath and TV for 3800 ptas a double (4800 ptas from July to mid-September). Its restaurant has a three-course menú for 850 ptas. *Hostal La Esteponera* (☎ 956 17 66 68), Calle Carteya 10 several blocks west of the La Perla, has doubles with shared bath for 1875 ptas plus IVA.

La Crema on Calle Real just off the north-west corner of Plaza de la Constitución is a good spot for breakfast – coffee and a large tostada add up to 200 ptas.

Getting There & Away

Bus La Línea is linked by buses every 30 minutes or so to/from Algeciras (40 minutes, 225 ptas). There are four daily buses to Málaga (three hours, 1225 ptas), stopping in Estepona, San Pedro de Alcántara, Marbella, Fuengirola and Torremolinos; five to Tarifa (485 ptas) and Cádiz (2½ hours, 1440 ptas); three to Sevilla (four hours, 2500 ptas); and two to Granada (2390 ptas). A bus leaves Monday to Friday at 6.30 am for Jimena de la Frontera and Ronda (990 ptas).

Car & Motorcycle Owing to the usually long vehicle queues at the Gibraltar border, many visitors to Gibraltar opt to park in La Línea then walk across the border. Parking meters in La Línea cost 115 ptas an hour or 680 ptas for 10 hours; they're free from 10.30 pm to 9.30 am. The underground Parking Fo Cona just off Avenida 20 de Abril charges 150 ptas an hour or 1000 ptas a day; another underground car park on Plaza de la Constitución is a little cheaper.

CÁDIZ PROVINCE

Gibraltar

Looming like some great ship off almost the southernmost tip of Spain, the British colony (officially 'dependent territory') of Gibraltar is such a compound of curiosities that a visit can hardly fail to tweak the interest buds.

The mere sight of the thing is impressive. Gibraltar is 5km long and 1.6km at its widest. Most of it is one huge lump of limestone, rising to 426m and almost sheer at its northern end and along its eastern side. To the ancient Greeks and Romans, Gibraltar was one of the two Pillars of Hercules, set up by the mythical hero to mark the edge of the known world. (The other pillar is the coastal mountain Jebel Musa in Morocco, 25km south across the storm-prone Strait of Gibraltar.)

History

About 50,000 years ago Gibraltar was home to Neanderthal humans, as skulls found there in 1848 and 1928 testify. The former was actually discovered eight years before the skull in Germany's Neander valley which gave these people their modern name.

Phoenicians and ancient Greeks left traces here, but Gibraltar really entered the history books in 711 AD when Tariq ibn Ziyad, the Muslim governor of Tangier, made it the initial bridgehead for the Islamic invasion of the Iberian Peninsula, landing with an army of some 10,000 men. The name Gibraltar is derived from Jebel Tariq (Tariq's Mountain).

The Almohad Muslims founded a town here in 1159 and Muslims held it most of the time until Castilla wrested it from them in 1462. Then in 1704 an Anglo-Dutch fleet captured Gibraltar during the War of the Spanish Succession. Spain ceded the Rock of Gibraltar to Britain by the Treaty of Utrecht in 1713, but didn't finally give up military attempts to regain it until the failure of the Great Siege of 1779-83. Today, Spain still wants Gibraltar back. Britain developed it into an important naval

base and in WWII – when the entire local population was evacuated to Britain, Madeira and Jamaica – Gibraltar became a base for allied landings in North Africa. The British garrison was withdrawn in the early 1990s but the British navy continues to use Gibraltar.

During the Franco period Gibraltar was an extremely sore point between Spain and Britain: Franco closed the border between them in 1967 and it was not re-opened until 1985, 10 years after the Spanish leader's death. In a 1969 referendum, Gibraltarians voted 12,138 to 44 in favour of British rather than Spanish sovereignty. That year a new constitution – which gave Gibraltar domestic self-government and its own parliament, the House of Assembly – committed Britain to respecting Gibraltarians' wishes over sovereignty.

Spain maintains pressure on Gibraltar by such methods as occasional bursts of extra-thorough customs and immigration procedures, which cause hours-long delays at the border. On the diplomatic front, Spain proposes a period of joint British-Spanish sovereignty leading to Gibraltar eventually becoming the 18th autonomous Spanish region, with greater autonomy than any of

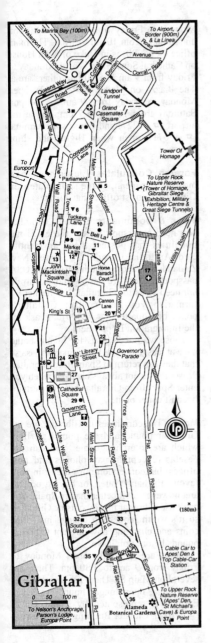

PLACES TO STAY
3 Emile Youth Hostel
5 Continental Hotel
18 Cannon Hotel
22 Eliott Hotel
24 Bristol Hotel
32 Toc H Hostel
34 Queen's Hotel
37 Rock Hotel

PLACES TO EAT
6 House of Sacarello
7 The Clipper
11 Viceroy of India
12 The English Tea Room
15 The Piazza
20 Three Roses Bar
21 Cannon Bar
23 Maxi Manger
31 Minister's Restaurant
35 Piccadilly Gardens

OTHER
1 Bus No 9
2 Health Centre
4 Touranfrica
8 Post Office
9 Bland Travel
10 Bell Books
13 Police Station
14 Bus No 10
16 Tourist Office
17 St Bernard's Hospital
19 Roman Catholic Cathedral
25 Gibraltar Museum
26 Bus No 3
27 Anglican Cathedral
28 Tourist Office
29 Gibraltar Bookshop
30 King's Chapel
33 Trafalgar Cemetery
36 Lower Cable-Car Station

the others. Britain continues to refuse any compromise over sovereignty.

Relations between Gibraltar and Spain have improved since the 1996 elections in which the Gibraltar Social Democrat Party, led by Peter Caruana, ousted the Gibraltar Socialist Labour Party under Joe Bossano, who had been in power since 1988. Caruana says he is prepared to enter talks with Britain and Spain over Gibraltar's future – something Bossano refused to do – but still

GIBRALTAR

fiercely opposes any concessions over sovereignty. Caruana's government is pushing to attract tourism, and has also taken steps to clean up Gibraltar's financial sector, previously considered a haven for money launderers. Smuggling, another bone of contention in the early and mid-1990s when scores of high-speed launches used Gibraltar as a base for moving illicit cigarettes and Moroccan drugs into Spain, seems to have been stopped.

Population & People

Gibraltar has around 30,000 people, of whom 75% are classed as Gibraltarians, 14% British, and 7% Moroccan. The Gibraltarians are of mixed Genoese, Jewish, Spanish and British ancestry, the Genoese element coming from Genoese ship repairers brought here by the British in the 18th century. The Moroccans are mostly short-term workers.

Language

Gibraltarians speak both English and Spanish and, at times, a curiously accented sing-song mix of the two, slipping back and forth from one to the other – often in mid-sentence. Signs are in English.

Orientation & Information

To reach Gibraltar by land you must pass through the Spanish border town of La Línea de la Concepción (see the Cádiz Province chapter). The international border is at the southern end of La Línea's Avenida 20 de Abril. Just south of the border, the road crosses the runway of Gibraltar airport, which stretches east-west across the neck of the peninsula. The town and harbours of Gibraltar lie along the foot of the Rock's less steep western side, facing the Bahía de Algeciras (or, as Gibraltarians call it, the Bay of Gibraltar).

Tourist Offices The Gibraltar Tourist Board has several very helpful information offices with plenty of good give-away material. One (☎ 50762) is in the customs and immigration building at the border, open Monday to Friday from 9 am to 4.30 pm, and Sunday from 10 am to 1 pm. The main office (☎ 45000) is in Duke of Kent House on Cathedral Square and is open Monday to Friday from 9 am to 5.30 pm; others are at The Piazza on Main St (☎ 74982), open Monday to Friday from 9 am to 5.30 pm, Saturday from 10 am to 2 pm; and at the airport (☎ 47227) and cruise ship terminal (☎ 47671), open when flights and ships arrive.

Foreign Consulates Eleven countries, mostly European, have consulates in Gibraltar. Tourist offices have lists.

Visas & Documents To enter Gibraltar you need a passport or, for those EU nationalities that possess them, an identity card. Australia, Canada, EU, Israel, New Zealand, Singapore, South Africa and USA passport-holders are among those who do *not* need visas for Gibraltar. For further information you can contact Gibraltar's police headquarters (☎ 72500) and ask for the Immigration Department.

Those who need visas for Spain should have at least a double-entry Spanish visa so that they can return to Spain from Gibraltar. Passports are not always checked when you enter Spain from Gibraltar but you certainly can't count on it.

Money The currencies in Gibraltar are the Gibraltar pound and the pound sterling, which are interchangeable. You can use pesetas (except in pay phones and post offices) but conversion rates aren't in your favour. Exchange rates for buying pesetas are, however, a bit better than in Spain. You can't use Gibraltar money outside Gibraltar, so it's worth requesting change in British coins and changing any unspent Gibraltar pounds before you leave.

Banks are generally open Monday to Friday from 9 am to 3.30 pm. There are several on Main St. There are also *bureaux de change*, open longer hours. American Express is represented by Bland Travel (☎ 77012), Cloister Building, Irish Town.

Post & Communications The main post office, open Monday to Friday from 9 am to 4.30 pm (in summer to 2.15 pm), and Saturday from 10 am to 1 pm, is at 104 Main St.

To phone Gibraltar from Spain, precede the five-digit local number with the code ☎ 9567; from other countries dial the international access code, then ☎ 350 (the Gibraltar country code) and the local number.

In Gibraltar you can make international as well as local calls from street pay phones. To phone Spain, just dial the nine-digit number. To phone other countries dial the international access code (☎ 00), then the country code, area code and number.

Bookshops Bell Books, 11 Bell Lane, and Gibraltar Bookshop, 300 Main St, are both good places where you can stock up on English-language reading material.

Medical & Emergency Services St Bernard's Hospital (☎ 79700) on Hospital Hill has 24-hour emergency facilities. There's also a health centre (☎ 77003) on Grand Casemates Square. The main station of the British-uniformed police (☎ 72500) is in the south of the town at New Mole House on Rosia Rd, but there's a more central station at 120 Irish Town. In an emergency you can call ☎ 199 for the police or an ambulance.

Electricity Electric current is the same as in Britain, 220V or 240V, with plugs of three flat pins.

Public Holidays Gibraltar observes the following public holidays: 1 January, Commonwealth Day (second Monday of March), Good Friday, Easter Monday, 1 May, Spring Bank Holiday (last Monday in May), Queen's Birthday (Monday after the second Saturday in June), Late Summer Bank Holiday (last Monday in August), Gibraltar National Day (10 September), 25 and 26 December.

Work Gibraltar is no longer an easy place to find paid work but it's better than anywhere in Spain, except Palma de Mallorca, for finding an unpaid yacht crew place. Yachting (Gibraltar) Ltd (☎ 73736) at Marina Bay runs a free crew register service, staff members say that in summer a couple of places a week normally come up on yachts cruising the Mediterranean. From November to January there's a chance of working your passage to the Caribbean.

The Town

Gibraltar's town centre, with its British shops, British pubs and British shoppers, is far from exotic but it has been spruced up in the last couple of years. Most Spanish and Islamic buildings were destroyed in 18th century sieges but British fortifications, gates and gun emplacements are all over the place; the *Guided Tour of Gibraltar* booklet by TJ Finlayson is good if you want to delve into details of the British heritage.

The **Gibraltar Museum**, on Bomb House Lane, contains very worthwhile historical, architectural and military displays and goes back to prehistoric times. Highlights include a well preserved Muslim bathhouse, and a detailed model of the Rock made in the 1860s by British officers. The museum is open Monday to Friday from 10 am to 6 pm, and Saturday from 10 am to 2 pm (£2).

The nearby Anglican **Cathedral of the Holy Trinity** was built in the 1820s and 1830s. The Catholic **Cathedral of St Mary the Crowned** on Main St stands on the site of Muslim Gibraltar's chief mosque. The **King's Chapel**, also on Main St, is part of a 16th century Franciscan convent which is now the governor's residence. Inside are buried the wife of the Spanish governor of 1648 and two 19th century British governors.

Many of the graves in the **Trafalgar Cemetery**, just south of Southport Gate, are of British sailors who died at Gibraltar after the Battle of Trafalgar (1805). A short distance south of here are the **Alameda Botanical Gardens**, entered from Europa Rd and open daily from 8 am to sunset (free). Just over 1km farther south, **Nelson's Anchorage** on Rosia Rd contains a 100-ton Victorian supergun, made in Britain in 1870 and overlooks Rosia Bay, where Nelson's body was brought ashore by *HMS Victory* – in a rum barrel, legend has it – after the Battle of Trafalgar. Nelson's Anchorage is open daily, except Sunday, from 9.30 am to 5 pm (£1, but free if you have an Upper Rock Nature Reserve ticket). A little farther south on Rosia Rd, the **Parson's Lodge** gun battery, atop a 40m cliff, is open Monday to Friday from 10 am to 5 pm (£2). Beneath the gun emplacements is a labyrinth of tunnels with former ammunition stores and living quarters.

Down at **Europa Point**, the southern tip of Gibraltar, are a lighthouse, the Christian Shrine of Our Lady of Europe and the Mosque of the Custodian of the Two Holy Mosques. This last, with a tall minaret, is claimed to be the largest mosque in a non-Islamic country. It was opened in 1997, cost £5 million and was paid for by King Fahd of Saudi Arabia. It's intended to be a focal point for Arabs travelling in southern Europe. Free guided tours are given: tourist offices can tell you the current opening hours.

Upper Rock Nature Reserve

Most of the upper parts of the Rock, starting just above the town, are now a nature reserve with spectacular views, a web of quiet roads and pathways and several interesting spots to visit. Once covered in trees, the Rock was virtually stripped of vegetation by the British garrison and grazing goats in the 18th and 19th centuries. Since then it has recovered to some extent and is home to 600 plant species. It's often a fine spot for observing the migrations of birds between Europe and Africa (see boxed text 'High Fliers At the Strait of Gibraltar').

The Upper Rock Nature Reserve is officially open daily from 9.30 am to 7 pm. From late afternoon you may find the reserve's entrance gates unstaffed and left open, which means you can enter free but must pay individually to visit any sights that are still open. Most stay open to 6.15 or 6.30 pm. Entry by

road, at £5 an adult, £2.50 a child and £1.50 a vehicle, includes all the sights mentioned in this section plus Nelson's Anchorage. Cable-car tickets (see the Getting Around section) include entry to the reserve, the Apes' Den and St Michael's Cave.

The upper rock's most famous inhabitants are Gibraltar's colony of **Barbary macaques**, the only wild primates (apart from *Homo sapiens*) in Europe. Some of these hang around the **Apes' Den** near the middle cable-car station, others can often be seen at the top cable car station and Great Siege Tunnels. Legend has it that when the apes (which may have been introduced from North Africa in the 18th century) disappear from Gibraltar, so will the British. When ape numbers were at a low ebb during WWII, the British brought in ape reinforcements from Africa. Recently their numbers have been increasing rapidly and a range of control measures from contraceptive implants to 'repatriation' to North Africa have been considered.

From the **top cable-car station**, there are views as far as Morocco in decent weather. You can also look down the sheer precipices of the Rock's eastern side to the biggest of the old **water catchments** which channelled rain into underground reservoirs. Today these have been replaced by desalination plants. In 1704, 500 Spanish soldiers scaled the eastern side of the Rock in an attempt to surprise the British occupiers. They spent a night in St Michael's Cave but were defeated once they came out of hiding.

About 15 minutes walk south down St Michael's Rd from the top cable car station, O'Hara's Rd leads up to the left to **O'Hara's Battery**, an emplacement of big guns on the Rock's summit.

St Michael's Cave, a few minutes further down St Michael's Rd (or 20 minutes up from the Apes' Den), is a big natural grotto with fine stalagmites and stalactites. It was once home to Neolithic inhabitants of the Rock. Today, apart from attracting tourists in droves, it's used for concerts, plays and even fashion shows. There's a café outside.

About 30 minutes walk north (downhill) from the top cable-car station is Princess Caroline's Battery, housing a **Military Heritage Centre**. From here one road leads down to the Princess Royal Battery – more gun emplacements – while another leads up to the **Great Siege Tunnels** (or Upper Galleries). These impressive galleries were hewn out of the rock by the British during the siege of 1779-83 to provide gun emplacements. They constitute only a tiny proportion of more than 70km of tunnels and galleries in the Rock, most of which are off limits to the public. General Eisenhower had an office in one such tunnel during WWII.

Worth a stop on Willis's Rd, which leads down to the town from Princess Caroline's Battery, are the **Gibraltar, A City Under Siege** exhibition, in the first British building on the Rock (originally an ammunition store), and the **Tower of Homage**, the remains of Gibraltar's Muslim castle built in 1333.

Dolphins

The Bahía de Algeciras has a sizeable year-round population of dolphins and at least six boats run dolphin-spotting trips. From about April to September most boats make two or more daily trips; at other times of year there's usually at least one in daily operation. Most of the boats go from Watergardens Quay or the adjacent Marina Bay, north-west of the town centre. Trips last about 2½ hours and the cost per adult ranges from £11.50 to £20. Children can go for about half price. You'll be unlucky if you don't get plenty of close-up dolphin contact, and you may even come across whales. Tourist offices have full details of the boats.

Organised Tours

Taxi drivers will take you on a 1½ hour 'Official Rock Tour' of Gibraltar's main sights for £20 plus the cost of entry to the Upper Rock Nature Reserve. Most drivers are knowledgeable. Many travel agents run tours of the same sights for £10. Several travel agents, including Tourafrica (☎ 77666), ICC

Building, Main St, and Bland Travel (see Money under Information), offer day trips to Tangier for £35 to £44.

Places to Stay

The independent *Emile Youth Hostel* (☎ 51106) at Montagu Bastionon Line Wall Rd, has 43 places in two to eight-person rooms, for £10 including continental breakfast. There are showers, a TV/sitting room and an outside patio. The *Toc H Hostel* (☎ 73431), a ramshackle old place tucked into the city walls at the southern end of Line Wall Rd, is the cheapest place with beds at £5 a night or £20 a week and cold showers. A reader wrote to tell us that the *Gibraltar Motorcycle Club* (☎ 79049, luisbike@gibnyex.gi), 6 East Side Road, has free bunk beds for travelling motorcyclists in a building with adjacent showers and toilets. A donation to club funds is invited.

The *Queen's Hotel* (☎ 74000) at 1 Boyd St has a restaurant, bar, games room, and singles/doubles at £16/24, or £20/36 with private bath or shower. Reduced rates of £14/20 and £16/24 are offered for students and young travellers. All rates include English breakfast. The *Cannon Hotel* (☎ 51711), at 9 Cannon Lane, also has decent rooms, each sharing a bathroom with one other room, for £20/30 including English breakfast.

Rooms at the *Bristol Hotel* (☎ 76800), 10 Cathedral Square, are pleasant enough and a decent size, with TV and bathroom, but nothing special for the price of £47/61 interior or £51/66 exterior. The *Continental Hotel* (☎ 76900), at 1 Engineer Lane, is cosier, with air-con rooms at £42/55 including continental breakfast.

Gibraltar has two competing luxury hotels with over 100 rooms each. The *Eliott Hotel* (☎ 70500), centrally placed at 2 Governor's Parade, charges £120 to £200 per room. The *Rock Hotel* (☎ 73000), up the hill a bit at 3 Europa Rd, has a bit more colonial history – past guests include Winston Churchill and Noel Coward – and singles/doubles from £65/85 to £105/110 include English breakfast. Both hotels have good restaurants and pools.

GIBRALTAR

If Gibraltar prices don't grab you there are some economical options in the Spanish border town of La Línea (see the Cádiz Province chapter).

Places to Eat

Most of the many pubs in town do typical British pub meals. One of the best is *The Clipper* at 78B Irish Town, where a generous serve of fish and chips and a pint of beer will set you back £6. *Three Roses Bar* at 60 Governor's St does an all-day breakfast of two eggs, sausage, bacon, fried bread, beans, tomato and mushrooms for £3.20. The *Cannon Bar*, Cannon Lane 27, does some of the best fish and chips in town, with big portions for £4.50. At the popular *Piccadilly Gardens* pub on Rosia Rd you can sit out in the garden and have a three-course lunch for £6.

Maxi Manger on Main St is a good fast-food spot with burgers (including a veggie version) for £1.75 and calamari or fish and chips for £3.50. For a restaurant meal, the chic *House of Sacarello*, 57 Irish Town, is a good bet, with good soups at around £2 and some excellent daily specials from £4.95 to £5.75. You can also linger over a £7.50 afternoon tea for two between 3 and 7.30 pm. The Indian food at the *Viceroy of India*, 9/11 Horse Barrack Court, is usually pretty good: it has a three-course lunch special for £6.75. À la carte there are vegetarian dishes for £2 to £3, and main courses from £6 to £10. *The Piazza*, 156 Main St, does decent burgers and pizzas for £4.50 to £6, and fish and meat main courses from £5.50 to £8. On Friday and Saturday nights it has live music (blues and country when we last checked). *Minister's Restaurant*, 310 Main St, does good servings of fish and seafood for £7.50 to £9, or fish, meat or pasta with chips or salad from £7.

The English Tea Room, 9 Market Lane, open from 9 am to 7 pm, isn't much to look at but the scones, jam and cream are great, and only £1.80 a serve (tea included!). There are also lunchtime specials from £3 to £6.50.

A little out of the centre, there's a line of pleasant waterside cafés and restaurants at Marina Bay. Among them is *Bianca's* and its restaurant is open from noon to 2.45 pm and 7.30 to 10.45 pm. It has fish and meat main dishes from £6 to £10 and pasta or burgers for around £5.

Things to Buy

British expats from the Costa del Sol come to Gibraltar to stock up on British goods at cheaper prices than in Spain. Gibraltar has lots of British high street chain stores, such as Marks & Spencer, Mothercare and The Body Shop (all on Main St) and Safeway (in the Europort development at the northern end of the main harbour). There are even a few Indian corner shops on streets such as Irish Town. Shops are normally open Monday to Friday from 9 am to 7.30 pm and on Saturday morning.

Getting There & Away

The border is open 24 hours daily.

Air GB Airways (☎ 79300, in Britain it's ☎ 0345 222111) flies daily to/from London. Return fares from London range from around £160 to more than double that, depending on season and offers. From Gibraltar, one-way/return fares are about £100/180. GB Airways also has flights to Casablanca most days for £99/146 one-way/return.

Monarch Airlines (☎ 47477, in Britain ☎ 01582-398333) flies up to four times a week to/from Luton. Fares range from £65 to £115 one way (return fares are double).

In Gibraltar the airline offices are at the airport; or book through travel agents.

Bus Excursion buses run Monday to Friday from bus stations in Costa del Sol resorts to Gibraltar, giving you about six hours in Gibraltar, for a return fare of, for example, 1350 ptas from Marbella. Otherwise there are no regular buses to Gibraltar itself. However, the bus station in La Línea (see the Cádiz Province chapter) is only a five-minute walk from the border, from which there are ample buses into Gibraltar town centre (see the Getting Around section).

Car & Motorcycle Vehicle queues at the border often make it less time-consuming to park in La Línea, then walk across the border. To take a car into Gibraltar you need an insurance certificate, registration document, nationality plate and driving licence. Your drive on the right, as in Spain. At the time of writing petrol in Gibraltar was about 10% cheaper than in Spain.

Ferry The ferry between Gibraltar and Tangier takes two hours, and normally runs three times a week each way. The fare is £18/30 one way/return per person and £40/80 per car. In Gibraltar, you can buy tickets at Tourafrica (☎ 77666), ICC Building on Main St. Ferries from Algeciras are more frequent and cheaper.

Getting Around

The 1.5km walk from the border to the town centre is quite fun as it crosses the airport runway. A left turn off Corral Rd will take you through the pedestrians-only Landport Tunnel (once the only land entry through Gibraltar's walls) into Grand Casemates Square. Alternatively, bus Nos 3 and 9 go from the border into town about every 15 minutes. No 9 goes to Market Place and runs between 8 am and 9 pm. No 3 runs between 7.15 am and 9.30 pm, stops at Cathedral Square and the bottom cable-car station, then goes up Europa Rd and on to Europa Point at the southern end of the Rock. Bus No 10 runs from the border to Europort (with a stop at the Safeway supermarket), then via Queens Way to Reclamation Rd near the town centre. On Sunday bus services are limited. All buses are 40p or 100 ptas a ride.

All of Gibraltar can be covered on foot and much of it (including the upper rock) by car or motorcycle, but there are other options worth considering. Most obvious is the cable car which, weather permitting, leaves its lower station on Red Sands Rd Monday to Saturday every few minutes between 9.30 am and 5.15 pm. Fares are £3.65/4.90 one way/return (£1.80/2.45 for under-11s), including entry to the Upper Rock Nature Reserve, Apes' Den and St Michael's Cave. For the Apes' Den, disembark at the middle station. You can get back on to go up to the top station.

Málaga Province

This southern province – many people's point of entry into Andalucía – is much more than the infamous Costa del Sol, Spain's most densely packed holiday coast. Málaga city is Andalucía's second biggest and one of its most vibrant, with a spectacularly festive August *feria*. Inland there are intriguing old towns such as Ronda and Antequera to explore, and lots of rugged hill country and old-fashioned white villages, with good walking in areas like the Sierra de las Nieves near Ronda and La Axarquía, east of Málaga.

MÁLAGA

Málaga, the capital of the Costa del Sol yet mercifully distinct from it, is ignored by many visitors who slip straight off from the airport to the resort towns. But this thriving, cosmopolitan, southern port city of 549,000 people is well worth investigating. Its centre, with the backdrop of a sparkling blue Mediterranean, has wide, leafy boulevards, some charmingly dilapidated streets and buildings, good museums and a handful of impressive monuments. A lively city with a liberal tradition, Málaga stays open late and inspires fierce devotion among its citizens.

History

Early Phoenician traders are credited with planting the area's first vineyards. The city flourished in the Muslim era, especially under the Granada taifa in the 11th century and the later Emirate of Granada. Its fall to the Christians in 1487 was a big nail in the emirate's coffin.

The expulsion of the Moriscos, who had been active in agriculture, contributed to famine in the 17th century but prosperity arrived in the 19th century with a dynamic middle class led by the Larios and Heredia families who founded textile factories, sugar mills, shipyards and steel mills. The popularity of Málaga dessert wine in Victorian England was also profitable until a bug

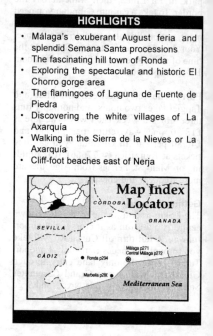

devastated the vineyards around the city. Málaga's first tourism drive helped to compensate: the city had already been popularised by the Romantic movement and in the 1920s it became the favourite winter resort of rich *madrileños*.

In the civil war, Málaga, which had a firm tradition of anarchism and syndicalism, was initially a Republican stronghold. Hundreds of Nationalist sympathisers were killed and churches and convents burnt. The city was then bombed by Italian planes before falling in February 1937 to the Nationalists. Particularly vicious reprisals followed.

In the 1960s Franco promoted tourism on the Costa del Sol and Málaga has since flourished; its industry is healthy, too, though youth unemployment is high.

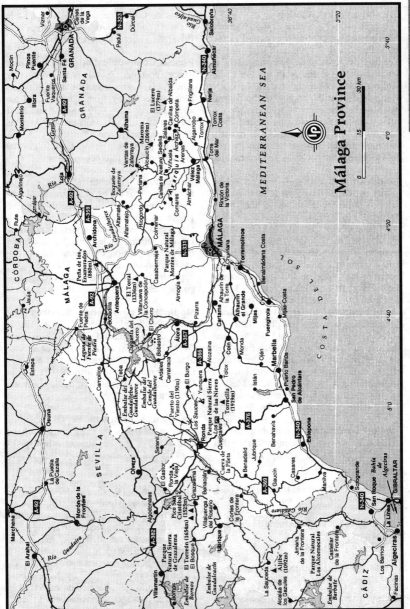

Málaga Province

MEDITERRANEAN SEA

Orientation & Information

The central thoroughfare is the Alameda Principal which continues eastward as the leafy Paseo del Parque and westward as Avenida de Andalucía. The main streets heading north off the Alameda are Calle Molina Lario, with the cathedral; Calle Marqués de Larios, ending at the central Plaza de la Constitución around which is what remains of the old quarter; and Calle Puerta del Mar, the centre of the modern shopping district. On the hill above Paseo del Parque are the Alcazaba and Gibralfaro.

Tourist Offices Málaga is well served by tourist offices. The Junta de Andalucía's helpful, multilingual tourist office (☎ 95 221 34 45) is at Pasaje Chinitas 4, an alley off Plaza de la Constitución. It's open Monday to Friday from 9 am to 7 pm, on Saturday from 10 am to 7 pm and Sunday from 10 am to 2 pm. The main municipal tourist office (☎ 95 260 44 10) is in a lovely old building at Avenida de Cervantes 1, just off Paseo del Parque. Its efficient staff have plenty of printed material to give away, though city maps cost 100 ptas. Hours are Monday to Friday from 8.15 am to 2 pm and 4.30 to 7 pm and on Saturday from 9.30 am to 1.30 pm. There are smaller tourist offices at the airport and bus station, plus information kiosks on Plaza de la Merced and outside the post office, and a couple of roving tourist information buses.

Foreign Consulates The nearest US and Irish consulates are in Fuengirola (see that section). Consulates in Málaga include:

Canada
  (☎ 95 222 33 46) Edificio Horizonte, 1st floor, Calle Cervantes
France
  (☎ 95 222 65 90) Calle Duquesa de Parcent 8
Germany
  (☎ 95 222 78 66) Paseo del Limonar 26
UK
  (☎ 95 221 75 71) Calle Duquesa de Parcent 8

Money There are plenty of banks with ATMs on Calle Puerta del Mar and Calle Marqués de Larios. American Express is at Rosaleda Viajero, Calle Especerías 10.

Post & Communications The main post office (postcode 29080) is at Avenida de Andalucía 1. It's open for most services Monday to Friday from 8 am to 8.30 pm and Saturday from 9.30 am to 2 pm. Near the post office, Ciber Málaga Café, Avenida de Andalucía 11, and Chat Chat Chat on Calle Medellín both charge from 500 to 800 ptas an hour for Internet connections.

Bookshops Atlante Mapas, Calle Echegaray 7, is an excellent source of city and hiking maps and Spanish-language guidebooks for most parts of Andalucía; it also sells a wide range of Lonely Planet titles. Librería Jabega, Calle Santa María 17, and Librería de Ocasión, Calle Sancha de Lara 9, has English-language novels. El Corte Inglés, opposite the post office, stocks English-language press, guides, novels and maps.

Medical & Emergency Services The Policía Nacional (☎ 95 221 13 02) are at Plaza de la Aduana 1. The Policía Local (☎ 95 260 00 92) are at Avenida de la Rosaleda 19 on the eastern side of the Río Guadalmedina. The Hospital Cruz Roja (☎ 95 225 04 50) is at Avenida Jorge Silvela 64, 1km north.

Dangers & Annoyances Take care of your valuables in the dark corners of the centre and at the bus station, where pickpockets and bag-snatchers operate.

Alcazaba

The Alcazaba (☎ 95 221 60 05) is the Muslim palace-fortress at the lower, western end of the hill that dominates the city centre. It looks splendid in spring when the jacaranda trees at its base are in full purple bloom. With a double wall and a large number of defensive towers, the Alcazaba was begun in 1057 by the fearsome Granada taifa ruler Badis. The entrance has staggered passages to make access difficult.

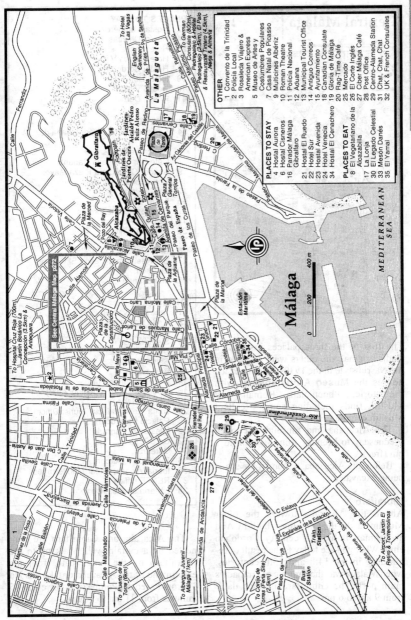

Málaga

MEDITERRANEAN SEA

0   200   400 m

See Central Málaga Map p272

OTHER
1 Convento de la Trinidad
2 Policía Local
3 Rosaleda Viajero &
   American Express
5 Museo de Artes y
   Costumbres Populares
7 Casa Natal de Picasso
9 Multicines Albéniz
10 Roman Theatre
11 Policía Nacional
12 Aduana
13 Municipal Tourist Office
14 Antiguo Correos
15 Ayuntamiento
18 Canadian Consulate
19 Gloria de Málaga
20 Rag-Time Café
25 Mercado
26 El Corte Inglés
27 Cíber Málaga Café
28 Post Office
29 Centro-Alameda Station
31 Chat, Chat, Chat
32 UK & French Consulates

PLACES TO STAY
4 Hostal Aurora
6 Hostal Cisneros
16 Parador Málaga
   Gibralfaro
21 Hostal El Ruedo
22 Hotel Sur
23 Hostal Avenida
24 Hotel Venecia
34 Hostal El Cenachero

PLACES TO EAT
8 El Vegetariano de la
   Alcazabilla
17 La Lonja
30 El Legado Celestial
33 Mesón Danés
35 El Yamal

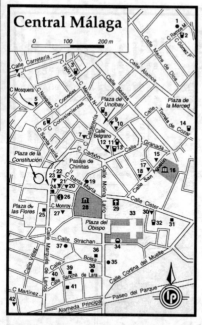

Central Málaga

0   100   200 m

PLACES TO STAY
22 Hostal Lampérez
24 Hostal Chinitas
25 Hotel Larios
31 Hotel Carlos V
36 Hostal Córdoba
39 Hotel Don Curro
40 Hostal Victoria
41 Hostal Derby

PLACES TO EAT
4 Sociedad Naturo-Vegetariana de Málaga
5 Mesón Las Bijas
7 Café Bar La Nueva Cabaña
9 Asador Cervecería Plaza Mayor
10 Cervecería Uncibay
12 La Cancela
15 La Tetería
17 Bar Restaurant Tormes
18 La Casa Abuela
20 Rincón Chinitas
21 Málaga Siempre Bar
23 Café Central
27 Bar Restaurant Mesón El Chinitas
30 El Jardín
42 Marisquerías

OTHER
1 Teatro Cervantes
2 Onda Passadena Jazz
3 ZZ Pub
6 Siempre Asi
8 Discoteca Anden
11 Salsa
13 Barsovia
14 Morrisey's Irish Pub
16 Museo Picasso (opening 2000)
19 Librería Jabega
26 Junta de Andalucía Tourist Office
28 Palacio Episcopal
29 Iglesia del Sagrario
32 Café Teatro
33 Catedral
34 Bus Stop to Airport
35 Iberia; Aviaco; Binter Mediterráneo
37 RENFE Office
38 Librería de Ocasión

The first of the three palaces inside is a Badis original; the others were restored in the Nasrid style in the 1930s. The Alcazaba houses the **Museo Arqueológico**, with prehistoric, Phoenician, Roman and Muslim finds including some excellent Muslim ceramics.

The Alcazaba and museum are open Wednesday to Monday from 8.30 am to 7 pm (free).

Below the Alcazaba, a Roman theatre is being excavated.

Gibralfaro

Above the Alcazaba towers the older Muslim castle, the Gibralfaro, built by Abd ar-Rahman I, the 8th century Cordoban emir. What you see today is the result of re-building in the 14th and 15th centuries, when Málaga was the Emirate of Granada's main port. The Gibralfaro is open daily from 9 am to 6 pm.

The Alcazaba and Gibralfaro are connected by a curtain wall. Walk up to the Gibralfaro by the rough path from the eastern end of the Alcazaba or take bus No 35 from Paseo del Parque (roughly every 45 minutes from 11 am to 7 pm).

Catedral

Málaga's cathedral on Calle Molina Lario was begun in the 16th century on the site of the former main mosque and building continued for two centuries. Like many of Málaga's old buildings, it's falling down but restoration has recently begun after a big public fund-raising effort. The cathedral is known locally as La Manquita (the One-Armed) owing to the fact that only the west tower was ever completed. Money allocated for the east tower was given instead to the campaign against the British in the American War of Independence. Recently, in belated thanks, the Costa del Sol's American Society handed over money towards the current repairs. The cathedral has an 18th century baroque façade but the inside is both Gothic and Renaissance. Of most interest are the finely carved 17th century wooden choir stalls by Pedro de Mena. The cathedral and attached museum are open Monday to Saturday from 10 am to 12.45 pm and 4 to 6.45 pm (200 ptas).

On the northern side of the cathedral is the separate, late Gothic **Iglesia del Sagrario** with a splendid portal and a gilded retablo.

Palacio Episcopal

Opposite the cathedral on Plaza del Obispo is the 18th century bishop's palace which has one of the most impressive façades in the city. Inside is a beautiful patio with an imperial-type staircase. The former palace is now used for art exhibitions.

Museo Picasso & Museo de Bellas Artes

The lovely 16th century Palacio de los Condes de Buenavista on Calle San Agustín is being converted into an important new museum devoted to Málaga-born Pablo Picasso. The museum will be based on a large donation of work by the artist's daughter-in-law Christine Ruiz-Picasso. and is due to open on 28 February 2000.

Meanwhile, Málaga's Museo de Bellas Artes (Fine Arts Museum), which had occupied the building since 1961, is to move

to another site. Debate about the site has raged in the city but, at the time of writing, the Convento de la Trinidad west of the Río Guadalmedina appeared to have been chosen. The museum's extensive collection concentrates on work by *malagueños* though others such as Ribera, Zurbarán, Murillo and Cano are also well represented.

Casa Natal de Picasso

Picasso fans might like to stop by the house where he was born at Plaza de la Merced 15. The recently restored house (☎ 95 221 50 05) is operated by the Fundación Picasso which organises cultural events in memory of the painter. But there's not a lot to see: a few Picasso sketches and paintings, articles and a video about his life. Most visitors are academics. Current opening times are Monday to Friday from 11 am to 2 pm and 5 to 8 pm.

Alameda Principal & Paseo del Parque

The Alameda Principal, now a busy thoroughfare, was created in the late 18th century as a boulevard on what were the sands of the Guadalmedina estuary. Until the Paseo del Parque was built it was the city's main gathering and strolling place. It's adorned with old trees from the Americas and lined with 18th and 19th century buildings.

In the 1890s the palm-lined Paseo del Parque, an extension of the Alameda, was built on land reclaimed from the sea. Over time the garden along its southern side, Paseo de España, has been filled with rare and exotic tropical plants, making a pleasant refuge from the bustle of the city. On the paseo's northern side are several notable buildings: the elegant 18th century **Aduana** (Customs House) fronted by rows of tall palms, which originally had the sea lapping at its doors (it's now government offices); the former **Casita del Jardinero**, the paseo gardener's cottage (now the municipal tourist office); the early 20th century **Antiguo Correos** (Old Post Office); and the striking 20th century neobaroque **Ayuntamiento** (City Hall).

Pasaje de Chinitas

In the late 19th century the bars in this passage off the eastern side of Plaza de la Constitución were popular after-work meeting places for Málaga's businessmen, who would later move on to the Café de Chinitas, one of the most famous of the flamenco *cafés cantante* (see Music in Facts about Andalucía). In the 1920s and 1930s, the still-going-strong Café de Chinitas attracted bullfighters, stage performers, artists and writers, including Federico García Lorca, whose friend Juan Breva, a famous singer of *malagueñas*, sang there frequently. Today, the Café de Chinitas is a fabric shop with a plaque above the door verifying its past.

Museo de Artes y Populares

The Museum of Popular Arts & Customs (☎ 95 221 71 37), housed in a 17th century inn on Pasillo de Santa Isabel, is a fun place to visit, especially for children. The collection focuses on everyday life and includes items connected with farming and fishing. Note the glass cabinets containing painted clay figures *(barros)* of the highwayman, the couple dancing, the rider from Ronda and other characters from malagueño folklore. Barros of this type, particularly the *biznagero* (jasmine seller) and *cenachero* (fishmonger), fascinated 19th and early 20th century travellers influenced by the Romantic movement. The museum is open Monday to Friday from 10 am to 1.30 pm and 4 to 7 pm (200 ptas, students and children under 14 free).

English Cemetery

The leafy English Cemetery, founded in 1829, is on Paseo de Reding, just beyond the Plaza de Toros. (Before 1829, non-Catholic bodies were buried at night upright in the sand at the foot of the beach. Corpses were liable to be ravaged by dogs, or washed out to sea or back to shore.) Some of the graves and monuments have fascinating inscriptions. A variety of people of many nationalities, from poets to consuls to children, are buried here. In the far corner,

the original walled inner cemetery contains many graves covered in cockle shells. Between here and the main gates is St George's Anglican church, which has regular Sunday services.

The cemetery is open daily from 8 am to 1 pm and 2.30 to 6 pm Monday to Friday.

Jardín Ornitológico y Botánico El Retiro

A few kilometres west of the city in Churriana, on the C-344 to Alhaurín de la Torre, are the lovely El Retiro gardens and bird park (☎ 95 262 16 00). The gardens were developed and landscaped by the Condes de Buenavista and other owners in the 18th century. They retain much of their original design which incorporated English, Italian baroque and French styles. There are marble classical statues, lovely fountains and buildings and an impressive collection of exotic birds, some in aviaries, some roaming freely. The gardens are open daily from 9 am to 6 pm. Entry is a steep 1250 ptas (children 750 ptas). To get there take one of the hourly buses bound for Alhaurín de la Torre from Málaga bus station.

Jardín Botánico La Concepción

Four kilometres north of the city centre, the wonderful, largely tropical La Concepción gardens (☎ 95 225 21 48) have a more modest entry fee (400 ptas, children 200 ptas). In the 1850s, Englishwoman Amalia Livermore and her Spanish husband, Jorge Loring Oyarzábal, began collecting plants from all over the world to establish the gardens. The gardens feature towering trees (including hundreds of palms) and spectacular splashes of colour provided by seasonal blooms: in spring, purple wisteria flowers creep up the trunks of exotic palms. Opening hours are Tuesday to Sunday from 10 am to 9 pm in summer (to 5.30 pm in winter). Visits are by 1½- hour guided tour, with the last beginning 1½ hours before closing time.

By car, take the N-331 Antequera road north from the Málaga ring road (N-340) to Km 166 and follow signs. On Saturday,

Sunday and holidays there are buses from Málaga's Alameda to La Concepción.

Language Courses

We've had good reports about Spanish courses run by the Universidad de Málaga (☎ 95 227 82 11, fax 95 227 97 12). Two-week intensive courses cost around 45,000 ptas, four-week courses 82,000 ptas and accommodation with a Spanish family (3000 ptas per day) can be arranged. For more information, write to Universidad de Málaga, Cursos de Español para Extranjeros, Apartado 310, 29080 Málaga. There are at least 24 private language schools in Málaga, several charging around 57,000 ptas a month; the main tourist offices can help with information.

Special Events

March/April

Semana Santa

Holy Week in Málaga is second only to Sevilla in splendour and solemnity. Each night from Palm Sunday to Good Friday, six or seven *cofradías* bear their holy images for several hours through the city, watched, and in some cases followed, by big crowds. Málaga's floats *(tronos)* are large and heavy and are borne on long poles extending in front and behind, with teams of up to 150 carriers (in contrast to Sevilla, where the bearers are underneath the float). On the Monday, the procession following the image of Jesús Cautivo (Christ taken Prisoner) is joined by as many as 25,000 people, some barefooted, hooded or with their ankles in chains. Events reach their climax on Good Friday. A good place to watch is the Alameda Principal, where the processions pass through between about 7 pm and midnight.

May

World Dance

The port area is turned into a massive dance venue for one Saturday night, with more than 100,000 people enjoying live international dance music.

Mid-August

Feria de Málaga

Málaga's nine-day August Fair, launched by a huge fireworks show at midnight on the opening Friday, is the biggest and most ebullient of Andalucía's summer ferias. From late morning till about 7 pm, especially on the two

GERRY REILLY

Up she goes – raising the throne of the Virgin, Easter Sunday, Cómpeta, La Axarquía

Saturdays, celebrations overwhelm the city centre, with music and dancing in the packed streets and bars and horses and riders in their finery parading round a circuit of streets. The action is thickest around Plaza Uncibay, Plaza de la Constitución and the streets to its north, and on Calle Marqués de Larios. At night the action switches to the large feria site at Cortijo de Torres, 4km south-west of the centre, with fairground rides and lots more music and dancing, including nightly concerts by pop, rock, flamenco and other performers. Special buses run from all over the city to the feria site. Málaga also stages its main bullfight season during the feria. Tourist offices have programs of feria events.

28 December
Fiesta Mayor de Verdiales
Thousands gather at Puerto de la Torre on the Almogía road on the north-western outskirts of the city, for a grand gathering of *verdiales* groups, who perform an exhilarating type of folk music and dance unique to the Málaga area. The music sounds like a kind of Celtic/Gypsy mix, with lots of high-pitched fiddle and tambourine-type percussion. It accompanies intricate, flag-waving dances and participants wear colourful, flowery hats. Bus No 21 from the Alameda Principal goes to Puerto de la Torre.

Places to Stay – Budget
Youth Hostel The *Albergue Juvenil Málaga* (☎ 95 230 85 00) at Plaza Pío XII, 1.5km west of the centre and a couple of blocks north of Avenida de Andalucía, is inconvenient for the centre but on the right side of town for the bus and train stations. It has 100 places, all in double rooms. Bus No 18 from the Alameda Principal along Avenida de Andalucía will take you most of the way.

Hostales Most of Málaga's hostales are in the blocks north and south of the Alameda Principal. Budget rooms are on the whole tatty and the cathedral bells may toll on the quarter-hour through the night, a recipe for disturbed sleep. Expect to pay more than the prices quoted during July, August and Semana Santa.

North of the Alameda *Hostal Chinitas* (☎ 95 221 46 83) at Pasaje Chinitas 2, off Plaza de la Constitución, is run by a friendly family and has clean, basic singles/doubles for 1700/3400 ptas plus IVA. Close by, *Hostal Lampérez* (☎ 95 221 94 84), at Calle Santa María 6, costs 1500/2500 ptas. Rooms vary; the bathroom is a bit grim.

West of Plaza de la Constitución, *Hostal Aurora* (☎ 95 222 40 04), Calle Muro de Puerta Nueva 1 off Calle Cisneros, has six clean, attractive rooms for 2300/4500 ptas plus IVA. The owners are welcoming. *Hostal Cisneros* (☎ 95 221 26 33), Calle Cisneros 7, is spotless and friendly. Rooms are 2500/4500 ptas, or 5500 ptas for doubles with bath, all plus IVA.

Close to the Alameda Principal, the friendly *Hostal Derby* (☎ 95 222 13 01), Calle San Juan de Dios 1, has spacious rooms with big windows and private bath from 3200/4500 ptas. One block north, Calle Bolsa has yet more possibilities. The homey *Hostal Córdoba* (☎ 95 221 44 69) at No 9 has rooms with shared bath from 1300/2500 ptas.

South of the Alameda *Hostal Avenida* (☎ 95 221 77 28), Alameda Principal 5, has clean, basic rooms with shared bath at 1500/2900 ptas plus IVA or doubles with private bath for 3850 ptas plus IVA. *Hostal El Ruedo* (☎ 95 221 58 20), Calle Trinidad Grund 3, one block south of the Alameda Principal, is an old place with friendly owners and rooms at 1700/3200 ptas. *Hostal El Cenachero* (☎ 95 222 40 88), Calle Barroso 5, is a good bet at 3200/4900 ptas for rooms with bath, or doubles for 3700 ptas with shared bath.

Places to Stay – Mid-Range
For all places, except Hotel Carlos V, add IVA to these prices. Expect to pay more in July and August. All have private bathroom and TV.

Just east of the cathedral, *Hotel Carlos V* (☎ 95 221 51 27), Calle Cister 10, has comfortable singles/doubles for 3600/7000 ptas. The popular *Hostal Victoria* (☎ 95 222 42 24), Calle Sancha de Lara 3, has 16 rooms at 4000/5900 ptas. On the southern side of the Alameda, *Hotel Venecia* (☎ 95 221 36 36), Alameda Principal 9, and *Hotel Sur* (☎ 95 222 48 03), Calle Trinidad Grund 13, have similar rates. About 4km east of the centre near the beach, *Hostal Pedregalejo* (☎ 95 229 32 18), Calle Conde de las Navas 9, has attractive, comfortable rooms for 4300/6300 ptas.

Places to Stay – Top End
Add IVA to all prices. In the centre, *Hotel Larios* (☎ 95 222 22 00), Calle Marqués de Larios 2, has doubles for 17,000 ptas (rising to a whopping 35,000 ptas during Semana Santa). The large *Hotel Don Curro* (☎ 95 222 72 00), Calle Sancha de Lara 9, has singles/doubles from 8500/12,000 ptas. One kilometre east of Paseo del Parque, *Hotel Las Vegas* (☎ 95 221 77 12), Paseo de Sancha 22, has rooms for 6900/9800 ptas year-round and the added attractions of a pool and proximity to the beach.

The *Parador Málaga Gibralfaro* (☎ 95 222 19 02), with an unbeatable location on the Gibralfaro hill, has recently been refurbished and also has a pool. Doubles are 16,500 ptas but there are winter discounts.

Places to Eat
Malagueño cuisine concentrates on fish fried quickly in olive oil. *Fritura malagueño* consists of fried fish, anchovies and squid. Cold soups are popular. As well as *gazpacho*, in the tomato season, and *sopa de ajo* (garlic soup), try *sopa de almendra con uvas* (almond soup with grapes).

Seafood Sample fish dishes at the *marisquerías* with outside tables on slightly seedy Calle Comisario, off the northern side of the Alameda Principal, or at *Rincón Chinitas* on Pasaje Chinitas, where raciones of fried fish cost 700 ptas or tortillitas 300 ptas. The more up-market *La Lonja*, Calle Cervantes 5, immediately east of the bullring, does a wide range of fish and seafood dishes. The seafront eateries at Pedregalejo, 4.5km east of the centre, do good fish, or you could continue 1km east to *Restaurante Tintero* on the seafront at Playas del Dedo,

El Palo, where plates of fish and seafood (most 600 ptas) are brought out by the waiters and you shout for what you want. The food is not exquisite (it's best when hot) but the place is lively and great fun.

Near Plaza de la Constitución *Café Central* on the busy east side of the plaza is a noisy local favourite; its coffee will satisfy even hardened caffeine addicts. Prices for food are reasonable and there's plenty of choice. Round the corner on Pasaje Chinitas, *Málaga Siempre Bar* serves up a good range of tapas (150 ptas including a glass of beer) and coffee. Nearby, *Bar Restaurante Mesón El Chinitas* on Calle Monroy is a fancy place with prices to match. The long menu lists many typical *andaluz* dishes (from 1250 to 2100 ptas), while the *menú* is 1975 ptas, all plus IVA.

Café Bar La Nueva Cabaña on Calle Calderería, open till late on weekdays and till 4 pm on weekends, is good for tea, coffee and pastries. *La Cancela*, nearby at Calle Belgrano 5, has an appetising menu at moderate prices.

There are several popular tapas bars on and around nearby Plaza de Uncibay. *Cervecería Uncibay* at No 5 has *embutidos* (sausages), cheeses, patés and *pulpo a la gallega* (Galician-style octopus), while *Asador Cervecería Plaza Mayor* at No 9 specialises in *asados* (roasted meats). A few streets north-west at Calle Mosquera 7, *Meson las Bijas* does *carnes a la brasa* (grilled meats), *revueltos* (scrambled egg concoctions), *migas* (see food glossary) and more.

Near the Catedral *El Jardín* on the corner of Calle Cister and Calle Cañón, with a pleasant terrace facing the cathedral, has a fancy interior and an elaborate *carta* with lots of seafood; menús are 1100 ptas and 1170 ptas, while platos combinados are 600 to 1000 ptas. Open daily from 8 am to late, it's a pleasant spot for your morning coffee and tostada. *La Casa Abuela* on the corner of Calle Echegaray and Calle San Agustín is an alternative-type place with herbal teas, pure juices and filled baguettes (300 to 400 ptas). *La Tetería* on Calle San Agustín, opposite the future Museo Picasso, does all manner of teas, including an '*antidepresivo*', plus crêpes, pastries and sorbets. Open daily from 4 pm until late, it's popular with students. *Bar Restaurante Tormes* at Calle San Agustín 13 is open for late breakfast, lunch and dinner; the three-course menú is 1100 ptas.

Near the Market The colourful *Mercado Central*, north of the Alameda Principal, built in the 19th century in a mudéjar-influenced style and retaining a 14th century arch, has terrific fresh produce. Nearby, there are loads of cafés on pedestrian Calle Herredería del Rey. These open early and pack up promptly at 1 pm. There are also some atmospheric *bars* serving local wine from barrels, among them one on the corner of Calles Puerta del Mar and Herredería del Rey.

South of the Alameda Head for this area if you're after something different from the usual fare. *El Yamal* at Calle Blasco de Garay 3 is a relaxed place cooking up excellent Moroccan food in traditional *tajines*, earthenware dishes with pointed lids: cous cous with vegetables costs 1100 ptas; and a tasty salad with hummus and flat bread is 600 ptas. It's closed Sunday evening. *Mesón Danés*, Calle Barroso 5, offers Spanish and Danish food; the menú is 950 ptas (closed Sunday).

Vegetarian Vegetarians should try *Sociedad Naturo-Vegetariana de Málaga*, at Calle Carretería 82 (1st floor), open for lunch. *El Vegetariano de la Alcazabilla*, Calle Pozo del Rey 5, opposite the Multicines Albéniz, has a good range of dishes, including a very nice Greek salad, wholemeal pasta, soyburgers and *empanadillas de espinacas* (spinach pies), all between 800 and 1100 ptas. On Calle Medellín behind the post office, *El Legado Celestial* is a vegetarian restaurant with a daily lunch and dinner buffet (800 ptas).

Entertainment

Three monthly publications – *Guía del Ocio* (200 ptas) available from kiosks, and *¿Qué Hacer? ¿Dónde Ir?* and *Málaga, Tan Cerca,* free from tourist offices – have entertainment listings. The Friday *Imagina* and Saturday *Fin de Semana* sections in *Sur* newspaper are also useful.

Live Music & Music Bars Nightlife in the centre clusters around Calle Granada, Plaza de Uncibay and Calle Beatas. *Barsovia* on little Calle Belgrano has recorded dance music (80s and 90s) and a dance floor that gets pretty crowded on weekends. It's open nightly till late. *Salsa*, on the corner of Calle Belgrano and Calle Méndez Núñez, has live salsa on Wednesday, from midnight to late, and occasional party nights. *Discoteca Anden* on Plaza Uncibay rages Thursday to Saturday from midnight to dawn. A few blocks further north, Calle Méndez Núñez becomes Calle Tejón y Rodríguez, where *ZZ Pub* has live music, mainly rock, several nights a week. Close by, *Siempre Asi*, Calle Convalecientes 5, a music bar with mostly Spanish music, has a good atmosphere and varied clientele (25 to 40). It's open Thursday to Sunday from 9.30 pm to 3.30 am. *Morrisey's Irish Pub* on Calle Granada, opposite the Iglesia de Santiago, has a relaxed atmosphere, low-key background music, and Irish beers. *Onda Passadena Jazz* on Calle Gómez Pallete, near Plaza de La Merced, has live jazz on Tuesday and live flamenco music on Thursday from 11 pm. Near the cathedral, *Café Teatro* on Calle Afligidos is a slightly offbeat place, good for a drink from 8.30 pm daily.

Rag-Time Café, Calle Reding 12 in La Malagueta, the area near the seafront immediately east of the centre, has blues, jazz or flamenco, depending on the night.

Pedregalejo, 4.5km east of the centre, with many bars and discos, buzzes until late on weekends and most nights in summer.

Other Málaga has several cinema complexes, such as *Multicines Astoria* on Plaza de la Merced, showing latest releases, and

Multicines Albéniz, Calle Alcazabilla 4, which screens international films with Spanish subtitles at 10 pm most nights (400 ptas).

The *Teatro Cervantes* on Calle Ramos Marín has a regular program of classical music, opera, dance and theatre.

Gloria de Málaga, Avenida Canovas del Castillo on the corner of Calle Cervantes, has a flamenco *tablao* most nights from 11 pm.

Getting There & Away

Air Málaga's busy airport (☎ 95 224 88 04, 95 204 88 04), the main international gateway to Andalucía, is 10km west of the centre, halfway to Torremolinos. See the introductory Getting There & Away chapter for information on international and domestic flights. The Málaga office of Iberia, Aviaco and Binter Mediterráneo (☎ 95 213 61 46) is at Calle Molina Lario 13. Air Europa (☎ 95 237 30 00) is at the airport.

The airport arrivals hall has a tourist office and ATMs giving cash pesetas on a wide variety of cards.

Bus The bus station (☎ 95 235 00 61) is on Paseo de los Tilos, 1km west of the centre. Lockers cost around 400 ptas a day.

There are frequent buses along the coast in both directions and several daily to inland towns including Antequera (470 ptas) and Ronda (1100 ptas). Other destinations include Sevilla (10 or more buses daily, 3½ hours, 2245 ptas), Córdoba (five daily, 2½ hours, 1515 ptas), Granada (up to 15 daily, 2½ hours, 1175 ptas), Murcia, Alicante, Valencia, Barcelona (18 hours, 8495 ptas), and Madrid (four or more daily, 8½ hours, 2629 to 4480 ptas). There are also buses to Germany, Switzerland, the UK, Portugal, France and the Netherlands.

Train The train station (☎ 95 236 02 02) is on Explanada de la Estación, around the corner from the bus station. The city centre RENFE office (☎ 95 221 41 27), Calle Strachan 2, is open Monday to Friday from 9 am to 1.30 pm and 4.30 to 7.30 pm. Lockers at the station cost around 400 ptas a day.

Talgo 200s (2200 ptas) take around two hours to get to Córdoba, to which there are also two InterCity trains (2¼ hours, 2000 ptas), two *regionales* (three hours, 1550 ptas) and two night trains (1900 to 2800 ptas). To Sevilla (three hours, 1825 ptas) there are four regionales daily, one requiring a change at Bobadilla. For Granada (three trains daily, three to four hours, 1520 to 2600 ptas) and Ronda you must change at Bobadilla.

Most days there are five trains to Madrid: three Talgo 200s (four hours, 6800 to 8000 ptas), one InterCity (6½ hours, 4800 ptas) and one 1st-class night train. For Valencia and Barcelona (14 hours, 6500 ptas) there are two or three 2nd-class trains daily, one of them overnight.

Car Rental Several agencies, many with cars for under 20,000 ptas a week, have desks at the airport – either in a room off the luggage-carousel hall or outside the arrivals hall.

Boat Trasmediterránea (☎ 95 222 48 83), Estación Marítima, Local E1, operates ferries daily (except Sunday from mid-September to mid-June) to/from Melilla. The trip takes 6½ hours and costs 3760 ptas for passengers and 15,355 ptas for a standard-size car. Buy your tickets at the Estación Marítima, more or less directly south of the town centre.

Getting Around

The Airport A taxi between the airport and city costs around 1200 ptas; from the airport to Fuengirola is 2600 ptas; and to Marbella it's about 5700 ptas.

Buses to the city centre (135 ptas) leave from the 'City Bus' stop outside the arrivals hall. They go about every half-hour between 6.30 am and 11.30 pm, stopping at Málaga's main bus and train stations en route. Going out to the airport you can pick up the buses on the southern side of the cathedral.

The Aeropuerto train station on the Málaga-Fuengirola line is a five-minute walk from the airport terminal: follow signs from the departures *(salidas)* hall. Trains run every half-hour from 7.15 am to 11.45 pm to Málaga's main station (11 minutes, 135 ptas) and the Centro-Alameda station on the west side of the Río Guadalmedina just south of Avenida de Andalucía. They also run every half-hour from 6.13 am to 10.43 pm to Torremolinos (10 minutes, 135 ptas) and Fuengirola (30 minutes, 230 ptas).

Departures from the city to the airport and beyond are every half-hour from 6 am to 10.30 pm. Fares are slightly higher on Saturday, Sunday and holidays.

Bus Useful buses around town (115 ptas) include No 4 from the train station to the centre and No 11 to Pedregalejo and El Palo from Paseo del Parque.

Taxi Taxis line up by the market on Calle Atarazanas and at the eastern end of Paseo del Parque. Fares within the centre, including to the train and bus stations, are around 500 ptas. Expect to pay 700 ptas to the Gibralfaro and 900 ptas to El Palo.

Costa del Sol

The much-maligned Costa del Sol might best be described as an international strip stuck on the bottom of Spain. It's home to perhaps 300,000 expatriates, particularly from Britain, Germany and Scandinavia. Comprising a string of resorts running south-west from Málaga towards Gibraltar, it is geared for, and incredibly popular with, package-deal tourists and the timeshare crowd, though it also manages to attract the jet set with some exclusive facilities. The Costa del Sol's recipe for success is sunshine, beaches (though with grey-brown sand, these are far from Andalucía's best), warm Mediterranean water and cheap package deals. There are plenty of nightlife and entertainment, and some good leisure attractions.

The resorts were once fishing villages but there's little evidence of that now. Instead, the Costa del Sol is arguably the finest example in Europe of how overdevelopment can ruin a spectacular landscape. It has become a series of townscapes from one end to the other, as *urbanización* after *urbanización* has raped the land which used to punctuate the towns. In summer all the towns heave with humanity.

Activities
The Costa del Sol is good for sport lovers, with nearly 40 golf clubs, several busy marinas, tennis and squash courts, riding schools, swimming pools and gymnasiums. Many beaches have facilities for water sports such as windsurfing, sailing, waterskiing and paragliding.

Accommodation
There's accommodation for every budget, including some 40 luxury hotels. But in August and the second half of July, it's an idea to ring ahead to avoid a weary trudge around seeing *completo* (full) signs. Prices given here are for the high season of July, August and, in some places, September. They usually come down sharply at other times.

The *costa* has about 15 camp sites, nearly all on or just off the N-340. If you want one near the beach, pick a stretch of the N-340 that runs along the coast.

Getting Around
A convenient train service links Málaga and its airport with Torremolinos, Arroyo de la Miel and Fuengirola and there are plenty of buses linking the costa towns. Bargain rental cars (16,000 to 20,000 ptas all-inclusive for a small car for a week) can be found from local firms in the main resorts.

TORREMOLINOS & AROUND
Margate-on-the-Med begins 5km southwest of Málaga airport. This concrete high-rise jungle is basically designed to squeeze as many paying customers as possible into the smallest possible space. Even in March there can be traffic jams of pedes-

Carretera de Confusión

Though a new *autopista* is being built from Málaga to Estepona, life on the Costa del Sol continues to revolve around the existing main road, the N-340, without which it is impossible to get from A to B. So pivotal is the N-340 to everyday life that even luxury hotels use the kilometre marks on it as their address. They may call it the CN-340 (Carretera Nacional 340), or the Carretera de Cádiz, or the Carretera Málaga-Cádiz, but they're all talking about the same road. It's a hair-raisingly busy road on which many drivers travel far too fast.

Many visitors don't spot their turn-off until the last minute, or miss it altogether, which leads to panic-stricken driving manouevres. The confusion is compounded by the fact that new bypasses mean there are now often two, in some places three, parallel roads all named N-340 or Carretera de Cádiz. The N-340 that's usually referred to in addresses is the one that forms Torremolinos' *inner* bypass, then runs through Fuengirola and Marbella. It is *not* the autovía which bypasses Torremolinos, Fuengirola and Marbella, as much as 4km from the coast in places, even though that road is also numbered N-340.

The Km numbers along the N-340 rise from west to east: Estepona is at Km 155 and central Marbella at Km 181. Km markers aside, undoubtedly the most useful sign for the motorist is 'Cambio de Sentido', indicating that you can change direction to get back to a turning you have missed. Meanwhile, beware of other motorists and watch out for cats, dogs and inebriated pedestrians.

Take special care when it's been raining, particularly after months of hot weather. You'd expect people to slow down in these conditions, but they don't.

The new autopista, due to open in 1999, will incorporate the existing Torremolinos, Fuengirola and Marbella bypasses and there will be tolls on some stretches, totalling about 1850 ptas (less in winter) for the Málaga-Estepona trip.

---

trians up and down the narrow lanes behind the main beach.

One of the few legacies of the past is an Islamic watchtower at the bottom end of Calle San Miguel, referred to in a 1947 decree as the Torre de los Molinos (Tower of the Mills), from which the resort takes its name. 'Torrie' led the Costa del Sol's mass tourist boom of the 1950s and 1960s. After that it lost ground to other resorts but has made an effort to spruce up in the 90s. A pleasant seafront walk, the Paseo Marítimo, extends for nearly 7km. Torremolinos does succeed in providing lots of inexpensive sun and fun for lots of people and, despite what you might have heard, there's even a bit of Spanish atmosphere too.

Orientation & Information

The coast here is oriented north-east to south-west. Coming from the Málaga direction, the main road through town is called first Calle Hoyo (where you'll find the bus station), then Avenida Palma de Mallorca after it passes Plaza Costa del Sol. Calle San Miguel, running most of the 500m from Plaza Costa del Sol down to the central beach, Playa del Bajondillo, is the main pedestrian artery. The train station is on Avenida Jesús Santos Rein, another pedestrian street which intersects Calle San Miguel 200m down. South-west of Playa del Bajondillo, around a small point, is Playa de la Carihuela, once the fishing quarter.

There are tourist offices in the ayuntamiento (☎ 95 237 95 51) on Plaza de la Independencia, a block inland from Plaza Costa del Sol; on Plaza de las Comunidades Autónomas (☎ 95 237 19 09), facing Playa del Bajondillo; and on Calle Borbollón Bajo in La Carihuela. All are open daily from 10 am to 2 pm except that the ayuntamiento office closes on Sunday. There's also a free tourist information line (☎ 900-18 14 70).

Things to See & Do

Beaches Torremolinos' beaches are wider, longer and a paler shade of grey-brown than most on the Costa del Sol – which is why they pull in so many thousands of people.

Aquapark Just inland of the N-340 (not the autovía) at Calle Cuba 10, Aquapark (☎ 95 238 88 88) has water slides, a wave pool etc in the typical water-fun-park mould. Opening hours vary with the seasons. A day ticket costs 1800 ptas (children 1125 ptas), with discounts for families of four or more.

Sea Life In the swish Puerto Deportivo (marina) at Benalmádena Costa, just west of Torremolinos, Sea Life (☎ 95 256 01 50) is a good modernistic aquarium of mainly Mediterranean marine creatures. A highlight is the walk-through shark and stingray tunnel. It's open daily from 10 am to 6 pm (975 ptas, children from four to 12 675 ptas). You can also visit a Mississippi river boat at the Puerto Deportivo.

Tivoli World The costa's biggest amusement park at Arroyo de la Miel, about 2km inland from Benalamádena Costa, is visited by about a million people a year. In addition to the multifarious rides and slides, Tivoli World (☎ 95 244 28 48) stages daily dance, music and children's shows and has a busy program of concerts by well-known Spanish performers. It's five minutes walk from Benalmádena-Arroyo de la Miel train station. In July and August it's open daily from 6 pm to 3 am; in early and late summer, it's open daily from 4 pm to 1 am; and during the rest of the year, it's open on Saturday, Sunday and holidays from 1 to 11 pm. Entry is 600 ptas, but you pay for your rides. A Supertivolino ticket (1500 ptas, 950 ptas in winter) gives unlimited rides on over 20 attractions.

Places to Stay

There are a couple of dozen hostales and hotels within a few minutes walk of the train and bus stations. The pleasant, 17-room *Hostal Micaela* (☎ 95 238 33 10), Calle Bajondillo 4, is close to Playa del Bajondillo and has doubles with bath for 4000 ptas plus IVA. Just across the Paseo Marítimo from the same beach, *Hostal Guadalupe* (☎ 95 238 19 37), Calle del Peligro 15, and *Pensión Beatriz* (☎ 95 238 51 10), next door, are smaller places charging 5000 ptas plus IVA. *Hostal Guillot* (☎ 95 238 01 44) at Pasaje Río Mundo 4, off Pasaje de Pizarro near Plaza Costa del Sol, is nowhere near as pleasant, but has doubles at 3800 ptas.

In La Carihuela, about 1.5km south-west of the centre, *Hostal Prudencio* (☎ 95 238 14 52), Calle Carmen 43, has 35 rooms, some looking directly on to the beach, at 3000/6000 ptas for singles/doubles. The nearby *Hostal Pedro* (☎ 238 54 79), also facing the beach at Calle Bulto 1, is smaller and cheaper. *Hotel Miami* (☎ 95 238 52 55), a few blocks back at Calle Aladino 14, has as much charm as the rest of Torremolinos put together. It's a quaint old villa turned into a small hotel with nice gardens, a pool and doubles for 6800 ptas.

The tourist offices can supply a list of further options, including more than 2000 apartments costing 5000 ptas or more a night for two people in high season. Alternatively, head for the nearest travel agent and, for a small fee, get them to book you somewhere.

Places to Eat

One of the best things about Torremolinos is that there's lots of good seafood. On Playa del Bajondillo, *Restaurante Los Pescadores Playa* does grilled fish and meat from 750 ptas. *Bodega Quitapeñas* on Cuesta del Tajo, near the tower, and *Bar La Bodega*, Calle San Miguel 40, are both popular with Spaniards for their seafood tapas and raciones from 500 to 800 ptas. *Restaurante Miramar* at the bottom of Calle San Miguel will serve you a Chinese menú for 675 ptas (775 ptas at night).

More eateries, many specialising in

seafood, line the Paseo Marítimo in La Carihuela. At the north-eastern end, *Restaurante La Marina* is popular for its 950 ptas menú. A few doors away is *Restaurante Juan*, one of the classiest places here. Farther along, *Restaurante El Roqueo* and *Restaurante Gauquín* are also good, both serving fish from 900 ptas.

There's no shortage of British bars with inexpensive British breakfasts, roast beef lunches for 700 ptas, fish and chips for 500 ptas, British beer and British football on TV.

Entertainment
Torremolinos' nightlife can be wild and there's a big gay and transvestite scene – most of the gay bars are on Calle Nogalera off Avenida Jesús Santos Rein. Discos are mainly on Avenida Palma de Mallorca.

Getting There & Away
From the bus station (☎ 95 238 24 19) on Calle Hoyo, buses run to Benalmádena Costa and Fuengirola (155 ptas) every 30 minutes, to Marbella (435 ptas) about hourly and to Ronda, La Línea, Tarifa, Cádiz and Granada a few times a day. Buses to Málaga (about every half-hour, 125 ptas) stop at the corner of Avenida Palma de Mallorca and Calle Emilio Esteban, 200m south-west of Plaza Costa del Sol.

Trains run to Torremolinos every half-hour, from 6 am to 10.30 pm, from Málaga city (20 minutes, 135 ptas) and the airport (10 minutes, 135 ptas), then continue to Benalmádena-Arroyo de la Miel and Fuengirola (20 minutes, 150 ptas).

FUENGIROLA
Fuengirola, 18km down the coast from Torremolinos, has more of a family scene but is, if anything, even more densely packed with buildings.

Orientation & Information
The narrow streets in the few blocks between the beach and Avenida Matías Sáenz de Tejada (the street the bus station is on) constitute what's left of the old town. The train station is a block farther inland on

Avenida Jesús Santos Rein. At the old town's centre is Plaza de la Constitución.

The tourist office (☎ 95 246 74 57) at Avenida Jesús Santos Rein 6, just along from the train station, is open Monday to Friday from 9.30 am to 2 pm and 4.30 to 7 pm and Saturday from 10 am to 1 pm.

There's a US consular agency (☎ 95 247 48 91) at Centro Comercial Las Rampas, Fase 2, Planta 1, Locales 12-G-7 and 12-G-8. The Irish consulate (☎ 95 247 51 08) is at Avenida de los Boliches 15.

Things to See & Do
When the beach palls, there's **Parque Acuático Mijas** (☎ 95 246 04 09) on the N-340 Fuengirola bypass, which is similar to Torremolinos' Aquapark but slightly cheaper; it's usually open from about May to October. At the south-west end of Fuengirola the 10th century Islamic **Castillo de Sohail** has recently been restored and opened to visitors. Unless the Río Fuengirola is flowing unusually strongly you can reach the castle across the sandbar at its mouth.

Special Events
The 16 July Virgen del Carmen celebrations in Los Boliches, a former fishing village that's now an eastern suburb of Fuengirola, are famous. In a two-hour procession 120 bearers carry a heavy *paso* (platform) holding the image of the virgin, from Los Boliches church into the sea. Fuengirola stages a lively feria for a week around 7 October.

Places to Stay
Fuengirola gets pretty full in August. The English-run *Pensión Coca* (☎ 95 247 41 89), Calle de la Cruz 3, close to both Plaza de la Constitución and the beach, has decent singles/doubles at 3600/5800 ptas (cheaper outside August). The friendly *Hostal Italia* (☎ 95 247 41 93), Calle de la Cruz 1, is bigger (35 rooms) and has doubles for 4580 ptas plus IVA. *Hostal Cuevas* (☎ 95 246 06 06), nearby at Calle Capitán 7, is a good, small place with doubles for 4200 ptas plus

IVA. *Hostal Sedeño* (☎ 95 247 47 88), also close at Calle Don Jacinto 1, is marginally cheaper and has a garden. *Hostal Marbella* (☎ 95 266 45 03), Calle Marbella 34, just south-west of Plaza de la Constitución, is friendly and clean, with singles/doubles for 3950/5950 ptas.

Places to Eat

On and just off Calle Moncayo, a block back from the beachfront Paseo Marítimo Rey de España in the centre, you can choose from a host of British bars and Italian, Chinese, Indonesian and even Spanish restaurants, many with menús for 800 or 900 ptas. On Paseo Marítimo Rey de España, there's a similar range and some menús for under 600 ptas. *Restaurante Portofino*, Paseo Marítimo Rey de España 29, near the end of Calle de la Cruz, is one of the best eateries, with fish and meat main courses from 1600 ptas. *El Tomate*, Calle Troncón 19, is a fine international restaurant with a good 1600-ptas menú. *Café Berlin*, attached to Hostal Marbella, Calle Marbella 34, does good German-based food at good prices.

Entertainment

Music bars and discos cluster along Calle Martínez Catena, opposite the port. *Pub Route 66*, a few blocks south-west at Calle Medina 16, has live blues or jazz several nights a week (entry 700 ptas). Sports fans should head for *Lineker's* bar in the port. Run by the brother of English footballer Gary Lineker, it has satellite coverage of all major international events and is open until 3 am. The *Irish Times* pub on Avenida Condes de San Isidro has a large patio which is great on a hot evening.

Getting There & Away

From the bus station (☎ 95 247 50 66) there are frequent buses to Torremolinos, Málaga (290 ptas) and Marbella (280 ptas), plus a few a day to Ronda (815 ptas), Sevilla (2100 ptas), Granada (1455 ptas), La Línea (930 ptas) and elsewhere.

Fuengirola is served by the same trains as

Torremolinos (230 ptas from Málaga or the airport).

MIJAS

Mijas, a village of Muslim origin which is 8km north of Fuengirola and 425m higher, was where foreign artists and writers settled in the 1950s and 1960s when their package-tour compatriots were pouring into Torremolinos. Since then villas and urban developments have spread wide over the surrounding hills. The village remains a pretty place with narrow streets, panoramic views and whitewashed houses covered with bougainvillea and jasmine. But it is also full of souvenir and craft shops and a gamut of restaurants and cafés. Busloads of tourists from the costa come here in search of 'the typical Andalucian village'.

The village's **Casa Museo**, opened in 1995, covers local traditions and recreates a traditional village house. The unusual rectangular **bullring** can only be entered by way of an overpriced bullfighting museum. The **Iglesia de la Concepción Inmaculada** on Plaza de la Constitución was built on the site of a mosque, mainly in mudéjar style.

There are a few hostales and hotels, if the mood takes you. Frequent buses run between Mijas and Fuengirola (95 ptas).

MARBELLA

Marbella, some 25km west of Fuengirola, has always been the glossiest resort on the Costa del Sol. Sheltered by the beautiful Sierra Blanca and with a genuinely picturesque *casco antiguo* (old town) of Muslim origins, it's still the most interesting place on the costa.

The building in the 1950s of the exclusive Marbella Club Hotel, just west of town, by the part-Spanish, part-Austrian Alfonso von Hohenlohe turned Marbella into a play-ground of the international set. For three decades oil-rich Arabs and other glitterati flocked to build their own luxury pieds-à-terre and to be seen here. In the 1980s, an economic slump and the rapid growth of urban developments with their own bars and restaurants sent Marbella into decline, but in 1991 Jesús Gil y Gil, a flamboyant, controversial businessman, won a landslide victory to become mayor. Gil increased the number of local police, who, using some notoriously heavy handed tactics, cleansed Marbella's streets of petty criminals, prostitutes and drug addicts. Avenues were lined with palms, marble pavements were laid, plazas spruced up and underground car parks built to deal with the traffic problem. Today, Marbella has regained its reputation as the quality resort of the Costa del Sol. The beaches are clean and the tourists are back. But Gil, who has assiduously courted the costa's new wave of wealthy Russians, has not managed to silence those who say that too much serious organised crime (mainly related to drug trafficking and money laundering) goes on, unchecked, beneath the surface.

Orientation & Information
The N-340 through town goes by the names Avenida Ramón y Cajal and, farther west, Avenida Ricardo Soriano. Many of Marbella's glossy shops are between these avenues and the beach. The old town is centred on Plaza de los Naranjos, north of Avenida Ramón y Cajal. The bus station is on the northern side of the N-340's Marbella bypass, about 1.2km from Plaza de los Naranjos.

The main tourist office (☎ 95 277 14 42) on Glorieta Fontanilla is open Monday to Friday from 9.30 am to 8 pm and Saturday from 10 am to 2 pm. There's a smaller office (☎ 95 282 35 50) at Plaza de los Naranjos 1, opening at 9 am and closing at the same times as the other office.

Central Hispano and Banco Argentaria on Avenida Ramón y Cajal, opposite Plaza de la Alameda, have ATMs. The post office (postcode 29600) is on Calle Finlandia.

The Policía Nacional (☎ 091) are on Avenida Doctor Viñals north of the town. The most central public medical clinic is the Ambulatorio Leganitos (☎ 95 277 81 24) on Plaza Leganitos. The Hospital Europa (☎ 95 277 42 00) is 1km east of the centre on

Avenida de Severo Ochoa and the big Hospital Costa del Sol (☎ 95 286 27 48) is 6km east at Km 187 on the N-340.

Things to See & Do
Pretty **Plaza de los Naranjos** is the heart of the largely pedestrianised casco antiguo, with the 16th century ayuntamiento on its northern side and a 17th century fountain to the south. Nearby on Plaza de la Iglesia is the **Iglesia de Nuestra Señora de la Encarnación**, begun in the 16th century and later redone in baroque style. A little farther east, the **Museo del Grabado Español Contemporáneo** (Museum of Contemporary Spanish Prints, ☎ 95 282 50 35), in a 16th century hospital on Calle Hospital Bazán, houses work by Picasso, Miró and Dalí. It's open Tuesday to Friday from 11 am to 2 pm and 5.30 to 8.15 pm, Monday from 11 am to 2 pm and Sunday from 11.30 am to 2.15 pm (300ptas). Just to the north, along streets such as Calle Arte and Calle Portada, are remains of Marbella's old **Muslim walls**.

Down to the east of the old town, in the watery Parque de la Represa, is the charming **Museo Bonsai** (☎ 95 286 29 26), the only museum in Spain devoted to this Japanese miniature-tree art; it's open daily from 10 am to 1.30 pm and 4 to 7 pm (400 ptas).

The lively **Monday market** takes place in the streets between the football stadium and Avenida General López Domínguez, east of the old town.

The best stretch of town beach is **Playa de Venus**, east of the Puerto Deportivo.

Organised Tours
Numerous travel agencies offer day trips to places like Ronda, Gibraltar and even Tangier, which cost 8000 to 10,000 ptas depending on the season.

Special Events
In mid-March Marbella subjects itself to a weekend motorcycle get-together, the Concentración Internacional Mototurística, which pulls in many thousands of machines and riders from around Spain. Marbella's

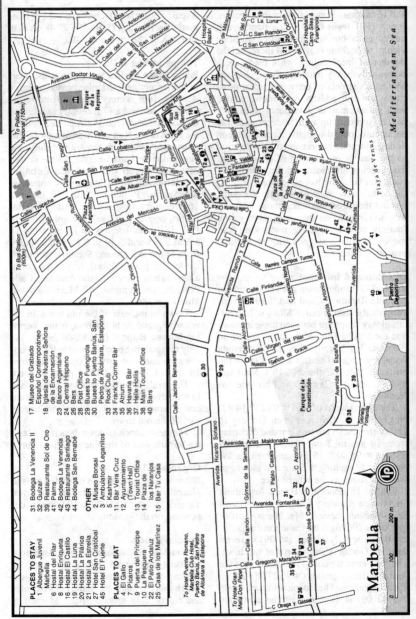

PLACES TO STAY
1 Albergue Juvenil Marbella
8 Hostal Pilar
16 Hostal Enriqueta
19 Hostal El Castillo
20 Hostal La Luna
21 Hostal La Pilárica
27 Hostal La Estrella
27 Hotel San Cristóbal
45 Hotel El Fuerte

PLACES TO EAT
4 El Gallo
7 Picaros
10 Puerta del Príncipe
22 La Pesquera
22 El Patio Andaluz
25 Casa de los Martínez
31 Bodega La Venencia II
32 Gulzar
39 Restaurante Sol de Oro
41 Palms
42 Bodega La Venencia
43 Restaurante Santiago
44 Bodega San Bernabé

OTHER
2 Museo Bonsai
3 Ambulatorio Leganitos
5 Bar Vera Cruz
12 Ayuntamiento (Town Hall)
13 Tourist Office
14 Plaza de los Naranjos
15 Bar Tu Casa
17 Museo del Grabado Español Contemporáneo
18 Iglesia de Nuestra Señora de la Encarnación
23 Banco Argentaria
24 Central Hispano
26 Bars
28 Post Office
29 Buses to Fuengirola
30 Buses to Puerto Banús, San Pedro de Alcántara, Estepona
33 Rock Club
34 Frank's Corner Bar
35 Atrium
36 Havana Bar
37 Helle Hollis
38 Main Tourist Office
40 Bars

To Hotel Puente Romano, Marbella Club Hotel, Puerto Banús, San Pedro de Alcántara & Estepona

To Hotel Gran Meliá Don Pepe

Marbella

0   100   200 m

Mediterranean Sea

Playa de Venus

Puerto Deportivo

big week-long feria happens around 11 June, with the daytime fun focused on the town centre and the after-dark action on an outlying fairground which seems to change site almost annually.

Places to Stay

Camping *Camping Marbella 191* (☎ 95 277 83 91), on the beach at N-340, Km 184.5, 3km east of the centre, charges 3000 ptas a site in the high season. There are three bigger and less expensive year-round camp sites within walking distance of the beach in the next 10km of the N-340 heading east.

Youth Hostel The modern *Albergue Juvenil Marbella* (☎ 95 277 14 91), above the old town at Calle Trapiche 2, has room for 100 people in rooms with two or three beds (half have private bath). There's a pool too.

Budget There are plenty of pensiones in the old town. *Hostal El Castillo* (☎ 95 277 17 39), near the remains of the Islamic walls at Plaza San Bernabé 2, has singles/doubles with bath for 2700/5000 ptas. The recently renovated *Hostal Enriqueta* (☎ 95 282 75 52), Calle Los Caballeros 18, has doubles/triples with bath for 5000/7500 ptas plus IVA. The British-run *Hostal del Pilar* (☎ 95 282 99 36) at Calle Mesoncillo 4 is deservedly popular with backpackers. Single, double and triple rooms with shared baths cost 1500 to 2000 ptas a person, depending on season, and there's a bar with a pool table. Big English breakfasts are served for 600 ptas.

Just south-east of the old town, small budget hostales cluster on narrow Calle San Cristóbal and nearby streets. Three of the best are: *Hostal La Luna* (☎ 95 282 57 78), Calle La Luna 7, where doubles with bath are 5000 ptas; *Hostal La Estrella* (☎ 95 277 94 72), Calle San Cristóbal 36, with doubles at 5500 ptas; and *Hostal La Pilárica* (☎ 95 277 42 52), Calle San Cristóbal 31, charging 4500 ptas or 4000 ptas with shared bath.

Mid-Range & Top End Above the hostal bracket you'll normally pay 10,000 ptas or more for a double in summer. One of the more economical hotels is *Hotel San Cristóbal* (☎ 95 277 12 50), Avenida Ramón y Cajal 3, with doubles at 10,400 ptas plus IVA; you'll probably be better off with a room at the back or side, away from the noisy avenue. Most of the ritzier hotels are along the coast to the east or west, but the 263-room *Hotel El Fuerte* (☎ 95 286 15 00), Avenida El Fuerte s/n, is close to Playa de Venus and has doubles at 15,000 ptas plus IVA. The five-star *Hotel Gran Meliá Don Pepe* (☎ 95 277 03 00) on Calle José Meliá, a little over 1km west of the centre, has doubles for 45,700 ptas plus IVA, a golf course, and tennis and squash courts.

The famous *Marbella Club Hotel* (☎ 95 282 22 11), with its large, verdant gardens, is at N-340, Km 178.5, 2km west of town on the Puerto Banús road. Doubles are 42,000 ptas plus IVA. *Hotel Puente Romano* (☎ 95 282 09 00), a bit farther west at N-340, Km 177.6, has singles/doubles for 35,700/45,000 ptas plus IVA. *Hotel Los Monteros* (☎ 95 277 17 00), N-340, Km 187 (29,000/36,000 ptas plus IVA) and *Hotel Don Carlos* (☎ 95 283 11 40), N-340, Km 192 (26,000/33,000 ptas plus IVA) are 6 and 11km east of town respectively.

Places to Eat

Old Town The restaurants around Plaza de los Naranjos are popular with visitors but, naturally, they're not cheap. For a local adventure head for *El Gallo* bar at Calle Lobatos 44 – egg and chips for 300 ptas and the cheapest *gambas pil pil* in town at 500 ptas (closed Tuesday). Or you can eat in the courtyard of *El Patio Andaluz*, a charming, dilapidated old coaching inn on Calle San Juan de Dios; sardines, *boquerones* and chips with wine will set you back just 800 ptas. Also popular with locals is *Casa de los Martínez* at Avenida Ramón y Cajal 7, where tapas cost around 150 ptas.

For something more up-market book a patio table at *Pícaros* (☎ 95 282 86 50), Calle Aduar 1. The chef is from New York and the décor and open-air *terraza* are beautiful. Main courses are from 900 to 2300 ptas plus IVA. It's open daily from 7.30 pm to 1 am but outside summer it closes on Monday. Alternatively you could head for Calle Huerta Chica, where the *Puerta del Príncipe* does good grilled meat and fish from 850 ptas. *La Pesquera* next door concentrates on seafood for similar prices.

Elsewhere *Bodega San Bernabé* on Calle Carlos Mackintosh, facing the leafy Plaza de la Alameda, is wonderfully traditional, with tapas of ham and cheese only. On the beach at the eastern side of the Puerto Deportivo, *Palms* specialises in interesting salads from 850 ptas. *Restaurante Santiago*, just behind this beach on Avenida Duque de Ahumada, is one of the best and most expensive seafood restaurants in town. *Bodega La Venencia*, nearby on Avenida Miguel Cano, serves great ham tapas and *montaditos* from 125 ptas, plus raciones and media-raciones, and has an equally good branch, *Bodega La Venencia II*, on Avenida Fontanilla farther west.

The best Indian restaurant in town is *Gulzar* on Calle Camilo José Cela, with main dishes from 750 ptas. It's open from 1 to 3 pm and 7 to 11.30 pm (closed Monday).

On Avenida Duque de Ahumada near the Glorieta de la Fontanilla tourist office, *Restaurante Sol de Oro* does a popular lunch menú, including wine, for 1000 ptas.

Entertainment

Bar Tu Casa, off Plaza de los Naranjos at Calle Valdés 2, is a convenient meeting place. The cosy Canadian-run *Bar Vera Cruz* at Calle Buitrago 7 is open from 7.30 pm to 3 am (closed Sunday). Nearby Calle Pantaleón has a string of *cervecerías* and other bars that buzz late into the night with a young crowd. The other place this crowd heads for after midnight is the Puerto Deportivo, where a line of music bars and discos throb till dawn in summer. The older set gravitates to the streets around Calle Camilo José Cela, where *Frank's Corner Bar*, the *Rock Club* (with live music, and drinks for 500 ptas-plus after midnight), the *Atrium* and *Havana Bar* are among the main hang-outs. *Kashmir*, in the north of the old town at Calle Rafina 8, puts on some live blues and jazz.

Getting There & Away

Bus Buses to Fuengirola (280 ptas), Puerto Banús (125 ptas), San Pedro de Alcántara and Estepona (255 ptas) leave about every 30 minutes and stop on Avenida Ricardo Soriano. Other services use the bus station (☎ 95 276 44 00) in the north of town. These include frequent buses to Benalmádena Costa, Torremolinos and Málaga (570 ptas), and a few a day to La Línea (695 ptas), Algeciras, Cádiz, Ronda (585 ptas), Sevilla (1820 ptas) and Granada (1735 ptas).

Car Helle Hollis (☎ 95 282 30 38), Calle Camilo José Cela 21, is one local firm with good prices on rental cars – a Seat Marbella costs from 15,900 to 19,900 ptas a month all inclusive, depending on season.

Getting Around

From the bus station, bus No 7 runs to Avenida Ricardo Soriano and No 2 stops on Calle Jacinto Benavente on the north-western edge of the old town. A taxi to the centre is 500 ptas. To walk, cross the bridge over the bypass and carry straight on down Calle La Florida and Avenida Trapich which leads down to the Albergue Juvenil Marbella.

OJÉN & AROUND

The picturesque mountain village of Ojén is 10km to the north of Marbella, with panoramic views along the way. There are few concessions to tourism here. Ojén was originally a Muslim settlement but most of that burnt down during the 1569 Morisco uprising. The present parish church, mudéjar in style, was built on the site of the old mosque. There's a festival of flamenco song in the first week of August.

About 4km north of Ojén, shortly past the 580m Puerto de Ojén on the Coín road, a left turn heads 6km west up an isolated valley to the *Refugio de Juanar* (☎ 95 288 10 00). This comfortable hotel has doubles at 9800 ptas plus IVA and is a starting point for some good walks in the forested Sierra Blanca, including to a marvellous 1000m-high *mirador* 2km away.

Several buses a day run from Marbella bus station to Ojén.

PUERTO BANÚS

The coastal strip between Marbella and Puerto Banús, 5km west, is known as the 'Golden Mile' because of its number of super-luxury properties – including King Fahd of Saudi Arabia's *Mar Mar* (complete with mosque and three palaces) overlooking the Istán junction. Puerto Banús is the flashiest marina on the Costa del Sol, often a port of call for gin palaces that moor in Monte Carlo at other times of year.

This is the land of stick-on hairy chests and gold medallions: there used to be a stall selling made-to-measure 'gold' chains. A visit gives a glimpse into how *some* people live. Some young travellers get work on the yachts – if they're not already working as time-share touts elsewhere. Puerto Banús is also a nightlife centre, though its prices are decidedly higher than anywhere else.

Jesús Gil y Gil, mayor of Marbella municipality, which includes Puerto Banús, has been prevented by the Spanish government from creating an artificial pleasure island of discos, restaurants and shops 500m offshore but wants to build an island marina instead.

Near the main, western entrance to the marina stands a glittering Islamic arch, a kind of tribute to the Arabs who brought lots of money to Marbella in the 1970s; near the far end looms a large Russian socialist realist statue, a gift to Gil y Gil from the mayor of Moscow whose compatriots have been flocking to the costa in the 1990s.

The main entrance has security gates to prevent access by unauthorised cars. Here you will find two banks with ATMs – Central Hispano and Banco Atlántico. By the control tower at the western end of the harbour – where the swankiest boats tie up – is the Aquarium de Puerto Banús (☎ 95 281 87 67), similar to Sea Life at Benalmádena Costa. It's open daily from 11 am to 6 pm (750 ptas, children 550 ptas).

Places to Eat & Drink

The marina is surrounded by glittery shops and restaurants which get less expensive as you move east. Towards the western end you'll find *Salduba Pub* and *Sinatra Bar*, two of the most popular bars. Just east is *The Red Pepper*, the oldest Greek restaurant in town, with a spectacular display of live seafood and most main courses over 2000 ptas. Farther east, *Don Leone* is the best Italian restaurant with a menú for 1950 ptas. A little farther along is *Pizzeria Picasso*, popular for its pizza and pasta from 675 to 950 ptas.

At night, *Old Joy's Pub*, just east of Pizzeria Picasso and behind it, the *Navy* are popular haunts. *Bang & Olufsen*, by the main entrance, has a classy late-night bar upstairs. For the liveliest disco try *La Comedia* on Calle de Ribera behind The Red Pepper.

SAN PEDRO DE ALCÁNTARA

Only a couple of kilometres west of Puerto Banús, San Pedro is still within Marbella municipality – as the huge Arco de San Pedro arch over the N-340 just west of the town, emblazoned with 'Marbella' in giant letters, testifies. The arch houses one of the town's two tourist offices (☎ 95 278 13 60), open daily from 10 am to midnight. The other (☎ 95 278 52 52; open Monday to Friday from 9 am to 8 pm and Saturday from 10 am to 2 pm) is at Calle Marqués del Duero 69, on one of the streets leading to the centre from the N-340.

It's difficult for San Pedro to compete as a resort when the beach – albeit one of the nicest on the costa – is a 1km hike from the town, down Avenida del Mar from the N-340 at the bottom of Calle Marqués del Duero.

The tourist offices will be able to provide you with a list of places to stay. A couple of blocks to the west, Calle Marqués del Duero and Avenida de la Constitución, which run parallel to each other, are lined with restaurants, banks and shops. There are also plenty of places where you can eat on the beach.

ESTEPONA

Estepona has controlled its development carefully and remains an agreeable seaside town. There's a nice strip of palms and greenery along the beachfront *paseo* and a pleasant oldish town centre. Estepona also has a sizeable fishing fleet, sharing the port beyond the lighthouse at the west end of town with a marina which (Puerto Banús beware!) the town leaders want to enlarge into the world's biggest.

The tourist office (☎ 95 280 09 13) at Avenida San Lorenzo 1 in the west of the centre is open Monday to Friday from 10 am to 9.30 pm and Saturday from 10 am to 1.30 pm. The bus station (☎ 95 280 02 49) is 400m west, on the seafront Avenida de España.

There are plenty of places to stay. *Hostal El Pilar* (☎ 95 280 00 18), Plaza Las Flores 10, overlooks the central square and has singles/doubles for 2100/3500 ptas (doubles with bath for 4500 ptas). Friendly *Pensión San Antonio* (☎ 95 280 14 76), a block east of the plaza at Calle Adolfo Suárez 9, has basic rooms for 1900/3500 ptas. On the seafront, *Hotel Buenavista* (☎ 95 280 01 37), Paseo Marítimo 180, has doubles with bath for 6500 ptas. *Las Dunas Beach Hotel & Spa* (☎ 95 279 43 45) on the beachfront at N-340, Km 163, 8km east of Estepona, is a recent addition to the costa's super-luxury hotels and has been an 'in place' with celebrities in the last couple of years.

A good place to start the search for food is Plaza Las Flores which is surrounded by tapas bars and restaurants. Nightlife focuses on the marina.

CASARES

Eight kilometres south-west of Estepona on the N-340 is the turn-off for Casares, 10km inland. Dubbed 'the hanging village' for the way it clings to the edge of a cliff below the well-preserved remains of a Muslim castle (from which there are wonderful views), it is well worth an excursion and the surrounding hills offer good hiking opportunities. On one side of the main square, Plaza de España, stands a statue of Blas Infante, a local lad who led an An-

dalucian nationalist movement in the early 20th century and was executed by the Spanish nationalists in the civil war.

Hostal Plaza (☎ 95 289 40 88) on Plaza de España has decent rooms with bath for 2700 ptas a double.

There are buses (except Sunday) from Estepona at 11 am, 1.30 pm and 7 pm. The last one back leaves Casares at 4.30 pm.

The Interior

The mountainous interior of Málaga province is a far cry from the coastal hulla-baloo. Here you'll find spectacular gorges and remote mountainous areas with good walking; one of Europe's two main breeding grounds for the spectacular greater flamingo; towns and villages of Muslim origin with winding, hilly streets and ancient castles; and traces of even earlier humanity in the form of impressive cave paintings and megalithic tombs.

EL CHORRO, ARDALES & AROUND

Fifty kilometres north-west of Málaga the Río Guadalhorce carves its way through the awesome Garganta del Chorro (El Chorro Gorge, also called the Desfiladero de los Gaitanes), up to 400m deep and in places as little as 10m wide. The gorge, about 4km long, is traversed not only by the main railway in and out of Málaga (with the aid of 12 tunnels and six bridges) but also by a footpath, the Camino del Rey, which for long stretches becomes a perilously decaying concrete catwalk clinging to the side of the gorge up to 100m above the river. El Chorro's often sheer walls are the biggest magnet for rock climbers in Andalucía.

The gorge apart, this craggy north-western area of the province is full of spectacular scenery, other walking possibilities and places of historic and natural interest. The pleasant and interesting small town of Ardales is the main centre for the area west of the gorge.

Getting There & Away

There are several buses a day by the Los Amarillos line from both Málaga and Ronda to Ardales and daily buses from Málaga to Teba. There's no bus service to El Chorro.

At the time of writing there was one train a day from Málaga at 1.35 pm (45 minutes, 455 ptas). From El Chorro to Málaga there are two trains a day (8.35 am and 2.52 pm). You can also reach El Chorro by train from Sevilla, Córdoba, Fuente de Piedra or (with an early morning train change at Bobadilla) from Ronda.

The main road into the area is the A-357 from Málaga to Ardales. You branch off it near Pizarra to reach El Chorro, passing through Álora. From El Burgo (see Around Ronda), a mostly unpaved 20km road leads north-east down the pretty valley of the Río Turón to Ardales.

El Chorro

El Chorro village is a tiny settlement above a dam on the Guadalhorce, just south of the gorge. Life revolves around its train station and the *Restaurante Estación*, better known as *Bar Isabel*, which is a renowned climbers' gathering spot.

The Swiss-run Finca La Campana (see Places to Stay & Eat) offers climbing courses and climbing, caving, walking and mountain bike trips and rents out mountain bikes for 1500 ptas a day.

Camino del Rey

The Camino del Rey (King's Path) is so named because Alfonso XIII reputedly walked it in 1921, when he opened the dams and reservoirs above the gorge which supply much of Málaga province's water. The camino has been in a state of alarming disrepair for years and has been officially closed since 1992 but there's nothing to stop adventurous folk with a head for heights from using parts of it – and plenty do. We can't actually recommend walking the Camino del Rey but we have done it and you can avoid its most perilous parts by walking along the railway instead.

The route is: from El Chorro village follow the road up the east side of the reservoir for some 600m to a point below a railway viaduct (where you can park a vehicle). Walk up to the railway and go about 2.25km north along it, through tunnel Nos 10, 9, 8 and 7 (No 9 has three separate sections). The tunnels have plenty of space at the side should a train come. Between tunnels Nos 10 and 9 the Camino del Rey starts along the cliff face to the left, but don't take it here – you'll see why when you glimpse its collapsed state across the gorge from the railway farther up. Between tunnels Nos 7 and 6 you have to cross the gorge by a narrow, concrete footbridge without parapets. Then walk along the catwalk up the gorge – there are a few small holes in the floor and the handrail is missing in parts – for 1.5km until you come to a dam at the foot of the small Embalse de Gaitanejo reservoir.

From here you can return the way you came or take a broad track up to the left. After 1.5km this meets a road which leads 600m down to the Restaurante El Mirador, from which it's a further 1km to the Parque Ardales camp site (see Ardales & Around).

Places to Stay & Eat

Refugio de Escalada La Garganta (☎ 95 249 51 19), just below El Chorro station, has beds for 600 ptas. If the door is closed ask at Apartamentos La Garganta. At the station, *Pensión Estación* (☎ 95 249 50 04) has four clean little singles/doubles for 2000/3500 ptas and *Restaurante Estación* does platos combinados from 375 to 550 ptas. *Apartamentos La Garganta* (☎ 95 249 51 19), a converted flour mill just south of the station, has rooms with small kitchen and bathroom at 4000 ptas (single or double), or 6000 ptas for up to five people. It has a pool and restaurant too. *Finca La Campana* (☎ 95 211 20 19), up a dirt road 2km from the station (signposted), has bunks for 1500 ptas, a double room for 3000 ptas and an apartment costing 4000 ptas for two people or 6000 ptas for four. There's a guest kitchen or prepared meals are available.

Bobastro

Back in the 9th century the rugged El Chorro area was the redoubt of a kind of Robin Hood of Al-Andalus, Omar ibn Hafsun, who resisted the authority – and armies – of the emirs of Córdoba for nearly 40 years from the hill fortress of Bobastro. Ibn Hafsun came from a landed family of *muwallads* (converts from Christianity to Islam) but turned to banditry after being disowned by his father for killing a neighbour. Quickly gaining followers and popular support – partly, it's said, because he defended the peasants against taxes and forced labour – he at one stage controlled territory from Cartagena to the Strait of Gibraltar.

To reach Bobastro from El Chorro village follow the road up the valley from the far (west) side of the dam and after 3km take the signposted Bobastro turning. Three kilometres up from here, an 'Iglesia Mozárabe' sign indicates the footpath (about 500m) to the remains of a remarkable little Mozarabic church cut out of the rock. The legend, supported by some historical sources, is that Ibn Hafsun converted to Christianity (thus becoming a Mozarab) before his death in 917 and was buried in this church. Mozarabs certainly played an important part in his uprising. When Bobastro was finally conquered in 927, Ibn Hafsun's remains were taken away for posthumous crucifixion outside Córdoba's Mezquita.

A further 2.5km up the road, after passing a curiously sited reservoir you reach the top of the hill which has faint traces of Ibn Hafsun's *alcázar* (fortress) on its highest point, the *Bar La Mesa,* and magnificent views.

Ardales & Around

If you continue westward past the Bobastro turn-off on the road from El Chorro, after 2.5km you reach a T-junction. A left turn here will take you south to Ardales (8km); a right turn leads to the Parque Ardales camp site (800m), the Restaurante El Mirador (1.6km), from which you can walk to the northern end of El Chorro gorge (see

under Camino del Rey) and other restaurants and walking trails near the picturesque Embalse del Conde del Guadalhorce.

Things to See & Do On Plaza Ayuntamiento, adjoining Ardales' central Plaza de San Isidro, the **Museo Municipal Cueva de Ardales** (☎ 95 245 80 87) is devoted to the Cueva de Ardales outside the town, with copies of its prehistoric rock paintings and carvings. It's open daily except Monday from 10.30 am to 2 pm and 5 to 7 pm (4 to 6 pm in winter; 100 ptas) and also provides tourist information. Up near the top of the town the **Iglesia de la Nuestra Señora de los Remedios** was originally a mosque and has a good *artesonado* ceiling. If the church isn't open ask at Plaza de la Iglesia 1, opposite, for the key. Above the church is **La Peña**, a crag with the remains of a 10th century fort probably built by Omar ibn Hafsun. For two-hour guided visits (700 ptas) to the **Cueva de Ardales** itself, contact in advance either the Ardales or the Parque Ardales tourist office (see later in this section). The caves contain 60 Palaeolithic paintings and carvings of animals, done between about 18,000 and 14,000 BC, and there are traces of later occupation and burials from about 8000 to after 3000 BC. The cave is 3km off the Málaga road from a turning 500m from the Ardales turn-off.

At Parque Ardales is the **Museo Parque Ardales** (200 ptas) combined with another tourist office (both ☎ 95 245 81 20), open daily, except Monday, from 10 am (11 am in winter) to 2 pm, and 4 to 6 pm. The museum has exhibits on Bobastro, the dams, the Camino del Rey and local geology, flora and fauna.

At the camp site you can rent a mountain bike for 300 ptas an hour (less per hour for longer periods) or a canoe for 700 ptas an hour.

Places to Stay *Parque Ardales* (☎ 95 211 24 01), 9km north of Ardales on the banks of the Embalse del Conde del Guadalhorce, has a large, shady camp site costing 1175 ptas plus IVA for two people with a car and small tent, and apartments for up to four people, with kitchen, at 8000 ptas plus IVA in the high season.

The friendly *Pensión Bobastro* (☎ 95 245 91 50) in the centre of Ardales at Plaza de San Isidro 13 has singles/doubles for 1500/3000 ptas. The prices are similar at *Pensión El Cruce* (☎ 95 245 90 12) at the Ardales junction on the main road, 500m from the centre.

Places to Eat The best food in Ardales – tapas and raciones – is at *Bar El Casino* on Plaza de San Isidro. Try the scrumptious *huevos con bechamel* or *pimientos rellenos de ternera*, respectively hard-boiled eggs in béchamel sauce and peppers with veal stuffing, both rolled in breadcrumbs then deep fried.

Several restaurants along the road beyond Parque Ardales are popular with locals on weekends and at holiday times. *Restaurante El Mirador*, 1km beyond Parque Ardales, has a terrace overlooking the reservoir and serves economical salads and omelettes as well as more expensive meaty options. One kilometre farther on across the dam, the popular *Mesón El Oasis* specialises in roast lamb and *carnes a la brasa* (800 to 1500 ptas).

Teba
Teba, another small town 18km north-west of Ardales across rolling country, is dominated by a hill-top Muslim castle, the **Castillo de la Estrella** (mainly ruined but worth a visit). On Plaza de España at the top of Calle San Francisco stands a **monument to Sir James Douglas**, a Scottish knight who died at Teba in 1330 fighting with Alfonso XI against the Muslims. Douglas was actually on his way to Jerusalem to get Robert the Bruce's heart consecrated there (a task entrusted to him by the dying Bruce) but had detoured to Spain for a spot of crusading. The casket in which Douglas was carrying the heart was recovered from the battlefield and sent to Scotland's Melrose Abbey where it (and the heart) still reside.

The short **Teba Gorge**, 2.5km east of town, is a noted bird-watching spot: Egyptian vultures, Bonelli's eagles and black kites all nest here. A path leads into the gorge from a bridge over the Río de la Venta on the Antequera road.

Hostal Hermanos Sevillano (☎ 95 274 80 11), Calle San Francisco 26, has singles/doubles for 1500/3000 ptas.

RONDA
Though just an hour or so's journey up from the Costa del Sol, Ronda is a world away from the coastal hustle. It's a pretty and historic town of 34,000 people, set astride the 100m-deep El Tajo gorge amid the beautiful Serranía de Ronda mountains. It attracts its quota of visitors but remains little changed by them. Many come from the coast just for the day. For Spaniards, May and September, when the weather is at its most agreeable, constitute the 'season' in Ronda.

The capital of a small Berber taifa after the collapse of the Córdoba caliphate, Ronda came under Sevillan rule in the mid-11th century. After the fall of Sevilla in 1248 Ronda regained a large measure of independence. Its near-impregnable position kept it out of Christian hands until 1485 when it fell to Fernando El Católico only because its governor and army had left to protect Malaga.

Orientation & Information
The old Muslim town known as La Ciudad stands on the southern side of El Tajo, with the newer town to the north. Three bridges cross the gorge, the main one being the Puente Nuevo which heads across from Plaza de España to Calle de Armiñán. Both parts of town come to an abrupt end on their western sides with cliffs plunging away to the valley of the Río Guadalevín far below. Places of historic and architectural interest are mostly concentrated in La Ciudad while most places to stay and eat, along with the bus and train stations, are in the new town.

The tourist office (☎ 95 287 12 72), Plaza de España 1, is open Monday to Friday

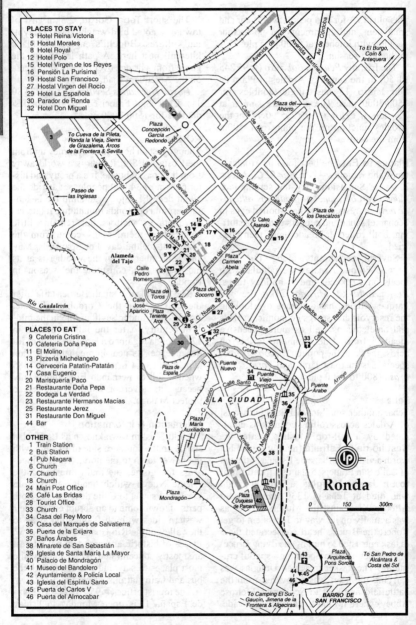

PLACES TO STAY
- 3 Hotel Reina Victoria
- 5 Hostal Morales
- 8 Hotel Royal
- 12 Hotel Polo
- 15 Hotel Virgen de los Reyes
- 16 Pensión La Purísima
- 19 Hostal San Francisco
- 27 Hostal Virgen del Rocío
- 29 Hotel La Española
- 30 Parador de Ronda
- 32 Hotel Don Miguel

PLACES TO EAT
- 9 Cafetería Cristina
- 10 Cafetería Doña Pepa
- 11 El Molino
- 13 Pizzería Michelangelo
- 14 Cervecería Patatín-Patatán
- 17 Casa Eugenio
- 20 Marisquería Paco
- 21 Restaurante Doña Pepa
- 22 Bodega La Verdad
- 23 Restaurante Hermanos Macías
- 25 Restaurante Jerez
- 31 Restaurante Don Miguel
- 44 Bar

OTHER
- 1 Train Station
- 2 Bus Station
- 4 Pub Niagara
- 6 Church
- 7 Church
- 18 Church
- 24 Main Post Office
- 26 Café Las Bridas
- 28 Tourist Office
- 33 Church
- 34 Casa del Rey Moro
- 35 Casa del Marqués de Salvatierra
- 36 Puerta de la Exijara
- 37 Baños Árabes
- 38 Minarete de San Sebastián
- 39 Iglesia de Santa María La Mayor
- 40 Palacio de Mondragón
- 41 Museo del Bandolero
- 42 Ayuntamiento & Policía Local
- 45 Iglesia del Espíritu Santo
- 45 Puerta de Carlos V
- 46 Puerta del Almocabar

Ronda

0   150   300m

from 10 am to 2 pm and from 4 to 6.30 pm and Saturday from 10.30 am to 2.30 pm (sometimes longer in summer).

Banks and ATMs are mainly on Calle Virgen de la Paz and Plaza Carmen Abela. The main post office (postcode 29400) is at Calle Virgen de la Paz 18-20. The Policía Local (☎ 092) are in the Ayuntamiento on Plaza Duquesa de Parcent.

Plaza de España & Puente Nuevo

Chapter 10 of Ernest Hemingway's *For Whom the Bell Tolls* tells how at the start of the civil war the 'fascists' of a small town were rounded up into the ayuntamiento, then clubbed and flailed as they were made to walk the gauntlet between two lines of townspeople 'in the plaza on the top of the cliff above the river'. At the end of the line the victims, dead or still alive, were thrown over the cliff. The episode was based on events in Ronda, though the actual perpetrators were, according to Hugh Thomas' authoritative *The Spanish Civil War*, a gang from Málaga. Thomas says 512 people were murdered in Ronda in the first month of the war.

The Parador de Ronda on Plaza de España was, before it became a hotel, the ayuntamiento.

The majestic Puente Nuevo (New Bridge) spanning El Tajo from Plaza de España is two centuries old. A Ronda tradition relates that its architect, Martín de Aldehuela, fell to his death in 1793 while trying to engrave the bridge's date on its side. The word *año* (year), accompanied by some incomplete hieroglyphics, beside the shield on the side of the bridge, may encourage you to disregard historians who say Aldehuela died in 1802, nine years after the bridge was opened.

La Ciudad

Though most of its Muslim buildings have been heavily modified over the centuries La Ciudad retains a typical *medina* character of narrow streets twisting between white buildings. Starting along Calle de Armiñán from the Puente Nuevo, the first street to the left, Calle Santo Domingo, leads down to the **Casa del Rey Moro** (House of the Moorish King). The house itself – built in the 18th century, supposedly over the remains of a Muslim palace – is closed. But for 500 ptas you can visit its terraced gardens which extend down into the gorge, as well as La Mina, an old underground stairway cut by slaves out of the rock right down to the river to enable emergency water supplies to be drawn (open daily from 10 am to 7 pm).

From the Casa del Rey Moro you can head back up towards the **Plaza María Auxiliadora** where there are fine views. Continue then to the **Palacio de Mondragón** on Plaza Mondragón. Thought to have been built for Abomelic, ruler of Ronda, in 1314, the palace was altered soon after the Christian conquest and Fernando and Isabel lodged here at some point. Inside, the ground floor has three courtyards, of which only the Patio Mudéjar preserves an Islamic character with its rich tiling, brick arches, marble columns and a horseshoe arch leading into a small clifftop garden with fountain and pool. Some rooms house the Museo de la Ciudad, mostly dealing with the prehistoric life of the Ronda area. The palace is open daily from 10 am to 7 pm (to 3 pm on Saturday and Sunday; 200 ptas).

A minute's walk beyond is Plaza Duquesa de Parcent where the **Iglesia de Santa María La Mayor** stands on the site of Muslim Ronda's main mosque. After the Christian conquest it was rebuilt as a church but the tower betrays Islamic origins and the galleries beside it, built for viewing festivities in the plaza, also date from Muslim times. Just inside the church entrance is an arch covered with Arabic inscriptions which was the mosque's *mihrab*. The church was begun in Gothic style but, as building went on over the centuries, tastes changed to the Renaissance style and finally to the 18th century baroque of the northern end. It's open daily from 10 am to 8 pm in summer (6 pm in winter; 200 ptas).

From Plaza Duquesa de Parcent you

could detour to the Barrio de San Francisco, the southern end of town. You'll find the imposing late 15th century **Iglesia del Espíritu Santo** (Church of the Holy Spirit), supposedly open from 10 am to 6 pm (75 ptas) although you'll have most luck in the morning, and a stretch of the old city walls pierced by two gates, the 16th century **Puerta de Carlos V** and the 13th century **Puerta del Almocabar**. The little bar on Plaza Arquitecto Pons Sorolla, facing the gates, displays a small photo of Ernest Hemingway, who once dropped in.

Back near Plaza Duquesa de Parcent at Calle Armiñán 65, the Museo Histórico-Popular de la Serranía, more often called the **Museo del Bandolero** (Bandit Museum), is dedicated to the banditry for which the Ronda area was once renowned (see the boxed text entitled Bandoleros, Guerrilleros & Treachery etc). It has guns, maps, press cuttings and lifesize figures of some of the most renowned outlaws, plus an audiovisual in Spanish; it's open daily from 10 am to 6 pm (to 8 pm in summer; 200 ptas). Just off the same street, to the north, the little **Minarete de San Sebastián** was built in Granada style, as part of a mosque, in the 14th century.

Beside the museum, steps lead down to an impressive stretch of the old **walls** along the eastern side of La Ciudad. You can follow them down and pass through the **Puerta de la Exijara**, the entry to Islamic Ronda's Jewish quarter. From here a path leads down the hillside to the beautiful and

Bandoleros, Guerrilleros & Treachery in the High Sierras

Andalucía's complicated sierras, full of ravines, caves, and hidden valleys, have for centuries been a refuge for those who don't get on with the authorities. As long ago as the 9th century the El Chorro area was the epicentre of prolonged, widespread opposition to Cordoban rule led by a sort of Islamic Robin Hood, Omar ibn Hafsun (see Bobastro in the El Chorro, Ardales & Around section).

In the 19th century the bandits *(bandoleros)* who preyed on the rich also became folk heroes. The most famous was El Tempranillo (the Early One), born in 1800 at Jauja, near Lucena in Córdoba province. By the age of 22 he claimed: 'The king may reign in Spain, but in the sierra I do.' El Tempranillo reputedly demanded an ounce of gold for each vehicle which crossed his domain.

The activities of these bandits led the government to set up the Guardia Civil, Spain's rural police force, in 1844. Many bandoleros were then forced into the service of the *caciques* (local landowners and political bosses), or even of the Guardia Civil itself. El Tempranillo met his end this way, murdered by an old comrade.

The last of the bandolero breed was Pasos Largos (Big Steps), a murderous, agile and clever poacher who haunted the area between El Burgo and Yunquera, east of Ronda. He was killed in 1934, officially in a cave shootout with the Guardia Civil, though some say his killer was a traitorous companion.

After the civil war the Andalucian sierras became the refuge of a new kind of outlaw: communist *guerrilleros* waging the last resistance to Franco. The Sierra Bermeja, north of Estepona, and the mountains of La Axarquía, east of Málaga, were among their hideouts. This little known chapter of Spanish history closed in the 1950s.

almost intact **Baños Árabes** (Arab Baths), built in the 13th and 14th centuries (open daily except Monday from 9 am to 2 pm and 4 to 6 pm; free). Just north of the baths is the old **Puente Árabe** over the Río Guadalevín. Immediately downstream at the start of the gorge is the **Puente Viejo** (or Puente Romano). Some say it's originally Roman, most think it's of Muslim pedigree. Either way it was rebuilt in 1616.

From the northern side of the Puente Viejo you can make your way back up to Plaza de España via a small park along the gorge's edge. Before doing so you might like to detour to the **Casa del Marqués de Salvatierra** at the foot of Calle Marqués de Salvatierra, an 18th century mansion open for guided visits (300 ptas) daily, except Sunday afternoon and Thursday, every half-hour from 11 am to 2 pm and 4 to 7 pm.

Plaza de Toros & Around
Ronda's elegant bullring on Calle Virgen de la Paz is a mecca for aficionados. Opened in 1785, it's one of the oldest bullrings in Spain, has one of the biggest arenas and has been the site of some of the most important events in bullfighting history (see boxed text). Open for visits daily from 10 am to 6 pm (275 ptas), it contains a small **Museo Taurino** with memorabilia such as early bullfight posters, bullfighting costumes worn by Pedro Romero and contemporary star Jesulín de Ubrique and photos of famous visitors including Ernest Hemingway and Orson Welles.

Behind the Plaza de Toros, there are some vertiginous cliff-top views from **Plaza Teniente Arce.** You can walk from here to the shady **Alameda del Tajo** park. The **Paseo de las Inglesas** path along the clifftop from the Alameda to the Hotel Reina Victoria was recently closed for repairs.

Walks
A path leads down into the valley at the foot of the gorge from Plaza María Auxiliadora in La Ciudad. A lone Islamic archway stands about halfway down the path. From the valley bottom a road leads south-east up to

the Barrio de San Francisco, or you can work your way north, crossing the river and find the path up to near the Hotel Reina Victoria.

Special Events
Ronda's famous old bullring stages relatively few fights but in early September it holds some of the most celebrated and unusual anywhere; the Corridas Goyescas, in which top matadors fight in early

Ronda's Fighting Romeros
Ronda can justly claim to be the home of bullfighting. A company of knights, the Real Maestranza de Caballería, was formed here in 1572 to supervise the activity. In the 18th and 19th centuries three generations of the Romero family established most of the basics of modern bullfighting on foot (previously it was on horseback as a kind of cavalry training-cum-sport for the nobility). Francisco Romero, born in 1698, invented the use of the cape to attract the bull, and the *muleta*, its cloth replacement in the kill. His son Juan introduced the matador's supporting team, the *cuadrilla*; and grandson Pedro (1754-1839) perfected a strict classical style, still known as the Ronda School, before becoming director of the country's first bullfighting college (in Sevilla) at the age of 77. Pedro's skill was such, it's said, that outlaws from the bandit-ridden mountains around Ronda would risk capture to see him in action.

19th-century-style costumes as in Goya's depictions of Ronda bullfights. The fights are the centrepiece of a general fiesta, the Feria de Pedro Romero, which includes plenty of music too.

Places to Stay – Budget

The good *Camping El Sur* (☎ 95 287 59 39) in a pleasant setting, 2km south-west of town on the Algeciras road, has a swimming pool and restaurant and is open all year. It charges 1650 ptas plus IVA for two adults with a car and tent.

The bright, clean and friendly *Pensión La Purísima* (☎ 95 287 10 50) at Calle de Sevilla 10 has nine rooms at 2000/3000 ptas. *Hostal Morales* (☎ 95 287 15 38), Calle de Sevilla 51, is also fair value at 1200/2400 ptas. *Hostal Virgen del Rocío* (☎ 95 287 74 25), Calle Nueva 18, has 11 doubles with bathroom for 3500 ptas plus IVA. The 16-room *Hostal San Francisco* (☎ 95 287 32 99), Calle María Cabrera 18, has singles/doubles with bathroom for 1800/3600 ptas plus IVA.

Places to Stay – Mid-Range

The 30-room *Hotel Virgen de los Reyes* (☎ 95 287 11 40), Calle Lorenzo Borrego Gómez 13, has solid singles/doubles with TV and small bathrooms for 3000/5000 ptas. *Hotel Royal* (☎ 95 287 11 41), Calle Virgen de la Paz 42, has similar standards and prices.

Hotel Polo (☎ 95 287 24 47), Calle Mariano Soubirón 8, is a bit better. Its 33 rooms at 6300/9000 ptas plus IVA have air-conditioning and there's a restaurant too.

If you're set on a room overlooking the gorge the least expensive option is *Hotel Don Miguel* (☎ 95 287 77 22), Calle Villanueva 8, where doubles are 9000 ptas plus IVA. *Hotel La Española* (☎ 95 287 10 52), well located at Calle José Aparicio 3, the narrow pedestrian street between the tourist office and bullring, has similar prices.

Places to Stay – Top End

The 90-room *Hotel Reina Victoria* (☎ 95 287 12 40), Avenida Doctor Fleming 25, was built by a British company in the 1900s when Ronda was a popular destination for outings from Gibraltar by the recently constructed railway from Algeciras. The air of slightly faded comfort recalls hill-station hotels in far-flung parts of the British empire. Singles/doubles with shower are 9000/16,800 ptas plus IVA; bigger rooms with bath, balcony and view are 11,000/16,800 ptas plus IVA. The hotel has fine cliff-top gardens.

The stylish modern *Parador de Ronda* (☎ 95 287 75 00), Plaza de España s/n, is right on the edge of the gorge with an almost-cliff-top pool. Standard singles/doubles are 14,800/18,500 ptas; doubles with balcony are 21,700 ptas (all plus IVA).

Places to Eat

Typical Ronda food is hearty mountain fare, with a strong emphasis on stews (*cocido*, *estofado* or *cazuela*), trout (*trucha*), game such as rabbit (*conejo*), partridge (*perdiz*) and quail (*codorniz*), and of course oxtail (*rabo de toro*).

Calle José Aparicio has a line of handy but touristy restaurants with ordinary three-course menús for around 900 ptas. *Restaurante Jerez,* on the corner of Calle Blas Infante, is better with soups and salads at 450 to 650 ptas, oxtail at 1600 ptas and partridge for 2200 ptas.

Restaurante Don Miguel on Plaza de España has tables overlooking El Tajo and serves huntin' and shootin' fare such as partridge stew or roast stag leg for 1500 to 2000 ptas.

You'll find a generally better-value range of options on and around Plaza del Socorro, a block north-east of the bullring. *Marisquería Paco* does good seafood and jamón tapas. *Restaurante Doña Pepa*, solid and old-fashioned in food and décor, has menús for 1300 and 1750 ptas and lots of à la carte choices. Its sibling, *Cafetería Doña Pepa*, a few doors along at Calle Marina 1, has slightly cheaper menús and raciones and is open for breakfast. Vegetarians have options at both these places. *Cafetería Cristina* in Pasaje del Correos, the arcade between the two, does platos combinados from only 500 ptas, and good pastries. *El Molino*, with tables on Plaza del Socorro, is popular for its pizzas and pasta at 500 to 700 ptas and platos combinados from 600 ptas.

Bodega La Verdad, at Calle Pedro Romero 5 just off Plaza del Socorro, is a good tapas joint, popular with young locals; a *fino* and a tapa shouldn't set you back more than 200 ptas. *Restaurante Hermanos Macías* on the same street does a reasonably priced *menú* with typical local offerings.

The bright *Cervecería Patatín-Patatán* at Calle Lorenzo Borrego Gómez 7, off the other side of Plaza del Socorro, has sherry and very tasty tapas, most priced between 75 and 150 ptas. The *filetito*, a small slice of steak with a choice of accompaniments, is a good bet, as are the plates of fried potatoes with sauce dips from 300 ptas. Busy *Pizzeria Michelangelo* next door serves up economical pizza and pasta for around 600 ptas.

Casa Eugenio at Calle de Sevilla 7 must have the cheapest platos combinados in town – bacon, egg and chips for 350 ptas.

Entertainment
Café Las Bridas at Calle Los Remedios 18 usually has live flamenco or rock on Friday and Saturday at around midnight. Entry is free. *Pub Niagara* on Avenida Doctor Fleming plays some good music.

Getting There & Away
Bus The bus station is at Plaza Concepción García Redondo 2. The Comes line (☎ 95 287 19 92) has buses to: Zahara de la Sierra (Monday to Friday at 7 am and 1 pm); Arcos de la Frontera, Jerez de la Frontera and Cádiz (three to five times daily); and Jimena de la Frontera and La Línea de la Concepción (990 ptas; Monday to Friday at 4 pm). Los Amarillos (☎ 95 287 22 64) goes to Sevilla (2½ hours, 1235 ptas) three to five times daily; Grazalema, Villaluenga del Rosario and Ubrique twice daily; and Málaga (two hours, 1075 ptas) six times daily. Portillo (☎ 95 287 22 62) runs to San Pedro de Alcántara, Marbella (585 ptas), Fuengirola and Torremolinos three to five

times daily. There are further services to other sierra towns and villages.

Train Ronda is on the scenic Bobadilla-Algeciras line, served by three or four trains each way daily. The station (☎ 95 287 16 73) is on Avenida de Andalucía. You need to change at Bobadilla for Sevilla (around three hours from Ronda, 1860 ptas), Málaga (2 to 2½ hours, 1130 ptas), Granada (3½ hours, 1550 ptas) and Córdoba (three hours, 1550 ptas).

Car & Motorcycle The modern A-376 winds up through the hills from San Pedro de Alcántara. You can also reach Ronda by even more scenic roads such as the A-366 from Coín which winds round the Sierra de las Nieves or the A-369 from San Roque, near Gibraltar, via Jimena de la Frontera.

Getting Around
It's less than 1km from the train station to most accommodation. Occasional town buses run to Plaza de España from Avenida Martínez Astein, across the road from the station.

AROUND RONDA
If you're in the mood for exploring some beautiful, rugged back country, dotted with isolated mountain towns and villages, Ronda is only the start. Fine hill country stretches in all directions from the town, including the Parque Natural Sierra de Grazalema to the west (see Cádiz Province). These green, damp and misty sierras are the western end of the wedge of ranges that twist across nearly all of Andalucía south of the Guadalquivir valley.

Cueva de la Pileta
Some of Spain's most fascinating and beautiful prehistoric rock art – paintings of animals, including a pregnant horse, fish, an archer and abstract symbols – is in this impressive cave some 15km south-west of Ronda. Visits will give you a genuine sense of exploration: the entrance is on a rocky hillside and you'll be guided by lamplight

by one of the Bullón family from the only farmhouse in the valley. A member of the family discovered the paintings, along with fossilised skeletons, pottery and other remains of its Palaeolithic occupants, in 1905 when searching for bat dung to use as fertiliser.

Cueva de la Pileta (☎ 95 216 73 43) is signposted from the Benaoján-Cortes de la Frontera road about 4km south of Benaoján. One-hour tours in Spanish are given daily at 10 and 11 am, noon and 1, 4 and 5 pm. They cost 600 to 800 ptas per person, depending on the size of the group.

Molino del Santo (☎ 95 216 71 51) at Barriada Estación s/n in Benaoján is an attractive, small British-run hotel in a converted water mill, with doubles for 9300 ptas plus IVA.

The nearest you can get to the cave by public transport is Benaoján. There are four daily trains from Ronda to Benaoján (20 minutes), and Los Amarillos buses (195 ptas) leaving Ronda Monday to Friday at 8.30 am and 1 pm.

Ronda la Vieja
Also called Acinipo, this ruined hill-top Roman town about 16km north-west of Ronda has fine views. The theatre has been partly reconstructed and a site plan you'll be given will help you decipher other buildings. It's open Tuesday to Friday from 10 am to 6 pm and on Saturday and Sunday from noon to 6 pm (free). You'll need your own wheels to get there: the turning north off the A-376 is about 6km from Ronda.

Parque Natural Sierra de las Nieves
This 180-sq km park south-east of Ronda encompasses some fine walking country in the craggy Sierra de las Nieves and Sierra de Tolox. These mountains are noted for their stands of the rare Spanish fir *(pinsapo)*, mainly on the damper northern slopes, and fauna including ibex, mouflon (wild sheep), deer, peregrine falcons and various eagles.

For information on the park and walking routes you can contact the tourist office in

Ronda or the tourist offices or ayuntamientos in towns along the A-366 around the north and east edges of the park: Calle Real 22, El Burgo (☎ 95 216 02 77); Calle del Pozo, Yunquera (☎ 95 248 25 01); Calle Coín 10, Alozaina (☎ 95 248 10 17); and Plaza Alta 5, Tolox (☎ 95 248 73 33).

A dirt road crosses the park from the A-376, about 15km south of Ronda, to the small town of Tolox, just outside the park's eastern boundary and 5km off the A-366. A turning north off the dirt road takes you to Los Quejigales picnic area about 9.6km in from the A-376 at an altitude of 1280m from where a day's hike would take you via the Puerto de los Pilones pass (1783m) to Torrecilla (1919m), the highest peak in these sierras, and back. Another walk from Los Quejigales goes north-east to the Los Sauces camping area, just outside the park, via the Puerto de los Quejigales and Peñón de Ronda. From Los Sauces a dirt road runs 9km north to El Burgo, which has remains of a Muslim castle. There are plenty of shorter walks from Los Quejigales, Tolox, El Burgo and Yunquera.

Places to Stay Camping is not allowed in the park but in addition to the *Zona de Acampada Los Sauces* (see earlier), there are also the *Zona de Acampada La Fuensanta* just outside El Burgo on the way to Los Sauces and *Camping Pinsapo Azul* (☎ 95 248 27 54) on the edge of the park near Yunquera charging around 400 ptas per person, per car and per tent.

In El Burgo, *Hostal Sierra de las Nieves* (☎ 95 216 01 17), Calle Comandante Benítez 26, has doubles with bathroom for 4000 ptas; the friendly *Posada del Canónigo* (☎ 95 216 01 85) in a restored mansion at Calle Mesones 24 has doubles with bath from 5000 to 6000 ptas. *Hostal Asencio* (☎ 95 248 27 16) at Calle Mesones 1 in Yunquera charges 4400 ptas plus IVA for doubles with bath, or 3600 ptas plus IVA with shared bathrooms. There are three places at Tolox with doubles between 3100 and 3600 ptas; they're open from mid-June to mid-October.

Getting There & Away Ferron Coín (☎ 95 235 54 90) runs buses between Ronda and Málaga via El Burgo and Yunquera three times daily (once on Sunday) and also has a Ronda-Tolox bus daily, except on Sunday and holidays. Portillo (☎ 95 236 01 91) runs daily buses from Málaga to Tolox.

Even if you don't enter the park proper, the A-366 is a scenic approach to Ronda, winding up through the villages and hills. It's worth stopping for the views from the Mirador del Guarda Forestal lookout between El Burgo and the 1190m Puerto del Viento pass leading to Ronda.

ANTEQUERA

Antequera (population 40,000), 50km north of Málaga, is an attractive town with a well preserved old heart, some fine buildings and two outstanding natural sites within 25km. It's set on the edge of a 540m-high plain with rugged, mountainous country to the south and east.

Some time around 2000 BC the area was inhabited by a people who erected some of Europe's largest megalithic dolmens (tombs of huge boulders). Later Antequera was a significant Roman town. In Muslim times it was a favourite spot of the emirs of Granada before it became the first of their towns to fall to Castilla in 1410.

Orientation & Information

The old heart of the town is below the north-western side of the hill-top Muslim Alcazaba. The main street, Calle Infante Don Fernando, begins here on Plaza San Sebastián and runs west. The bus and train stations are north-west of the centre: the bus station at Campillo Alto s/n is about 1km from Plaza San Sebastián and the train station at Calle Divina Pastora 8 is about 2km out, along Avenida de la Estación.

The tourist office (☎ 95 270 25 05) is in the centre at Plaza San Sebastián 7 on the corner of Calle Encarnación. It's open Monday to Saturday from 9.30 am to 1.30 pm and 4 to 7 pm and on Sunday and holidays from 10 am to 2 pm. The post office is a couple of blocks east at Calle Nájera 23.

Things to See

The Muslim castle, the **Alcazaba**, affords great views over the town and surrounding country, and its gardens sport a nice line in topiary. It's open daily, except Monday, from 10 am to 2 pm (free). Also up here is an impressive gate, the **Arco de los Gigantes**, built in 1585 and incorporating stones with Roman inscriptions. You'll also find the 16th century Renaissance **Colegiata de Santa María la Mayor** church (open the same hours as the Alcazaba).

In the town below, the pride of the **Museo Municipal** in the 18th century Palacio de Nájera on Plaza Coso Viejo is a 1.5m bronze Roman statue of a boy, 'Efebo', found on a local farm in the 1970s. The museum is open Monday to Friday from 10 am to 1.30 pm, Saturday from 10 am to 1 pm and Sunday from 11 am to 1 pm (200 ptas).

The finest of Antequera's many churches is the **Iglesia del Carmen**, on Plaza del Carmen a couple of blocks east of the museum. This 16th century mudéjar construction has a lavish 18th century baroque interior. It's open Monday from 11.30 am to 2 pm (other days from 10 am to 2 pm plus Saturday from 4 to 7 pm; 200 ptas).

In many ways the most impressive of Antequera's monuments are the **Cueva de Menga** and **Cueva de Viera** dolmens, about 1.5km from the centre on the road leading north-east to the N-331. Around 2500 or 2000 BC the locals managed to quarry dozens of huge blocks of stone from nearby hills and transport them here to construct tombs, originally covered in earth, for their chieftains, who were probably buried with their weapons and treasures. Menga, the larger of the two mentioned, is 25m long, 4m high and composed of 31 slabs, the largest of which weighs 180 tonnes. At midsummer the sun rising behind the 'head' on the landmark Peña de los Enamorados mountain to the north-east shines directly into the mouth of this dolmen. Menga and Viera are open daily, except Monday, from 10 am to 2 pm and also from 3 to 5.30 pm Tuesday to Friday (free). A third big dolmen, the **Cueva del Romeral**, is 5km from the centre. Continue past Menga and Viera, and turn left along the old bypass after about 2km; cross the railway, then take the first track on the left.

Special Events
Antequera is a rather sober place by Andalucian standards but it lets its hair down for its Real Feria de Agosto in the second week of August.

Places to Stay
The no-frills *Camas El Gallo* (☎ 95 284 21 04) at Calle Nueva 2 just south of Plaza San Sebastián has small singles/doubles for 1300/2200 ptas. Half a kilometre west, *Hostal Reyes* (☎ 95 284 10 28), Calle Tercia 4 off Calle Infante Don Fernando, has singles/doubles with shared bath at 1450/2900 ptas and doubles with private bath at 4000 ptas plus IVA. *Pensión Madrona* (☎ 95 284 00 14), also fairly central at Calle Calzada 31, has doubles with bath for 3800 ptas plus IVA. *Hostal Manzanito* (☎ 95 284 10 23), Plaza San Sebastián 4, could hardly be more central and charges 2600/4500 ptas plus IVA for singles/doubles. The larger *Hostal Colón* (☎ 95 284 00 10), Calle Infante Don Fernando 29, has rooms costing from 3200 to 5000 ptas plus IVA a double. The *Parador de Antequera* (☎ 95 284 02 61), Paseo García del Olmo s/n, in a quiet area north of the bullring, has nice gardens and doubles for 12,500 ptas plus IVA.

Places to Eat
Bar Manzanito on Plaza San Sebastián has reasonably priced meals. *Mesón Papabellotas* on Calle Encarnación facing the lovely old Plaza Coso Viejo is more expensive; you could just have a drink and tapas and admire the interesting old photos. *Copa-Así* at Calle Lucena 10, off the west end of Plaza San Sebastián, does good value tapas for 50 to 100 ptas (closed Thursday). *Hostal Madrona* (see Places to Stay) has a good, economical restaurant; there are other places around the nearby *mercado* (market) on Plaza Abastos. *La*

Espuela in the 19th century bullring at the western end of Calle Infante Don Fernando has good local cooking and a fairly economical menú.

Getting There & Away
There are several daily buses to/from Málaga, about four to/from Estepa, Osuna and Sevilla (Prado de San Sebastián) and three each to/from Granada and Córdoba.

Three trains a day run to/from Granada, three to/from Sevilla (one with a change at Bobadilla) and two each (with a change at Bobadilla) to/from Málaga and Córdoba.

AROUND ANTEQUERA
El Torcal
Millions of years of wind and water action have sculpted this mountain (1336m) south of Antequera into some of the most weird and wonderful rock formations you'll see anywhere. Twelve sq km of gnarled, serrated and pillared limestone – formed as seabed 150 million years ago – constitute the protected Paraje Natural Torcal de Antequera. There are some deep ravines and cliffs on most sides. The El Torcal visitor centre (☎ 95 203 13 89) is open daily from 10 am to 2 pm and 4 to 6 pm.

A few walking trails of varied lengths set off from the visitor centre. At weekends and holidays some get pretty busy. You're also free to set off on your own, though this probably isn't sensible when it's cloudy. El Torcal harbours 664 plant species, including 20 types of orchid, and 82 species of bird and 22 mammals (including ibex) have been recorded here.But the real stars are the rocks themselves.

Camping is not allowed in the Paraje Natural. There's an intermittently functioning camp site on the road from Antequera.

Getting There & Away You really need a vehicle or else you'll have to walk either to or from Antequera (16 km). From Monday to Friday only there's a bus at 1 pm from Antequera to Villanueva de la Concepción which will drop you at the Cruce del Torcal junction. From here it's a 4km uphill walk to the visitor centre. The return bus leaves Villanueva at 4.15 pm, passing the Cruce a few minutes later.

Drivers from Antequera should head south down Calle Picadero near the western end of Calle Infante Don Fernando, then follow the C-3310 towards Villanueva de la Concepción. Twelve kilometres from the town a turn uphill to the right leads 4km to the car park and visitor centre.

Laguna de Fuente de Piedra

When it's not dried up by drought, Fuente de Piedra, just south of the A-92 about 20km north-west of Antequera, is the biggest natural lake in Andalucía and one of Europe's two main breeding grounds for the spectacular greater flamingo (the other place is the Camargue in France). In 1996, 1997 and 1998, after wet winters, record numbers of flamingo chicks – more than 13,000 each year – hatched here from around 16,000 nesting pairs. The birds arrive in January or February, with the chicks hatching in April and May, and stay till about August when the lake, which rarely is more than 1m deep, no longer contains enough water to support them. The flamingoes share the lake with thousands of other water fowl.

The Centro de Información Fuente de Piedra (☎ 95 211 10 50) at the lake and on the edge of Fuente de Piedra village, is open daily, except Monday, from 9 am to 2 pm and 4 to 7 pm. However, you may fiind that most of the flamingoes cluster on the far side of the lake, a walk or drive of 6 or 7km away. Camping La Laguna (☎ 95 273 52 94), on the edge of Fuente de Piedra village with lake views, is open all year and inexpensive. Hostal La Laguna (☎ 95 273 52 92) at Km 135 on the A-92 at Fuente de Piedra has doubles for 5000 ptas.

Getting There & Away Buses run between Antequera bus station and Fuente de Piedra village seven times a day Monday to Friday, five times on Saturday and three times on Sunday.

Fuente de Piedra train station, about 500m from the lake, is on the Málaga-Córdoba line, with two trains each way daily. Schedules don't permit a day-trip from Málaga or Antequera.

East of Málaga

The coast east of Málaga, sometimes described as the Costa del Sol Oriental, is less developed than the coast west of the city. Along the grey-sand beaches is a string of medium-sized resort towns: Rincón de la Victoria, Torre del Mar, Torrox Costa and Nerja. The first two are mainly popular with Spaniards while Torrox is favoured by Germans and Nerja preferred by the British. All have hostales, hotels and holiday apartments – Nerja has the biggest range – and there are several camp sites too.

Behind the coast the attractive region known as La Axarquía climbs to the Sierras de Alhama, Tejeda and Almijara along the border of Granada province. A 400 sq km area of these mountains was due to be declared Andalucía's 23rd parque natural in late 1998.

A series of crumbling old towers along this coast, many built after the Reconquista to provide a watching place for Muslim raiders from North Africa, adds a romantic touch to the landscape.

RINCÓN DE LA VICTORIA

Rincón's **Las Cuevas del Tesoro** (Treasure Caves – gold was supposedly hidden here by Muslim emirs who used them as a refuge) is worth a stop. The series of underground caverns has stalagmites, stalactites, underground pools and some Palaeolithic wall paintings, though these are off-limits to visitors. Opening hours are Monday to Friday from 10 am to 2 pm and from 3 to 6 pm and on weekends from 10 am to 6 pm.

TORRE DEL MAR

Despite the ugly line of apartments facing

its seafront, Torre del Mar is a likeable place with more local flavour than the coastal towns farther east. Its pleasant beachfront promenade with pretty views along the coast and up into the hills dotted with whitewashed houses continues a couple of kilometres east to Playa La Caleta, which has a marina. Torre fills up with Spanish holiday-makers in July and August. There's a tourist office (☎ 95 254 11 04) at Avenida Andalucía 119 on the main road through town, a few blocks west of the central boulevard, Paseo de Larios.

La Cueva on Paseo de Larios does excellent seafood tapas and raciones. *Las Yucas*, on Avenida de Andalucía a little east of Paseo de Larios, does good-value fancy sandwiches and bocadillos (from 400 ptas). At the seafront end of Paseo de Larios is a line of bars and discos known as El Copo, which kick on all night on Friday and Saturday and attract crowds from far afield.

NERJA

Nerja, 56km east of Málaga with the Sierra de Almijara rising close behind it, is older, whiter and more charming than the preceding towns, though it's inundated by tourism, which has pushed it far beyond its old confines since the 1960s. Nerja has a large foreign community, mainly English.

There are good coastal views from the Balcón de Europa lookout point in the centre. The tourist office (☎ 95 252 15 31), nearby at Puerta del Mar 4, has booklets on walks in the area. The best beach is Playa Burriana, on the eastern side of town. The Book Centre at Calle Granada 30, with books in English and other languages, is well worth a browse. Nerja's annual feria (around 10 October) is one of the last of the year.

Places to Stay

The pleasant *Nerja Camping* (☎ 95 252 97 14), about 4km east of town on the N-340, charges 2000 ptas for two people, a tent and a car.

In August you should try to arrive early in the day to ensure a room. A good, economical choice among the couple of dozen

hostales and pensiones is *Hostal Mena* (☎ 95 252 05 41), Calle El Barrio 15, a short distance west of the tourist office. Its 14 rooms are 1000/2000 ptas for singles/doubles with shared bath or 1250/2500 ptas with private bath (add about 60% in the high season). A bit more expensive, with doubles from about 3000 to 5000 ptas depending on the season, are *Hostal Atenbeni* (☎ 95 252 13 41) at Calle Diputación Provincial 12 (one block north of Calle El Barrio); *Hostal Alhambra* (☎ 95 252 21 74) on the corner of Calle Antonio Millón and Calle Chaparil, a block west of Calle El Barrio; and *Hostal Nerjasol* (☎ 95 252 22 21), Calle Arropieros 4, four blocks north of the tourist office.

Hotel Cala Bella (☎ 95 252 07 00) and *Hotel Portofino* (☎ 95 252 01 50) on Puerta del Mar, close to the tourist office, have some rooms with good beach views. Rooms cost 6000 ptas a double in the high season at the Cala Bella and 8000 ptas at the Portofino, both plus IVA. The half-dozen top-end places include the *Hotel Balcón de Europa* (☎ 95 252 08 00), next to the Balcón itself and with its own little beach (doubles 14,900 ptas plus IVA in the high season), and the *Parador de Nerja* (☎ 95 252 00 50), Calle Almuñécar 8 above Playa Burriana (18,000 ptas plus IVA).

Places to Eat

There are dozens of places to eat in town but one of the best feeds to be had is at the open-air *Merendero Ayo*, towards the eastern end of Playa Burriana, where a plate of paella, cooked on the spot in great sizzling pans, is 675 ptas. There are reasonably priced salads and more expensive fish and meat.

In town, *Haveli* is a good, medium-priced Indian restaurant with a roof terrace at Calle Cristo 44, north off Puerta del Mar. There are over 85 dishes to choose from. Try the Sunday buffet lunch (1400 ptas). *Osteria di' Mamma Rosa* in Edificio Corona on Calle Chaparil, about a 10-minute walk west of Puerta del Mar, is another good medium-priced option. The more expensive *Carabeo 34*, at Calle Carabeo 34, east off

Puerta del Mar, has stunning Mediterranean views and serves up excellent meals and tapas (closed Monday). The classy *Casa Luque* at Plaza Cavana 2, behind the Iglesia del Salvador (the church near the Balcón), does pricey Spanish and Basque food.

At Km 288.5 on the N-340, 3km west of Nerja, *Restaurante La Restinga*, with a thatched conical roof and its own little beach, serves up wonderful but pricey seafood and fish dishes. The *paella marinera* (2000 ptas) is loaded with succulent bites of fish and seafood while the *mejillones* (mussels; 700 ptas) are superbly cooked in a light tomato salsa.

Entertainment

Nerja has a new *Casa de la Cultura*, with a small theatre and cinema, on Calle Granada. There are several places with touristy flamenco shows. Of the town's handful of discos, *Jimmy's,* on Calle Antonio Millón, is a local favourite.

Getting There & Away

Alsina Graells (☎ 95 252 15 04), on the N-340 near the top of Calle Pintada which runs up from near the tourist office, has around 12 daily buses to/from Málaga, eight to/from Almuñécar, several to/from Almería and two to/from Granada.

AROUND NERJA

The area's really big tourist attraction is the **Cueva de Nerja**, 3km east of the town, just off the N-340. This enormous cavern, like some vast underground cathedral, remains impressive despite the crowds that continually traipse through it. Hollowed out by water around 5 million years ago, it was inhabited by Stone Age hunters around 15,000 BC. Unfortunately their rock paintings are off-limits to visitors but there are still lots of impressive stalactites, stalagmites and rock formations to admire. Every July, Spanish and international ballet and music stars perform in the cave as part of the Festival Cueva de Nerja . The cave is open daily from 10.30 am to 2 pm and 3.30 to 6 pm (500 ptas). About 11 buses a day

run from Nerja; others run from Málaga and even Marbella.

Farther east the coast becomes more rugged and scenic and with your own wheels you can head out to some good **beaches** reached by tracks down from the N-340 around 8 to 10km from Nerja. **Playa del Cañuelo**, immediately before the border with Granada province, is one of the best, with a couple of simple summer-only restaurants.

Seven kilometres north of Nerja and linked to it by several buses daily (except Sunday) is the very pretty white village of **Frigiliana**. El Fuerte, the hill that climbs above the village, was the scene of the final bloody defeat of the Moriscos of La Axarquía in their 1569 rebellion (see the La Axarquía section). The hill is topped by scanty remains of a ruined fort from which some of the Moriscos reputedly threw themselves rather than be killed or captured by the Spanish. It's said that bones and rusted weapons from this encounter still lie among the scrub on El Fuerte.

Frigiliana's lone hostal, *Las Chinas* (☎ 95 253 30 73) at Plaza Capitán Cortés 14, has doubles for 4000 ptas.

LA AXARQUÍA

La Axarquía was one of Andalucía's forgotten areas until a decade or so ago, when northern European expatriates became interested in parts of it. Since then, rural tourism has taken off. The chief attractions are the area's hill and mountain scenery, its pretty, unspoiled, white villages, the strong, sweet wine made from sun-dried grapes and good walking (best in April and May and from mid-September to late October).

La Axarquía is riven by deep valleys lined with terraces and irrigation channels that go back to Muslim times. Nearly all the villages that dot the olive, almond and vine-planted hillsides are of Muslim origin, with narrow, higgledy-piggledy streets. La Axarquía joined the 1569 Morisco rebellion (see Las Alpujarras in the Granada Province chapter) and afterwards its inhabitants were replaced with Christians from farther north.

Signposted routes with names like Ruta del Sol y del Vino and Ruta Mudéjar link groups of villages in one-day drives along the snaking mountain roads. You can pick up information at the tourist offices in Nerja or Torre del Mar. RurALandalus (see Accommodation in Facts for the Visitor) has a number of self-catering houses and apartments in La Axarquía, mostly at around 1800 ptas a person per night.

Two good Spanish walking guides are *Sendas y Caminos por los Campos de la Axarquía* (Interguías Clave) and *Andar por La Axarquía* (El Búho Viajero); one place to look for them locally is Papelería Ariza at Avenida Constitución 57 in Cómpeta.

Western Axarquía

The 'capital' of La Axarquía, **Vélez Málaga**, 4km north of Torre del Mar, is busy but unspectacular though its restored hill-top Muslim castle is worth a look. From Vélez the A-335 heads north past the Embalse de la Viñuela reservoir and up through the **Boquete de Zafarraya**, a dramatic cleft in the mountains, to Alhama de Granada. One bus a day each way between Málaga, Torre del Mar and Granada makes its way over this road.

Westward, **Comares** is spectacularly set atop a conical hill. It has a history of rebellion against Muslim and Christian rulers, having been a stronghold of Omar ibn Hafsun (see El Chorro, Ardales & Around). Some of the most dramatic Axarquía scenery is up around the highest villages, **Alfarnate** (925m) and **Alfarnatejo** (858m), where rugged crags such as Tajo de Gomer and Tajo de Doña Ana rise to the south. Both villages are a couple of kilometres off a road crossing to Loja in Granada province. The *Antigua Venta de Alfarnate* at the Alfarnate junction is probably the oldest inn in Andalucía, dating from 1690. It's full of mementoes of past visitors including some of the bandits who used to roam these hills and who, on occasions, took it over.

Places to Stay *Camping Presa de la Viñuela* (☎ 95 255 44 37, 95 203 01 27) on

the west bank of the Embalse de la Viñuela charges 1775 ptas plus IVA for two people with a car and tent. *Camping El Mirador de la Axarquía* (☎ 95 250 92 09) at Comares is cheaper (1100 ptas plus IVA). Both are open all year.

Casa San José (☎ 95 227 62 29) in Alfarnate has singles/doubles for around 1800/3600 ptas. At Alfarnatejo, *Cortijo Pulgarín Bajo* (☎ 95 246 23 05) has rooms in an attractive 19th century farmhouse. The modern *Hotel Atalaya* (☎ 95 250 92 08) at Calle Encinilla s/n, Comares, has singles/doubles with private bath for 2500/4340 ptas and a restaurant. *Hotel de La Viñuela* (☎ 95 251 91 93) has a fine site on the eastern bank of the Embalse de la Viñuela and very comfortable rooms at 5120/10,240 ptas, including breakfast, and a restaurant. Near Periana, a few kilometres above the embalse, the *Villa Turística de la Axarquía* (☎ 95 253 62 22), Carril del Cortijo Blanco s/n, has rooms for 3250/6500 ptas plus IVA, including breakfast; it has a pool and horse stables.

Cómpeta & Around

The highest mountains in the area stretch east from the Boquete de Zafarraya. The typically pretty mountain village of Cómpeta, whose charms are attracting a growing population of northern Europeans, is one of the best bases for a stay in La Axarquía. It has some of La Axarquía's best local wine and quite a range of places to stay and eat. Its popular Noche del Vino (Night of the Wine), 15 August, features a programme of flamenco and sevillana music and dance in the central Plaza Almijara, and limitless free wine. Marco Polo, Calle José Antonio 3, just off Plaza Almijara, sells English-language books.

Árchez, a few kilometres down the valley from Cómpeta, has a beautifully decorated Almohad-style minaret next to its church. A scenic road winding west through the villages of Salares, Sedella and Canillas de Aceituno eventually links up with the A-335 north of Vélez Málaga. Another road leads south-west to **Arenas**

where a steep but driveable track climbs to the ruined Muslim **Castillo de Bentomiz**, crowning a hill top with fine panoramas. In early October Arenas stages the Feria de la Mula, dedicated to that rapidly disappearing beast of burden, the mule.

Walks The best map for walking in the mountains is the SGE's 1:50,000 *Zafarraya*, sold at Marco Polo in Cómpeta, as is *25 Walks in and around Cómpeta & Canillas de Albaida*, by Albert & Dini Kraaijenzank, which covers a range of day-walks from Cómpeta and its smaller neighbouring village 3km north-west.

Maroma (2069m), the highest peak hereabouts, can be climbed from Canillas de Albaida, Salares, Sedella, Canillas de Accituno or the El Alcázar picnic area, a 5km drive from Alcaucín. In each case it's a demanding eight to 10 hours walk, with an ascent and descent of 1200 to 1400m.

Perhaps the most exhilarating walk in the area is up the dramatically peaked **El Lucero** (1779m). From its summit on a clear day, there are stupendous views as far as Granada in one direction and the mountains of Morocco in the other. This is another full day's walking with an ascent of 1150m from Cómpeta. It is possible to drive as far up as the Puerto Blanquillo pass (1200m) on a sometimes rough mountain track from Canillas de Albaida, in 40 minutes or so. A walker's route from Cómpeta to Puerto Blanquillo is described in the Kraaijenzank guide. From Puerto Blanquillo it's a fairly easy walk up to the Puerto de Cómpeta pass (1400m). You then descend the dirt road on the far side (with a quarry on your right). One kilometre down from the Puerto de Cómpeta, take a small path across a stream (or stream bed) to the right. The turn-off is marked by a small cairn and post and a green and white paint mark on a stone just over the stream. This path will lead you to the top of El Lucero in about 1½ hours. El Lucero is topped by the ruins of a Guardia Civil post built to watch for anti-Franco rebels after the civil war.

A couple of pleasant, less demanding outings are to the **Fábrica de Luz de Canillas de Albaida** and the **Fábrica de Luz de Cómpeta**, each 6 or 7km from Cómpeta. The *fábricas de luz* are tiny, ruined hydroelectric installations set in deep, luxuriantly vegetated river valleys among the hills. From the Fábrica de Luz de Cómpeta you can walk on to the abandoned hamlet of **Acebuchal** and, if you wish, round the lower slopes of El Fuerte to Frigiliana (see Around Nerja).

Places to Stay The attractive stone-built *Hostal Alberdini* (☎ 95 251 62 41) has spectacular views from La Lomilla, 1km south-east of Cómpeta (turn right at the Venta de Palma bar on the Torrox road). Singles/doubles with bathroom are 3000/5000 ptas (discounts for more than one night)and there's a good, reasonably priced restaurant. *Hostal Los Montes* (☎ 95 251 60 15) on Cómpeta's Plaza Almijara has singles/doubles for 1500/3000 ptas. In Sedella, *Hostal Casa Pintá* (☎ 95 250 88 77) has rooms with bathroom for 3500/5000 ptas and a restaurant and pool.

Places to Eat In Cómpeta, *Café Bar Perico* on Plaza Almijara does decent standard fare with omelettes and revueltos at 400 to 750 ptas and fish and meat mains from 650 to 1650 ptas. *El Pilón* on nearby Calle Laberinto does terrific Spanish and international food including prawn and avocado salad (650 ptas) or *solomillo a la pimienta verde* (pork sirloin in green pepper sauce, 950 ptas) and Indian or Thai specials. The *Museo del Vino*, Avenida Constitución 6, serves jamón and sausage raciones for 500 to 1975 ptas and wine from the barrel. It also sells good regional crafts. Next door, *Restaurante Asador Museo del Vino* specialises in excellent carnes a la brasa, from chicken or pork chops at 650 ptas to leg of lamb at 2200 ptas.

Getting There & Away Three buses a day (two on Saturday, Sunday and holidays) run from Málaga to Cómpeta and Canillas de Albaida, via Torre del Mar.

Córdoba Province

The big draw in this central northern province is the city of Córdoba itself, which was the capital of Al-Andalus when Al-Andalus was at its political and cultural peak. Córdoba's Mezquita (Mosque) is one of the most magnificent Islamic buildings. The city lies in the fertile valley of the Río Guadalquivir, which runs east-west across the middle of the province. To the north rises the Sierra Morena. To the south is the rolling agricultural area called La Campiña, rising to the Sierras Subbéticas in the south-east.

CÓRDOBA

Lying on a sweep of the Río Guadalquivir with countryside stretching far in every direction around it, Córdoba (population 306,000) almost seems a city in the middle of nowhere. It is by far the biggest and most prosperous place in an otherwise rural province, and feels both provincial and sophisticated. Its labyrinthine, well preserved old quarter, centred on the Mezquita, is fascinating to explore. By contrast, the modern heart of the city, farther north, brings you back to the 20th century with its bustle, shops and traffic. To get some idea of what being *cordobés* is about, you need to experience both parts of the city. Somehow the combination casts a spell which the old quarter alone, being rather peripheral to the daily lives of many Cordobans, cannot quite manage.

The most popular time to visit Córdoba is from about mid-April to mid-June, when the skies are big and blue but the heat is tolerable, the city's many trees are in leaf, and the old town's splendid patios are at their best, dripping with foliage and blooms. Among several festivals at this time is the Concurso de Patios, when many patios are open to the public.

History

The thriving Roman colony of Corduba,

HIGHLIGHTS

- The Mezquita, one of the great Islamic buildings
- Spring flowers and greenery in Córdoba's patios, the Alcázar gardens, and in the countryside almost everywhere
- Wandering the labyrinthine Jewish and Muslim quarters of old Córdoba
- Medina Azahara, Andalucía's most impressive archaeological site
- The mountainous south-east, with its dramatically sited villages and the architectural treasures of Priego de Córdoba

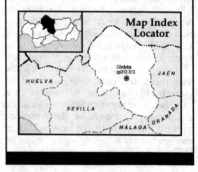

Map Index Locator

Córdoba pp312-313

HUELVA   JAÉN

SEVILLA

MÁLAGA   GRANADA

founded in 169 BC, became the capital of Hispania Ulterior, one of the two initial Roman provinces on the peninsula. After a reorganisation in the 1st century BC, Corduba was the capital of Baetica province (covering most of today's Andalucía plus south-western Castilla-La Mancha and southern Extremadura). This major cultural centre was the birthplace of the famous Latin writers Seneca and Lucan.

In 711 AD Córdoba fell to the Islamic invaders and soon became the capital of Muslim Spain. At first it was subordinate to the Omayyad caliphate in Damascus but, after this, was overthrown by the Abbasids in 750. A survivor – by legend the only survivor – made his way to Córdoba and set

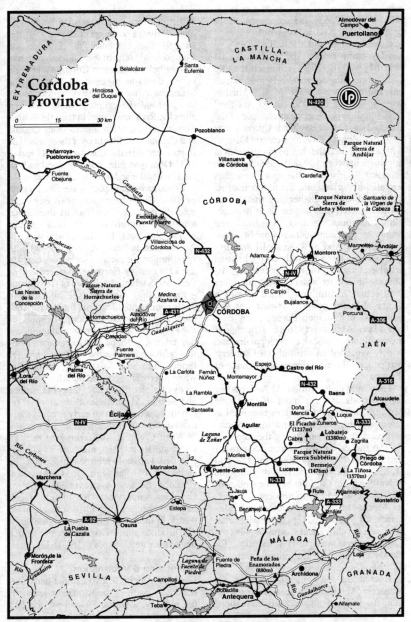

himself up in 756 as the independent emir of Al-Andalus, Abd ar-Rahman I.

Córdoba's – and Islamic Spain's – heyday came under Abd ar-Rahman III (912-61) who in 929 gave himself the title Caliph (meaning supreme religious, political and military leader of the Muslim world), setting the seal on Al-Andalus' long-standing *de facto* independence of the Abbasid caliphs in Baghdad. Córdoba was now the biggest city in western Europe, with a population that has been estimated at anywhere between 100,000 and 500,000. Its economy flourished on the agriculture of its irrigated hinterland and the products of its skilled artisans – leather and metalwork, textiles, glazed tiles and more. It had dazzling mosques, patios, gardens and fountains, plus aqueducts and public baths. The court of Abd ar-Rahman III was frequented by Jewish, Arab and Christian scholars, and Córdoba's university, its famous library, its observatories and other intellectual institutions turned it into a centre of learning whose impact was still being felt in Christian Europe many centuries later. Abulcasis (936-1013), author of a 30-volume medical encyclopaedia and widely regarded as the father of surgery, was perhaps the most remarkable scholar of this age.

The Omayyads unified Al-Andalus for long periods and for most of their rule Muslims, Jews and Christians coexisted in reasonable harmony, despite frequent discontent and rebellion among the ruled. At its peak, the caliphate encompassed most of the Iberian Peninsula south of the Río Duero, plus the Balearic Islands and some of North Africa. Córdoba became a place of pilgrimage for Muslims who could not get to Mecca or Jerusalem. One of Mohammed's arm bones, kept in the Mezquita, became a psychological weapon against the Christians and was partly responsible for the development of the opposing cult of Santiago (St James).

Towards the end of the 10th century, Al-Mansour (Almanzor), a fearsome general, took the reins of power from the caliphs and struck terror into Christian Spain with over 50 forays *(razzias)* in 20 years. He destroyed the cathedral at Santiago de Compostela, home of the Santiago cult, and had its bells brought to Córdoba and hung upside-down as gigantic oil lamps in the Mezquita. After the death of Al-Mansour's son in 1008 the caliphate descended into anarchy. Rival claimants to the title, Berber troops and Christian armies from Castilla and Cataluña all fought over the spoils. The Berbers terrorised and looted the city and in 1031 Omayyad rule ended for good and Al-Andalus collapsed into dozens of *taifas*.

Córdoba became part of the Sevilla taifa in 1069 and has been overshadowed by that upstart city ever since. But its intellectual traditions continued. The 11th century philosopher-poets Ibn Hazm (who wrote in Arabic) and Judah Ha-Levi (Hebrew) both spent important parts of their lives here. In the 12th century Córdoba produced two of the most celebrated scholars of Al-Andalus – the Muslim Averroës (see Literature in Facts about Andalucía) and the Jewish Maimonides (1135-1204), author of *Guide for the Perplexed*. Both were men of multifarious talents, perhaps best remembered for their philosophical efforts to harmonise religious faith with Aristotelian reason. But while Averroës supported the Almohads and enjoyed high office under them in Córdoba and Sevilla, Maimonides fled Almohad religious intolerance at an early age and spent most of his career in Egypt.

When Córdoba was taken by Castilla's Fernando III in 1236, much of its population fled. Fernando returned the bells to the cathedral of Santiago de Compostela. Córdoba became a provincial town of shrinking importance, a situation which began to change only with the coming of industry in the late 19th century – though it did produce one of the greatest Spanish poets, Luis de Góngora (1561-1627).

Orientation & Information

Córdoba is a city of two distinct parts. Immediately north of the Río Guadalquivir is the old city, a warren of narrow, winding streets focused on the Mezquita just a short block from the river. Within the old city, the area north-west of the Mezquita was the Judería (Jewish quarter) and the Muslim quarter was north and east of the Mezquita. The Mozarabic (Christian) quarter was farther to the north-east. Nearly all the sightseeing interest is concentrated in the old town.

The main square of the city is Plaza Tendillas, 500m north of the Mezquita, with the main shopping streets to its north and west. Some 500m west of Plaza Tendillas is a park strip running north towards the railway station, 1km from Plaza Tendillas. A new bus station is due to open behind the train station, probably in 1999, but until then bus companies all have their own terminals scattered west of the centre.

Maps Librería Luque, Calle Conde de Gondomar 13, sells Michelin, CNIG and Córdoba city maps at about half the prices charged by the tourist shops in the old city.

Tourist Offices The Junta de Andalucía tourist office (☎ 957 47 12 35) faces the western side of the Mezquita at Calle de Torrijos 10 and is housed in a 16th century chapel with a fine portal. In summer it's open Monday to Saturday from 9 am to 8 pm and Sunday and holidays from 10 am to 2 pm. In other seasons it closes earlier Monday to Saturday (5 pm in winter). The office has free maps and plenty of other information. The staff speak several languages. The municipal tourist office (☎ 957 20 05 22) is on Plaza de Judá Levi, a block west of the Mezquita. Its hours are Monday to Friday from 9 am to 2 pm and 4.30 to 6.30 pm, Saturday 8.30 am to 2.30 pm and Sunday from 9 am to 2 pm. The staff are helpful but speak only Spanish.

There's also a Punto de Información Turística (Tourist Information Point) at the train station, open Monday to Saturday from 10 am to 2 pm and 4 to 8 pm.

Money The main concentration of banks and ATMs is in the new town, around Plaza

---

Opening Hours

Opening hours for Córdoba's sights rarely remain static. It's worth checking with the tourist offices for the latest times as most places except the Mezquita are closed on Monday. Closing times are generally earlier in winter than summer.

Tendillas and Avenida del Gran Capitán. There's an ATM at the train station.

Post & Communications The main post office (postcode 14080) on Calle José Cruz Conde is open Monday to Friday from 8.30 am to 8.30 pm, Saturday from 9.30 am to 2 pm.

Bookshops Librería Luque, Calle Conde de Gondomar 13, has a decent selection of novels and guides in English downstairs.

Medical & Emergency Services The main general hospital, Hospital Reina Sofía (☎ 957 21 70 00), is 1.5km south-west of the Mezquita at Avenida de Menéndez Pidal s/n. The Hospital Cruz Roja (Red Cross Hospital; ☎ 957 29 34 11) is more central at Avenida Doctor Fleming s/n. For an ambulance call ☎ 061.

The Policía Nacional (☎ 957 47 75 00, ☎ 091 in emergency) are at Avenida Doctor Fleming 2.

Mezquita
This astonishing building can seem a little bewildering at first. Because of the Christian alterations made to the original Islamic structure, and the darkness they impose, you need a bit of imagination to picture the building as it was in Muslim times, open to and in harmony with its surroundings. The Mezquita has some truly beautiful architectural features, among them the famous rows of two-tier arches assembled in mesmerising stripes of red brick and white stone, and

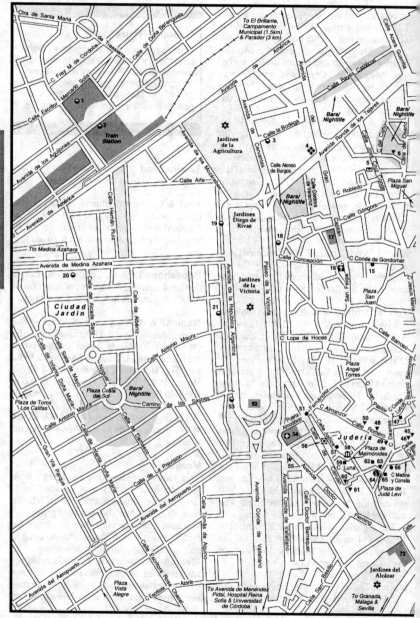

Ctra de Santa María

C Frey M de Córdoba

de Trassierra

Calle de Doña Berenguela

Calle Escritor

Mercado Solís

1

2

Train Station

Calle de los Aguarones

Avenida de los Aguaones

Avenida de América

Calle Hernán Ruiz

Calle Arfe

Calle de los Mozárabes

Avenida de los Mozárabes

Tto Medina Azahara

Avenida de Medina Azahara

20

Ciudad Jardín

Calle del Albéñiz

Calle del Alcalde Sanz

Calle Siete de Mayo

Calle de Infanta Doña María

Noguer

21

Calle Antonio Maura

Plaza Costa del Sol

Bars/ Nightlife

Plaza de Toros Los Califas

Calle Antonio Maura

Gran Vía Parque

Camino de los Sastres

Calle de Dámasio

Calle de Infanta Doña María

Calle de la Previsión

Avenida del Aeropuerto

Calle Tomás de Aquino

Avenida del Aeropuerto

C Escritora Rosa Chacel

Azorín

Plaza Vista Alegre

To El Brillante, Campamento Municipal (1.5km) & Parador (3 km)

Avenida de América

Calle la Bodega

3

Calle Alonso de Burgos

Avenida de Cervantes

Jardines de la Agricultura

4

Calle Córdoba de Veracruz

Bars/ Nightlife

19

Jardines Diego de Rivas

18

17

Calle Concepción

Jardines de la Victoria

Paseo de la Victoria

Avenida de la República Argentina

C Lope de Hoces

Plaza Angel Torres

52

53

51

Puerta Almodóvar

54

56

55

Avenida

Calle Conde de Vallellano

Avenida Conde de Vallellano

Calle Doctor Barraquer

To Avenida de Menéndez Pidal, Hospital Reina Sofía & Universidad de Córdoba

Avenida del Gran Capitán

Gran Capitán

Calle Reyes Católicos

Bars/ Nightlife

Calle Acera Guerrita

Calle Ronda de los Tejares

Bars/ Nightlife

Calle Osario

Calle José Cruz Conde

Calle del Cairo

6

5

Plaza San Miguel

C Robledo

Calle Góngora

C Conde de Gondomar

16

15

Plaza San Juan

San Felipe

Plaza San Juan

Calle Jesús María

Calle Barroso

Calle Buen Pastor

C Almanzor

Calle Fernández

Juderia

50 48

49

C Romero

Deanes

Calle Judíos

58

57

59

C Luna

60

61

Plaza de Maimónides

62 63

64

65

66

C Medina y Corrella

Plaza de Judá Leví

Fleming

Conde Luque

Calle Blanco Belmonte

Calle Manríquez

47

45

46

Jardines del Alcázar

73

To Granada, Málaga & Sevilla

Calle San Basilio

Doctor

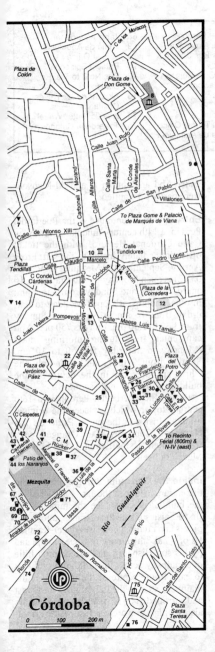

Córdoba

0   100   200 m

PLACES TO STAY
13 Pensión San Francisco
23 Hostal La Fuente
25 Hostal El Portillo
31 Hostal Maestre
32 Hostal Los Arcos
33 Hotel Maestre
34 Hostal Santa Ana
35 Hostal Mari
36 Hostal Trinidad
37 Huéspedes Martínez Rücker
38 Hotel El Conquistador
39 Hostal Rey Heredia
40 Hotel Los Omeyas
42 Hotel Marisa
47 Hostal Séneca
52 Hotel Meliá Córdoba
59 Hotel Amistad Córdoba
62 Albergue Juvenil Córdoba
65 Hotel González
71 Hostal El Triunfo
76 Hotel Hesperia Córdoba

PLACES TO EAT
6 Restaurante Da Vinci
7 Casa El Pisto (Taberna San Miguel)
11 Taberna Salinas
12 Mercado
14 Simago
24 Bar San Francisco
26 Taberna Sociedad de Plateros
28 Taberna El Potro
29 Bar Callejón
41 Bar Santos
43 Taberna El Paseíllo
45 Self-Service Los Patios
46 El Caballo Rojo
48 Restaurante El Rincón de Carmen
49 Casa Pepe de la Judería
50 El Churrasco
60 Mesón la Muralla
61 Mesón de la Luna
63 Café Bar Judá Levi
67 Restaurante Bandolero

OTHER
1 New Bus Station (opening approx
   1999)
2 Bus No 3 to Centre
3 Autotransportes San Sebastián
4 El Corte Inglés
5 Post Office
8 Palacio de Viana
9 Centro de Idiomas Klack
10 Roman Temple
15 Librería Luque
16 Iglesia de San Nicolás de la Villa
17 Gran Teatro de Córdoba

(Continued on next page)

CÓRDOBA PROVINCE

18	Auto-Transportes López	44	Puerta del Perdón	68	Tablao Cardenal
19	Bus No 0-1	51	Puerta de Almodóvar	69	Junta de Andalucía
20	Alsina Graells/Bacoma	53	Secorbus Bus Station &		Tourist Office
	Bus Station		Europcar	70	Palacio Episcopal
21	Empresa Carrera Bus	54	Hospital Cruz Roja	72	Bus No 3 to Train
	Station	55	Policía Nacional		Station
22	Museo Arqueológico	56	Sinagoga	73	Alcázar de los Reyes
27	Museo de Bellas Artes &	57	Zoco		Cristianos
	Museo Julio Romero de	58	Museo Taurino	74	Islamic Water Wheel
	Torres	64	Municipal Tourist Office	75	Torre de la Calahorra
30	Posada del Potro	66	Filmoteca de Andalucía		

the more elaborate arches, domes and mosaic and stucco decoration in and around the splendid *mihrab* (prayer niche).

From the outside the building looks like a fortress, with thick stone walls punctuated by ornately decorated gates; it is low-slung except for the protruding roofs of the cathedral within and the lower domes along the south wall.

History Abd ar-Rahman I founded the Mezquita in 785 on the site of a church which for 50 years had been partitioned between Muslims and Christians. He purchased the Christian half from the Christian community. Abd ar-Rahman II in the 9th century and Al-Hakim II in the 960s extended the Mezquita southwards to cater for Córdoba's expanding population. Al-Hakim II also added the existing mihrab and, to solve the lighting problem caused by the Mezquita's increased size, had a number of domes with skylights built above the area in front of the mihrab. Because they were made of stone, which made them heavier than the wooden roofs of the rest of the Mezquita – these domes rested on stronger, more elaborate arches supporting their star-patterned ribs. Under Al-Mansour, further extensions were made to the east and the mihrab lost its central position in the south wall.

What you see today is the building's final Islamic form with one marked alteration – a 16th century cathedral right in the middle (hence the often-used description 'Mezquita-Catedral'). For this the extensions made

under Abd ar-Rahman II and Al-Mansour were partly dismantled.

Entry The main entrance is the Puerta del Perdón, a 14th century mudéjar gateway on Calle Cardenal Herrero, with the ticket office immediately inside to the left. From April to September the Mezquita (☎ 957 47 05 12) is open Monday to Saturday from 10 am to 7.30 pm and Sunday from 2 to 7 pm; in other months, it's open Monday to Saturday from 10 am to 5 pm, and Sunday from 3.30 to 5.30 pm. Entry is 750 ptas. You can enter free during morning mass (Monday to Saturday from 9 to 10 am, Sunday from 9 to 11 am), but only the Christian cathedral in the centre of the building will be lit at these times.

Beside the Puerta del Perdón is a 16th century tower which replaced the original minaret. Inside is the pretty **Patio de los Naranjos** (Courtyard of the Orange Trees), from which a small door leads into the Mezquita itself.

Inside the Mezquita Straight ahead from the entrance door in the far (south) wall of the building you can see the mihrab. The first 12 aisles inside the entrance, a forest of pillars and arches, comprise Abd ar-Rahman I's original 8th century mosque, completed by his son Hisham I and extending a little over halfway across the building from west to east. In the centre of the building is the main Christian cathedral, aligned east-west and surrounded on all sides by more Islamic aisles, pillars and arches. Just past the right-hand (western) end of the cathedral begins the approach to the mihrab, marked by heavier, more elaborate arches.

The bay immediately in front of the mihrab and the bay to each side form the **maksura**, where the Caliphs and their retinues would have prayed (today enclosed by railings). The maksura and mihrab are acclaimed as the artistic pinnacle of the building. Each of the three bays of the maksura has a skylit dome with star-pattern stone vaulting: the mosaic decoration on the central bay is particularly beautiful. In the central bay is the horseshoe-arched entrance to the mihrab itself. The arch and its rectangular frame *(alfiz)* were superbly decorated with floral-motif mosaics by Byzantine craftsmen, rich stucco work, and mosaic inscriptions from the Qur'an – all in gold, purple, green, blue and red. The **mihrab** itself, which you cannot enter, is octagonal with a shell-shaped dome. The mihrab served both to amplify the voice of the prayer leader and to indicate the direction of Mecca.

Wandering around the rest of the Mezquita, it's possible to lose yourself in the aisles with views of only the incredible columns and arches, uninterrupted by the Christian alterations. In Muslim times the Mezquita would have been better lit, with doors open along its sides.

Columns, Capitals & Arches Abd ar-Rahman I's section of the Mezquita incorporated columns and capitals – of various coloured marbles, granite and alabaster – from the site's previous Visigothic church, from Roman buildings in Córdoba and farther afield, and even from ancient Carthage. The columns were of differing heights so the tall ones had to be sunk into the floor. They support two tiers of arches, giving an effect reminiscent of Roman aqueducts and/or date palms. The use of bicoloured materials for the arches was inspired. Subsequent alterations required more columns, most of which were made by Cordoban craftsmen. The final Islamic building had 1300 columns, of which 850 remain.

Christian Alterations After Fernando III took Córdoba in 1236, the Mezquita was turned into a cathedral. Early modifications, such as the mudéjar tiling added in the 1370s to the Mozarabic and Almohad Capilla Real (nine bays north and one east of the mihrab), were carried out with restraint. But in the 16th century the centre of the Mezquita was ripped out to allow construction of the Capilla Mayor and coro (choir) designed by Hernán Ruiz the Elder. The Capilla Mayor has a rich 17th century jasper and marble retablo; the coro's fine mahogany stalls were carved in the 18th century by Pedro, Duque Cornejo y Roldán.

If you conceive of the whole building as a cathedral, the forests of Islamic arches and pillars provide a magnificent setting for the central structures. But if you think of it as a mosque, the Christian additions undeniably destroy the whole conception of the place. Legend has it that when Carlos I, who had overridden the wishes of Córdoba's city council in giving permission for the Capilla Mayor and coro to be built, saw the results he was horrified, exclaiming: 'You have destroyed something that was unique in the world'.

There are further chapels: one next to the mihrab and others lining the east and west walls of the building.

Palacio Episcopal
Parts of the Bishops' Palace, facing the western side of the Mezquita on Calle de Torrijos, date back to the 14th century. It stands on the site of the caliphs' palace and now houses the **Palacio de Congresos y Exposiciones**, which stages some interesting exhibitions, and the **Museo Obispado de Bellas Artes** with a collection of religious art including some excellent medieval woodcarving.

Judería
The Judería extends west and north-west from the Mezquita, almost to the beginning of Avenida del Gran Capitán. A pleasure to get lost in (like the old Islamic quarter to its east), it's a maze of narrow streets and small

plazas, of whitewashed buildings with flowers dripping from window boxes and of wrought-iron doorways giving glimpses of plant-filled patios. The tourist shops and restaurants around the Mezquita thin out pretty rapidly within one or two blocks.

In a 16th century mansion on Plaza de Maimónides is the **Museo Taurino** (Bull-fighting Museum; ☎ 957 20 10 56), which celebrates Córdoba's legendary *toreros*: there are rooms dedicated to El Cordobés and Manolete, even with the skin, tail and ear of Islero, the bull that fatally gored Manolete at Linares in 1947. The museum is open Tuesday to Saturday from 10 am to 2 pm and 6 to 8 pm (October to April, 5 to 7 pm) and Sunday and holidays from 9.30 am to 3 pm. The cost is 425 ptas (free on Friday).

Just up Calle Judíos from the Museo Taurino are a statue of the famous Córdoba-born scholar Maimonides; the **Zoco** or Souk, a craft centre built around a patio, with fairly up-market silver and leather goods for sale, and artisans at work; and the small 14th century **Sinagoga** (☎ 957 20 29 28), one of Spain's few surviving medieval synagogues. It retains its original women's gallery and the mudéjar stucco work on the upper part of its walls. The opening hours are Tuesday to Saturday from 10 am to 2 pm and 3.30 to 5.30 pm and Sunday and holidays from 10 am to 1.30 pm (free for EU citizens, 50 ptas for others).

Just to the left at the top of Calle Judíos is the **Puerta de Almodóvar**, an Islamic gate in a restored stretch of the old city walls.

Alcázar de los Reyes Cristianos

The Castle of the Christian Monarchs (☎ 957 42 01 51), south-west of the Mezquita, began as a palace and fort for Alfonso X in the 13th century. Isabel and Fernando received Columbus here on one occasion, and from 1490 to 1821 the Inquisition operated from here. A square mudéjar building with three of its four watchtowers still standing, the Alcázar has been much altered and is currently undergoing renovations which mean you can't explore the towers and ramparts. But its extensive and

beautiful gardens, full of fish ponds, fountains, orange trees, flowers and topiary, are among the most beautiful in Andalucía. The alcázar also houses a royal bathhouse and a museum, with some Roman mosaics of most interest.

The opening hours are Tuesday to Saturday from 10 am to 2 pm and 6 to 8 pm (October to April from 4.30 to 6.30 pm) and Sunday and holidays from 9.30 am to 3 pm. The cost until renovations are completed is 300 ptas (free on Friday).

Río Guadalquivir & Torre de la Calahorra

The Guadalquivir is not particularly impressive, except when it's swollen by winter rains. Just south of the Mezquita, it's crossed by the much-restored **Puente Romano** (Roman Bridge). Just downstream from the bridge are the remains of a few Islamic water mills and, near the north bank, a restored **Islamic water wheel** which raised water to the caliphs' palace on the site of the Palacio Episcopal.

At the southern end of the Puente Romano is the **Torre de la Calahorra** (☎ 957 29 39 29), a 14th century tower now housing a curious museum highlighting the intellectual achievements of Islamic Córdoba and focusing rather rose-tintedly on its reputation for religious tolerance. A 55-minute earphone commentary, available in several languages, guides you through the displays while preaching an 'all religions are one' kind of message. In one room, lifesize figures of Averroës, Maimonides, the Andalucian Muslim mystic Ibn al-Arabi (c 1169-1240) and the Castilian king Alfonso X expound on themes of tolerance and understanding of other religions. The museum also contains excellent models of the Mezquita and Granada's Alhambra. Its message appears to sit rather oddly with the fact that its founder, the French philosopher and politician Roger Garaudy, was fined in a Paris court in 1998 for racial defamation and denying a crime against humanity in his book *The Founding Myths of Israeli Politics*. Garaudy, a former communist who converted to Islam in 1982 and became an ardent pro-Palestinian, questioned the existence of the Nazi gas chambers and has claimed that Nazi killing of the Jews did not amount to genocide. (His supporters would claim that he is against all religious extremism and that his motive for questioning the nature of the Nazi crimes was because they were used as a justification for the creation of the state of Israel.)

The Torre de la Calahorra is open daily from 10 am to 2.30 pm and 5.30 to 8.30 pm (October to April, 10 am to 6 pm) and entry costs 500 ptas (400 ptas for pensioners and student or Euro<26 cardholders).

Museo Arqueológico

Córdoba's Archaeological Museum (☎ 957 47 40 11), in a Renaissance mansion with a large patio on Plaza de Jerónimo Páez, has an extensive collection ranging from Palaeolithic to Islamic times. A reclining stone lion takes pride of place in the Iberian section. The Roman period is well represented with large, intricate mosaics, elegant ceramics and tinted glass bowls. The rooms upstairs are devoted to medieval Córdoba, including bronze animals from the caliphs' out-of-town palace at Medina Azahara. The museum's hours are Tuesday from 3 to 8 pm, Wednesday to Saturday from 9 am to 8 pm and Sunday and holidays from 9 am to 3 pm (free with an EU passport, 250 ptas otherwise).

Plaza del Potro

This attractive plaza 400m north-east of the Mezquita is mentioned in *Don Quijote*, whose author, Miguel Cervantes, lived for a spell in a nearby street. The plaza's heyday was during the 16th and 17th centuries when it was a hangout for traders and adventurers. In the centre of the square is a lovely 16th century stone fountain topped by a rearing colt *(potro)*. On the western side of the square is **Posada del Potro**, formerly an inn but now an art gallery. Opposite, the former Hospital de la Caridad houses two art museums. The **Museo de Bellas Artes** has a fairly modest collection

of paintings by mainly Cordoban artists. The baroque room has a couple of Valdés Leals. Among the most arresting of its more modern works are a few canvases by Julio Romero de Torres (1880-1930), a local painter who has the **Museo Julio Romero de Torres**, across the courtyard, to himself. This includes a wonderful collection of his dark, sensual portraits of Cordoban women. The Museo de Bellas Artes has the same hours and prices as the Museo Arqueológico. The Romero de Torres museum opens Tuesday to Saturday from 10 am to 2 pm and 6 to 8 pm (October to April, 5 to 7 pm) and Sunday and holidays from 9.30 am to 3 pm (425 ptas; free on Friday).

Plaza de la Corredera

This handsome square 200m north of Plaza del Potro was the site of Córdoba's Roman amphitheatre and later of Inquisition burnings and bullfights. Today, under restoration from its recent dilapidated condition, it's the site of Córdoba's food market and a lively Saturday flea market.

Palacio de Viana

This Renaissance palace (☎ 957 48 01 34) at Plaza de Don Gome 2, 500m north of Plaza de la Corredera, is famous for its garden and 12 patios, some of which are outstandingly beautiful. Occupied by aristocrats until a couple of decades ago, the palace is also packed with a rich collection of antique furniture, tapestries (some by Goya), ceramics, art, Cordoban leatherwork and more. The opening hours are Monday to Saturday (closed Wednesday) from 10 am to 1 pm and 4 to 6 pm and Sunday from 10 am to 2 pm. Entry is 500 ptas.

Other Sights

As you're roaming around Córdoba's old quarters, you'll notice several beautiful churches. Most of these were built soon after the Reconquista and are Gothic in style. The **Iglesia de San Nicolás de la Villa** at the southern end of Avenida del Gran Capitán, with its octagonal tower, is one of the most impressive.

A ruined **Roman temple** has been partly restored, with 11 columns standing, on Calle Claudio Marcelo.

Language Courses
Centro de Idiomas Klack (☎/fax 957 49 13 03; klack@arrakis.es), Calle Manchado 9, runs courses that last from two to 16 weeks for 32,000 to 197,000 ptas. For information on courses at the university contact the Servicio de Lenguas y Traducción Técnica (☎ 957 21 89 97; fax 957 21 89 96), Universidad de Córdoba, Avenida de Menéndez Pidal, 14071 Córdoba.

Organised Tours
Córdoba Vision (☎ 957 23 17 34), Calle Rafael Márquez Mazzantini 5, operates tours in and around the city. City tours of 2½ hours including the Mezquita and Judería are 2650 ptas. Book at major hotels and agents around town.

Special Events
Semana Santa is celebrated with typical Andalucian fervour and is one of Córdoba's biggest festivals. Every evening from Palm Sunday to Good Friday, between six and 12 pasos and their processions file through the city, passing along the *carrera oficial* (official course) – Calle Claudio Marcelo, Plaza Tendillas and Calle José Cruz Conde – between about 8 pm and midnight. The climax is the *madrugada* of Good Friday, when six pasos pass along the carrera oficial between 4 and 6 am.

Spring and early summer is the chief festival time for Córdoba. Events include:

Late April/early May
Cruces de Mayo – plazas and patios are decked with crosses made entirely of flowers which become a focus for wine and tapas stalls, music and merrymaking; prizes are given for the most beautiful crosses

Hidden Havens Of Delight
Concealed behind heavy wooden doors or partly hidden by wrought-iron gates are many examples of a beautiful Cordoban tradition.

For centuries, the patios of Córdoba have provided shade during the searing heat of summer, a haven of peace and quiet and a place to entertain. In Roman times they were meeting places. In Islamic times they were used for rest and recreation.

In the first half of May, you'll notice 'patio' signs in the streets and alleyways, which means that you're invited to enter and enjoy the patios when they're at their best, with new blooms proliferating. Many of these patios will have been entered in the annual award competition, the Concurso de Patios Cordobeses. You can get a map of patios open for viewing from the tourist office but, if you don't have a lot of time, the patios near Calle San Basilio, about 400m west of the Mezquita, are some of the best.

During the competition, the patios are generally open Monday to Friday from 5 pm to midnight and Saturday and Sunday from noon to midnight. Entry is usually free but sometimes there is a container for donations.

If you're not here in May, the Palacio de Viana, which has 12 lovely patios, is open year round.

First half of May
Concurso & Festival de Patios Cordobeses – see the boxed text Hidden Havens of Delight; at the same time there's a busy cultural programme which, every three years, includes the Concurso Nacional de Arte Flamenco, an important flamenco competition, with performances by big and small names. The next concurso will be held in 2001

Last week of May/first days of June
Feria de Nuestra Señora de la Salud – 10 days of party time for Córdoba with concerts, a big fairground in the El Arenal area, south-east of the city centre, the main bullfighting season in the Los Califas ring on Gran Via Parque, and a general celebratory atmosphere

Late June/first half of July
Festival Internacional de Guitarra (International Guitar Festival) – a two-week celebration of the guitar with live performances of classical, flamenco, rock, blues and more; top names play in the Alcázar gardens at night

Places to Stay

Many of Córdoba's lodgings are built around the charming patios for which the city is famous. There are plenty of places within a few blocks of the Mezquita – some middle and top-end places are just across the street from it. Cheaper places are chiefly in the streets to the east. It's best to ring ahead at peak times, including Semana Santa and during the festivals from late April to early June. Single rooms for a decent price are in short supply.

Places to Stay – Budget

Camping The *Campamento Municipal* (☎ 957 28 21 65) is at Avenida del Brillante 50 (the road to Villaviciosa) in the north of the city, about 1.5km north of the train station. Open year round, it charges 532 ptas per adult and per car and 377 to 532 ptas per tent, all plus IVA.

Youth Hostel Córdoba's ultramodern youth hostel, the *Albergue Juvenil Córdoba* (☎ 957 29 01 66), perfectly positioned on Plaza de Judá Levi, has room for 94 people in double, triple and four-person rooms.

Hostales *Huéspedes Martínez Rücker* (☎ 957 47 25 62), Calle Martínez Rücker 14, with a pretty patio and nice singles/doubles for 1750/3500 ptas, is particularly friendly and only a stone's throw east of the Mezquita. *Hostal Trinidad* (☎ 957 48 79 05), Calle Corregidor Luis de la Cerda 58, is equally well placed and has rooms for 1400/2700 ptas. Two blocks farther east at Calle Cardenal González 25, *Hostal Santa Ana* (☎ 957 48 58 37) has one single at 1750 ptas and doubles at 3500 ptas, or 4500 ptas with bath; the rooms upstairs are more appealing. Nearby at Calle Horno de Porras 6, *Hostal Mari* (☎ 957 48 60 04; mirstation@jet.es) has singles doubles for 1800/3500 ptas.

Heading north a little, the friendly *Hostal Rey Heredia* (☎ 957 47 41 82), Calle Rey Heredia 26, has rooms, with shared bath, around a plant-filled patio for 1500/3000 ptas.

There are some good hostales a little more to the north-east, farther from the main tourist masses. *Pensión San Francisco* (☎ 957 47 27 16), Calle de San Fernando 24, has one small single at 2000 ptas and doubles at 4500 ptas, or 5000 ptas with private bath. *Hostal La Fuente* (☎ 957 48 78 27), Calle de San Fernando 51, has compact singles at 2000 ptas and doubles with bath at 5500 ptas; it's been recently refurbished (the shower pressure is excellent!), has a courtyard for sitting out and a café which serves a decent breakfast. *Hostal El Portillo* (☎ 957 47 20 91), just west off Calle de San Fernando at Calle Cabezas 2, is a friendly and pretty place where rooms come with shared bath for 3000 ptas a double. Close by at Calle Romero Barros 14, *Hostal Los Arcos* (☎ 957 48 56 43) has modern rooms around a pretty courtyard for 2000/3500 ptas, or 4500 ptas with attached bath. Next door at No 16, *Hostal Maestre* (☎ 957 47 53 95) has plenty of clean, spacious rooms with private bath at 2500/4500 ptas.

A short distance north of the Mezquita, *Hostal Séneca* (☎ 957 47 32 34), Calle Conde y Luque 7, is charming, with friendly management, a *típico* patio and a breakfast room; rooms with shared bath cost 2450/4600 ptas while those with attached bath cost 5600 ptas – including breakfast. Phone ahead.

Places to Stay – Mid-Range

Hostal El Triunfo (☎ 957 47 55 00), Calle Corregidor Luis de la Cerda 79, on the southern side of the Mezquita, has singles/doubles with air-con and TV for 3700/6200 ptas plus IVA. There's a restaurant too. *Hotel Marisa* (☎ 957 47 31 42), facing the Mezquita at Calle Cardenal Herrero 6, has all mod cons; rooms with bath cost 4400/8200 ptas plus IVA. Half a block from the Mezquita at Calle Encarnación 17, *Hotel Los Omeyas* (☎ 957 49 22 67) is attractive with doubles at 7000 ptas plus IVA. *Hotel González* (☎ 47 98 19), Calle Manríquez 3, is well placed a block west of the Mezquita and has doubles for 9850 ptas plus IVA. It has a courtyard restaurant. To the east, *Hotel Maestre* (☎ 957 47 24 10) at Calle Romero Barros 4, on the corner of Calle de San Fernando, has bright rooms with attached bath for 3500/ 6000 ptas.

Places to Stay – Top End

Add IVA to all prices quoted. *Hotel El Conquistador* (☎ 957 48 11 02), Calle Magistral González Francés 15, facing the eastern side of the Mezquita, has very comfortable doubles for 15,500 ptas. In the Judería the attractive *Hotel Amistad Córdoba* (☎ 957 42 03 35), Plaza de Maimónides 3, occupying two converted mansions with a mudéjar courtyard, has singles/doubles for 12,300/ 15,000 ptas, but from Friday to Sunday doubles come down to 9800 ptas. On the southern side of the Río Guadalquivir – close to the Torre de la Calahorra, *Hotel Hesperia Córdoba* (☎ 957 42 10 42), Avenida de la Confederación s/n, charges 15,800 ptas and has views across to the old town and the additional attraction of a large swimming pool and terrace. The luxurious *Hotel Meliá Córdoba* (☎ 957 29 80 66) is just outside the Judería at the southern end of the Jardines de la Victoria, with doubles for 16,900 ptas.

Córdoba's modern *Parador* (☎ 957 27 59 00), Avenida de la Arruzafa s/n, is 3km north of the centre on the site of Abd ar-Rahman I's country palace where Europe's first palm trees were planted – *arruzafa* is Arabic for 'garden of the palm trees'. Doubles cost 16,500 ptas (14,500 ptas in July and August).

Places to Eat

A couple of dishes are common to most Cordoban restaurants. *Salmorejo* is a type of gazpacho with chopped hard-boiled eggs floating on top. *Rabo de toro*, ox tail stew, is another favourite. Some of the top places to eat feature recipes from Al-Andalus such as garlic soup with raisins, honeyed lamb, fried aubergine and meats stuffed with dates and pine nuts. The local tipple is wine from nearby Montilla and Moriles; and is very similar to sherry and made by the same process but without being fortified. Like sherry, it comes as *fino*, *amontillado* or *oloroso* and there's also the sweet Pedro Ximénez variety made from raisins.

There are loads of places to eat right by the Mezquita, some expensive, some mediocre and some awful. Some better-value places are a short walk west into the Judería. A longer walk east or north will produce even better options for the budget-conscious and/or inquisitive.

Around the Mezquita *Self-Service Los Patios*, right opposite the Mezquita at Calle Cardenal Herrero 14, has a good choice of functional main courses and desserts with nothing over 700 ptas plus IVA. A typical main dish is fried *merluza* (hake) and salad. The lovely covered patio offers respite from the heat in summer. *Taberna El Paseillo*, Calle Cardenal Herrero 16, does a three-course menú del día including bread and a drink for 1250 ptas. *El Caballo Rojo*, Calle Cardenal Herrero 28, specialises in Mozarabic food from the time of the caliphs. The menú is a hefty 2950 ptas plus IVA and mains start at about 1600 ptas, but here you're guaranteed something different from the usual fare. There's also good food at *Restaurante Bandolero*, Calle de Torrijos 6 on the west side of the Mezquita. It has media-raciones from 250 ptas and platos combinados from 975 to 1100 ptas; á la carte, you could expect to pay 3000 to 4000 ptas for three courses with drinks. Delicious items on the menu include red peppers stuffed with seafood (1500 ptas) and seafood soup (975 ptas). You can sit in the bar or in the open-air patio.

The basic little *Bar Santos* on Calle Magistral González Francés on the east side of the Mezquita does bocadillos for 200 to 300 ptas and raciones for 500 ptas.

Judería *Casa Pepe de la Judería*, Calle Romero 1, does excellent tapas and raciones, such as *puntillitas* (fried young squid, 500 ptas a media-ración) and croquetas caseras, in its bar. It also has a good restaurant with typical main dishes in the 1500 ptas zone. A few doors up the street, *Restaurante El Rincón de Carmen* has an open-air patio with a menú for 1500 ptas and an attached café that does good snacks and breakfasts. Comfy cane chairs and relaxed background music provide relief to the footsore. *El Churrasco*, Calle Romero 16, is one of Córdoba's very best restaurants. The food is rich, the portions are generous and the service is attentive with prices to match. The menú is 3000 ptas; most mains are around 2000 ptas, though *churrasco* pork fillet and some fish dishes are as little as 1200 ptas.

Café Bar Judá Levi on Plaza Judá Levi is a pleasant place to sit. It is popular for its ice creams, and does platos combinados from 700 ptas. A short stroll beyond here, in the city walls on Calle de la Luna, *Mesón de la Luna* and *Mesón la Muralla* share a courtyard and both have menús from 1200 to 1900 ptas which feature local specialities.

East of the Mezquita There are several good-value places in this area. *Taberna Sociedad de Plateros*, Calle San Francisco 6, is a popular tavern with a good range of tapas and raciones (nothing over 700 ptas).

A breakfast café con leche and tostada here is 210 ptas. Round the corner on Calle de San Fernando, *Bar San Francisco* has a menú for 975 ptas. Just east, on pedestrian Calle Enrique Romero de Torres, are two bar/restaurants with tables outside looking on to Plaza del Potro. This is a fine place to sit on a balmy evening at sunset. *Bar Callejón* has egg dishes and omelettes for around 400 ptas, or a three-course menú with a drink for 1000 ptas. *Taberna El Potro* next door is more expensive.

The homely *Taberna Salinas*, a little farther north at Calle Tundidores 3, offers good, inexpensive Cordoban fare – bacalao with bitter oranges makes an interesting change. Other options include a good revuelto de ajetes, gambas y jamón (scrambled eggs with garlic shoots, prawns and ham) and chuletas de cordero (lamb chops), while vegetarians could go for dishes such as setas en salsa (wild mushrooms in a sauce) or pisto (fried vegetables). All these are between 625 and 725 ptas. The restaurant is open Monday to Saturday for lunch and dinner.

City Centre *Casa El Pisto* (officially *Taberna San Miguel*) at Plaza San Miguel 1, just north of Plaza Tendillas, is a popular and atmospheric old watering hole with a great range of tapas (200 to 275 ptas), media-raciones (500 to 900 ptas) and raciones, and good Moriles wine. You can stand at the bar or eat at tables in the back. We enjoyed the gambas rebozadas (fried battered prawns, 750 ptas a media-ración) and the montaditos de lomo (265 ptas each). El Pisto is open Monday to Saturday from noon to 4 pm and 8 pm to midnight. A little farther north, *Restaurante Da Vinci*, Plaza de Chirinos 6, does reasonable pizzas and pasta from 575 to 900 ptas, plus more expensive carnes a la brasa and fish. There are several other reasonably priced eateries on Plaza Tendillas and Calle Claudio Marcelo.

Self-Catering There's a *food market* (*mercado*) on the southern side of Plaza de la Corredera, open Monday to Saturday but busiest on Saturday. *Simago* is a handy supermarket on Calle Jesús María, just south of Plaza Tendillas.

Entertainment
For information about what's on, look for *Salir* magazine in the tourist offices or newsagents, or consult the daily newspaper *Córdoba*.

Córdoba's lively music bars and late-night bars are scattered around in three or four areas, all in the north or west of town. There are a few such places on Calle del Caño and Calle del Osario, 300m north of Plaza Tendillas, but more around Calle Reyes Católicos, a little farther north, and on streets such as Calle Córdova de Veracruz and Calle Alonso de Burgos, south of Avenida Ronda de los Tejares and west of Avenida del Gran Capitán. Another nightlife area is the Ciudad Jardín suburb around Plaza Costa del Sol, 350m west of Avenida de la República Argentina. Finally, there's the northern El Brillante suburb, especially along Avenida del Brillante (the continuation of Avenida del Gran Capitán) and in the El Tablero urbanisation. There's generally little action anywhere early in the week.

Most bars in the old town close at about midnight. But there's a fairly good and authentic flamenco show from Tuesday to Saturday night at *Tablao Cardenal* (☎ 957 48 31 12), Calle de Torrijos 10 facing the western side of the Mezquita. It starts at 10.30 pm and costs 2400 ptas including one drink.

The *Gran Teatro de Córdoba* (☎ 957 48 02 37), Avenida del Gran Capitán 3, has a busy programme ranging from varied concerts and theatre to dance and film festivals. The *Filmoteca de Andalucía* (☎ 957 47 20 18), in an alley just west of the Mezquita at Calle Medina y Corella 5, regularly shows subtitled (not dubbed) foreign films.

Things to Buy
Córdoba is known for its leather goods, silver jewellery (particularly filigree), and attractive pottery in distinctive, green, blue and black on a white background. Plenty of these crafts can be had, at a price, in the tourist shops around the Mezquita, but the central shopping district around Plaza Tendillas has some of the same at less inflated prices. The Zoco on Calle Judíos in the Judería has good but pricey products.

Plaza de la Corredera has a few shops selling boots, music and bric-a-brac but becomes a lively *mercadillo* on Saturday morning and to a lesser extent on Wednesday and Thursday.

Calle José Cruz Conde is the smartest central shopping street. The excellent El Corte Inglés department store is on the corner of Avenida del Gran Capitán and Avenida Ronda de los Tejares.

Getting There & Away
Córdoba newspaper has fairly up-to-date transport information in its back pages.

Bus A new bus station, behind the train station, is due to open some time (maybe in 1999), but until then the different bus lines use at least half a dozen different stations.

The major one is the Alsina Graells and Bacoma bus station at Avenida de Medina Azahara 29, 500m west of Avenida de la República Argentina. There are a few consigna lockers here (300 ptas for 24 hours). Alsina Graells (☎ 957 23 64 74) has at least 10 daily buses to Sevilla (1200 ptas), seven to Granada (1765 ptas), five to Málaga (1515 ptas), three to Écija, four to Jaén and others to the Costa del Sol, Algeciras, Cádiz, Motril, Almería (2995 ptas) and Murcia. From this station Bacoma (☎ 957 45 65 14) runs buses to Baeza, Úbeda, Alicante, Valencia and Barcelona.

Empresa Carrera (☎ 957 23 14 01), Avenida de la República Argentina 30, serves Córdoba province south of Córdoba, with several daily buses each to Priego de Córdoba, Aguilar, Baena, Montilla and Cabra, and at least two a day to Luque, Zuheros and Iznájar.

Auto-Transportes López (☎ 957 47 45 92), Paseo de la Victoria 15, runs buses to Extremadura and north-western Córdoba province. Autotransportes San Sebastián (☎ 957 47 04 28), Calle La Bodega 1, heads west to Palma del Río and Hornachuelos. Empresa Ramírez (☎ 957 41 01 00), Avenida de la República Argentina 26, serves Montoro and Andújar, to the east. Buses to Madrid (at least six daily; 1580 ptas) are run by Secorbus (☎ 957 46 80 40), Camino de los Sastres 1.

Train Córdoba's modern train station (☎ 957 40 02 02) is on Avenida de América, 1km north-west of Plaza Tendillas. There are consigna lockers (300 to 600 ptas for 24 hours depending on size) outside the rear exit.

About 20 trains a day run to/from Sevilla, ranging from Andalucía Exprés regional trains (1¼ hours; 1050 ptas) to AVEs (45 minutes; 2300 to 2700 ptas). To/from Madrid, several daily AVEs take 1¾ hours (5900 to 7000 ptas); other options range from a middle-of-the-night Estrella (6¼ hours; 3500 ptas) and an afternoon Inter-City (4¼ hours; 3700 ptas) to various Talgos taking two hours or so for 4800 to 5700 ptas.

There are several daily trains to Málaga (about 2¼ hours; 1900 to 2200 ptas) and Cádiz, and one each to Jaén and Huelva. For Granada you need to take a Málaga train and change at Bobadilla; it takes four hours and the fare is about 1800 ptas.

Car Car rental firms include Avis (☎ 957 47 68 62), Plaza de Colón 35; Europcar (☎ 957 23 34 60), Camino de los Sastres 1 and at the train station; and Hertz (☎ 957 40 20 60) at the train station.

Getting Around
Bus City buses cost 110 ptas. Bus No 3 from behind the train station (and in front of the new bus station when it opens) runs to Plaza Tendillas and down Calle de San Fernando, 300m east of the Mezquita. You can pick it up on Ronda de Isasa, just south of the Mezquita, for the return trip, on which it also stops on Paseo de la Victoria, within walking distance of many of the existing

bus stations. No 14 from the Alsina Graells and Bacoma bus station will take you 600m to Paseo de la Victoria – but no nearer to anywhere useful.

Car & Motorcycle Córdoba's one-way system is not much fun, nor is finding a place to park in the old city. Fortunately the routes to many hotels and hostales are fairly well signposted: the signs also display a 'P' if the establishment has parking space.

Taxi In the city centre, cabs congregate at the north-eastern corner of Plaza Tendillas. Fares are around 450 ptas from the train station or Alsina Graells bus station to the centre or Mezquita.

AROUND CÓRDOBA
Medina Azahara
In 936 Abd ar-Rahman III decided his new caliphate needed a new capital and duly had one built 8km west of Córdoba at the foot of the Sierra Morena. Records state that 10,000 labourers worked on its construction, setting 6000 stone blocks a day, and by 945 Abd ar-Rahman was able to install himself and his retinue. Stretching about 1.5km from east to west and 700m from north to south, the new city was called Medina Azahara, or Madinat al-Zahra, after the caliph's wife Azahara. It was undoubtedly a magnificent place (though the chronicler who wrote that it required 3750 slaves to run it and that the fish in its ponds ate 12,000 loaves of bread a day was very likely an exaggerator). Its glory was short-lived, however. Al-Mansour transferred the seat of government to a new palace-complex of his own, east of the city, in 981. Then, between 1010 and 1013, Medina Azahara was wrecked by Berber soldiers who occupied it during the anarchic collapse of the caliphate. Over succeeding centuries its ruins were plundered repeatedly for building material. Excavation of the site began in 1922.

Though less than one-tenth of the city has been excavated, and what's open to visitors is only about a quarter of that, Medina

Azahara (☎ 957 32 91 30) is still an intriguing place to visit and its location in pleasant countryside adds to the appeal. It's open Tuesday to Saturday from 10 am to 2 pm and 6 to 8.30 pm (October to April, 4 to 6.30 pm) and Sunday from 10 am to 2 pm. Entry is free with an EU passport, 250 ptas otherwise.

The uppermost of the terraces on which the city was built – immediately in front of the site entrance – was the site of the Dar al-Mulk, or caliph's residence (not open to visitors at our last check). The visitor route takes you down a path and through the northern gate of the city to the **Dar al-Wuzara** (House of the Viziers), a substantial partly-restored building which would have been used by the caliphs' administrative advisers. It has several horseshoe arches and is fronted by a square garden. Down to the east from here is a **portico**, a row of arches in a red and white striped design similar to that of the Córdoba Mezquita, which fronted a military parade ground. From here you follow the path downhill, with views over the ruins of Medina Azahara's caliphal **mosque**, to the most impressive building on the site, the much-restored **Salón de Abd ar-Rahman III**, facing a large garden. This was the caliph's throne hall, where he would have conducted affairs of state. The salón is a three-aisled affair with beautiful horseshoe arching. Its floral, geometric and calligraphic decoration of carved stone (still being pieced together by the reconstructors) was of a lavishness unprecedented in the Islamic world. Richard Fletcher writes in *Moorish Spain* that in the centre of the hall stood a bowl containing mercury: when the caliph wished to impress visitors, he would have a slave rock the bowl so that light reflected from the mercury would flash around the hall like lightning.

Getting There & Away If you're driving, take Avenida de Medina Azahara west from the city centre, leading out on to the A-431. The turn-off to Medina Azahara is signposted some 5km from the city centre. If

you haven't got wheels, Córdoba Vision (see Organised Tours under Córdoba) runs tours to Medina Azahara twice daily (except Sunday afternoon and Monday) for 2150 ptas. A taxi costs around 4000 ptas for the return trip. The nearest you can get by bus is the Cruce de Medina Azahara, the turnoff from A-431, from which it's a 3km slightly uphill walk to the site. City bus No 0-1 from the northern end of Avenida de la República Argentina will drop you there. You can phone ☎ 957 25 57 04 for schedule information in Spanish.

SOUTH OF CÓRDOBA

Córdoba city apart, the province is well off the tracks of most tourists. But if you like exploring back roads and small towns and villages, there's plenty of picturesque scope. While the main road to/from the south, the N-331 to Antequera and Málaga, crosses mainly unspectacular, rolling *campiña* country, the south-east of the province is mountainous and beautiful. There's plenty of historical and architectural interest too for those who like delving into details. Many of the towns and villages across the south of the province – which straddled the Muslim-Christian frontier from the 13th to 15th centuries – are ancient places crowned by hill-top castles. The Junta de Andalucía tourist office in Córdoba has comprehensive brochures on the region, but in Spanish only.

Towards Málaga

Just east of the N-331 and on the Córdoba-Málaga railway, 45km from Córdoba, **Montilla** is the main production centre for Córdoba's sherry-like wines. You can visit Bodegas Alvear (☎ 957 65 01 00) at Avenida María Auxiliadora 1, but you should call first for times. There are several hotels and hostales.

Nature lovers with their own transport could detour to the **Laguna de Zoñar**, 4km south-west of Aguilar by the A-309, which has a high winter and spring population of water birds. Conservation efforts here have saved the western European population of the white-headed duck *(pato malvasía)*, a polygamous creature which can hardly walk on land because of its underdeveloped feet designed for diving. Since 1977 its numbers here have jumped from 50 to over 700. The Centro de Información El Lagar (☎ 957 66 11 52) here is open daily except Monday from 10 am to 6 pm.

Farther south, **Lucena** is an industrial town with furniture, wrought iron and lighting showrooms lining the N-331. **Cabra**, 10 km east off the N-331, is one of the best places to detour to – it has a pretty old quarter, the Barrio del Cerro, and some handsome old mansions and churches, including the red-marble-columned Iglesia de la Asunción which retains much of the plan of the mosque that it once was. There's an archaeological museum in the Casa de la Cultura on Calle Martín Belda. Winding roads lead 15km east from Cabra up to 1217m El Picacho in the mountainous Parque Natural Sierra Subbética. There are great panoramas from up here and the hill is topped by a chapel, the **Ermita de Nuestra Señora de la Sierra**, which attracts numerous *romerías* including the celebrated Romería de los Gitanos on a Sunday in mid-June, when Gypsies (and others) from around Spain gather to honour the Virgen de la Sierra – and sing, play and dance a great deal of flamenco. *Fonda Guerrero* (☎ 957 52 05 07), Calle Pepita Jiménez 5 in Cabra, has rooms with bath for 3800 ptas a double. There's also *Hostal San José* (☎ 957 52 03 68), Avenida Fuente del Río 12.

Towards Granada

The handsome old town of **Baena**, 62km south-east of Córdoba on the N-432 to Granada, is noted for its high-quality olive oil and for its Semana Santa celebrations in which rival teams of hundreds of drummers try to outdo each other in volume and stamina. Beyond Baena the mountains of Sistema Subbética start to rise up from the campiña. The picturesque castle-topped mountain villages of **Luque** and **Zuheros**, both a few kilometres south off the N-432,

have accommodation and can act as bases for walks in the rugged hills and wooded river valleys of the Parque Natural Sierra Subbética, which begins immediately to their south. (Try to get the CNIG 1:50,000 map *Parque Natural Sierras Subbéticas* if you fancy walking in these sierras). In Zuheros, the good *Hotel Zuhayra* (☎ 957 69 46 93), Calle Mirador 10, has doubles with bath for 6000 ptas plus IVA.

Priego de Córdoba

Some 18km south of the Granada road, along the A-333, the sizeable town of Priego de Córdoba is another possible base for exploring the Parque Natural Sierra Subbética and an attractive place in its own right. Surrounded by fine hill country – walking targets include 1570m La Tiñosa and 1476m Bermejo, both rising to the south-west – the town goes back a long way but its chief glory is a series of baroque churches, built in the 18th century when the town blossomed on the profits of a textile industry.

Information Free guided tours of the town are available from the helpful tourist office (☎ 957 54 09 47) in the Centro Cultural Alonso Lozano Sidro at Carrera de las Monjas 16, a short walk west of the central Plaza de la Constitución. It's open Monday to Friday from 10 am to 1 pm and Saturday and Sunday from 11 am to 1 pm. Priego's churches are normally open daily from about 6.30 to 9 pm, plus 11 am to 1 pm on Saturday and Sunday. You can arrange a tour outside the tourist office's and the churches' opening hours by calling the office, or the guide on ☎ 957 70 06 25. The tourist office building also houses the town's museum.

Things to See The highlight church is the **Parroquia de la Asunción** on Plaza de Abad Palomino about 200m north-east of Plaza de la Constitución. Founded in the 16th century, it was rebuilt in baroque style in the 18th century by Jerónimo Sánchez de Rueda. The main part of the church is ornate enough but the Sagrario chapel is one of the supreme baroque works in Andalucía, an extraordinarily lavish confection of white stucco and sculpture with a beautiful windowed dome.

Behind La Asunción are the winding streets of the old Muslim quarter, the **Barrio de La Villa**, where the Andalucian love affair with potted geraniums reaches its ultimate expression on beautiful Calle Real. The Barrio de La Villa gives on to the Balcón del Adarve, a walkway along the edge of the cliff on which the barrio stands.

Other sumptuous baroque churches include the **Iglesia de San Pedro** on Plaza San Pedro, the **Ermita de la Aurora** on Carrera de Álvarez, and the **Iglesia de San Francisco** on Calle Buen Suceso.

Also not to be missed is the **Fuente del Rey** at the end of Calle del Río, a wonderfully elegant 1780s fountain which would be more at home in the gardens of Versailles than a small town in provincial Andalucía. Composed of three curvaceous pools, with water flowing from one to the next, it's fed by 139 spouts, the upper ones in the form of grotesque stone faces. Sculptural groups in the pools show a lion fighting a dragon, and Neptune and Anfitrite.

Places to Stay & Eat *Camping Cortijo Las Palmas* (☎ 957 72 00 02), open from mid-April to mid-September, is a few kilometres west at Km 5 on the Carcabuey-Zagrilla road. It charges 300 ptas plus IVA per person, per tent and per car.

The welcoming *Hostal Rafi* (☎ 957 54 07 49), just east of Plaza de la Constitución at Calle Isabel La Católica 4, has good rooms

with bath at 4300 ptas a double and a restaurant. The basic *Hostal Andalucía* (☎ 957 54 01 74), also central at Calle del Río 13, has rooms with bath for 3000 ptas a double or with shared bath for 2400 ptas. The *Río Piscina* (☎ 957 70 01 86) is down on the east edge of town at Carretera Monturque-Alcalá La Real Km 44, with doubles at 5750 ptas plus IVA, and a pool. The modern but Muslim-style *Villa Turística de Priego* (☎ 957 70 35 03) is 7km north on the road to Zagrilla, with attractive self-catering apartments at 8560 ptas plus IVA a double. It has a pool and a restaurant.

For food in town, there are cafés around Plaza de la Constitución and the streets to its east or you could try *El Aljibe* restaurant by the Parroquia de la Asunción.

Getting There & Away Priego's bus station is about 1km west of Plaza de la Constitución on Calle Nuestra Señora de los Remedios. There are up to 13 daily buses to Córdoba, two or more buses to Granada and others to Cabra, Baena and elsewhere.

South of Priego

The A-333 winds south from Priego – take the road signed 'Lagunillas, Rute' off the Loja road leaving the town centre – through handsome hill country whose lower slopes are strung with line upon line of mature olive trees. **Iznájar**, 26km from Priego, overlooks the Embalse de Iznájar reservoir from an imposing crag topped by a Muslim castle and a 16th century church. South of here the A-333 hits the A-92 Granada-Sevilla highway.

Granada Province

As well as the world-famous city of Granada, this eastern province includes Andalucía's highest mountains (in the Sierra Nevada) and the beautiful Las Alpujarras valleys to their south.

Granada city is surrounded by a fertile plain called La Vega which is traversed by the Río Genil. To the south-west are further *sierras* bordering Málaga province's Axarquía region. In the north-east is the Altiplano, a large expanse of high, dry and often desolate country, with a rather lunar landscape breaking out into mountains here and there.

GRANADA

At first, modern Granada with its traffic-choked main streets and high-rise apartment blocks seems a disappointing world away from its Muslim past. However, the famous Alhambra, dominating the skyline from its hill-top perch, and the fascinating Albayzín, the old Islamic quarter which also rises above the modern city, are highlights of a visit to Andalucía.

The city has more to offer. Its setting, with the backdrop of the often snow-clad Sierra Nevada, is magnificent; its greenness is a delight in often parched Andalucía and its climate pleasant, especially in spring and autumn. Granada also has some impressive and historic post-Reconquista buildings and, thanks to its university, a vibrant youthful population, a buzzing cultural life, some excellent bars and a hopping nightlife.

A wealthy city of 246,000 people, Granada has an international feel, mostly due to its high numbers of tourists. It seems to absorb tourism well except during peak periods inside the Alhambra and Capilla Real. In tandem with this wealth subsists an underclass: you'll see quite a few beggars.

History

An Iberian tribe, the Túrdulos, settled here in the 5th century BC. The Romans arrived late in the 3rd century BC, settled in the vicinity

Map Index Locator

JAÉN

CÓRDOBA

Granada pp332-333
Central Granada p342
Alhambra p336

MÁLAGA

ALMERÍA

GRANADA PROVINCE

of the Alcazaba (part of the Alhambra) and Albayzín, and called their town Illiberis. The Visigoths built city walls and laid the foundations of the Alcazaba. Muslim forces, with the help of the city's Jews, took the city in 711. It was ruled from Córdoba until 1031 and later from Sevilla by the Almoravids and then the Almohads. The Islamic city came to be called Karnattah, from which 'Granada' is derived (*granada* also happens to be the Spanish for pomegranate, the fruit which is on the city's coat of arms).

After the fall of Córdoba (1236) and Sevilla (1248) to Christian Castilla, Muslims sought refuge in Granada, where the founder of the Nasrid dynasty, Mohammed ibn Yousouf ibn Nasr (also called Mohammed al-Ahmar), had recently established an

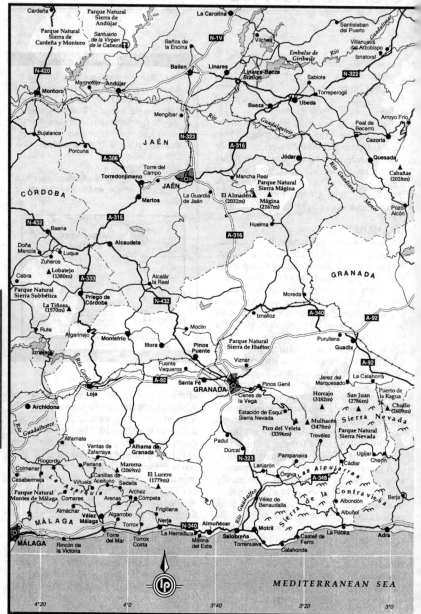

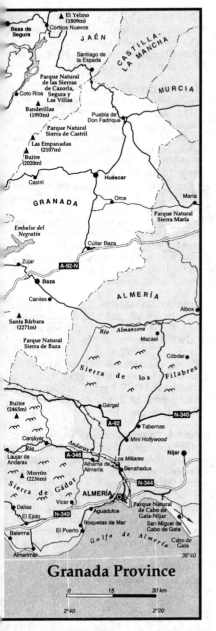

Granada Province

```
0        15        30 km
```

independent emirate. Stretching from the Strait of Gibraltar to east of Almería, this emirate became the final remnant of Al-Andalus, ruled by the Nasrids from the lavish Alhambra palace for 250 years. The Nasrids actually helped Fernando III take Sevilla and paid tribute to Castilla from this time until 1476. However, throughout their rule they played Castilla and Aragón (the peninsula's other main Christian state) off against each other, at times also seeking assistance from the Merenid rulers of Morocco.

Granada became one of the richest and most populous cities in medieval Europe, flourishing on the talents of its big population of traders and artisans. Two centuries of artistic and scientific splendour peaked under Yousouf I and Mohammed V in the 14th century.

But by the late 15th century the economy had stagnated, the rulers led a life of hedonism inside the Alhambra and violent rivalry developed over the succession. One faction supported the emir, Abu al-Hasan, and his harem favourite, Zoraya (actually a Christian from the north). The other faction backed Boabdil, Abu al-Hasan's son by his wife Aixa. In 1482 Boabdil rebelled, setting off a confused civil war. The Christian armies which invaded the Granada emirate that year took full advantage. The scene had been set for war by Abu al-Hasan's refusal to pay tribute to Castilla from 1476, and the unification of Castilla and Aragón through the marriage of Isabel and Fernando.

Capturing Boabdil in 1483 the Catholic Monarchs extracted from him a promise to surrender much of the emirate if they would help him regain Granada. Following Abu al-Hasan's death in 1485, Boabdil won control of the city. The Christians pushed across the rest of the emirate, besieging towns and devastating the countryside, and in 1491 they finally laid siege to Granada from the newly built town of Santa Fé.

After eight months Boabdil agreed to surrender the city in return for the Alpujarras valleys, 30,000 gold coins plus political and religious freedom for his subjects. To forestall trouble from hawkish factions in the city he allowed Castilian troops into the Alhambra on the night of 1-2 January 1492. The next day Isabel and Fernando entered the city ceremonially in Muslim dress. They set up court in the Alhambra for several years.

Under Isabel and Fernando, Granada became a dynamic Castilian city but religious persecution soured the scene. Jews were expelled from Spain soon after the city's conquest and persecution of Muslims led to revolts across the former emirate and finally their expulsion from Spain in the early 17th century (see the History section in Facts about Andalucía).

By the early 17th century, Granada, having lost much of its talented populace, had fallen into a decline which was only arrested by the interest drummed up by the Romantic movement in the 1830s. This set the stage for the restoration of Granada's Islamic heritage and the arrival of tourism. Many historic buildings were, however, torn down to make way for wide thoroughfares.

Early 20th century Granada frowned on liberalism, leading to the horrors unleashed after the Nationalists took the city at the start of the civil war in 1936. An estimated 4000 *granadinos* with left or liberal connections were killed, among them Federico García Lorca, Granada and Andalucía's most famous writer. Granada still has a reputation for conservatism.

Orientation & Information

The two main streets, Gran Vía de Colón and Calle Reyes Católicos, meet at Plaza Isabel La Católica. North-east of here, Calle Reyes Católicos passes through Plaza Nueva to Plaza Santa Ana, from where Carrera del Darro leads up to the Albayzín. To the south, Calle Reyes Católicos extends to Puerta Real, Granada's main plaza. From here, Acera del Darro heads south-east across the Río Genil.

The Alhambra, atop the hill north-east of the centre, overlooks Carrera del Darro and the Albayzín. Cuesta de Gomérez leads up to the Alhambra from Plaza Nueva.

Most major sights are within walking distance of the city centre though there are buses if you get fed up with walking uphill. The bus station (north-west) and train station (west) are out of the city centre but have plenty of buses heading there.

Tourist Offices Granada's provincial tourist office (☎ 958 22 66 88) is on Plaza de Mariana Pineda, east of Puerta Real. The helpful English-speaking staff have plenty of free information on Granada and the province. Opening hours are Monday to Friday from 9.30 am to 7 pm and Saturday from 10 am to 2 pm. The Junta de Andalucía has a more central tourist office (☎ 958 22 59 90) in the Corral del Carbón on Calle Mariana Pineda. Its staff are busier and charge for city maps and other printed material. Bus and train information is posted outside. Hours are Monday to Friday from 9 am to 7 pm, Saturday from 10 am to 2 pm. There are also two tourist offices in the Alhambra complex.

Foreign Consulates There's a British consulate (☎ 958 22 14 60, weekday mornings ☎ 958 27 47 24) at Carmen de San Cristóbal, Carretera de Murcia s/n.

Money There are several banks with ATMs on Gran Vía de Colón, Plaza Isabel La Católica and Calle Reyes Católicos. American Express (☎ 958 22 45 12) is at Calle Reyes Católicos 31.

Post & Communications The main post office (postcode 18080) is at Puerta Real s/n. It's open for most services Monday to Friday from 8.30 am to 8.30 pm, Saturday from 9.30 am to 2 pm.

Net (☎ 958 22 69 19), Calle Santa Escolástica 13, is one of several places offering public Internet access, which costs 400 ptas an hour. It's open Monday to Saturday from 9 am to 11 pm and Sunday from 4 pm to 11 pm.

Internet Resources The following Web sites are worth checking out:

Guía de Granada
    www.moebius.es/ii/granada/

Granada en la Red
www.lingolex.com/granada.htm; www.lingolex.com/granada.htm£english (links to several good Granada sites, in English and Spanish; includes online bookshop with Granada-related titles)

Books & Bookshops *Tales of the Alhambra* by Washington Irving is a great read. Books in English are available from Librería Urbano at Calle Tablas 6, south-west off Plaza de la Trinidad; Librería Continental on Puerta Real; Librería Atlantida, Gran Vía de Colón 9; and El Corte Inglés.

Medical & Emergency Services For urgent medical help, the Cruz Roja (Red Cross; ☎ 958 22 22 22) is at Cuesta de Escoriaza 8, near Paseo de la Bomba and the Río Genil. The Hospital Universitario San Juan de Dios (☎ 958 24 11 00) is fairly central at Calle San Juan de Dios 15.

The Policía Local (☎ 092) are at Plaza del Carmen 5. The Policía Nacional (☎ 091) are at Calle de la Duquesa 15.

Capilla Real
The Royal Chapel (☎ 958 22 92 39) on Calle Oficios, adjoining the cathedral, is Granada's outstanding Christian building. It was built in elaborate Isabelline Gothic style, commissioned by the Catholic Monarchs as their mausoleum, but was not finished until 1521 so they were their temporarily interned in the Convento de San Francisco. The monarchs lie with three relatives in simple lead coffins in the crypt beneath their marble monuments in the chancel, enclosed by a stunning gilded wrought iron screen constructed in 1520 by Maestro Bartolomé of Jaén. The coffins, from left to right, belong to Felipe El Hermoso (the Handsome; husband of the monarchs' daughter Juana la Loca), Fernando, Isabel, Juana la Loca (the Mad) and Miguel, the eldest grandchild of Isabel and Fernando. The carved effigies reclining above the crypt were a tribute by Carlos I to his parents and grandparents. The slightly lower of the two monuments, representing Isabel and Fernando, is the work of a Tuscan, Domenico Fancelli. The other monument, to Felipe and Juana, is higher, apparently because Felipe was the son of the Holy Roman Emperor, Maximilian. This is the work (1520) of Bartolomé Ordóñez from Burgos. The chancel's densely decorated plateresque *retablo* (1522) is by Felipe de Vigarni. Note its kneeling figures of Isabel and Fernando, attributed to Diego de Siloé, and the paintings below depicting the defeat of the Muslims and subsequent conversions to Christianity. Cardinal Cisneros is there too.

In the sacristy is a museum with an impressive collection including Isabel's sceptre and silver crown and Fernando's sword. Isabel's personal art collection, mainly Flemish, occupies one room; there is also Botticelli's *Prayer in the Garden of Olives* and two fine statues of the kneeling monarchs by Vigarni.

The Capilla Real is open Monday to Saturday from 10.30 am to 1 pm and from 4 to 7 pm (3.30 to 6.30 pm in winter) and on Sunday from 11 am to 1 pm. Entry is 300 ptas.

Catedral
Adjoining the Capilla Real is a chunky Gothic/Renaissance cathedral with a cavernous interior. Building began in 1521, directed by Diego de Siloé from 1528 to 1563, but was not finished until the 18th century. The main façade on Plaza de las Pasiegas, with four heavy buttresses and an arched doorway, was designed by Alonso Cano (whose statue stands to the south-east). The lavish Puerta del Perdón on the north-west façade has statues carved by de Siloé. Much of the interior is also his work, including the gilded and painted Capilla Mayor. The Catholic Monarchs at prayer were carved by Pedro de Mena in the 17th century (each side of the main altar, above the lovely carved and painted pulpits) and the busts of Adam and Eve are by Cano.

The cathedral is open for tourist visits (300 ptas) Monday to Saturday from 10.30 am to 1.30 pm and daily from 4 to 7 pm (3.30 to 6.30 pm in winter). Entry is from Gran Vía de Colón.

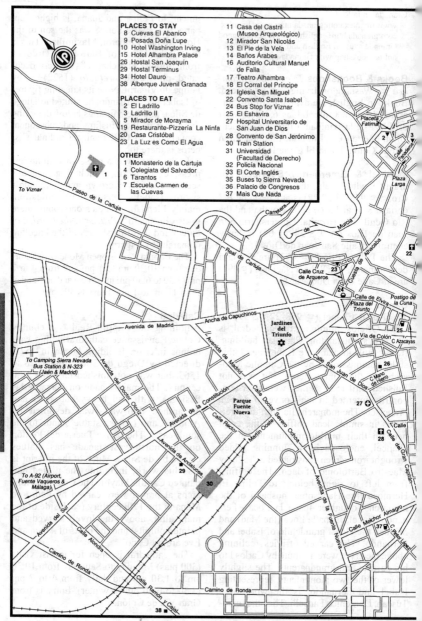

PLACES TO STAY
8 Cuevas El Abanico
9 Posada Doña Lupe
10 Hotel Washington Irving
15 Hotel Alhambra Palace
26 Hostal San Joaquín
29 Hostal Terminus
34 Hotel Dauro
38 Alberque Juvenil Granada

PLACES TO EAT
2 El Ladrillo
3 Ladrillo II
5 Mirador de Morayma
19 Restaurante-Pizzería La Ninfa
20 Casa Cristóbal
23 La Luz es Como El Agua

OTHER
1 Monasterio de la Cartuja
4 Colegiata del Salvador
6 Tarantos
7 Escuela Carmen de
   las Cuevas

11 Casa del Castril
   (Museo Arqueológico)
12 Mirador San Nicolás
13 El Pie de la Vela
14 Baños Árabes
16 Auditorio Cultural Manuel
   de Falla
17 Teatro Alhambra
18 El Corral del Príncipe
21 Iglesia San Miguel
22 Convento Santa Isabel
24 Bus Stop for Viznar
25 El Eshavira
27 Hospital Universitario de
   San Juan de Dios
28 Convento de San Jerónimo
30 Train Station
31 Universidad
   (Facultad de Derecho)
32 Policía Nacional
33 El Corte Inglés
35 Buses to Sierra Nevada
36 Palacio de Congresos
37 Mais Que Nada

GRANADA PROVINCE

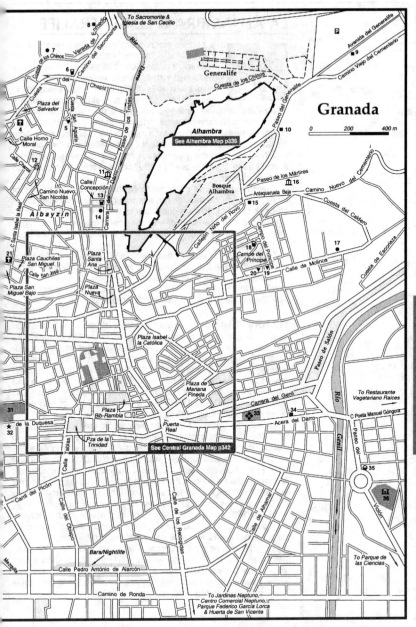

To Sacromonte &
Iglesia de San Cecilio

Avenida del Generalife

P

9

Camino Viejo del Cementerio

Vereda de Enmedio

7

Camino del Sacromonte

6

Cuesta de los Chinos

del

Chapiz

Plaza del
Salvador

Cuesta San Agustín

4

Calle Homo
Moral

5

Generalife

Río Darro

Paseo de los Tristes

Cuesta de los Chinos

Alhambra
See Alhambra Map p335

Paseo del Generalife

10

Granada

0   200   400 m

Camino Nuevo del Cementerio

Calle Chaves

12

11

Calle
Concepción

13

14

Carrera

Camino Nuevo
San Nicolás

Paseo del Darro

Bosque
Alhambra

Paseo de los Mártires

16

Antequeruela Baja   Camino   Nuevo   del

15

Cuesta del Caldero

Cuesta de Escoriaza

A l b a y z í n

C Santa Isabel la Real

21

Plaza Cauchiles
San Miguel

Calle San José

Plaza San
Miguel Bajo

Plaza
Santa
Ana

Plaza
Nueva

Callejón Niño del Rollo

Campo del Príncipe

18

Campo del
Príncipe

20   19

17

Calle de Molinos

Plaza Isabel
la Católica

Plaza de
Mariana
Pineda

Carrera del Genil

Paseo de Salón

Río Genil

To Restaurante
Vegetariano Raices

C Poeta Manuel Góngora

31

32

de la Duquesa

Plaza
Bib-Rambla

Puerta
Real

Pza de la
Trinidad

Calle Tablas

See Central Granada Map p342

33

34

Acera del Darro

35

36

To Parque de
las Ciencias

Carril del Picón

Calle del Obispo

Calle de los Racogidas

Calle de Alhamar

Paseo del Violón

Marquês

Bars/Nightlife

Calle Pedro António de Alarcón

Camino de Ronda

To Jardines Neptuno,
Centro Comercial Neptuno,
Parque Federico García Lorca
& Huerta de San Vicente

LA ALHAMBRA & EL GENERALIFE

Nothing can prepare you for the delights of the Alhambra. Perched on top of La Sabika, this monument is the stuff of fairytales. It may initially disappoint with its simple, unadorned red fortress towers and walls, though its Sierra Nevada backdrop and the cypress and elms among which it nestles are undeniably magnificent. Inside the marvellously decorated Palacio Nazaries (Nasrid Palace) and the Generalife (the Alhambra's gardens), you're in for a treat. Water is an art form in both places and even around the exterior of the Alhambra the sound of running water and the greenness contribute to a sense of calm – a world away from the bustle of the city and the general dryness of much of Spain.

This tranquillity can be completely shattered by the hordes of tourists who traipse through (an average of 5000 a day even in the off-peak season), so it's a good idea to visit first thing in the morning, late in the afternoon or – a magical experience – at night. (Note that only the major rooms of the Palacio Nazaries are open for night visits.)

The Alhambra proper has two main parts, the Alcazaba (fortress) and the Palacio Nazaries. Also within it are the Palacio de Carlos V, the Iglesia de Santa María de la Alhambra, two hotels, a few restaurants, souvenir shops and refreshment stalls. The Generalife is a short walk to the north-east.

History The Alhambra, from the Arabic *al-qala'at al-hamra* (red castle), began life as a fortress as early as the 9th century. The Nasrids of the 13th and 14th centuries turned it into a fortress-palace complex adjoined by a small city (medina), of which nothing remains. The founder of the Nasrid dynasty, Mohammed ibn Yousouf ibn Nasr, set up home on the hill top, restoring and expanding the Alcazaba. His 14th century successors, Yousouf I and Mohammed V, built the Palacio Nazaries: Mohammed V was responsible for much of the palace's decoration.

In 1492 the Catholic Monarchs moved into the Palacio Nazaries after their conquest of Granada. They appointed a Muslim to restore the decoration of the Palacio Nazaries and in time the palace mosque was replaced with a church and the Convento de San Francisco was built. Carlos I, grandson of the Catholic Monarchs, had a wing of the Palacio Nazaries destroyed to make space for a huge Renaissance palace, which is called the Palacio de Carlos V, (using Carlos' title as Holy Roman Emperor).

In the 18th century the Alhambra was abandoned to thieves and beggars and during the Napoleonic occupation it was used as a barracks and narrowly escaped being blown up. In 1870 it was declared a national monument as a result of the huge interest taken in it by Romantic writers such as Washington Irving, who wrote his wonderful *Tales of the Alhambra* in his study in some palace rooms during his stay in the 1820s. Since then it has been salvaged and heavily restored.

Information The Alhambra Bus (No 2) from Plaza Nueva (leaving every 35 minutes, every 12 minutes from July to mid-September) heads up to the Alhambra ticket office. The Tren Alhambra (100 ptas), a little road train, runs every 15 minutes between the Alhambra ticket office/car parks and the Palacio de Carlos V.

Walking up Cuesta de Gomérez from Plaza Nueva you soon reach the **Puerta de las Granadas** (Gate of the Pomegranates), a solid gateway with three carved stone pomegranates, built by Carlos I. Above the gate is the Bosque Alhambra (woods). A path to the left climbs to the austere **Puerta de la Justicia** (Gate of Justice) constructed by Yousouf I in 1348 and originally the main entrance to the Alhambra. From the gate, a passage leads to the Plaza de los Aljibes, where there is a tourist office and the ticket office for night visits to the Palacio Nazaries.

Renaissance fountain which stands in the Puerta de las Granadas *(photograph by Bethune Carmichael)*

The main ticket office is 800m south-east of the Puerta de la Justicia outside the Generalife and adjacent to the Alhambra car parks. If you're on foot, don't take the path up to the Puerta de la Justicia but continue ahead outside the Alhambra walls. Just past La Mimbre restaurant you'll see the main ticket office and entrance; there's another tourist office here.

From April to September, the Alhambra and Generalife are open Monday to Saturday from 9 am to 8 pm and Sunday from 9 am to 6 pm; the Palacio Nazaries is also open on Tuesday, Thursday and Saturday from 10 pm to midnight. Hours from October to March are 9 am to 6 pm daily, with the Palacio Nazaries also open on Saturday from 8 to 10 pm. You can buy tickets until one hour before closing time unless the 8000 tickets for the day have already been sold. Tickets cost 725 ptas but are free for disabled people and children under eight.

At busy times you may have to queue two hours to buy tickets. Tickets are stamped with a half-hour time slot and you must enter the Palacio Nazaries within this time, though you can spend as long as you like once there. But in high season, even if you buy your ticket at 8.30 am you may have to wait several hours before you can enter the Palacio Nazaries. You can book a time for your visit on ☎ 958 22 09 12 (fax 958 21 05 84) from one week to a year ahead.

Ticketing arrangements change from time to time as the authorities strive to cope with the huge numbers of visitors and ticket purchase points are planned for the city centre .

Alcazaba What remains of the Alcazaba are the ramparts and several towers, the most important and tallest being the Torre de la Vela (watchtower). Here, a narrow, winding staircase leads to the top terrace which has splendid views of the city and surrounds. The cross and banners of the Reconquista were raised here in January 1492. The tower's bell rings on festive occasions only, but in the past it tolled to control the irrigation system of the Vega.

Palacio Nazaries This is what all the fuss is about. The Nasrid Palace (also called the Casa Real or Royal House), with its intricately-carved stucco walls, fine knotted wooden ceilings,

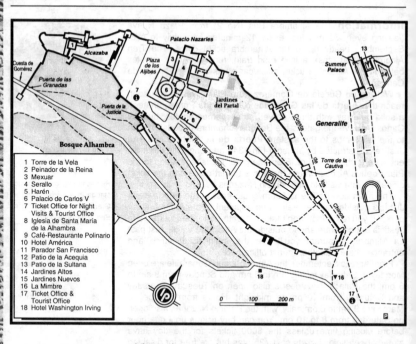

Map legend:
1 Torre de la Vela
2 Peinador de la Reina
3 Mexuar
4 Serallo
5 Harén
6 Palacio de Carlos V
7 Ticket Office for Night Visits & Tourist Office
8 Iglesia de Santa María de la Alhambra
9 Café-Restaurante Polinario
10 Hotel América
11 Parador San Francisco
12 Patio de la Acequia
13 Patio de la Sultana
14 Jardines Altos
15 Jardines Nuevos
16 La Mimbre
17 Ticket Office & Tourist Office
18 Hotel Washington Irving

Detail from the Cuarto Dorado
(photograph by Damien Simonis)

elaborate honeycomb vaulting and beautifully proportioned rooms and courtyards, stands in marked contrast to the austere walls and towers of the Alcazaba. Arab inscriptions recur in the stucco work. Routes through the palace sometimes change from what follows, depending on restoration work.

Mexuar These rooms, through which you normally enter the palace, date from the 14th century and were used for bureaucratic and judicial purposes. The general public would not have been allowed beyond them. The first room, the council chamber, has been much altered and contains both Muslim and Christian motifs. At its far end is a small, lavishly decorated room (originally a prayer room) that overlooks the Río Darro. From here you pass into the Patio del Mexuar or Patio del Cuarto Dorado, with a small fountain and the mudéjar Cuarto Dorado (Golden Room) on the left. Opposite the Cuarto Dorado is the entrance to the Serallo through a beautiful façade of glazed tiles, stucco work and carved wood.

Serallo This was the official residence of the emir or sultan. Its rooms surround the Patio de los Arrayanes (Patio of the Myrtles) named after the hedges that flank its rectangular pool and fountains. Finely carved arches sit atop marble pillars to form porticos

BETHUNE CARMICHAEL

DAMIEN SIMONIS

Left & Right: Details from the Patio de los Leones

BETHUNE CARMICHAEL

Muslim tilework

DAMIEN SIMONIS

DAMIEN SIMONIS

Left & Right: Details from the Cuarto Dorado

Patio de los Arrayanes (Patio of the Myrtles) from Torre de Comare

DAMIEN SIMONIS

Muslim tilework

BETHUNE CARMICHAEL

Detail of the Cuarto Dorado with characteristic high archways

DAVID WATERMAN

at the northern and southern ends of the patio. Through the north portico is the Sala de la Barca (Hall of the Boat) with a beautiful inverted boat-shaped wooden ceiling. This room leads into the impressive, square Salón de Embajadores (Hall of the Ambassadors), where the sultans would have conducted their negotiations with Christian emissaries. Its domed cedar ceiling is remarkable and the repeating patterns of the stuccoed and tiled walls mesmerising. The southern end of the patio is marred by the gloomy grey walls of the Palacio de Carlos V.

Harén The harem was built during Mohammed V's reign and surrounds the celebrated Patio de los Leones with its fountain feeding water through the mouths of 12 stone lions. The patio's gallery, including the beautiful structures protruding at its eastern and western ends, is supported by 124 slender marble columns.

The lion fountain in front of the Sala de los Reyes, Patio de los Leones *(photograph by Damien Simonis)*

Of the four halls bordering the patio, the **Sala de los Abencerrajes** on the southern side is legendary for the murders of the noble Abencerraj family, whose head, the story goes, dared to dally with Zoraya, Abu al-Hasan's harem favourite. (Historians say the Abencerrajes also favoured Boabdil in the palace power struggle.) The room's highlight is its high-domed ceiling with stalactite vaulting which produces a star-like effect and windows which give the room a wonderful light.

At the eastern end of the patio is the **Sala de los Reyes** (Hall of the Kings) with paintings, attributed to 14th century Christian artists, of royalty and medieval scenes and motifs on its leather-lined ceiling. The name of the room comes from the painting on the central part of the ceiling, thought to depict 10 Nasrid emirs. On the northern side of the patio is the **Sala de las Dos Hermanas** (Hall of the Two Sisters), as beautiful and richly decorated as the Sala de los Abencerrajes, and named after the two slabs of white marble either side of its fountain. This was the room of the sultan's favourite paramour. At its far end is the enchanting **Sala de los Ajimeces**, the favoured lady's dressing room and bedroom, with low-slung windows through which she could catch the view of the Albayzín and mountains while reclining on ottomans and cushions. In Islamic times, buildings did not mar the view.

Other Sections From the Sala de las Dos Hermanas a passageway leads through deserted rooms which were decorated by Carlos I and later used by Washington Irving. The Peinador de la Reina (Queen's Dressing Room), the last of these, was a dressing room for Isabel, wife of Carlos I. From here you descend to the Patio de los Cipreses (Patio of the Cypresses), off which are the richly decorated, but closed, Baños Reales (Royal Baths).

Outside the palace is a group of recent gardens, the **Partal**, graded in terraces and bordered by the palace towers and ramparts. From here there is an exit to the Palacio de Carlos V, or you can continue along a path to the Generalife.

Detail of the exterior of Palacio de Carlos V *(photograph by Damien Simonis)*

Palacio de Carlos V This huge Renaissance palace, also called the Casa Real Nueva, is the dominant Christian building in the Alhambra. Begun in 1527 by Pedro Machuca, a Toledo architect who studied under Michelangelo, it was never completed. The building is square but contains a surprising two-tiered circular courtyard with 32 columns. The main, western façade features three porticos divided by pairs of fluted columns and carvings of horsemen, angels and other mythological figures. Were the palace in a different setting its merits would be more readily appreciated, but here it seems intrusive.

The palace houses two museums. On the ground floor, the **Museo de la Alhambra** concentrates on the Muslim period with a wonderful collection of artefacts from the Alhambra, the province of Granada, and Córdoba. Detailed explanatory texts in English and Spanish fill out the picture. Its highlight is the elegant Alhambra Vase, decorated with gazelles. The museum (free) is open Tuesday to Saturday from 9 am to 2.30 pm.

The **Museo de Bellas Artes** upstairs has an impressive collection of paintings and sculptures. Most notable are the carved wooden relief of the Virgin and child by Diego de Siloé; a small, enamelled screen of around 1500 that belonged to El Gran Capitán (Gonzalo Fernández de Córdoba), the military right-hand man of Isabel and Fernando; and various pieces by Alonso Cano. Hours are Tuesday to Saturday from 10 am to 2 pm (free).

Other Christian Buildings The Iglesia de Santa María was built between 1581 and 1617 on the site of the former palace mosque. The Convento de San Francisco, now a parador, was erected upon an Islamic palace. Isabel and Fernando were laid to rest in a sepulchre (in what's now the parador's patio) before being transferred to the Capilla Real. The outdoor terrace bar is a fine setting for refreshments.

El Generalife The name means 'Garden of the Architect'. These palace gardens on the hillside facing the Palacio Nazaries have a beautiful, soothing composition of walkways, terraces, patios, fountains and trimmed hedges, tall, long-established trees, especially cypresses and, in season, flowers of every imaginable hue. The Muslim rulers' summer palace is in the farthest corner. Within the palace, the Patio de la Acequia (Court of the Long Pond) has a long pool framed by flower beds and fountains whose shapes sensuously echo the arched porticos at each end. Off the Patio de la Acequia is the Patio de la Sultana, almost as lovely and with the trunk of a 700-year old cypress tree, where Abu al-Hasan supposedly caught his lover, Zoraya, with the head of the Abencerraj clan, leading to the murders in the Sala de los Abencerrajes of the Palacio Nazaries. Above here are the modern Jardines Altos (Upper Gardens), and a stairway with cascading waterfalls. Back towards the entrance are the Jardines Nuevos (New Gardens). A pleasant alternative route back to town is along Cuesta de los Chinos which runs down a gully between the Generalife and the Alhambra proper to the Río Darro.

La Madraza
Opposite the Capilla Real remains part of the old Muslim university, La Madraza, also called the Casa del Cabildo Antiguo, as it was later used as a town hall. Now with a painted baroque façade, the much-altered building retains an octagonal domed prayer room with stucco lacework and pretty tiles. The building is now part of the modern university but you can see it at most times during the day.

Corral del Carbón
This place's name (Coal Yard) disguises its original function as a 14th century caravanserai, or inn for merchants, commonplace in the oriental world but not in Spain. The building has since had a chequered history, being used as an inn for coal dealers (hence its modern name) and later a theatre. It houses a tourist office and government-run crafts shop (Artespaña). To find it, cross Calle Reyes Católicos from the Capilla Real and look for the sign pointing down an alley. You can't miss the lovely Islamic façade with its elaborate horseshoe arch.

Alcaicería
The Alcaicería was the Muslim silk exchange but what you see now is a restoration, after a 19th century fire, filled with tourist shops. Take a look before the shops open, when it still manages to convey some charm in the early morning light and quiet. The buildings, separated by narrow alleys, are just south-west of the Capilla Real.

Albayzín
A wander around the hilly streets and narrow, aged alleys of Granada's old Muslim quarter is a must. The Albayzín covers much of the hill that faces the Alhambra across the Darro valley. Its name derives from 1227, when Muslims from Baeza populated the district after their city was conquered by the Christians. It became a densely populated residential area and for a few decades after the Reconquista it survived as the Muslim quarter. Muslim ramparts, cisterns, gates, fountains and houses remain and many of the Albayzín's churches and *cármenes* (large walled villas with gardens) stand on the sites of, or incorporate the remains of, Islamic buildings.

Carrera del Darro One way to approach the Albayzín is up Carrera del Darro from Plaza Nueva. On Plaza Santa Ana is the **Iglesia de Santa Ana**, which incorporates a former mosque's minaret in its belltower, as do several churches in the Albayzín. Stop at Carrera del Darro 31 to see the remains of the 11th century **Baños Árabes** (Muslim Baths; ☎ 958 22 23 39), open Tuesday to Saturday from 10 am to 2 pm. Entry (free) is through a pretty patio.

At Carrera del Darro 43 is the Renaissance Casa del Castril, home to the **Museo Arqueológico** (☎ 958 22 56 40) which has some interesting finds from the province. On the upper floor, the Islamic room has some lovely *azulejos*, carved wood and fine ceramics. As you leave this room you're greeted with a splendid vista of the Alhambra. The museum is open Tuesday to Sunday from 10 am to 2 pm (250 ptas, EU passport holders free).

Paseo de los Tristes & Cuesta del Chapiz Shortly after the museum, Carrera del Darro becomes Paseo de los Tristes (also called Paseo del Padre Manjón), with a number of cafés and restaurants with outdoor tables. This is a good spot to take in the view of the Alhambra's fortifications directly above.

Upper Albayzín From the north-eastern end of Paseo de los Tristes, Cuesta del Chapiz heads north and uphill, then curves west into Plaza del Salvador, where the **Colegiata del Salvador**, a 16th century church, still contains the Islamic courtyard of the mosque it replaced; it's open daily from 10 am to 1 pm and 4 to 7 pm (100 ptas). From here Calle Panaderos leads to **Plaza Larga** with an Islamic gateway at the top end of the Albayzín's surviving Muslim ramparts and lively bars offering cheap *menús*. From Calle Panaderos, Calle

Horno Moral and Calle Charca lead to the **Mirador San Nicolás** with fantastic views of the Alhambra and the Sierra Nevada – you can't miss the trail at sunset!

Descent from Mirador San Nicolás
Descending from the *mirador* along Camino Nuevo San Nicolás, which becomes Calle Santa Isabel la Real, you pass the **Convento Santa Isabel**, a former Islamic palace. Its church, open daily from 10 am to 6 pm, has a mudéjar ceiling. Nearby is Plaza San Miguel Bajo where the **Iglesia San Miguel** occupies the site of a former mosque. To wend your way back to the centre, follow Plaza Cauchiles San Miguel and then Calle San José. Calle San José ends near the top end of picturesque **Calle Calderería Nueva** with its *teterías* (Arabic-style tea shops), a stone's throw from Plaza Nueva. Alternatively, enjoy getting lost – but not too late at night.

Sacromonte
Camino del Sacromonte leads from Cuesta del Chapiz up Sacromonte hill to the **Iglesia de San Cecilio**, passing by caves dug into the hillside; these caves have been occupied by Gypsies since the 18th century.

Plaza Bib-Rambla & Around
Just south-west of the Alcaicería is the large, pleasant Plaza Bib-Rambla with restaurants, flower stalls, toy shops and a central fountain with statues of giants. This plaza used to be the scene of Inquisition lashings and burnings, jousting and bullfights. Today buskers, mime artists and street sellers provide gentler entertainment.

A block south-west is the pedestrianised Calle de los Mesones, with modern shops. At its north-western end is leafy Plaza de la Trinidad from which Calle de la Duquesa leads past the university founded by Carlos I (now the Law Faculty, with the main modern campus north of the centre) to the 16th century **Convento de San Jerónimo** (☎ 958 27 93 37) on Calle del Gran Capitán. This features more work by the talented and ubiquitous Diego de Siloé, including the

larger of the convent's two cloisters and much of the attached church. Either side of the church's altar are statues of El Gran Capitán and his wife María; El Gran Capitán is reputedly buried beneath the altar. The convent is open daily from 10 am to 1.30 pm and 4 to 7 pm (3 to 6.30 pm in winter; 300 ptas).

Monasteria de La Cartuja
The impressive, ornate La Cartuja Monastery (☎ 958 16 19 32) is a 20 minute walk north of the Convento de San Jerónimo (or take bus No 8 from Gran Vía de Colón). The monastery, with an imposing, sand-coloured stone exterior, was built between the 16th and 18th centuries. Its baroque interior oozes wealth, especially the astonishingly lavish sacristy decorated in brown and white marble and stucco, and the adjacent sanctuary *(sanctum sanctorum)*, a riot of colour and patterns with its twisted marble columns, loads of statues, paintings, gilt and beautiful frescoed cupola. In contrast, four dark chapels off the cloister display bizarre paintings of martyrdom and the Inquisition. The monastery (300 ptas) is open daily from 10 am to 1 pm (to noon on Sunday) and 4 to 8 pm (3.30 to 6 pm in winter).

Huerta de San Vicente
This house, where Federico García Lorca spent summers and wrote some of his well known works, is a 15 minute walk from the centre and was once surrounded by orchards. Today the new Parque Federico García Lorca separates it from whizzing traffic in an attempt to recreate the tranquil environment that inspired Lorca. The house contains some original furnishings, including Lorca's desk and piano, some of his drawings and other memorabilia, and exhibitions connected with his life and work. To find it head down Calle de las Recogidas from Puerta Real and cross Camino de Ronda. A block farther along is Calle del Arabial; the park is to the right. Huerta de San Vicente (☎ 958 25 84 66) is open Tuesday to Sunday from 10 am to 1 pm and

5 to 8 pm (4 to 7 pm in winter), with guided tours in Spanish on the hour. Entry is 300 ptas, free on Wednesday. See Around Granada for more Lorca sites.

Parque de las Ciencias

Granada's well-equipped new science museum (☎ 958 13 19 00), 2km south of the centre at Avenida del Mediterráneo s/n, has plenty of hands-on exhibits and a special room for children to explore basic scientific principles. Hours are Tuesday to Saturday from 10 am to 7 pm (to 3 pm on Sunday; 350 ptas). The planetarium has sessions roughly every hour (200 ptas).

Language Courses

With its attractions and youthful population, Granada is a good city in which to study Spanish. The university offers a variety of intensive programmes, popular with young Americans, with a four-week 80-hour course costing 58,000 ptas. For more information contact Universidad de Granada, Centro de Lenguas Modernas, Cursos Para Extranjeros, Placeta del Hospicio Viejo s/n (Realejo), 18071 Granada (☎ 958 22 07 90; fax 958 22 08 44). The Escuela Carmen de las Cuevas (☎ 958 22 10 62; fax 958 22 04 76, info@carmencuevas.com) in the Albayzín is another good choice; it offers Spanish language classes at all levels plus courses in history, literature, art, and flamenco dance, guitar and song. A four-week intensive language course costs 73,000 ptas (66,300 ptas in the low seasons). Its postal address is Cuesta de los Chinos 15, 18010 Granada.

Organised Tours

Granavisión (☎ 958 13 58 04) does guided tours of the Alhambra and Generalife (3700 ptas), Granada Histórica tours (3900 ptas), flamenco shows (3800 ptas) and excursions further afield. Phone direct or book through any travel agent.

Special Events

Semana Santa and the Corpus Christi *feria* nine weeks later are the big two. Benches are set up in Plaza del Carmen to view the Semana Santa processions. At Corpus Christi, fairgrounds, drinking, sevillana dancing and bullfights are the go. Other festivals include:

2 January
> *Día de la Toma* (Day of the Conquest) commemorates the taking of Granada by the Catholic Monarchs.

Late March/early April
> *Espárrago Rock*, a weekend alternative music festival held at Granada's Feria de Muestras in the Armilla district, 3km south of the centre, attracts around 16,000 people. With three stages and a huge dance tent, the festival boasts ska, rap, rock, flamenco, punk, reggae, indie and more. There are usually one or two big-name bands. Call ☎ 958 22 98 03 for information.

3 May
> *Día de la Cruz* (Day of the Cross) sees squares, patios and balconies adorned with floral crosses (the Cruces de Mayo), while horse riders, polka-dot dresses and sevillana dancing add to the colour.

Late June/early July
> *Festival Internacional de Música y Danza* is an international music and dance festival with performances (some free) in the Generalife, Palacio de Carlos V and other historical sites; for information and tickets, head to the Junta de Andalucía tourist office in the Corral de Carbón (tickets are also sold at El Corte Inglés).

November
> *Festival Internacional de Jazz* (for information, ask at Calle Gran Capitán 24).

Places to Stay

There should be no problem finding a room in Granada except during Semana Santa. The prices are no higher than elsewhere in Andalucía. The most expensive places are in and around the Alhambra. Unless stated otherwise, you can expect to pay more than the prices quoted during Semana Santa, July and August.

Places to Stay – Budget

There are some good budget options in Granada.

Camping There are several camping grounds within about 5km of Granada, all accessible by bus. All charge around 500 ptas

GRANADA PROVINCE

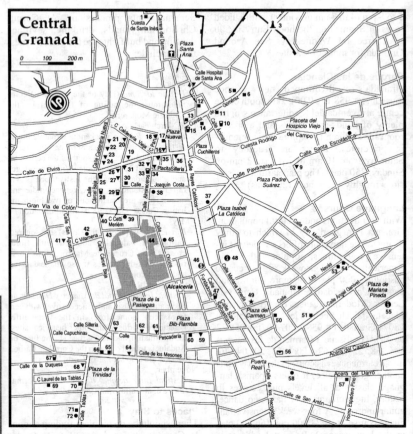

Central Granada

0   100   200 m

per adult, 450 ptas per tent, and 500 to 600 ptas per vehicle. The closest and biggest, though closed from November to February and now less tranquil with the new bus station close by, is *Camping Sierra Nevada* (☎ 958 15 00 62) at Avenida de Madrid 107, 3km north-west of the centre. There are big clean bathrooms, a pool and a laundry. Take bus No 3 from Gran Vía de Colón in the centre. Year-round camping grounds include:

Camping Granada (☎ 958 34 05 48), Cerro de la Cruz s/n, Peligros, 4km north of Granada (take exit 123 from the N-323)

Camping María Eugenia (☎ 958 20 06 06), Carretera A-92 Km 286, in the Vega en route to Santa Fé

Camping Los Álamos (☎ 958 20 84 79), Carretera A-92 Km 290, also in the Vega en route to Santa Fé

Youth Hostel The *Albergue Juvenil Granada* (☎ 958 27 26 38) is at Calle Ramón y Cajal 2, just off Camino de Ronda, 1.7km west of the centre and a 600m walk south-west of the train station. It's a large, modern, white building with 60 or so double rooms with bath, and a pool.

PLACES TO STAY		
1	Palacio Santa Inés	
5	Hostal Navarro Ramos	
6	Hostal Landázuri	
11	Hostal Gomérez	
12	Hostal Vienna	
13	Hostal Britz	
14	Hostal Austria	
29	Hotel Inglaterra	
50	Hostal-Residencia Lisboa	
51	Hostal Fabiola	
52	Hotel Navás	
53	Hotel Dauro II	
54	Hostal Roma	
57	Hotel Montecarlo	
60	Hotel Los Tilos	
65	Pensión Romero	
66	Huéspedes Capuchinas	
69	Hostal Lima	
70	Hostal Zurita	
71	Hotel Reina Cristina	

PLACES TO EAT	
4	Pilar del Toro
9	Seis Peniques
16	Mardini
17	Restaurante León

18	Boabdil
19	Samarcanda
20	El Panadero Loco
21	Medina Zahara
22	Naturii Albayzín
23	Kasbah
25	La Nueva Bodega
26	Café/Bar Nueva Riviera
30	Mesón Andaluz
31	Café/Bar Almireceros
33	Antigua Castañeda
34	Bodegas Castañeda
35	Café Bar Al Andalus
39	Vía Colón
59	Café Bib-Rambla
61	Pizzeria Gallio
62	Cunini
63	El Cepillo
64	Mesón El Patio
68	Bar/Cervecería Reca

OTHER	
2	Iglesia de Santa Ana
3	Puerta de las Granadas
7	Universidad - Centro de Lenguas Modernas
8	Net

10	Café Aljibe
15	Gran Taberna
24	Bar Avellano
27	Granada 10
28	Hannigan & Sons
32	La Taberna del Irlandés
36	Iberia & Aviaco Office
37	Jamones Castellano
38	Librería Atlantida
40	Mercado
41	Panadería Moises
42	Catedral
43	Capilla Real
44	La Madraza (Casa del Cabildo Antiguo)
45	American Express
46	Alcaicería
47	La Sabanilla
48	Corral del Carbóne Tourist Office (Junta de Andalucía) & Artespaña
49	Policía Local
55	Provincial Tourist Office
56	Main Post Office
58	Librería Continental
67	Pub Librería
72	Librería Urbano

Bus No 3 from the bus station will get you fairly close – get off at the Constitución 4 bus stop and walk 400m west along Avenida de la Constitución and Avenida del Sur, then about the same distance south along Camino de Ronda. Alternatively you can continue on bus No 3 to the cathedral stop in the centre of town and pick up bus No 11: it runs a circular route and will drop you in front of the hostel.

Hostales & Pensiones Cheap hostales are mainly located near Plaza Nueva, around Plaza de la Trinidad and near Plaza del Carmen. One exception, handy for the Alhambra, is Posada Doña Lupe (☎ 958 22 14 73), Avenida del Generalife s/n, with more than 40 rooms. Management is friendly, English is spoken, food is available and there is a small, clean pool on a large roof terrace. Clean singles/doubles/triples with bathroom cost 1000/1950/2925 ptas, or 700 ptas per person if you provide bedding. These are interior rooms with windows on to corridors. Better doubles are 3900 ptas and 4950 ptas plus IVA. All prices include a light breakfast. The Alhambra Bus from Plaza Nueva stops outside.

Near Plaza Nueva There's plenty of choice on Cuesta de Gomérez, which runs from Plaza Nueva towards the Alhambra. Most places have parking for 1000 ptas a day. The friendly *Hostal Britz* (☎ 958 22 36 52) at No 1 has clean, adequate singles /doubles for 2300/3500 ptas, or 3600/5000 ptas with bath. *Hostal Gomérez* (☎ 958 22 44 37), No 10, has a lively, helpful owner who speaks English, French and Italian. The nine well-kept rooms cost 1500/2500 ptas.

Hostal Vienna (☎ 958 22 18 59), Calle Hospital de Santa Ana 2 (first left off Cuesta de Gomérez coming from Calle Reyes Católicos) is a popular choice. Rooms vary and some have private bathrooms. Tolerable singles, reasonable doubles and good triples without bath cost 1500/3000/4000 ptas. The management is obliging and they speak

GRANADA PROVINCE

English and German. The same people run *Hostal Austria* (☎ 958 22 70 75), Cuesta de Gomérez 4, where all rooms have bathrooms. Singles/doubles cost from 2000 3000 to 2500/4500 ptas.

Hostal Landázuri (☎ 958 22 14 06), Cuesta de Gomérez 24, is a good bet: the rooms with bath at 3000/4075 ptas are nothing special but the triples at 6000 ptas are excellent, the location is handy, the management is really friendly and there's a pretty enclosed garden and a terrace with views of the Alcazaba. There's an attached cafeteria too. *Hostal Navarro Ramos* (☎ 958 25 05 55), Cuesta de Gomérez 21, has better and cheaper doubles, with bath, at 3500 ptas but no areas for sitting outside.

Near Puerta Real (Plaza del Carmen)
Hostal Fabiola (☎ 958 22 35 72), Calle Ángel Ganivet 5 (3rd floor) is a friendly family-run place. The 19 good rooms, some with balcony and all with private bathroom, cost 1800/3500/5000 ptas for singles/ doubles /triples. Two blocks north at Plaza del Carmen 27, the friendly *Hostal-Residencia Lisboa* (☎ 958 22 14 13) has singles/doubles for 3300/4700 ptas with bath (2150/3250 ptas without). *Hostal Roma* (☎ 958 22 62 77), Calle Las Navás 1, has good, clean singles with shower for 2500 ptas and doubles from 3000 to 4500 ptas.

Near Plaza de la Tinidad
Some of the many hostales in this area fill up with university students in term-time. The following should have rooms year-round. The good, family-run *Pensión Romero* (☎ 958 26 60 79) at Calle Sillería 1, on the corner of Calle de los Mesones, has rooms for 1500/2700 ptas, some with balconies. *Hostal Zurita* (☎ 958 27 50 20), Plaza de la Trinidad 7, has good-value rooms for 1875/3750 ptas, and doubles with bathroom for 4500 ptas. There's off-street parking for 1000 ptas a day. The same family runs *Hostal Lima* (☎ 958 29 50 29) just around the corner at Calle Laurel de las Tablas 17, where the pleasant rooms with bath and TV cost

3000/5000 ptas. *Huéspedes Capuchinas* (☎ 958 26 53 94), Calle Capuchinas 2 (2nd floor), has five clean rooms with shared bathrooms for 1800/3600 ptas.

Elsewhere *Hostal Terminus* (☎ 958 20 03 11), Avenida de Andaluces 10, a stone's throw from the train station, has basic rooms with shared bathroom for 1500/2500 ptas. *Hostal San Joaquín* (☎ 958 28 28 79), Calle Mano de Hierro 14, between the centre of town and the train station and near the Hospital Universitario de San Juan de Dios, is a rambling place set around a couple of leafy patios. It's run by a jovial, elderly couple. The spacious, clean but a touch shabby rooms, all with bath, cost 2000 ptas per person.

Places to Stay – Mid-Range
Many mid-range hotels are on or near the busy Acera del Darro. Others are near Plaza Nueva, or in the Alhambra area. You can even stay in a cave! Add IVA to all prices given here.

Hotel Montecarlo (☎ 958 25 79 00), Acera del Darro 44, has good singles/ doubles with all mod cons for 4700/6800 ptas. *Hotel Los Tilos* (☎ 958 26 67 12), Plaza Bib-Rambla 4, charges 4700/7000 ptas. Up the scale a bit, *Hotel Navás* (☎ 958 22 59 59), Calle Las Navás 24, charges 7350/ 10,850 ptas. *Hotel Dauro* (☎ 958 22 21 55), Acera del Darro 19, and *Hotel Dauro II* (☎ 958 22 15 81), Calle Las Navás 5, both charge 8000/11,500 ptas.

The central *Hotel Macia* (☎ 958 22 75 36), Plaza Nueva 4, has comfortable rooms at 5000/8000 ptas. *Hotel Reina Cristina* (☎ 958 25 32 11), just off Plaza de la Trinidad at Calle Tablas 4, is in a renovated old building which once belonged to the Rosales family who were friends of Lorca. The writer spent his last days here before being arrested by the Nationalists. Rooms cost 7200/10,750 ptas year-round.

Hotel América (☎ 958 22 74 71), Calle Real de Alhambra 53, is within the Alhambra grounds but only open from March to October (6,500/11,000 ptas). It has only 13 rooms: reserve well in advance. *Hotel Washington Irving* (☎ 958 22 75 50), Paseo del Generalife 2, near the Bosque Alhambra, has been around since the last century. Rooms are 8000/10,500 ptas.

Another possibility is the comfortable cave lodgings at *Cuevas El Abanico* (☎ 958 22 61 99), Vereda de Enmedio 89, Sacromonte. You can choose from one or two-bedroom caves – all these caves have heating in winter and kitchens which are equipped. Single or doubles cost 7500 ptas, while caves for four people cost 10,500 ptas. There's a minimum stay of two nights.

Places to Stay – Top End
Again, add IVA to these prices. *Parador San Francisco* (☎ 958 22 14 40), Calle Real de Alhambra s/n, is the top hotel in Granada. The converted monastery can't be beaten for its location within the Alhambra and historical connections. Singles/doubles cost 26,400/33,000 ptas; book well ahead. The distinctive neo-Islamic *Hotel Alhambra Palace* (☎ 958 22 14 68), Peña Partida 2, close to the Bosque Alhambra, has wonderful views over the city. Standard rooms are 16,000/20,500 ptas.

Bang in the centre, *Hotel Inglaterra* (☎ 958 22 15 58), Calle Cetti Meriém 4, has 36 rooms with all mod cons at 12,000/14,000 ptas. *Palacio de Santa Inés* (☎ 958 22 23 62), Cuesta de Santa Inés 9, is the only accommodation we know of in the Albayzín. It's in a restored early 16th century building with a stunning mudéjar *artesonado* ceiling in the upstairs salón. The six rooms cost 9500/12,500 ptas; there are also five suites with equipped kitchen from 18,000 to 20,000 ptas.

Places to Eat
Granadino cuisine uses the seafood and tropical fruits from the nearby coast, the meats and sausages of the interior (particularly from Las Alpujarras) and the excellent fresh vegetables from the Vega's market gardens (the broad beans are considered especially tasty and the asparagus is excellent). A hint of the Muslim past is evident in desserts,

pastries such as syrup cakes, aniseed doughnuts, almond meringues and avocado ice cream, and in *granizados* (sorbets) – Muslim rulers liked their ices to be made with snow from the sierras.

Granadinos enjoy hearty soups and stews flavoured with herbs like fennel. *Rabo de toro* (ox tail stew) and *habas con jamón* (broad beans with ham) are *platos típicos*. Granada's most famous dish, *tortilla Sacromonte*, is an omelette combining *jamón*, prawns or oysters, greens and offal (traditionally, calf brains and bull testicles!).

Bar flies will be pleased to find that tapas are often free at night. Food and drink prices are higher in choice locations such as in and around the Alhambra, Plaza Bib-Rambla, Plaza Nueva and some of the tea shops *(teterías)* on Calle Calderería Nueva.

Near Plaza Nueva Two blocks west of Plaza Nueva, *La Nueva Bodega*, Calle Cetti Meriém 3, and *Café/Bar Nueva Riviera*, next door, have similar fare and prices and seem to be run by the same outfit. Menús start at 850 ptas; vegetarians can be accommodated. Excellent spinach soup (425 ptas) and bacalao and trout with mushrooms (each 925 ptas) enliven the menu.

Across the road on the corner of Calle de Elvira, *Mesón Andaluz* is slightly more expensive with most mains for around 1300 ptas and *menús* from 1200 ptas, all plus IVA. Round the corner on Calle de Elvira, *Boabdil* has reasonable food, with menús from 725 ptas. A line of blackboards out the front advertises the options.

Back towards Plaza Nueva, *Restaurante León*, Calle Pan 3, is popular, with *menús* from 850 to 1300 ptas plus IVA. Classier food in a more *típico* setting can be had at *Bodegas Castañeda* (an institution among locals and tourists alike) and *Antigua Castañeda*. The two are almost side by side on Calle Almireceros and Calle de Elvira. Both places have barrels of potent *costa* wine from the Sierra de la Contraviesa and offer delicious, beautifully presented food. Try the montaditos (280 ptas), slices of bread with toppings such as smoked salmon with avocado and caviar. More elaborate meals cost around 1700 ptas. Down the scale but good value, especially for breakfast, is *Café/Bar Almireceros* on Calle Almireceros opposite Bodegas Castañeda.

Behind the east side of Plaza Nueva at Calle Hospital de Santa Ana 12, *Pilar del Toro* is an upmarket restaurant with comfy cane chairs in an attractive covered patio – nice for a morning coffee and tostada (220 ptas). If you're after a 700-ptas menú, head for *Seis Peniques* on Plaza Padre Suárez at Calle Pavaneras, a five minute walk southeast of Plaza Nueva.

Vía Colón, at Gran Vía de Colón 13, is a smart, popular café-bar serving up fancy bocadillos (450 ptas), other snacks and typical granadino meals (1400 ptas).

Basic groceries, hams and cheeses can be bought at *Jamones Castellano* on the corner of Calle Almireceros and Calle Joaquín Costa.

For fresh fruit and veggies, the produce *mercado* spills down Calle San Agustín, a block west of the cathedral. A new covered market is being built here. Opposite, on Calle Villamena, *Panadería Moises* is a good little bakery.

Alhambra Even the kiosks inside the Alhambra complex charge marked-up prices. *Café/Restaurante Polinario* has bocadillos and a buffet lunch at 1350 ptas plus IVA. *Parador San Francisco* has a pricey restaurant but also a terrace bar out the back with a lovely view, open daily from 11 am to 11 pm. Teas and coffees cost 205 ptas and bocadillos cost from 720 ptas.

La Mimbre on the corner of Avenida del Generalife and Cuesta de los Chinos has outdoor tables in a leafy garden under the walls of the Alhambra. It specialises in granadino fare, with main dishes from 950 to 1700 ptas and a menú at around 1500 ptas.

Albayzín A couple of blocks from Plaza Nueva, atmospheric Calle Calderería Nueva has several restaurants, teterías, health food shops and takeaway food places. *Kasbah*,

one of the more popular teterías, makes a relaxed stop for time out from sightseeing: try a pot of one of the numerous teas on offer (275 ptas) or a wine or even a martini: snacks include bocadillos, crepes and fancy cakes. The bakery and health food shop at Calle Calderería Nueva 14, *El Panadero Loco*, stocks good wholemeal breads and cakes. It's closed on Sunday.

Near the top of the Albayzín, Plaza Larga and nearby Calle Panaderos have lively cafés and bars which have cheap *menús at* around 750 ptas. A couple of blocks farther north, the tables at *El Ladrillo* on Placeta Fatima spill into the street in fine weather. It's a popular, fun, seafood place which is open for both lunch and dinner. The big platters of seafood called *barcos* go for 1200 ptas. *Ladrillo II* on Calle Panaderos does the same food.

For a splash-out, try the highly regarded *Mirador de Morayma*, Calle Pianista Carrillo 2, off Cuesta San Agustín on the west side of Cuesta del Chapiz. It occupies a lovely *carmen* (walled villa).

On the west edge of the Albayzín, Plaza San Miguel Bajo has a couple of lively bars with meals and tapas, popular with students. Down from here, close to Plaza del Triunfo at Calle Cruz de Arqueros 3, *La Luz es Como el Agua* is a relaxed, alternative sort of place run by a multilingual Belgian who's a good source of information about Granada's flamenco scene. She, or her cook, dishes up good pastas and salads Wednesday to Saturday from 8 pm to 1 am, Sunday from 2 to 5.30 pm.

Plaza Bib-Rambla & Around *Café Bib-Rambla*, with tables on the plaza, is a great place for breakfast. You can choose from seven types of bread and seven toppings. Coffee and toast with butter and excellent marmalade cost 400 ptas (less at the bar inside). They do home-made ice creams and granizados too! *Pizzeria Gallio*, Plaza Bib-Rambla 10, does tasty Italian food. Try pizza Florentina, with spinach and béchamel sauce (785 ptas plus IVA). Drinks are expensive.

A little to the west on Calle Pescadería is *Cunini*, an expensive seafood restaurant with tables outside – again, prices are lower at the bar. A few doors away, *El Cepillo* is a popular cheaper seafood restaurant; it gets packed at lunchtime. Menús are 775 ptas and it's closed on Sunday.

Plaza de la Trinidad & Around
Bar/Cervecería Reca on the plaza is full to overflowing at peak times. A beer and a tapa, consisting of a couple of bites of seafood, fried eggplant, a dumpling and spicy salsa, will set you back 175 ptas. Raciones are 500 to 1000 ptas. *Mesón El Patio*, Calle de los Mesones 50, is mid-priced with the usual Spanish/granadino mix of food and a pleasant patio. Tasty cured olives and warm bread precede your meal. A breakfast of coffee, juice, bread, eggs and bacon costs 500 ptas but you can't have it before 10 am.

Campo del Príncipe South of the Alhambra is Campo del Príncipe, which is another area that buzzes at night. At No 14, *Restaurante-Pizzería La Ninfa* is a bright, cheerful

place on two floors. Good pizzas come out of a wood-fired oven and the excellent pasta, like *nioqui al cuatro quesos* (gnocchi with four cheeses, 900 ptas), is home-made. A few doors west, *Casa Cristóbal* has menús from 850 ptas and does wonderful sangría.

Entertainment
Available at kiosks at the beginning of each month, the excellent *Guía del Ocio* lists entertainment and places to eat, including tapas bars. *Ideal*, Granada's daily newspaper, has entertainment listings too.

Bars, Live Music & Discos Granada is reputed to have a sedate nightlife but you can easily dance the night away here as in most places in Spain. Keep your eye open for posters advertising live music and nontouristy flamenco.

Around Plaza Nueva The streets just west of Plaza Nueva are lively on weekend nights. *Bodegas Castañeda* and *Antigua Castañeda* (see Places to Eat), with free tapas, make a good start to the evening.

GRANADA PROVINCE

Where to Find Authentic Flamenco

It's difficult to see flamenco that's not geared to tourists – but some shows are more authentic than others and attract Spaniards as well as foreigners. These include the almost-nightly ones (in summer only) at *El Corral del Príncipe* (☎ 958 22 80 88) on Campo del Príncipe (4000 ptas), and the Friday and Saturday midnight shows at *Tarantos* (☎ 958 22 45 25 day, ☎ 958 22 24 92 night) in a cave at Camino del Sacromonte 9 (3500 ptas). Tarantos' 10 pm shows attract more foreigners. *Jardines Neptuno* (☎ 958 52 25 33) on Calle del Arabial, southwest of the centre, has a tourist-oriented flamenco performance at 10.15 pm daily (3500 ptas).

For all these places, you can pre-book tickets at the venues or through hotels and travel agents. Some will pick you up. The quality of the show depends on who is performing. If some of the top professionals who kick around Granada are dancing, you're in for a good show. If not, you may be disappointed!

Flamenco dancers and singers perform in some of Granada's more highbrow venues – see Other Entertainment. *El Eshavira* and *Mais Que Nada* (see Bars, Live Music & Discos) have live flamenco some nights.

Some travellers go to the Sacromonte caves to see impromptu flamenco but it is extremely touristy and a bit of a rip-off. Watch your back if you go up there alone at night.

Nearby, there are popular bars with good music on Placita Sillería and Calle Joaquín Costa, while *La Taberna del Irlandés* on Calle Almireceros offers Tetley's Bitter, Guinness and Fosters as well as Spanish tipples.

Another Irish pub, *Hannigan & Sons*, Calle Cetti Meriém 1, provides competition. Also close by, *Bar Avellano* on the corner of Calle de Elvira and Calle Cárcel Baja has great music – African, blues and pop classics. It's best after midnight at weekends. *Granada 10*, the disco on Calle Cárcel Baja, has varied dance music. It opens about midnight and gets going about 2 am. Don't look too scruffy! The 1000 ptas cover charge includes a *copa*; subsequent drinks are expensive. You can take in a movie beforehand as the place also functions as a cinema with screenings at 6, 8 and 10 pm.

Cafe Aljibe, Calle Ánimas 7, just above Plaza Cuchilleros on the southern side of Plaza Nueva, is great for late live music, though this is only sporadic. The bar opens nightly from 10 pm. Nearby, *Gran Taberna* on the corner of Plaza Nueva and Cuesta de Gomérez is another central bar popular at night. *La Sabinilla* at Calle San Sebastían 14, near the Alcaicería, is Granada's oldest bar: though showing its age, it's still worth a visit.

Elsewhere Don't miss *El Eshavira*, a basement jazz and flamenco club down a dark alley at Postigo de la Cuna 2, off Calle Azacayas towards the northern end of Calle de Elvira. The bar is open most nights from 10 pm, with live music on Wednesday, Thursday and Sunday. There's a cover charge if a relatively big name is playing. *Mais Que Nada* at Calle Pintor López Mezquita 3, 1km or so west of the centre, has live flamenco, jazz or Brazilian music some nights.

Al Pie de la Vela, on Carrera del Darro near Calle Concepción, with crazy lighting, is another popular bar. There are more places to check out farther up on Paseo de los Tristes.

Pub Libería, Calle de la Duquesa 8 near Plaza de la Trinidad, celebrates the blues. A talented young four-piece band was playing when we visited. Entry is free and the music starts about 11 pm on Thursday and Friday. The place is a student hangout, with a pool table. It's open for a drink from late afternoon most days.

From about 11 pm on weekends you can't miss the crowds heading for Calle Pedro António de Alarcón, a kilometre or so south-west of the centre, where a string of disco-bars offers cheap deals on drinks with free tapas.

Some of the Sacromonte caves turn into lively discos during university terms.

Other Entertainment The notice board in the foyer of La Madraza on Calle Oficios, opposite the Capilla Real, has large posters which list forthcoming cultural events. The *municipal band* often performs at noon on Sunday on Plaza de las Pasiegas, between the cathedral and Plaza Bib-Rambla.

Auditorio Manuel de Falla (☎ 958 22 00 22), Paseo de los Mártires s/n, near the Alhambra, is the venue for orchestral concerts a couple of nights a week from around 9 pm.

The *Teatro Alhambra* (☎ 958 22 04 47) Calle de Molinos 56, has an ongoing program of theatre and concerts (sometimes flamenco). In winter, there are cultural programmes such as Música En Los Monumentos with concerts several times monthly in historic buildings.

Things to Buy

A distinctive local craft is marquetry *(taracea)*, used on boxes, tables, chess sets and more – the best have shell, silver or mother-of-pearl inlays. Other *granadino* crafts include embossed leather, guitars, wrought iron, brass and copperwork, basket weaving, textiles and, of course, pottery. Places to look include the Alcaicería, the Albayzín and Cuesta de Gomérez.

You can watch marquetry experts at work in the shop opposite the Iglesia de Santa María in the Alhambra, and in a shop on Cuesta de Gomérez. There are at least two

GRANADA PROVINCE

guitar makers on Cuesta de Gomérez. The government-run Artespaña in the Corral del Carbón has a good range of granadino handicrafts.

Granada is also a good place to buy ethnic clothes and jewellery, especially around Plaza de la Trinidad. For general shopping, head to El Corte Inglés department store on Acera del Darro, or the big Centro Comercial Neptuno on the corner of Calle del Arabial and Calle Neptuno, a 15-minute walk south-west of the centre.

Getting There & Away

Air Aviaco, which shares the Iberia office (π 958 22 75 92) at Plaza Isabel La Católica 2, has daily flights to/from Madrid and Barcelona. Air Europa (π 902 24 00 42) has daily flights (except Saturday) to/from Barcelona (17,050 ptas one-way, from 17,150 ptas return). You can buy tickets at Halcón Viajes, Calle de las Recogidas 2.

Bus Granada's bus station is at Carretera de Jaen s/n, the continuation of Avenida de Madrid, 3km north-west of the centre. All services operate from here except for a few to nearby destinations such as Fuente Vaqueros, Viznar and the Estación de Esquí Sierra Nevada (see those sections). Consigna lockers cost 300 ptas and there's a large cafeteria. Alsina Graells (π 958 18 50 10) runs to Las Alpujarras (see that section), Córdoba (eight daily, 3½ hours, 1735 ptas), Sevilla (nine daily, four hours, 2710 ptas), Málaga (14 daily, 2½ hours, 1165 ptas), Jaén, Baeza, Úbeda, Cazorla, Almería, Almuñécar, Nerja and Torre del Mar. There are at least nine daily buses to Madrid (six hours, 1945 ptas).

Bacoma (π 958 15 75 57) has daily services to Alicante, Valencia and Barcelona. Buses to Guadix (1½ hours) and Mojácar are run by Autedia (π 958 15 36 36).

Train The station (π 958 27 12 72) is 1.5km west of the centre on Avenida de Andaluces, off Avenida de la Constitución. Consigna lockers cost 600 ptas for 24 hours. Three

trains run daily to/from Antequera (1¾ hours, 970 ptas) and Sevilla (four hours, 2280 ptas), and to/from Almería (2¾ hours, 1550 ptas) via Guadix. For Málaga (1520 to 2600 ptas) and Córdoba (1900 to 2400 ptas), there are two or three trains daily. All four-hour trips involve a change at Bobadilla. For Linares-Baeza there are at least four daily trains.

To Madrid there's a daily Talgo at 3.40 pm (six hours, 3200 ptas) and a night train (9½ hours, 3000 ptas). One train daily goes to Valencia and Barcelona.

Car Car rental is expensive. ATA Rent A Car on Plaza Cuchilleros has weekly rentals from 36,540 ptas plus IVA, including insurance.

Getting Around

To/From the Airport The airport (π 958 44 64 11) is 17km west of the city on the A-92. Five airport buses leave from Plaza Isabel La Católica daily (except Saturday). Call π 958 13 13 09 for information. A taxi will set you back 2500 ptas.

Bus City buses charge 125 ptas. The tourist offices have a handy map showing routes. Bus No 3 runs from outside the bus station to the centre. You may have to wait up to 20 minutes. Get off at the Catedral stop – you can't see the cathedral itself from the bus. To reach the centre from the train station, walk straight ahead to Avenida de la Constitución and pick up bus No 3 or 11 going to the right (south-east).

Taxi Taxis line up on Plaza Nueva. Most fares within the city are 400 to 600 ptas.

AROUND GRANADA

Granada is surrounded by a fertile plain known as La Vega, planted with poplar groves and crops ranging from potatoes and maize to melons and tobacco. The Vega has always been vital to the city and was an inspiration to Federico García Lorca, who was born and was killed here.

Fuente Vaqueros

The house where Lorca was born in 1898, in this village 17km west of Granada, is now the **Casa Museo Federico García Lorca** (☎ 958 51 64 53). The place really makes his spirit come alive, with numerous charming photos, posters and costumes for plays that he wrote and directed, and paintings illustrating some of his poems. A short video captures him in action with the touring Teatro Barraca.

The museum is open for guided tours in Spanish (200 ptas) from Tuesday to Sunday, hourly from 10 am to 1 pm and 4 to 6 pm (6 to 8 pm from July to September). To get there take a Ureña company bus from outside Granada train station. On summer weekdays this service runs almost hourly from 9 am to 9 pm in both directions; on weekends it's every two hours. There are fewer buses in winter. There's a timetable at the roundabout in the village centre.

Viznar

To follow the Lorca trail to the bitter end you have to make your way out to this village 8km north-east of the city. When the Spanish Civil War broke out and the city was taken over by the Nationalists in 1936, García Lorca took refuge in a friend's house. He was soon discovered, arrested and taken with hundreds of others to Viznar to be shot.

Outside the village, on the road to Alfacar, is the **Parque Lorca**, with a granite block marking the spot where the writer is believed to have been killed. His body has never been found.

The *Albergue Juvenil Viznar* (☎ 958 54 33 07) at Camino de la Fuente Grande s/n is a good, modern youth hostel, with its own swimming pool.

Buses to Viznar leave from Plaza del Triunfo on weekdays at 12.30, 2.45 and 8 pm, returning from Viznar at 7.45 am, 12.30 and 4 pm. On Saturday there's one bus, at 1.30 pm from Granada and 8.30 am from Viznar. There are no buses on Sunday. Call Martín Perez (☎ 958 15 12 49, ☎ 958 16 26 41) to check the schedule.

West of Granada

The A-92 runs west from Granada towards Sevilla and Málaga.

MONTEFRÍO

This small town provides fine panoramas from its hill-top position 25km north of the A-92. There's a tourist office (☎ 958 33 60 04) at Plaza de España 1 which can tell you about the Peña de los Gitanos Stone and Copper Age site, 8km east, with megalithic tombs, some carved with animals. In the town, the neoclassical Iglesia de la Encarnación has an unusually large 30m-wide dome. The hill is topped by the 16th century Iglesia de la Villa, designed by Diego de Siloé, and the remains of a Muslim fort. There are cheap, basic rooms and food at *Bar La Fonda* (☎ 958 33 60 16) near the tourist office.

LOJA

The main town along the A-92 before Málaga province, Loja has the remains of a Muslim castle, a few churches worth looking at, including the 16th century Iglesia de San Gabriel designed by Diego de Siloé, and several hostales and hotels. There's a tourist office (☎ 958 32 39 49) at Calle Duque de Valencia 1.

ALHAMA DE GRANADA

An alternative route from Granada to the Málaga area runs south-westward via this picturesque ancient spa town of 6000 people, 53km from Granada. Alhama stands at the top of a ravine *(tajo)* where the Río Alham carves through otherwise rolling countryside. There's a tourist office (☎ 958 36 06 86) in the 15th century Hospital de la Reina on Calle Vendederas, uphill from and east of the central Plaza de la Constitución.

Things to See & Do

The Town The centre, with narrow zig-zagging streets, is obviously of Muslim origin. A much modified Muslim castle on

Plaza de la Constitución is private property and closed. Nearby, close to the edge of the gorge is the pretty 16th century **Iglesia del Carmen**, restored in the 1970s after severe civil war damage. It has some fine stone carving. The late Gothic **Iglesia de la Encarnación**, with its big tower, on Plaza de los Presos near the tourist office, was a gift to Alhama from the Catholic Monarchs whose 1482 conquest of the town was a key step in the war against Granada. It has a mudéjar pulpit and ceiling. There's a **Roman bridge** over the Río Alhama, about 1km below the town near the modern bridge on the road to Granada.

Balneario Beside the modern bridge over the Río Alhama is the turn-off to the Balneario (Spa), 1km or so down a road through a minor gorge. The thermal, therapeutic springs have been channelled into baths since Roman times. Around 12.30 pm daily during the spa's opening season (10 June to 10 October), you can go inside the Hotel Balneario to look at the horseshoe-arched Muslim bathhouse (100 ptas). In the woodland park in front of the hotel is a public open-air pool with lovely hot waters, open daily in season from 11 am to 2 pm and 4.30 to 7.30 pm (500 ptas, tickets from the hotel).

Places to Stay & Eat
Hostal San José (☎ 958 35 01 56), Plaza de la Constitución 27, has reasonable rooms at 2800 ptas plus IVA a double or 3500 ptas plus IVA with bathroom. At the Balneario, *Hotel Baño Nuevo* (☎ 958 35 00 11) has doubles for 4700 ptas plus IVA and *Hotel Balneario* (same phone number) charges 8900 ptas plus IVA. Both are open in season.

Among several eateries on Plaza de la Constitución, *Café-Bar Andaluz* at No 8 is decent value: a ración of boquerones is 650 ptas and a good sopa de mariscos is 350 ptas.

Getting There & Away
Alsina Graells runs three daily buses (two on Saturday, one on Sunday) to/from Granada and one to/from Málaga via Torre del Mar.

East of Granada

The A-92 east from Granada travels forested mountainous country before entering a strange, arid landscape, at times lunar, at times steppe-like.

GUADIX
Just south of the A-92, 55km from Granada, the dusty and rather shabby town of Guadix (population 20,000) is famous for its cave dwellings – not prehistoric remnants but modern-day homes of ordinary townsfolk, nearly half of whom inhabit the town's cave quarter, known as the Ermita Nueva or Barrio de Santiago. Cave dwelling is a fairly widespread practice in eastern Granada but Guadix has the biggest concentration of underground homes. There's a tourist office (☎ 958 66 26 65) near the centre at Carretera de Granada s/n.

Things to See
Your average late 20th century cave has a whitewashed wall across the entrance and a chimney – often with TV aerial. Some have many rooms and all mod cons and are even second homes for city dwellers. The caves maintain a comfortable temperature of around 18°C all year. The habit of living in caves apparently goes back to when Muslims were expelled from the old town after the Reconquista. A **Cueva Museo** on Plaza de la Ermita Nueva recreates typical cave life and is open Monday to Friday from 10 am to 2 pm and 4 to 6 pm and on Saturday from 10 am to 2 pm.

Guadix has an interesting 16th-century sandstone **catedral** designed by Diego de Siloé, with an 18th century baroque façade and choirstalls. It's open Monday to Saturday from 11 am to 1 pm and 4.30 to 7 pm and on Sunday from 10.30 am to 2 pm.

Also have a look at the remains of the Muslim fort, the **Alcazaba**, with views over the Ermita Nueva. It's open daily except Sunday from 9.30 am to 1.30 pm and 3.30 to 6.30 pm (closed Saturday afternoon).

GRANADA PROVINCE

Places to Stay

Cuevas Pedro Antonio de Alarcón (☎ 958 66 49 86), a modern cave hotel on Barriada San Torcuato, near the train station about 1km from the centre, has comfortable, modern two-room grottoes at 6000/7600 ptas plus IVA for singles/doubles, or 10,200 ptas plus IVA for four. It has a pool and a good restaurant too. Doubles with bath are 5500 ptas plus IVA in the good central *Hotel Comercio* (☎ 958 66 05 00), Calle Mira de Amezcua 3, and 5150 ptas plus IVA at *Pensión Mulhacén* (☎ 958 66 07 50), Avenida Buenos Aires 41 on the Murcia road near the edge of Guadix.

Getting There & Away

Guadix is about 1½ hours from both Granada and Almería by several daily buses or by three daily trains. The bus station is about five minutes walk from the centre, the train station 20 minutes away.

LA CALAHORRA

Those with their own wheels travelling between Guadix and Almería could detour to this impressive hill-top castle, looming 4km south of the A-92, 16km south-east of Guadix. It was built in 1509-12 by Rodrigo de Mendoza, son of Cardinal de Mendoza, who was chief adviser to the Catholic Monarchs during the war against Granada. Within the forbidding walls, topped by domed corner towers, is an amazingly elegant Italian Renaissance courtyard with arches, a staircase of Carrara marble and bedrooms with fine coffered ceilings. The castle is open on Wednesday only, from 10 am to 1 pm and 4 to 6 pm. There are two hostales in La Calahorra village.

BAZA

This market town of 21,000 people is 44km north-east of Guadix and something of a rival to it. Like Guadix, Baza dates back to Iberian times. Its **Museo Arqueológico** on Plaza Mayor contains a copy of the *Dama de Baza*, a life-size statue of an Iberian goddess unearthed locally in 1971 (the original is in Madrid). Also on the square is the

16th century **Colegiata de Santa María** church, with an 18th century brick tower.

The good, central *Hostal Mariquita* (☎ 958 70 10 12), Calle Caños Dorados 10, has doubles at 3500 ptas plus IVA or 4000 ptas plus IVA with bath; the comfortable *Hostal Anabel* (☎ 958 86 09 98), also central at Calle María de Luna s/n, charges 5000 ptas plus IVA. Both have restaurants.

Baza is served by several daily Autedia buses from Guadix and Granada. From here drivers could head north to Cazorla in Jaén province by the A-315 or reach the northern part of the Parque Natural de Cazorla via Huéscar and Puebla de Don Fadrique on the A-330.

Sierra Nevada & Las Alpujarras

The Sierra Nevada mountain range, which includes mainland Spain's highest peak, Mulhacén (3478m), forms an almost year-round snowy, south-eastern backdrop to Granada. The range extends about 75km from west to east, crossing from Granada into Almería province. All its highest peaks (3000m or more) are towards the Granada end.

Between the Sierra Nevada and the lower Sierra de la Contraviesa, which rises from the Mediterranean, lies one of the oddest and most picturesque crannies of Andalucía: the 70km-long valley – or jumble of valleys – known as Las Alpujarras or La Alpujarra. Here arid hillsides split by deep ravines alternate with oasis-like steep, white villages by rapid streams and surrounded by gardens, orchards and woodlands of chestnut, oak, poplar and pine.

Of the infinite number of walking routes in the Sierra Nevada area, most of the more attractive possibilities are on the southern side, in and above Las Alpujarras. The best map of the western half of the Sierra Nevada and Las Alpujarras is the CNIG's 1:50,000 *Sierra Nevada*, though it doesn't

GERRY REILLY

DAMIEN SIMONIS

GERRY REILLY

GRANADA
Top: Mountain *finca*
Middle: La Alhambra from Mirador de San Nicolás (Albaicín)
Bottom: Water as art: the Patio de la Acequía, El Generalife

Top: Rural Scene in Andalucía
Bottom: Cabo de Gata, Almería

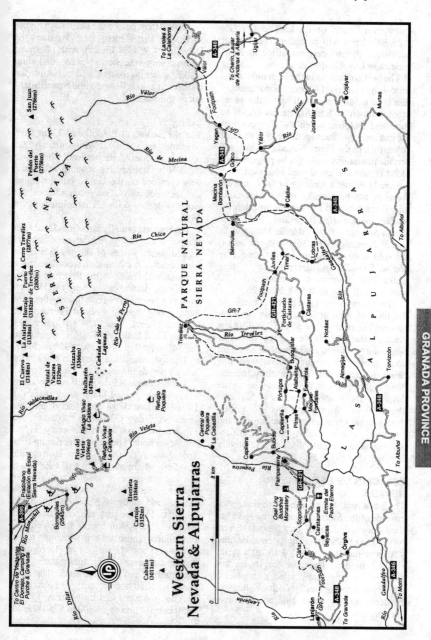

Western Sierra Nevada & Alpujarras

GRANADA PROVINCE

show every path or track. The CNIG's 1:25,000 sheets will be better. You can get both from the information office in Pampaneira in Las Alpujarras.

The best conditions in the high mountains (mid-July to early October) unfortunately don't coincide very well with the ideal months down in Las Alpujarras (April to June and October, when the temperatures are just right and the vegetation is at its most colourful). In the Sierra Nevada – which are serious mountains – always be prepared for cloud or rain and come well equipped.

Lonely Planet's *Walking in Spain* covers some of the best walks in the Alpujarras and Sierra Nevada. For readers of Spanish, *Andar por La Alpujarra* and *Andar por Sierra Nevada – Baja y Media Montaña*, in Libros Penthalon's El Búho Viajero series, are sold in several shops in the Alpujarras and in Granada and describe lots of fine walks. For information on mountain *refugios* for walkers call ☎ 958 24 83 26.

The Sierra Nevada is a protected area. At the time of writing its status was *parque natural* but nearly half of the 1710-sq km Parque Natural Sierra Nevada was due to be upgraded to *parque nacional*. The exact boundaries of the parque nacional were still being discussed but will certainly include most higher parts of the range. The alpine desert of these upper reaches is home to about 60 endemic plant species, among them unique varieties of violet, crocus and narcissus and several types of gentian. Among wild animals, ibex are relatively common (but shy).

ESTACIÒN DE ESQUÍ SIERRA NEVADA

The main road from Granada to the northern side of the Sierra Nevada – the A-395 to the Estación de Esquí Sierra Nevada (Sierra Nevada Ski Station) – is unspectacular until you near the ski station, with high peaks rising behind it. The pine forests on this flank of the range are riddled with processionary caterpillar nests and look likely to be decimated by these pine needle-eating creatures.

About 10km before the ski station on the A-395 is the Centro de Visitantes El Dornajo (☎ 958 34 06 25), with plenty of information on the Sierra Nevada, including walks, other activities and refugios for walkers. It also sells maps and Spanish-language guidebooks.

Skiing

The ski station, at Pradollano, 33km from Granada, is Spain's most southerly ski resort and one of its biggest. The resort itself is an uninspiring modern affair and very crowded on weekends, but the skiing and facilities were good enough to host the world Alpine skiing championships in 1996.

The season normally lasts from December to April or early May – though conditions are unpredictable. Prices of ski passes and accommodation are lowest on weekdays in the 'promotional seasons' (the first half of December and after about 25 April) and highest from just before Christmas to just after New Year, during the last week of February and Semana Santa, and on all Saturdays, Sundays and holidays. There's an information office (☎ 958 24 91 19, ☎ 958 24 91 11) on Plaza de Andalucía, the main plaza in the bottom part of the resort.

The resort has 45 downhill runs totalling 61km – five graded black (very difficult), 18 red (difficult), 18 blue (easy) and four green (very easy). The two cable cars and 17 chairlifts and T-bars can carry 31,965 people an hour. The cable cars run up from Pradollano (2100m) to Borreguiles (2645m), where other lifts will take you to the higher slopes, some of which start almost at the top of 3396m Pico del Veleta, the second highest peak in the Sierra Nevada. The longest run, Águila, drops 1175m in its 5.9km course from Veleta to Pradollano. There are cross-country routes too, and a snowboard run at Borreguiles. Nonskiers' areas offer tobogganing and snowmobile and dog-sled rides. The cable cars cost 1050 ptas (return) for nonskiers.

A ski pass *(forfait)* costs from 3000 to 3650 ptas for one day, 5800 to 6750 ptas for two days or 8300 to 9900 ptas for three days. Skis, boots and sticks can be rented at numerous places for 2500/4500/5500 ptas for one/two/three days.

The resort has at least four ski schools, with a six-hour weekend group class costing around 7500 ptas and a 15-hour Monday to Friday class costing 11,500 to 14,500 ptas. Private classes cost from around 3500 ptas an hour for one person to 5000 ptas for four people. The Escuela Internacional de Esquí (☎ 958 48 01 42) does daily 2½-hour group classes for 1700 ptas per person. Wax Surfers (☎ 958 48 01 84) offers snowboard and boot rental for 2500 ptas a day and snowboard classes at similar rates to ski school. (For skiing and accommodation packages, see Places to Stay & Eat.)

Walking

From the ski station in July and August you can walk up Pico del Veleta in three or four hours – a paved road actually runs up there but it's closed at the Borreguiles turn-off about a quarter of the way up from Pradollano. From Veleta to the top of Mulhacén is about another five hours walk and you would need to spend a night in a *refugio* if you want to do both peaks. See Mulhacén in the Las Alpujarras section for information on refugios and on ascents from the south.

Other Activities

Mountain biking, horse riding and paragliding can be arranged at the ski resort in summer.

Places to Stay & Eat

Accommodation reservations are highly advisable in the ski season. Outside the ski season only a few hotels stay open.

The small *Camping El Purche* (☎ 958 34 04 07), 15km from the ski station and 2km off the road from Granada, is open all year, charging around 2000 ptas for two people with a tent and car. The *Albergue Juvenil Sierra Nevada* youth hostel (☎ 958 48 03 05) near the top of the ski station has 206 places in rooms holding two to six and is

open all year. The resort has around 15 hotels, with doubles costing 5700 to 7200 ptas plus IVA at the cheapest, the *Hotel Telecabina* (☎ 958 24 91 20). *Hostal El Ciervo* (☎ 958 48 04 09), *Hotel El Parador* (☎ 958 48 06 61) and *Hotel Ziryab* (☎ 958 48 05 12) have doubles for around 10,000 ptas.

If you're here to ski, the best deals are packages which you should try to book at least two weeks ahead through the resort's central booking service (☎ 958 24 91 11). Per person, a two-night package with two days' ski passes included costs 11,540 ptas at the youth hostel (accommodation only), from 13,500 to 24,000 ptas including breakfast at the cheapest hotels or 19,000 to 36,000 ptas at the most expensive.

The ski station has dozens of restaurants, cafés and bars, including a couple up at Borreguiles, one with a self-service buffet.

Entertainment

In the ski season the ski resort has a thriving nightlife, with numerous lively bars and a few discos.

Getting There & Away

Autocares Bonal (☎ 958 27 31 00) runs a bus to the ski resort daily at 8 or 9 am from Bar Ventorrillo on Paseo del Violón near the Palacio de Congresos in Granada. The bus returns from Pradollano at about 5 pm. In the ski season there are two buses a day and four at weekends. The one-way/return fare is 365/700 ptas. A taxi from Granada costs about 6000 ptas.

The road crossing right over the Sierra Nevada from the ski station to Capileira in Las Alpujarras – reaching altitudes of over 3200m – is now closed to unauthorised vehicles from the Borreguiles turn-off, some 4km up from the top of Pradollano.

RUTA INTEGRAL DE LOS TRES MIL

A succession of 3000m-plus peaks can be bagged in a tough hike of four or more days, known as the Ruta Integral de los Tres Mil. This runs from Jerez del Marquesado, south of Guadix and 66km east of Granada (served by daily Autedia buses from Granada), to Lanjarón, 45km south of Granada. There's a visitor information centre (☎ 958 34 51 81) at Los Morolillos near Jerez. Many walkers spend the first night at the Refugio Postero Alto (also called Refugio Ballesteros; ☎ 958 34 51 54; open all year) above Jerez del Marquesado at 1880m. The second night is often spent camping below 3129m Puntal de Vacares, the third night at the Refugio Poqueira (see Mulhacén in the Las Alpujarras section) and the fourth night camping or in one of the dilapidated refugios near the top of the Río Lanjarón valley.

LAS ALPUJARRAS

For centuries one of Spain's most isolated corners, Las Alpujarras has experienced a burst of tourism in the last decade or two. But it remains, almost throughout, a world apart, with a sense of timelessness and mystery that's born, in part, of a bizarre history which saw a flourishing Muslim community replaced en masse by Christian settlers in the 16th century. Reminders of the Muslim past are ubiquitous in the form of the Alpujarras' Berber-style villages and the terracing and irrigation of the land. Four centuries of Christian habitation have seen some unique folklore and customs evolve. Tourism has made little difference to the lives of many, who still have to work their steep fields by hand using donkeys as pack animals.

Some of the higher villages on the Sierra Nevada side of the Alpujarras are within the Parque Natural Sierra Nevada, while the upper reaches of the sierra are within the Parque Nacional Sierra Nevada.

History

The Alpujarras rose to prominence in the 10th and 11th centuries as a great silkworm farm, supplying the silk workshops of

The Houses of Las Alpujarras

Travellers who have been to Morocco may notice a resemblance between villages in the Alpujarras and those in the Atlas Mountains. In fact the building style was introduced by Berber settlers in the Alpujarras during Muslim times.

Most houses have two storeys, with the lower one used for storage and animals. The characteristic *terraos*, or flat roofs, with their protruding chimney pots, consist of a layer of *launa* (a type of clay) packed on to flat stones which are laid on beams of chestnut, ash or pine. Nowadays there's often a layer of plastic between the stones and the launa for extra waterproofing. Whitewash is a fairly modern introduction too but a few poorer villages remain stone-coloured as all villages used to be.

GERRY REILLY

GRANADA PROVINCE

Almería with silk thread – from the unravelled cocoons of mulberry-leaf-eating caterpillars of the silk moth. This activity arose hand in hand with a wave of Berber migrants to the area. Later, silk made from Alpujarras thread was one of the economic backbones of Nasrid Granada. Together with successful irrigation and agriculture, silk production supported a population of probably over 150,000 in at least 400 villages and hamlets by the late 15th century.

By the terms of his surrender to Fernando and Isabel in 1492, Boabdil, the last Granada Emir, was awarded the Alpujarras as a personal fiefdom. He settled at Laujar de Andarax in the Almerian Alpujarras but left for Africa the next year. As Christian promises of religious and cultural tolerance gave way to forced mass conversions and land expropriations, in 1500 Muslims across the former emirate rebelled, with the Alpujarras in the thick of things. When the revolt failed, Muslims were given the choice of exile or conversion. Most converted – to become known as Moriscos – but the change was barely skin deep. The Christians contented themselves with repressing outward signs of Islamic culture until a particularly repressive decree by Felipe II in 1567, which forbade the use of Arabic names, dress and even of the language, finally brought a new revolt in the Alpujarras in 1568. Led by a Morisco named Aben Humeya and aided by North African Muslims, the rebellion again spread across southern Andalucía. In the Alpujarras two years of vicious guerrilla war ensued, ending only after Don Juan of Austria, Felipe's half-brother, was brought in to quash the insurrection and Aben Humeya was assassinated by his cousin Aben Aboo.

Almost the whole Alpujarras population was deported as land labour to western Andalucía and parts of Castilla, and some 270 villages and hamlets were repeopled with settlers from northern Spain. The rest of the villages were abandoned. According to Gerald Brenan (see Books), two Morisco families from each village had to remain and teach irrigation and silkworm breeding to the newcomers. But over the centuries, the silk industry fell by the wayside and swathes of the Alpujarras' woodlands were lost to mining and cereal growing. The Alpujarras returned to the footnotes of history.

Books
Englishman Gerald Brenan lived for several years, in the 1920s and 30s, in Yegen, with 'a good many books and a little money'. His *South From Granada* provides a wealth of fascinating detail on what was then a very isolated and superstitious corner of Spain. One of Brenan's friends was hauled up before the local mayor by three men who thought he was a *mantequero*, a monster of outwardly human appearance that feeds on human fat. Brenan also recounts visits by Virginia Woolf and other literati.

Special Events
The Alpujarras calendar is replete with village fiestas (tourist offices have lists). Among the most interesting are the Moros y Cristianos (Moors and Christians) festivities in several villages, which recreate events of the 1568-70 rebellion. The best known, and certainly among the most colourful and noisy, are those at Válor, Aben Humeya's birthplace, on 14 and 15 September. With costumed 'armies' of 50 or so on each side, the festivities continue intermittently from midday to evening.

On 5 August or the Sunday before it, villagers from Capileira and Trevélez stage *romerías* (pilgrimages) to the top of Mulhacén to honour the Virgen de las Nieves (Virgin of the Snows).

Walks
There's a wealth of good walks linking valley villages or heading up into the Sierra Nevada. Some are discussed below in the sections on Pampaneira, Bubión & Capileira; Mulhacén; Pitres & Around; and Trevélez. An alternative to heading up the valleys or mountains is to walk between the valley villages, most of which are linked by footpaths as well as roads. One route is part

of the GR-7 long-distance footpath which runs across Europe from Greece to Algeciras via Las Alpujarras. The section from the Puerto de la Ragua pass in the eastern Sierra Nevada, through Las Alpujarras to Lanjarón ,is marked by posts with red and white rings and runs through Bayárcal, Laroles, Mairena, Nechite, Válor, Yegen, Golco, Mecina Bombarón, Bérchules, Cádiar, Lobras, Juviles, Trevélez, Busquístar, Pórtugos, Atalbéitar, Pitres, Capilerilla, Bubión, Pampaneira, Soportújar and Cañar. This section could be done in six days or so.

Accommodation
It's worth trying to book ahead for rooms in the Alpujarras during Semana Santa and from June to September. In addition to the hotels and hostales, many villages have apartments and houses for short-term rental – look for signs or ask around. Organisations with a number of houses and apartments in different villages include Rustic Blue (see Walking under Pampaneira, Bubión & Capileira, below) and RurALandalus and Red Andaluza de Alojamientos Rurales (see Accommodation in Facts for the Visitor). Prices for two or three people generally range upwards from around 6000 ptas a night or 30,000 ptas a week.

Food & Drink
Apart from a couple of new-wave eateries in the more touristed villages, Alpujarras food is straightforward, hearty country fare, with lots of good meat and also local trout. Trevélez is famous for its *jamón serrano*, but many other villages produce good hams too. The *plato alpujarreño*, which you'll find on almost every menu, consists of fried potatoes, fried eggs, sausage, ham and maybe a black pudding, usually for around 700 ptas.

Alpujarras or *costa* wine comes mainly from the Sierra de la Contraviesa and tends to be strong and fairly raw.

Getting There & Away
Bus Buses to the Alpujarras are run by Alsina Graells (☎ 958 78 50 02 in Órgiva).

From Granada, buses run three times daily to Lanjarón, Órgiva (1½ hours), Pampaneira (two hours), Bubión, Capileira and Pitres (2¾ hours. At the time of writing these left Granada at 10.30 am, noon and 5.15 pm), with the last two continuing to Trevélez (3¼ hours) and Bérchules (3¾ hours). The return buses start from Bérchules at 5 am and 5 pm and from Pitres at 3.30 pm. There is also a twice-daily Granada-Ugíjar service via Lanjarón, Órgiva, Torvizcón, Cádiar and Yegen; a daily Málaga-Lanjarón service via Órgiva (except Sunday); a daily Almería-Ugíjar bus via Berja (except Sunday); and a daily Almería-Bérchules service via Adra, Ugíjar and Yegen (except Sunday). Other daily services link Lanjarón, Órgiva and other villages with Bérchules, Ugíjar and Berja, Almería province.

Car & Motorcycle The main road into the Alpujarras from the west is the A-348 (marked C-333 on some signs). The GR-421 turns north off the A-348 just west of Órgiva to wind along the northern slopes of the Alpujarras, rejoining it a few kilometres north of Cádiar. The only petrol station on the GR-421 is between Pampaneira and Pitres. The A-348 continues east to Ugíjar and on into Almerían Alpujarras. Coming from the Motril direction, turn east off the N-323 on to the A-346 to Órgiva, just north of Vélez de Benaudalla.

'Ruta Pintoresca' (Picturesque Route) signs here and there indicate driveable tracks up into the hills.

Lanjarón
Unless you're here to bathe in and imbibe its mineral-rich curative waters, there's little reason for more than a brief stop in the Alpujarras' westernmost town (population 4000). You could browse the stalls which sell woven baskets along the main street, Avenida de Andalucía. Though Lanjarón has a good setting on the southern slopes of the Sierra Nevada, it's a mostly modern place straggling along the A-348, and lacks most of the charm of other parts of the

Alpujarras. The Lanjarón mineral water bottling plant, which turns out 400,000L a day, and the spa *(balneario)*, which opens from May to November, are towards the western end of Avenida Andalucía. The Alsina Graells bus stop is towards the eastern end. There are numerous hostales and hotels, with doubles for between 3000 and 8000 ptas, on the same street (mostly west of the bus stop), though only a few stay open in winter.

Órgiva

The main town of the western Alpujarras, Órgiva (sometimes spelt Órjiva; population 5000) is a scruffy spot with traffic clogging the A-348 around its central traffic lights. But it's a bustling place, at its most interesting on Thursday mornings when both locals and the Alpujarras international community – which has a strong alternative/New Age component – descends on Órgiva to buy and sell everything from vegetables and wholefoods to hippie art and jewellery at a colourful market by the Río Chico on the Lanjarón side of town.

From the Alsina Graells bus stop and office on Avenida González Robles walk up the street and round the corner to the right and you'll come to the traffic lights. There are banks, some with ATMs, on and near Calle Doctor Fleming which heads uphill from the lights, and a post office (postcode 18400) towards the top of the town at Calle Mulhacén 5 (follow signs from the top of Calle Doctor Fleming). The Policía Local (☎ 958 78 52 12) are at Calle Doctor Fleming 1.

The landmark 16th century twin-towered **Iglesia de Nuestra Señora de la Expectación** stands at the foot of Calle Doctor Fleming.

Places to Stay & Eat *Camping Órgiva* (☎ 958 78 43 07) has a pool and restaurant but only a small area for camping. Two adults with a car and tent pay around 1900 ptas. It's open all year and is 2km south of the centre on the A-348 running down to the Río Guadalfeo.

Pensión Alma Alpujarreña (☎ 958 78 40 85), Avenida González Robles 49, just below the traffic lights, has singles/doubles for 2000/4000 ptas (doubles with bath 5000 ptas) and a three-course *menú*, including a drink, for 1200 ptas, .

Hostal Mirasol (☎ 958 78 51 59) at Avenida González Robles 3, overlooking the Thursday market site, has adequate singles/doubles with bathroom for 2000/4000 ptas plus IVA. The adjacent *Hotel Mirasol* (☎ 958 78 51 08) has newer, more comfortable rooms with TV for 5000/8000 ptas plus IVA. The two share a decent restaurant where a three-course dinner costs around 1700 ptas. *Hotel Taray* (☎ 958 78 45 25), 1.5km south of the centre on the A-348, has doubles for 8000 ptas plus IVA.

La Zahona bakery on Calle Doctor Fleming does good cakes and pastries which go well with a drink at the pavement tables of *Café Heladería Galindo*, which shares the same premises. The Galindo also has pizzas for 950 ptas. You can get wholemeal bread *(pan integral)* in the daily *mercado* at the top of Calle Doctor Fleming.

For raciones and tapas, try *Café Bar El Semáforo* on Avenida González Robles just west of the traffic lights.

Pampaneira, Bubión & Capileira

These villages clinging to the side of the deep Barranco de Poqueira ravine 14 to 20km north-east of Órgiva, are three of the prettiest, most dramatically sited and most touristed in Las Alpujarras. Their whitewashed stone houses seem to clamber over each other in an effort not to slide into the gorge, while streets decked with flowery balconies climb haphazardly in-between.

Capileira, the highest of the three at 1440m, is the best base for walks in the surrounding valleys and mountains. If you're staying in one of the other two villages you could use the buses to reach it, though their timing isn't great for morning starts.

Information The Centro de Visitantes de Pampaneira (☎ 958 76 31 27) on Pampaneira's square, Plaza de la Libertad, has a wealth of information on the Alpujarras and Sierra Nevada – including maps for sale – and can put you in the picture about walks and mountain refuges. It's open Wednesday to Saturday from 10 am to 2 pm and 4 to 6 pm (other days 10 am to 3 pm) and English is spoken. A small information kiosk by the main road in Capileira gives out a useful village map.

There's an ATM just outside the car park entrance in Pampaneira and at La General bank on Calle Doctor Castilla in Capileira. All three villages have supermarkets.

Things to See The villages – like many others in the Alpujarras – have solid 16th century **mudéjar churches** (open only at mass times, which are posted on the doors). They also have small **weaving workshops** which you can poke your head into and plentiful craft shops, some selling pottery from all over Andalucía as well as the more homespun Alpujarras cotton rugs.

Given the somewhat Himalayan character of the Poqueira landscape, it's not entirely surprising that there's a small Tibetan Buddhist monastery, **Osel Ling** (Place of Clear Light) about 1550m up on the far side of the valley from Pampaneira. The monastery welcomes visitors at certain times (call ☎ 958 34 31 34 for hours). You can walk to it from any of the villages or drive up from the turn-off marked 'Ruta Pintoresca' and 'Camino Forestal a la Casa 4340m Altitud 995m' opposite the Ermita del Padre Eterno, a wayside chapel on the GR-421 5km below Pampaneira.

Walks Eight trails ranging from four to 23km (1½ to eight hours) have been marked out in the Barranco de Poqueira with little colour-coded posts. Their outlines are shown on rather rough maps posted in prominent places in the villages. Most routes start from Capileira, though No 1 (6km, 2½ hours) is a circuit from Pampaneira and No 6 (14km, 4½ hours) is a circuit from Bubión.

Route No 4 from Capileira (8km, 2½ hours) takes you up to the hamlet of La Ce-

badilla, then down the western side of the valley and back up to Capileira. To find its start, walk down to the end of Calle Cubo at the northern end of Capileira, turn right at Apartamentos Vista Veleta and keep going. Route Nos 7 and 8 both continue up the valley from La Cebadilla to altitudes of around 2100m before returning. Nos 2 and 5 start at the end of Calle Cerezo in Capileira.

You can walk from Capileira to Trevélez in about five hours by taking the broad track heading to the right 4km up the Mulhacén road from the village, a couple of hundred metres after the 8km marker. The turning is marked by a wooden post with red and white paint rings and red and white paint on a rock a few metres along the track.

Nevadensis (nevadensis@arrakis.es, ☎ 958 76 31 27), which runs the information office at Pampaneira, and Rustic Blue (☎ 958 76 33 81), Barrio de la Ermita, Bubión (by the main road at the bottom of Bubión), offer a range of guided hikes and treks, with vehicle drop-off and pick-up when needed. With Nevadensis, day walks cost from 2300 to 4000 ptas a person (the top price is to ascend Mulhacén); a four-day Integral de Sierra Nevada trek, across the highest parts of the range, is 32,500 ptas. Most of Nevadensis' trips are on offer year-round, with a minimum of five people usually needed.

Other Activities Nevadensis and Rustic Blue can set you up with horse riding (around 4000 ptas for two hours or 8000 ptas a day) or, in winter, ski touring. Rustic Blue also offers long-distance horse treks and courses in sevillana dancing, painting, photography and vegetarian and nonvegetarian cooking. Nevadensis arranges mountain biking, climbing, paragliding, canyoning and 4WD trips too.

For horse riding you could also contact Dallas Sierra Trails (☎ 958 76 30 38), which has stables 2km above Capileira.

Places to Stay & Eat There are some good accommodation and eating options in the three villages.

Pampaneira Two good hostales face each other across Calle José Antonio at the entrance to the village. *Hostal Pampaneira* (☎ 958 76 30 02) has singles/doubles with bathroom for 2000/3000 ptas and the cheapest restaurant in the village (trout 550 ptas, pork chops 650 ptas). *Hostal Ruta del Mulhacén* (☎ 958 76 30 10) has singles/doubles with bathroom for 2900/4000 ptas and uninterrupted valley views from some rooms. Of the three restaurants just along the street on Plaza de la Libertad, *Restaurante Casa Diego*, with a pleasant upstairs terrace, is a good choice. Main dishes are from 650 to 1100 ptas (trout with ham, and local ham and eggs, are among the cheaper options). Omelettes are 300 to 450 ptas and there's also a 900 ptas three-course menú. *Bar Belezmín* has a few vegetarian dishes.

Bubión *Hostal Las Terrazas* (☎ 958 76 30 34) at Plaza del Sol 7 below the main road has pleasant though smallish singles doubles with bath for 2350/3300 ptas and apartments in nearby buildings at 5000 to 10,000 ptas for two to six people – all plus IVA. The *Villa Turística de Bubión* (☎ 958 76 31 11), just off the main road at the top of the village, has comfortable self-catering apartments with fireplaces for two to six people (12,000 ptas plus IVA for two or three people). There's a restaurant too.

Places to eat are chiefly along the main road. *Restaurante Teide* is good, with a three-course menú, including a drink, for 1100 ptas .There are several à la carte mains, including trout with ham, for under 800 ptas, and vegetarian options such as fennel-stuffed aubergines for 675 ptas (all plus IVA). Up the road are a few convivial bars such as the pub-like *Restaurante Fuenfría*, with a terrace across the road, and *Taberna Boabdil*.

Capileira *Mesón Hostal Poqueira* (☎ 958 76 30 48), just off the main road at Calle Doctor Castilla 6, has good singles/doubles with bath for 2400/4000 ptas, and a popular restaurant. *Hostal Atalaya* (☎ 958 76 30 25), 100m down the main road at Calle

Perchel 3, has similar prices but is smaller and less appealing. Or there's the slightly dearer *Hostal Paco López* (☎ 958 76 30 11), just up the main road at Carretera de la Sierra 5. *Café Bar Rosendo* (☎ 958 76 30 70) a little farther up the road has apartments for three to six people at 6000 to 10,800 ptas; *Hotel Finca Los Llanos* (☎ 958 76 30 71) at the top of the village has classier apartments – from 10,000 ptas plus IVA for two people.

There are plenty of places to eat. *Bar El Tilo* on Plaza Calvario, just down from the far end of Calle Doctor Castilla, has good-value raciones such as patatas a lo pobre (400 ptas), pollo en salsa (500 ptas) or pork chops (550 ptas). *Casa Íbero* below the church (follow signs from the end of Calle Doctor Castilla) makes good, original international food ranging from vegetarian or ham-and-chicken croquettes (650 ptas) to several couscous dishes (700 to 1100 ptas) or lamb with ginger sauce (1100 ptas). It's open for lunch and dinner except Sunday night and Monday.

Mulhacén
Rising above the top of the Poqueira valley are the Sierra Nevada's two highest peaks – Mulhacén (3478m) and Pico del Veleta (3396m). Mulhacén, the highest peak in mainland Spain, is named after Moulay Abu al-Hasan, father of the ill-fated Boabdil.

The road climbing over the Sierra Nevada from Capileira to the Estación de Esquí Sierra Nevada is closed to unauthorised vehicles some 12km from Capileira at about the 2500m mark (in winter snow may prevent you driving even that far). The first 5km from Capileira is paved. The upper part of the road passes 400m below the top of Mulhacén then heads westward for a few kilometres before climbing north to over 3200m then descending to the ski station.

Very strong hikers could make it from Capileira to the summit of Mulhacén in a long day (with over 2000m of ascent), but a better plan is to overnight at the *Refugio Poqueira* (☎ 958 34 33 49), (87 places) towards the top of the Poqueira valley at

2500m. The refugio is open all year (book a day or two ahead) at 1000 ptas per person and has both a guests' kitchen and prepared meals available (breakfast 550 ptas, dinner 1600 ptas). Blankets are provided and there are showers. From the refugio you can reach the top of Mulhacén in about three hours. Two 12-bed *refugios vivac* (just a shelter for your sleeping bag) are higher up, near the road: the Refugio Vivac La Caldera is beneath the western side of Mulhacén and the Refugio Vivac La Cariguela is beneath the southern side of Veleta.

An alternative walker's approach to Mulhacén and other high peaks is from Trevélez to their south-east, by the Trevélez valley and the Cañada de Siete Lagunas, a lake-dotted basin below the eastern side of Mulhacén. The important thing to remember on this route is to steer clear of the boggy bottom of the valley of the Río Culo de Perro (Dog's Arse River). Again, it's possible to reach the peak in one hard day but it's better to camp in the cañada, five or six hours up from Trevélez.

For approaches from the north, see the earlier Estación de Esquí Sierra Nevada and Ruta Integral de los Tres Mil sections.

Pitres & Around

Pitres is almost as pretty as the Poqueira gorge villages but less touristed. It has a bank (no ATM) on the main square.

Camping El Balcón de Pitres (☎ 958 76 61 11), by the GR-421 on the western side of the village, opens from March to October and charges 1700 ptas plus IVA for two adults with a car and tent. It has a decent restaurant and a pool. *Refugio Los Albergues* (☎ 958 34 31 76), two minutes walk (signposted) down a path from the GR-421 on the eastern side of the village, is a small privately run hikers' hostel, with 12 places in a bunk dorm at 1000 ptas, one double room for 3000 ptas, an equipped kitchen, hot showers and interesting outdoor toilets. It's closed from 10 January to 15 February. The friendly German owner is full of information on the area and its many good walks, including a good route around the

three small villages below Pitres which are grouped with it in what's still called La Tahá de Pitres, one of the units into which the Alpujarras were divided under the Granada emirate.

Fonda Sierra Nevada (☎ 958 76 60 17) on Pitres' plaza has singles/doubles at 1700/3400 ptas. There are also a few middle-range hostales and hotels, with doubles between 5000 and 7000 ptas plus IVA, on or just off the GR-421 in Pitres and nearby Pórtugos and Busquístar. There's a handful of cafés and restaurants around Pitres' plaza.

Trevélez

Trevélez (population 800; altitude 1476m), set in a gash in the mountainside almost as impressive as the Poqueira gorge, is the most famous Alpujarras village for three reasons: it's a frequent starting point for ascents of the high Sierra Nevada peaks; it claims to be the highest village in Spain (Taüll in Cataluña, at 1495m, might have something to say about that, though the Trevélez *municipio* is certainly the highest on the mainland as it includes Mulhacén); and it produces some of the country's best *jamón serrano*. Hams are trucked in from far and wide for curing in Trevélez's dry mountain air.

First impressions of the village are disappointing, as you're confronted by a welter of jamón and souvenir shops along the main road, but a wander into the upper parts reveals a lively village of typical Alpujarran quaintness. The La General bank just above the main road at the foot of the village has an ATM.

Walking Aside from being a starting point for Mulhacén and walks to other Alpujarras villages, Trevélez is also one end of an old pack animal route up the Trevélez valley and over the 2800m Puerto de Trevélez pass to the pretty town of Jerez del Marquesado, 22km north-east. This could be walked in a long day or you could overnight at the *Refugio Postero Alto* above Jerez (see the earlier Ruta Integral de los Tres Mil section).

Places to Stay & Eat *Restaurante González* (☎ 958 85 85 33) on Plaza de Don Francisco Abellán, by the main road at the foot of the village, has doubles with shared bathrooms for 2500 ptas and a good restaurant with a four-course *menú* for 950 ptas or chicken, trout or a plato alpujarreño for 700 to 800 ptas. *Hostal Regina* (☎ 958 85 85 64), nearby at Plaza de Don Francisco Abellán 12, has comfier singles/doubles with bath for 2800/5000 ptas or doubles with shared bath for 3900 ptas. Between these two places, *Restaurante Álvarez* and *Bar La Alpujarra* also have rooms.

Hostal Fernando (☎ 958 85 85 65), Pista del Barrio Medio s/n, by the road going up towards the top of the village, has decent doubles with bath for 3200 ptas, or two-person apartments with terraces for 4200 ptas. Past here, the road reaches Plaza Barrio Medio, where there are signs to the *Hotel La Fragua* (☎ 958 85 86 26), Calle San Antonio 4, which has Trevélez's most comfortable rooms at 5500 ptas with bath. Its restaurant, *Mesón La Fragua*, a short walk away, offers relatively exotic fare such as partridge in walnut sauce (1400 ptas) as well as trout, ham and pork. Just below the hotel and restaurant, *Café Bar Castellón* on Calle Cárcel has rooms with shared baths for 1250/2500 ptas.

Mesón Haraicel just above Plaza de Don Francisco Abellán has a few outside tables and good food, with several trout and meat main courses for 775 to 850 ptas. Also good is *Mesón Joaquín* by the main road on the west side of the village. A three-course *menú,* including a drink, costs 900 ptas.

Jamón de Trevélez crops up on every menu. If you're tempted to buy some to take away, the shops up in the village tend to be cheaper than those on the main road. You should be able to get 1kg for 1000 ptas or less (double for the special ibérico and pata negra varieties).

East of Trevélez
The east side of the Trevélez valley is one of the greenest parts of the Alpujarras, covered with evergreen oak and pine. Seven kilometres south of Trévelez the GR-421 crosses the low Portichuelo de Cástaras pass and turns east into a barer landscape. Yet there are still oases of greenery around the villages. These central and eastern parts of the Alpujarras are in their own way just as impressive as the west, but pull in far fewer tourists.

Bérchules, 17km from Trevélez, is an attractive village in a green valley which stretches a long way back into the hills. *Casa Resu* (☎ 958 76 90 92) in the centre at Calle Iglesia 18 has basic singles/doubles for 1000/2000 ptas. *Hotel Los Bérchules* (☎ 958 85 25 30) on the main road has doubles for 5000 ptas.

Cádiar (population 2000), in the bottom of the valley 8km south of Bérchules, is one of the bigger Alpujarras villages and more appealing than it looks from afar. *Hostal Montoro* (☎ 958 76 80 68), Calle San Isidro 20, has doubles with bath for just 1900 ptas plus IVA. The *Alquería de Morayma* (☎ 958 3433 03), 2km south of Cádiar, is a beautifully renovated old farmhouse with a good, inexpensive restaurant and a library of Alpujarras information. Singles/doubles in rooms and apartments, some with a small kitchen, are from 4800/6000 ptas to 6700/8300 ptas plus IVA. The friendly owners offer a variety of interesting walks and excursions, many of them focused on the traditional events of the Alpujarras calendar.

Twelve kilometres east of Bérchules is **Yegen**, where Gerald Brenan made his home in the 1920s. His house, just off the main plaza with the fountain, has a plaque. Yegen is a typically pretty Alpujarras village to stroll around and could be a good walking or touring base. Parts of the valley below have a particularly moonlike quality. *Café-Bar La Fuente* on the plaza has singles/doubles for 1300/2600 ptas. *El Tinao* (☎ 958 85 12 12) on the main road has good rooms with bath for 2000/3500 ptas, and four and six-person apartments and houses for 5000 to 8000 ptas, plus food, in its bar and *comedor.* It also rents out bicycles. *El Rincón de Yegen* (☎ 958 85 12 70), by the road on the eastern edge of the village, has more rooms and apartments and a restaurant.

Válor, a quiet place between two ravines 5km east of Yegen, was the birthplace of Aben Humeya, leader of the 1568 rebellion, and is today the setting for the best known of the Alpujarras' Moros y Cristianos festivals. *Hostal Las Perdices* (☎ 958 85 18 21) on Calle Torrecilla in the centre has good rooms with bath for 3000 ptas a double.

Ugíjar (population 2600), 7km south-east of Válor, is the main market town hereabouts, with two hostales. From Cherín, 6km east, the scenic A-337 heads north over the 1993m Puerto de la Ragua pass (sometimes snowbound in winter) to La Calahorra. East of Cherín, the Alpujarras and the A-348 continue into Almería province.

The Coast

Granada's 80km coastline is rugged and cliff-lined, with the coastal N-340 highway winding up and down between scattered towns and villages. The tourism industry calls this the Costa Tropical because of the crops such as sugar cane, custard apples, avocados and mangos that are grown where the coastal plain broadens out a bit. The N-323 from Granada arrives near the coast just west of Motril after threading through an impressive gorge carved by the Río Guadalfeo. East of uninspiring Motril, the mountains often come right down to the sea, the settlements are mostly drab and the beaches pebbly. If you're driving from the east, the C-333 to Las Alpujarras heads north across the Sierra de la Contraviesa from La Rábita.

West of Motril the terrain is a bit less abrupt and there are a few quite attractive beach towns. La Herradura and the nearby Marina del Este form a minor scuba-diving centre. The views you'll get from the N-340 as it winds west into Málaga province are spectacular.

SALOBREÑA

Salobreña's huddle of white houses rises on a crag between the N-340 and the sea, 2km west of the N-323 junction. At the top is an impressive Muslim castle and below is a long and wide dark-sand beach. It's a low-key place for most of the year but gets pretty lively in July and August.

Orientation & Information

From the N-340, Avenida Federico García Lorca skirts the eastern and lower part of the town as it heads a kilometre or so south to the seafront. Just 200m along on Plaza de Goya is the helpful tourist office (☎ 958 61 03 14) , which offers maps (100 ptas) with suggested walking itineraries through the old town. It's open Monday to Saturday from 9.30 am to 1.30 pm and Monday to Friday from 4.30 to 7 pm (5 to 8 pm in summer). The Alsina Graells bus stop is diagonally across the street from the tourist office.

Market days are Tuesday and Friday.

Things to See

A 20-minute walk uphill from the tourist office, the **Castillo Árabe** (Arab Castle; ☎ 958 61 01 11) dates from the 13th century, though the site was fortified as early as the 10th century. The castle, a beautiful sight when floodlit at night, was used as a summer residence by the Granada emirs. Legend has it that Emir Mohammed IX had his three daughters, Zaida, Zoraida and Zorahaida, held captive here too; Washington Irving gives a version of this story in his *Tales of the Alhambra*. The inner Alcazaba, a setting for many cultural events, retains much of its Nasrid structure. You can walk along parts of the surrounding parapets. The castle is open for visits (200 ptas) Monday to Friday from 10 am to 1.30 pm and 4 to 8 pm.

Immediately below the castle is the 16th century mudéjar **Iglesia de Nuestra Señora del Rosario** with a striking arched doorway. The old Muslim town (the original Albayzín and the later Broval and Boveda districts) spills out below the castle, ending on one side in steep cliffs. There's a mirador in the Albayzín and another on Paseo de las Flores below the castle.

The **Museo Arqueológico** (☎ 958 61 06 30) in the library on Calle Ángel Ganivet in the south-west of town is worth a visit. A model and visual aids illustrate how Salobreña was practically an island until river sediments formed a fertile delta around the rocky outcrop on which the town was built. The museum (free) is open Monday to Friday from 10 am to 2 pm.

Special Events
Semana Santa processions through the steep old town streets attract a lot of visitors. The Día de la Cruz (Day of the Cross) on 3 May is a lively, colourful affair with horse riders, polka-dot dresses and sevillana dancing, as in Granada. The feria takes place in the last week of June. Around 20 August, the one-day Lucero de Alba features rock and flamenco acts in the Alcazaba and elsewhere.

Places to Stay
The camp site on the beach has disappeared but there are half a dozen hostales, all pretty cheap. *Pensión Mari Carmen* (☎ 958 61 09 06), Calle Nueva 30, and *Pensión Arnedo* (☎ 958 61 02 27), Calle Nueva 15, both about a 10 minute walk west of Plaza de Goya, have reasonable doubles with shared bath for less than 3000 ptas. *Hotel Salambina* (☎ 958 61 00 37) just west of town at N-340, Km 341, has better rooms from 4500 to 5390 ptas a double, depending on the season. The slightly flashier *Hotel Salobreña* (☎ 958 61 02 61) at N-340, Km 345, has comfy doubles from 6600 to 8100 ptas.

Places to Eat
Little *Restaurante Pesetas* on Calle Bóveda, the street opposite the Iglesia de Nuestra Señora del Rosario, serves up good tapas and meals. The popular *La Bodega*, with outdoor tables on Plaza de Goya, does a *menú* for 1200 ptas. A couple of hundred metres down Avenida Federico García Lorca, on Plaza Ramírez de Madrid, *Mesón de la Villa* is another good bet. There are

several restaurants, *chiringuitos*, bars and even a spot of nightlife on and near the beachfront. *Restaurante El Peñón*, by the big rock which divides Salobreña's main beach, does good seafood dishes.

Getting There & Away
Alsina Graells (☎ 958 18 50 10) has plenty of buses along the coast in both directions (Málaga 865 ptas, Almeria 1045 ptas), and at least six daily to Granada (670 ptas). There are also daily buses to Sevilla, Córdoba, Jaén, Úbeda, Lanjarón and Madrid.

ALMUÑÉCAR
Fifteen kilometres west of Salobreña, Almuñécar may appear uninviting but there's an attractive old section aroud its 16th century castle. Popular with Spanish tourists and home to a small community of northern Europeans, it's bright and not too expensive, though the beaches are pebbly.

History
The Phoenicians set up a colony called Sexi here in the 8th century BC and the Roman Sexi Firmum Iulium was well established by the 3rd century AD. Abd ar-Rahman I arrived here from Damascus in 755 and went on to found the emirate of Córdoba. Later, the town served as a coastal fortress for the Granada emirate. From here, Boabdil, with 1130 supporters, left Spain for North Africa in 1493.

Orientation & Information
The bus station is at Avenida Juan Carlos I 1, just south of the N-340. Plaza de la Constitución, the main plaza of the old part of town, is a few minutes walk south-west. The little Plaza de la Rosa is a couple of minutes farther south-east. The tourist office (☎ 958 63 11 25) is at the other end of town in the pretty neo-mudéjar Palacete la Najarra on Avenida de Europa, just back from the eastern end of Playa de San Cristóbal. It's open daily from 10 am to 2 pm and from 4 to 7 pm (5 to 8 pm in summer).

Almuñécar's beachfront is divided by a rocky outcrop, the Peñón del Santo, with

Playa de San Cristóbal, the best of the beaches, to the west and Playa de la Caletilla, Playa Puerta del Mar and Playa Fuente de Piedra to the east. Farther east is the separate Playa de Velilla with lots of apartment blocks but quite a good beach.

Things to See
On Playa de San Cristóbal is an aviary with 120 types of tropical bird, the **Parque Ornitológico Loro Sexi** – open daily from 10 am to 2 pm (300 ptas). The **Museo Arqueológico**, in 1st century Roman galleries called the Cueva de Siete Palacios, has local Phoenician, Roman and Islamic finds plus a rare 3500-year-old Egyptian amphora. It's open Tuesday to Sunday from 10.30 to 1.30 pm and 4 to 6 pm (6 to 8 pm in summer). Opposite the tourist office in the Parque El Majuelo is the **Factoría de Salazones Romana**, the remains of a Roman *garum* sauce factory. Farther afield, off Avenida del Mediterráneo and about a half-hour walk west of the old town, you'll find the **Tumbas Fenicias Puente de Noy**, a Phoenician and Roman necropolis. The two-tiered Roman **Acueducto de la Carrera** is situated on the north side of the N-340 near the Río Seco, west of the Carretera Suspiro del Moro. In the town centre, near the seafront, the **Castillo Árabe**, also known as the Castillo San Miguel, built over Muslim and Roman fortifications by the conquering Christians, contains the **Museo de la Ciudad**. The museum gives a potted history of the town and was due to reopen in 1998.

Places to Stay
There are two year-round camping grounds on the N-340 east of the centre. *Camping Carambolo* (☎ 958 63 03 22) at Km 315 is the cheaper of the two and farther from the beach. Farther out, at Km 317.5, *Camping El Paraíso* (☎ 958 63 23 70) is on the coast side of the N-340. The summer sites at nearby La Herradura are better situated.

Budget hostales are in the streets between the bus station and Plaza de la Rosa. Among them, though only open in July and August,

is the basic but clean *Hostal Victoria* (☎ 958 63 00 22) at Plaza de la Victoria 6, which has doubles with bath for 3700 ptas. The better *Hotel Victoria II* (☎ 958 63 17 34), Plaza de la Victoria 22, has singles/doubles from 1800/3200 ptas to 3000/4800 ptas. Almost next door in a distinctive neo-Muslim building, the good *Hostal Plaza Damasco* (☎ 958 63 01 65), Calle Cerrajeros 8, has doubles from 3000 to 5000 ptas. Also in this price range but on Avenida de Europa close to Playa de San Cristóbal are the *Hostal Tropical* (☎ 958 63 34 58) and *Hotel Goya* (☎ 958 63 05 50). Right by Playa de San Cristóbal, opposite the big monument to Abd ar-Rahman I, is the more upmarket *Hotel Casablanca* (☎ 958 63 55 75), Plaza San Cristóbal 4, with comfortable doubles at 9000 ptas plus IVA.

Places to Eat
Plaza de la Constitución has a few popular restaurants with tables outside. At Calle Real 15, between Plaza de la Constitución and Plaza de la Rosa, *Bodega Francisco* is a *típico* bar with a long tapas list and an 850 ptas *menú*. Just east of Plaza de la Rosa is Plaza Kelibia, which has several bars with tables on the plaza: *La Trastienda* has excellent tapas. Nearby at Plaza de Damasco 5, *Pizzería Il Grillo* serves up good Italian food. Directly south of Plaza de la Rosa, Acera del Mar has more places to eat. Or you could head for the restaurants opposite the seafront on Paseo de las Flores and Paseo de San Cristóbal: *Hotel Casablanca's* restaurant, with tables on the plaza at the eastern end of Paseo de los Flores, does a *menú* for 850 ptas and serves up tasty meat dishes.

Entertainment
Plaza Kelibia and Acera del Mar buzz at night. The *Auditorium Martín Recuerda*, in the Casa de la Cultura on Calle Puerta de Granada, hosts musical events, theatre, poetry readings and a cine club. *Venta Luciano*, 3km north of Almuñécar on the Carretera Suspiro del Moro (a scenic road to Granada via Otívar), has an all-you-can-eat-and-drink barbecue followed by a

flamenco show (3300 ptas, 4300 ptas with transport) in summer on Tuesday and Friday from 9 pm and in winter on Friday from 8 pm. Book on ☎ 958 63 13 79 or at hotels and travel agents in town.

Getting There & Away
Several buses a day run along the coast to Nerja, Málaga and Almería, and inland to Granada. There's also one bus daily to Lanjarón, Orgiva, Jaén, Úbeda, Cádiz and Córdoba, and two to Sevilla.

MARINA DEL ESTE
West of Almuñecar, the N-340 winds between the mountains and the coast for 7km to La Herradura. Shortly before is the turn-off to Marina del Este on the Punta de la Mona promontory. The 4km road winds uphill then descends steeply to the coast and the beautiful marina with its exclusive feel.

There are a couple of diving outfits: Club Nautique (☎ 958 82 75 14) charges 5000 ptas for a dive including the boat and equipment, or 45,000 ptas for a four-day PADI course. Shortly before the marina is Alcázar (☎ 958 64 01 82), a sports club in a large neo-Muslim building with loads of facilities – ask about paragliding. Close by is Club Hípico (☎ 929-57 00 02), a riding school that rents out horses.

El Barco, with main dishes from 1000 to 2000 ptas, does excellent seafood. In summer, *Tradewinds* is a lively spot for a drink and tapas from 6 pm until late.

LA HERRADURA
The little resort town of La Herradura, named for its pretty, horseshoe-shaped bay, is popular locally for water sports (it has a windsurfing school and a couple of dive outfits) and good seafront restaurants. Its sheltered beach is packed in July and August. In January the town hosts the Andrés Segovia international classical guitar competition.

Orientation & Information
The Alsina Graells bus stop is at the top of Calle Acera del Pilar, right by the N-340.

Calle Acera del Pilar heads south to the seafront Paseo Andrés Segovia, also called Paseo Marítimo, which runs right along the bay. The town, with a few shops and services, spills down the gentle slope between the N-340 and the beach, and along the land side of Paseo Andrés Segovia. On this street, head to Windsurf La Herradura (☎ 958 64 01 43) for windsurfer, dinghy and canoe rentals, or Granada Sub (☎ 958 64 02 81) for diving.

Places to Stay
Two summer camping grounds, *Camping La Herradura* (☎ 958 64 00 56) and *Nuevo Camping La Herradura* (☎ 958 64 06 34), are opposite the beach on Paseo Andrés Segovia. Nuevo Camping is the more expensive at 2300 ptas plus IVA for two adults, a tent and a car. On the same street, *Hostal Peña Parda* (☎ 958 64 00 66), at the west end, and *Hostal La Caleta* (☎ 958 82 70 07), towards the east end, have good restaurants and both charge 6000 ptas plus IVA for doubles with bath in summer. *Hotel Tryp Los Fenicios* (☎ 958 82 79 00), a few doors east of Hostal La Caleta, has doubles from 10,750 ptas to 15,200 ptas, both plus IVA, depending on the season.

Places to Eat
Most restaurants on Paseo Andrés Segovia serve good food at reasonable prices, though they mark up drinks. The Italian-owned *Los Faroles*, east of Calle Acera del Pilar, does good pasta at around 600 ptas, and meat or fish dishes for less than 1000 ptas. You can buy decent wines from all over Europe by the glass, and a tapa comes free with your drink. Next door, *Casa Antonio & Evelyn* has a mixed menu; try one of their excellent soups, or jabalí (wild boar). Also at the east end of Paseo Andrés Segovia, *Café Luciano*, open from 1 pm, is a relaxed place to linger over a coffee.

Getting There & Away
Plenty of Alsina Graells buses head east and west along the coast and a few go to Granada.

Jaén Province

There are two particularly good reasons to venture on from Granada or Córdoba to the back-country province of Jaén. One is the large Parque Natural de Cazorla in the north-east, perhaps the most beautiful of Andalucía's mountain regions. The other is an architectural heritage dominated by the Renaissance master Andrés de Vandelvira, at its best in Úbeda but also impressive in Baeza and Jaén.

Crossed by the Río Guadalquivir, which rises in the Cazorla park, the Jaén landscape alternates between rolling agricultural *campiña* country, covered with olive trees, and impressive mountain ranges. The Desfiladero de Despeñaperros pass – a gap in the Sierra Morena on Jaén's northern border – has, from time immemorial, been the most important northern gateway to Andalucía.

Food

Jaén food is pretty traditional but richly varied. It's based on local products such as olive oil, seasonal vegetables (including wild mushrooms), eggs, pork, ham, chicken, game, trout and bacalao (traditionally the only sea fish available in interior Andalucía). Escabeche marinade is used to preserve perishables.

In the Cazorla region, venison (of *ciervo*, red deer, or *gamo*, fallow deer) and wild boar *(jabalí)* are widely available. You may even come across mouflon (wild sheep). Partridge salad *(ensalada de perdiz)* and *choto* (the local name for veal) are other favourites and there's a wide range of egg *revueltos*. *Lomo de orza* is seasoned pork loin, fried then conserved in oil in a clay pot called an *orza*.

Rin-rán is a traditional concoction of bacalao, potato and dried red peppers mashed up together. *Carruécano* is pumpkin fried with garlic and chillies.

Many bars have the endearingly traditional habit of serving free tapas with drinks.

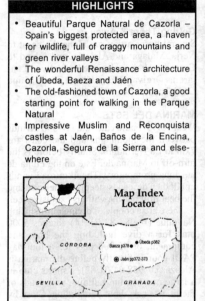

JAÉN

The provincial capital (population 105,000), 574m up among rugged mountains and olive groves, would rate as a thrilling city for few people, but it has enough to hold you for a day or so.

Castilla's Fernando III El Santo took Jaén from the Emirate of Granada after a six-month siege in 1246. The emir agreed to pay to Castilla half his annual income in tribute but won Fernando's agreement to respect the emirate's frontiers. However, in the late 15th century the Catholic Monarchs made Jaén a base for their successful final war against the Granada emirate. Centuries of decline set in after the Reconquista, with

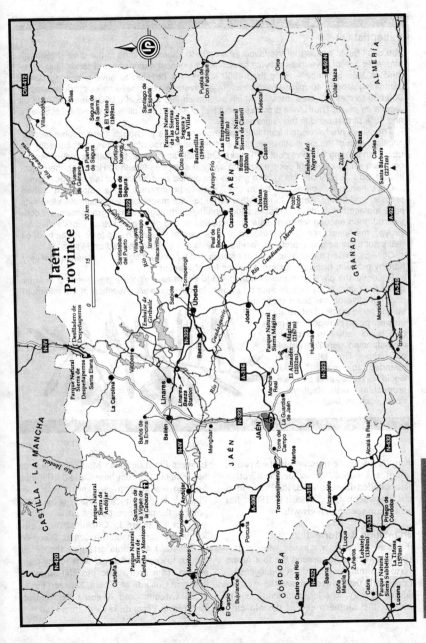

Essential Oil

You can't fail to notice that the favoured crop in the Jaén campiña is the olive *(aceituna)*. Line after line of olive trees *(olivos)* stretch across almost every scrap of fertile land. One-third of Jaén province – more than 4500 sq km – is devoted to olive groves *(olivares)* containing around 40 million olive trees. In an average year these trees produce around 900,000 tonnes of olives, most of which are turned into some 200,000 tonnes of olive oil *(aceite de oliva)*. Thus, Jaén provides about half of Andalucía's olive oil, one-third of Spain's and 10% of that used in the entire world.

The olives are harvested from late November to January. Though there's some mechanisation, a lot of the job is still done by the traditional method of spreading nets beneath the tree, then beating the olives out with sticks. On small family plots, this can be quite a festive occasion with six or eight people bashing away at each tree together. However, the majority of Jaén's (and Andalucía's) olive groves are owned by a handful of large landowners.

Once harvested, olives are taken to oil mills to be mashed into a pulp which is then pressed and finally filtered. In recent years up-to-date machinery and stainless steel vats have replaced mule-driven presses squeezing the oil through esparto-grass mats. Oil considered good enough for immediate consumption is sold as virgin olive oil *(aceite de oliva virgen)*, the finest grade of oil. Refined olive oil *(aceite de oliva refinado)* is made from oil that's not quite so good, and plain *aceite de oliva* is a blend of refined and virgin oil.

Olive oil is used throughout Spain for salads and for frying. Virgin oil is considered a very healthy product, being cholesterol-free and full of vitamins.

Recently, the olive community of Jaén – and Spain as a whole – has been up in arms about EU plans to change its support system for olive growers. Abolition of the minimum price for olive oil has been suggested and there is talk of future aid to growers being provided on a per-tree basis rather than on the long-standing per-kilogram-of-oil basis. The latter idea, intended to combat fraud, would hurt areas of large-scale production with high-yield trees, such as Jaén.

many *jiennenses* emigrating to the Spanish colonies – hence the existence of other places called Jaén, in Peru, the Philippines and elsewhere. Only since the 1960s has Jaén again seen much growth.

Orientation & Information

Old Jaén, with narrow, winding, often pedestrian streets, huddles around the foot of the Cerro de Santa Catalina, the wooded, castle-topped hill that towers above the western side of the city. The large cathedral stands towards the southern end of the old city,

between Plaza de Santa María and Plaza de San Francisco. From here Calle de Bernabé Soriano leads north-east and downhill to Plaza de la Constitución, which is the focal point of the newer part of the city.

From Plaza de la Constitución, Calle Roldán y Marín (which becomes Paseo de la Estación), the main artery of the newer part of town, heads north-west to the train station, 1km away. The bus station is on Plaza de Coca de la Piñera, between Paseo de la Estación and Avenida de Madrid, 250m from Plaza de la Constitución.

Tourist Offices The Junta de Andalucía tourist office (☎ 953 22 27 37) at Calle del Arquitecto Berges 1 is a couple of minutes walk from the bus station. It's open Monday to Friday from 9 am to 7 pm and Saturday from 9 am to 2 pm. The staff are helpful and also have information on the province.

The Oficina Municipal de Turismo (☎ 953 21 91 16) in the Palacio Municipal de Cultura at Calle de la Maestra 16, near the cathedral, is open Monday to Friday from 9 am to 2 pm.

Money There's no shortage of banks or ATMs around Plaza de la Constitución and on Calle Roldán y Marín.

Post & Communications The main post office (postcode 23080) on Plaza de los Jardinillos is open Monday to Friday from 8.30 am to 8.30 pm and Saturday from 9.30 am to 2 pm.

Bookshop Librería Metrópolis in the old town at Calle del Cerón 19 is handy for maps and Spanish-language guidebooks.

Medical & Emergency Services The main general hospital is the Hospital Ciudad de Jaén (☎ 953 22 24 08) on Avenida del Ejército Español. The Cruz Roja is on ☎ 953 25 15 40.

The Policía Municipal (☎ 953 21 91 05) are on Carrera de Jesús, just behind the Ayuntamiento. The Policía Nacional (☎ 953 26 18 50) are at Calle del Arquitecto Berges 11.

Catedral

Jaén's huge cathedral was built mostly in the 16th and 17th centuries, and mainly to the designs of Andrés de Vandelvira, on the site of Muslim Jaén's main mosque. Its highlight is the superb twin-towered **south-west façade** on Plaza de Santa María, which is more baroque than Renaissance, with an array of 17th century statuary, much of it by Sevilla's Pedro Roldán.

The vast but dark interior is open Monday to Saturday from 8.30 am to 1 pm and 4 to 7 pm (5 to 8 pm in summer) and on Sunday and holidays from 8.30 am to 1.30 pm and from 5 to 7 pm. Directly behind the main altar, the **Capilla Mayor** (or Capilla del Santo Rostro) houses the Reliquia del Santo Rostro de Cristo, a cloth with an image of Christ's face, with which St Veronica is believed to have wiped Christ's face on the road to Calvary. On Fridays at 11.30 am and 5 pm long queues of the faithful wait to kiss the cloth.

Centro Cultural Palacio de Villardompardo

This handsome Renaissance palace on Plaza de Santa Luisa de Marillac, 500m north-west of the cathedral, houses two museums and what's claimed to be the largest Islamic bathhouse open to visitors in Spain. All three sections (☎ 953 23 62 92) are open Tuesday to Friday from 10 am to 2 pm and from 5 to 8 pm and Saturday and on Sunday from 10.30 am to 2 pm (closed on Monday and holidays). Entry is 100 ptas (free with an EU passport or national identity card).

The **Baños Árabes** (Arab Baths), in the bowels of the building, are beautified by numerous horseshoe arches and star-shaped skylights. The most impressive room is the *sala templada* (temperate room). Built in the 11th century, and turned into a tannery by the Christians, the baths disappeared in the 16th century when the Conde de Villardompardo had a palace built over the site. They were not rediscovered until 1913.

The **Museo Internacional de Arte Naïf** (International Museum of Naïf Art), opened in 1988, is the first of its kind in Spain. Much of the large collection was donated by Manuel Moral Mozas of Torre del Campo, Jaén. The work tends to be very colourful (the paintings from Haiti are the most vivid) and does not use perspective. Village life and the countryside are constant themes.

The collections of old carts and fine 19th century clothes are the most eye-catching items in the Museo de Artes y Costumbres Populares (Museum of Popular Art &

JAÉN PROVINCE

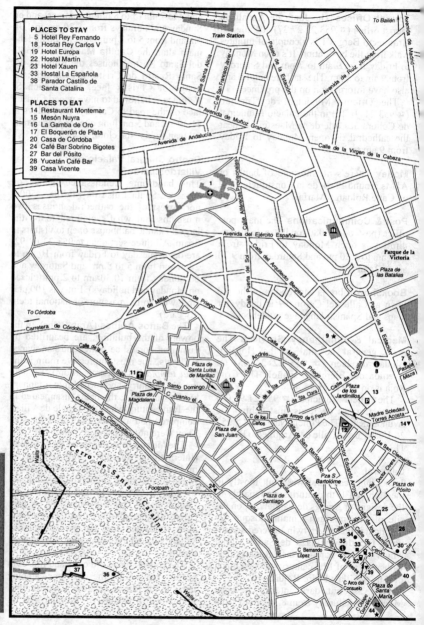

PLACES TO STAY
5 Hotel Rey Fernando
18 Hostal Rey Carlos V
19 Hotel Europa
22 Hostal Martín
23 Hotel Xauen
33 Hostal La Española
38 Parador Castillo de
   Santa Catalina

PLACES TO EAT
14 Restaurant Montemar
15 Mesón Nuyra
16 La Gamba de Oro
17 El Boquerón de Plata
20 Casa de Córdoba
24 Café Bar Sobrino Bigotes
27 Bar del Pósito
28 Yucatán Café Bar
39 Casa Vicente

OTHER
1 Hospital Ciudad de Jaén
2 Museo Provincial
3 Autos del Pino
4 Bus Station
6 Taxi Stand
7 Viajes Sacromonte
8 Junta de Andalucía
  Tourist Office
9 Policía Nacional
10 Centro Cultural Palacio
   de Villardompardo
11 Iglesia de la Magdalena
12 Main Post Office
13 Parking
21 Café-Pub Iroquai
25 Parking San Francisco
26 Diputación Provincial
29 Iglesia de San Ildefonso
30 Taxi Stand
31 La Manchega
32 El Gorrión
34 Librería Metrópolis
35 Oficina Municipal
   de Turismo
36 Cross
37 Castillo de Santa Catalina
40 Catedral
41 Palacio de los Vélez
42 Palacio de los
   Covaleda-Nicuesa
43 Ayuntamiento
44 Policía Municipal

Customs), devoted to pre-industrial Jaén province.

Iglesia de la Magdalena

Jaén's oldest church stands a short walk west of the Palacio de Villardompardo along Calle Santo Domingo. Originally a mosque, it has a Gothic main façade and interior. Its tower is the mosque's minaret, reworked in the 16th century. You can enter the church daily from 6 to 8 pm: the outstanding feature inside is the *retablo* by Jacobo Florentino. Behind the church is a lovely Islamic courtyard with Roman tombstones and a pool used for ritual ablutions in Muslim times.

Iglesia de San Ildefonso

Jaén's second-biggest church (after the cathedral) and 'home' of its patron saint, the Virgen de la Capilla, stands on Plaza de San Ildefonso, 200m north-east of the cathedral. San Ildefonso was founded in the 13th century but remodelled several times. An inscription on the bottom (north-east) end of its exterior marks the spot where the Virgin is believed to have appeared on 10 June 1430. Inside, her much-venerated image stands in the Capilla de Nuesta Señora de la Capilla. The church is open daily from 8.30 am to noon and from 6 to 9 pm.

Museo Provincial

Jaén's Provincial Museum (☎ 953 25 06 00), Paseo de la Estación 27, has a good archaeological section, which covers the cultures of Jaén province from pre-3000 BC hunter-gatherers to Muslim times. The highlight of the museum is a fine collection of 5th century BC Iberian sculpture, showing a clear Greek influence.

The museum is open Tuesday to Friday from 10 am to 2 pm and 4 to 7.30 pm and Saturday and Sunday from 10 am to 2 pm. (closed Monday and holidays). Entry is 100 ptas (free with an EU passport or national identity card).

Castillo de Santa Catalina

Undoubtedly Jaén's most exhilarating spot

JAÉN PROVINCE

is this originally Muslim castle perched atop the Cerro de Santa Catalina. If you don't have a vehicle for the circuitous 4km drive up from the city centre, you can take a taxi (800 ptas) or walk (about an hour) using a steep path that leaves the Carretera de Circunvalación almost opposite the top of Calle de Buenavista.

The castle was, according to tradition, handed over to Fernando III in 1246 by the Emir of Granada and later rebuilt by the Christians. It's open daily, except Wednesday, from 10 am to 1.30 pm (free). Inside you can check out the keep, a chapel and some underground water tanks.

Past the castle at the end of the ridge stands a large cross on the site where Fernando III had a cross placed after his victory in 1246. The views over the city and the olive groves beyond are magnificent.

If you have walked up you deserve to treat yourself to a drink in Parador Castillo de Santa Catalina next to the castle.

Special Events

Semana Santa is celebrated in a big way, with processions through the old city by 13 *cofradías*. The week climaxes in the early hours of Good Friday. Jaén's biggest bash is the Feria y Fiestas de San Lucas with concerts, funfairs, bullfights and general merrymaking for about 10 days up to the saint's day, 18 October.

Places to Stay

Mosquitoes can be a nuisance in Jaén hotels, especially the cheaper ones. Prices in several places rise a bit during Semana Santa and the feria.

Hostal Rey Carlos V (☎ 953 22 20 91), Avenida de Madrid 4, is the nearest hostal to the bus station, but on a noisy street and the staff don't always answer the door. Basic singles/doubles are 2300/3200 ptas.

Hostal Martín (☎ 953 24 36 78), Calle Cuatro Torres 5 in a narrow street just east of Plaza de la Constitución, is shabby but adequate, with basic rooms for 2000/3000 ptas.

Hostal La Española (☎ 953 23 02 54), near the cathedral at Calle Bernardo López

9, has the most character of the cheapies – it's a sizeable old house on a narrow street, with an interestingly tilted wooden spiral staircase. Singles/doubles with shared bath are 1600/3000 ptas (doubles with private shower and toilet are 4000 ptas). We found the hot water supplies sporadic.

A step up in quality is *Hotel Europa* (☎ 953 22 27 00), Plaza de Belén 1, just off Avenida de Granada, where decent rooms with air-conditioning, TV and bath cost 5000/7490 ptas. There's also a garage.

Better still is *Hotel Xauen*, Plaza del Deán Mazas 3, (☎ 953 24 07 89), just off Plaza de la Constitución. Rooms here, again with air-con, TV and bath, are 5200/7000 ptas plus IVA.

Hotel Rey Fernando (☎ 953 25 18 40), next to the bus station at Plaza de Coca de la Piñera 7, has doubles for 9100 ptas plus IVA.

If money is not an object and you have a vehicle, stay at the *Parador Castillo de Santa Catalina* (☎ 953 23 00 00), which has an incomparable site atop the Cerro de Santa Catalina. Built in 1965 in imitation of the castillo next door, the parador has spacious, comfortable singles/doubles at 13,200/16,500 ptas plus IVA, a pool and Islamic-style decorative touches.

Places to Eat

Several of the atmospheric old bars on Calle de Arco del Consuelo and Calle Bernardo López, near the cathedral, serve decent raciones and tapas. One, *La Manchega*, also does *platos combinados* for 500 ptas.

Nearby and in a restored mansion, *Casa Vicente* on Calle Francisco Martín Mora is one of the best restaurants in town. Its specialities are pork and venison; a three-course à la carte meal will be around 2500 to 3000 ptas.

Yucatán Café Bar on Calle de Bernabé Soriano isn't a bad place for breakfast. It also serves reasonable platos combinados for up to 795 ptas. On Plaza del Pósito, down the steps, *Bar del Pósito* is a cosy, quite trendy little place with good music, raciones and outside tables.

Restaurant Montemar, Calle Roldán y Marín 7, serves up lots of Jaén specialities, with a three-course *menú del día* with wine for 1500 ptas, or à la carte main dishes from 850 ptas.

Opposite Restaurant Montemar, short Calle Nueva is packed with good places to eat and drink. *El Boquerón de Plata* (The Silver Anchovy) and *La Gamba de Oro* (The Golden Shrimp) both, naturally, specialise in seafood. They're bright, lively places serving excellent raciones which you can eat at the bar or a table (most at El Boquerón de Plata are 750 to 1000 ptas, while at La Gamba de Oro they are a bit dearer). *Mesón Nuyra* on Pasaje Nuyra, a passageway off Calle Nueva, is a bit more formal. Salads are 1100 to 1600 ptas, and fish and meat main dishes are 1500 to 2000 ptas.

Casa de Córdoba on Plaza de Belén, directly opposite the Hotel Europa, is always busy and has a restaurant at the back of the bar. Its speciality is *solomillo a la pimienta* (pepper steak) for 1000 ptas, though there's a *menú* for the same price.

The *Parador de Santa Catalina* has an excellent restaurant where a three-course meal will set you back about 3500 ptas plus drinks. The menu includes many Jaén specialities.

Entertainment
Downtown Jaén is fairly sleepy but there's a clutch of atmospheric old bars along narrow Calle de Arco del Consuelo and Calle Bernardo López, north-west of the cathedral. Among them are *El Gorrión* on Arco del Consuelo and *La Manchega*, with entrances on both streets. Several of the establishments on Calle Nueva (see Places to Eat) are also excellent for a drink and tapas.

One relatively central music bar is *Café-Pub Iroquai* at Calle Las Bernardas 38, which sometimes has live bands. Other similar places are mainly along Paseo de la Estación and in the university zone near the train station: *Pub Inn*, Paseo de la Estación 23; *Talismán*, Avenida de Muñoz Grandes 5; *Pub St Louis*, Calle de San Francisco Javier 5, with Celtic music; *Club de Jazz*

Chubby Cheek, Calle de San Francisco Javier 7; and *Café Latino*, Calle Santa Alicia 3.

Things to Buy
The main shopping streets are Calle Roldán y Marín, Paseo de la Estación and Calle de San Clemente (off Plaza de la Constitución). A big flea market (*mercadillo*) happens on Thursday mornings at the Recinto Ferial on Avenida de Granada.

Getting There & Away
Bus The bus station (☎ 953 25 01 06) is on Plaza de Coca de la Piñera, 250m north of Plaza de la Constitución. Alsina Graells runs 11 or more daily buses to Granada (1½ hours, 900 ptas), seven or more to Baeza (45 minutes, 450 ptas) and Úbeda (1¼ hours, 535 ptas), and two to Cazorla (two hours, 930 ptas) at noon at 4.30 pm. The Ureña line travels up to eight times daily to Córdoba and three times daily to Sevilla. Other buses head for Guadix, Málaga, Almería, Madrid, Valencia, Barcelona and many smaller places in Jaén province.

Train Jaén station (☎ 953 27 02 02) at the northern end of Paseo de la Estación is at the end of a branch line. Most days there are only four departures. One train leaves at 7.45 am for Córdoba (1½ hours, 1105 ptas), Sevilla (three hours, 2125 ptas) and Cádiz. Two go to Madrid.

Car & Motorcycle Jaén is 92km north of Granada by the fast N-323. This road continues to Bailén where it meets the Córdoba-Madrid N-IV. To/from Córdoba, you can choose between the A-316 and N-432 via Martos and Baena, and the A-306 via Porcuna. North-eastward, the A-316 heads to Baeza and Úbeda.

Parking San Francisco near Plaza de San Francisco is always open, charging 100 ptas an hour or 1400 ptas for 24 hours.

Rental Viajes Sacromonte (☎ 953 22 22 12) in Pasaje Maza, an arcade at Paseo de la Estación 12, is an agent for several major car rental companies. Autos del Pino (☎ 953 25 09 01), Calle de la Luna 6, may have cheaper cars.

Getting Around

There's a bus stop around the corner from the train station on Paseo de la Estación: bus No 1 will take you to Plaza de la Constitución, the central point for all city buses, for 150 ptas.

Taxis congregate on Plaza de San Francisco and Plaza de Coca de la Piñera.

THE NORTH-WEST

The N-IV Córdoba-Madrid highway slices across the north-west of Jaén province. If you're travelling this way there are several places worth your time, on and off the highway.

Parque Natural Sierra de Andújar

This 608sq km natural park north of Andújar is claimed to have the biggest expanses of natural vegetation in the Sierra Morena. It has evergreen oaks in sunny areas, gall oaks in shady ones, plus plenty of scrub and bull-breeding ranches. It's home to a few wolves and lynx plus deer, wild boar, mouflon and various birds of prey. Tourist information is available in the ayuntamiento (☎ 953 50 12 50) on the central Plaza de España in Andújar.

Within the park, a 31km drive north of Andújar, is the Santuario de la Virgen de la Cabeza. The 13th century shrine, largely rebuilt after an eight-month siege by Republicans in the civil war, is the scene of one of Spain's biggest religious celebrations, the Romería de la Virgen de la Cabeza. On the last Sunday of April half a million people converge here to witness the Virgin's image – known as La Morenita (The Little Brown One) – being carried around the Cerro del Cabezo for about four hours from about 11 am. It's a festive, emotive occasion, when children and items of clothing are passed over the crowd to priests who touch them to the virgin's mantle. A small hotel and a hostal near the sanctuary could be bases for exploring the park at normal times of year. There's also a range of accommodation in Andújar.

At least four buses a day run from Jaén to Andújar and there are buses from Andújar to the sanctuary on Saturday and Sunday.

Baños de la Encina

One of Andalucía's finest Muslim castles dominates the quiet ridge-top town of Baños de la Encina, a few kilometres north of unexciting Bailén. Built in 967 on the orders of the Cordoban caliph Al-Hakim II, the oval castle has 14 wall towers and a large keep entered through a double horseshoe arch. It fell to the Christians in 1212 just after the battle of Las Navas de Tolosa. Tourist information – and the key to the castle – are available at the 16th century ayuntamiento (☎ 953 61 30 04), on the village's main square, Plaza de la Constitución, open Monday to Friday from 8.30 am to 1.30 pm. Baños de la Encina has several other churches and mansions which make a ramble through its old streets worthwhile – including the Ermita del Cristo del Llanowith spectacular rococo decoration reminiscent of the Alhambra.

Desfiladero de Despeñaperros

About 40km north-east of Bailén, the N-IV threads through a deep, rocky gorge, its two carriageways at times as much as 1km apart, and leaves Andalucía. This is the Desfiladero de Despeñaperros (Defile of the Overthrow of the Dogs), a name owed to the historic defeat of the Muslims at Las Navas de Tolosa a few kilometres south (see the boxed text Las Navas de Tolosa). The gorge and surrounding area form the Parque Natural Sierra de Despeñaperros, with an office (☎ 953 12 50 18) in the village of Santa Elena.

A few buses run daily from Jaén, Baeza and Úbeda to the Desfiladero de Despeñaperros and beyond.

BAEZA

Standing on the northern side of Guadalquivir valley, 48km north-east of Jaén, this relaxed country town (population

Las Navas de Tolosa

After the rout of the Castilian army by the Almohads at Alarcos in 1195, and subsequent papal diplomacy, some Christian states on the Iberian Peninsula united to fight the Muslims. Subsequently, in one of the key events of the Reconquista, they forced open the gates of Andalucía.

In 1212 three Christian armies, led by Alfonso VIII of Castilla, Pere II of Aragón and Sancho VII 'El Fuerte' of Navarra, with the help of a few French crusaders, marched south. Waiting for them on the plain of Las Navas de Tolosa, south of the Desfiladero de Despeñaperros, the key pass through the Sierra Morena between La Mancha and Andalucía, were the Almohad forces of Mohammed II al-Nasir.

The Muslims had blocked a narrow canyon where they could ambush the Christians. But a mysterious shepherd called Martín Alhaga appeared and guided the northern armies through an alternative defile unknown to the Almohads.

On 16 July the opposing armies met on Las Navas de Tolosa and the Christians scored an overwhelming victory. Mohammed abandoned his standard on the battlefield and later Alfonso VIII reported to the Pope that the Christian armies camped on the battlefield had needed no other fuel for their fires than their enemies' discarded spears and arrows.

Many arrowheads and hatchets have been found at what is thought to have been the site of battle, Mesa del Rey, 4 or 5km south of Santa Elena.

16,000) is packed with gorgeous Gothic and Renaissance buildings.

The seat of a bishopric under the Visigoths, Baeza developed into a trade centre renowned for its bazaars during the Muslim period. In 1227 it became the first sizeable Andalucian town to fall to the Christians when it was conquered by Fernando III. Its heyday was during the 16th century when its textile and grain industries were booming. The Baeza nobility, having finally ended centuries of feuding, ploughed much of the profit into grand buildings.

Orientation & Information

The heart of town is composed of Plaza de España and the long, wide Paseo de la Constitución stretching to its south-west.

The tourist office (☎ 953 74 04 44) is in a beautiful 16th century building on Plaza del Pópulo, just south-west of Paseo de la Constitución. It's open Monday to Friday from 8.30 am to 2.30 pm and Saturday from 10 am to 12.30 pm.

The bus station is about 700m east of Plaza de España on Paseo Arco del Agua

(now officially called Avenida Alcalde Puche Pardo).

You'll find banks and ATMs on Paseo de la Constitución and Calle San Pablo.

Things to See

You could walk round the sequence of sights described here in a leisurely day. The opening hours of some buildings are unpredictable.

Plaza de España & Paseo de la Constitución On Plaza de España stands the Torre de los Aliatares, one of the few remaining bits of Muslim Bayyasa, whose walled *alcázar* it helped to fortify. Somehow this tower survived Isabel la Católica's 1476 order to demolish Baeza's fortifications in order to end the feuds between the town's Benavide and Carvajal noble families.

Paseo de la Constitución, once Baeza's market place and bullring, is lined with attractive arcades.

Plaza del Pópulo This beautiful square, a few steps west of Paseo de la Constitución,

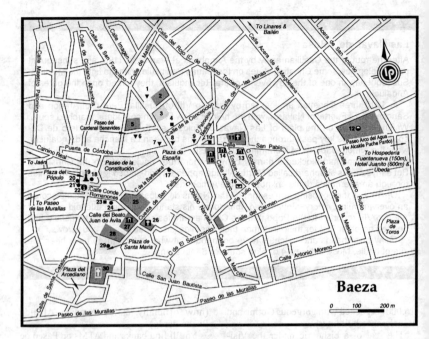

Baeza

0   100   200 m

PLACES TO STAY
- 4 Hotel Baeza & Restaurante La Cazuela
- 10 Hostal Comercio
- 23 Hostal El Patio

PLACES TO EAT
- 1 Restaurante Vandelvira
- 6 Restaurante Sali
- 7 Cafetería Mercantil
- 8 La Góndola
- 9 Cafetería Churrería Benjamín

OTHER
- 2 Convento de San Francisco
- 3 Market
- 5 Ayuntamiento
- 11 Iglesia de San Pablo
- 12 Bus Station
- 13 Casa Cabrera
- 14 Palacio Cerón
- 15 Palacio de los Salcedo
- 16 Post Office
- 17 Torre de los Aliatares
- 18 Antigua Carnicería
- 19 Fuente de los Leones
- 20 Puerta de Jaén
- 21 Arco de Villalar
- 22 Casa del Pópulo; Tourist Office
- 24 Peña Flamenca
- 25 Antigua Universidad
- 26 Iglesia de la Santa Cruz
- 27 Palacio de Jabalquinto
- 28 Universidad Internacional de Andalucía
- 29 Fuente de Santa María
- 30 Catedral

is also named Plaza de los Leones after the **Fuente de los Leones** (Fountain of the Lions) in its centre. Constructed with carvings from the Iberian and Roman village of Cástulo, 15km west of Baeza, the fountain is topped by a statue that is traditionally believed to represent Imilce, an Iberian princess from Cástulo who was the wife of the Carthaginian leader Hannibal. The statue, whoever it represents, bears a suitably enigmatic smile.

On the southern side of the plaza is the lovely plateresque Casa del Pópulo, built in about 1540. Formerly the Audiencia Civil (Civil Court), it now houses Baeza's tourist office. It adjoins the 1526 Arco de Villalar

(Villalar Arch), next to which is the originally Muslim Puerta de Jaén (Jaén Gate).

On the eastern side of the plaza stands the Antigua Carnicería (Old Slaughterhouse), a fine 1548 edifice with a Renaissance gallery and the large two-headed Habsburg eagle shield of Carlos I.

If you have time to spare you could go through the Puerta de Jaén and along the street to the Paseo de las Murallas, a path-cum-road, with good views over the surrounding country, which loops southeast round the old city walls to a point near the cathedral.

Antigua Universidad Baeza's Old University stands a short walk south-east of Plaza del Pópulo on Calle del Beato Juan de Ávila. Founded in 1538, the university was a fount of often progressive ideas which ran counter to the conservative tendencies of Baeza's dominant families. It was closed in 1824 and since 1875 the building has housed a high school. You can usually enter Monday to Friday from 9 am to 2 pm. The main patio has two floors of elegant Renaissance arches and a plaque outside one classroom telling us that the poet Antonio Machado taught French there from 1912 to 1919.

Palacio de Jabalquinto Round the corner on Cuesta de San Felipe is the finest of Baeza's noble mansions. Probably built in the early 16th century for one of the Benavides clan, it has a spectacular façade in the flamboyant Isabelline Gothic style, topped by a Renaissance gallery. The patio was recently under restoration but is normally open Monday to Friday from 11 am to 1 pm and 5 to 7 pm (free). It, too, is Renaissance-style, with marble columns, two tiers of elegant arches, a fountain and orange trees. A majestic baroque stairway ascends from one side.

Iglesia de la Santa Cruz Across the square from the Palacio de Jabalquinto, the mid-13th century Church of the Holy Cross, with round-arched portals and semicircular apse at the far end, is a rare Andalucian example of Romanesque architecture. It's

supposedly open Monday to Saturday from 11 am to 1 pm and Sunday and holidays from noon to 2 pm, though these times are not very reliable. There are some 15th century paintings inside.

Plaza de Santa María This pleasant plaza south-west of the Palacio de Jabalquinto is dominated by the cathedral. Also worth a pause are the **Fuente de Santa María** and the **Universidad Internacional de Andalucía** on the plaza's northern side. The pretty *fuente* (fountain), built in 1569 by baezano Ginés Martínez, is in the form of a miniature Roman triumphal arch. The university, which mainly conducts short courses for postgraduates, is housed in the sober 17th century former Seminario (Seminary) de San Felipe Neri.

Catedral Baeza's cathedral is a bit of an aesthetic hotch-potch, but with interesting parts. The predominant style is 16th century Renaissance, shown in the main façade on Plaza de Santa María and the basic design of the three-nave interior (by Andrés de Vandelvira and Jerónimo del Prado). The oldest feature is the 13th century Gothic-*mudéjar* Puerta de la Luna (Moon Doorway) at the west end, above which is a nice 14th century Gothic rose window. The Puerta del Perdón (Pardon Doorway) on the southern side is 15th century Gothic.

The cathedral is open daily from 10.30 am to 1 pm and 5 to 7 pm (free, but donations are welcome). There's a lavish baroque *retablo* on the main altar and a 13th century Romanesque-Gothic Crucifixion sculpture – rare in Andalucía – high on the retablo of the adjacent Capilla del Sagrario. At the west end, the **reja** on the Antiguo Coro (Old Choir) is one of the finest works of Jaén's 16th century wrought iron supremo, Maestro Bartolomé. The centre of the reja, from the bottom up, depicts with pleasing simplicity St Andrew, the coronation of the Virgin (holding the infant Jesus) and the Crucifixion. To the right of the reja you can pop 100 ptas into a slot by an unremarkable painting: the painting slides noisily aside, a recording of holy music plays and the 18th century Custodia del Corpus, a large silver monstrance used in Baeza's Corpus Christi processions, is revealed in all its glory.

The cathedral's **cloister** has four mudéjar chapels with Arabic inscriptions. At the time of writing it was closed for repairs, as was the tower.

Ayuntamiento A block north of Paseo de la Constitución at Paseo del Cardenal Benavides 9, the ayuntamiento (town hall) has a marvellous plateresque façade with four finely carved balcony portals on the upper storey separated by the coats of arms of Felipe II (in the middle), the magistrate Juan de Borja, who had the place built, and the town. It was originally a courthouse and prison (entered by the right and left-hand doors respectively).

Convento de San Francisco The San Francisco convent on Calle de San Francisco, a short walk from the Ayuntamiento, was apparently one of Andrés de Vandelvira's masterpieces, conceived as the funerary chapel of the Benavides family. But it stood in ruins for a long time after it was devastated by an earthquake and sacked by French troops in the early 19th century. It's now partly restored and, at the east end, girders trace the outline of its dome over a space adorned with Renaissance carvings. The cloister, occupied by the Restaurante Vandelvira, is also worth a look.

Calle San Pablo This street leading east from Plaza de España is lined by several handsome 16th century mansions including No 18, the Palacio de los Salcedo; No 24, the Palacio Cerón (also called the Nuevo Casino), with a nice arched two-tier patio; and No 30, the Casa Cabrera, with a good plateresque front. Across the street from the Casa Cabrera is the 15th century Gothic Iglesia de San Pablo.

Special Events
There are Semana Santa and Corpus Christi

processions and Baeza stages an annual feria from 10 to 15 August. Most renowned is the Romería de La Yedra. On the morning of 7 September the image of the Virgen del Rosell is carried from the Iglesia de San Pablo through the streets of Baeza accompanied by a singing and dancing crowd. In the afternoon, a colourful procession of riders and decorated carts follows the image to the village of La Yedra, 4km north, to continue celebrations there.

Places to Stay
Some prices go up a few hundred pesetas from about June to September.

The friendly *Hostal El Patio* (☎ 953 74 02 00), Calle Conde Romanones 13, occupies a 17th century mansion with a fountained and pillared (but covered) patio which boasts one of the most extensive lounge suites you've ever seen. Good, modernised singles/doubles are 1500/2500 ptas, or 2000/3000 ptas with shower, and there are doubles with bath for 3500 ptas.

Another friendly place, *Hostal Comercio* (☎ 953 74 01 00), Calle San Pablo 21, has decent singles/doubles with shower and toilet for 1700/2900 ptas (singles with shared toilet for 1500 ptas, doubles with bath for 3300 ptas). There's heating in winter and plenty of hot water. Antonio Machado stayed in room 215 in 1912.

The most upmarket place in town is the *Hotel Baeza* (☎ 953 74 81 30), Calle de la Concepción 3, in the old Hospital de la Purísima Concepción – very much modernised but still with a large, arcaded central patio. Cosy, air-conditioned singles/doubles cost 6300/9600 ptas plus IVA, including breakfast.

Hospedería Fuentenueva (☎ 953 74 31 00), about 300m beyond the bus station at Paseo Arco del Agua s/n, used to be a women's prison but now it's a beautifully restored and relaxed small hotel. The 12 rooms, which are comfortable, bright and mostly large, have marble bathrooms and cost 5700/8000 ptas plus IVA, including breakfast.

Hotel Juanito (☎ 953 74 00 40), 450m

farther along Paseo Arco del Agua, next to a petrol station, offers rooms with bath, air-conditioning, heating and TV for 4600/5400 ptas plus IVA. Its restaurant is the most famous in the province (see Places to Eat).

Places to Eat

Cafetería Churrería Benjamín, Calle Patrocinio Biedma 1 on the corner of Calle San Pablo, is a fine place for a breakfast of good crisp churros y chocolate.

Cafetería Mercantil on Plaza de España is busy from morning to night with amiable baezano men and serves a long list of tapas and generous raciones for 900 to 1200 ptas (100 ptas less if you eat at the bar). This is your chance to sample bull or lamb testicles (*criadillas*) or brains (*sesos*), but there are plenty more straightforward things too!

La Góndola, nearby on Plaza de España, will serve you pizza and pasta for 550 to 900 ptas, or half an oven-roasted chicken for 650 ptas.

Nearby, in the Hotel Baeza, the popular *Restaurante La Cazuela* is a step up in quality but moderately priced. Raciones and platos combinados go for 700 to 1100 ptas, or there's a three-course *menú* for 1400 ptas (all plus IVA).

Restaurante Sali at Paseo del Cardenal Benavides 9 does a three-course menú del día with lots of choice for 1600 ptas. À la carte main dishes range from chicken or *lomo* at 800 or 900 ptas to solomillo pimienta for 2300 ptas.

Restaurante Vandelvira, in part of the re-modelled Convento de San Francisco, Calle de San Francisco 14, has even classier airs. The *menú* is 2100 ptas and most à la carte mains are 1500 to 2000 ptas. If you want to splurge you might go for the partridge salad (1550 ptas) followed by solomillo al carbón (2200 ptas).

The restaurant of the *Hospedería Fuentenueva* on Paseo Arco del Agua is good. A three-course lunch costs 2100 ptas including drinks and its bar-café has some tasty snacks such as suelas (sizeable toasted sandwiches) for 525 ptas.

People come from far and wide to *Restaurante Juanito* (☎ 953 74 00 40) in the Hotel Juanito on Paseo Arco del Agua, where Juan Antonio Salcedo and his wife Luisa have been dishing up traditional Jaén fare for four decades. A three-course meal is likely to set you back 4000 ptas or more, plus drinks. Specialities include *alcachofas Luisa* (Luisa's artichokes) or partridge salad as starters, and choto frito, lomo de orza, or partridge/quail/pheasant in escabeche to follow. Juanito is closed Sunday and Monday evenings.

Getting There & Away

From the bus station (☎ 953 74 04 68), Alsina Graells runs up to 12 daily buses to Jaén (45 minutes, 450 ptas), up to 16 to Úbeda, buses to Cazorla daily at 1 and 5.30 pm, and at least five daily to Granada. Other buses go to Madrid, Córdoba, Sevilla and Málaga.

The nearest train station is Linares-Baeza (☎ 953 65 02 02), 13km north-west, from where a few trains a day leave for Granada, Córdoba, Sevilla, Málaga, Cádiz, Almería, Madrid and Barcelona. There are connecting buses for most trains from Monday to Saturday.

ÚBEDA

Just 9km east through the olive groves from Baeza, with which it has a neighbourly rivalry, Úbeda is a bigger place (population 32,000) with an even larger stock of marvellous buildings from bygone centuries. Úbeda's Plaza Vázquez de Molina is the finest ensemble of Renaissance buildings in Andalucía.

History

Úbeda was taken from the Muslims by Fernando III in 1234. In the 14th century a group of local knights earned the title Lions of Úbeda for their heroics during the conquest of Algeciras, which is why lions are a common motif on the town's buildings. But just as in Baeza, the town's leading post-Reconquista families, among them the Molinas, the de la Cuevas and the Cobos, spent a deal of energy quarrelling with each

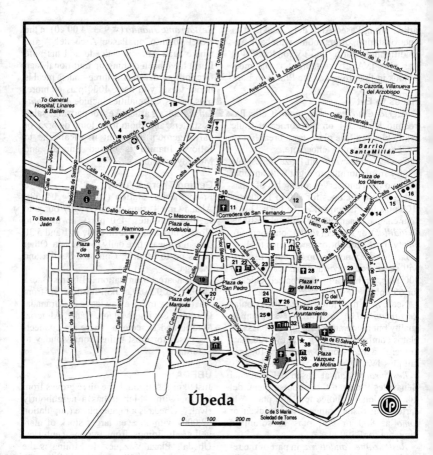

Úbeda

0   100   200 m

other and getting tangled up with the factions competing for the Castilian throne.

In 1506 most of Úbeda's fortifications were knocked down, on Isabel la Católica's orders, to put an end to these quarrels. The Cobos and Molinas had now patched things up enough to intermarry and one of their line, Francisco de los Cobos y Molina, rose to be first secretary to emperor Carlos I; his nephew Juan Vázquez de Molina succeeded him in the job and kept it under Felipe II.

High office exposed these men to international culture just as the Renaissance was

reaching Spain from Italy. Much of the wealth that they and a flourishing local agriculture brought to 16th century Úbeda was spent on the profusion of lavish Renaissance mansions and churches that remain its chief glory.

Orientation & Information

The old town in the south-east is a warren of narrow, winding streets and expansive plazas which contains most of the architecture which is the reason for visiting Úbeda. The drab new town in the west and north

PLACES TO STAY		7	Bus Station	28	Iglesia de San Pablo
1	Hotel La Paz	8	Hospital de Santiago &	29	Museo de San Juan de la
4	Hostal Castillo		Tourist Office		Cruz
5	Hostal Sevilla	10	Post Office	30	Capilla de El Salvador
9	Hostal Victoria	11	Iglesia de la Santísima	32	Museo de Alfarería
19	Palacio de la Rambla		Trinidad		Artesana
31	Parador Condestable	12	Market	33	Palacio de Vázquez de
	Dávalos & Palacio del	14	Alfarería Góngora		Molina & Ayuntamiento
	Deán Ortega	15	Alfarería Paco Tito	34	Casa de las Torres
		16	Potters' Workshops	35	Santa María de los
PLACES TO EAT		17	Museo de Úbeda		Reales Alcázares
2	Restaurante El Gallo Rojo	18	Pub Siglo XV	36	Cárcel del Obispo
3	Churrería Cafetería	21	Iglesia de San Pedro	37	Statue of Andrés de
13	Mesón Gabino	22	Palacio de los Condes de		Vandelvira
20	Restaurante El Marqués		Guadiana?	38	Antiguo Pósito & Policía
26	Restaurante Mesón	23	Artesanía Blanco		Nacional
	Navarro	24	Palacio de Vela de los	39	Palacio del Marqués de
			Cobos		Mancera
OTHER		25	Alfarería Tito	40	Mirador
6	Centro de Salud	27	Antiguo Ayuntamiento		

contains the cheaper accommodation and bus station. Plaza de Andalucía marks the boundary between the two parts of town.

The tourist office (☎ 953 75 08 97) is in the Hospital de Santiago on Calle Obispo Cobos, 400m west of Plaza de Andalucía. It's inconvenient for the old town but fairly close to the bus station and most budget accommodation. It's open Monday to Saturday from 8 am to 3 pm.

The post office (postcode 23400) at Calle Trinidad 4 is open Monday to Friday from 8.30 am to 2.30 pm and Saturday from 9.30 am to 1 pm. You'll find the biggest concentration of banks and ATMs on Plaza de Andalucía and nearby Calle Rastro.

There's a Centro de Salud (Health Centre ☎ 953 75 11 03), with an emergency section, in the new part of town on Calle Explanada; and a general hospital (☎ 953 79 71 00) on the north-western edge of town at Carretera de Linares Km 1. The Policía Nacional (☎ 091) occupy the Antiguo Pósito on Plaza Vázquez de Molina.

Plaza Vázquez de Molina
Almost entirely surrounded by beautiful stone buildings from the 15th and 16th centuries, this 180m-long plaza is Úbeda's

crown jewel. After dark, floodlighting makes it even more picturesque than by day. A mirador, 150m east of the plaza along Baja de El Salvador, affords fine views with the Cazorla mountains in the distance to the east.

Capilla de El Salvador Facing along the plaza from its eastern end, this church was Andrés de Vandelvira's first commission in Úbeda. Founded by Francisco de los Cobos y Molina as a funerary chapel for his family, it today belongs to the Sevilla-based Duques de Medinaceli, descendants of the Cobos and one of Andalucía's major landowning families. Vandelvira built the chapel in the 1540s to basic designs by Diego de Siloé. But he added plenty of his own touches, including the portals and the sacristy.

The main façade on Plaza Vázquez de Molina is a pre-eminent example of plateresque, modelled on Siloé's Puerta del Perdón at Granada's cathedral. The portal is topped by a carving of the transfiguration of Christ, flanked by statues of St Peter and St Paul. On the underside of the arch immediately above the door, the French sculptor Esteban Jamete placed representations of Greek gods – a Renaissance touch which

JAÉN PROVINCE

Andrés de Vandelvira

Born in 1509 at Alcaraz, 150km north-east of Úbeda, Andrés de Vandelvira almost single-handedly brought the Renaissance to then-wealthy towns of the Jaén region. Influenced by the pioneering Spanish Renaissance architect Diego de Siloé, Vandelvira designed a string of marvellous stone buildings in Úbeda, Baeza, Jaén and elsewhere, which form one of the outstanding groupings of Renaissance architecture in Spain.

His work spanned all three main phases of Spanish Renaissance architecture and three of Úbeda's finest buildings illustrate this neatly. In buildings of the ornamental early phase known as plateresque, such as the Capilla de El Salvador, a predilection for sculpted coats of arms lingered from the Isabelline Gothic era. A much purer line and more classical proportions emerge in the later Palacio de Vázquez de Molina. In his last building, the Hospital de Santiago (completed the year he died, 1575), Vandelvira displays almost as much sobriety as did Juan de Herrera in El Escorial, the paradigm of the austere Spanish late Renaissance.

would have been inconceivable a few decades earlier. A Gothic penchant for heraldry lingers, however, in the sculptures flanking the portal. To the left, soldiers bear the five-lion coat of arms of Francisco de los Cobos y Molina; to the right, two women hold the shield of his wife María Manrique.

The church's side portals, though smaller, also bear intricate carving including, on the northern Portada del Evangelio, Santiago Matamoros incarnated as Carlos I, beneath a medallion of Christ.

To enter the church, knock on the sacristy door along the street past the Portada del Evangelio (the door has a five-lion shield above it), and you'll be shown around by the caretaker (who, at the end of the tour, will appreciate a donation towards upkeep). You first enter the sacristy, designed by Vandelvira and with much classical sculpture by Esteban Jamete. There's also a portrait of Francisco de los Cobos y Molina.

The richly decorated chancel of the main church is modelled on Siloé's Capilla Mayor in Granada's cathedral, with a frescoed dome. The main *retablo*, by Alonso Berruguete, was badly damaged in the civil war and only one statue, the *Transfiguración del Monte Tabor*, is original.

A fine 1557 reja – some say it's by Jaén's

Maestro Bartolomé – divides the chancel from the nave, beneath which is the Cobos family crypt, which contains the tomb of Francisco de los Cobos y Molina.

Palacio del Deán Ortega Next to the Capilla de El Salvador stands what was the abode of its chaplains. Their quarters amounted to one of Vandelvira's finest palaces and were at least as big as their church. Partly remodelled in the 17th century, the mansion became Úbeda's parador in 1930 and its typically Vandelvira two-tier courtyard is about the most elegant spot for a drink (beer is 250 ptas) or snack in town.

Palacio de Vázquez de Molina This Vandelvira mansion, now Úbeda's ayuntamiento, dominates the west end of Plaza Vázquez de Molina. The harmonious proportions of its façade make it perhaps the most magnificent building in Úbeda. Vandelvira built it in about 1562 for Juan Vázquez de Molina, whose coat of arms surmounts the doorway.

The uncluttered and deeply Italian-influenced façade is divided into three discrete tiers by slender cornices. Esteban Jamete's caryatids separating the oval windows of the top level continue the lines of the pilasters flanking the rectangular windows of the middle tier.

You can enter any day from 10.30 am to 2 pm and 4.30 to 9 pm to admire the fine patio, with two storeys of rounded arches on slender pillars.

In one side of the building the Museo de Alfarería Artesana is devoted to Úbeda pottery, a craft which dates back to Muslim times. It's open daily except Monday from 10.30 am to 2 pm and 5 to 9 pm (free).

Santa María de los Reales Alcázares Facing the Palacio de Vázquez de Molina, this large church is one of Úbeda's finest but has recently been closed for restoration. Built over Muslim Úbeda's main mosque, it has a Renaissance façade but is mainly 15th century Gothic. Inside are rejas by Maestro Bartolomé and a lovely Gothic cloister occupying what was the mosque's ritual ablutions courtyard.

Other Buildings Next door to Santa María stands the Cárcel del Obispo (Bishop's Prison), where nuns who stepped out of line used to be incarcerated. It is now a courthouse *(juzgados)*. Under the trees in front is a statue of Andrés de Vandelvira, the man who made Úbeda worth visiting. By the statue, fronting the main plaza, the 16th century Antiguo Pósito, originally a communal store for grain surpluses, is now a police station. Calle de Santa María Soledad de Torres Acosta leads south from here into the area that was the Muslim alcázar.

North of Plaza Vázquez de Molina

Plaza del Ayuntamiento You can leave the Palacio de Vázquez de Molina by its north side on to this broad plaza where the **Palacio de Vela de los Cobos**, with handsome middle-floor windows and top-floor gallery, was built by Vandelvira for another of the Cobos clan, Francisco Vela de los Cobos.

Calle Real, once Úbeda's main commercial street, leads north from here. Three blocks up stands the 17th century Palacio de los Condes de Guadiana, one of the town's best mansions, with a tower and some fine carving round the windows and balconies.

Plaza 1° de Marzo A couple of blocks north-east of Plaza del Ayuntamiento, this used to be the market square, bullring and site of Inquisition burnings. The kiosk in the south-eastern corner stands where heretics met their fate. Local worthies could watch the merry events from the gallery of the elegantly proportioned Antiguo Ayuntamiento (Old Town Hall) in the south-west corner, built in the 16th century. Along the top (north) side of the square is the Iglesia de San Pablo, with a fine late Gothic portal (1511). Its western front dates from the 13th century and the tower at the east end is plateresque (1537). You can enter the church daily between 7 and 9 pm: look for the 1530s Capilla de Camarero Vago, by Vandelvira, and some good rejas.

Just north of Plaza 1° de Marzo at Calle Cervantes 4, a 14th century mudéjar house with an attractive patio houses the Museo de Úbeda, with archaeological exhibits from neolithic to Muslim times. It's open daily except Monday from 10 am to 2 pm and 5 to 9 pm (free).

Museo de San Juan de la Cruz This museum, in the 17th century Oratorio de San Juan de la Cruz on Calle del Carmen, a block east of Plaza 1° de Marzo, is devoted to the 16th century mystic, poet and religious reformer St John of the Cross (San Juan de la Cruz). It's open daily except Monday from 11 am to 1 pm and 5 to 7 pm. Visits (free) are guided by Spanish-speaking monks and last about half an hour.

St John of the Cross, born in Castilla y León in 1542, founded the breakaway monastic order of Carmelitos Descalzos (Barefoot Carmelites – they wore sandals instead of shoes) in an effort to return to the austerity and contemplative life from which he felt mainstream Carmelites had lapsed. St John's campaign provoked hefty opposition from the mainstream Carmelites, and he was imprisoned several times. After a stint as rector of a monastery in Baeza, St John came to Úbeda in September 1591, suffering from gangrene in his leg, and died here three months later.

St John wrote of the 'dark night of the soul', leading to the bright dawn of experience of God, and taught that mysticism was basically understanding and accepting the way things are.

On the museum's ground floor you'll visit the chapel where St John was originally buried; an effigy now lies on the spot. Upstairs, you see the room in which he died – with some of his bones in a glass case. Other rooms hold prints recording the key events of his life, early editions of some of his writings, and art connected with his life and teachings. There's also a reconstructed monk's cell with a rather lifelike figure of St John sitting at a writing table he used. In a cabinet there are letters written by him and a couple of fingers from his right hand!

Hospital de Santiago

Vandelvira's final work is the farthest from the heart of old Úbeda but one of his masterpieces. Commissioned by Diego de los Cobos, bishop of Jaén, the Hospital de Santiago was begun in 1562 and completed in 1575. This sober, grand-scale, late Renaissance building has been described as the Escorial of Andalucía.

The lack of decoration focuses attention on the building's fine proportions, from the long façade crowned by a tower at each end to the classic Vandelvira two-level patio with marble columns. Off the patio are a chapel, badly damaged in the civil war but now restored as an auditorium, and a staircase with colourful original frescos.

Open daily from 8 am to 3 pm and 3.30 to 10 pm, the hospital now houses Úbeda's tourist office, the municipal dance school and, upstairs, a Museo de Semana Santa with material on Úbeda's Holy Week festivities.

Special Events

Úbeda's major festivities are the Fiestas de San Miguel from 27 September to 4 October, with firework displays, parades, concerts, a bullfight season and more. Semana Santa processions are colourful.

Places to Stay

Hostal Victoria (☎ 953 75 29 52), just 200m west of Plaza de Andalucía at Calle Alaminos 5, has good singles/doubles, with bath, TV, air-conditioning and heating, for 2400/4300 ptas. Farther from the centre and under the same ownership, *Hostal Castillo* (☎ 953 75 04 30), Avenida Ramón y Cajal 20, has similar rooms without TV for the same price, plus rooms with a washbasin for 2000/3300 ptas.

Hostal Sevilla (☎ 953 75 06 12), Avenida Ramón y Cajal 9, has clean, fairly modern rooms with bath and heating for 2000/3800 ptas (a little less without TV).

Hotel La Paz (☎ 953 75 21 40), Calle Andalucía 1 just off Avenida Ramón y Cajal, looks bland but the rooms are a surprise – all individually decorated and some large and stylish. Doubles with bathroom, TV and air-conditioning are 6800 ptas. The few singles (2000 to 2500 ptas) are small.

In the old town, the 30-room *Parador Condestable Dávalos* (☎ 953 75 03 45) on Plaza Vázquez de Molina is the comfortably modernised Palacio del Deán Ortega. The privilege of staying here costs 14,400/18,000 ptas plus IVA for singles/doubles in high season.

The *Palacio de la Rambla* (☎ 953 75 01 96) at Plaza del Marqués 1 is another refined hotel in a 16th century palace with large singles/doubles for 10,000/14,000 ptas plus IVA, breakfast included. Still the home of the Marquesa de la Rambla, the eight-room hotel centres on a lovely Vandelvira patio and has a pleasant garden.

Places to Eat

The restaurant at the *Hostal Castillo*, Avenida Ramón y Cajal 20, does a good three-course *menú*, with salad and a drink, for 1000 ptas. The *Churrería Cafetería* just up the street is a bustling breakfast spot.

Restaurante El Gallo Rojo at Calle Manuel Barraca 3, just off the top end of

Avenida Ramón y Cajal, is one of the best places in the new part of town. It does a three-course *menú* with lots of choice and a drink for 1100 ptas. À la carte meat and fish main dishes range from 800 to 1800 ptas, though there are tortillas for less.

In the old town, *Restaurante El Marqués* on Plaza del Marqués, 150m downhill from Plaza de Andalucía, does reasonable-value platos combinados for 700 to 1000 ptas (but 20% more if you eat them at a table). There's also a four-course *menú*, with drink, for 2140 ptas. *Restaurante Mesón Navarro*, Plaza del Ayuntamiento 2 (the sign just says 'Restaurante Mesón'), has a bar at the front, good for a range of raciones, media-raciones and *bocadillos*, and a restaurant serving typical local fare in the back. At the bar many raciones are 1000 ptas or more (plus 20% if eaten at a table) but you can get a tortilla española for 600 ptas.

Mesón Gabino on Calle Fuente Seca is a cellar-type restaurant with old stone pillars and decent food, including tortillas at 400 to 800 ptas and meat and fish main dishes for 800 to 2000 ptas.

The best place is the restaurant in the *Parador Condestable Dávalos* on Plaza Vázquez de Molina. Lunch or dinner costs around 3500 ptas but that's a fair price for some of the excellent local dishes, such as carruécano, green peppers stuffed with partridge, local turkey and some scrumptious desserts.

Entertainment
Pub Siglo XV bar on Calle Prior Blanca is an atmospheric place with old stone pillars and sometimes live flamenco or other music.

Things to Buy
The typical green glaze on Úbeda's varied and attractive pottery, and the tradition of embroidering coloured patterns into esparto-grass mats *(ubedíes)*, both date from Muslim times.

Several workshops in the San Millán barrio, the potters' quarter north-east of the old town, sell pottery and the potters are

often willing to explain some of the ancient techniques they use. Alfarería Paco Tito at Calle Valencia 22 is one of the best known but several others on the same street, and Alfarería Góngora, nearby at Cuesta de la Merced 32, are worth a look. Alfarería Tito also has a large shop at Plaza del Ayuntamiento 12.

For esparto mats and baskets, visit Artesanía Blanco at Calle Real 47 in the old town.

The main shopping streets are Calle Mesones and Calle Obispo Cobos, between Plaza de Andalucía and the Hospital de Santiago.

Getting There & Away
Bus The bus station (☎ 953 75 21 57) is at Calle San José 6, near most budget lodgings but 1km west of the heart of the old town. Alsina Graells runs to Baeza up to 16 times daily, to Jaén (1¼ hours, 535 ptas) up to 12 times, to Cazorla three or four times and to Granada up to seven times. Bacoma goes to Córdoba and Sevilla three times daily. Other buses head to Málaga, Madrid, Valencia, Barcelona and small places around Jaén province.

Train The nearest station is Linares-Baeza (☎ 953 65 02 02), 21km north-west, which you can reach by Linares-bound buses. See the Baeza section for information on trains.

CAZORLA
Cazorla (population 9000), 45km south-east of Úbeda, is the main gateway to the Parque Natural de Cazorla, which begins in the hills above the town. It's also an attractive old place in its own right, with an imposing castle, narrow streets climbing the steep hillside beneath the dramatic Peña de los Halcones (Falcon Crag), and a range of good places to stay, eat and drink. It can get very crowded during Spanish holiday times and on fine weekends from spring to autumn.

Orientation & Information
The A-319/C-328 from the west winds up

into Cazorla as Calle Hilario Marco, which ends at Plaza de la Constitución, the main square of the northern, newer part of town. The second important plaza is Plaza de la Corredera, 150m south of Plaza de la Constitución along Calle Doctor Muñoz, which probably qualifies as Cazorla's main street. Plaza de Santa María, 300m farther south-east through narrow streets, and lower down, is the heart of the oldest part of town.

The Oficina de Turismo Municipal (☎ 953 71 01 12) at Paseo del Santo Cristo 17, 200m north of Plaza de la Constitución, has some information on the parque natural as well as Cazorla town. Quercus (☎ 953 72 01 15) at Calle Juan Domingo 2 (just off Plaza de la Constitución) provides some tourist information as well as selling maps and Spanish-language guidebooks. It also offers excursions into the park (see the Parque Natural de Cazorla section).

The post office (postcode 23470) is at Calle Mariano Extremera 2 behind the ayuntamiento, just off Plaza de la Corredera. There are several banks with ATMs on Plaza de la Constitución, Calle Doctor Muñoz and Plaza de la Corredera.

The Policía Local (☎ 953 72 01 81) are in the Ayuntamiento just off Plaza de la Corredera. The health centre, Centro de Salud Dr José Saldedocano (☎ 953 72 10 61), is at Calle Ximénez de Rada 1.

Things to See

Plaza de la Corredera The 17th century Iglesia de San José at the northern end of the plaza contains six copies of El Greco paintings by Rafael del Real. In the plaza's top corner, with its landmark clock tower, stands the ayuntamiento, a former monastery. A theatre occupies the monastery's old church. About 200m up Calle del Carmen from here, the Iglesia del Carmen is Cazorla's best-looking church – a mainly 17th and 18th century construction, though it has a plateresque tower.

Plaza de Santa María Calle Gómez Calderón heads south from the ayunta-

miento to the Balcón de Zabaleta, a lookout with fine views over the town and the Castillo de la Yedra. Down to the left is the lovely Plaza de Santa María (or Plaza Vieja). The large, ruined Iglesia de Santa María at the plaza's far end was built by Andrés de Vandelvira in the 16th century. Constructed over a river which also runs under the plaza, the church was wrecked by Napoleonic troops in reprisal for Cazorla's tenacious resistance to them and is now used as an open-air concert venue. Also on the plaza is a 400-year-old fountain, the Fuente de las Cadenas.

Castillo de la Yedra A short walk up from Plaza de Santa María, the impressive Castle of the Ivy (also called the Castillo de las Cuatro Esquinas) is of Roman origin, though it was largely built by the Muslims, then restored in the 15th century. It houses the Museo del Alto Guadalquivir (Museum of the Upper Guadalquivir) which contains some interesting art and relics of local life – including a chapel which has a lifesize Romanesque-Byzantine Crucifixion sculpture, models of old oil mills and a reconstructed traditional Cazorla kitchen.

From 15 June to 15 September it's open Tuesday to Saturday from 9 am to 3 pm and Sunday from 10 am to 12.30 pm (other times of year, Tuesday to Saturday from 10 am to 1 pm and 4 to 7 pm and Sunday 10 am to 12.30 pm). It closes on holidays. Entry is free with an EU passport or national identity card.

Special Events

Cazorla's main fiesta, from 17 to 21 September, features bullfights, music and, on the 17th, a procession around town bearing a 17th century painting of the Cristo del Consuelo which was rescued from the destruction of the Iglesia de Santa María. On 14 May, in a *romería* called La Caracolá, the image of San Isicio (a Christian apostle supposedly stoned to death at Cazorla in Roman times), is carried from the Ermita de San Isicio to the Iglesia de San José, and the streets are lit with oil lamps.

Places to Stay

Tiny *Camping Cortijo San Isicio* (☎ 953 72 12 80), off the Úbeda road about 2km from Cazorla, has room for just 54 people, charging 1400 ptas plus IVA for two adults with a tent and car. You should find it open from March to early November.

The *Albergue Juvenil Cazorla* (☎ 953 72 03 29) at Plaza Mauricio Martínez 6, 200m uphill from Plaza de la Corredera, is a spick-and-span youth hostel, with a pool, in a former 16th century convent. It has places for 97 people in rooms holding between two and six. The top-floor doubles, with old wood-beamed ceilings, are as attractive as any budget room in town.

The clean, friendly *Hostal Betis* (☎ 953 72 05 40), Plaza de la Corredera 19, has singles for 1200 to 1500 ptas and doubles for 2500 or 2700 ptas. Some rooms overlook the plaza. *Pensión Taxi* (☎ 953 72 05 25), just off Plaza de la Constitución at Travesía de San Anton 7, is another friendly place; singles/doubles with shared bathrooms are 1500/3000 ptas. *La Cueva de Juan Pedro* (☎ 953 72 12 25) on Plaza de Santa María has a few rooms with bath for 1500/3000 ptas. One of the doubles has a kitchen.

Hostal Guadalquivir (☎ 953 72 02 68), Calle Nueva 6 just off Calle Doctor Muñoz, is a step up in quality – a friendly, family-run place where prettily decorated doubles with bath cost 3800 to 4000 ptas plus IVA. Some rooms are being upgraded and will cost a few hundred pesetas more; a lift and cafetería will be installed.

Hotel Andalucía (☎ 953 72 12 68), Calle Martínez Falero 48, looks dull but has nice, sizeable rooms with bath and TV at the decent price of 3400/4400 ptas for singles/doubles.

Hotel Peña de los Halcones (☎ 953 72 02 11), 400m uphill from Plaza de la Corredera at Travesía del Camino de La Iruela 2, has good-sized, pine-furnished rooms, with air-conditioning, bath and TV for 5000/6400 ptas plus IVA. Some have great views over the town or crags. The hotel has a restaurant, café and pool.

A few other hotels are a bit of a hike down Calle Hilario Marco. The small *Hotel Parque* (☎ 953 72 18 06), Calle Hilario Marco 62, and the 23-room *Hotel Don Diego* (☎ 953 72 05 31), almost opposite at No 163, have doubles with bath for around 5000 ptas.

Rooms at the *Villa Turística de Cazorla* (☎ 953 71 01 00) on Ladera de San Isicio have a kitchen and fireplace and cost 10,200 ptas plus IVA. There's a restaurant and pool too.

Places to Eat

In late summer or autumn, after rain, locals disappear into the woods to gather large, deliciously edible mushrooms that they call *nízcanos* or *níscalos*. If these are available, go for them.

Mesón Don Chema, Calle Escaleras del Mercado 2, down a lane off Calle Doctor Muñoz, has pizzeria-like check tablecloths and colourful chairs, but the antlers on the walls give a truer hint of its good, typical local fare. There's a wide choice and prices are middling, with revueltos, meat, fish and various raciones for between 700 and 1500 ptas.

If a pizza is actually what you're after, *La Forchetta*, Calle de las Escuelas 2, just down from Plaza de la Constitución, serves them for 450 to 700 ptas, plus pasta at similar prices (closed Tuesday). Nearby on Plaza del Mercado, *Restaurante La Sarga* is one of the more upmarket eateries, serving a four-course *menú* for 1700 ptas, and individual mains for around 1200 to 1500 ptas (closed Tuesday). Specialities include venison stew (caldereta de gamo*)*.

Over on Plaza de Santa María, the ancient, wood-beamed *La Cueva de Juan Pedro*, hung with countless clumps of garlic and drying peppers, serves up very traditional Cazorla fare such as rabbit, trout, rin-rán, wild boar, venison and even mouflon. All are available as raciones, prepared in a variety of ways, for 900 ptas.

Several of the bars on Cazorla's three main plazas serve fine tapas and raciones – among them *Café-Bar Las Vegas*, Plaza de la Corredera 17, where besides *lomo de jabalí* (loin of wild boar) there's an item called *gloria bendita* (blessed glory), which is a tasty prawn-and-capsicum revuelto. The Las Vegas also has the town's best breakfast tostadas. *La Montería*, Plaza de la Corredera 18, has tapas of *choto con ajo* (veal with garlic) and venison. Other good tapas stops include the bright *Café-Bar Rojas* on Plaza de la Constitución and the down-to-earth *Taberna Quinito* on Plaza de Santa María.

There's a daily *market* on Plaza del Mercado.

Entertainment
Aside from its tapas bars (see Places to Eat), Cazorla has a number of music bars which get lively on weekend nights – among them *Disco-Bar La Rana Verde* on Calle San Juan above the youth hostel, *Pub Yedra*, Plaza de la Constitución 4, *Pub Glass*, Travesía de San Antón 1, and *Pub Liberty*, Calle Hilario Marco 4.

Getting There & Away
Bus Alsina Graells runs two daily buses to/from Úbeda, Baeza, Jaén (two hours, 930 ptas) and Granada. The main stop in Cazorla is Plaza de la Constitución. In Cazorla, Quercus has timetable information. When we checked, the buses to Cazorla left Granada at 10.30 am and 3 pm, Jaén 1½ hours later, Baeza 2½ hours later and Úbeda three hours later. Departures from Cazorla were at 5.30 pm daily, as well as at 7 am Monday to Saturday and at 8 am Sunday and holidays. A couple of other daily buses run just between Úbeda and Cazorla.

Car & Motorcycle From Úbeda, take the N-322 east then turn south-east on to the A-315 at Torreperogil, then east on to the A-319/C-328 at Peal de Becerro.

AROUND CAZORLA
The footpaths and dirt roads working their way between the pine forests, open meadowlands, rocky crags, streams and valleys of the Sierra de Cazorla, rising immediately east of Cazorla, offer heaps of scope for day walks or drives. As well as fine panoramas, walkers may see deer, ibex, mouflon or wild boar.

La Iruela, Riogazas & El Chorro
The village of La Iruela, 100m higher than Cazorla on the hill to the east, is less than 1km from Plaza de la Corredera – up Calle del Carmen and its continuation, Camino de la Iruela. The picturesque ruins of La Iruela's Knights Templar castle stand atop a sheer crag at the far (eastern) end of the village.

If you turn right along Carretera Virgen de la Cabeza soon after entering La Iruela from Cazorla (a sign says 'Ermita' and 'Merendero de Riogazas'), you reach the Merenderos de Cazorla mirador, with fine views over Cazorla, after about 700m. Here a track which is just driveable heads 500m left up to a white church visible from Cazorla – the Ermita de la Virgen de la Cabeza.

Some 3km farther along the road, which becomes dirt, from the Merenderos de Cazorla, is the Riogazas entry point to the natural park. About 4.5km beyond that is El Chorro, a gorge which is an excellent spot for watching Egyptian and griffon vultures.

Just beyond El Chorro, the road meets another dirt road coming up from the south-west. A left turn here (initially southward) will wind you round over the Puerto Lorente pass to a junction after 12km, where you can fork right for the Nacimiento del Guadalquivir (see the Parque Natural de Cazorla section), or left down the Guadalquivir valley to Puente de las Herrerías.

Hotel de Montaña Riogazas (☎ 953 12 40 35), at Km 4.5 on the road from La Iruela to El Chorro, is an old hunting lodge converted into an attractive little hotel with 10 simple, pleasant rooms, a dining room and pool. It's open daily from July to September (Friday to Sunday at other times), with singles/doubles for around 3500/5500 ptas.

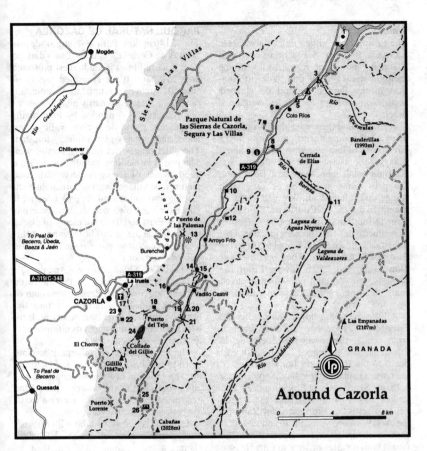

Around Cazorla

0   4   8 km

PLACES TO STAY

2 Hotel Paraíso de
   Bujaraiza
3 Camping Fuente de la
   Pascuala
4 Camping Llanos de
   Arance
5 Camping Chopera Coto
   Ríos
6 Hotel San Fernando;
   Hostal Mirasierra;
   Apartamentos El Pinar
7 Hotel de Montaña
   La Hortizuela

10 Hotel Noguera de la Sierpe
12 Hotel Río
18 Parador El Adelantado
20 Complejo Turístico
    Puente de las Herrerías
22 Hotel de Montaña
    Riogazas

OTHER

1 Parque Cinegético
   Collado del Almendral
8 Piscifactoría
9 Centro de Interpretación
   Torre del Vinagre
11 Hydroelectric Station

13 Mirador Paso del Aire
14 Central Hidroeléctrico
    Cerrada del Utrero
15 Cascada de Linarejos
16 Empalme del Valle
17 Ermita de la Virgen
    de la Cabeza
19 Fuente del Oso
21 Puente de las Herrerías
23 Riogazas Entry Point
24 Loma de los Castellones
25 Nacimiento del
    Guadalquivir
26 Cañada de las Fuentes

Walks

The Ermita de la Virgen de la Cabeza (see La Iruela, Riogazas & El Chorro, above) is a starting point for many walks in the parque natural (you'll find more information in the Parque Natural de Cazorla section on some of the places mentioned here).

A path behind the ermita climbs along the edge of the pine forest, then ascends a stream bed to join a north-south path about 1.5km (300m ascent) from the ermita. Heading south then south-east from here, the path loops around some crags and brings you, after about 3km and 250m of ascent, to the 1550m **Puerto del Tejo** pass, three to four hours from Cazorla.

At Puerto del Tejo there's a junction. One track heads down through pine forest to the **Parador El Adelantado** hotel, a little over 1km away and 250m lower. From the parador you can continue down a paved road leading north-eastward towards Vadillo Castril.

A little over 3km down this road is the **Fuente del Oso**, a shady roadside fountain from which the marked Sendero de la Fuente del Oso path goes 1.4km south-east down to the **Puente de las Herrerías** in the upper Guadalquivir valley. Another easy path, the Sendero de El Empalme del Valle, strikes 1.5km north-west from the Fuente del Oso across to **Empalme del Valle** on the A-319, where you can, if you arrive in time, pick up afternoon buses down the Guadalquivir valley or back to Cazorla (see Getting There & Away under Parque Natural de Cazorla).

The southward option from Puerto del Tejo runs fairly level to **Loma de los Castellones**, a grassy area frequented by deer. Farther south-westward is the **Collado del Gilillo**, a 1750m pass beneath 1847m **Gilillo**, the highest peak in this area, about 4km from Puerto del Tejo. It's a short detour to the top of Gilillo. The north-west-ward path from the collado leads 3km down to Riogazas on the La Iruela-El Chorro road. You should get back to Cazorla seven or eight hours after leaving it.

PARQUE NATURAL DE CAZORLA

The 2140sq km Parque Natural de las Sierras de Cazorla, Segura y Las Villas (to give it its full title) is the biggest protected area in Spain. It's a crumpled region of several rugged, complicated mountain ranges – not extraordinarily high, but memorably beautiful – divided by high plains called *navas* and deep river valleys and lakes, and in many places thickly forested. The chief ranges run roughly north-south. The park's attractions include fine walks, a good chance of seeing some wildlife, and picturesque villages with historical interest. Getting into and around the park is easier if you have your own wheels, but some bus services exist and there are plenty of places to stay inside the park. Those without vehicles can reach the more remote areas on guided excursions.

The Río Guadalquivir, Andalucía's longest river, rises between the Sierra de Cazorla and Sierra del Pozo in the south of the park and flows northward into the Embalse del Tranco de Beas reservoir, from which it turns west towards its ultimate destination, the Atlantic Ocean.

The best times to visit the park are late April to late June, September and October: the vegetation is at its most colourful and you avoid most of the winter rain and the heat of July and August. In winter a lot of the park is often covered in snow.

The park is hugely popular with Spanish tourists and attracts an estimated 600,000 visitors a year – some 50,000 of them in Semana Santa. The other peak periods are July and August, and weekends from April to October.

Maps & Guides

Lonely Planet's *Walking in Spain* details some of the best Cazorla walks.

A new guide-booklet and map to Cazorla, to be published by Editorial Alpina in 1998, will probably be the best overall Spanish-language guide and map. Libros Pen-thalon's *Plano Topográfico de las Sierras de Cazorla, Segura y Las Villas* is a compilation of several SGE 1:50,000 sheets but

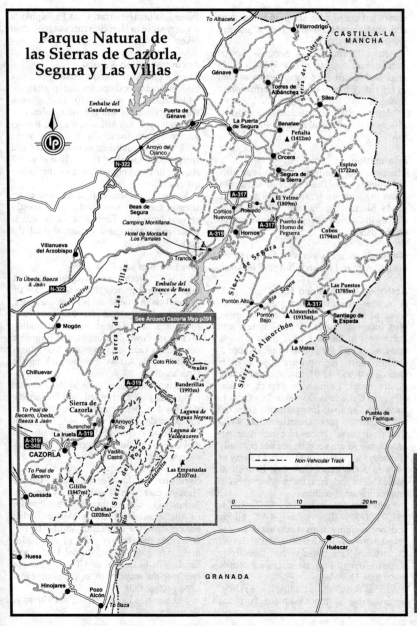

Parque Natural de las Sierras de Cazorla, Segura y Las Villas

To Albacete

Villarrodrigo

CASTILLA-LA MANCHA

Sierra del Calderón

Génave

Torres de Albánchez

Siles

Embalse del Guadalmena

Puerta de Génave

La Puerta de Segura

Benatae

Peñalta (1412m)

Arroyo del Ojanco

N-322

Orcera

Espino (1722m)

Segura de la Sierra

A-317

El Robledo

El Yelmo (1809m)

Beas de Segura

Cortijos Nuevos

A-317

Camping Montillana

Hotel de Montaña Los Parrales

A-319

Hornos

Puerto de Horno de Peguera

Cobos (1794m)

Villanueva del Arzobispo

Tranco

Sierra de Segura

To Úbeda, Baeza & Jaén

N-322

Río Guadalquivir

Sierra de Las Villas

Embalse del Tranco de Beas

Las Puestos (1785m)

Pontón Alto

Río Segura

A-317

Pontón Bajo

Almorchón (1915m)

Santiago de la Espada

La Matea

See Around Cazorla Map p391

Mogón

Río Aguamulas

Coto Ríos

A-319

Sierra del Almorchón

Chilluevar

Banderillas (1993m)

Sierra de Cazorla

Río Borosa

Laguna de Aguas Negras

Puebla de Don Fadrique

To Peal de Becerro, Úbeda, Baeza & Jaén

Burenchel

Arroyo Frío

Laguna de Valdeazores

A-319 / C-348

La Iruela

A-319

CAZORLA

Vadillo Castril

Río del Pozo

Sierra del Pozo

Río Guadalentín

To Peal de Becerro

Gilillo (1847m)

Las Empanadas (2107m)

Non-Vehicular Track

Quesada

Cabañas (2028m)

0   10   20 km

Huesa

Huéscar

GRANADA

Hinojares

Pozo Alcón

To Baza

somewhat out of date, showing some paths and tracks which no longer exist and not showing some that do.

Anaya Touring Club's *Ecoguía Sierras de Cazorla, Segura y Las Villas* (1997) maps and describes 16 varied walks, as well as providing plenty of other information in Spanish.

Maps and guides are sold at tourist offices in the park and at some shops in the town.

Information
The main park information centre is at Torre del Vinagre (see The Centre of the Park). There are seasonal tourist offices at Segura de la Sierra, Orcera and Siles. Tourist offices in Cazorla also provide information on the park.

Money There are banks with ATMs in Burunchel, Arroyo Frío and Cortijos Nuevos.

Activities & Organised Tours
A number of outfits offer guided trips to some of the park's less accessible areas, plus other activities. Several hotels and camp sites in the park have links to these and can arrange for you to be picked up.

The most high-profile operator is Quercus (☎ 953 72 01 15), some of whose guides speak English or French. It has offices at Calle Juan Domingo 2 in Cazorla and at the Centro de Interpretación Torre del Vinagre in the park. Quercus offers 4WD trips from these centres to *zonas restringidas* (areas where vehicles are not normally allowed) for 2900 to 3400 ptas a half-day or 4400 to 5000 ptas a full day, as well as guided hikes and *'caza fotográfica'* (photographic hunting) outings.

Excursiones Bujarkay (☎ 953 71 30 11, 953, 71 30 58) offers walking, 4WD, biking and horse-riding trips with local guides *(guías nativos)*. It's based at Calle Borosa 81 in Coto Ríos but also has a roadside kiosk in Arroyo Frío. Its prices are a little lower than Quercus'.

Various activities, including horse riding, are available at the Complejo Turístico

Puente de las Herrerías. Casa El Rápido, a grocery store in Hornos, rents out mountain bikes.

Accommodation & Food
There's plenty of accommodation but few budget places, except for camp sites, of which there are at least 10. During peak visitor periods it's worth booking ahead.

Camping is not allowed outside the organised camp sites. These don't always stick to their published opening dates and from about October to April it's worth ringing or checking with one of the tourist offices.

Virtually all hotels, hostales and camp sites in the park have restaurants, mostly serving local fare. There's also a variety of other restaurants and kiosks around the park.

The South of the Park
The A-319 from Cazorla enters the park after 7km at Burunchel, then winds 5km up to the 1200m Puerto de las Palomas pass, with the breezy Mirador Paso del Aire lookout a little farther on. Five winding kilometres downhill from here is Empalme del Valle, a junction where the A-319 turns north towards Arroyo Frío to pick up the Guadalquivir.

Accommodation options in the southern part of the park are limited, and the farthest that the bus penetrates into this area is Empalme del Valle.

See Around Cazorla for some walks and driving routes in the areas of the park nearest to Cazorla.

Sendero de la Cerrada del Utrero
Heading east from Empalme del Valle, after 2.5km you reach the turning to the Parador El Adelantado hotel. One kilometre farther on, opposite the turning to Vadillo Castril village, is the starting point of two paths: the Sendero de la Cerrada del Utrero and Sendero de la Central de Utrero (when we checked, the maps of these paths appeared to be juxtaposed).

The Sendero de la Cerrada del Utrero is

Cazorla Fauna & Flora

In the hills or forests of the Parque Natural de Cazorla you stand a chance of seeing ibex, mouflon, red or fallow deer and wild boar. You may even run across deer or boar near some of the main roads.

The ibex lives mainly on rocky heights and has made a fair recovery from an outbreak of scabies in the late 1980s which decimated its population.

The other four animals prefer forests. All five species are subject to controlled hunting. The mouflon and the fallow deer were introduced for hunting though, ironically, the roe deer, native to the area, was hunted out of existence.

Some 140 species of birds nest in the park. Rocky crags are the favoured haunt of the golden eagle, Bonelli's eagle, griffon vulture, Egyptian vulture, eagle owl and peregrine falcon. In the forests you may spot buzzard, short-toed eagle, booted eagle, goshawk, sparrowhawk, hobby or great spotted woodpecker. The lammergeier is something of an emblem of the park but you'll be very lucky to see this bird – it disappeared in 1986 from its only Spanish habitat outside the Pyrenees, but efforts are being made to reintroduce it to the park.

The park's rich vegetation is a delight. In spring the wildflowers are magnificent and parts of the park seem to be a red carpet of poppies. In autumn the deciduous trees provide another feast of colour.

Of the park's 2300 plant species, 24 are unique, including the beautiful Cazorla violet (*violeta de Cazorla* in Spanish), a very bright violet colour, and the Cazorla geranium (*geranio cazorlense*). Both like rock crevices in the drier areas.

The Savin – a type of cedar

Among the trees, the tall laricot pine (*pino laricio* or *pino salgareño*) generally likes the higher terrain; the umbrella pine (*pino resinero*) is mainly found between about 1300 and 1700m. The Aleppo pine (*pino carrasco*) prefers to grow at lower levels. These last two trees were introduced in the 18th and 19th centuries after many of the native oaks had been floated downriver to be made into ships at Cádiz or Cartagena. Some holm oak and gall oak woodlands remain, however. If you know your trees you'll find many other species including wild olive, juniper, poplar, ash, willow, maple – these last four notably in river valleys – and, higher up, the savin.

Lammergeier – Europe's largest bird of prey

Ibex – a true mountain species; related to domesticated goats

JAÉN PROVINCE

a loop walk of 2km which takes you around under some imposing red and black cliffs to the Cascada de Linarejos waterfall, which falls a long way into a pool just below a small dam on the Guadalquivir. Most of the year, when the river is low, you can cross the river to the waterfall and explore the paths on that side: one follows the Guadalquivir down the deep valley towards the Central Hidroeléctrico Cerrada del Utrero, a small power station on the Guadalquivir beside the A-319. The main sendero continues above the Embalse de la Cerrada del Utrero, the narrow reservoir formed on the Guadalquivir by the dam, and returns to the road at a bridge 300m below your starting point.

The Sendero de la Central de Utrero is a 1km downhill walk to the Central Hidroeléctrico Cerrada del Utrero.

Puente de las Herrerías, Nacimiento del Guadalquivir & Cabañas Some 400m along the road past the Vadillo Castril turning, a turning to the right (south) leads up the upper Guadalquivir valley to Puente de las Herrerías and the Nacimiento (Source) del Guadalquivir. The large Complejo Turístico Puente de las Herrerías camp site begins 2km up this road. At its far end the road crosses the river by the Puente de las Herrerías and becomes dirt – bumpy in places but quite passable for ordinary cars. It's a beautiful drive up the wooded valley with the river bubbling to one side and rugged crags rising all around. Eleven kilometres past the Puente de las Herrerías is a junction with signs to 'Quesada 28' to the right and 'Nacimiento' to the left. Three kilometres in the Quesada direction a track, from which vehicles are banned, branches 4.5km right (north) up towards Gililio. Nine kilometres farther on towards Quesada, another right turn leads to El Chorro and La Iruela.

A couple of hundred metres up the left-hand road from the Quesada-Nacimiento junction, a 'Nacimiento del Guadalquivir' sign points down some steps towards the river on your left. A plaque on the far bank marks the official source of the Guadalquivir. Apparently in dry periods you can identify the stream emerging from underground, but if there has been rain it will be overwhelmed by another stream coming down from higher in the hills.

The road heads past the Nacimiento to the Cañada de las Fuentes picnic area then, 8km farther on, it passes close beneath 2028m-high Cabañas, one of the highest peaks in the park. You can ascend Cabañas in a two-hour round-trip walk from the road. The route loops round the southern end of the hill and approaches the summit, which offers superb views, from the south-east.

Sierra del Pozo, Barranco del Guadalentín, & Las Empanadas There are other good walks in the south of the park: in the Sierra del Pozo, which rises above the east side of upper Guadalquivir valley; in the Barranco del Guadalentín ravine, down to the east of the Sierra del Pozo; and up 2107m Las Empanadas, the park's highest peak, on its eastern edge. You approach these areas by continuing along the paved road past the turning for Puente de las Herrerías and the Nacimiento del Guadalquivir. In the next 7km the road winds 400m upward through the Sierra del Pozo, becoming dirt after about 4.5km.

Places to Stay The *Complejo Turístico Puente de las Herrerías* (☎ 953 72 70 90) is the largest camp site in the park, with room for about 1000 people at 425 ptas per adult/tent/car. It also has cabañas, a restaurant and a bar, and you can arrange activities such as horse riding, canoeing, canyoning and climbing. It's open from about mid-April to early December.

The *Parador El Adelantado* or *Parador de Cazorla* (☎ 953 72 70 75) offers all the usual parador comforts in a pine forest setting, with a grassy garden and fine pool. The 33 rooms cost 13,500 ptas, but only nine of them have outside views.

The Centre of the Park
From Empalme del Valle the A-319 heads

north down the Guadalquivir valley to the unspectacular villages of Arroyo Frío (6km) and Coto Ríos (22km) and the Embalse del Tranco de Beas. The main concentration of accommodation and visitor facilities in the park is dotted along this road and the most popular day hike, up the Río Borosa, is accessible from it. The bus from Cazorla goes as far as Coto Ríos.

Torre del Vinagre Sixteen kilometres from Empalme del Valle, the roadside Centro de Interpretación Torre del Vinagre was built as a hunting lodge for Spain's high and mighty, including Franco, in the 1950s. Today it offers displays and information on the park and is open daily, except winter Mondays, from 11 am to 2 pm and 5 to 8 pm (the afternoon session is 4 to 7 pm in spring and autumn, and 4 to 6 pm in winter). In an adjoining building is a Museo de Caza (Hunting Museum) with stuffed specimens of park wildlife and some impressive antlers and tusks. Just up the road is a botanical garden with the park's flora. It's open Monday to Friday from 9 am to 2.30 pm and Saturday, Sunday and holidays from 11 am to 2 pm and 4 to 6 pm.

Río Borosa Walk Though it gets busy at weekends and holiday times, this seven or eight-hour walk (return) is popular for good reason. It follows the tumbling, lushly vegetated course of the Río Borosa upstream, via a gorge and two tunnels (a torch is highly beneficial) to two beautiful mountain lakes – an ascent of 500m in the course of about 11km. Using the bus to Torre del Vinagre, you can do it as a day trip from Cazorla.

A road signed 'Central Eléctrica', east off the A-319 opposite the *centro de interpretación*, crosses the Guadalquivir and within 1km reaches a *piscifactoría*, where trout are reared, with parking areas close by. Shortly past the piscifactoría the road crosses the Borosa and immediately on your right is the marked start of the walk. Initially it's a track up the northern bank of the river. The track criss-crosses the Borosa a

couple of times before arriving, after about 3km, at a grassy area on the northern side of the river, the Vado de los Rosales. Here you leave the main track to follow the path through the Cerrada de Elías gorge, a little over 1km long, which closes in dramatically, forcing the path to criss-cross the river by footbridges and to take to wooden walkways along the walls.

At the end of the Cerrada de Elías the path rejoins the main track for about 3km up to a hydroelectric station. You could take a detour along a footpath to the 170m Salto de los Órganos waterfall on the river, but the main route goes to the left of the power station where a sign indicates the path to the *túneles*. This zig-zags steeply upwards to the tunnels. There's enough room at their sides to avoid getting wet as you go through. From the second tunnel you emerge at the Laguna de Aguas Negras (an hour from the power station). A track to the second lake, Laguna de Valdeazores, starts about 800m up the right (west) side of Laguna de Aguas Negras. Both lakes attract a variety of water birds.

Río Aguamulas Walk Soon after the turning to Coto Ríos, a dirt road east off the A-319 crosses the Guadalquivir and winds about 18km along the eastern bank of the Embalse del Tranco de Beas. This area is good for spotting wildlife. Several tracks (closed to vehicles) lead up into the forests above the reservoir, including one which, just after the Aguamulas control point 3km off the A-319, follows the Río Aguamulas upstream for about 10km. You can continue by path for a couple of kilometres to the Nacimiento del Aguamulas – a total ascent of some 500m. Banderillas, 1993m, towers above the upper stages of the walk.

Parque Cinegético Collado del Almendral & Tranco Between the A-319 and the embalse, 7km north of the Coto Ríos turning, the parque cinegético is a large enclosed area where ibex, mouflon and deer are kept. A 1km footpath leads from the parking area to three miradores where you might see some animals – your chances are highest at dawn and dusk.

Fifteen kilometres beyond the parque cinegético the A-319 crosses the dam which holds back the waters of the embalse. The small village of Tranco stands on the northern side of the dam.

Places to Stay Arroyo Frío has two modern, medium-size hotels, the *Hotel Cazorla Valle* (☎ 953 72 71 00) and the *Hotel Montaña* (☎ 953 72 70 11), with doubles between 6300 and 7000 ptas plus IVA. At the north end of the village the *Complejo Turístico Los Enebros* (☎ 953 72 71 10) has a hotel, apartments, wooden cabins and a small camp site. In the hotel singles/doubles with bath, TV and heating are 5500/7000 ptas plus IVA, breakfast included. The apartments cost 14,000 ptas plus IVA for six people, while the cabins range from 8500 ptas for two people to 14,000 ptas for six, plus IVA. There are also two pools and a playground.

RurALandalus (see Accommodation in Facts for the Visitor) has several *casas rurales* in Arroyo Frío for 1900 to 3000 ptas a person.

About 1km north of Arroyo Frío, a turning to the east leads 2km to the comfortable, pine-panelled, 21-room *Hotel Río* (☎ 953 71 30 33), with doubles with bath for 6800 ptas plus IVA, and a pool.

Five kilometres farther along the A-319 is the *Hotel Noguera de la Sierpe* (☎ 953 71 30 21), a favourite of the hunting community and decked with trophies (some of which, such as the entire stuffed lion in the lobby, are clearly not of local origin). The rooms (6000/8500 ptas plus IVA for singles/doubles, breakfast included) are comfortable without being exactly cosy. The large gardens contain a swimming pool and a small lake. There's also a horse-breeding ranch here.

Two kilometres north of the Centro de Interpretación Torre del Vinagre is the turning to the 27-room *Hotel de Montaña La Hortizuela* (☎ 953 71 31 50), a friendly hotel of terracotta tiles and wrought-iron balconies

in a tranquil setting 1km off the main road. The rooms are medium-sized with small bathrooms and cost 4000/5000 ptas plus IVA. The hotel has a good restaurant and a garden with pool.

A further 1km north on the A-319 are the comfortable, modern *Hotel San Fernando* (☎ 953 71 30 69), with doubles at 9000 ptas plus IVA, and the older *Hostal Mirasierra* (☎ 953 71 30 44), where singles/doubles with bath are 3800/4800 ptas plus IVA; both have pools. Adjoining the Mirasierra is *Apartamentos El Pinar* (☎ 953 71 30 68) which has four-person apartments for 8000 ptas.

Within the next 4km on (or just off) the A-319 are three medium-sized camp sites beside the Guadalquivir: first *Camping Chopera Coto Ríos* (☎ 953 71 30 05), with a rather tight but shady site by the side road into Coto Ríos; then *Camping Llanos de Arance* (☎ 953 71 31 39), just across the Guadalquivir; and finally *Camping Fuente de la Pascuala* (☎ 953 71 30 28), beside the A-319. All charge around 1300 ptas for two adults with a car and tent.

Just before the Parque Cinegético Collado del Almendral, *Hotel Paraíso de Bujaraiza* (☎ 953 12 41 14) is on the shores of the embalse and has doubles with bath for a reasonable 4500 ptas plus IVA.

North of Tranco along the road towards Hornos are the *Hotel de Montaña Los Parrales* (☎ 953 12 61 70), overlooking the embalse, with a pool and doubles with bath for 5000 ptas, and *Camping Montillana* (☎ 953 49 51 19), open from March to October.

The North of the Park
North of the Embalse del Tranco the main valley widens out and the hills are less rugged.

Hornos Twelve kilometres north of the dam at Tranco, the A-319 runs into a T-junction from which the A-317 winds 4km up to Hornos, a small village atop a high rock outcrop with panoramic views. Hornos' castle, which dates from Islamic times, looks more impressive from a distance than it really is.

El Yelmo The A-317 winds 45km across the Sierra de Segura from Hornos to the small town of Santiago de la Espada near the park's eastern boundary. About 10km out of Hornos is the Puerto de Horno de Peguera pass and junction. One kilometre up the road to the left (which leads towards Siles), a dirt road turns left at some ruined houses to the top of El Yelmo (1809m), one of the most distinctive mountains in the northern part of the park. It's little more than 2km and an ascent of 350m, to the top. At a fork after 1km, go right (the left fork goes down to El Robledo and Cortijos Nuevos). Both the climb and the summit of El Yelmo afford superb long-distance views. You should see griffon vultures wheeling around the skies. The road is OK for cars, if narrow, but is also a good walk.

Segura de la Sierra Easily the most spectacular and interesting village in the park, Segura de la Sierra sits atop a 1100m hill crowned by a castle which dominates the countryside. By road it's 20km north of Hornos: turn east off the A-317 4km after the village of Cortijos Nuevos.

Segura, a small place of just 2200 people and a few narrow streets, is possibly of Phoenician origin, and the Romans mined silver in the area. In Muslim times it was briefly the capital of a small taifa. When taken in 1214 by the Knights of Santiago, it was one of the very first Christian conquests in Andalucía.

As you approach the upper, older part of the village, there's a tourist office (☎ 953 48 02 80), open in Semana Santa and summer only, beside the Puerta Nueva, an arch which was one of four gates in Segura's outer Muslim walls. If the tourist office is open, ask about access to any buildings you want to visit – especially the key for the castle (see the next paragraph). Through the Puerta Nueva is the Iglesia de Nuestra Señora del Collado, the parish church, built about 1400 but much reconstructed since.

The deconsecrated Iglesia de los Jesuitas, adjoining it from below, has a good Renaissance façade. Continue down from here, then left along Calle Caballeros Santiaguistas, to the Baño Moro (Muslim Bath), built about 1150, probably for the taifa ruler Ibn ben Hamusk. There are three rooms for cold, temperate and hot baths, a barrel vault with skylights, and horseshoe arches. Nearby is the Puerta Catena, the best preserved of Segura's four Muslim gates.

To visit the castle at the top of the village you first have to borrow the foot-long key from the tourist office, in exchange for your passport. If the tourist office is closed, ask for the key in the Café-Bar Casino back down the hill.

If you're walking up to the castle, take the first narrow street up to the right after the parish church, Calle de las Ordenanzas del Común. After a few minutes you'll come out beside Segura's tiny, sort-of-rectangular bullring, with the castle track heading up to the right. Alternatively, you can drive most of the way up by heading past the parish church and round the perimeter of the village.

The main feature of the castle is its three-storey keep from which there are great views across to El Yelmo and far to the west. There's also a chapel with supposedly marvellous acoustics, but even the foot-long key wouldn't open that for us. The castle's origins are Muslim or earlier. The first documented restoration was made by the Knights of Santiago, the latest in the 1970s. The castle took its most recent knocks in a siege during the Napoleonic wars.

Places to Stay & Eat In Hornos, *Bar El Cruce* (☎ 953 49 50 35) at Puerta Nueva 45, the entrance to the village, has half a dozen decent rooms with bath at 3500 ptas a double, and good food. Round the corner into the village, *El Mirador* restaurant (☎ 953 49 50 19) has eight rooms with bath for 3700 ptas.

Camping El Robledo (☎ 953 12 61 56) is at El Robledo, about 4km east of Cortijos Nuevos on a road leading up to El Yelmo.

The only accommodation in Segura de la Sierra is the *Mesón Jorge Manrique* (☎ 953 48 03 80) at Calle de las Ordenanzas del Común 2, with just a few rooms at 1800/3500 ptas for singles/doubles, or 4000 ptas for a double with private bath. It has a small restaurant with most dishes at 1100 ptas or less.

Getting There & Away

Bus Carcesa (☎ 953 72 11 42) runs buses daily, except Sunday, from Cazorla's Plaza de la Constitución to Empalme del Valle, Arroyo Frío, Torre del Vinagre and Coto Ríos. Quercus in Cazorla can give you the latest timetable. At our last check, the buses left Cazorla in summer at 6.30 am and 2 pm; and during the rest of the year from Monday to Friday at 5.45 am and 3 pm and Saturday at 6.30 am and 2.30 pm. The run to Coto Ríos takes 1¼ hours. Buses back to Cazorla

left Coto Ríos at 8 am (7 am Monday to Friday outside summer) and 4.30 pm.

No buses link the northern part of the park with the centre and south, but coming from Jaén, Baeza or Úbeda, you could get an Alsina Graells bus to La Puerta de Segura (leaving Jaén daily at 9.30 am). From the same stop in La Puerta de Segura, Gil San (☎ 953 49 60 27) runs a bus daily, except Sunday and holidays at 12.30 pm to Segura de la Sierra and Cortijos Nuevos.

Car & Motorcycle Approaches to the park include the A-319 from Cazorla, roads into the north from Villanueva del Arzobispo and Puente de Génave on the N-322, and the A-317 to Santiago de la Espada from Puebla de Don Fadrique in northern Granada province.

There are at least seven petrol stations in the park.

Almería Province

Andalucía's easternmost province is its sunniest, with over 3000 hours of sunshine a year. It's also the most parched part of Spain, with large expanses of rocky semidesert, particularly north and east of Almería city. On the hilly Cabo de Gata promontory, this stark landscape meets the coast in majestic fashion with excellent, often isolated beaches strung between dramatic cliffs and headlands.

Remote and for a long time forgotten and impoverished, the province has used its main natural resource – sunshine – to stage a bit of a comeback in recent decades through tourism and intensive cultivation of vegetables, fruit and flowers in plastic greenhouses, which you can't fail to notice.

ALMERÍA

Almería hasn't figured among Spain's great cities for almost 1000 years, but it's a likeable and lively enough place to linger for a night or so. The large Islamic fort dominating the city, the Alcazaba, is the chief reminder of Almería's distant heyday. As the chief port of the Córdoba caliphate and capital of an 11th century *taifa*, the Islamic city of Al-Mariyat grew wealthy on trade and a textile industry which wove silk from the silkworms of the Alpujarras. The city was taken by the Catholic Monarchs in 1489 and its Muslim populace was expelled a year later. Devastated by an earthquake in 1522, Almería only began to recover in the 19th century. Today it's a mostly modern place of 171,000 people and the hub of a mining and horticultural region.

Orientation & Information

The city centre lies between the Alcazaba on the west and Rambla de Belén, a *paseo* created from a dry river bed, on the east. Paseo de Almería, cutting north-west from Rambla de Belén to the intersection called Puerta de Purchena, is the main artery. The bus station is 400m east of Rambla de

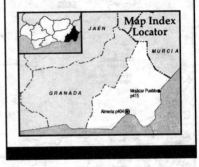

Belén, on Plaza Barcelona, with the train station 200m to its south, on Plaza de la Estación.

The helpful tourist office (☎ 950 27 43 55) at Parque de Nicolás Salmerón s/n is open Monday to Friday from 9 am to 7 pm, Saturday and Sunday from 9 am to 1 pm. It has details of several foreign consulates in the city.

There are numerous banks on Paseo de Almería. The post office (postcode 04080) is at Plaza de Juan Cassinello 1.

The Policía Local (☎ 950 21 00 19) are at Calle Santos Zárate 11. The main public hospital is the Hospital Torrecárdenas (☎ 950 21 21 19) on Pasaje Torrecárdenas in the north of the city.

Librería Cajal, Calle Navarro Rodrigo 14, has a good stock of maps and Spanish guidebooks.

Alcazaba

Though earthquakes and other ravages of time have spared little of its apparently once

401

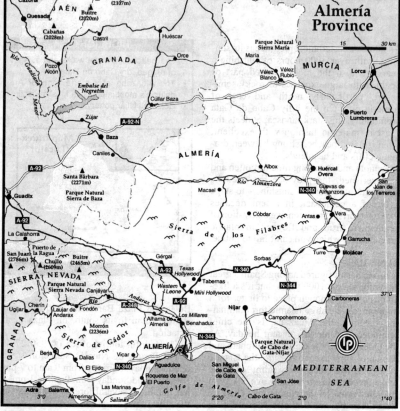

Alhambra-like internal splendour, the hilltop Alcazaba's hefty walls and towers still dominate the city and command great views. The entrance is from Calle Almanzor, up the hill west of Calle de la Reina. It's open daily: from mid-June to September, 10 am to 2 pm and 5 to 8.30 pm; otherwise 9 am to 1.30 pm and 3.30 to 6.30 pm (free with an EU passport, 250 ptas for others).

The Alcazaba was founded in the first half of the 10th century by the Córdoba caliph Abd ar-Rahman III. It consists of three compounds. The lowest, the **Primer Recinto**, reached through the Puerta de Justicia gate from the ticket office, is today mainly gardens. Originally it served as a military camp and refuge for the population in time of siege. From its top corner, the **Muralla de Jairán** – built in the 11th century by Jairán, the first ruler of the Almería taifa – descends the valley on the north side of the Alcazaba and climbs the Cerro de San Cristóbal on the far side.

The **Segundo Recinto** was the heart of the Alcazaba. By the wall at its east end is the Ermita de San Juan chapel, converted from a mosque by the Catholic Monarchs. You can also make out the remains of the soldiers' and queen's bathhouses and, on the north side of the recinto, the Muslim rulers' palace, the Palacio de Almotacin. The Ventana de la Odalisca (Concubine's Window) here gets its name from a slave girl who, the legend goes, jumped to her death from it after her Christian prisoner lover had been thrown from it when caught attempting to escape.

The **Tercer Recinto**, at the north-west end of the Alcazaba, is a fortress added by the Catholic Monarchs. Its thick stone walls and sturdy round towers are in much better shape than the rest of the Alcazaba. The Torre del Homenaje, ahead as you enter, bears the Catholic Monarchs' insignia on its façade.

Estación Experimental de Zonas Aridas

Down in the valley north of the Alcazaba, you'll notice a number of pens containing gazelles and other un-Spanish wildlife. This is a research centre into threatened Saharan fauna. You can visit by booking with the office (☎ 950 27 64 00) at Calle General Segura 1.

Catedral

Almería's weighty cathedral is at the heart of the old part of the city, a tangle of narrow streets below the Alcazaba. Begun in 1524 to replace a predecessor wrecked by the 1522 earthquake, it's mainly a mixture of late Gothic and Renaissance styles. Its fortress-like appearance – with six towers – was dictated by raids by pirates from North Africa. The north façade on Plaza de la Catedral is an elaborate mid-16th century creation by Juan de Orea.

The spacious interior has a Gothic ribbed ceiling and makes use of jasper and local marble in some of its baroque and neoclassical trimmings. The chapel behind the main altar contains the tomb of Bishop Villalán, founder of the cathedral, whose broken-nosed image is another work of de Orea, as are the choir, with its walnut stalls,

and the Sacristía Mayor with its fine carved stone roof, windows and arches.

The cathedral is open for tourist visits Monday to Friday from 10 am to 5 pm, Saturday from 10 am to 1 pm (300 ptas).

Museums & Exhibitions

The **Centro Andaluz de la Fotografía** (Andalucian Photography Centre; ☎ 950 26 94 33), in the Escuela de Artes on Plaza Pablo Cazard, puts on good photo exhibitions in a beautiful patio – open Monday to Friday from 9 am to 2 pm and 4 to 9 pm, Saturday 6 to 9 pm (free).

Almería's city museum is closed pending the construction of a new building on Plaza de la Estación. In the meantime its **Sala de Prehistoria**, with finds from the important Los Millares site, is in the Biblioteca Pública on Calle Hermanos Machado, open Tuesday to Saturday from 9 am to 2 pm; and the **Sala de Historia Antigua**, with the Iberian and Roman collections, is in the Archivo Histórico Provincial at Calle Infanta 12, open Monday to Friday from 10 am to 1 pm, plus Monday and Wednesday from 5.30 to 7.30 pm.

Beach

Almería has a long, grey-sand beach fronting the mainly pedestrianised Paseo Marítimo, east of the centre.

Places to Stay – Budget

Camping *Camping La Garrofa* (☎ 950 23 57 70) is on the coast 4km west of town on the Aguadulce road. It's open all year with room for 200 people at 465 ptas plus IVA per adult, per car and per tent.

Youth Hostel The *Albergue Juvenil Almería* (☎ 950 26 97 88) at Calle Isla de Fuerteventura s/n has room for 170 people, nearly all in double rooms. It's 1.5km east of the centre, off Calle Úbeda which is three blocks north up Calle Estadio from Avenida del Cabo de Gata. Bus No 1 'Universidad' from the east end of Rambla del Obispo Orbera runs along Avenida del Cabo de Gata; ask the driver for the Albergue Juvenil.

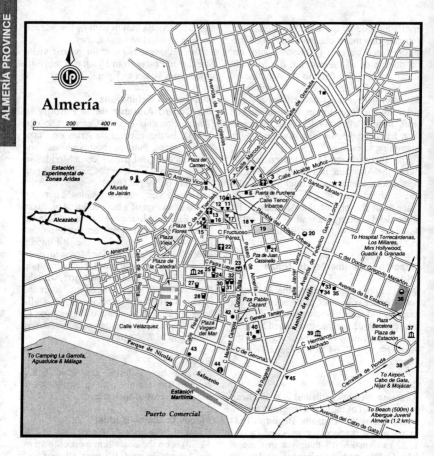

Hostales & Hotels *Hostal-Residencia Americano* (☎ 950 25 80 11), Avenida de la Estación 6, is a good choice and is near the bus and train stations. Plain but clean, well-kept and decent-sized singles/doubles cost from 2200/4200 ptas, with washbasin, to 2800/ 5000 ptas, with bath.

Hostal Universal (☎ 950 23 55 57), in the centre of town at Puerta de Purchena 3, has about 20 simple but sizeable rooms, with shared bathrooms, which cost 1500/3000 ptas. The building was once a minor mansion, which is indicated by the broad staircase and the spacious lobby full of draping plants.

The better *Hostal Sevilla* (☎ 950 23 00 09), nearby at Calle de Granada 23, has rooms with TV and bath for 3200/5000 ptas. *Hostal Bristol* (☎ 950 23 15 95), Plaza San Sebastián 8, has doubles with bath for 5500 ptas. *Hostal Maribel* (☎ 950 23 51 73), Avenida de Federico García Lorca 153, 600m north-east of Puerta de Purchena, has clean if small singles/ doubles for 2000/4100 ptas (2300/4500 ptas with bath).

PLACES TO STAY	33	Cafetería Santa Rita La Rambla	26	Archivo Histórico Provincial
1 Hostal Maribel	34	Portocarrero Café	27	Vértice Pub
5 Hostal Sevilla	45	Cafetería Central	28	Vhada
6 Hostal Bristol			29	Catedral
8 Hotel Residencia La Perla		OTHER	30	Velvet
10 Hostal Universal	2	Policía Local	31	El Cafetín
14 Hotel Residencia Torreluz	3	RENFE Office	32	Taberna Postigo
15 Hotel Complejo Torreluz	4	Templo de San Sebastián	36	Bus Station
16 Hotel Torreluz	9	Christ Statue	37	Museo de Almería (Future Site)
35 Hostal-Residencia Americano	13	Templo de Santiago	38	Train Station
40 Hotel Residencia Costasol	19	Mercado	39	Biblioteca Pública
	20	Buses to Albergue Juvenil Almería & Airport	41	Office of Estación Experimental de Zonas Áridas
PLACES TO EAT	21	Librería Cajal	42	Centro Andaluz de la Fotografía
7 Restauran Alfareros	22	Iglesia de San Pedro	43	Trasmediterránea Office
11 Marisquería El Alcázar	23	Post Office	44	Tourist Office
12 Cervecería Baviera	24	Irish Tavern		
17 Bodega Las Botas	25	Georgia Pub Jazz Club		
18 Restaurant Sol de Almería				

Places to Stay – Mid-Range & Top End

In this range you get private bath, TV, air-conditioning in summer and heating in winter. *Hotel Residencia La Perla* (☎ 950 23 88 77) at Plaza del Carmen 7, just off Puerta de Purchena, has singles/doubles for 4825/7500 ptas plus IVA. *Hotel Residencia Costasol* (☎ 950 23 40 11), Paseo de Almería 58, has good rooms for 7600/9500 ptas plus IVA, and a restaurant.

Plaza Flores has a group of three sizeable places (all ☎ 950 23 43 99) to suit most pockets; the *Hotel Complejo Torreluz* at No 6, the *Hotel Residencia Torreluz* at No 1 and the *Hotel Torreluz* at No 5. Doubles are, respectively, 7345, 9300 and 16,615 ptas plus IVA.

Places to Eat

The cafés lining the Puerta de Purchena end of Paseo de Almería are better for a spot of breakfast, a coffee or maybe tapas than for a full meal. For more substantial eating, the simple, friendly *Restauran Alfareros* at Calle Marcos 6, also near Puerta de Purchena, has a good three-course lunch and dinner menú, including wine and a decent choice of fish and meat main courses, for 950 ptas. It's open daily. There's also a handful of good places on Calle Tenor Iribarne, just off Paseo de Almería. *Marisquería El Alcázar* is good

for fish and seafood: most raciones are 800 to 1000 ptas at a table, or about 20% less at the bar. On the same street, *Cervecería Baviera* has a three-course menú for 1000 ptas, while round the corner at Calle Fructuoso Pérez 3, *Bodega Las Botas* is an atmospheric sherry bar doing varied tapas and raciones and a menú for 2000 ptas.

Restaurant Sol de Almería on Calle Circunvalación, by the covered mercado (market), offers several daily menús for around 900 ptas, including a drink. Some are only two-course but they're quite substantial. It's open lunchtime and evenings from 7.30 to 10 pm. The *mercado* itself is a good source of fresh food of all kinds.

A few glossy but not over-expensive places line up on Avenida de Federico García Lorca beside the Rambla de Belén. The bright *Cafetería Central* does platos combinados from 975 ptas and main dishes from 600 to 1900 ptas. The *Portocarrero Café* and *Cafetería Santa Rita La Rambla* are nice for a lighter bite.

Entertainment

There are a dozen or two music bars and discos on streets like Calle Padre Luque, Calle San Pedro, Calle Guzmán and Calle Real, between the post office and the cathedral. Some open from late afternoon.

Getting There & Away

Air Almería airport (☎ 950 22 41 14) receives charter flights from several European countries and has daily scheduled services to/from Barcelona and Madrid by Aviaco and to/from Melilla by Binter Mediterráneo (both airlines are on ☎ 950 21 37 90 at the airport) Pauknair (☎ 950 21 37 88 at airport) flies Monday to Friday to/from Barcelona and Melilla, with Málaga connections at Melilla. You can pick up one-way international fares from agencies such as Viajes Cemo (☎ 950 21 38 47) or Viajes Mundial (☎ 950 21 37 45) at the airport.

Bus Daily departures from the bus station (☎ 950 21 00 29) include nine or more to Guadix (1½ hours); five or more to Granada (2¼ hours, 1285 ptas); eight to Málaga (3¼ hours, 1915 ptas); and three to Sevilla (6¼ hours). There's also at least one bus a day each to Jaén, Úbeda, Córdoba, Cádiz, Madrid, Murcia, Cartagena, Valencia, Barcelona and – except Sunday – Ugíjar (via Berja) and Bérchules (via Adra).

For buses to places within Almería province, see destination sections.

Train You can buy tickets at the town centre RENFE office (☎ 950 23 18 22), Calle Alcalde Muñoz 7, open daily from 9.30 am to 1 pm plus Monday to Friday from 4.30 to 8 pm, as well as at the station (☎ 950 25 11 35). Direct trains run to/from Granada (2¾ hours, 1550 ptas) three times daily and to/from Madrid twice daily. All trains go through Guadix (1½ hours). You can connect for other destinations at Linares-Baeza or Granada.

Car & Motorcycle East of Almería, the N-344 is a faster and better road than the N-340. The original N-344 passing through the city centre and the newer northern bypass, also numbered N-344, meet 19km east of Almería.

There are several car-rental agencies in the city, and desks at the airport.

Boat From the Estación Marítima, Trasmediterránea sails to Melilla six days a week and three times daily from mid-June to the end of August. The trip takes up to eight hours. The cheapest passenger accommodation, a *butaca* (seat), is 3760 ptas one way; a car is 15,355 ptas. You can buy tickets at the Estación Marítima or the Trasmediterránea office (☎ 950 23 61 55), Parque de Nicolás Salmerón 19. Ferri Maroc (☎ 950 27 48 00), at the Estación Marítima, runs a slightly more expensive service, with similar frequency, to Nador, the Moroccan town neighbouring Melilla.

Getting Around

The airport is 9km east of the city off the N-344: the No 14 'El Alquián' bus runs between the city (east end of Rambla del Obispo Orbera) and airport every 30 to 45 minutes from 7 am to 9.30 pm.

AROUND ALMERÍA
West of Almería

Aguadulce, 11km from Almería, and **Roquetas de Mar**, 8km farther around the coast, are run-of-the-mill coastal resorts with a sizeable package trade. The *salinas* (salt lagoons) beginning at Las Marinas, 4km south of Roquetas, are a good place to see greater flamingos and other water birds in autumn, winter or spring.

A vast area west of Almería – and a lesser one to its east – are covered in plastic greenhouses which, with the aid of fertiliser and water pumped up from wells as deep as 100m, have turned a barren wilderness into one of Europe's most intensive horticultural zones. Most of the produce is trucked out to northern Europe. It's an oppressive sight but one that has finally, since the 1970s, brought wealth to at least a part of Almería province. The 'capital' of *plasticultura* is the sprawling town of **El Ejido**, bypassed by the N-340 west of Almería.

Los Millares

Archaeology fans will enjoy a trip out to this site, about 20km north-west of Almería on the N-324 between the villages of Gádor and Santa Fé de Mondújar. Los Millares, occupied from about 2700 to 1800 BC, was the site of what is thought to be Spain's first metalworking culture. Its people – who may have numbered up to 2000 – made pottery and jewellery, hunted, bred domestic animals and grew crops in what must then have been a much more fertile landscape. But it was their ability to smelt and shape copper that makes Los Millares a crucial stepping stone between the Stone and Bronze ages. The large site, almost 1km long on a spur above the beds of the Río Andarax and the Rambla de Huéchar, is still being excavated. It contains remains of four lines of sturdy defensive walls (reflecting successive enlargements of the village), round dwelling huts, a foundry and over 100 tombs. The tombs typically comprise a domed chamber reached by a low corridor: a few have been reconstructed but most are in a ruined state.

At our last check, Los Millares was open Wednesday to Saturday from 9.30 am to 2.30 pm and 4 to 6 pm, Sunday and holidays from 9.30 am to 2.30 pm – but it's advisable to check the latest hours at the Almería tourist office or by ringing the site (☎ 908-95 70 65).

In your own vehicle, take the A-92 north from Almería to Benahadux, then head north-west on the A-348. Signs indicate the Los Millares turning, shortly before Alhama de Almería. You might be able to get a bus bound for Alhama de Almería (daily from Almería at 8.30 am, and Monday to Friday at 1.15 and 2 pm) to drop you at the Los Millares turn-off, a few hundred metres from the site. But you may have to walk into Alhama, about 4km, to get a bus back – these are not very frequent and almost nonexistent on weekends.

Mini Hollywood

North of Benahadux, the Almería landscape takes on a particularly desertified aspect, with canyons and rocky wastes that look straight out of the Arizona badlands. In the 1960s and 70s, makers of Western movies spotted the resemblance and shot dozens of films here – many now deservedly forgotten, but some classics. Locals played Indians, outlaws and US cavalry while Clint Eastwood, Raquel Welch, Charles Bronson and co did the talking bits. The big-time movie industry then moved on, but left behind three Wild West town sets which are now open as tourist attractions. Occasionally, film stars still appear here. In 1998 directors Gene Quintano and Bill Corcoran brought Kris Kristofeferson, Willie Nelson and up-and-coming Spanish actor Jordi Mollá to the Almería desert for the shooting of new Westerns.

Mini Hollywood (☎ 950 36 52 36), the best known and best kept of the Wild West towns, is 24km from Almería on the N-340 to Tabernas. Parts of more than 100 films, including *A Fistful of Dollars*, *The Magnificent Seven* and *The Good, the Bad and the Ugly*, were shot here. Mini Hollywood is normally open daily from April to October from 10 am to 9 pm, and daily except Monday in other months from 10 am to 7 pm. Entry is 995 ptas (children 600 ptas), and at noon and 5 pm a mock bank holdup and shootout is staged. Also here, and open the same hours, is a 250,000 sq m Reserva Zoológica (☎ 950 36 29 31), with lions, elephants, brown bears, giraffes and 100-odd other species of African and Iberian fauna. It costs 1195 ptas (children 650 ptas), or there are combined tickets for both attractions at 1800 ptas (children 950 ptas).

Three kilometres farther along the N-340 towards Tabernas, then a few minutes along a track to the north, **Texas Hollywood** (☎ 950 16 54 58) boasts not only a Western town but also a stockaded fort, a Mexican pueblo and Indian tepees. There's also **Western Leone** (☎ 950 16 54 05), about 1km north on the A-92 from the N-340. Both places claim a hand in some of the same films as were shot at Mini Hollywood.

You really need your own vehicle to reach any of these sites. Buses from Almería to Tabernas (up to eight daily each way) may well be willing to drop you at Mini Hollywood or the Texas Hollywood turn-off, but are unlikely to stop for you on the way back. The same applies to Guadix-bound buses for Western Leone.

Níjar

Some of Andalucía's most attractive and unusual glazed pottery, and colourful striped cotton rugs known as *jarapas*, are made in this small town 4km north of the N-344, 31km north-east of Almería. It's well worth a detour if you're passing this way – though bus schedules make a day trip from Almería impossible. Shops selling the products, many of which are quite affordable, line the main street, Avenida García Lorca. There are three hostales.

THE ALMERIAN ALPUJARRAS

West of the small spa town of Alhama de Almería near Los Millares, the A-348 winds up the valley of the Río Andarax into the Almerian Alpujarras (see the Las Alpujarras section in Granada Province for an introduction to this series of valleys along the south side of the Sierra Nevada; the Almerian side is much less visited than the Granada side). The landscape is at first amazingly barren, with lines of arid serrated ridges stretching to infinity – but somehow supporting a surprising number of villages – then becomes gradually more vegetated as you approach Fondón, where *Camping Puente Colgante* (☎ 950 51 42 90) is open all year.

For information on walkers' *refugios* in the Almerian section of the Sierra Nevada you can call ☎ 950 27 70 12.

Laujar de Andarax

This pleasant village of 1800 people is the 'capital' of the Almerian Alpujarras and a good place for a stop. Laujar is where Boabdil, the last emir of Granada, settled briefly after losing Granada; later it was the headquarters of Aben Humeya, the first leader of the 1568-70 Morisco uprising, and the place where he was assassinated by his cousin Aben Aboo.

Just beyond the western edge of Laujar on the A-348, the Parque Natural Sierra Nevada maintains an information office, the Centro de Visitantes Laujar de Andarax (☎ 950 51 35 48).

Things to See & Do The handsome **Casa Consistorial** (Town Hall) on the central Plaza Mayor de la Alpujarra was built in 1792 with a façade of three tiers of arches. The large 17th century brick **Iglesia de la Encarnación**, just up the hill on the site of the old mosque, has a minaret-like square tower and a lavish golden retablo. From the village a signposted road leads about 1km north to **El Nacimiento**, a series of waterfalls in a deep, steep valley. There are a couple of restaurants near the falls, which are also the starting point for some walking trails which the Centro de Visitantes can tell you about.

Places to Stay The good *Hostal Fernández* (☎ 950 51 31 28), Calle General Mola 4, just off Plaza Mayor de la Alpujarra, has doubles for 3300 ptas with shared bathrooms. *Fonda Nuevo Andarax* (☎ 950 51 31 13), Calle Canalejas 27, about 300m west of the plaza along the main street, is cheaper. *Hotel Almirez* (☎ 950 51 35 61), 1km west of town on the A-348, is the most comfortable; doubles with bath are 4600 ptas and it has a restaurant.

Getting There & Away Two Alsina Graells buses a day run to Laujar from Almería. At the time of writing there were no direct buses linking Laujar with the Granada Alpujarras: you had to get one bus to Berja, then another on to Ugíjar or beyond.

CABO DE GATA

The stark landscape of eastern Almería meets the Mediterranean most dramatically where the Sierra del Cabo de Gata, of volcanic origin, plunges towards azure and turquoise waters around this promontory east of Almería city. Some of Spain's most beautiful and least crowded beaches are strung between cliffs and capes of awesome grandeur and the whole area has an elemental feel that's virtually unique on the Spanish Mediterranean. With just 100mm of rain in an average year, Cabo de Gata is the driest place in Europe. The arid landscape, dotted with low white houses, sometimes seems like a piece of North Africa transported to Europe. Though Cabo de Gata is certainly not undiscovered, it's far enough from the beaten track to feel positively deserted compared with many other Andalucian beach areas. There are no real towns here, just a scattering of villages which – with a couple of exceptions in July and August – remain very low-key.

It's possible to walk along, or not far from, the coast all the way from Retamar in the north-west to Agua Amarga in the north-east, but in summer bear in mind that there's very little shade. The west side of the promontory is straight and flat, with a sandy beach stretching most of its length; the south and east are more rugged, though still with plenty of good beaches. There's good snorkelling in several places.

It's worth calling ahead for accommodation anywhere on Cabo de Gata during Semana Santa and in July and August. Camping is only officially allowed in the four organised camp sites.

The IGN 1:50,000 map *Parque Natural Cabo de Gata-Níjar* is the best for the area.

Getting There & Away

Bus Schedules of buses from Almería bus station at the time of writing were:

Agua Amarga – Monday and Friday at 7.45 pm by Autocares Bergarsan (☎ 950 26 42 92)

La Isleta del Moro – Monday at 6.30 pm, Saturday at 2.15 pm, by Autocares Bernardo (☎ 950 25 04 22); on other days drivers of San José buses might be persuaded to detour

Las Negras & Rodalquilar – Monday to Friday at 5.30 pm, Saturday at 1.30 pm, by Tomás Marín Amat (☎ 950 22 81 78)

San José – Monday to Friday at 1.15 and 6.30 pm, Saturday at 2.15 pm, by Autocares Bernardo (☎ 950 25 04 22); from about June

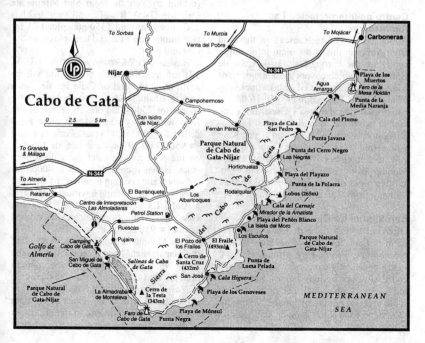

to September, an extra bus on Saturday and one on Sunday
San Miguel de Cabo de Gata – four or more daily by Autocares Becerra (☎ 950 22 44 03)

From Mojácar there's only one bus on Thursday and two on Saturday to Carboneras, 9km north of Agua Amarga.

Car & Motorcycle The road from Almería to Cabo de Gata turns south off the N-344, 15km east of Almería. After 8km, at Ruescas, one road forks south for San Miguel de Cabo de Gata while another heads across to the east side of the promontory. The east is also reachable by roads from Carboneras and Campohermoso to the north. The only petrol station on Cabo de Gata is halfway along the Ruescas-San José road.

San José has a couple of car rental agencies.

Centro de Interpretación Las Almoladeras

About 2.5km before Ruescas on the road from Almería, this is the main information centre for the Parque Natural de Cabo de Gata-Níjar, which covers the 60km or so of coast around Cabo de Gata, plus a thick strip of hinterland. The centre (☎ 950 16 04 35) has displays on the area's fauna, flora and human activities, as well as tourist information, and is well worth a stop if you have your own wheels. In Semana Santa and from July to September it's open daily, except Monday, from 10 am to 2 pm and 5 to 9 pm; at other times of year, it's open daily except Monday from 9.30 am to 3.30 pm.

San Miguel de Cabo de Gata

Often called just Cabo de Gata, this is the main village on the west side of the promontory. Fronted by a long, straight, sandy beach, it's composed largely of one and two-storey holiday homes, but has an old nucleus with a small fishing fleet at the south end and retains an amiable village atmosphere. Caja Rural bank on Calle Iglesia has an ATM.

South of the village are the **Salinas de Cabo de Gata** salt-extraction lagoons. In spring, many greater flamingos and other water birds call in here while migrating from Africa or the Doñana area to breeding grounds farther north (France's Camargue, in the case of the flamingos). A few flamingos and many others stay on here to breed, then others arrive in summer: by late August there can be 1000 flamingos here. Autumn brings the biggest numbers of migratory birds as they call in on their return south. A good place to watch the birds is the hide in a wood-fenced area just off the road 3km south of the village. You should see a good variety of birds any time of year, except winter, when the salinas are drained after the autumn salt harvest.

Places to Stay & Eat *Camping Cabo de Gata* (☎ 950 16 04 43) is near the beach, 2km down a side road just south of Ruescas (6.5km by vehicle from San Miguel de Cabo de Gata). It's open all year and has 250 sites at around 1350 ptas plus IVA for two adults with a car and tent, plus a restaurant and pool.

Restaurante Mediterráneo (☎ 950 37 11 37) towards the south end of the village seafront, at the end of Calle Iglesia, has a handful of singles/doubles with shared bathrooms for 2500/4000 ptas. It serves decent food with many seafood and meat main dishes for 700 to 1000 ptas. *Pizzeria Pedro* (☎ 950 37 00 10) on Calle Islas de Tabarca, on the right as you enter the village from Ruescas, has four basic rooms at 4000 ptas a double, and cooking facilities. Its sign just says 'Pizzeria'. Behind a wrought-iron gate at Calle La Sardina 2, on the left as you enter the village from Ruescas, is a good *hostal* (☎ 950 37 00 36 or ☎ 950 37 70 77, ask for Manolo or Mari). It was so new that the management hadn't yet chosen a name for it when we visited. Five nice, modern doubles with bathroom go for 5000 ptas.

Hostal Las Dunas (☎ 950 37 00 72) at Calle Barrio Nuevo 58, about 250m from the beach at the north end of the village, is a clean, modern place where singles/

doubles with bath are 4500/6500 ptas plus IVA.

Faro de Cabo de Gata & Around
The salt collected from the salinas is piled up in great heaps at **La Almadraba de Monteleva**, a drab village at their southern end. Beyond here the coast becomes rapidly more rugged and the road winds 4km up round the cliffs to the Faro de Cabo de Gata, the lighthouse on the promontory's southern tip. A turning by Bar José y María, just before the lighthouse, leads up to **Punta Negra**, 3.5km east, with an old Arab watchtower atop some very high cliffs and awesome views. Here the road ends but a walking track continues to Playa de Mónsul (about 1½ hours away), Playa de los Genoveses and San José.

Places to Stay & Eat *Hotel Las Salinas* (☎ 950 37 01 03) at La Almadraba de Monteleva is the most upmarket place on this side of Cabo de Gata, with doubles at 10,500 ptas plus IVA. The good *Restaurant Morales* is next door. *Bar José y María*, near the lighthouse, does platos combinados costing from 600 ptas and seafood raciones from 700 ptas.

San José & Around
San José, spreading around a bay towards the south end of the east side of Cabo de Gata, is the largest settlement on the promontory. Though it becomes a mildly chic little resort in summer, out of season its permanent population of 175 seems decidedly sparse as most of the holiday villas and flats stand empty. Despite gradual growth, it's still a small and pleasant place, with sandy streets and no high-rise development.

Orientation & Information The road from the north becomes San José's main street, Calle Correo, with the beach a couple of blocks down to the left. On Calle Correo you'll find a natural park and tourist information office (☎ 950 38 02 99), open in Semana Santa, July and August daily from 10.30 am to 10 pm, at other times daily

except Sunday from 10.30 am to 2 pm. It sells maps. Also on Calle Correo in the centre of town are an ATM and a Spar supermarket. Farther on up the hill is the post office (postcode 04118). You can change money at Molincar opposite Spar. Lavandería Pascal, a self-service laundromat, is on Paseo Marítimo behind Restaurante Carolina y Vanessa.

Beaches San José has a sandy central beach, with a harbour at its east end, but two of the finest beaches on Cabo de Gata lie along a dirt road to the south-west, well away from human settlement. **Playa de los Genoveses**, a broad strip of fine yellow sand about 1km long, with shallow waters, and rocky headlands at each end, is 4.5km from San José. **Playa de Mónsul**, 2.5km farther on, is a shorter length of fine grey sand backed by huge lumps of volcanic rock. Two kilometres beyond Playa de Mónsul, the road is blocked to vehicles – but not to walkers – as it climbs up to Punta Negra.

Activities The information office can tell you about bicycle rental, horse riding, boat trips, Landrover tours, windsurfing and diving.

Places to Stay – Budget *Camping Tau* (☎ 950 38 01 66), open from April to September, has a shady site about 300m from the beach, with room for 185 people, at around 450 ptas per person, per tent and per car. To find it, follow the 'Albergue' sign pointing left along Camino de Cala Higuera as you enter San José from the north, and go about 800m.

The *Albergue Juvenil de San José* (☎ 950 38 03 53) at Calle Montemar s/n is a friendly, non-Inturjoven youth hostel run by the local municipality. It has room for 86 people in bunk rooms holding two to eight, at 1000 to 1300 ptas a night depending on the season. It opens from Semana Santa to 1 October, and also for Christmas-New Year and long weekends. There's a small terrace café. To find it, head towards Camping Tau but turn right after crossing a dry river bed, then take the first left up the hill.

If you're looking for a bit of a hideaway, a fine choice is the friendly *Refugio Mediterráneo de Gata* (☎ 950 52 56 25) on Cala Higuera, a pebbly bay about 1.25km by dirt road beyond Camping Tau. The accommodation consists of eight rustic but cosy rooms for two or three people, some with kitchen, costing from 3000 to 6000 ptas. There's also a summer terrace bar with food. To get there, continue past Camping Tau to a T-junction with a wooden fence in front of you, then go right and follow the 'Bungalow' signs.

On Calle Correo in the village centre, *Café Bar Fonda Costa Rica* (☎ 950 38 01 03) has eight decent doubles with bath for 5500 ptas plus IVA.

Places to Stay – Mid-Range & Top End
Hostal Bahía (☎ 950 38 03 07), on Calle Correo in the centre, has 16 attractive, clean singles/doubles with bathroom and TV, in a bright, modern building, for 5000/7500 ptas. There are three larger places, with similar prices, at the entrance to San José from the north: *Hostal Las Gaviotas* (☎ 950 38 00 10) and *Hostal Ágades* (☎ 950 38 03 90), beside the main road, and *Hostal Puerto Genovés* (☎ 950 38 03 20), on Calle Arrastre just off to the east.

Top of the range is the often-full eight-room *Hotel San José* (☎ 950 38 01 16) in Barriada de San José, up the hill past the post office. Doubles are 15,000 ptas plus IVA.

If you fancy staying a while, consider renting an apartment. There are plenty available and two people can pay as little as 2000 ptas a day for a 10-day stay off season, though it costs more like 6000 ptas in high summer.

Places to Eat *Restaurante El Emigrante*, across Calle Correo from Hostal Bahía is clean and attractive with good service and good food. Fish and meat mains are around 850 to 1100 ptas, tortillas are 350 to 500 ptas, and a big mixed salad is 400 ptas. *Restaurante Carolina y Vanessa* on Calle

Correo in the centre does platos combinados for 750 to 900 ptas.

Just back from the far end of the beach, *Cafetería Restaurante El Ancla* is a popular seafood restaurant, with most main dishes costing between 1100 and 2000 ptas, though some shellfish dishes cost less. Just beyond, near the harbour, there's a line of eateries with outdoor tables including two Italian places (pizza or pasta 600 to 900 ptas) and *La Cueva* with fish mains in the 1200 to 1600 ptas region.

The Hotel San José's *Restaurant El Borany* is reckoned to be the best place for a splurge.

San José to Las Negras
The rugged coast north-east of San José allows only two small settlements, the odd old fort and a few beaches before the slightly bigger village of Las Negras, 17km away as the crow flies. The road spends most of its time ducking inland and though you can walk off-road most of the way, you're also off-coast much of the time.

The hamlet of **Los Escullos** has a short, mainly sandy beach and a restored old fort, the Castillo de San Felipe. You can walk here from San José along a track which branches off the road to Cala Higuera. The large, moderately shaded *Camping Los Escullos* (☎ 950 38 98 11), 900m back from the beach, is open all year and has a pool and supermarket. High-season cost for two adults with a car and tent is 2180 ptas plus IVA. There are two reasonable middle-range hotels: *Hotel Los Escullos* (☎ 950 38 97 33) by the beach with about 20 rooms at 8000 or 9000 pts, and *Casa Emilio* (☎ 950 38 97 32) just behind it with eight singles/doubles for 4000/6000 ptas. All three places have restaurants.

La Isleta del Moro, 2km farther north-east, is a tiny *pueblo* with a couple of fishing boats and Playa del Peñón Blanco stretching to the east. *Hostal Isleta del Moro* (☎ 950 38 97 13) has rooms with bath for 3000/5000 ptas, and a restaurant with fresh seafood. *Casa Café de la Loma* (☎ 950 52 52 11) on a small hill above the village, run by a friendly English-speaking young German, has a few rooms at 3000/4500 ptas for singles/doubles, or 5800 ptas for a double with bath, and a vegetarian restaurant in summer. Tai-chi or drama workshops and similar activities sometimes happen here.

From here, the road climbs to the **Mirador de la Amatista** lookout point before heading inland past the former gold-mining village of Rodalquilar. Walkers, unless they want to detour down to the small Cala del Carnaje beach or up Lobos hill (265m) – both reached from a turn marked 'La Polacra' just past Rodalquilar – must stick to the road as far as the turning for Playa del Playazo, 300m after the La Polacra turning. It's 2km along a level track to **Playa del Playazo**, a beach with good sand between two headlands, one topped by the Castillo de San Ramón (now a private home). From here walkers can continue close to the coast as far as Las Negras.

Las Negras is another small village, on a pebbly beach, with a few bars and cafés and several holiday apartments and houses to let. *Camping Nautico La Caleta* (☎ 950 52 52 37), open all year, is 1km south in a separate cove with little shade – but a nice swimming pool. Summer prices are 495 ptas per adult, 500 ptas per car and 550 ptas per tent, plus IVA. *Restaurante La Palma* on the village beach serves good medium-priced food.

Las Negras to Agua Amarga
There's no road along this cliff-lined and most secluded stretch of the Cabo de Gata coast but walkers can take an up-and-down path of about 11km, which gives access to several beaches. The nudist **Playa de Cala San Pedro**, with its ruined fort, is about 4km from Las Negras. **Cala del Plomo** is about 3.5km farther on.

Drivers from Las Negras to Agua Amarga must head inland through Hortichuelas. From the bus shelter on the east side of the road in the village of Fernán Pérez, a road – paved for the first couple of hundred metres, then with a reasonable dirt surface – heads

north-east across country. Keep to the main track at all turnings and after 10km you'll reach a paved road running down to Agua Amarga from the N-341.

Agua Amarga
The most northerly settlement on the east side of Cabo de Gata, Agua Amarga (sometimes spelt Aguamarga) is a rather pleasant fishing-cum-tourist settlement stretched along a straight sandy beach. It has a supermarket and post office.

Three kilometres up the road to the east, there's a turning to a clifftop lighthouse, the Faro de la Mesa Roldán (1.25km), which has an old watchtower for a neighbour. The views up here are marvellous. From the car park by the turning you can walk down to the nudist Playa de los Muertos. The road continues north through Carboneras, a minor resort with a big cement factory, to Mojácar, 30km from Agua Amarga.

Places to Stay & Eat *Hostal Restaurante La Palmera* (☎ 950 13 82 08) at the east end of the beach has 10 pleasant rooms with bath for 10,000 ptas plus IVA (a bit less if you can do without a sea view). On Calle La Lomilla just up from the west end of the beach, *Restaurante-Hostal René y Michèle 'El Family'* (☎ 950 13 80 14) has nine lovely double rooms with bath for 10,000 ptas including a big breakfast, plus a pool and an excellent four-course menú for 2000 ptas including drinks. The rooms are half-price from mid-September to February. The restaurant opens nightly at 7 pm, also Saturday and Sunday at 1 pm. There are also houses and apartments for rent in Agua Amarga.

Restaurante Ajoblanco, near the middle of the village on Calle Ferrocarril Minero, has most main dishes at 950 ptas or more but does baguettes for 275 to 600 ptas. *Chiringuito Las Tarahis* at the west end of the beach does tortillas from 500 ptas and fish and meat dishes from 1200 ptas.

MOJÁCAR
Mojácar, up the coast north-east from Cabo de Gata and 85km from Almería, is two

towns: the old Mojácar Pueblo, a jumble of white cube-shaped houses perched on a hilltop 2km inland, and the new Mojácar Playa, a modern coastal resort strip 7km long but only a couple of blocks wide. Though even the Pueblo is dominated by tourism, it remains picturesque, especially in the dim after-dark lighting. Mojácar Playa has been developed in a less intense way than other Spanish package tourism honeypots. It has few high-rise buildings, a good, long, clean beach, and quite a lively summer scene. The whole place is pretty quiet from October to Semana Santa.

The Pueblo goes back at least to Muslim times. From the 13th century it found itself on the Granada emirate's eastern frontier and suffered several Christian attacks, including a notorious massacre in 1435, finally succumbing to the Catholic Monarchs in 1488. Tucked away in an isolated corner of one of Spain's most backward regions, it was decaying and almost abandoned by the mid-20th century before the mayor started luring artists and others by offering give-away property. Mojácar became chic, then a holiday resort. Today its two parts have a permanent population of around 4000.

Orientation & Information
Mojácar Playa and Mojácar Pueblo are joined by a road which heads uphill from a junction known as El Cruce, by the Parque Comercial shopping centre towards the north end of Mojácar Playa.

The tourist office (☎ 950 47 51 62) is on Calle Glorieta, just below Mojácar Pueblo's main square, Plaza Nueva, in the same building as the post office and Policía Local (☎ 950 47 20 00). It's open Monday to Friday from about 10 am to 2 pm and 5 to 7 pm, Saturday from 10 am to 1 pm (from about October to Semana Santa, the Monday to Friday hours are 9 am to 3 pm). Banesto, next door, has an ATM, as has Banco de Andalucía in the Parque Comercial at El Cruce. There's another post office in the Parque Comercial too. The postcode for all Mojácar is 04638.

Things to See & Do
Seeing the Pueblo is mainly a matter of wandering the quaint winding streets with their flower-decked balconies and nosing into the craft shops, galleries and boutiques. **El Castillo**, at the very top of the village, is private property (and not a castle), but there are good views from a walkway around it. The fortress-style **Iglesia de Santa María** on Calle Iglesia, just up from Plaza Nueva, dates from 1560 and may have been a mosque. The **Puerta de la Ciudad** gate on Calle La Guardia is one of the few vestiges of Muslim Mojácar.

The most touching spot is the **Fuente Público** (Public Fountain) on Calle La Fuente in the lower part of the Pueblo. Though remodelled in modern times, the fountain maintains the Spanish Muslim tradition of turning water into art. Flowing from 12 spouts into marble troughs, the water tinkles along a courtyard decked with hanging plants. An inscription records the speech made, according to legend, on this spot in 1488 by Alavez, the last Islamic governor of Mojácar, to Garcilaso, the envoy of the conquering Catholic Monarchs. It translates, in part, as follows:

I am just as much a Spaniard as you. Though my people have lived in Spain for more than 700 years, you say to us 'You are foreigners, go back to the sea'. In Africa an inhospitable coast awaits us, which will surely tell us, as you do – and certainly with more reason – 'You are foreigners: cross the sea by which you came and go back to your own land'. Treat us like brothers, not enemies, and let us continue working the land of our ancestors.

Special Events
The Moros y Cristianos festival, on the weekend nearest 10 June, re-enacts the Christian conquest of Mojácar, along with dances, processions and other festive goings-on.

Places to Stay
Mojácar Pueblo *Camping El Quinto* (☎ 950 47 85 41) is 2km west of the Pueblo, on the Turre road. *Pensión Casa Justa* (☎ 950 47 83

72), Calle Morote 7, is good value with rooms at 2000/4000 ptas all year, or 5000 ptas for doubles with bath. *Hostal La Esquinica* (☎ 950 47 50 09), nearby at Calle Cano 1, charges 1750/3500 ptas. *Pensión La Luna* (☎ 950 47 80 32), Calle Estación Nueva 15, is a more comfortable place with 10 individually decorated doubles with bath for 6000 ptas, including breakfast. Other good meals are also available.

Hotel Mamabel's (☎ 950 47 24 48) at Calle Embajadores 3 has just four excellent rooms – big, characterfully decorated, with sea views and bath – for 6500 ptas. *Pensión El Torreón* (☎ 950 47 52 59), Calle Jazmín s/n, has great views from its bougainvillea-draped balcony, and just five good rooms, with shared bath, at 6000 ptas a double. According to a persistent Mojácar belief, Walt Disney was born in this house in about 1901. Originally named José Guirao, he emigrated as a child with his parents to the

US – as did a number of Mojácar folk in those hard times. When young José's parents died, he was adopted by a Californian family called Disney, and renamed Walt.

At the foot of the village, *Hostal Simón* (☎ 950 47 87 69) charges 6000 ptas for doubles with bathroom, and has meals available.

Mojácar Playa Almost everything here is on the main road running along the back of the beach. The shady *Camping El Cantal* (☎ 950 47 82 04), 1km south of El Cruce at the El Cantal bus stop, is open all year with room for 800 people at around 2050 ptas plus IVA for two adults with a car and tent. *Hotel Bahía* (☎ 950 47 80 10), just to its south, has doubles for 4000 ptas, or 5000 ptas with bathroom. You may find it closed in winter.

Hotel El Puntazo (☎ 950 47 82 65), 2km south of El Cruce, is a decent medium-sized

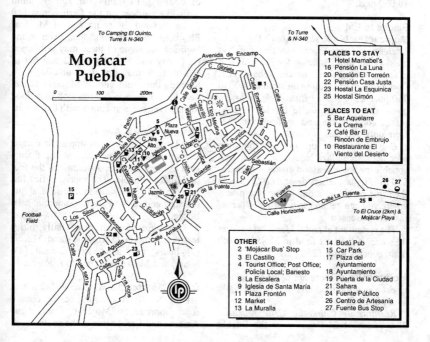

PLACES TO STAY
1 Hotel Mamabel's
16 Pensión La Luna
20 Pensión El Torreón
22 Pensión Casa Justa
23 Hostal La Esquinica
25 Hostal Simón

PLACES TO EAT
5 Bar Aquelarre
6 La Crema
7 Café Bar El Rincón de Embrujo
10 Restaurante El Viento del Desierto

OTHER
2 'Mojácar Bus' Stop
3 El Castillo
4 Tourist Office; Post Office; Policía Local; Banesto
8 La Escalera
9 Iglesia de Santa María
11 Plaza Frontón
12 Market
13 La Muralla
14 Budú Pub
15 Car Park
17 Plaza del Ayuntamiento
18 Ayuntamiento
19 Puerta de la Ciudad
21 Sahara
24 Centro de Artesanía
26 Centro de Artesanía
27 Fuente Bus Stop

hotel with doubles from 6730 to 10,200 ptas, all with bath, TV and breakfast. The best have air-conditioning and balconies. There are also four-person apartments for 9500 ptas, and a pool and restaurant.

Hotel Rancho del Mar (☎ 950 47 86 15) and *Hostal Provencal* (☎ 950 47 83 08), both about 1km north of El Cruce, have doubles for 6000 ptas plus IVA. *Hotel Playa Río Abajo* (☎ 950 47 89 28) at the north end of town has 19 nice rooms in chalets in a pleasant garden fronting the beach for 6500 ptas, or 8500 ptas with TV and a beach view. The hotel has its own pool, restaurant and bar. From La Rumina bus stop, head towards the beach and you'll find it.

Mojácar's *Parador* (☎ 950 47 82 50), a few hundred metres south of El Cruce, is a modern affair with nice gardens. Doubles are 14,500 ptas plus IVA. *Hotel Virgen del Mar* (☎ 950 47 22 22), 2km south, is another of the better places, with doubles at 10,000 ptas.

Places to Eat

Mojácar Pueblo *Restaurante El Viento del Desierto* on Plaza Frontón by the church is good value with fish soup for 375 ptas and main courses such as chicken kebabs, beef Bourguignon or rabbit in mustard for 600 to 750 ptas. *Café Bar El Rincón de Embrujo,* down the street at Calle Iglesia 4, does platos combinados and seafood raciones from only 500 ptas.

Bar Aquelarre, up in the shopping precinct above Plaza Nueva, serves up reasonable meat and seafood dishes – some for 550 to 750 ptas, others dearer. *La Crema* in the same precinct, is one of the few places where you can get an early coffee or breakfast out of season.

The restaurant at *Hotel Mamabel's* serves up some of the best food in Mojácar, with main courses from 1250 ptas.

Mojácar Playa There are dozens of places to eat along the road and beach, especially south of El Cruce.

Restaurante Chino La Gran Muralla, 2km south of El Cruce near the Pueblo Indalo bus stop, has fair-value set meals from 625 to 1750 ptas. *Antonella*, with a fine position just above the beach near the Cueva del Lobo bus stop, pulls in the customers with its medium-priced pizzas and pasta. Out of season it usually opens evenings only. *Mesón Casa Egea*, towards the south end of Mojácar Playa, at the Las Ventánicas bus stop, is popular for its fish and meat main courses costing from about 500 to 800 ptas.

Entertainment

Lively bars in Mojácar Pueblo include *La Escalera* on Calle Horno, *Budú Pub* on Calle Estación Nueva, *La Muralla* on Calle Aire Alto and *Sahara* on Calle Cuesta de la Fuente. To burn up some energy after midnight you can head down the hill to one of Mojácar's open-air discos such as *Master Disco*, halfway between Mojácar Pueblo and Playa, *Pascha*, on the beach just north of Camping El Cantal, or *Tuareg*, amid oasis-like gardens on the Carboneras road 3.5km beyond the south end of Mojácar Playa. But bear in mind that, even in the high season, some of these may only open on Friday and Saturday nights and out of season they may not open at all. *Tito's*, towards the south end of Mojácar Playa, near the Las Ventánicas bus stop, is a good lounge-type bar, sometimes with live music.

Getting There & Away

Bus Long-distance buses stop at the Parque Comercial at El Cruce and at the Fuente stop by the Centro de Artesanía at the foot of Mojácar Pueblo. The tourist office has timetables. Cafetería San Bernabé at the seaward end of the Parque Comercial sells tickets.

There are at least three daily buses to/from Almería (1¾ hours) and Murcia (2½ hours), two each to/from Granada (4½ hours) and Madrid, and one to Alicante.

Car & Motorcycle Mojácar is 14km east off the N-340. A winding, scenic coastal road approaches Mojácar from Agua Amarga and Carboneras to the south.

Getting Around

The 'Mojácar Bus' service runs from near the tourist office in Mojácar Pueblo down to El Cruce, to the southern end of Mojácar Playa (Hotel Indalo stop), to the northern end of Mojácar Playa (La Rumina stop) and then back to El Cruce and the Pueblo. It goes about every half-hour from 9 am to 11 pm in summer, and about every hour from 10 am to 6.30 pm in winter.

THE NORTH

Those who want to get well off the beaten track could head for the Los Vélez area in the far north of the province. In **Vélez Rubio**, just north of the A-92 (the main road to Granada from Murcia), the large Iglesia de la Encarnación is the most lavish baroque building in Almería. North of here, 1km before Vélez Blanco, a signposted path leads 1km off the road to the **Cueva de los Letreros**, with prehistoric cave paintings of animals, humans and a figure known as the Indalo, whose outstretched arms supporting a semicircle have become a symbol of Almería (they may represent a shaman and serpent, or a rainbow god). For a close look you can get a key from the petrol station at the turning, or from the information kiosk opposite.

Vélez Blanco itself has a picturesque former Muslim quarter, the Barrio de la Morería, and is crowned by an impressive 16th century castle whose original marble Renaissance patio, bought by a rich American in 1903, now adorns the Metropolitan Museum of Art in New York. **María**, a few kilometres west of Vélez Blanco, is a base for walks in the wooded, mountainous Parque Natural Sierra María, which reaches altitudes of over 2000m.

For tourist or walking information, contact the tourist office on Calle San Pedro in Vélez Rubio (☎ 950 41 01 48), the ayuntamiento in Vélez Blanco (Calle Corredera 38, ☎ 950 41 50 01) or the roadside park visitor centre (☎ 950 52 70 05) 2km west of María. All three of these small towns have cheap or medium-priced hostales and are served by one daily bus from Almería.

Language Guide

Spanish, or Castilian (*castellano*), as it is often and more precisely called, is spoken throughout Andalucia. English isn't as widely spoken as many travellers often expect, though you are more likely to find people who speak some English in the main cities and tourist areas. Generally, however, you'll be better received if you try to communicate in the local language.

Andalucian Colloquial Pronunciation
Pronunciation of Spanish isn't difficult, given that many Spanish sounds are similar to their English counterparts, and there's a clear and consistent relationship between pronunciation and spelling. However, few Andalucians pronounce Castilian as it is used in other parts of Spain or as it is taught to foreigners. Local accents vary too but if you stick to the following rules you should have very few problems making yourself understood.

Vowels Unlike English, each of the vowels has a uniform pronunciation which doesn't vary. For example, the letter **a** has one pronunciation rather than the numerous pronunciations we find in English, such as in 'cake', 'care', 'cat', 'cart' and 'call'. Many words have a written accent. This acute accent (as in días) indicates a stressed syllable; it doesn't change the sound of the vowel. Vowels are pronounced clearly even if they are in unstressed positions or at the end of a word.

a somewhere between the 'a' in 'cat' and the 'a' in 'cart'
e as in 'met'
i somewhere between the 'i' in 'marine' and the 'i' in 'flip'
o similar to the 'o' in 'hot'
u as in 'put'

Consonants Some consonants are the same as their English counterparts. The pronunciation of other consonants varies according to which vowel follows. The Spanish alphabet also contains the letter **ñ**, which is not found in the English alphabet. Until recently, the clusters **ch** and **ll** were also officially separate consonants, and you're likely to encounter many situations – eg in lists and dictionaries – in which they are still treated that way.

b soft, as the 'v' in 'van'; also (less commonly) as in 'book' when word-initial or when preceded by a nasal such as 'm' or 'n'
c when followed by 'e' or 'i' it's pronounced as 's', (not 'th' as in standard Castilian)
ch as in 'choose'
d sometimes not pronounced at all
g as in 'go' when initial or before 'a', 'o' or 'u'; elsewhere much softer. Before 'e' or 'i' it's a harsh, breathy sound, similar to the 'ch' in Scottish *loch*
h always silent
j a harsh, guttural sound similar to the 'ch' in Scottish *loch*
ll similar to the 'y' in 'yellow'
ñ a nasal sound like the 'ni' in 'onion' or the 'ny' in 'canyon'
q always followed by a silent 'u' and either 'e' (as in 'que') and 'i' (as in 'aquí'); the combined sound of 'qu' is like the 'k' in 'kick'
r a rolled 'r' sound; longer and stronger when initial or doubled
s often not pronounced at all, especially at the end of a word; thus *pescados* (fish) is pronounced *pecao* in Andalucia
v same as 'b'
x as the 'x' in 'taxi' when between two vowels; as the 's' in 'say' when it precedes a consonant
z pronounced as 's' (not 'th' as in standard Castilian)

Semiconsonant Andalucian Spanish also has the semiconsonant **y**. This is pronounced as **i** when it's at the end of a word or when it stands alone as a conjunction. As a consonant, its sound is somewhere between the 'y' in 'yonder' and the 'g' in 'beige', depending on the region.

Greetings & Civilities

Hello.	*¡Hola!*
Goodbye.	*¡Adiós!*
Yes.	*Sí.*
No.	*No.*
Please.	*Por favor.*
Thank you.	*Gracias.*
That's fine/	*De nada.*
You're welcome.	
Excuse me.	*Perdón/Perdone.*
Sorry/Excuse me.	*Lo siento/*
	Discúlpeme.

Useful Phrases

Do you speak English?	*¿Habla inglés?*
Does anyone speak English?	*¿Hay alguien que hable inglés?*
I (don't) understand.	*(No) Entiendo.*
Just a minute.	*Un momento.*
Could you write it down, please?	*¿Puede escribirlo, por favor?*
How much is it?	*¿Cuánto cuesta/vale?*

Getting Around

What time does the ... leave/arrive?	*¿A qué hora sale/ llega el ...?*
boat	*barco*
bus (city)	*autobús/bus*
bus (intercity)	*autocar*
train	*tren*
metro/ underground	*metro*

next	*próximo*
first	*primer*
last	*último*
1st/2nd class	*primera/segunda clase*

I'd like a ... ticket.	*Quisiera un billete ...*
one-way	*sencillo*
return	*de ida y vuelta*

Where is the bus stop?	*¿Dónde está la parada de autobús?*
I want to go to ...	*Quiero ir a ...*
Can you show me (on the map)?	*¿Me puede indicar (en el mapa)?*
Go straight ahead.	*Siga/Vaya todo derecho.*
Turn left.	*Gire a la izquierda.*
Turn right.	*Gire a la derecha.*
near	*cerca*
far	*lejos*

Around Town

I'm looking for ...	*Estoy buscando ...*
a bank	*un banco*
the city centre	*el centro de la ciudad*
the embassy	*la embajada*
my hotel	*mi hotel*
the market	*el mercado*
the police	*la policía*
the post office	*los correos*
public toilets	*los servicios/ aseos públicos*
a telephone	*un teléfono*
the tourist office	*la oficina de turismo*

the beach	*la playa*
the bridge	*el puente*
the castle	*el castillo*
the cathedral	*la catedral*
the church	*la iglesia*
the hospital	*el hospital*
the lake	*el lago*
the main square	*la plaza mayor*
the mosque	*la mezquita*
the old city	*la ciudad antigua/ el casco antiguo*
the palace	*el palacio*
the ruins	*las ruinas*
the sea	*el mar*
the square	*la plaza*
the tower	*el torre*

Accommodation

Where is a cheap hotel?	*¿Dónde hay un hotel barato?*
What's the address?	*¿Cuál es la dirección?*
Could you write it down, please?	*¿Puede escribirla, por favor?*

LANGUAGE

Do you have any rooms available?	*¿Tiene habitaciones libres?*
I'd like ...	*Quisiera ...*
a bed	*una cama*
a single room	*una habitación individual*
a double room	*una habitación doble*
a room with a bathroom	*una habitación con baño*
to share a dorm	*compartir un dormitorio*
How much is it ...?	*¿Cuánto cuesta ...?*
per night	*por noche*
per person	*por persona*
Can I see it?	*¿Puedo verla?*
Where is the bathroom?	*¿Dónde está el baño?*

Food

breakfast	*desayuno*
lunch	*almuerzo/comida*
dinner	*cena*
I'd like the set lunch.	*Quisiera el menú del día.*
Is service included in the bill?	*¿El servicio está incluido en la cuenta?*
I'm a vegetarian.	*Soy vegetariano/ vegetariana.* (m/f)

Time & Dates

What time is it?	*¿Qué hora es?*
today	*hoy*
tomorrow	*mañana*
in the morning	*de la mañana*
in the afternoon	*de la tarde*
in the evening	*de la noche*
Monday	*lunes*
Tuesday	*martes*
Wednesday	*miércoles*
Thursday	*jueves*
Friday	*viernes*
Saturday	*sábado*
Sunday	*domingo*

January	*enero*
February	*febrero*
March	*marzo*
April	*abril*
May	*mayo*
June	*junio*
July	*julio*
August	*agosto*
September	*setiembre/septiembre*
October	*octubre*
November	*noviembre*
December	*diciembre*

Health

I'm ...	*Soy...*
diabetic	*diabético/a*
epileptic	*epiléptico/a*
asthmatic	*asmático/a*
I'm allergic to ...	*Soy alérgico/a a ...*
antibiotics	*los antibióticos*
penicillin	*la penicilina*
antiseptic	*antiséptico*
aspirin	*aspirina*
condoms	*preservativos/ condones*
contraceptive	*anticonceptivo*
diarrhoea	*diarrea*
medicine	*medicamento*
nausea	*náusea*
sunblock cream	*crema protectora contra el sol*
tampons	*tampones*

Numbers

0	*cero*
1	*uno, una*
2	*dos*
3	*tres*
4	*cuatro*
5	*cinco*
6	*seis*
7	*siete*
8	*ocho*
9	*nueve*
10	*diez*
11	*once*
12	*doce*
13	*trece*

LANGUAGE

14	*catorce*
15	*quince*
16	*dieciséis*
17	*diecisiete*
18	*dieciocho*
19	*diecinueve*
20	*veinte*
21	*veintiuno*
22	*veintidós*
23	*veintitrés*
30	*treinta*
31	*treinta y uno*
40	*cuarenta*
50	*cincuenta*

60	*sesenta*
70	*setenta*
80	*ochenta*
90	*noventa*
100	*cien/ciento*
1000	*mil*

| one million | *un millón* |

Emergencies

Help!	*¡Socorro!/Auxilio!*
Call a doctor!	*¡Llame a un doctor!*
Call the police!	*¡Llame a la policía!*
Go away!	*¡Vete!*

LANGUAGE

Glossary

See also the Food & Wine section for a glossary of food and eating terms.

abierto – open
aficionado – enthusiast
albergue juvenil – youth hostel; not to be confused with hostal
alameda – avenue or boulevarde originally planted with poplar (*álamo*) trees
alcázar – Muslim-era fortress
alcalde – mayor
alfiz – rectangular frame about the top of an arch in Islamic architecture
altar mayor – high altar
alud – avalanche
alumbrados – enlightened ones (16th century religious free-thinkers)
años de hambre – years of hunger (1940s)
apartado de correos – post office box
apnea – snorkelling
armadura – wooden **mudéjar** ceiling, especially one like an inverted ship's hull
arroyo – stream
artesonado – **mudéjar** wooden ceiling with interlaced beams leaving a pattern of spaces for decoration
auto de fe – elaborate execution ceremony staged by the Inquisition
autonomía – autonomous community or region; Spain's 50 provincias are grouped into 17 of these
autopista – tollway
autovía – toll-free dual-carriage highway
AVE – Tren de Alta Velocidad Español; high-speed train
ayuntamiento – city or town hall
azulejo – glazed tile

baezano – person from Baeza
bailaor/a – flamenco dancer
baile – flamenco dance
bakalao – ear-splitting Spanish techno music (not to be confused with *bacalao*, salted cod)
barrio – district, quarter (of a town or city)
biblioteca – library

bici todo terreno – mountain bike
bodega – a cellar (especially a wine cellar); also means a winery, or a traditional wine bar likely to serve wine from the barrel
bota – sherry cask or animal-skin wine vessel
botijo – jug, usually an earthenware one
BTT – abbreviation for *bici todo terreno*
buceo – scuba diving
bulería – upbeat type of flamenco song

cajero automático – automatic teller machine (ATM)
calle – street
callejón – lane
camas – beds
cambio – in general, change; also currency exchange
caña – a small beer in a glass
cantaor/a – flamenco singer
cante jondo – literally 'deep song', the essence of flamenco
capilla – chapel
capilla mayor – chapel containing the high altar of a church
carmen – walled villa with gardens, in Granada
carnaval – carnival; a period of fancy-dress parades and merrymaking in many places, usually ending on the Tuesday 47 days before Easter Sunday
carretera – highway
carta – menu
casa rural – a village or country house or farmstead with rooms to let
casco – literally, helmet; often used to refer to the old part of a city (more correctly, *casco antiguo*)
castellano – Spanish language
castillo – castle
catedral – cathedral
caza – hunting
cercanías – local trains serving suburbs and nearby towns
cerrado – closed
cervecería – beer bar

churrigueresque – ornate style of baroque architecture named after the brothers Alberto and José Churriguera

claustro – cloister

cofradía – same as *hermandad*

colegiata – collegiate church

comarca – a district; or a grouping of municipios

comedor – dining room

comisaría – National Police station

comunidad autónoma – same as *autonomía*

consejo de gobierno – Cabinet of the Junta de Andalucía

consigna – left-luggage office or lockers

converso – Jew who converted to Christianity in medieval Spain

copas – drinks (literally, glasses); to go out for a few drinks: *ir de copas*

coplas – flamenco songs

cordillera – mountain chain

coro – choir (part of a church, usually in the middle)

Correos – post office

corrida de toros – bullfight

cortijo –farmhouse

cortes – parliament

costa – coast

costumbristas – 19th century Andalucian painters and writers who dealt with local customs and manners

cuenta – bill (check)

cuesta – lane (usually on a hill)

custodia – monstrance

dehesa – woodland pastures with evergreen oaks

dolmen – prehistoric megalithic tomb

ducha – shower

duende – the spirit or magic possessed by great flamenco performers

duro – literally, hard; also a common name for a 5 ptas coin

embalse – reservoir

embarcadero – pier or landing stage

encierro – running of bulls Pamplona-style (also happens in many other places around Spain)

entrada – entrance

ermita – hermitage or chapel

escalada – climbing

estación de autobuses – bus station

estación de esquí – ski station or resort

estación de ferrocarril – train station

estípite – pilaster

faro – lighthouse

feria – fair; can refer to trade fairs as well as to city, town or village fairs which are basically several days of merrymaking

ferrocarril – railway

fiesta – festival, public holiday or party

finca – farmhouse

fin de semana – weekend

flamenco – means flamingo and Flemish as well as flamenco music and dance

fonda – basic eatery and inn combined

gaditano – person from Cádiz

garum – a spicy, vitamin-rich sauce made from fish entrails in Roman Andalucía, used as a seasoning or tonic

gitano – Gypsy

glorieta – big roundabout

hermandad – brotherhood, in particular one that takes part in religious processions

hispalense – person from Sevilla

hostal – simple guesthouse-like or small hotel-like accommodation; not a youth hostel

humedal – wetland

iglesia – church

infanta – princess

infante – prince

IVA – impuesto sobre el valor añadido , or value-added tax

jardín – garden

jiennense – person from Jaén

jornalero – landless, seasonally employed agricultural labourers

judería – Jewish barrio in medieval Spain

Junta de Andalucía – executive government of Andalucia

latifundio – huge estate

latifundista – owner of vast estates

lavabo – washbasin
librería – bookshop
lidia – the art of bullfighting
lista de correos – poste restante
literas – couchette (on a train) or sleeping carriage
llegada – arrival

madrileño – a person from Madrid
madrugada – the 'early hours', from around 3 am to dawn – a pretty lively time in some Spanish cities!
manchego – La Manchan; a person from La Mancha
marcha – action, life, 'the scene'
marismas – wetlands
marisquería – seafood eatery
medina – Arabic word for town or inner city
menú del día – fixed-price meal available at lunchtime, sometimes in the evening
mercadillo – flea market
mercado – market
meseta – high tableland of central Spain
mezquita – mosque
mihrab – prayer niche in a mosque indicating the direction of Mecca
mirador – lookout point
morería – former Islamic quarter in a town
Morisco – a Muslim converted (often only superficially) to Christianity in medieval Spain
moro – 'Moor' or Muslim (usually in a medieval context)
movida – similar to *marcha* ; a *zona de movida* is an area of a town where lively bars and maybe discos are clustered
Mozarab – Christian living under Muslim rule in medieval Spain
mudéjar – a Muslim living under Christian rule in medieval Spain; also refers to their decorative style of architecture
muelle – wharf or pier
municipio – municipality, Spain's basic local administrative unit
museo – museum
muwallad – Christians who converted to Islam, in medieval Spain
nao – sailing ship for carrying merchandise

oficina de turismo – tourist office
onubense – person from Huelva

palermo – person from Palos de la Frontera
palo – literally a stick; also refers to the catagories of flamenco song
papelería – stationer's shop
parador – luxurious state-owned hotel, often in historic building
paso – literally, a step; also means the platform an image is carried on in a religious procession
peña – a club, usually supporters of a football club or flamenco *aficionados*; sometimes a dining club
pícaros – dice tricksters and card sharps; rogues
pinsapares – forest of Spanish firs
piscina – swimming pool
plateresque – early phase of Renaissance architecture noted for its intricately decorated façades
plato combinado – literally 'combined plate', a largeish serve of meat/seafood/omelette with trimmings
playa – beach
plaza de toros – bullring
porrón – jug with a long, thin spout through which you (try to) pour wine into your mouth
presa – dam
pronunciamento – pronouncement of insurrection, military rising
provincia – province; Spain is divided into 50 of them
pueblo – village
puente – bridge; also means the extra day or two off that many people take when a holiday falls close to a weekend
puerta – gate or door
puerto – port or mountain pass

quinto real – the royal fifth – the 20% of the bullion from the New World to which the Spanish Crown was entitled

ración – meal-sized serve of tapas
rastro – flea market, car-boot (trunk) sale
REAJ – Red Española de Albergues Juveniles; Spanish HI youth hostel network

Reconquista – the Christian reconquest of the Iberian Peninsula from the Muslims (8th to 15th centuries)

refugio – shelter or refuge, especially a mountain refuge with basic accommodation for hikers

reja – grille, especially a wrought-iron one dividing a chapel from the rest of a church

RENFE – Red Nacional de los Ferrocarriles Españoles, the national rail network

retablo – altarpiece

río – river

ría – estuary

romería – festive pilgrimage or procession

ronda – ring road

s/m – on menus, an abbreviation for *según mercado*, meaning 'according to market price'

s/n – sin numero (without number), sometimes seen in addresses

sacristía – sacristy, the part of a church in which vestments, sacred objects and other valuables are kept

saeta – outburst of adoration by an onlooker at Santa Semana processions

salida – exit or departure

salinas – salt lagoons

Semana Santa – Holy Week, the week leading up to Easter Sunday

señorio – feudal estate

sevillana – a popular Andalucian dance; also a female from Sevilla

sevillano – citizen of Sevilla

sida – AIDS

sierra – mountain range

Siglo de Oro – Golden Century; artistic period of the 17th century, literary period from mid-16th to mid-17th century

supermercado – supermarket

taifa – small Muslim kingdom in medieval Spain

tapas – bar snacks traditionally served on a saucer or lid (tapa)

taquilla – ticket window

tarjeta de crédito – credit card

tarjeta de residencia – residence card

tarjeta telefónica – phonecard

techumbre – roof or, specifically, a common type of *armadura*

terraza – terrace; often means an outdoor table in a bar or café

tertulia – informal discussion group or other regular social gathering

tetería – teahouse, usually in Middle Eastern style with low seats round low tables

tienda – shop or tent

tocaor/a – flamenco guitarist

torno – revolving counter in a convent where nuns sell cakes, sweets and other products to the public without being seen

trascoro – screen behind the *coro*

trono – literally, throne; can also mean the platform on which an image is carried in a religious procession

turismo – means both tourism and saloon car; *el turismo* can also mean the tourist office

turismo rural – rural tourism; usually refers to accommodation in casas rurales and associated activities such as walking and horse riding

ubetense – person from Úbeda

urbanización – suburban housing development

v.o. (versión original) – a foreign-language film subtitled in Spanish

valle – valley

zoco – large market in Muslim cities

zona de acampada – country camp site with no facilities, no supervision and no charge

Index

MAPS

TEXT

BOXED TEXT

LONELY PLANET PHRASEBOOKS

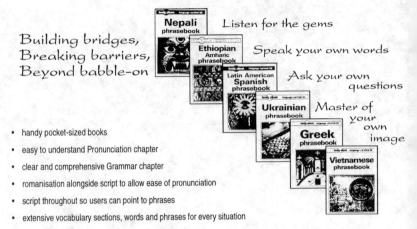

Listen for the gems

Speak your own words

Ask your own questions

Master of your own image

Building bridges,
Breaking barriers,
Beyond babble-on

- handy pocket-sized books
- easy to understand Pronunciation chapter
- clear and comprehensive Grammar chapter
- romanisation alongside script to allow ease of pronunciation
- script throughout so users can point to phrases
- extensive vocabulary sections, words and phrases for every situation
- full of cultural information and tips for the traveller

'...vital for a real DIY spirit and attitude in language learning' – Backpacker

'the phrasebooks have good cultural backgrounders and offer solid advice for challenging situations in remote locations' – San Francisco Examiner

'...they are unbeatable for their coverage of the world's more obscure languages' – The Geographical Magazine

---

Arabic (Egyptian)
Arabic (Moroccan)
Australia
  Australian English, Aboriginal and Torres Strait languages
Baltic States
  Estonian, Latvian, Lithuanian
Bengali
Brazilian
Burmese
Cantonese
Central Asia
Central Europe
  Czech, French, German, Hungarian, Italian and Slovak
Eastern Europe
  Bulgarian, Czech, Hungarian, Polish, Romanian and Slovak
Ethiopian (Amharic)
Fijian
French
German
Greek

Hindi/Urdu
Indonesian
Italian
Japanese
Korean
Lao
Latin American Spanish
Malay
Mandarin
Mediterranean Europe
  Albanian, Croatian, Greek, Italian, Macedonian, Maltese, Serbian and Slovene
Mongolian
Nepali
Papua New Guinea
Pilipino (Tagalog)
Quechua
Russian
Scandinavian Europe
  Danish, Finnish, Icelandic, Norwegian and Swedish

South-East Asia
  Burmese, Indonesian, Khmer, Lao, Malay, Tagalog (Pilipino), Thai and Vietnamese
Spanish (Castilian)
  Basque, Catalan and Galician
Sri Lanka
Swahili
Thai
Thai Hill Tribes
Tibetan
Turkish
Ukrainian
USA
  US English, Vernacular, Native American languages and Hawaiian
Vietnamese
Western Europe
  Basque, Catalan, Dutch, French, German, Irish, Italian, Portuguese, Scottish Gaelic, Spanish (Castilian) and Welsh

LONELY PLANET JOURNEYS

JOURNEYS is a unique collection of travel writing – published by the company that understands travel better than anyone else. It is a series for anyone who has ever experienced – or dreamed of – the magical moment when they encountered a strange culture or saw a place for the first time. They are tales to read while you're planning a trip, while you're on the road or while you're in an armchair, in front of a fire.

JOURNEYS books catch the spirit of a place, illuminate a culture, recount a crazy adventure, or introduce a fascinating way of life. They always entertain, and always enrich the experience of travel.

THE GATES OF DAMASCUS
Lieve Joris
Translated by Sam Garrett

This best-selling book is a beautifully drawn portrait of day-to-day life in modern Syria. Through her intimate contact with local people, Lieve Joris draws us into the fascinating world that lies behind the gates of Damascus. Hala's husband is a political prisoner, jailed for his opposition to the Assad regime; through the author's friendship with Hala we see how Syrian politics impacts on the lives of ordinary people.

Lieve Joris, who was born in Belgium, is one of Europe's leading travel writers. In addition to an award-winning book on Hungary, she has published widely acclaimed accounts of her journeys to the Middle East and Africa. *The Gates of Damascus* is her fifth book.

'Expands the boundaries of travel writing' – Times Literary Supplement

---

KINGDOM OF THE FILM STARS
Journey into Jordan
Annie Caulfield

Kingdom of the Film Stars is a travel book and a love story. With honesty and humour, Annie Caulfield writes of travelling in Jordan and falling in love with a Bedouin. Her book offers fascinating insights into the country – from the traditional tent life of nomadic tribes to the first woman MP's battle with fundamentalist colleagues. *Kingdom of the Film Stars* unpicks some of the tight-woven Western myths about the Arab world, presenting cultural and political issues within the intimate framework of a compelling love story.

Annie Caulfield, who was born in Ireland and currently lives in London, is an award-winning playwright and journalist. She has travelled widely in the Middle East.

'Annie Caulfield is a remarkable traveller. Her story is fresh, courageous, moving, witty and sexy!' – Dawn French

LONELY PLANET TRAVEL ATLASES

Lonely Planet has long been famous for the number and quality of its guidebook maps. Now we've gone one step further and produced a handy companion series: Lonely Planet travel atlases – maps of a country produced in book form.

Unlike other maps, which look good but lead travellers astray, our travel atlases have been researched on the road by Lonely Planet's experienced team of writers. All details are carefully checked to ensure the atlas corresponds with the equivalent Lonely Planet guidebook.

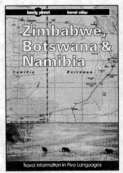

The handy atlas format means no holes, wrinkles, torn sections or constant folding and unfolding. These atlases can survive long periods on the road, unlike cumbersome fold-out maps. The comprehensive index ensures easy reference.

- full-colour throughout
- maps researched and checked by Lonely Planet authors
- place names correspond with Lonely Planet guidebooks
  – no confusing spelling differences
- legend and travelling information in English, French, German, Japanese and Spanish
- size: 230 x 160 mm

Available now:
Chile & Easter Island • Egypt • India & Bangladesh • Israel & the Palestinian Territories •Jordan, Syria & Lebanon • Kenya • Laos • Portugal • South Africa, Lesotho & Swaziland • Thailand • Turkey • Vietnam • Zimbabwe, Botswana & Namibia

---

LONELY PLANET TV SERIES & VIDEOS

Lonely Planet travel guides have been brought to life on television screens around the world. Like our guides, the programmes are based on the joy of independent travel, and look honestly at some of the most exciting, picturesque and frustrating places in the world. Each show is presented by one of three travellers from Australia, England or the USA and combines an innovative mixture of video, Super-8 film, atmospheric soundscapes and original music.

Videos of each episode – containing additional footage not shown on television – are available from good book and video shops, but the availability of individual videos varies with regional screening schedules.

Video destinations include: Alaska • American Rockies • Australia – The South-East • Baja California & the Copper Canyon • Brazil • Central Asia • Chile & Easter Island • Corsica, Sicily & Sardinia – The Mediterranean Islands • East Africa (Tanzania & Zanzibar) • Ecuador & the Galapagos Islands • Greenland & Iceland • Indonesia • Israel & the Sinai Desert • Jamaica • Japan • La Ruta Maya • Morocco • New York • North India • Pacific Islands (Fiji, Solomon Islands & Vanuatu) • South India • South West China • Turkey • Vietnam • West Africa • Zimbabwe, Botswana & Namibia

The Lonely Planet TV series is produced by:
Pilot Productions
The Old Studio
18 Middle Row
London W10 5AT UK

For video availability and ordering information contact your nearest Lonely Planet office.

Music from the TV series is available on CD & cassette.

PLANET TALK

Lonely Planet's FREE quarterly newsletter

We love hearing from you and think you'd like to hear from us.

*When...*is the right time to see reindeer in Finland?
*Where...*can you hear the best palm-wine music in Ghana?
*How...*do you get from Asunción to Areguá by steam train?
*What...*is the best way to see India?

For the answer to these and many other questions read PLANET TALK.

Every issue is packed with up-to-date travel news and advice including:

- a letter from Lonely Planet co-founders Tony and Maureen Wheeler
- go behind the scenes on the road with a Lonely Planet author
- feature article on an important and topical travel issue
- a selection of recent letters from travellers
- details on forthcoming Lonely Planet promotions
- complete list of Lonely Planet products

To join our mailing list contact any Lonely Planet office.

Also available: Lonely Planet T-shirts. 100% heavyweight cotton.

LONELY PLANET ONLINE

Get the latest travel information before you leave or while you're on the road

Whether you've just begun planning your next trip, or you're chasing down specific info on currency regulations or visa requirements, check out Lonely Planet Online for up-to-the minute travel information.

As well as travel profiles of your favourite destinations (including maps and photos), you'll find current reports from our researchers and other travellers, updates on health and visas, travel advisories, and discussion of the ecological and political issues you need to be aware of as you travel.

There's also an online travellers' forum where you can share your experience of life on the road, meet travel companions and ask other travellers for their recommendations and advice. We also have plenty of links to other online sites useful to independent travellers.

And of course we have a complete and up-to-date list of all Lonely Planet travel products including guides, phrasebooks, atlases, Journeys and videos and a simple online ordering facility if you can't find the book you want elsewhere.

www.lonelyplanet.com
or
AOL keyword: lp

LONELY PLANET PRODUCTS

Lonely Planet is known worldwide for publishing practical, reliable and no-nonsense travel information in our guides and on our web site. The Lonely Planet list covers just about every accessible part of the world. Currently there are nine series: *travel guides, shoestring guides, walking guides, city guides, phrasebooks, audio packs, travel atlases, Journeys – a unique collection of travel writing and Pisces Books - diving and snorkeling guides.*

EUROPE

Amsterdam • Andalucia • Austria • Baltic States phrasebook • Berlin • Britain • Canary Islands• Central Europe on a shoestring • Central Europe phrasebook • Czech & Slovak Republics • Denmark • Dublin • Eastern Europe on a shoestring • Eastern Europe phrasebook • Estonia, Latvia & Lithuania • Finland • France • French phrasebook • Germany • German phrasebook • Greece • Greek phrasebook • Hungary • Iceland, Greenland & the Faroe Islands • Ireland • Italian phrasebook • Italy • Lisbon • London • Mediterranean Europe on a shoestring • Mediterranean Europe phrasebook • Paris • Poland • Portugal • Portugal travel atlas • Prague • Romania & Moldova • Russia, Ukraine & Belarus • Russian phrasebook • Scandinavian & Baltic Europe on a shoestring • Scandinavian Europe phrasebook • Slovenia • Spain • Spanish phrasebook • St Petersburg • Switzerland • Trekking in Spain • Ukrainian phrasebook • Vienna • Walking in Britain • Walking in Italy • Walking in Switzerland • Western Europe on a shoestring • Western Europe phrasebook

Travel Literature: The Olive Grove: Travels in Greece

NORTH AMERICA

Alaska • Backpacking in Alaska • Baja California • California & Nevada • Canada • Chicago • Deep South• Florida • Hawaii • Honolulu • Los Angeles • Mexico • Mexico City • Miami • New England • New Orleans • New York City • New York, New Jersey & Pennsylvania • Pacific Northwest USA • Rocky Mountain States • San Francisco • Seattle • Southwest USA • USA phrasebook • Washington, DC & the Capital Region

Travel Literature: Drive thru America

CENTRAL AMERICA & THE CARIBBEAN

• Bahamas and Turks & Caicos • Bermuda • Central America on a shoestring • Costa Rica • Cuba • Eastern Caribbean • Guatemala, Belize & Yucatán: La Ruta Maya • Jamaica

Travel Literature Green Dreams: Travels in Central America

SOUTH AMERICA

Argentina, Uruguay & Paraguay • Bolivia • Brazil • Brazilian phrasebook • Buenos Aires • Chile & Easter Island • Chile & Easter Island travel atlas • Colombia Ecuador & the Galápagos Islands • Latin American Spanish phrasebook • Peru • Quechua phrasebook • Rio de Janeiro • South America on a shoestring • Trekking in the Patagonian Andes • Venezuela

Travel Literature: Full Circle: A South American Journey

ISLANDS OF THE INDIAN OCEAN

Madagascar & Comoros • Maldives • Mauritius, Réunion & Seychelles

AFRICA

Africa - the South • Africa on a shoestring • Arabic (Moroccan) phrasebook • Cairo • Cape Town • Central Africa • East Africa • Egypt • Egypt travel atlas• Ethiopian (Amharic) phrasebook • The Gambia & Senegal • Kenya • Kenya travel atlas • Malawi, Mozambique & Zambia • Morocco • North Africa • South Africa, Lesotho & Swaziland • South Africa, Lesotho & Swaziland travel atlas • Swahili phrasebook • Tunisia • Trekking in East Africa • West Africa • Zimbabwe, Botswana & Namibia • Zimbabwe, Botswana & Namibia travel atlas

Travel Literature: Mali Blues • The Rainbird: A Central African Journey • Songs to an African Sunset: A Zimbabwean Story

MAIL ORDER

Lonely Planet products are distributed worldwide. They are also available by mail order from Lonely Planet, so if you have difficulty finding a title please write to us. North American and South American residents should write to 150 Linden St, Oakland CA 94607, USA; European and African residents should write to 10a Spring Place, London NW5 3BH; and residents of other countries to PO Box 617, Hawthorn, Victoria 3122, Australia.

NORTH-EAST ASIA

Beijing • Cantonese phrasebook • China • Hong Kong • Hong Kong, Macau & Guangzhou • Japan • Japanese phrasebook • Japanese audio pack • Korea • Korean phrasebook • Kyoto • Mandarin phrasebook • Mongolia • Mongolian phrasebook • North-East Asia on a shoestring • Seoul • Taiwan • Tibet • Tibet phrasebook • Tokyo
Travel Literature: Lost Japan

MIDDLE EAST & CENTRAL ASIA

Arab Gulf States • Arabic (Egyptian) phrasebook • Central Asia • Central Asia phrasebook • Iran • Israel & the Palestinian Territories • Israel & the Palestinian Territories travel atlas • Istanbul • Jerusalem • Jordan & Syria • Jordan, Syria & Lebanon travel atlas • Lebanon • Middle East • Turkey • Turkish phrasebook • Turkey travel atlas • Yemen
Travel Literature: The Gates of Damascus • Kingdom of the Film Stars: Journey into Jordan

ALSO AVAILABLE:

Brief Encounters • Travel with Children • Traveller's Tales• Not the Only Planet

INDIAN SUBCONTINENT

Bangladesh • Bengali phrasebook • Bhutan • Delhi • Goa • Hindi/Urdu phrasebook • India • India & Bangladesh travel atlas • Indian Himalaya • Karakoram Highway • Nepal • Nepali phrasebook • Pakistan • Rajasthan • South India • Sri Lanka • Sri Lanka phrasebook • Trekking in the Indian Himalaya • Trekking in the Karakoram & Hindukush • Trekking in the Nepal Himalaya
Travel Literature: In Rajasthan • Shopping for Buddhas

SOUTH-EAST ASIA

Bali & Lombok • Bangkok • Burmese phrasebook • Cambodia • Ho Chi Minh City • Indonesia • Indonesian phrasebook • Indonesian audio pack • Indonesia's Eastern Islands • Jakarta • Java • Laos • Lao phrasebook • Laos travel atlas • Malay phrasebook • Malaysia, Singapore & Brunei • Myanmar (Burma) • Philippines • Pilipino phrasebook • Singapore • South-East Asia on a shoestring • South-East Asia phrasebook • South-West China • Thailand • Thailand's Islands & Beaches • Thailand travel atlas • Thai phrasebook • Thai audio pack • Thai Hill Tribes phrasebook • Vietnam • Vietnamese phrasebook • Vietnam travel atlas

AUSTRALIA & THE PACIFIC

Australia • Australian phrasebook • Bushwalking in Australia • Bushwalking in Papua New Guinea • Fiji • Fijian phrasebook • Islands of Australia's Great Barrier Reef • Melbourne • Micronesia • New Caledonia • New South Wales • New Zealand • Northern Territory • Outback Australia • Papua New Guinea • Papua New Guinea phrasebook • Queensland • Rarotonga & the Cook Islands • Samoa • Solomon Islands • South Australia • Sydney • Tahiti & French Polynesia • Tasmania • Tonga • Tramping in New Zealand • Vanuatu • Victoria • Western Australia
Travel Literature: Islands in the Clouds • Sean & David's Long Drive

ANTARCTICA

Antarctica

THE LONELY PLANET STORY

Lonely Planet published its first book in 1973 in response to the numerous 'How did you do it?' questions Maureen and Tony Wheeler were asked after driving, busing, hitching, sailing and railing their way from England to Australia.

Written at a kitchen table and hand collated, trimmed and stapled, *Across Asia on the Cheap* became an instant local bestseller, inspiring thoughts of another book.

Eighteen months in South-East Asia resulted in their second guide, *South-East Asia on a shoestring*, which they put together in a backstreet Chinese hotel in Singapore in 1975. The 'yellow bible', as it quickly became known to backpackers around the world, soon became *the* guide to the region. It has sold well over half a million copies and is now in its 9th edition, still retaining its familiar yellow cover.

Today there are over 350 titles, including travel guides, walking guides, language kits & phrasebooks, travel atlases and travel literature. The company is the largest independent travel publisher in the world. Although Lonely Planet initially specialised in guides to Asia, today there are few corners of the globe that have not been covered.

The emphasis continues to be on travel for independent travellers. Tony and Maureen still travel for several months of each year and play an active part in the writing, updating and quality control of Lonely Planet's guides.

They have been joined by over 80 authors and 200 staff at our offices in Melbourne (Australia), Oakland (USA), London (UK) and Paris (France). Travellers themselves also make a valuable contribution to the guides through the feedback we receive in thousands of letters each year and on our web site.

The people at Lonely Planet strongly believe that travellers can make a positive contribution to the countries they visit, both through their appreciation of the countries' culture, wildlife and natural features, and through the money they spend. In addition, the company makes a direct contribution to the countries and regions it covers. Since 1986 a percentage of the income from each book has been donated to ventures such as famine relief in Africa; aid projects in India; agricultural projects in Central America; Greenpeace's efforts to halt French nuclear testing in the Pacific; and Amnesty International.

'I hope we send people out with the right attitude about travel. You realise when you travel that there are so many different perspectives about the world, so we hope these books will make people more interested in what they see. Guidebooks can't really guide people. All you can do is point them in the right direction.'

– Tony Wheeler

---

lonely planet

LONELY PLANET PUBLICATIONS

Australia
PO Box 617, Hawthorn 3122, Victoria
tel: (03) 9819 1877 fax: (03) 9819 6459
e-mail: talk2us@lonelyplanet.com.au

USA
150 Linden St
Oakland, CA 94607
tel: (510) 893 8555 TOLL FREE: 800 275-8555
fax: (510) 893 8572
e-mail: info@lonelyplanet.com

UK
10a Spring Place,
London NW5 3BH
tel: (0171) 428 4800 fax: (0171) 428 4828
e-mail: go@lonelyplanet.co.uk

France:
1 rue du Dahomey, 75011 Paris
tel: 01 55 25 33 00 fax: 01 55 25 33 01
e-mail: bip@lonelyplanet.fr

World Wide Web: http://www.lonelyplanet.com
or *AOL keyword: lp*